INDIAN POLITY

For us democracy is not a gift, but the fundamental right of every citizen; for those in power democracy is a sacred trust. Those who violate this trust, commit sacrilege against the nation.

— President Smt. Droupadi Murmu,
Message to the Nation on the eve of Republic day
July 25, 2022.

Other books by the same author

1. New Comparative Government
2. Indian National Congress Since Independence
3. Select World Constitution

Published by :
Lotus Press Publishers & Distributors

INDIAN POLITY

(An Advanced Study of the Development and Working of India's Political System)

J.C. Johari
M.A., LL.B., Ph.D.

Third Edition

(Thoroughly Revised and Enlarged)

4735/22, Prakash Deep Building
Ansari Road, Darya Ganj,
New Delhi - 110002

Lotus Press : Publishers & Distributors
Unit No. 220, 2nd Floor, 4735/22, Prakash Deep Building,
Ansari Road, Darya Ganj, New Delhi-110002
3 K 41325510, 98118-38000
E-mail : lotuspress1984@gmail.com
Visit us: www.lotuspress.co.in

INDIAN POLITY
(An Advanced Study of the Development and Working of India's Political System)

ISBN: 81-89093-68-1

Printed & Published by : **Lotus Press Publishers & Distributors,** New Delhi-02

Preface to the Third Edition

Many important developments have taken place in the sphere of Indian political system like grant of Indian citizenship to the Non-Resident Indians with certain qualifications, Punchchi Commission Report on Centre-State Relations (2010), the ninety-seventh Constitutional Amendment of 2012 and the Fourteenth Presidential poll held in July 2012. I have taken note of all of them and revised the matter at appropriate places. I hope that this edition will meet the requirements of its readers well and thereby my efforts be suitably rewarded.

—J.C.Johari

Preface to the Second Edition

The first edition of this book was well received at the hands of its readers. Keeping in view the suggestions and comments of a good number of my friends, I have thoroughly revised and enlarged it. Some chapters have been added to discuss constitutional development and freedom movement so as to enable the readers to acquaint themselves with the course of the development of India's political system. Besides, chapters on Federal System and Parliament have been suitably enlarged and updated so that the readers may have a thorough understanding of the operation of our political system. The role of Judiciary and Election Commission has been reinterpreted in the light of latest developments. The themes of political corruption, political criminalisation and electronic governance and information technology have been included so as to cover the hitherto untouched issues of Indian politics. Adequate attention has been paid to the study of other significant issues of Indian politics like casteism, communalism and regionalism.

I hope that this book in the form of a detailed study of Indian polity shall meet the requirements of the students offering this course for the university or competitive examinations and thereby my labours shall be suitably rewarded.

—J.C.Johari

Preface to the First Edition

A study of the Indian Polity covering its Constitution, government and politics has an importance of its own. The political system is operated by the representatives of the people who, though rank politicians, have to operate within the parameters set by the provisions of the Constitution as well as the provisions of the statutes framed by the Legislature. From time to time, the provisions of the Constitution and the statutory arrangements are amended to meet the requirements of the day as well as to subserve the purpose of the men-in-power. But Judiciary plays the role of the custodian of the fundamental law of the land. In a federal set up, Union-State relations ever remain in a state of tension and the situation is further complicated by the operation of party system. But Judiciary comes to our rescue. It not only resolves the tangled issues, it also compels the popularly elected organs of the State to operate within restraints. Owing to this, our republican and democratic system with federal and parliamentary form of government is saved from being malfunctional or dysfunctional.

The study of Indian Polity is, for this reason, both interesting and perplexing to an average student of this subject. I have, therefore, made an attempt to place it in a concise form for the benefit of the students offering this course at the graduate levels or preparing for various competitive examinations. Every care has been taken to make the expressions lucid and to arrive at plausible conclusions in a detached manner. The views of eminent writers have been quoted and important case-law has been referred to where appropriate. All relevant topics have been discussed in the light of latest Constitution Amendment Acts as well as latest political developments. I shall feel obliged to the readers who convey their critical comments or suggestions to me in the light of which necessary changes shall be made in the next edition or print of this book.

— **J.C. Johari**

Contents

List of Tables and Charts

1

Geography, Economy, Society and Political Culture

India is not only a big country, she is also known as a subcontinent. Pakistan came into being as a result of India's partition in 1947. Known as the largest democracy in the world, India is the most 'developed' country among all the 'developing' countries of the globe. The success of democratic experiment in India should naturally be a source of inspiration for her immediate neighbours. With a population of about 100 millions (nearly the population of all African and Latin-American countries combined), she is the largest democracy with adult franchise since the late 1940 when it emerged as a sovereign nation-state after the termination of the British rule in 1947. About a dozen major languages and hundreds of dialects are spoken in India. Hindus constitute the largest chunk of the population, but followers of other faiths like Islam, Christianity and Buddhism also live here like citizens of a democratic and secular country. To a foreign scholar the durability of Indian democracy "is especially intriguing considering the diversity of Indian society."[1]

Land and People

India is the second most populous and the seventh largest country in the world. It has a land frontier of 152,000 km and a coastline of 6,083 km. The mighty Himalayas and other lofty mountains-Muztagh Ata, Aghil and Kunlun mountains to the north of Kashmir and Zaskar mountains to the east of Himachal Pradesh and north of Uttar

1. Atul Kohli: "India" in Mark Kesselman, Joel Krieger and W.A. Joseph (eds). *Democracies at the Corss-roads* (Lexington: D.C. Heath and Co., 1996) p. 289.

Pradesh-form India's northern boundary excluding the Nepal region. In the north India is adjoined by Nepal, Bhutan and China. In the east a series of mountain ranges and a belt of dense forests cuts her from Burma (Now Myanmar). The border States of Assam, Meghalaya, West Bengal, Tripura and Mizoram touch Bangladesh. In the extreme north-west she is bounded by Afghanistan. The border States of Jammu-Kashmir, Punjab, Rajasthan and Gujarat touch Pakistan in the West. South of the Tropic of Cancer, this country tapers off into the Indian Ocean between the Arabian Sea in the west and the Bay of Bengal in the east. The Gulf of Mannar and the Palk Strait separate India from Sri Lanka. The Andaman and Nocobar Islands in the Bay of Bengal and Lakshadweep in the Arabian Sea are parts of the territory of India.

The mainland comprises three well-defined regions -the great mountain zone, the Indo-Gangetic plains, and the Southern Peninsula. The Himalayas comprise three almost parallel ranges interspersed with large plateaus and valleys some of which, like the valleys of Kashmir and Kullu, are fertile, extensive and of great scenic beauty. Some of the highest peaks of the world like Everest and Kailash exist in these ranges. The mountain wall extends over a distance of about 2,400 km with a varying depth of 240 to 230 km. In the east between India on the one side and Burma (now Myanmar) and Bangladesh on the other the hill ranges are much lower. The Indo-Gangetic plains, about 2,400 km long and 240 to 320 km broad, are formed by the basin of three distinct river systems-the Indus, the Ganga and the Brahmaputra. They are one of the world's greatest stretches of flat alluvium and also one of the most densely populated areas on earth. Finally, the peninsular plateau is marked off from the Indo-Gangetic plains by a mass of mountains and hill ranges varying from 460 to 1,220 metres in height. Prominent among these are the Aravalli, Vindhya, Satpura, Maikala and Ajanta. The peninsula is flanked on one side by the Eastern Ghats where the average elevation is about 610 metres and on the other by Western Ghats where it is generally from 915 to 1,220 metres rising in places to cover 2,440 metres. Between the Western Ghats and the Arabian Sea lies a narrow coastal strip, while between the Eastern Ghats and the Bay of Bengal there is a broader coastal area. The southern point of the plateau is formed by the Nilgiri hills where the Eastern and Western Ghats meet.

A look at the map of India shows that in the north she is bounded by the great Himalayas and in the south by the Indian Ocean. The total area of the Indian Ocean is 74.92 million sq.km, that is approximately equal to the total area of Africa and Asia. The celebrated naval strategist, Admiral Alfred Mahan, was prophetic when he wrote: "Whoever controls the Indian Ocean dominates Asia. This Ocean is key to the seven seas. In the 21st century, the destiny of the world will be decided on its waters." In 1945 an eminent Indian historian and diplomat rightly pointed out: "While to other countries, the Indian Ocean is only one of the important oceanic areas, to India it is the vital sea. Her lifelines are concentrated in that area. Her future is dependent on the freedom of that vast winter surface. No industrial development, no commercial growth, no stable political structure is possible for her unless the Indian Ocean is free and her own shores are protected."[2]

India is a heavily populated country. According to the rough estimates of 2001, she has crossed the point of 100 crores. As such, now she is next to China, and is ranked as the second country in the world in respect of demographic make-up. The population figures of 2001 excludes population of areas under the unlawful occupation of Pakistan and China where census could not be taken. The total area of the country represents provisional 'Geographical Areas' as on 31 March 1982, supplied by the Survey of India. The area includes 78,114 sq. km under illegal occupation of Pakistan, 5,180 sq.km illegally handed over by Pakistan to China and 37,555sq. km under illegal occupation of China in Ladakh district.

The people of India are marked by great diversity in respects of religions, languages, dialects, racial and ethnic make-up and the like. The Hindus constitute majority of the population and the Sikhs, the Buddhists and the Jains, though they profess their own orders, are construed as belonging to the great Hindu fold. The Muslims, the Christians and the Parsis are the minorities from religious point of view. Besides, there are a very large number of castes and sub-castes whose total reaches the figure of 3,743 according to second Backward Classes Commission (Mandal Commission) Report of 1980. The Hindu society is broadly segmented into four broad castes-Brahmins, Kshattriyas, Vaishyas and Sudras or the 'untouchables', also known as 'Harijans'. But the further fragmentation of castes is very complicated and perplexing. Hinduism embraces many beliefs and practices from the highest to the lowest order. Its

---

2. K.M. Panikkar: *India and the Indian Ocean,* p. 85.

Area and Population of States and Union Territories (2001)

(According to rank)

	State/Union Territory	Capital	Population	Area (Sq. Kms)
	2	3	4	5
1.	Uttar Pradesh	Lucknow	16,60,52,859	2,38,566
2.	Maharashtra	Mumbai	9,67,52,247	3,07,762
3.	Bihar	Patna	8,28,78,796	94,163
4.	West Bengal	Kolkata	8,02,21,171	87,853
5.	Andhra Pradesh	Hyderabad	7,57,27,541	2,76,814
6.	Tamil Nadu	Chennai	6,21,10,839	1,30,069
7.	Madhya Pradesh	Bhopal	6,03,85,118	3,07,650
8.	Rajasthan	Jaipur	5,64,73,122	3,42,214
9.	Karnataka	Bangalore	5,27,33,958	1,91,733
10.	Gujarat	Ahmedabad	5,05,96,992	1,95,984
11.	Orissa	Bhubaneshwar	3,67,06,920	1,55,782
12.	Kerala	Thiruvanant-hapuram	3,18,38,619	38,864
13.	Jharkhand	Ranchi	2,69,09,428	79,714
14.	Assam	Dispur	2,66,38,407	78,523
15.	Punjab	Chandigarh	2,42,89,296	50,362
16.	Haryana	Chandigarh	2,10,82,989	44,222
17.	Chhattisgarh	Raipur	2,07,95,956	1,35191
18.	Delhi	Delhi	1,37,82,976	1,485
19.	Jammu & Kashmir	Srinagar	1,00,69,917	22,2236
20.	Uttarakhand	Dehradun	84,79,562	53,483
21.	Himachal Pradesh	Shimla	60,77,248	55,673
22.	Tripura	Agartala	31,91,168	10,477
23.	Manipur	Imphal	23,88,634	22,356
24.	Meghalaya	Shillong	23,06,069	22,489
25.	Nagaland	Kohima	19,88,636	16,527
26.	Goa	Panaji	13,43,998	3,702
27.	Arunachal Pradesh	Itanagar	10,91,117	83,578
28.	Punducherry	Punducherry	9,73,829	480
29.	Chandigarh	Chandigarh	9,00,914	114
30.	Mizoram	Aizol	8,91,058	21,087

31.	Sikkim	Gangtok	5,40,493	7,299
32.	Andaman & Nicobar Islands	Port Blair	3,56,265	8,293
33.	Dadra & Nagar Haveli	Silvassa	2,20,451	491
34.	Daman & Diu	Daman	1,58,059	112
35.	Lakshadweep	Kavaratti	60,595	32

N.B. The population of India includes the estimated population of Kachch district, Morvi, Maliya-Miyana and Wankaner talukas of Rajkot district, Jodiya taluka of Jamnagar district of Gujarat and entire Kinnaur district of Himachal Pradesh often opposed to or contradicting each other.

essental spirit seems to be to live and let live". According to Gandhiji, Hinduism is a relentless pursuit after truth.

Bharat is the original name of this country. It is given in the Vishnu Purana that the country south of the Himalayas and north of the vast sea (Indian Ocean) is Bharat and all born in it are called Bharatiyas. Similar references are traceable in the Rig Veda, the Mahabharata, the Ramayana, and other Sanskrit texts, all pointing out the cultural and political unity of India from the encircling northern mountains to the southern ocean.[3] By virtue of being the land of the Aryans, it also got the name of Aryavrata. Subsequently it became Hindustan (Hindostan) by virtue of being the land of the Hindus. The original word is Sindhu that became Hindu by virtue of its perversion at the hands of Muslim conquerors. It "would be interesting to note that the river Sindhu, which in Sanskrit means a vast mass of water like the ocean, was pronounced as Indus by the Greeks and later as 'Hindu' by the Persians. That is how the name 'India' came to be used for the land of the Indus. The name 'Hindustan' came from the word 'Hindu' which was the pronunciation in Persian of the word 'Sindhu'.[4]

Racial and ethnic variations may also be noted. While the people of the north claim themselves as belonging to the Aryan race, the people of the south proudly claim themselves to be of the Dravidian stock. Besides, the tribal people living mostly in the north-eastern

3. Vasant Sathe: *Towards Social Revolution*, pp. 39-40.

4. Jawaharlal Nehru: *The Discovery of India*, p. 77.

parts of the country have their distinct ethnic claims. Although the Constitution of India recognises 22 major languages of the country spoken by a sizeable number of people, there are innumerable dialects some which as Bhojpuri and Rajasthani claim themselves as a separate language of the land. On account of this we may take note of great variety in the cultural sphere. It is rightly said that the inhabitants of this country show an enormous variety of distinct racial and ethnic types. Corresponding to this complexity, the racial composition is the wealth of different cultural patterns, ranging from the primitiveness of semi-nomadic forest dwellers to the highly advanced stage of civilisation represented by the inhabitants of the great industrialised cities, such as Bombay (Mumbai) and Calcutta (Kolkata). Moreover, there are major religious and linguistic divisions and the differences between the populations of many parts of India are far more fundamental than those between the individual nations of Europe.[5]

However, the astonishing point is 'India's unity in the midst of diversity'. As Nehru realises: "The Pathan and the Tamil are two extreme examples; the others lie somewhere in between. All of them have their distinctive features, all of them have still more the distinguishing mark of India. It is fascinating to find how the Bengalis, the Marathas, the Gujaratis, the Tamils, the Andhras, the Oriyas, the Assamese, the Canarese, the Malayalis, the Sindhis, the Punjabis, the Pathans, the Kashmiris, the Rajputs and the great central block comprising the Hindustani-speaking people have retained their peculiar characteristics for hundreds of years, have still more or less the same virtues and failings of which old traditions on record tell us, and yet have been throughout these ages distinctively Indian, with the same national heritage and the same set of moral and mental qualities. There was something living and dynamic about this heritage which showed itself in ways of living and a philosophical attitude of life and its problems. Ancient India, like ancient China, was a world in itself, a culture and a civilisation which gave shape to all things. Foreign influences poured in and often influenced that culture and were absorbed. Disruptive tendencies gave rise immediately to an attempt to find a synthesis.

5. According to Linguistic Survey of India, there are 179 languages and 544 dialects.

Some kind of a dream of unity has occupied the mind of India since the dawn of civilisation."[6]

Socio-Cultural Diversity and Political Unity

Indian civilisation is very old. In most ancient times Indians could make marvellous researches in the fields of science, mathematics, astrology, astronomy, literature, philosophy, architecture, engineering, fine arts, medicine etc. The rishis (seers) produced the Vedas and the Upanisadas. Different schools of philosophy like Nyaya, Samkhya and Vaisheshek came into being. We may refer to the immortal contributions of Gautama, Kapila, Kanada, Gemini, Aryabhata, Bhaskara, Panini, Charka, Dhanvantri, Valmiki, etc. in this connection. The great seers wanted to discover and explain the secrets behind all the wonders; they kept on searching and inquiring till they felt that they had arrived at the truth. In course of time, different functions created a caste system having four main folds- the Brahmins or the worshippers, the Kshattriyas or the warriors (defenders), the Vaishyas or the traders, and the Sudras or the social servants. This division was based on the *guna* (quality) and *karma* (action) which automatically implied the principle of merit and specialisation. In course of time, the caste system became very rigid and its membership flowed from the fact of birth in a particular caste. More unfortunate than this rigid stratification was the evolution of a tendency to put four castes in an hierarchical order with the Brahmins followed by the Kshattriyas at the top, the Vaishyas in the middle and the Sudras at the bottom and treating them as 'untouchables'. The system in the beginning had its inherent advantages but when it "got stratified and began stagnating, then the urge for gaining new knowledge was lost probably because of an easy life and the preacher class acquired a dominant position. Then, it joined hands with the ruling class to evolve theories and customs in order to keep the rest of the society frightened and suppressed through blind faith."[7]

The fourfold division of the Hindu society into the form of different castes became more complicated with the emergence of sub-castes within each fold. The number went on increasing. Towards the end

6. Nehru, *op. cit.*, p. 63.

7. Vasant Sathe, *op. cit.*, p. 43.

of the twelfth century India came under the rule of the Muslim invaders. Not as much as a result of the influx of the Muslims from West Asia as owing to religious conversions on a large scale, the number of the followers of Islam increased. In course of time the interaction between the two cultures had its definite impact as a result of which both absorbed the basic qualities of each other. Not only the ways of the Sakas and the Huns but also of the Muslims became parts of the Indian culture. In the seventeenth century India saw the advent of the European Christians like the Portuguese, the French and the British. The British succeeded in establishing their imperial hold over this country and thus the layer of Christianity had its confluence with the Indian culture. It shows that the Indian social and cultural pattern has a composite character in which the merits of all faiths and professions have a harmonious confluence. The foundation and the unifying force is the 'Indian tradition' that believes in absorbing the merits of others and creating a synthesis of diverse ways of life. It may be described as the Brahmanical tradition.As Prof. Embree observes: "It is not Hinduism but one element of it, Brahmanical ideology, that has been a unifier in Indian civilization and a powerful force in maintaining its integrity in the face of tremendous onslaughts of two other great civilizations, the Islamic and the European."[8]

Herein lies the secret of India's deep and underlying fundamental unity in the midst of great social and cultural diversity. Different social, religious and cultural orders adopted the ways of synthesisation and harmonization and they never thought in terms of such distinct political entities as a result of which Christendom disintegrated and different nation-states came into being in Europe. Ashok and Akbar became 'great' emperors by following the policy of tolerance. If any ruler (as Aurangzeb) adopted ways violative of the principle of 'syncretism', it caused disintegration of the empire. Ellenborough made a point by arguing that "the Company's government could gain the whole Mughal inheritance but he must write and act for India, not for England."[9] Then, antedating Disraeli by thirty years, he envisioned the assumption of the imperial title by the Queen (Victoria) with all the chiefs and rulers of this country

---

8. A.T. Embree: "Indian Civilisation and Two Regional Cultures" in Paul Wallace (ed.): *Region and Nation in India*, p. 22.

9. *Ibid.*, p. 34.

becoming her feudatories. It shows that the British rulers after the termination of the Company rule in 1858 "also saw themselves as the inheritors of Ashoka and Akbar and increased the use of this nationalist use of history."[10]

The founding fathers of the Indian nationalist movement "correctly perceived that there was a possibility of creating one great Indian nation because India was not like Europe, Punjab was not like Spain and Madras was not like England, even though the English argued that the differences between the Indian regions were as great."[11] The British rulers unified the whole country politically. The leaders of the Indian National Congress strengthened the forces of nationalism on the basis of social and cultural harmony of the country. The country as a whole cried for 'swaraj' under the leadership of Mahatma Gandhi. And yet the British policy of 'divide and rule' could make its success because of the growing line of separatism and exclusivism so obdurately followed by the leaders of the Aligarh movement. A great nationalist of the country and once known as the 'ambassador of Hindu-Muslim unity' Jinnah had a change after 1928 and he put coping stone on this edifice by presenting the case of 'two nations' (Hindu and Muslim) that entailed the doom of India's political unity in 1947. And yet this fact should not be overlooked that, in spite of this partition, the life of the people of the two countries is marked by social and cultural links. This point is equally applicable to Bangladesh that came into being in 1971 as a result of the falsification of two-nation theory.

Economy

In spite of being rich in terms of natural resources and manpower, India is ranked among the economically backward countries of the world. The reason for this should be traced in her political subjugation and economic exploitation by the British colonial power. Apart from this, it should also be noted that her natural resources have not yet been fully exploited and that her economy is still predominantly agricultural. About half of this country's national income is derived from agriculture and some

10. *Ibid.*, p. 35.

11. *Ibid.*, p. 34.

allied activities which absorb nearly three-fourths of its working force. But the matter of satisfaction is that the natural resources of the country are capable of greater utilisation and, more important than this, since independence the aim has been to diversify the economy of the country by accelerating the pace of industrial development, to increase agricultural productivity and to achieve all-round progress through the machinery of planning.

India has adopted the pattern of mixed economy. The peopl have the right to private property. But the enjoyment and exercis of this right may be restricted or regulated by the state in the publi interest. As such, we have a 'private sector' of economy that is i the hands of the individuals. On the other hand, there is the publi sector that may be designated as the 'state sector'. Art.39 of th Directive Principles of State Policy enjoins that "the ownership an control of the material resources of the community are so distribute as best to subserve the common good and that the operation of th economic system does not result in the concentration of wealth an means of production to the common detriment." The Second Fiv Year Plan summed up the objectives of the planned developmen in the phrase 'socialist pattern of society'. It implied that "the basi criterion for determining the lines of advance must not be privat profit but social gain."

The Indian leaders well realised that a developing country lik ours had no alternative to entering the field of industrial an commercial enterprise if it wished to increase its productivity an the general standard of living. Thus, the vast expansion of the publi sector has not come out fortuitously, it is the result of planne development and the adoption of a particular social and economi philosophy. This economic argument "aims at the achievement of rapid growth of the economic infrastructure which, at the sam time, would guide private sector in its development. The socia argument seeks to prevent concentration of wealth and income i private hands and gives the State a commanding position in th economy."[12]

It may, however, be noted that in spite of many economi activities under state control, the general character of India

---

12. R.B Jain: *Contemporary Issues in Indian Administration*, p. 21

economy is liberalistic. In the total national output the share of the public sector is still less than 20 per cent. With the exception of some basic industries, all other important industries as cotton textiles, jute, sugar, cement, leather, vegetable oils etc. are in the private sector. It is more for the sake of winning votes than for rendering economic services to the people that some industry is nationalised in the public interest. For instance, the nationalisation of life insurance in 1955 and of scheduled banks in 1969 were done just to demonstrate socialistic professions of the government. Agriculture is the principal economic activity in the country and it is in the private sector. Moreover, the success of the private sector and the failure of the public sector should also be kept in view which enables a leading Indian economist to point out that "as of now, there is no evidence that, despite the growth of a large public sector, India has moved to any significant extent closer to a socialist society in any meaningful sense of the term. If the present trends are not going to be reversed, it is possible that India will witness in the closing decade of this century a considerably enlarged private sector with further erosion of the role of planning in the traditional sense of the term."[13]

It, however, does not imply that the government has been neglectful towards the growth of monopoly trends in the country. It is a fact that since independence monopoly houses have grown rapidly and with it the concentration of economic power in the country has also increased. The Committee on Distribution of Income and Levels of Living (under the chairmanship of P.C. Mahalanobis) admitted in its report (1960) that the working of planned economy had contributed to this serious development. The Monopolies Inquiry Commission confirmed that there were 75 big business houses in 1963-64 controlling 44 per cent of the paid up capital of all non-government and non-banking companies of the country. In absolute terms they had control over capital worth Rs. 2,606 crores. Another committee headed by Prof. Subimal Dutt (called Industrial Licensing and Policy Inquiry Committee) showed its agreement with the rise of 20 big business houses with the Tatas

13. Sukhomoy Chakravarty: "Policy Making in Mixed Economy-The Indian Case" in PR. Brahmanand and V.R. Panchmukhi (ed.s): *The Development Process of the Indian Economy*, p. 733.

at the top possessing the assets of Rs. 520.6 crores. Since then monopoly trends appear to have become stronger and the grip of big business on the economy of the country seems to have increased in spite of all measures of the government taken to control them. For instance, each of the 20 big business houses in 1983 had control over capital assets worth Rs. 292 crores or more, while the assets of the Birlas could touch the figure of 2,831 crores of rupees. It shows that the Monopolies and Restrictive Trade Practices Act (1970) had failed to achieve the desired purpose.

It would, therefore, be wrong to agree with any social and economic theorist who, after taking into his account the growth of public sector and the professions and economic planning, characterises it as 'state capitalism'. Instead we may endorse the view of Prof. Chakravarty that "adherence to a mixed economy does not imply that it will grow into that many people once thought to be its rationale, i.e., a socialist pattern of society. In fact, a mixed economy is an unstable blend of different features which is dynamically compatible with different outcomes."[14]

It should also be taken into account that, as the experience shows, "the so-called nationalised sector, known broadly as the public sector, has provided greater scope for economic inefficiency, heavy losses and a strain on public resources. The simplistic denunciation of the entire private sector as exploitative, anti-national and capitalist and eulogising the pubic sector managed by paid servants in the name of socialism and therefore sacrosanct, have proved to be a highly disastrous feature which has somehow cast a spell on the entire economic system."[15]

The way for the growth of public sector was opened after the Indian National Congress adopted the goal of 'socialist pattern of society' at its Awadi session in 1955 and then the government of Nehru adopted the Industrial Policy Resolution in 1956. It was declared that the state "will progressively assume predominance and direct responsibility for setting up new industrial undertakings and for developing transport facilities." The objectives of seting up public enterprises were:

---

14. *Ibid.*, p. 731.

15. Sathe, *op. cit.*, p. 187.

(*i*) to promote rapid economic development through creation and expansion of infra-structure,

(*ii*) to generate financial resources for development,

(*iii*) to promote redistribution of national income and wealth,

(*iv*) to create employment opportunities,

(*v*) to promote balanced regional growth,

(*vi*) to encourage the development of small-scale and ancillary industries, and

(*vii*) to promote exports on the one side and import substitution on the other.

These objectives were to be achieved through the process of planning. As a former member of the Planning Commission visualised: "Securing rapid economic growth and expansion of employment, reduction of disparities in income and wealth, prevention of concentration of economic power, and creation of values and attitudes have been among the objectives of the plans."[16]

In course of time, it appeared that the public sector had developed shortcomings. Such undertakings had to suffer mounting losses owing to over-staffing and inefficiency. After 1990 the waves of liberalisation and globalisation had their effect on the Indian economy. So the government of Narsimha Rao on the advice of Finance Minister Manmohan Singh adopted the Liberalisation, Privatisation and Globalisation (LPG) model that unleashed the era of economic reforms in the country. It signified more emphasis on the growth of private sector and invitation to foreign investments. The government of Vajpayee moved ahead in the same direction of economic reforms. It implemented the policy of disinvestment in the public sector with greater zeal. The economic policy-makers realised what Prof. J.M. Keynes had said in 1926: "The world is not so governed from above that private and social interests always coincide... It is not a correct deduction from the principles of economics that enlightened self-interest always operates in the public interest. Nor is it true that self-interest is generally enlightened."

16. B.S. Minhas: *Planning and the Poor*, p. vii

The main features of the new economic policy introduced in 1991 by the government of Rao may be pointed out as under:

1. Areas hitherto reserved for the public sector have been opened to private sector and the Government intends to transfer loss-making units to the private sector.
2. The Government has removed the shackles whereby the private sector may set up its industrial units and the ceiling of the money to be invested (as imposed by the Monopolies and Restriction of Trade Practices Act) has also been lifted.
3. Direct foreign investment upto 51 per cent of equity has been permitted in high priority areas.
4. Greater autonomy has been given to public sector undertakings so as to make them more professional.
5. The economy of the country has been opened to other countries so as to encourage more exports.

But the critics take it as mortgaging of Indian economy to great global agencies like International Monetary Fund and World Bank. It is said that India has lost her economic sovereignty and by allowing the entry of foreign investments and multi-national corporations we have done a lot of injustice to the native industries. But the defenders of the new policy have their own argument. In their view, it would enable India to make astonishing development as has happened in countries like China, Japan, South Korea, Taiwan and Malaysia.

This economic policy covered the decade of 1991-2000 and now it is known as the era of 'first generation reforms'. The government of Vajpayee had Yashwant Sinha as its Finance Minister who added some new points and so came the phase of 'second generation reforms'. It is also known as 'rethinking on the development strategy in India'. In March 2000 Sinha laid stress on these points:

1. To strengthen the foundation of the growth of our rural economy, especially agriculture and allied activities.
2. To nurture the revolutionary potential of the new knowledge-based industries as infotech, biotechnology and pharmaceuticals.
3. To strengthen and modernise traditional industries as textiles and leather.

4. To remove hurdles in the making of power, roads, ports, railways, airways, telecommunication etc.,
5. To accord highest priority to human resource development and social programmes in the spheres of education and public health,
6. To strengthen our role in world economy through rapid growth of exports, higher foreign investments and prudent external debt management.
7. To establish a credible framework of fiscal discipline.

The model of development set up by the government of Nehru on the advice of P.C. Mahalanobis has now been replaced to a great extent. The fundamental idea however, is the same 'growth with social justice and equity'. A new term 'social sector' has been invented which implies rendering of basic minimum services to the people like universal primary education, primary health care, safe drinking water, shelter for all, family welfare, sanitation, rural development etc., It was visualised in the Tenth Five Year Plan (2002-2007): "Although growth has strong direct poverty reducing effects, the frictions and rigidity in the Indian economy can make the process less effective and the Tenth Plan must therefore be formulated in a manner which explicity addresses the need to ensure equity and social justice."

India's corporate sector is one of the major driving forces of its economic growth. From major multinational corporations to small and medium enterprises and ranging across a wide diversity of sectors including manufacturing, construction and telecom services, corporate sector has played a significant role in the economic development of the country. The growth and development of corporate sector was enabled by the liberal reforms introduced in the country from time to time. To meet the expectations of the corporate sector and its stockholders in the changing national and global business environment, the Ministry of Corporate Affairs has expanded its efforts through a number of initiatives to bring about 'good governance'. These initiatives aim at improving the legislative framework and administrative set up to enable every incorporation and exit of the companies, convenient compliance of regulations with transparency and accountability in corporate governance.

Growth of Corporate Sector in India

Year	*No. of Companies (limited by shares)*	*Paid up Capital (in crores of rupees)*	*Percentage of Contribution of the GDP*
1982	72,402	18,935.5	11.1
1987	1,40,670	43,967.5	14.0
1992	2,50,361	84,642.3	12.9
1997	4,50,950	1,90,518.6	13.8
2002	5,89,246	4,05,753.2	17.8
2003	6,12,155	4,57,058.7	18.7
2004	6,41,512	4,98,790.8	18.1
2005	6,79,649	6,54,021.6	21.0
2006	7,72,169	6,19,152.0	16.7
2007	7,43,678	7,06,560.0	16.49
2008	7,69,145	9,24,028.0	18.68
2009	7,86,774	10,03,887	18.1

Source: *India—A Reference Annual*, 2012, p. 484.

Political Culture

A brief discussion of the political culture has now become an important part of the study of political system of a country in view of this realization that "every political system is embedded in a particular pattern of orientation to political actions."[17] The political culture of a people refers to their beliefs, convictions, views and commitments in relation to political values and institutions. According to Sidney Verba, it "consists of the system of empirical beliefs, expressive symbols of values which define the situation in which political action takes place. It provides the subjective orientation to politics."[18] That is, it "refers to the

17. G.A. Almond: "Comparative Political System" in *Journal of Politics*, Vol.18, 1956.

18. Sidney Verba: "Comparative Political Culture" in Pye and Verba (eds): *Political Culture and Political Development*, p. 513

system of beliefs about patterns of political interaction and political institutions. It refers not to what is happening in the world of politics but what people believe about these happenings."[19] It is, therefore, obvious that the concept of political culture suggests that the traditions of a society, the spirit of its public institutions, the passions and the collective reasoning of its citizenry, and the style and operating code of its leaders are not just random products of historical experience but fit together as a part of a meaningful whole and constitute an intellectual web of relations. For the individual the political culture provides controlling the collectivity; it gives a systematic structure of values and rational considerations which ensures coherence in the performance of institutions and organizations."[20]

Indian political culture has the peculiarity of being traditional in some, modern in some other, and also a curious hotch-potch of the two in certain other respects. People's attachment with the bonds of casteism, communalism, parochialism, linguism, tribalism and the like constitutes a clear case of traditionalism in the Indian political culture, while movements for more and more educational and social reforms, for opportunities of employment, and for democratization of the decision-making process constitute instances of the modern political culture that is a definite result of the dispersion of power in post-independence era. With the inauguration of a democratic and secular system in the country under the Constitution, social and political institutions have come so close to each other that one has affected the other to a considerable extent.

The element of tradition in the political culture of India may be noted in several important directions. For instance, most of the people living particularly in the poor and backward parts of the country have faith in caste and communal ties with the result that election campaigns are conducted on the lines of wooing their votes. If the element of tradition prevails in the rural and relatively backward parts of the country, the element of modernity in India's

---

19. *Ibid.*, p. 516.

20. L.W.Pye: "Introduction: Political Culture and Political Development", *Ibid.*, p. 7.

political culture may be seen in the language of the Constitution, the system of law and justice in the courts, composition and functioning of the legislative bodies, running of administrative machinery, role of the press and mass media, and working of the political parties. In other words, modernity "expresses itself in policies and interests, programmes and plans, arguments and representations, discussions and demonstrations, deliberations and decisions."[21]

In a democratic, secular and socialist system of India, the phenomenon of elite versus mass political culture may also be taken note of. While the elite political culture is a legacy of the foreign colonial rule, the emerging mass political culture is a consequence of the freedom struggle. The former may also be called 'defensive political culture' in view of the fact that it is very critical of the success of a popular system in which decision-making process is shared by more and more people of the country. It has been the ruling culture of the country and its manifestation may be noticed in its unwillingness to share power with the common lot. Naturally, the leaders of the emerging mass culture condemn the class of the elites as the 'band of exploiters' and strive as well as struggle for their participation in the avenues of power. They take inspiration from the forces of tradition, but they also desire to take advantage of the advanced political and administrative apparatus of the country. To them government is no longer a thing to be feared, it is an instrument that they should handle themselves for their political ends. As Weiner says: "Under the new democratic structure political leadership is often torn between attractions of the older pattern of aloofness and the new requirement of intimacy with citizens. One important consequence of this change and of the greater developmental activities pursued by the government is that the punitive image of government which was so prevalent in the pre-independence era is rapidly being replaced by a more instrumental view. Rural people are developing high expectations with respect to the services government can perform for them."[22]

---

21. W.H. Morris–Jones: "India's Political Idioms" in C.H. Phillips (ed). *Politics and Society in India*, pp. 133-54.
22. Myron Weiner: "India–Two Political Cultures" in Pye and Verba (eds), *op. cit.*, pp. 219-20.

Both kinds of political culture are neither wholly traditional nor wholly modern, they are a complex amalgam of tradition and modernity and, for this reason, both feed and fatten on each other. Those subscribing to the elite culture have realized that they have to make rapport with the emerging mass culture and those subscribing to the 'mass culture' have taken it for granted that they cannot remain in positions of power and influence without having some kind of rapport with the elite culture of the country. Though several factors as religion, caste, language, ethnicity etc. divide people, the politicians of diverse 'hues' join together in a common search for prestige and power. Different kinds of loyalties cut across each other and politics plays the role of a great unifier. When such persons manage to secure control of the national government, they face the formidable task of making the emerging mass political culture acceptable to the national elite while, at the same time, they make intelligent modification in their own 'mass culture' so that it is "truly conducive both to modernization and a stable democratic system."[23]

It is a fact that the pattern of Indian political culture lacks homogeneity. According to Rajni Kothari, there are a series of regional, caste and community cultures, political cultures, and a national political culture on the top of all of them. In other words, there are two levels of cultural orientations in politics-one is at the level of society, individual, elite which cuts across all the divisions of region and language and to that extent there is an all-India frame. But there are also specific folk orientations towards authority, towards symbolism, towards power which are in some ways much more real, because people live in folk cultures. The whole spectrum ranges from looking at authority with a sense of reverence mixed with awe to that of openly challenging it and attempting to grab it for the realization of specific political ends.

Power must be grabbed by any means-by muscle power, by money power, or by the power of 'personality'. It is for this reason that while some use their purse to grab power, others adopt ways of the 'criminals' for the same purpose. The result is that high public offices become a source of attraction for seeking selfish ends in the name

---

23. *Ibid.*, p. 244.

of 'social service'. Pragmatism of the worst sort informs politica behaviour which enables a foreign writer to comment: "Instead ther is growing in public life a struggle for power by men who ar concerned with patronage and power for its own sake. The result i a bitter struggle for the fishes and loaves of office, and intens factionalism within the growing party based not on differences i policy but on competing personal loyalties and ambitions. Thus, th party functionaries are less concerned with the specific politics an ideology of the people than they are with access to power."[24]

The saintly tradition has its own part in the making of India political culture. The people pay great regard to those who renounc all worldly pleasures for the sake of doing social service. They ar virtually adored and their words have an electrical effect on th behaviour of the people. They treat politics not as a struggle fc power but as a mode of public service. This can be traced in the rol of Mahatma Gandhi, Vinoba Bhave and Jayaprakash Narayan. Bu politics has its own part too behind its outward renunciation i some cases. Some shrewd leaders assume the form of saints fc being successful in the field of politics. The heads of the religiou places become the 'masters' and 'controllers' of the politicians of particular sort and it is also possible that the 'saints' and th 'swamis' adopt ways where struggle against power becomes a mas for struggle for power.

In short, the political culture of India represents a peculia blending of three 'idioms'—tradition, modernity and saintliness. Th presence, the confrontation and, indeed, the mixing of all the thre "dominates the Indian political scene and gives it a distinctive tone." The three 'idioms' may also be described as the three 'languages' Indian politics and their simultaneous flow may be traced in th operation of what Rajni Kothari calls, the 'Congress system'. Morri Jones observes that "Congress is one of the great meeting-places all the three languages of politics."[26] What is, however, a matter great anxiety is that in recent times the trend of 'amoral politics' emerging. This brand of politics is characterised by a decline of th

---

24. Weiner, *op. cit.*, p. 232.

25. Morris–Jones, *op. cit.*, p. 64.

26. *Ibid.*, p. 67.

political values associated with democratic institutions. Some leaders have been publicly crying for practising 'value-based politics' with a view to give a setback to the rising trend of 'criminalisation' of politics. "Many politicians and their children are in league with black marketeers or other criminal elements and yet are rarely penalised for their transgressions." [27] Such politicians are considered to be 'free looters' interested only in 'plunder and power' and they may also be called 'half-educated money-making simpletons'.[28]

The decline of 'creative leadership' may also be taken into account owing to which the use of extra-constitutional and blatantly unconstitutional means is becoming an accepted part of people's political behaviour. A new conviction is growing that only violence pays. Thus, the techniques of *ahimsa* and *satyagraha,* as evolved and practised by Gandhiji, are becoming more and more irrelevant and their practice is now very much adulterated with the vices of fraud and hypocrisy. The acceptance of the patron-client relationship rooted in 'amoral politics' is becoming a part of the political culture. It substantiates the view that "self-interest provides the necessary political cement when neither a traditional governing elite nor a ruling group based upon ideological class interest is available."[29]

Three important conclusions may be drawn from it. First, political struggles in a relatively poor democracy are especially likely to be contentious. Given the multi-cultural nature of India, many of these struggles readily become ethnic conflicts; the lines of conflict are sometimes defined along religion, at other times, along language or territorial attachments. Second, the growing contentiousness among groups is political in the sense that mobilised groups seek to influence who rules and what the rulers do. In other words, numerous mobilised groups want more of what is valued in society,

---

27. Y.K. Malik: "India-Social Structure and Political Culture" in Craig Baxter and others (eds): *Government and Politics in South Asia*, p. 54.

28. Arun Shourie: "The State as Private Property" *in Economic and Political Weekly* (Bombay), March 1980, p. 508.

29. J.C. Scott: "Corruption, Machine Politics and Political Change" in *American Political Science Review* (December, 1969) p. 1151.

namely, wealth, status and power, and expect the government to fulfil their demand. And, third, "although growing conflicts often push Indian politics to the brink, somehow India's democracy in the nearly fifty years since independence has managed to pull back, absorb the crises, and muddle through, albeit with a strained democratic system."[30]

30. Atul Kohli, *op. cit.*, p. 288.

2

Constitutional Development
(1773–1935)

Despite the fact that the system of imperialism or colonialism is patently based on the twin facts of economic exploitation and political subjugation, its zealous architects resort to the technique of implementing legislative measures so as to offer a desperate justification for their blunders and heinous crimes. The main purpose behind it is to pose their 'rule of sword' as the 'rule of law'. Statutes after statutes are enforced to establish 'supremacy of law' over 'supremacy of man' with the definite motive of putting a mask on the misdeeds of the empire-builders.[1] But the facts remain facts and the growing tide of nationalism in the subject country exposes the hollowness of the tall claims of the bearers of 'white man's burden'. Paradigms after paradigms are constructed to somehow maintain the balance between the interests of the empire and the demands of the dependent people. So happened in India first under the rule of the East India Company and then under the British Crown. An English historian frankly admits. "To disguise the blunders and crimes of the English East India Company and to maintain that the British administration were always swayed by impeccable motives and unerring statesmanship is to produce unrealistic and impossible picture, for we are dealing after all with the human agency."[2]

Regulating Act of 1773

The East India Company, a trading organisation of the English capitalist class, came into being when Queen Elizabeth I granted its Charter on 31st December, 1600. It was given for a period of 15

1. Lenin is right in saying that empire "is a bread and butter issue. If you want to avoid civil war, you must become imperialists." Cited in R.J.C. Young: *Post-Colonialism: An Historical Introduction*, p.22.

2. P.E. Roberts: *History of British Rule in India*, p.24.

years, but it could be terminated by giving a notice of two years. By the terms of the Charter, the Company was authorised "to traffic and trade freely into and from the East Indies, in the countries, and parts of Asia and Africa, and into and from all islands, ports, havens, cities, creeks, towns and places of Asia and Africa and America, or any of them beyond the Cape of Bona Esperanza to the Streights of Magellan. "In 1609 King James I renewed the Charter 'for ever', though it could be terminated by giving a notice of at least three years.

From time to time, the British Government granted concessions to the Company. For instance, in 1615 it was authorised to issue commissions to its captains. In 1623 it was authorised to grant commissions to its Presidents and Chief Officers for the punishment of offences committed by the servants of the Company. The city of Bombay (now Mumbai) was under the rule of the Portuguese, but it was gifted by King Alfonso XVI to King Charles II of England who had married his younger sister. In 1668 this city was given away to the East India Company by the King of England. In 1683 the Company was given the power to declare war and make peace with any other power. It also got the power to raise, arm, train and muster a sufficiently strong army. The Charter of 1686 authorised the Company to appoint Admirals and other naval officers. it shows that with the passage of time, the Company had more and more powers which enabled it to implement its policy of territorial conquests and annexations in India.

The Mysore and the Maratha wars entailed favourable results to the Company. Gradually, a big portion of South India came under the control of the Company and so the two provinces of Bombay and Madras were carved out and placed under the charge of the Governors. The victory of the Company in the battle of Plassey (1757) established its hold over the province of Bengal. Then, by its victory in the battle of Buxar (1764) it got rights of civil administration in the provinces of Bengal, Bihar and Orissa. The victory of Bengal was, indeed, a great achievement that ascribed to Lord Clive the title of being the 'founder of the English rule in India.' He became the Governor of Bengal and there he introduced the system of 'double government'[3]. Now the leaders of the new

---

3. The system of 'dual government' signified the separation of civil administration (*Diwani*) from matters of defence, police and administration of criminal justice (*Nizamat*). The problem arose

industrial class in England like Fox, Sheridan and Burke thought in terms of establishing their effective control over the affairs of the Company. "It represented an offensive not so much against an individual as against a system."[4] The affairs of the Company had become unmanageable and the dyarchical system of Bengal was doing havoc to the people. Since the matter was taken up by the Parliament of England, a Secret Committee was set up to study the whole case. It submitted its report in May, 1773. On the basis of its recommendations, the Regulating Act came into being. Its main provisions were:

1. It gave the right of vote for the election of the Directors of the Company to the share-holders holding stock worth one thousand pounds for 12 months preceding the date of election. They were to be elected for a term of four years, one-fourth of them to retire after every year.
2. The Governor of Bengal was made the Governor-General and so the Governors of Bombay and Madras came under his control. He was given an Executive Council of four members.[5] They were to be appointed by the Court of Directors of the Company, but their names were to be approved by the British Crown. They were vested with the whole civil and military government of the said Presidency, and also the ordering, the management, and Governments of territorial acquisitions and revenues in the Kingdoms of Bihar, Bengal and Orissa.

---

when Emperor Shah Alam in a decree signed on 12 August, 1765 granted the Diwani functions to the Company. After some time, the Company also got Nizamat from the Nawab of Bengal. But the authority of the Nawab continued as a shadow to put all responsibility on him. Two Indian Diwans were appointed-one having the charge of Nizamat and the other one having the charge of revenue collection. Both were under the nominal authority of the Nawab but under the real control of the Company. It was a trick played by Clive to pose that Bengal was not under the exclusive control of the Company. It proved a sham and made the role of the Company unpopular.

4. Rajni Palme Dutt: *India Today*, p. 115.
5. By this Act, Warren Hastings, the then Governor of Bengal, was appointed as the Governor-General and the Act itself specified the names of four Executive Councillors, namely, Clavering, Monson, Francis and Barwell.

3. The Governor-General-in-Council was given the power to make rules, ordinances and regulations for the good order and civil government of Company's settlement at Fort William and factories and places subordinate to it.

4. The Governors-in-Council of Bombay and Madras were required to pay obedience to the orders of the Governor-General of Bengal. They were required to submit to the Governor-General-in-Council advice and intelligence on transactions and matters relating to the government, revenues and interests of the Company.

5. It provided for Supreme Court at Calcutta with a Chief Justice and three puisne judges. Sir E. Impay was appointed as its first Chief Justice. It was given the power to try civil, criminal, admiralty and ecclesiastical cases.

But it had some defects which may be put as under:

1. It vitiated the composition of the Home Government of the Company. The raising of the qualifications of the voters among the proprietors turned the Court of Directors more or less into a permanent oligarchy.

2. It did not specify the jurisdictions of the Governor-General-in-Council and of the Supreme Court as a result of which situations of conflict arose which could be solved by the Judicature Act of 1781.

3. It weakened the position of the Governor-General. The decisions of the Executive Council were to be taken by the majority of votes. In the event of a tie, he had the right to cast his vote. He could not set aside the view of the majority of the members of his Council.

4. Specific provisions were not made whereby the Governor-General-in-Council could exercise effective control over the presidencies of Bombay and Madras.

5. It made the Supreme Court so powerful that it claimed to have jurisdiction over the revenue collectors of the Company for the wrongs done by them in their official capacity. It also claimed its authority to try judicial officers of the Company for the wrongs done by them in their official capacity.

As late as in 1918 the authors of the Report on Constitutional Reforms pointed out that this Act "created a Governor-General who was powerless before his own Council and an executive that was powerless before a Supreme Court itself immune from all responsibility for peace and welfare of the country–a system that was made workable by the genius and fortitude of one great man."[6]

However, this Act has its own importance in the constitutional history of India. It established the control of the British Parliament over the affairs of the Company that increased more and more with the passage of time. It was mentioned in this Act that the work of the Company in India would be reviewed after every 20 years. It implied that the Parliament got the power to terminate its rule after any twenty years on the ground of an adverse report of the reviewers. It "definitely recognised the political functions of the Company, because it asserted for the first time the right of the Parliament to dictate the form of government what was considered till then the private possession of the Company (by an important section of the people of England); and because, it is the first of a long series of Parliamentary statutes that altered the form of government in India."[7]

Judicature Act of 1781

As pointed out above, this Act removed some of the defects of the Regulating Act. It exempted the actions of the public servants of the Company done by them in their official capacity from the jurisdiction of the Supreme Court. So were exempted the Revenue Collectors and the judicial officers of the Company. The Governor-General and the members of his Executive Council were exempted from the jurisdiction of the Supreme Court, both individually and collectively, for anything counselled, ordered or done by them in their public capacity. The Court was to have full jurisdiction over the inhabitants of Calcutta and determine all kinds of suits and actions against them. The Company was to maintain registers containing the names and occupations of its Indian employees. The Governor-General-in-Council was given the power to make

---

6. *Montfort Report* (1918), para 14.

7. G.N. Singh: *Landmarks in Indian Constitutional and National Development,* pp. 14-15.

regulations for the Provincial Courts and Councils. Appeals were to be taken from the Provincial Courts to the Governor-General-in-Council.

Pitt's India Act of 1784

This amending act could not remove all the shortcomings of the Regulating Act. In April 1783 Dundas, a member of the Opposition, moved a bill whereby the Crown was to have the powers to recall the principal servants of the Company. The control of the Presidency of Bengal over the Presidencies of Bombay and Madras was to be increased. The Governor-General was to have the power of acting on his own responsibility in opposition to the opinions of his Executive Councillors. He was to be empowered to hold the office of the Commander-in-Chief. But this bill could not be passed. Then, in November 1783 came the Fox India Bill. It proposed to abolish the Board of Directors and the Court of Proprietors and instead set up two other bodies. Seven Commissioners or Directors were to administer the revenues and territories of India. They were to appoint or dismiss all persons in the service of the Company. They were to be named in the Act itself and were irremoveable except on an address from either House of Parliament. Vacancies were to be filled by the Crown. Nine Assistant Directors were to be nominated from amongst the proprietors with largest holdings in the Company. They were to be appointed for a term of five years and vacancies were to be filled by the Court of Proprietors. It was passed by the House of Commons, but it was defeated in the House of Lords.

But the bill moved by Pitt, the Younger, was passed by the Parliament in August, 1784. He took the precaution of banking on the pleasure of King George III as well as neutralising the opposition of the Company. It is owing to this fact that while the bill of Fox fell through in the Lords, the bill of Pitt had its safe passage. Its main provisions were:

1. It provided for a Board of Control of six Privy Councillors with comprehensive powers of supervision and control over Indian administration.
2. A Secret Committee consisting of three Directors was appointed to take the place of the Court of Directors in political and military matters.

3. The Directors were to retain the right of making appointments to different offices in India.
4. The Court of Proprietors was deprived of its right of over-riding the decisions of the Court of Directors.
5. The Governor-General-in-Council was given the power to superintend, control and direct the administration of several presidencies.
6. The number of the Executive Councillors was reduced from 4 to 3 so that Governor-General could act a little independently of the hold of his Councillors.
7. The Governor-General was to be appointed by the Court of Directors with the approval of the Crown, but no such approval was required in matters relating to the appointment of Governors of the Presidencies and the Executive Councillors of the Governor-General and the Governors. It made some improvement of course. Now a body of six Privy Councillors headed by the Chancellor of Exchequer could have a watch at the day-to-day activities of the administration of the Company in India. The Governor-General could act a little independently if two of the Councillors were on his side.

And yet some deficiencies persisted. The Act of 1786 made the Governor-General (Cornwallis at that time) the Commander-in-Chief of the Indian forces. He was also given the power to override the view of his Executive Council on his own responsibility. Then came the Declaratory Act of 1788. It vested full powers in the Board of Control headed by a Privy Councillor (Dundas at that time) and provided that the Directors should place annual accounts of the Company before the Parliament.

Charter Acts of 1793, 1813, 1833 and 1853

As given in the Regulating Act, the administration of the Company was renewed after every twenty years. The life of the Charter was extended or renewed again and again, but in the revised arrangement some important modifications were also made. For this sake, we should study their main provisions. The Charter Act of 1793 was a very long one having these important provisions:

1. The Governor-General and Governors were given the power to over-ride their Councils. The control of the Governor-General over the presidencies of Madras and Bombay was emphasised. It was laid down that when a Governor-General visited a Presidency, he superseded the Governor.

2. The Governor-General was given the power to appoint a Vice-President of his Executive Council from the members of the Council. The Vice-President was to act in place of the Governor-General when the latter was absent.

3. The Commander-in-Chief was not to be a member of the Council of the Governor-General unless he was specially appointed to be a member by the Court of Directors.

4. No leave or absence out of India was to be allowed to the Governor-General, Governors, the Commander-in-Chief and a few other high officials during their tenure of office.

5. It was provided that the payment of the members and the staff of the Board of Control should be made out of the Indian revenues. The two junior members of the Board of Control need not be Privy Councillors.

6. The Act tried to regulate the finances of the Company. A particular amount was assumed to be the annual surplus of the Company. Out of the annual surplus, five pounds were to go to the liquidation of the debts of the Company, and a similar amount was to be absorbed in increasing the dividend from 8 per cent to 10 per cent.

The Charter Act of 1793 renewed the Charter of the Company for 20 years. When the time for the renewal of the Charter arrived, there was a lot of agitation. The people demanded the ending of the commercial monopoly of the Company. Stalwarts like Warren Hastings, Malcolm and Munro defended the monopoly of the Company Ultimately the Charter Act of 1813 was passed. It had these provisions:

1. It renewed the charter of the East India Company for 20 years. The Company was deprived of its monopoly of trade with India. But she was to enjoy her monopoly of trade with China for 20 years. The Indian trade was thrown open to all British merchants and Indian subjects, although they had to work under certain limitations.

2. Maintenance of forces was to be the first charge on the revenues of the Company, payment of interest was the second charge, and the maintenance of the civil and commercial establishment was the third charge. Provisions were also made for the reduction of the debt of the Company. The Company was required to keep its commercial and territorial accounts separately.
3. It was provided that not more than 29 thousand troops were to be maintained out of the revenues of the Company. The Company was authorised to make laws, regulations and articles of war for the Indian troops. It was also authorised to provide for the holding of the Court Martial.
4. The Act provided for the religious learning and education of the people of India. A sum of Rs. 100,000 a year was to be set apart and applied to the revival and improvement of literature and the encouragement of the learned natives of India and for the introduction and promotion of a knowledge of the sciences among the inhabitants of the British territories in India.
5. The Act also made provision for the training of the civil and military servants of the Company.

The Charter of the Company had been given in 1813. When the time for its renewal drew nearer, there was a lot of agitation for the abolition of the Company and the taking over of the administration of India by the Crown. There was a searching parliamentary enquiry. Lord Macaulay gave a memorable speech in Parliament advocating the retention of the Company as an organ of the Government of India. The great Reform Act had been passed in 1832. The Parliament was in a mood of reform. The Charter Act of 1833, that was said to be the outcome of much enquiry and consideration, was a great landmark[8] with these provisions:

1. The Act of 1813 had abolished the monopoly of the Company as regards Indian trade, but had allowed the Company the monopoly of Chinese trade. That monopoly was also abolished in 1833. After 1833, the Company was to have no commercial functions. It was to have only political functions.

8. A.B. Keith: *The Constitutional History of India, 1600-1935*, p. 131.

2. The President of the Board of Control became minister for Indian Affairs. He was to have two Assistant Commissioners and they were to be his assistants and not colleagues. His secretary occupied a position of great influence because he was usually in Parliament and spoke for his chief when the latter sat in the House of Lords.

3. This Act centralised the administration of the country. The Governor-General of Bengal became the Governor-General of India. The Governor-General-in-Council was given the power to control, superintend, and direct the civil and military affairs of the Company. Bombay, Madras and Bengal and other districts were placed under the complete control of the Governor-General-in-Council. All revenues were to be raised under the authority of the Central Government and it was to have complete control over the expenditure. Provincial Governments were to spend only that money which was approved for them.

4. This Act brought about complete legislative centralisation. The Presidencies of Bombay and Madras lost their right to make their laws. The Governor-General-in-Council became the only law-making authority in Inda. It could make laws almost on all subjects. These laws were applicable to all things and to all persons in British India. They were enforceable by all the courts in India. No one could refuse to enforce them. The Govenor-General-in-Council could make Articles of War and Code of Military discipline, and provide for the administration of justice. The Law Member was to be consulted whenever a new law was to be passed. The laws passed by the Government of India were to be called Act. Before 1833, the enactments of the Bombay, Madras and Bengal Councils were known as Regulations.

5. The Act added one more member to the Executive Council of the Governor-General. He was to be known as the Law Member. His work was purely legislative. He attended meetings of the Government of India by special invitation. He had no vote in the Council. The quorum of three was fixed for legislative work and of two for administrative work. In these provisions, one may find the faint beginnings of a Legislative Council as distinct from the Executive Council.

6. The number of members of the Council of the Governors of Bombay and Madras was reduced to two. Bombay and Madras were to keep their separate armies under their Commanders-in-Chief, but they were to be under the control of the Central Government.

7. It provided for the codification of the law in India. Before 1833, laws were "so imperfect that in many cases it was quite impossible to ascertain what the law was." It authorised the Governor-General to appoint the Indian Law Commissioners to study, collect and codify various rules and regulations prevalent in India. The Law Member was to be its Chairman. As a result of the labours of the Indian Law Commission, the Indian Penal Code and the Codes of Civil and Criminal Procedures were enacted.

8. It declared that no Indian subject of the Company in India was to be debarred from holding any office under the Company " by reason of his religion, place of birth, descent and colour."

9. The Europeans were permitted to come to India to settle. But they had to register themselves on landing in India. Bishops of Calcutta, Madras and Bombay were to be appointed for the benefit of the Christians in India. The Bishop of Calcutta became the Metropolitan Bishop in India.

10. The Act proposed to divide the Presidency of Bengal into two Presidencies, viz., Presidency of Agra and Presidency of Bengal. However, this provision was suspended by an Act of 1835 which authorised the appointment of a Lieutenant-Governor for the North-Western Provinces.

Critics point out that the Act of 1833 was passed before "empty benches and an uninterested audience" of the House of Commons. But the Calcutta Gazette of October 1833 hailed the Charter's renewal by calling for a general 'illumination and a display of fire-works,' which were granted, and brought much satisfaction to a populace always agreeably avid for "tamashas."[9]

Thus, there was established in India one central legislative authority in place of three Councils which had existed before. The new Council was armed with authority to pass Laws and

---

9. Thomas and Garrat: *British Rule in India*, p. 302.

Regulations for the whole of the British territories in India. It continued to exist with some changes and modifications till 1861, when it again gave way to the prevalent desire for local Legislative Councils. During that time it passed a considerable number of Acts, some of general application throughout the empire, but the greater portion having a limited and partial operation. Local Legislatures had been tried and superseded by an Imperial Legislature, which in its turn was found inadequate to the political necessities of the country. An attempt was made to increase its usefulness and authority in 1853. But in 1861 a new system was introduced by which local Legislatures were re-established, not to supersede, but to work in harmony with and to certain extent in subordination to the Legislative Council of the Viceroy.

The Charter Act of 1853 was the last of its kind. The separation of the executive and the legislative functions was carried a step further by the provision of additional members for the purpose of legislation.

1. The Law Member was made a full member of the Executive Council of the Governor-General.
2. The Governor-General was given powers to nominate a Vice-President of is Council.
3. Discussion of measures which had already begun, was thrown open to the public. Different legislative measures were entrusted to select committees for examination. Thus, the framework of the central legislature was completed. The assent of the Governor-General was made necessary for all legislative proposals.
4. Provinces were allowed to send one representative each to the Central Legislative Council. No measure concerning any Province was to be considered unless the representative from that Province was present. The Chief Justice of the Supreme Court of Calcutta was to be an ex-officio member of the Council and one more member was to be appointed. The Governor-General was given the power of appointing two more civil servants as members of the Council. But the power was never exercised. The Council in its legislative capacity was to consist of 12 members. These were the Governor-General, Commander-in-Chief, 4 members of the Council, and 6 legislative members. Out of 6 members, 4 were the

representatives from the provinces and other two were the Chief Justice and a puisne Judge.

5. Provision was made for the appointment of a separate Governor for the Presidency of Bengal, and until that was made, the Court of Directors might authorise the Governor-General of India-in-Council to appoint a covenanted servant of ten year's standing as the Lieutenant-Governor of the Province. The latter appointment was made as it was cheaper of the two.
6. Power was given to the Court of Directors to constitute a new Presidency. Power was also given to alter and regulate from time to time the limits of the various provinces. This power was used to create the Punjab into a Lieutenant-Governorship in 1850.
7. The Act authorised the Crown to appoint a Law Commission in England. The Law Commission was required to examine and put into shape the mass of reports and drafts of the Acts by the Indian Law Commission and to recommend what legislation was necessary. It renewed the power of the Company and allowed it to retain possession of the Indian territories "in trust for Her Majesty, her heirs and successors" only until Parliament shall otherwise provide. It marked the beginning of a parliamentary system in India.

The great defect of the Act of 1853 was that no Indian element was associated with the Legislative Council. Its knowledge of the local conditions outside Bengal was not adequate for making laws for other provinces. According to Sir Syed Ahmed Khan, this system deprived the people of India of the means of entering any protest against any unpopular measure. The Government also got no opportunity of explaining their aims and intentions which were consequently misunderstood. In his Minute of 1860, Sir Bartle Frere advocated the need for including Indians in the Legislative Council in order to do away with "the perilous experiment of continuing to legislate for milions of people with few means of knowing except by rebellion, whether the laws suit them or not."

The horrible consequences of the revolt of 1857 entailed the end of the Company's rule and with it the termination of the notorious system of dual government. The real rulers of Britain were no longer interested in keeping the East India Company as an intermediary in spite of the fact that its leading statesmen like Clive, Hastings,

Wellesely and Bentinck had rendered remarkable services 'more magnificent than that of the Romans'.[10] While speaking in the House of Commons on 12 February, 1858 Prime Minister Lord Palmerston said: " The indisposition to make changes is wise and useful. As a general principle, it is wise and nations do themselves great mischief by rapid and ill-considered alterations of their institutions. But equally unwise and equally injurious is to cling to existing arrangements simply because they exist, and not to admit changes which can be made with advantage to the nation. What can be more cumbrous than the existing system of Indian administration which is called by the name of the Dual Government?"

Government of India Act of 1858

The Charter of 1853 was not renewed for 20 years as was the case with the earlier Charters. It left the door open for the Home Government to step in and take over the administration of India from the hands of the East India Company. The Mutiny of 1857 gave an impetus to the demand that a trading Company should not be allowed to continue to exercise political power. The government decided to put an end to the political functions of the Company. Against this decision, the Company protested in a dignified and weighty petition drawn up by John Stuart Mill. They proudly claimed at the same period at which a succession of administrations under the control of Parliament were losing to the Crown of Great Britain another empire on opposite side of the Atlantic. Prime Minister Lord Palmerston rejected it on the ground that he wanted responsible government in India. His bill to this effect was passed by the House of Commons, but it was defeated in the Lords. Then, his successor Lord Derby moved the bill again. It was passed by the Parliament and assented to by Queen Victoria on 2 August, 1858. It had these important provisions:

1. The Government of India passed from the hands of the English East India Company to the Crown. The Military and Naval forces of the Company were transferred to the Crown.

2. The Board of Control and the Court of Directors were abolished and their powers were transferred to the Secretary of State for India and his India Council. He was given the power to

10. J.C. Marshman: *The History of India*, Vol, II, p. 457.

superintend, control and direct the Indian affairs. He was to sit in Parliament and was to be assisted by a Parliamentary Under-Secretary. He was a cabinet minister of England.

3. The Act created an India Council of fifteen members. Seven of them were to be elected by the Court of Directors and the remaining eight were to be appointed by the Crown. More than half the members of the India Council were to be those persons who had lived in India for at least ten years and had not left India for more than ten years preceding the date of appointment. Members of the India Council were to hold office during good behaviour. Each member was to be paid £1,200 a year out of Indian revenues.

4. The Secretary of State for India was to be the President of the India Council. He was given a vote and a casting vote in the case of a tie. The Council met twice a week. The Secretary of State was given power to divide the India Council into Committees for the convenience of business. If a majority of the Council was opposed to a proposal, the Secretary of State was given power to over-ride them. But he had to give reasons for so doing. In matters of grant or appropriation of Indian revenues, he was not allowed to act against the majority of his Council. Control over Civil and Military servants of the Crown was given to India Council. It was to make appointments to the Councils of the Governor-General and Governors.

5. The India Council was a body of permanent Civil Servants chosen for their knowledge of Indian administration to safeguard the Indian revenues against a British Secretary of State for India. This India Council was to see that there was no tampering with the Indian Civil Service for political reasons.

6. It transferred the Government of India into the hands of Parliament and the latter acquired full, formal and legal control over Indian affairs. Questions on Indian administration could be asked from the Secretary of State. Resolutions could be moved. Indian affairs could be discussed on the occassion of adjournment or at the time of rising for parliamentary recess. Bills could be introduced and votes of confidence moved.

7. Every year, the Secretary of State was to present to the House of Commons a report on the moral and material progress of

India. Rules and regulations made in India or by the Secretary of State under authority delegated by Parliament were to be laid on the table of the House of Commons.

8. The Secretary of State-in-Council laid down certain directions for the guidance of Government of India in its dealings with England. All projects of legislation, all measures concerning revenues, construction of public works and railways, creation of new jobs, any question of policy or any problem involving new expenditure of State.
9. The Act declared the Secretary of State for India a corporate body who could sue and be sued in England and in India.
10. The Act divided the patronage between the Crown, the Secretary of State-in-Council and the authorities in India. Appointments to the covenanted Civil Service were to be made by open competition according to rules made by Secretary of State-in-Council with the help of Civil Service Commissioners.

It is pointed out that concentration of powers of the Court of Directors and the Board of Control into the hands of the Secretary of State led to important consequences. To serve two masters may be a different business, but it had its advantages also. On account of the eternal rivalry between the Court of Directors and Board of Control, a shrewd and able Governor-General could and often did play one against the other and had his way. The same rivalry between the authorities stood in the ways of formulating a strong and rigorous policy to which the Indian Government did not subscribe. Under the new set-up, the Secretary of State exercised his large powers practically without any control. He also exercised a greater degree of influence. The Act of 1853 vested the India Council with large powers also gradually fell into the hands of the Secretary of State and enabled him to exercise an effective control over the Viceroy and his Council. Prof. H.H. Dodwell points out that although the changes of 1858 "are usually ascribed to the occurrence of the Indian mutiny, as a matter of fact, the mutiny did not so much produce the change of Government as fix its date. Even in 1853 men had begun to foresee and prepare for the abolition of the Company. In 1853 the Crown had been given the power of nominating a number of the Directors. Its authority was gradually overshadowing that of the Company and even if no mutiny had happened, the change of 1858 would certainly have come to pass in a comparatively few more years. In many respects, the change was hardly more than a change of form. The Government of India continued to follow along the lines of progress already laid down."[11]

Queen's Proclamation of 1858

The assumption of the Government of India by the Crown was announced to the Princes and people of India by Queen Victoria in her Proclamation of 1st November, 1858. This was done in India by Lord Canning at Allahabad as the first Viceroy.[12] and Governor-General for the Crown. It is stated that Queen Victoria rejected the first Proclamation submitted to her and requested that the revised draft "should breathe feelings of generosity, benevolence and religious toleration." The second one was drafted on those lines. Its contents were as follows:

1. The Indian Princes were assured the preservation of their existing territories by the declaration that the British Government did not desire any extension of its territories. The British Government disclaimed all desire for an extension of territory, and promised to respect "the dignity and honour" of the native Princes. The Government deliberately and openly gave up the policy of lapse. The feudatory chiefs were granted Sanads or Charters empowering them to adopt heirs. Although the existence of the native States was guaranteed, their rights were limited and defined. They would not have any relation with foreign powers or with one another except through the British Government. Their military forces were strictly limited, although they were given full control over their internal affairs.
2. The Queen charged and enjoined upon all those in authority in India to abstain from all interference in the religious belief and worship of the Indians on pain of her highest displeasure. She ordered that in framing and administrating law, due regard should be paid to customs, ancient rites and usage of India.

---

11. Dodwell: *India*, pp. 133-34.
12. The term 'Viceroy' was commonly applied to the Governor-General of India after transfer of the Government to the Crown. This term was first used in the Queen's Proclamation of 1858 and Lord Canning was described as "the first Viceroy and Governor-General of India."

3. Indian subjects of Her Majesty were declared to be equal to British subjects in other parts of the Empire. Equal rights and opportunities were guaranteed to the Indians along with other British subjects. The Queen declared it to be her will that " so far as may be, our subjects, of whatever race or creed, be freely and impartially admitted to offices in our service, the duties of which they may be qualified by their education, ability, and integrity duly to discharge."
4. Pardon and amnesty were offered to all those Indians who were still in arms against the British Government and who were not guilty of the murder of British subjects.
5. The treaties of the East India Company were declared to be in force.
6. The Proclamation ended with a promise of measures for the material and moral improvement of the Indian people in whose "prosperity will be our strength, in their contentment our security and in their gratitude our best reward."

The Proclamation of 1858 remained the basis of British policy in India. It laid down the principles on the basis of which the British Government was to govern the people of India. It was the most momentous Declaration. "It sealed the unity of Indian Government and opened a new era.... This memorable Proclamation, justly called Magna Carta of India, was published in every large town throughout the country and translated into the vernacular languages."

Indian Councils Acts of 1861 And 1892

The Act of 1858 was exclusively concerned with the machinery of the Home Government. It did not touch the administratiev set-up in India. It was necessary that something should be done to reform the Indian machinery also. The shock of the Indian Mutiny had forced the Government of India and British Government to consider ways and means of establishing closer contacts with the Indian public opinion so that a similar tragedy may not repeat itself again. Sir Syed Ahmed Khan suggested the nomination of non-official Indians on the Council of the Governor-General. Sir Bartle Frere, the Governor of Bombay, summed up the point of view of Canning in these words: "Unless you have some barometer or safety valve in the shape of a deliberative Council, I believe, you will always be liable to very unlooked for and dangerous explosions."

The constitution and powers of the Legislative Council left much to be desired. It had the powers to legislate for the whole of India. It dealt with both small and great matters. It was not fitted to do its job on account of its ignorance of the conditions prevailing in different parts of the country. There was a feeling in the presidencies of Madras and Bombay that they were being overridden by the Bengal Council. Moreover, the Legislative Council had become a sort of debating society or a Parliament on a small scale. It had arrogated to itself all the functions and privileges of a representative body. It had adopted all the formalities of parliamentary procedure in the making of its laws.

After the exchange of views between the Government of India and the Home Government, the Indian Councils Act of 1861 was passed. Its main provisions were:

1. As regards the Central Government, a fifth member was added to the Executive Council of the Viceroy. He was to be "a gentleman of legal profession, a jurist rather than a technical lawyer."

2. The Act empowered the Governor-General to delegate special business to individual members of the Executive Council and henceforward the various members of the Council had their own portfolios and dealt on their own initiative with all but the most important matters. The most important matters were placed before the Governor-General, and if any difference of opinion appeared, were considered by the whole Council. He was authorised to nominate a President who was to preside over the meeting of the Executive Council in his absence.

3. The Governor-General was given the power of making rules and regulations for the conduct of the business of the Executive Council. The Executive Council was to be strengthened by the addition of not less than 6, and not more than 12, members nominated by the Governor-General for the purpose of legislation. Not less than half of the additional members were to be non-officials. They were to hold office for two years.

4. The function of the Council was strictly limited to legislation and the Act expressly forbade the transaction of any other business. It was empowered "to make laws and regulations for all persons whether British or native, foreigners or others, and for all places and things whatever within the said

territories, for all servants of the Government of Indi (afterwards extended to all British subjects) within th dominions of princes and states in alliance with Her Majesty

5. The Governments of Bombay and Madras were given the powe of nominating the Advocate-General and not less than 4 an not more than 8 additional members of the Executive Counc for purpose of legislation. These additional members were t hold office for two years. The business of the Council was t be strictly legislative. The assent of the Governor-General wa made necessary for all legislation passed or amended by th Governments of Madras and Bombay.

6. No distinction was made between the Central and Provincia subjects. But measures concerning public debt, finance currency, post-office, telegraph, religion, patents an copyrights were to be ordinarily considered by the Centra Government.

7. The Governor-General was given the power to create ne provinces for legislative purposes and to appoint Lieutenan Governors for them. He was authorised to divide or alter th limits of any Presidency, Province or territory.

This Act is important in the constitutional history of India fc two chief reasons. Firstly, because it enabled the Governor-Genera to associate the people of the land with work of legislation, an secondly, by vesting legislative powers in the Government c Bombay and Madras and by making provision for the institutio of similar legislative councils in other provinces, it "laid th foundations of the policy of legislative devolution which resulted i the grant of almost complete internal autonomy to the provinces i 1937."[13] It made the Governor-General omnipotent, brought th whole of India under his control, vested powers of emergency i the Governor-General, put restrictions on the right of the peopl regarding free discussion and introduction of motions other tha those of legislation, and tried to unify India by bringing both th Regulation and non-Regulation provinces under the supreme contr of the Governor-General, who himself was to abide by the Crowr the authority of Parliament and its enactments.

---

13. Bisheshwar Prasad: *The Origin of Provincial Autonomy*, p. 39.

It is pointed out that the Act of 1861 was retrograde in certain respects as it deprived the Legislative Council of any independent power. It ceased to exercise any control or check upon the executive, and even its legislative functions were circumscribed by too many restrictions. But in spite of all its defects, the Indian Councils Act of 1861 must always be regarded as memorable one. It gave the frame-work of the Government of India which it has retained up till now, and all the subsequent changes have been made within that frame-work. It was ushered in one of the great developments that distinguished the subsequent reforms of administration in this country, viz., the admission of Indians into the higher counsels of the Government. Although not expressly provided for in the Act, there was no definition of the non-official element of the Legislative Council, which accordingly could include Indians.

The Indian Councils Act of 1861 marked the close of a chapter. Its main interest lay in the gradual construction and consolidation of the mechanical framework of Government. The three separate Presidencies had come into a common system. Much of the intervening spaces had been brought under British rule. The legislative and administrative authority of Governor-General-in-Council was asserted over all the provinces and extended to all the inhabitants. The principle of recognizing local needs and welcoming local knowledge was admitted. Local Councils were recreated and a few non-official and even Indian members were introduced for the purpose of advice. However, out of anxiety to prevent the authority of the executive from being impaired by any other rival institution without administrative responsibility, it was expressly declared that Councils were to be merely legislative committees of the Government and did not contain the germs of responsible institutions.[14]

---

14. Certain changes took place after 1861. The Government of India Act, 1865 extended the legislative powers of the Governor-General's Council to all British subjects in Native States, whether servants of the Crown or not. It empowered the Governor-General-in-Council to define and alter, by proclamation, the territorial limits of the various Presidencies and Lieutenants-Governorships. The Indian Councils Act, 1869 empowered the Governor-General's Council to make laws for all native Indian subjects of the Crown in any part of the world, whether in India or not. An Act of 1873 formally dissolved the East India Company from January 1, 1874.

The process of constitutional development went on.[15] Lord Dufferin set up a Committee in 1881 with Sir George Chesney as President to consider the question of the reforms. He sent a despatch to the Home Government containing his own proposals. The despatch proposed that the Councils in India be changed into petty Parliaments. As consultative bodies, they had to help government with advice and suggestions. The non-officials were to have majority. Two-fifths of the non-official members were to be elected. However, the heads of the governments were given the right to over-rule the Councils and thus prevent the passing of the bills they did not like. If the executive government considered certain bills necessary, it could get them passed independently. The new legislatures were to be given access to all papers and be free to offer any suggestions. Debates on such advice or suggestions were allowed. "The main aim was to give a still wider share in the administration of public affairs to such Indian gentlemen as by their influence, their requirements, and the confidence they inspired in their own countrymen, are marked out as fitted to assist with their counsel the responsible rulers of the country."

In spite of the proposals of the Government of India, the Conservative Government in England did not move in the matter immediately. Even when a Bill for that purpose was introduced in the House of Lords in 1890, it was allowed to linger on. Thus the Indian Councils Act was passed in 1892. Its main provisions were:

---

15. The Royal Titles Act, 1876 formally recognised the transfer of the Government of India from the Company to the Crown. It empowered the Queen of England to "make an addition to the Royal Style and Titles appertaining to the Imperial Crown and its Dependencies." On 28th April, 1876, Queen Victoria assumed the title of "Empress of India" by a proclamation. By the Indian Councils Act of 1870, the Governor-General-in-India was empowered to pass regulations without reference to the Legislative Council. It also repeated and clearly defined the power of the Viceroy to override the decision of the majority of the Council and to adopt and carry into execution or suspend or reject, even against the opinion of the majority, any measure affecting "the safety, tranquillity or interests of the British possession in India, or any part thereof." The Act of 1874 provided for the addition of a sixth ordinary member to the Viceroy's Council, "the member for Public Works."

1. It enlarged the functions of the Legislative Councils. They were authorised to discuss the annual financial statement under certain conditions and restrictions.

2. The members of the Councils were given the right of addressing questions to the government on matters of public interest. A previous notice of 6 days was to be given to the government for asking a question. The President might disallow any question without giving any reason. Questions on matters of public interest could be asked "subject to such conditions and restrictions as may be prescribed in rules made by the Governor-General or the provincial Governors."

3. The number of additional members in the Councils was increased. It was not to be less than ten and not more than sixteen in the case of Supreme Legislative Council and not less than eight and not more than twenty in the case of Madras and Bombay. The maximum number for Bengal was fixed at twenty, and for North-Western Province and Oudh fifteen. Two-fifths of the additional members were to be non-officials.

4. The Government agreed to allow elections to be held in India under the rules, though the members so elected could take their seats only after being nominated by the Government.

5. The Governor-General could appoint the maximum number of ten non-official members as follows: Five were directly appointed by the Governor-General to represent different classes and interests. Four were appointed to represent the provinces, (one being elected by the non-official members of each of the four Provincial Legislative Councils). One was appointed to represent the Calcutta Chambers of Commerce. As regards the twenty members to be added to the Councils of Madras and Bombay, eleven were non-officials and they were nominated by Municipalities, University Senates and various trading associations.

But this Act had certain defects:

1. It did not give anything substantial to the people of India. The system of elections was a roundabout one. The people who got into the legislatures by this system did not represent the people in the real sense of the word. They could not sit in the Councils as a matter of right of elections.

2. The functions of the Legislative Councils were strictly circumscribed. The members could not ask supplementary questions. The President could disallow asking of any question, and there was no remedy against his ruling. The Councils did not get any substantial control over the budget.

3. The number of non-official members was very small. Out of 24 members at the Centre, 14 were officials, 4 were elected non-officials and 5 were nominated non-officials.

4. Punjab was not given any representation either in the Viceroy's Council or in the local Council.

5. The rights and privileges granted to the members of the Legislative Councils were strictly circumscribed. The budget could be discussed but not until after the estimates had already been settled by the executive. There was practically no chance for the non-official members to amend the bills introduced by the Government. The bill had to be passed in the form in which it had been previously approved by the Government of India or the Secretary of State for India. Under the circumstances, debates in the legislatures were a mere formal ceremony. They were considered to be a farce by certain critics.

6. The Provincial Councils were too small in size to represent the people of the provinces. In the case of Bengal, 7 elected members represented 70 million people. There were certain sections of the provinces which were given practically no representation at all. However, one might conclude by saying that though the Act of 1892 fell far short of the demands made by the Indian National Congress, it was an advance upon the existing state of things. By conceding the principle of elections and by giving the Legislative Councils some control over the Executive, it paved the way for future progress on those lines which were destined to place in the hands of the Indians a large measure of control over the administration of the country.

Indian Councils Act of 1909

The people of India were not happy with the measure of reforms given by the Indian Councils Act of 1892. Even those persons who were favourably inclined towards the Act of 1892 found that in actual working it was hollow The bitterness and discontentment in the country went on increasing with the lapse of years. The regime of Lord Curzon (1899-1905) added to the discontentment in the country. The people resented his autocratic and bureaucratic attitude.

The victory of the Liberals in the elections of 1906 filled the Indians with hope. But to their utter disappointment, the Liberals did not take our national movement seriously. They had heard little about it except from Henry Cotton and W. Wedderburn. Lord Morley, the new Secretary of State for India, did not bring with him a new attitude towards India. By 1906, the idea was gaining ground among the Indians that the constitutional programme of the Indian National Congress will take them nowhere. The result of this was that a large number of secret societies came into existence. They believed in secrecy and violence. They were the worshippers of the cult of bombs (humorously called sweets). These people believed that the only way to extort concessions from the British was to frighten them. They believed in a policy of intimidation and outrage. They carried out political dacoities and perpetrated murders. In August, 1906, Lord Minto wrote thus: "We, the Government of India, cannot shut our eyes to present conditions. The political atmosphere is full of charge. Questions are before us which we cannot afford to ignore and which we must attempt to answer and to me it would appear all important that the initiative should emanate from us, that the Government of India should not be put in the position of appearing to have its hands forced by agitation in this country or by pressure from Home—that we should be the first to recognise surrounding conditions and to place before His Majesty's Government the opinions which personal experience and a close touch with the every-day life of India entitle us to hold."

Lord Minto forwarded his recommendations to Lord Morley in 1907. His object was to give to the loyal and moderate educated classes a greater share in the Government of India. He suggested the formation of Advisory Councils in addition to the Legislative Councils. The Imperial Advisory Council was to include a few chiefs. His main suggestions were:

1. A Council of Chiefs, small in number to begin with to deal with questions affecting Native States and their relation with British India, for the express purpose of recognizing the loyalty of Ruling Chiefs and enlisting their interest in Imperial affairs;

2. The enlargement of the Imperial and Provincial Legislative Councils on a more representative basis, and greater opportunities for debate in those Councils;
3. Increased popular representation in District Councils and greater power to be given to them;
4. The appointment of Native Member to the Viceroy's Councils, probably to the Legislative Department;
5. The creation of a Department of Education in place of the Supply Department;
6. Also probably the addition of a Member to the Executive Councils of the two Presidencies, and that such Member would be a native;
7. The establishment of an Executive Council of four members for Bengal and the United Provinces, one of each such Councillors being a Native;
8. Cancellation of the suggestion for Advisory Councils.

Lord Morley accepted generally the proposals of the Government, but he rejected the proposal for the institution of Advisory Councils and the Chamber of Princes.[16]

The Government of India recommended to the Home Government to accept the principle of giving separate representation to the Muslims. It is true that Lord Morley at the outset did not accept proposals of the Government of India on this point but ultimately he gave way. The Hindus protested, but without any effect. The Government accepted the claim of the Muslims to separate representation.

In December, 1908, Lord Morley introduced his famous bill in the House of Lords. It was passed by the Parliament and became Indian Councils Act of 1909. Its main provisions were:

1. It enlarged the size of the Legislative Councils. The additional members of the Governor-General's Council were increased up to a maximum of 60, those of Madras, Bengal, U.P., Bombay and Bihar and Orissa to a maximum of 50 and those of the Punjab, Burma and Assam to 30.

16. Mary Countess of Minto: *India—Minto and Morley*, pp. 214-215.

2. It provided that the Imperial Legislative Council was to consist of 37 officials and 32 non-officials. Out of the 37 officials, 28 were to be nominated by the Governor-General and the rest were to be ex-officio. The ex-officio members were to be the Governor-General, 7 ordinary members of the Council, and one extraordinay member. Out of the 32 members, 5 were to be nominated by the Governor-General and the rest were to be elected.

3. The Act did not provide for any official majority in the Provincial Legislative Councils. The majority of the members were non-officials. However, this does not mean that there were non-official elected majorities in the Provincial Councils. Some of the non-officials were nominated by the Governor and the Government could always depend upon the unflinching loyalty of the nominated or elected members. The Government could manage to have a working majority in the Provincial Legislative Councils with the help of the officials and the nominated non-officials.

4. It provided for separate or special electorates for the due representation of the different communities, classes and interests. The remaining seats were allotted to the municipalities and district boards which were called general electorates.

5. The functions of the Legislative Councils were increased. Elaborate rules were made for the discussion of the budget in the Imperial Legislative Council. Every member was given the right to move a resolution relating to any alteration in taxation, any new loan or any additional grant to local Governments proposed or mentioned in the financial statement or explanatory memorandum. The Council was not permitted to discuss expenditure on interest on debt, ecclesiastical expenditure, and State Railways, etc.

6. The members were given the right of asking questions and supplementary questions for the purpose of further elucidating any point. But the Member-in-charge of department might refuse to answer the supplementary question off-hand. He could demand some time for the same.

7. The members were given the power to move resolutions in the Councils. The resolutions were to be in the form of definite

recommendation to the Government. They must be clearly and precisely expressed and must raise definite issues. The resolutions were not to contain arguments, inferences, ironical expressions, etc. The President was authorised to disallow any resolution or part of a resolution without giving any reason for the same.

8. Rules were also framed under the Act for the discussion of matters of general public interest in the Legislative Councils. No discussion was permitted on any subject not within the legislative competence of the particular Legislature, any matter affecting the relations of the Government of India with a Foreign Power or a native state, and any matter under adjudication by a court of law.

9. It raised the number of the members of the Executive Council in Bombay, Bengal and Madras to 4. It also empowered the Government to constitute an Executive Council for a Lieutenant-Governor's province.

10. In the Provinces, the University Senates, landlords, District Boards, Municipalities and Chambers of Commerce were to elect members. Muslims were given separate representation. The Muslim members of the Legislatures were to be elected by the Muslims themselves.

The reforms of 1909 could not come up to the expectations of the Indians. What the people of India demanded was that there should be set up a responsible government in the country. But the key feature of the reforms of 1909 was "benevolent depotism."

1. The reforms led to a lot of confusion. While parliamentary reforms were introduced, no responsibility was given. The result was thoughtless and irresponsible criticism of the Government. Indian leaders made legislatures the platforms for denunciation of the Government.

2. The reforms introduced the system of elections. But the number of voters was very small. In some cases, the number of voters in a constituency did not exceed 9 or 10.

3. The system of elections was indirect. The people elected members of local bodies. The latter elected members of an electoral college. The electoral college elected members of the provincial legislature and the members of the provincial

legislatures elected members of the Imperial legislature. The result was that there was no connection between the people and the members sitting in the legislatures.

4. It introduced separate electorates for Muslims. The evil did not end there. In 1919, the Sikhs also got separate electorates. The Act of 1935 gave separate representation to Indian Christians, Anglo-Indians, Europeans and Harijans. It cannot be denied that one of the effects of communal representation was the partition of the country in 1947.

According to Jawaharlal Nehru, " A political barrier was created round them (the Muslims), isolating them from the rest of India and reversing the unifying and amalgamating process which had been going on for centuries. This barrier was a small one at first for the electorates were very limited. but with every extension of the franchise it grew and affected the whole structure of political and social life, like some canker which corrupted the entire system. It poisoned the municipal and local self-government and ultimately it led to fantastic divisions. There came into existence (much later) separate Muslim Trade Unions and students' organisations and merchants chambers....these electorates, first introduced among the Muslims, spread to other minorities and groups till India became a mosaic of these separatist compartments....Out of them (communal electorates) have grown all manner of separatist tendencies and finally the demand for the splitting up of India."[17]

The Reforms of 1909 gave to the people "the shadow rather than substance." They granted influence and not power and according to George Washington of America, "influence is not government." A.C. Mazumdar described the reforms as "mere moonshine." The authors of the Montford Report (1919) admitted: "We have at present in India neither the best of the old system, nor the best of the new."

Proposals for Constitutional Reforms

The Reforms of 1909 were hailed by a great moderate leader like Surendernath Banerjea as 'crowning triumph of our constitutional agitation' and Gokhale appreciated them for "affording the Indian people an occassion to have a responsible

---

17. Nehru: *The Discovery of India*, pp. 295-296.

association with the Indian administration."[18] It cannot be lost sight of that, by this time, a definite change had occurred in the viewpoint of the English rulers. Their 'policy of association' hinted in the Royal Proclamation of 1858, embodied in the Indian Councils Act of 1861 and then reinforced by the Indian Councils Act of 1892 had yielded some dividends. Lord Morley, the then Secretary of State for India, through Viceroy Minto sought some suggestions from Gokhale to be considered for constitutional reforms in future. The great moderate leader obliged and so his ' political testament' came in 1915 that appeared in a published form two years after. Nineteen members of the Imperial Legislative Assembly submitted their memorandum in June, 1916. The two leading political parties of the country incorporated their views in the Congress-League Scheme adopted at their Lucknow session in December. 1916. Besides, some suggestions were contained in the Despatches of the Government of India in 1911 and 1916. The Punjab Chiefs Association and the Round Table Group of Lionel Curtis made their own contribution in this regard. It all prepared ground for the Montford Report of 1918. A brief discussion of all of them may be had in this manner.

Government Despatches

It its despatch of August 25, 1911, the Government of India recommended to the Secretary of State the transfer of capital of India from Calcutta to Delhi, the creation of Governor-in -Council for Bengal, a Lieutenant-Governor-in-Council for Bihar, Chhota Nagpur and Orissa, the restoration of the Chief Commissionership of Assam and the cancellation of the partition of Bengal. In para 3 of the same Despatch, it was stated that "the maintenance of British rule in India depends on the ultimate supremacy of the Governor-General-in-Council and the Indian Councils Act of 1909 itself bears testimony to the impossibility of allowing matters of vital concern to be decided by a majority of non-official votes in the Imperial Legislative Council. Neverthless it is certain that, in the course of time, the just demands of Indians for a larger share in the government of the country will have to be satisfied and the question will be how

---

18. J.S.Hoyland: *Gokhale: His Life and Speeches*, p.130. Even an English writer like W.H.Morris-Jones observes: "The atmosphere may not have been wholly parliamentary, but the change, as compared with the pre-1919 period, was marked enough." *Parliament in India*, p.50.

this devolution of power can be conceded, without impairing the supreme authority of the Governor-General-in-Council. The only possible solution of the difficulty would appear to be gradually to give to the provinces a larger measure of self-government. Until at last India would consist of a number of administrations. Autonomous in all provincial affairs, with the Government of India above them all, and possessing power to interfere in case of mis-government, but ordinarily restricting their functions to matters of Imperial concern." Lord Crewe, the Secretary of State, sent his approval to the Governor-General-in-Council.

Congress Schemes

At its Karachi session of 1913, the Indian National Congress passed a resolution asking for the reconstitution of the India Council of the Secretary of State. It was proposed that the total number of the members of the Council should not be less than 9 of which not less than one-third were to be elected by a constituency consisting of the elected members of the Imperial and Provincial Councils. The remaining portion of the nominated councillors was to consist of officials who had served in India for not less than ten years and who had not been away from it for more than two years at the time of appointment. The work of the India Council was to be purely advisory and not administrative. Its members were to hold office for five years. The salary of the Secretary of State for India was to be paid out of the British revenues. But no action was taken on this resolution by the Government.

At the Lucknow Congress session of 1916, the following demands were made for giving India a place in the coming Federal Council of the Empire:

1. "India must cease to be dependency and be raised to the status of a self-governing state as an equal partner with equal rights and responsibilities as an independent unit of the Empire.
2. "In any scheme of readjustment after the war, India should have a fair representation in the Federal Council like the Colonies of the Empire.
3. "India must be governed from Delhi and Simla, and not from Whitehall or Downing Street. The Council of the Secretary of State should be either abolished or its constitution so modified as to admit of substantial Indian representation on it. Of the

two Under-Secretaries of State for India, one should be an Indian, and the salary of the Secretary of State should be placed on the British Estimates as in the case of Secretary for the Colonies. The Secretary of State for India should, however, have no more powers over the Government of India than those exercised by the Secretary for the Colonies in the case of the Dominions. India must have complete autonomy—financial, legislative as well as administrative.

4. "The Government of India is the most vital point in the proposed reforms. It is the fountain-head of all the local administrations, and unless we can ensure its progressive character, any effective reforms of the Local Government would be impossible. Thus the services must be completely separated from the State, and no member of any service should be a member of the Government.

5. "The Executive Government must vest in a Governor-General and ministers, half of whom should be Indians elected by the Imperial Legislative Council and members of that body.

6. "The annual budget should be introduced in the Legislative Council as a Money Bill, and except the military estimates, the entire budget should be subject to the vote of the Council.

7. "The Provincial Governments should be perfectly autonomous, each province developing and enjoying its own resources, subject only to contribution towards the maintenance of the Supreme Government.

8. "A Provincial Administration should be vested, as in the case of the Supreme Government, in a Governor with cabinet not less than one half of whom should be Indians, elected by the non-official elected Indian members of the Legislative Council.

9. "India should have a national militia to which all the races should be eligible under proper safeguards; all should be allowed to volunteer for service under such conditions as may be found necessary for the maintenance of efficiency and discipline. The commissioned ranks of the army should be thrown open to His Majesty's Indian subjects.

10. "All local bodies should have elected chairmen of their own."

In 1916, the Government of India sent their Despatch to Chamberlain, Secretary of State for India, in which they made their suggestions regarding the concessions to be given to Indians. The Despatch was never published but we have in Lord Zetland's biography of Curzon the nature and contents of the proposals. This is what Zetland says: "In their representations to the Secretary of State the Government of India had been careful not to commit themselves to any specific form of self-government. The special circumstances of India, they pointed out, differed so widely from those of any other part of the Empire that they could scarcely expect an Indian constitution to model itself on those of the British Dominions. All that they contemplated was a gradual progress towards a large measure of control by her own people which would ultimately result in a form of self-government, differing in many ways enjoyed by other parts of the Empire but evolved on lines which had taken into account India's past history and the special circumstances and traditions of her component peoples."

Memorandum of Punjab Chiefs Association

A Memorandum was submitted by the Punjab Chiefs Association to the Lieutenant-Governor of the Punjab regarding the post-war reforms. The following suggestions were made to the Government:-

1. Local Self-Government should be developed and improved by the appointment of non-officials as presidents of municipalities and district boards.
2. An Advisory Committee should be established in each Division to advise the Commissioner.
3. The Provincial Council should be enlarged by the increase in the number of members so as to give definite and adequate representation to important minorities.
4. Besides the president, the number of Indians and Europeans in the Council should be equal.
5. The Provincial Legislative Council should be given the right of electing two members for the Imperial Legislative Council instead of one as at present.
6. The Administration of Civil and Criminal Justice should be entrusted gradually to honorary agency, provided that men of ability and character are available. Competent men may be entrusted even with the powers of an Assistant Sessions Judge.

7. Submontane and Hilly districts where there is no prospect of canal irrigation, should be permanently settlec. Districts benefited by irrigation should be settled for 40 years.
8. One or more educational institutions should be opened for the sons or orphans of military men who are serving or have served the Government.

The above were the recommendations for the Punjab, but the following were meant for the whole of India:

1. The Commissions should be opened to Indians and youngmen of good families should be given preference. Better arrangements must be made for their training.
2. The system and principle of internal defence introduced by the Defence of India Force Bill should be made permanent
3. Rules under the Arms Act should be so modified as to remove the present racial distinction.
4. Indians should be given a proper place in any scheme of imperial federation which may be formed after the war.
5. Indentured labour should be abolished.
6. Indian industries should be encouraged and saved as far as possible from the harmful effects of extraneous competition.
7. Special Jagirs, liberal land grants and pensions should be given to the survivors and heirs of men who have served in the present war.

Memorandum of the Nineteen (1916)

When the Imperial Legislature met at Simla in September 1916, its members resented the submission of the draft proposals by the Government of India to the Secretary of State without consulting them. The result was that nineteen elected members of the Council including Jinnah, Surendranath Bannerjea, Srinivas Shastri, etc. submitted a Memorandum in which they put down their own views regarding the nature of the reforms that could satisfy the aspirations of Indians.

1. The Reforms of 1909 were utterly inadequate, for they transferred no real control into the hands of the Indians. They hoped that the Indian problem be looked from "a new angle of vision" after the war. What India expected was not any reward

for services rendered, but a change in her status in the British Empire where she should be recognised as a comrade in equal partnership.

2. Half of the members of the Executive Councils should be Indians. The European half should be recruited from the ranks of men trained and educated in the public life of England so that India may have the benefit of a wider outlook and larger experience outside the world.
3. The elected members of the legislature must have an effective control over the selection of the Indian Executive Councillors.
4. All the Legislative Councils in India should have substantial majority of elected members. Franchise should be broadened and extended directly to the people. Provision should be made for an adequate representation of minorities, whether Hindu or Muslim.
5. The total membership of the Imperial Legislative Council should be increased. It should not be less than 150. The number might be 100 for major provinces and between 60 and 75 for minor ones. The budget should be passed in the form of money bills and fiscal autonomy be granted to India.
6. The Imperial and Provincial Legislatures should have jurisdiction in matters concerning central and provincial spheres respectively. But the departments of Foreign Affairs and Military Affairs, and the declaration of war or making of peace or treaty be reserved with the Government of India. Besides, the Governor-General-in-Council and the Governor-in-Council should have the right of veto but this power should be exercised subject to certain conditions and limitations.
7. The India Council of the Secretary of State should be abolished and the status of the Secretary for India be the same as that of the Minister-in-Charge of Colonies. His salary should be made a charge on the British revenues.
8. In case an Imperial Federation was established, India should be placed on a footing of equality with other self-governing dominions.
9. Provincial Governments should be granted the largest measure of autonomy. The United Pronvices and other major provinces should have Governors recruited directly from England. They should have Executive Councils also.

10. Full independence in the matter of local self-government should be granted immediately. Indians should be given arms on conditions analogous to those of the Europeans, and they be also allowed to offer themselves as volunteers in the army.
11. Indians should be given Commissions in the army on conditions similar to those of the Europeans.

Congress-League Scheme (1916)

The Memorandum of the Nineteen was published in October 1916, the famous Congress-League Scheme came in December of the same year. The scheme was approved by the Congress on 29th December and by the Muslim League on 31st December, 1916 in their sessions held at Lucknow. Its main provisions were:

1. The existing system of Government did not "satisfy the legitimate aspirations of the people" and consequently His Majesty the King Emperor should issue a proclamation announcing "that it is the aim and intention of British policy to confer self-government on India at an early date."
2. The strength of the Provincial Legislature should be not less than 125 members in major provinces and from 50 to 75 in the minor ones. Of these, four-fifths should be elected and one-fifth nominated. The members should be elected directly by the people for five years with as broad a franchise as possible. Muslims should be represented through special electorates in the proportion given in the scheme. No resolution or bill would be introduced by a non-official member if that affected a particular community and four-fifths of the members of that community in the provincial legislature opposed it. The provincial head should not preside over the Provincial Legislature. Its president should be elected by the members of the legislature. The right of asking supplementary questions should be given to all and not only to the member who put the question.
3. The divided heads of revenue should be abolished and provinces should make contributions to the Central exchequer. Extensive powers of control should be given to the Provincial Legislature including the right to raise loans, impose and alter taxation, and vote on the budget.
4. The right of moving resolutions on all matters within the purview of the provincial administration should be allowed.

Ordinarily, a resolution passed by the Legislature should be binding on the Government. But the Governor might veto the resolution. In case the resolution was passed once again within a year, it had to be carried out. The right of moving motion for adjournment to discuss a definite matter of urgent public importance should be granted in case not less than one-eighth of the members present asked for it.

5. The consent of the Governor should not be required for introducing a bill in the Provincial Legislature. Both the Governor and the Governor-General should be given the power to veto the bills passed by a provincial legislature.
6. The Governor was to be the head of every province, and "ordinarily" he should belong to the Indian Civil Service. In every province, there should be an Executive Council, half of whose members should be Indians elected by the elected members of the Provincial Legislature. The recruitment of executive councillors from the I.C.S. should be avoided as far as possible.
7. As regards the Imperial Legislative Council, its membership should be raised to 150. It should resemble the provincial legislature in the matter of proportion of elected and nominated members and power of asking questions and supplementaries, introducing bills, passing resolutions and adjournment motions. One-third of the Indian elected members should be Muslims. The elected members of the Imperial Legislative Council should be elected by the elected members of the Provincial Legislatures. The Budget should be submitted for the vote of the legislature. Members should hold office for five years. Military affairs and foreign and political relations of India including the right of declaration of war, making of peace and treaties, should be excluded from the jurisdiction of the Imperial Legislature.
8. Half the members of the Executive Council of the Governor-General should be those Indians who were elected by the elected members of the Imperial Legislature. Ordinarily, the members of the Indian Civil Service should not be appointed to these posts.
9. The Government of India should be independent of the control of Secretary of State in legislative and administrative matters. A system of independent audit of accounts of the Government should be established.

10. The India Council of the Secretary of State should be abolished and he be assisted by two permanent Under-Secretaries out of which one should be an Indian. The salary of Secretary of State should be a charge on the British revenues. His status should be the same as that of Secretary of State for Colonies. India should be given adequate and equal representation in any body that might be constituted to control imperial affairs.

The authors of the Report on Indian Constitutional Reforms regarded the Congress-League scheme as "the latest, most complete, and most authoritative presentation of the claims of the leading Indian political organisations."

The scheme perpetuated the system of communal representation. It is interesting to note that the Muslims were to have separate representation even in those provinces where they were in a majority. They were at the same time given weightage over and above their numerical strength in those provinces where they were in a minority. The scheme provided no connecting rod between the executive and legislative wheels of the machine which would enable them to work in collaboration with each other. This was bound to result in friction. "Parliamentary government avoids deadlocks by making the executive responsible to the legislature. Presidential government limits deadlcoks, because all the organs of the state must ultimately submit to a superior tribunal, the electorate of the nation. But a legislature elected by the people, coupled with a governor appointed by a distant power, is a contrivance for fomenting dissensions and making them perpetual."

The provision that the resolution of the legislature should be binding on the executive put the latter in the awkward position of carrying out what it did not approve of. But the only other alternative was that the executive should remain in power so long as it enjoyed the confidence of the House. That implied the establishment of responsible government to which the British Government had not committed itself. As a critic observes: "The fact was that in regard to communal adjustment, the Congress, generally speaking, suffered from self-delusion. Nothing could be more head-strong than to hope for the disappearance of separate electorate after 10 years of its birth. The evil could easily be nipped in the bud, but it was allowed to grow till it served an easy stepping stone for the demand of Pakistan. A diplomatic blunder of high magnitude was committed in conceding the right of separate Muslim representation through members of the community themselves."[19]

Gokhale's Political Testament

Before his death in 1915, Gokhale had prepared on the request of Lord Willingdon, a scheme of reforms to be given to India after the War. The so-called "Gokhale's Political Testament" was published in August 1917. Its main points were:

1. There should be the grant of provincial autonomy and the lessening of the control of the Government of India in the provincial sphere.
2. The Executive Council or Cabinet of the Governor should consist of 6 members, three of whom should be Indians. The Legislative Council should consist of 75 to 100 members, of whom not less than four-fifths should be elected.
3. The Provincial Government should work under the control of the Provincial Legislative Council, but otherwise it should have complete charge of the internal administration of the Province.
4. The Provinces should have greater fiscal autonomy, but they should make contributions to the central revenues.
5. The Legislative Council of the Viceroy should be known as the Legislative Assembly of India. It should consist of about 100 members, the majority of whom should be nominated members or officials. It should have "increased opportunities of influencing the policy of Government by discussion, questions connected with the Army and Navy.
6. The Government of India should be made free in fiscal affairs from the control of the Secretary of State whose powers should be curtailed in other matters also. His Council should be abolished and he himself be put on the same footing as the Secretary of State for Colonies.
7. Indians should be admitted to the ranks of commissioned officers both in the army and navy and proper facilities should be provided for their instruction.

19. Lal Bahadur: *The Muslim League*, p. 96.

8. If German East Africa was conquered from the Germans, it should be handed over to the Government of India after the war and reserved for Indian colonisation.

The Round Table Group of Curtis and Duke Memorandum

The Round Table group was started by Lionel Curtis and his friends in South Africa after 1906 and it played a very significant part in bringing various elements in the Union together. Encouraged by its results, the members thought of extending the scope of the studies and in that connection visited New Zealand, Australia and Canada. By means of discussion and criticism, the groups contributed to the study of the means by which the various parts of the British Empire could be brought together and the problems arising out of this huge combination of the states could be tackled satisfactorily. Curtis requested that a member of the group who had expert knowledge about India, should present before the group his own views on the position of India in the British Commonwealth. Sir William Duke who had been the Lieutenant-Governor of Bengal, took up the task and placed before the group his famous Memorandum. His scheme was printed and distributed among the members of the gathering who met at Oxford for three days to discuss its pros and cons. The draft was completely recast in the light of the discussions. The revised draft, however, was sent to Lord Chelmsford in India in May 1916.

The visit of Curtis to India and particularly his stay with big Englishmen and at the Government House and also his association with persons like Sir Valentine Chirol who was regarded by the patriotic Indians as the greatest foe of their country, created misgivings in the minds of the public. This led to a lengthy controversy. Curtis had no intention to enter into duels but merely desired to study, in a dispassionate manner, the nature of the future constitutional advance for India. But the press campaign forced him to come forward to explain and justify his position and that of the Round Table groups on whose behalf he was carrying on all this work. His conclusion was that no further advance on the road to "responsible government" could be made on the basis of the Minto-Morley Reforms. If an attempt was made, that was bound to result in disaster. He said that he had been convinced that India must be represented in the Imperial Parliament, whose scheme the Round Table groups were preparing

1. As regards the nature of the future constitutional advance of India, he stated that more and more independence should be given to the provinces and Government of India should not touch the subjects handed over to the provinces.
2. To achieve that goal, the first necessary step was to get rid of the official vote in the Provincial Legislative Councils. But this did not imply that there should be no officials in the Councils. "Let members of the Government sit in the Council and speak. Let them be free to summon any other official they please to take part in the debates. But let voting be confined to members who are not officials." The great advantage of the system was that the time of the highly paid officials was not to be wasted merely for the purpose of recording their votes which the Government wanted them to do so. The end to be achieved was that the councils should be made responsible in the true sense of the word for certain branches of administration and legislation.
3. The Governor of the Province was to summon that member of the Council who was most likely to command a majority of its members and entrust him with the task of forming a provincial government for the transferred parts of the administration. The leader was to select three colleagues who were to form the government along with the Leader. The Governor might help him with advice.
4. The ministers were to manage their own departments in their own way and were to be responsible for them also. They were to remain in power so long as they enjoyed the confidence of the Council. If they lost, then they were either to resign or ask the Governor to dissolve the Council.
5. He discussed the merits and demerits of the system of dyarchy propounded by him and came to the conclusion that it was the best alternative under the circumstances. He emphasised the fact that responsible government was to be first introduced in the provinces and then at the centre.

Not only did Curtis propound his own views in the above letters, he profoundly influenced both Lord Chelmsford and Montagu. He also played an important part in the drafting of the Joint Address that was presented to the Viceroy and the Secretary of State for India by the Europeans and Indians in November, 1917. Lord

Ampthill referred to the part played by Lionel Curtis in his speech in the House of Lords on December 16, 1919 thus: "The incredible fact is that but for the chance visit to India of a globe-trotting doctrinaire, with a positive mania for constitution-mongering, nobody in the world would even have thought of so peculiar a notion as that of 'Dyarchy'."

Montagu's August Declaration and Montford Report

On August 20, 1917, Montagu, the then Secretary of State for India, made the following statement in the House of Commons regarding the goal of British Government in India: "The policy of His Majesty's Government, with which the Government of India are in complete accord, is that of the increasing association of Indians in every branch of the administration and gradual development of self-governing institutions with a view to the progressive realisation of responsible Government in India as an integral part of the British Empire...They have decided that substantial steps in this direction should be taken as soon as possible, and that it is of the highest importance as a preliminary to considering what these steps should be that there should be a free and informal exchange of opinion between those in authority at Home and in India. I would add that progress in this policy can only be achieved by successive stages. The British Government and the Government of India, on whom the responsibility lies for the welfare and advancement of Indian peoples, must be judges of the time and measure of each advance, and they must be guided by the co-operation received from those upon whom new opportunities of service will be conferred and by the extent to which it is found that confidence can be reposed in their sense of responsibility."

The importance of the Declaration lies in the fact that it stated in categorical terms as to what exactly was going to be the goal of the British in India. It can be put on the same footing as the Queen's Proclamation of 1858. While the authors of Report on the Indian Constitutional Reforms regarded it as "the most momentous utterance ever made in India's chequered history", which marked "the end of one epoch, and the beginning of a new one". Pradhan declared that it was a "revolutionary pronouncement." To quote him again, "with the announcement of August 20, 1917, modern India has entered on a new era in the history." According to G.N. Singh, the August Declaration "created once again a division in the ranks of Indian Nationalists. The Moderates welcomed the declaration as the 'Magna Charta of India'...The Extremists, on the other hand, regarded the announcement as unsatisfactory both in language and substance and decided to continue agitation both for the release of the internees and for the better recognition of Indian claims and aspirations."

Montagu visited Delhi, Madras, Calcutta and Simla. He was the guest with some of the important ruling princes of Patiala, Gwalior, Bikaner, Bharatpur, Dholpur, Jaipur, Bhopal and Alwar. He exchanged his views with all those who came into contact with him and tried to develop in his mind the nature of the reform to be given to India. He met Lionel Curtis many a time, discussed with him the reforms-scheme and was gratified to find that Curtis agreed with him. It is this co-operation that enabled them to sign a joint report on April 22, 1918.

After dealing with the past development and the existing machinery of administration in Part I of the Report, the authors laid down the following four principles on which the proposals were to be based:

1. "There should be, as far as possible, complete popular control in local bodies and the largest possible independence for them of outside control."
2. "The provinces are the domain in which the earlier steps towards the progressive realisation of responsible government should be taken. Some measure of responsibility should be given at once, and our aim is to give complete responsibility as soon as conditions permit. This involves at once giving the provinces the largest measure of independence, legislative, administrative and financial, of the Government of India which is compatible with the due discharge by the latter of its own responsibilities."
3. "The Government of India must remain wholly responsible to Parliament, and saving such responsibility its authority in essential matters must remain undisputable pending experience of the effect of the changes now to be introduced in the provinces. In the meantime the Indian Legislative Council should be enlarged and made more representative and its opportunities of criticising Government increased."

4. **"In proportion as the foregoing changes take effect, the control of Parliament and the Secretary of State over the Government of India and Provincial governments must be relaxed."**

It was with a view to implement these general principles that the Report made following detailed recommendations:

1. **As regards the provinces, some measure of responsible Government was to be established thereby the transfer of some departments into the hands of Indian Ministry who were to be responsible to the Legislative Council. They were to be appointed by the Governor and hold office during the term of the Legislature. They were to be under the control of the Governor who was also in charge of the reserved departments.**
2. The Provincial Legislative Council was to have a substantial majority of elected members. Nominated official members were to possess freedom of speech and vote, except on those occasions when the Government thought it necessary to require their support. The Governor was to preside over the meetings of the Legislative Council, but he was authorised to appoint a vice-president. Any member of the Council could ask a supplementary question. This privilege was not to be restricted to the man who originally put the question. The Governor was given the power of dissolution. He was also given the power to certify a Bll or veto a Bill. The Governor-General could reserve provincial Acts.
3. The resources of the Central and Provincial Governments were to be completely separated. The divided heads were to be abolished. In order to make up the deficit of the Central Government, the provincial governments were to make contributions to the Central Revenues.
4. The Report recommended the creation of a Privy Council for India. Appointments to it were to be made by the King Emperor for life. Its function was to advise the Governor-General on question of policy and administration.
5. A bicameral system was to be introduced at the Centre. The lower house known as the Legislative Assembly was to consist of about 100 members, out of which two-thirds were to be elected. Out of the one-third who were to be nominated, not less than one-third were to be non-officials. These non-official

seats were to be filled with a view to give representation to minorities and special interests.

6. The Council of State was to consist of 50 members, excluding the Governor-General. The latter was to be its President but he was given the power of appointing a vice-president who was normally to be its president. Out of the 29 nominated members not more than 25 were to be officials and 4 non-officials. Official members were to be eligible for nomination to both the houses. But elected members of the Council of State were to vacate the seats they held in the provincial council of the Legislative Assembly. While the tenure of office of the Assembly was to be 3 years, that of the Council of State was fixed at 5 years.

7. Resolutions passed in the Legislature were to be merely advisory in character. The Government was to give effect to them only so far as they reconciled with its responsibility for the peace, order and good gcvernment of the country.

8. It was further recommended that ten years after the first meeting of the Councils, a Commission should be appointed. The names of the Commissioners were to be submitted by the Secretary of State of India to both Houses of Parliament for approval by a resolution. The Commission was to consider whether it was possible to establish complete responsible government in any province or provinces, or to recommend the transfer of more powers into the hands of the responsible ministers or withdraw those that had been transferred already.

9. It was recommended that a Council of Princes should be established. A few more recommendations regarding the relations of the Indian States with the Government of India were made.

These, in brief, were the recommendations made by the Report on Indian Constitutional Reforms, which was published in July 1918. In spite of the best intentions of the Secretary of State for India, the Report was received with mixed feelings of approval and condemnation. The Moderate leaders like Surendra nath Banerjea and Dinshaw Wacha were unanimous in declaring the Reforms to be a substantial instalment of responsible government and an honest endeavour to meet the legitimate aspirations of educated

India. Not only did the Moderates absent themselves from the Bombay session of the Congress, Banerjea moved in September 1918, a resolution in the Imperial Legislative Council approving of the Reform Scheme and recommending the appointment of a committee of non-official members of the Legislative Council. The resolution was carried with an overwhelming majority.

The Extremists in the Congress were very critical of the Reforms Scheme. A few days before the publication of the Report, one of the leaders of the Left Wing Party as represented by Home Rule Leaguers, condemned the proposals in advance as they originated with foreigners. Other Extremist leaders condemned them as soon as the Report was published. An Extremist gathering in Madras declared that "the Scheme is so radically wrong in principle and in detail that in our opinion it is impossible to modify or improve it." Mrs. Annie Besant remarked that "the scheme is unworthy to be offered by England or to be accepted by India." Tilak also declared the Scheme to be "entirely unacceptable."

Congress Session

A special session of the Indian National Congress was held at Bombay in the last week of August 1918 to discuss the Reforms Proposals. After a few days' discussions, the Congress re-affirmed the principles contained in the Congress-League Scheme. It was declared that the people of India were fit for responsible government and nothing less than self-government would satisfy their legitimate aspirations. It asked for simultaneous advance both in the provinces and the Government of India.

The following demands were passed at the session of the Indian National Congress held at Delhi in December 1918:

1. Full responsible government should be given to the provinces.
2. Non-official Europeans should not be given separate communal representation. But even if that was conceded, that must be in accordance with their total population.
3. The final authority in all internal matters should be the Supreme Legislative Assembly as voicing the will of the Indian nation.

The European community in India was dissatisfied for quite different reasons. The European Association issued a manifesto which expressed alarm at the double weakening of their position as a result of the Indianisation of the services and the changes in the administrative machinery of the country. The Europeans employed in Government service also became uncertain of their future. The Indian Civil Service started agitation with a view to decide the question of their retirement, pensions, etc., in case they found the conditions under the reforms unbearable. Likewise, the non-Brahmins of Southern India complained that their claims for separate representation had been unjustly ignored on theoretical grounds. The Mohammedans were somewhat disappointed at what the Reforms Scheme gave them. Some of them complained that they had secured more in the Congress-League Scheme or the Lucknow Pact than that offered to them by the Government. A few more unfortunate incidents added to the uneasiness of the Muslims in general.

Unmindful of the reception of his Report at home or in India, the Secretary of State and the Government proceeded with their work. The report had suggested the appointment of two Committees, viz., Franchise and Functions Committees, and in October 1918, the constitution and terms of reference of the two committees were published. Lord Southborough, whom S.N. Banerjee called "an ideal chairman", was to preside over both the committees which were to meet in joint session whenever necessary. The Franchise Committee consisted of Sir H.G. Sly, Sahibzada Aftab Ahmed Khan, W.M. Hailey, Surendranath Banerjea, Malcolm Hogg and Srinivas Shastri. Although Banerjea regarded it as a "representative of all interests, European and Indian, official and non-officials", yet the Left Wing Party grumbled because they were not represented on it. A similar complaint was made by the non-Brahmins of Madras.

As regards the terms of reference, the Franchise Committee was to advise the Government on the franchises and constituencies in each province with the object of securing as broad a franchise and as representative a council as the circumstances in each province permitted. It was to devise means for direct elections as far as possible. It was to advise as to how far the devices of territorial representation or occupational representation were to be employed in order to give adequate and effective representation to the various interests and the minorities. It was to propose a complete scheme for the size and composition of each Provincial Council and also advise as to the number of nominated official members.

The Franchise Committee was to recommend the best means of constituting the Indian Legislative Assembly in such a way that the proportion of the elected and nominated members was not changed, although the total strength could be altered. It was to make suggestions regarding the desirability and practicability of direct or indirect elections for the Assembly and also prepare a detailed statement for the same. As regards the Council of State, the Committee was to prepare a scheme for election of its members and also consider the question of six special constituencies.

The Committee on the Division of Functions consisted of H. Feethan (Chairman), H.F.W. Gillman, Khan Bahadur Maulvi Rahim Baksh, Dr. Tej Bahadur Sapru, Chimanlal Harilal Setalvad, H.L. Stephenson and J.P. Thompson. With a view to give the provinces the largest measure of legislative, administrative and financial independence of the Government of India, the Committee was to advise as to what functions were to be transferred by the Government of India to the provinces (Provincial List) and what amount of control was still to be retained by the Government of India for the discharge of its responsibility. It was also to recommend as to what departments could be transferred to the popular ministers and how much of control was still to be exercised by the Governor in this sphere.

The Committees finished their work and presented their reports to the Government of India on March 10, 1919. The latter sent their own recommendations regarding the subject in their despatch to the Secretary of State, dated April 16, 1919. The Despatch contained 130 paras of their own comments on the subject and also about 19 pages of the Minute of Dissent of Sir Sankaran Nair. The Government also sent the revised lists of All-India, Provincial and Transferred subjects to the Home Government.

In spite of the stout opposition at the hands of men like Sydenham and Ampthill, the Bill was passed by the House of Lords on December 18, 1919 and it received the Royal Assent on December 23. On the same day, a Royal Proclamation was issued by King George V to the Indian Princes and the people of India. It was hoped that the new Act "will take its place among the great historic measures passed by the Parliament of this Realm for the better government of India and for the greater contentment of her people". On the same occasion, he sent a happy news to the Princes of India that he had agreed to the establishment of a Chamber of Princes. He also assured them that their privileges, rights and dignity will be maintained in the future. He announced his intention to send the Prince of Wales to India to inaugurate the new Chamber of Princes and the new constitution in British India. He hoped that when the Prince of Wales visited the country, mutual goodwill and confidence would prevail among the Indians. He concluded with a prayer to "Almighty God that by His wisdom and under His guidance India may be led to greater prosperity and contentment and may grow to the fullness of political freedom."

Government of India Act of 1919

Thus came the constitution of 1919. Its Preamble is very important and ran as follows: "Whereas, it is the declared policy of the Parliament to provide for the increasing association of Indians in every branch of Indian administration, and for gradual development of self-governing institutions with a view to the progressive realization of responsible government in British India as an integral part of the Empire:"

Its main provisions may be put as under:

1. It made many changes in the administration of India. Formerly, the Secretary of State for India used to be paid out of the Indian revenues. It provided that in future he was to be paid out of the British revenues. However, some of the functions of the Secretary of State for India were taken away from him, and given to a High Commissioner for India who was appointed by the Government of India and paid by the Government of India. He acted as the agent of the Governor-General-in-Council. The control of the Secretary of State was reduced in the provincial sphere in so far as the transferred departments were concerned. But in the case of the Central Government of India, it remained as complete as before. The Secretary of State possessed and exercised the power of superintendence, direction and control over the affairs of India.

2. It set up a bicameral legislature at the Centre in place of the Imperial Legislative Council consisting of one House. The names of the two Houses were the Central Legislative Assembly and the Council of State. The Council of State

consisted of 60 members out of which 33 were elected and 27 were nominated by the Governor-General. The Central Legislative Assembly consisted of 145 members, out of which 103 were elected and the rest were nominated. Out of the 103 elected members, 51 were elected by the general constituencies, 32 by communal constituencies (30 by Muslims and 2 by Sikhs), and 20 by special constituencies (7 by land-holders, 9 by Europeans and 4 by Indian Commerce).

3. The life of the Central Legislative Assembly was 3 years and the Council of State 5 years but it could be extended by the Governor-General. It is to be noted that the last Assembly sat for 11 years. The first president of the Assembly was to be nominated by the Government, but the subsequent presidents were to be elected by the members of the Assembly.

4. As regards the franchise for both Houses of the Central Legislature, it was very much restricted. In the case of the Council of State, voters were assessed either to income-tax on an annual income of not less than Rs. 10,000 to 20,000 or to land revenue of Rs. 750 to Rs. 5,000. In addition, those who had previous experience in public work or who were recognized as men of high scholarship or academic worth were entitled to have their names enrolled on the electoral roll of general constituencies for the Council of State. As regards the qualifications of the voters for the Central Legislative Assembly, those were either the payment of municipal taxes amounting to not less than Rs. 15 to Rs. 20 per annum, or occupation or ownership of a house of the annual rental value of Rs. 180 or assessment to income-tax on the annual income of not less than Rs. 2,000 to Rs. 5,000 or assessment to land revenue for Rs. 50 to Rs. 150 per annum, varying from province to province.

5. The Governor-General was given the power to summon, prorogue and dissolve the chambers. He had also the right of addressing the members of the two Houses.

6. The Central Legislature was given wide powers. It could make laws for the whole of British India, for the subjects of His Majesty and Services of the Crown in other parts of India, for the Indian subjects of His Majesty wherever they may happen to be, and for all persons employed in His Majesty's defence

forces. It could also repeal or amend laws for the time being in force in British India, or applicable to the persons mentioned in the preceding sentence. However, the previous sanction of the Secretary of State-in-Council was required to pass any legislation for abolishing any High Court. The Indian Legislature had no power to amend or repeal any parliamentary statute relating to British India or to do anything affecting the authority of Parliament or the unwritten laws or constitution of the United Kingdom. The previous sanction of the Governor-General was required to introduce bills concerning the following subjects:

(*i*) The public debt or public revenues of India.

(*ii*) Religion or religious rites and usages of the British subjects in India.

(*iii*) Discipline or maintenance of His Majesty's military, naval and air forces.

(*iv*) Relations of the Government of India with foreign States or Indian States.

(*v*) Any measure which repealed or amended any Act of a legislature or any ordinance made by the Governor-General, etc.

7. Members of both Houses of the Central Legislature were given the right of putting interpellations and supplementary questions, of moving resolutions and making motions of adjournment, and of introducing projects of legislation according to the rules. The members were given the right to freedom of speech in the two chambers.

8. As regards the Central Budget, the Government submitted proposals for appropriation, in the form of demands for grant, to the vote of the Indian Legislative Assembly. However, there were certain non-votable items in the Budget. These items were not open to discussion in either chamber, "unless the Governor-General otherwise directs." All other items of expenditure were submitted to the vote of Assembly which "could assent or refuse its assent to any demand or may reduce the amount referred to in any demand by a reduction of the whole grant. If the Governor-General was satisfied that any demand which had been refused by the Assembly was

essential for the discharge of his responsibilities, he could restore the grant even if it was rejected by the Assembly. In cases of emergency, he was empowered "to authorize such expenditure as may, in his opinion, be necessary for the safety or tranquillity of British India or any part thereof."

9. It has been rightly pointed out that the Act of 1919 introduced responsive and not responsible Government at the Centre. The members of the Executive Council of the Governor-General were nominated members. The people had neither any hand in their appointment nor in their removal.

10. The new Act provided for two lists of subjects, Central subjects and Provincial subjects. The principle underlying this division was that matters in regard to which uniformity in legislation was necessary or desirable for the whole of India or for more than one province, should be regarded as central, while others in which only a particular province was interested, should be treated as provincial. The Central subjects were Defence, Foreign and Political Relations, Public Debt, Tariffs and Customs, Post and Telegraph, Patents and Copy-right, Currency and Coinage, Communications, Commerce and Shipping, Civil and Criminal Law and Procedure, major Ports, etc. The Provincial subjects were Local Self-Government, Public Health and Sanitation and Medical Administration, Education, Public Works, Water Supply and Irrigation, Land Revenue Administration, Famine Relief, Agriculture, Forests, Cooperative Societies, Law and Order, etc. As regards the residuary subjects, they were divided between the centre and the provinces on the same principle on which the lists were drawn up.

11. The size of the provincial Legislative Councils was considerably enlarged. While about 70 per cent of the members of the provincial legislatures were to be elected, about 30 per cent were to be nominated by the Governor. Some of these nominated members were officials and the others non-officials. The Legislative Council sat ordinarily for 3 years, but it could be dissolved earlier by the Governor. The latter could also extend its life. The members were given the right of asking questions and supplementary questions. They could reject the budget, although the Governor could restore it, if necessary.

12. It introduced dyarchy in the Provinces. Under this system, the subjects to be dealt with by the Provincial Governments were divided into two parts—Transferred and Reserved subjects. The Reserved subjects were administered by the Governor with the help of the Executive Council and the Transferred subjects were dealt with by the Governor with the help of the ministers. While the members of the Executive Council were to be nominated by the Governor, the ministers were to be appointed by the Governor from amongst the members of the legislature. The following were the Reserved subjects: Administration of Justice, Police, Irrigation and Canals, Drainage and Embankments, Water Storage and Water Power, Land Revenue Administration, Land Improvement and Agricultural Loans, Famine Relief, Control of Newspapers, Books and Printing Presses, Prisons and Reformatories, Borrowing money on the credit of the province, Forests, except in Bombay and Burma, Factory inspection, Settlement of labour disputes, Industrial Insurance and Housing. The Transferred subjects were: Local Self-Government including matters relating to Municipal Corporations and District Boards, Public Health, Sanitation and Medical Administration, including Hospitals and Ayslums and provision for Medical Education; Education of Indians with some exceptions; Public Works, including Roads, Bridges and Municipal Tramways, but excluding Irrigation, Agriculture and Fisheries, Co-operative Societies, Excise, Forests in Bombay and Burma only; Development of Industries, including Industrial Research and Technical Education. The provincial Governor was not a constitutional head. He was given some special responsibilities. He was authorized to over-rule his ministers and the members of the Executive Council if it was considered necessary for the discharge of his special responsibilities. The Governor was expected to encourage joint deliberation between the ministers and the members of the Executive Council. Provision was made for the temporary administration of Transferred subjects in the case of an emergency. If no minister was in charge of a transferred subject, the Governor himself assumed temporary charge of it till a minister was appointed. The Governor-General-in-Council with the previous sanction of the Secretary of State-in-Council could revoke or suspend the

transfer of all or any subjects in the province and in that case they would relapse into the position of reserved subjects and be administered by the Governor-in-Council.

Working of Dyarchy

The most significant as well as shocking feature of the Montford Reforms was the introduction of 'dyarchy' in the provinces. In a strict sense, dyarchy means a double set of government in which the two halves are cut off from each other. The Act of 1919 divided the subjects of provincial administration into 'reserved' and 'transferred' categories. All important items were included in the category of reserved subjects (as public order, finance, land revenue, police, jails, courts, canals and irrigation, English education etc.) and their administration was to be given to the Executive Councillors (or very senior officers of the Indian Civil Service) who were to be appointed by the Governor and who were not made accountable to the legislature. The subjects of the transferred category being of lesser importance (as local self-government, agriculture, public health, Inidan education etc.) were to be given to the Ministers appointed by the Governor and responsible to the legislature. While the Act did not specify the number of the Executive Councillors and the Ministers, a convention grew that their number could be from 3 to 4 and from 2 to 3 respectively. The administration of the reserved subjects could not be entrusted to the Ministers, though the administration of the transferred subjects could be given to the Executive Councillors in case the ministers were not available.

Obviously, dyarchy was a crude mixture of bureaucracy and democracy. The authors of the Act had hoped that in time to come the system would develop into a full-fledged responsible government. As an Indian writer says: "Dyarchy is a system which aims at assigning matters to ministers chosen from and accountable to the legislative council for their proper administration, while other subjects are administered by the members of the Executive Council who are selected independently of the legislature, and are not responsible to that body. It is admittedly a half-way house between autocracy and responsible government, its basis is the gradual training of the ministers, the legislature and the electorate by the exercise of responsiblities proportionate to their capacities for the time being."[20]

---

20. A. Appadorai: *Dyarchy in Practice*, p. 36.

The system of dyarchy was introduced in the provinces, but it did not work satisfactorily. Many factors were responsible for the failure of the system:

1. The very principle of dyarchy was faulty. The division of administration into two parts, each independent of the other, is opposed to political theory and practice of governments. The state is like an organism and the two parts cannot be separated completely. However, the actual division of subjects under the Act of 1919 was haphazard.

2. There was no love lost between the two halves of the Government. The ministers were the representatives of the people. The members of the Executive Council belonged to the bureaucracy. They usually never pulled together. There was constant friction. Sometimes the ministers and the Executive Councillors condemned each other in the public. As a result of this, the work of administration suffered. As a rule, the Governor backed the members of the Executive Council, because he himself belonged to the same service to which they belonged.

3. The position of the ministers was very weak. They had to serve two masters—the Governor and the Legislative Council. A minister was appointed by the Governor and could be dismissed at his will. He was responsible to the Legislature for the administration of his Department. He could be turned out by the Legislature by a vote of no-confidence. From the point of view of practical politics, the ministers cared more for the Governor than for the Legislature. There were no strong parties in the provincial legislatures. The result was that no minister had a majority to back him in office. The Governors did not care to encourage the principle of joint responsibility amongst the ministers. The ministers never worked as a team.

4. The position of the permanent services created many difficulties. The appointment, salary, suspension, dismissal and transfer of the members of All-India services was under the control of the Secretary of State for India. These persons continued to be under the control of the Secretary of State for India even if they were appointed in the Transferred Departments. They did not care for the ministers.

The ministers had no power to choose their own subordinates when vacancies occurred in their Departments. Most of the important jobs were reserved for the members of the All-India Services.

5. Another cause of the failure of dyarchy was the reservation of the Department of Finance in the hands of a Member of the Executive Council. All the nation-building Departments were given to the ministers, but they were given no money for the same. The result was that the ministers had to depend upon the sweet-will of the Finance Secretary. As a member of the Indian Civil Service, the Finance Secretary had no sympathy with the aspirations of the Indians as represented by ministers. He cared more for the needs of the Reserved Departments than for the Transferred Departments.

The reforms of 1919 were in the nature of a half-way house. The Indians knew that they were going to get more in future. The result was that the people of India were not in a mood to give the reforms a fair trial. Regarding the working of dyarchy, Sir H. Butler says: 'In India it has almost become a term of abuse." The view of A. Appadorai is: "Dyarchy was introduced with high hopes and it must be said that, on a theoretical analysis and if worked under ideal conditions, it is not without merits. It is the strictly logical solution of a situation in which it is desired to base the authority of Government in different matters on two different sources--a situation in which a complete transfer of responsibility is considered impossible by a ruling power. It is thus a bridge between autocracy and responsibility."[21]

Demand for RTC and Muddiman Committee Report (1924)

The Reforms of 1919 were considered to be utterly inadequate by the Indians. The Indian National Congress at its annual session held at Amritsar in December 1919 condemned the Reforms as "inadequate, unsatisfactory and disappointing." While it asked the British Government to take early steps to establish full responsible government in India in accordance with the principle of self-determination, it resolved to work the Reforms "so far as may be possible" with a view to bring about the early establishment of responsible government in India.

---

21. Appadorai, *op. cit.*, p. 36.

Sir William Vincent, the Home Member, suggested the following formula which was adopted by the Assembly: "That this Assembly recommends to the Governor-General-in-Council that should convey to the Secretary of State of India the view of this Assembly that the progress made by India on the path of responsible government warrants a re-examination and revision of the Constitution at an earlier date than 1929." On 18 February, 1924, Pandit Motilal Nehru, leader of the Swarajist Party, moved the following amendment and the same was carried: "This Assembly recommends to the Governor-General-in-Council to take steps to have the Government of India Act revised with a view to establish Full Responsible Government in India and for the said purpose—

(a) to summon at an early date a representative Round Table Conference to recommend with due regard to the protection of the rights and interests of important minorities the scheme of a constitution for India: and

(b) after dissolving the Central Legislature to place the said scheme for approval before a newly elected Indian Legislature for its approval and submit the same to the British Parliament to be embodied in a statute."

The Government of India did not accept the resolution of the Assembly, but set up a Committee under the Chairmanship of Sir Alexander Muddiman with T.B. Sapru and M.A. Jinnah as its members to enquire into the difficulties arising from, or defects inherent in, the working of the Government of India Act and the Rules thereunder in regard to the Central Government and the Governments of Governors' Provinces.

The Muddiman Committee did not submit a unanimous report. The majority view was that the existing constitution was working in most of the provinces and was affording valuable political experience. As the new constitution had been in existence only for a short period, it was not possible to say definitely as to whether it would succeed ultimately or not. However, detailed recommendations were made for improving machinery of the Government. The minority view was that dyarchy had absolutely failed and could not succeed at all in the future. It was only a fundamental change of the constitution which could bring about an improvement.

In September, 1925, the report of the Muddiman Committee was discussed in the Central Assembly. The Government of India proposed to accept the principle underlying majority report and proceed with the consideration of its recommendations. Motilal Nehru moved the following amendment which was carried in the Assembly in spite of the opposition of the Government: "That immediate steps should be taken to move His Majesty's Government to make a declaration in Parliament embodying such fundamental changes in the constitution of India as would make government fully responsible; and that a Round Table Conference or Convention, representative of all interests, should be held to frame a detailed scheme which should be placed before the Legislative Assembly for approval, and afterwards submitted to the British Parliament to be embodied in a statute."

Simon Commission

In November 1927 was appointed the Simon Commission. It consisted of seven members and was presided over by Sir John Simon. All of its members were Englishmen. The Commission was boycotted by the Indians on the ground that it had no Indian member. The excuse given for not appointing any Indian on the Commission was that the intention of the framers of the Act of 1919 was to confine the Commission to members of Parliament. However, the Act did not lay down any such restriction. But even if the British Government wanted to restrict the nomination to the members of Parliament, there were two Indian members at that time. Lord Sinha was a member of the House of Lords and Shapurji Saklatwala was in the House of Commons.

The Simon commission was appointed "for the purpose of inquiring into the working of system of Government, the growth of education and development of representative institutions in British India and matters connected therewith" and reporting "as to whether and to what extent it is desirable to establish the principle of responsible Government then existing therein, including the question whether the establishment of second chambers of the local legislatures, is or is not desirable." As the inquiry was coming to a close, the Commissioners "were increasingly impressed by the impossibility of considering the constitutional problems of British India without taking into account the relation between British India and the Indian States." With the approval of the British Government, the Commission also considered the relations between British India and the Indian States.

The Simon Commission was boycotted not only by the Congress and other representative organisations, but also by other distinguished leaders of India. Resolutions were passed condemning the constitution of the Commission. The day on which the Commission landed in India, there was a "hartal" all over the country. Wherever the members of the Commission went, they were greeted with black flags and cries of "Simon Go Back". The Central Assembly was invited to form a Committee to co-operate with the Commission, but it refused to do so. A large number of persons were arrested and prosecuted.

The Report of the Simon Commission was published in May 1930. First of all, the Report considered as to what should be the ultimate constitutional framework of all India and what should be the place of provinces in that. The Report declared that the framework could not be of a unitary type. It must be federal, not merely in response to the growth of provincial loyalties, but primarily because it must embrace all India and it was only in a Federation that the Indian States could be expected in course of time to unite with British India. Its main recommedations were :

1. The dyarchy should be abolished in the provinces and the whole field of provincial administration should be entrusted to ministers responsible to their legislatures. "Each province should as far as possible be the mistress in her own house."
2. The question of making Sind and Orissa as separate provinces should be given further expert examination. However, it should be decided forthwith to separate Burma from the Government of India. The North-West Frontier Province was considered to be ripe for the first step in constitutional advance. That province should be given a Legislative Council and its representation in the Central Legislature should be strengthened.
3. With regard to the Centre, the Report made recommendations which aimed at preparing the way for an All-India Federation. The Central Legislature was to be refashioned on the federal principle. The members of the Federal Assembly or the Lower House were to be representatives not of sections of the people of India at large but of the provinces. They were to be elected by the Provincial Councils. The elections and nominations to the Council of State were also to be on a provincial basis. The

distribution of seats among the various provinces for the Assembly was to be roughly on population basis. Each province was to have 3 members in the Council of State.

4. So far as the Central Executive was concerned, there was a note of "gradualness" in the Report. No substantial change was recommended. The whole Government was to continue as official Government. There was to be no Government responsible to the Legislature. There was to be no dyarchy at the Centre. It was pointed out that there was the need for keeping the Centre strong and stable while the Provincial Councils were learning by experience to bear the full weight of new and heavy responsibilities.

5. An All-India Federation was to be set up in the distant future. The idea that "the federation of Greater India can be artificially hastened or that, when it comes, it will spring into being at a bound" was set aside. For the present, only one new step was recommended. In order to "foster the sense of need for further developments and bring more nearly within the range of realization other steps which are as yet too distant and too dim to be entered upon and described", a Council for Greater India should be set up representing both British India and the States, discuss in a consultative capacity all matters of common concern, a list of which should be drawn up and scheduled.

The view of P.E. Roberts is that the Simon Commission Report "will always stand out as one of the greatest of India State papers. The impressive unanimity of the commissioners, who from their known party antecedents must clearly have sacrificed all but their deepest convictions to attain it, ought to have commended their sagacious and temperately worded conclusions to men of goodwill."[22] However, the Report was condemned by the Indians. The British Government itself had also partly forestalled it and ultimately side-tracked it, although some of its recommendations were ultimately embodied in the Act of 1935. According to Dr. A.B. Keith, "It was probably foolish of Indian opinion to repudiate the report out and out. If it had been accepted, the British Government could hardly have failed to work on it, and responsible government in the

22. P.E. Roberts, *op.cit.*, p.598.

provinces would have been achieved much earlier than it could be under any later scheme. Moreover, the pressure of such Governments on the Centre would doubtless have operated strongly in the direction of inducing the British Government to aim at federation and the States to come to terms with Indian political leaders. It is noteworthy that the Commission endeavoured to suggest that responsible government in India need not follow rigidly existing models, a fact which at once rendered it suspect in the eyes of Indian politicians, whose views on these topics have throughout shown a remarkable lack of ingenuity and a determination slavishly to copy Western models hardly compatible with the national spirit by which they are animated."[23]

Nehru Report (1928)

The Indians condemned the appointment of an all-white Simon Commission and Lord Birkenhead, while justifying the exclusion of Indians from the Commission, challenged the latter to produce an agreed constitution and submit the same to the British Parliament for consideration. This challenge was accepted by the Indians and an all—Parties Conference was held at Delhi in February-March, 1928. This Conference was presided over by Dr. M.A. Ansari. The Conference appointed a Committee under the Chairmanship of Pandit Motilal Nehru to consider and determine the principles of a constitution for India. Sir Tej Bahadur Sapru (Liberal), Sir Ali Imam, and Shoab Qureshi (Muslim League), M.S. Aney and M.R. Jayakar (Hindu Maha Sabha), Sardar Mangal Singh (Akali Dal), G. R. Pradhan (Dalit), N.M. Joshi (Labour) and Subhash Chandra Bose were its members. The Committee produced a report with these provisions:

1. It laid down generally that all treaties made between the East India Company and the Indian States and all such subsequent treaties so far as they were enforced, shall be binding on the Commonwealth of India and that the Commonwealth shall exercise the same right in relation to and discharge the same obligations towards the Indian States as the Government of India exercised and discharged previously. In regard to matters of justifiable character, in case of differences between Commonwealth and Indian States on any matter arising out

23. A.B. Keith, *op.cit.*, p 203-04.

of treaties, engagements, Sanads or similar other documents, the Governor-General-in-Council may, with the consent of the state concerned, refer such matters to the Supreme Court for its decision.

2. As regards the communal question the report made many wise recommendations. It proposed joint electorates with reservation of seats for minorities on population basis with the right to contest additional seats. No seats were to be reserved for any community in Punjab and Bengal. Full protection was to be given to the religious and cultural interests of the Muslim community. New provinces on linguistic basis were to be created with a view to the "planning of Muslim-majority provinces against Hindu-majority provinces."

3. It enumerated fundamental rights which were to be embodied in the statute.

   (*i*) It was to be declared that all powers of the Government and all authority are derived from the people.

   (*ii*) No person shall be deprived of his liberty, nor shall his dwelling or property be entered, sequestered or confiscated, save in accordance with law.

   (*iii*) Freedom of conscience and free profession and practice of religions will be guaranteed to every person.

   (*iv*) The right to free expression of opinion and the right to assemble peacefully and without arms and to form associations or unions shall be guaranteed for purposes not opposed to public order or morality.

   (*v*) All citizens shall have the right to free elementary education.

   (*vi*) All citizens shall be equal before law and possess equal civic rights. There shall be no penal law of a discriminative nature.

   (*vii*) No person shall be punished for any act which is not punishable under the law at the time it was committed. No corporal punishment or other punishment involving torture of any kind shall be lawful.

   (*viii*) Every citizen shall have the right to a writ of Habeas Corpus.

(*ix*) There shall be no state religion for the Commonwealth of India or for any province, nor shall any state endow any religion or give preference to any religion.

(*x*) No person attending any school receiving state-aid or other public money shall be compelled to attend religious instruction that may be given in the school.

(*xi*) No person shall by reason of his religion, caste or creed be prejudiced in any way in regard to public employment, office of power or honour and the exercise of any trade or calling.

(*xii*) All citizens shall have an equal right of access to, and use of, public roads, public wells and all other places of public resort.

(*xiii*) Freedom of combination and association for maintenance and improvement of labour and economic conditions shall be guaranteed to everyone and of all occupations. All agreements and measures tending to restrict or obstruct such freedom shall be illegal.

(*xiv*) No breach of contract or service or abetment shall be made a criminal offence.

(*xv*) Parliament shall make suitable laws for the maintenance of health and fitness for work of all citizens, securing of a living wage for every worker, the protection of motherhood, welfare of children, and the economic consequences of old age infirmity and unemployment.

(*xvi*) Every citizen shall have the right to keep and bear arms in accordance with the regulations made in that behalf.

(*xvii*) Men and women shall have equal rights as citizens.

4. It provided for a parliament of two houses, viz., Senate and House of Representatives. The Governor-General was to be appointed by the British Government. He was to be paid out of the Indian revenues and his salary was not to be altered during his continuance in office. The Senate was to consist of 200 members elected by provincial councils. The House of Representatives was to consist of 500 members. It was to be elected on an adult franchise basis. The life of the Senate was to be seven years and that of the House of Representatives 5 years.

5. The Governor-General was to act on the advice of the Executive Government. The Prime Minister was to be appointed by the Governor-General and other Ministers were to be appointed on the advice of the Prime Minister. The Executive Government was to be collectively responsible to the Parliament. The Governor-General-in-Council was to appoint High Commissioners and other foreign representatives similar to those appointed by him in Canada and other Dominions. He was also to appoint Auditor-General of India.

6. The Governor of every province was to be appointed by the King of England. He was to be paid out of the provincial revenues. Provision was also to be made for a Legislative Council elected on an adult-franchise basis. The Provincial Council was to sit for 5 years. However, it could be dissolved earlier by the Governor. The latter could also extend its life under special circumstances. Provision was made for a President and Vice-President of the Legislative Council.

7. The Governor was to act on the advice of the provincial Executive Council whose strength was not to exceed 5. The Governor-General was to select the Chief Minister and the other members of the Executive Council were to be appointed by him on the advice of the Chief Minister.

8. Provision was to be made for a Supreme Court. It was to consist of a Lord President and other Justices. The members of the Supreme Court were to be appointed by the Governor-General-in-Council, but were not to be removed from office except on an address from both houses of Parliament praying for such removal on the ground of misbehaviour or incapacity. The Supreme Court was to have both original and appellate jurisdiction. Provision was also to be made for taking of appeals to the King-in-Council under certain circumstances.

9. The Governor-General-in-Council was to appoint a Committee of Defence consisting of the Minister of Defence, Minister of Foreign Affairs, Commander-in-Chief, Commander of Air Forces, Commander of Naval Forces, Chief of the General Staff and two other experts. The Prime Minister was to be the Chairman of the Committee. The functions of that Committee were to advise the Government and the various departments concerned on questions of defence and general policy.

10. As regards the civil services, all officers of public services at the time of the establishment of Commonwealth, were to become officers of the Commonwealth. The Governor-General was to appoint a Public Service Commission. All officers of the Army Services were to retain all their existing rights regarding their salaries, allowances and pensions. They were also to get compensation for any loss incurred by them.

The Nehru Report was submitted on August 10, 1928 at the All-Parties Conference held at Lucknow. It could not be passed. It was revised and then discussed at the Calcutta meet on December 22, 1928. But it could not be passed owing to communal differences.

The Muslims criticized the Nehru Report on the ground that there was no provision for separate electorates for the Muslims in it and they were determined to retain what was given to them in the Acts of 1909 and 1919. The Nerhu Report was intended to serve as a fitting reply to the racial arrogance of Lord Birkenhead, but it ultimately resulted in national humiliation. Mahatma Gandhi admitted this fact in these words: "The Nehru constitution having lapsed, the communal solution has naturally lapsed."

Jinnah's Fourteen Points (1929)

Jinnah summoned a meeting of the All-India Muslim League at Delhi in March 1929 and put forward his Fourteen Points as the minimum Muslim demands for any political settlement. While rejecting the Nehru Report, the resolution of the League laid down as under:

"That no scheme for the future constitution of the Government of India will be acceptable to the Musalmans of India until and unless the following basic principles are given effect to and provisions are embodied therein to safeguard their rights and interests:

1. "The form of the future constitution should be federal with the residuary powers vested in the provinces.
2. "A uniform measure of autonomy shall be granted to all the provinces.
3. "All legislatures in the country and other elected bodies shall be constituted on the definite principle of adequate and

effective representation of minorities in every province without reducing the majority in any province to a minority or even equality.

4. "In Central Legislature Muslim representation shall be one-third.
5. "Representation of communal groups shall continue to be by separate electorates as at present, provided it shall be open to any community, at any time, to abandon its separate electorate in favour of joint electorates.
6. "Any territorial re-distribution that might at any time be necessary shall not in any way affect the Muslim majority in the Punjab, Bengal and North-West Frontier Province.
7. "Full religious liberty, *i.e.*, liberty of belief, worship and observance, propaganda, association and education shall be guaranteed to all communities.
8. "No bill or resolution or any part thereof shall be passed in any legislature or any elected body if three-fourths of the members of any community in that particular body oppose such a bill, resolution or part thereof on the ground that it would be injurious to the interests of that community, or in the alternative such other method is devised as may be found possible and practicable to deal with such cases.
9. "Sind should be separated from the Bombay Presidency.
10. "Reforms should be introduced in the N.W.F. Province and Baluchistan on the same footing as in other provinces.
11. "Provision should be made in the constitution giving Muslims adequate share along with other Indians in all the services of the state and in local self-government bodies having due regard to the requirements of efficiency.
12. "The constitution should embody adequate safeguards for the protection of Muslim culture and for the promotion of Muslim education, language, religion, personal laws and Muslim charitable institutions and for their due share in the grants-in-aid given by the state and by the self-governing bodies.
13. "No Cabinet either central or provincial should be formed without there being a proportion of at least one-third Muslim Ministers.

14. "No change shall be made in the constitution of the Central Legislature except with the concurrence of the States constituting the Indian Federation."

These points were discussed at the session of the Muslim League held at Delhi in March, 1929. On account of the vehement opposition of the groups of Shafi and Agha Khan, no decision could be taken, for both condemned the Nehru Report as the 'death warrant of the Muslims'. A small section of the Muslim nationalists led by Maulana Abul Kalam Azad could not have its way. Thus, the programme of Jinnah "became the charter of demands of the Muslims outside the Nationalist group."[24]

Round Table Conferences, Communal Award and Poona Pact

A change in the British attitude took place with the installation of the Labour government under Prime Minister Ramsay MacDonald with Capt. Wedgewood Benn as the Secretary of State for India. The Prime Minister desired to solve the communal problem of India by inviting prominet Indian leaders to a conference in London. The first conference was held from 16 November, 1930 to 19 January, 1931. The representatives of the Muslim League, the Hindu Maha Sabha, the Indian Liberal Federation, the Scheduled Castes Federation and the Indian princes took part in it, but no decision could be taken as the Congress leaders were detained in the country in connection with the civil disobedience movement. The second conference was held there from 7 September to 1 December, 1931. At this meet, Mahatma Gandhi (with Madan Mohan Malaviya and Sarojini Naidu) took part. In his bold speech, he insisted that the communal problem could be solved only by the Indian leaders in their own country without the intervention of foreign power that assiduously pursued the policy of divide and rule. It could be done by the role of the Indian National Congress as this was the only national and secular organisation of the country. But the leaders of the communal organisations adhered to their point of having reservation of seats in the legislative bodies and so no decision could be taken to solve the tangled issue of communal politics.

---

24. Rajendra Prasad: *India Divided*, p. 132.

Prime Minister MacDonald issued his award on 16 August 1932 specifying reservation of seats in favour of Muslims, Christians, Anglo-Indians, Europeans, Tribals, Sikhs, Marathas and women. It is known as the Communal Award. Surprisingly, the Muslims were given more than appropriate reservation of seats. For instance, in the Legislative Council of United Provinces, out of 228 seats, 66 seats were reserved for them, while 132 general seats were also open for them. For the first time, seats were reserved for the Depressed Castes or Classes (Dalits) in various provinces whose total figure was 71. They were also given separate electorates. At that time Gandhiji was interned in the Yervada jail of Poona. On 18 September, he went on a hunger strike with the demand for omitting the reservation of seats in favour of the Dalits as it would cut them off from the Hindu society. On 24th September, a pact was made with Dr. B.R. Ambedkar. It provided that the number of seats reserved for the Depressed Castes should be enhanced to 148 and that they should be given joint electorates in place of separate electorates.

The third round table conference was held there from 17 November to 24 December, 1932. Now the Labour government was replaced by the Conservative government. It was thinly attended. The leaders of the Labour Party boycotted it. No leader of the Indian National Congress was invited as Congress had been declared an illegal organisation by Viceroy Lord Willingdon in January, 1932. A Joint Select Committee of 16 members of the British Parliament under the chairmanship of Lord Linlithgow was constituted which studied the deliberations of the two conferences and examined a number of witnesses. Then, the British government released a White Paper. The leaders of the Congress rejected the proposals of the White Paper. The Muslim League rejected the proposal of an all-India Federation, though it accepted the plan of provincial autonomy. The provisions of the White Paper had their place in the Government of India Act, 1935 which was described by Nehru as the 'charter of slavery'. Clement Attlee of the Labour party commented that 'mistrust was the keynote of this Act." In the view of the national leaders, "the cardinal objection to this Act was that it was the product neither of self-determination, nor even of joint determination, but of other determination."[25]

---

25. P.B. Sitaramayya: *The History of the Indian National Congress*, Vol. II, p. 12.

3

Constitutional Development (1935–47)

A change occurred in the trend of India's constitutional development after 1930. The provisions of the Nehru Report (1928), of the Fourteen Points of Jinnah (1929), of the Simon Commission Report (1930) and the deliberations of the three Round Table Conferences (1930-32) had their definite impact on this trend. The Indian States were given representation in the Round Table Conferences which made it essential that in any scheme of constitutional reforms, their case should also be taken into account. For the first time, in the proposed federal system, seats were given to the States in both houses of federal legislature and the subjects of administration were explicitly distributed between the Centre and the units. Most notable is the fact that so far each statute made by the British Parliament came into effect in full, but the Act of 1935 created the peculiar case as its scheme of federation remained unimplemented owing to its inherent defects. It was scrapped in 1939. The provisions of provincial autonomy came into effect. The astounding success of the Congress in the elections of 1937 forced the leaders of the Muslim League to demand partition of the country. So an English writer observes: "The years 1937-39 were notable for a great success, a great failure, and a great mistake. The success was the Congress ministries, for which both the Government and the ministries share the credit. The failure was the inability of the Government to persuade the princes to join the federation."[1]

Government of India Act of 1935

So came this Act in the form of a very long document with these important features:

---

1. Percival Spear: *India: A Modern History* p. 393.

1. It provided for an All-India Federation. All the provinces were to join the Indian Federation. Entry into the Federation was to be a purely voluntary action on the part of each State, however small and insignificant that State might be. At the time of joining the Federation, the ruler of the State was to execute an Instrument of Accession in favour of the Crown. On acceptance of that Instrument, the State was to become a unit of the Federation. While the provinces were to be alike in respect of the position of the quantum of Legislative and Executive powers in the Federation, the States were to differ regarding the extent of their powers in the Federation.

2. The Indian States were to send 125 members to the Federal Assembly and 104 members to the Council of State. The provinces were to send 250 members to the Federal Assembly and 156 members to the Council of State. The members from the Indian States were to be nominated by the rulers, but those from the provinces were to be elected on communal lines. The functions of the Crown with regard to the Indian States were to be performed in India by his representative who, in fact, was the Viceroy himself.

3. It provided for dyarchy at the Centre. The dyarchy in the provinces was abolished, but it was introduced at the Centre. Certain Federal subjects were reserved in the hands of the Governor-General to be administered by him with the assistance of not more than 3 Executive Councillors to be appointed by him. Those subjects were Defence, External Affairs, Ecclesiastical Affairs and the Administration of Tribal Areas. In the administration of the other Federal subjects, the Governor-General was to be aided and advised by a Council of Ministers whose number was not to exceed 10. The Federal Ministry was to be formed on the usual cabinet lines except that it was to include the representatives of the States who were the nominees of their rulers and the representatives of the important minorities. In spite of the composite character of the Ministry, their responsibility was to be collective. The Ministry was to be responsible to the Federal Legislature. "The position assigned under the new Constitution to the Council of Federal Ministers is ornamental, without being useful, onerous without ever being helpful to the people they

are supposed to represent, responsibility without power, position without authority, name without any real influence."[2]

4. The Federal Legislature was to be bicameral, consisting of the Federal Assembly and the Council of State. The Federal Assembly was to have a life of 5 years from the date of its first meeting. On the expiry of that period, it was to be automatically dissolved. However, the Governor-General was given the power to extend its life. The Council of State was to be a permanent body of which one-third members were to retire after every 3 years. The members from the States were to be nominated by the rulers. The representatives from British India were to be elected. The Hindu, Muslim and Sikh members were to be elected on communal lines. While the members of Council of State were to be directly elected, those of Federal Assembly were to be indirectly elected.

5. The powers of the Legislatures were severely restricted. There were certain subjects on which neither the Federal Legislature nor the Provincial Legislatures could legislate. The Federal Legislature was debarred from making any law affecting the Sovereign or the Royal Family or the succession to the throne or suzerainty of the Crown or any part of India, or the law of British nationality, or the Army Act, the Air Force Act, or the law of Prize Courts. The Federal Legislature could not make any law amending any of the provisions of the Act of 1935, or any Order-in-Council made under it, or any rules made thereunder by the Secretary of State or by the Governor-General or a Governor in his discretion or in the exercise of his individual judgement. It could not make any law affecting the prerogative rights of the Crown to grant special leave to appeal to the Privy Council except in so far as that was expressly permitted by the Act. It could not pass any legislation which discriminated against the British interests in commercial and other spheres. Moreover, there were subjects of vital importance on which initiation of legislation required previous sanction of the Governor-General in respect of Federal legislation, and the Governor in respect of Provincial legislation.

---

2. K.T. Shah: *Federal Structure in India,* p. 223.

5. The Governor-General was empowered to summon a joint sitting of the two Houses of the Federal Legislature when a Bill passed by one chamber was rejected by the other, or was amended in a form to which the first chamber was not agreeable. After a Bill was passed by both the chambers of the Federal Legislature, the Governor-General, in his discretion, could assent to it, or veto it or send it back for re-consideration or reserve it for His Majesty's consideration. The Act assented to by the Governor-General could be disallowed within a year by the King-in-Council.
6. It provided for the establishment of a Federal Court with jurisdiction over the States and the Provinces. The Court was to consist of a Chief Justice and two puisne Judges. It was given both original and appellate jurisdiction. It was the duty of the Federal Court to interpret the Constitution and to see that the provinces and the Federal Government acted only within those spheres which were reserved for them by the Constitution. However, the last word in this matter was to be given by the Privy Council in London.
7. The Act of 1935 abolished the India Council of the Secretary of State. The Secretary of State was given advisers who could or could not be consulted, or whose advice could or could not be followed, except in regard to their advice in respect of the Services.
8. But the most important feature of the Act was the provision for Provincial Autonomy. This was in accordance with the August declaration of 1917. The Act of 1919 had placed a little control in the provincial field into the hands of the Indian ministers. This Act was a definite improvement on the Act of 1919 inasmuch as there were no reserved subjects with the Governor. All ministers under a premier were collectively responsible to the Legislature. However, the Governor was given many powers which he could exercise in his discretion and in his individual judgement.

The Home Government

The office of the Secretary of State for India was created by the Act of 1858 when the Board of Control and the Court of Directors were abolished after the Mutiny. The Secretary of State was a member of the British Parliament and also a member of the British

Cabinet. Up to 1919, he was paid out of the Indian revenues but the Act of 1919 provided that in future he was to be paid from the British Treasury. He was assisted in his work by a Parliamentary Under-Secretary, a Permanent Under Secretary, an Advisory Body and the India Office.

Under the Act of 1919, the Secretary of State enjoyed numerous powers. He was authorized to superintend, direct and control the affairs of the Government of India. Both the Governor-General and the Governors were required to pay due obedience to his orders. It changed the position to a considerable extent. It granted what is known as Provincial Autonomy. As the Indian ministers came to have a lot of control over provincial administration, the control of the Secretary of State diminished over the provinces. Likewise, the establishment of dyarchy at the Centre by the Act of 1935 also lessened the control of the Secretary of State over the Government of India. The control of the Secretary of State came in only when the Governors or the Governor-General acted in their individual judgement and decided to do things against the advice of the ministers, the control of the Secretary of State appeared again.

As the discretionary powers of the Governor-General and the Governors were very large, the control of the Secretary of State also remained substantial. The Secretary of State exercised control over the Reserved Departments of Defence, External Affairs, Administration of Tribal Areas, and Ecclesiastical Affairs, the Federal Railway Authority, and the Reserve Bank of India. He could control the whole administrative machinery of India by giving appropriate directions to the Central and Provincial administrations. He had many powers with regard to the services. He appointed officers belonging to the Indian Civil Service, Indian Police Service and the Irrigation Service. He determined the conditions of service of all such persons. He was the constitutional adviser of the Crown with regard to the Indian affairs. He advised the King in the exercise of all his powers of appointment and the vetoing of any Bill which could have been reserved by the Governor-General for the consideration of His Majesty or which may have been even assented to by the Governor-General.

The Secretary of State was required to submit all the draft Instruments of Instructions to be issued to the Governor-General and the Governors, before Parliament for its approval. He was also to submit before Parliament all Orders-in-Council to be issued by His Majesty under the powers granted by the Act. He was the agent of Parliament and was also responsible to Parliament for the Indian affairs. It was his duty to supply the British Parliament all the information regarding Indian affairs and also to answer all questions regarding the same.

The Secretary of State was assisted by an Advisory Body. This Advisory Body was formerly known as the India Council and was set up by the Act of 1858 to assist the Secretary of State for India in the discharge to his duties. Under the Act of 1919, the India Council consisted of not less than 8 and not more than 12 members. The Secretary of State-in-Council was a corporate body which could sue and be sued and conducted business in the United Kingdom in relation to the Government of India. Ordinarily, the Secretary of State was not bound by the advice of the India Council. But in matters relating to grants from the revenues of India, making of contracts, and rules and regulations connected with the Civil Service, he was bound by the majority view of the India Council.

This India Council was abolished and now the Secretary of State was to appoint not less than 3 and not more than 6 advisers. At least half of these persons were to be those who had held office in India for at least 14 years and who had not left India for more than 2 years at the time of their appointment. They were to hold office for 5 years only. They could not sit in Parliament. Their function was merely advisory and as a rule the Secretary of State was not bound by their advice. However, in matters relating to rules and regulations concerning the Civil Services, the Secretary of State was required to secure the concurrence of at least one-half of the advisers.

Federal Government

Under the Act of 1935, the Governor-General was the corner-stone of the entire constitution of India. It was he who gave unity and direction to its various, diverse and often conflicting elements. It was he who was expected to keep the ship of the State on an even keel and to protect the British vested interests in India. It is desirable to discuss his position under the Act of 1935. Appointed by the King on the advice of the British Prime Minister, the

Governor-General acted in three different capacities. Ordinarily, he was to act according to the advice of the Council of Ministers. When he did that, he acted as a constitutional head like the King of England or the Governor-General of Canada. In certain cases, he acted in his individual judgement. While doing so, he was to consult his Ministers, but could or could not act upon their advice. This he did in the performance of his special responsibilities:

1. Safeguarding the financial stability and the credit of India.
2. The prevention of any grave menace to the peace or tranquillity of India or any part of India.
3. Safeguarding the legitimate interests of the minorities.
4. Safeguarding the legitimate rights of the public servants and their dependants.
5. Prevention of commercial discrimination.
6. Prevention of discriminatory taxation against goods of British origin or Burmese origin.
7. Safeguarding the interests of the Indian States and the dignity of their rulers.
8. The securing of the due discharge of his discretionary powers.

While acting in his discretion, the Governor-General did not even consult the ministers in the following matters:

1. He was in charge of the Reserved Departments of Defence, External Affairs, Ecclesiastical Affairs and Administration of Tribal Areas.
2. He could appoint and dismiss the Council of Ministers and also preside over its meetings.
3. He could issue two kinds of ordinances. One type of ordinance he could issue at any time and that lasted for 6 months. The other kind of ordinance was issued when the Legislature was not sitting.
4. The previous sanction of the Governor-General was required for the introduction of certain bills in the Federal Legislature and the Provincial Legislatures. He was authorised to stop the discussion of any Bill at any time by the Legislature. He could withhold his assent to a Bill passed by the Legislature

or send the same back for reconsideration, or reserve the same for the consideration of His Majesty.

5. The Governor-General could in his discretion send any instructions to the Governors and it was the special responsibility of the latter to carry them out.
6. He could suspend the Constitution.
7. He was given the power to summon, prorogue or dissolve the Federal Assembly. He could summon both Houses for a joint sitting. He could address the Legislatures or send message regarding a certain bill.

As regards his control over the States, his special responsibilities allowed him to interfere freely in any matter of a federated state. Moreover, if it appeared to the Governor-General that the ruler of any federated state had in any way failed to fulfil his obligations to the Federal Government, he could issue in his discretion such directions to the ruler as he thought fit.

It is clear from above that the Governor-General had comprehensive powers which dealt with every field of administration. His powers were extensive both in the legislative and executive departments. His control over the federal finance was about 80 per cent of the whole. There was no sphere in which he was not in a position to dictate. The counsellors were merely his creatures. It is rightly said that "there is hardly any aspect of Government over which the Governor-General will not wield complete dictatorial authority. Not only will the Federal Legislature be an ineffective and powerless body as explained by the innumerable discretionary powers vested in the Governor-General, but the executive machinery of the Federation will also be under the complete and unquestioned sway of the Governor-General. The Federal Government will thus be in reality a one man's rule, unsurpassed in many respects by oriental despotism or modern dictatorships."[3]

Government of the Provinces

The position of the Governors under the Act of 1935 resembled that of the Governor-General, although it differed a little on account

3. Shafat Ahmad Khan: *The Indian Federation*, p. 43.

of the introduction of 'Provincial Autonomy. The Governor was appointed by the King by a Commission under the Royal Sign Manual. His office was constituted by Letters Patent. His salary was fixed by the Act. The job of a Governor was the prize post which usually went to those members of the Indian Civil Service who had brilliant record of service.

The Governors were authorised to act in their individual judgement. While doing so, they had to listen to the advice of the ministers but they could or could not act upon their advice. The Governors acted in individual judgement while performing their special responsibilities which were as follows:

1. Prevention of any grave menace to the peace or tranquillity of the province or any part thereof.
2. Safeguarding the rights and legitimate interests of the public servants and their dependants.
3. Safeguarding the rights and interests of the Indian States and the dignity of their rulers.
4. Safeguarding the legitimate interests of the minorities.
5. Administration of partially-excluded areas.
6. Prevention of commercial discrimination against Englishmen and their goods.
7. Execution of the orders and directions of the Governor-General issued by him in his discretion.
8. It was the duty of the Governor of C.P. to see that a reasonable share of the provincial revenues was spent for the benefit of the people of Berar.
9. It was the duty of the Governor of Sind to secure the proper administration of the Lloyd Barrage and Canal's Scheme.

The Governors acted in their discretion in these matters:

1. They could appoint and dismiss ministers. They presided over the meetings of the Council of Ministers. By doing so, they could influence the deliberations and conclusions of the Ministers.
2. They could issue two kinds of ordinances. One kind of ordinance could be issued by them at any time and that lasted

for six months. The other type of ordinance was issued only when the Legislature was not sitting. They could stop the discussion of any Bill in the Legislature at any time. Even when the Bill was passed, the Governors could veto the same or send the same back for reconsideration by the Legislature. They could reserve the same Bill for the assent of the Governor-General.

3. They appointed members of the Provincial Public Service Commission. They were given large powers regarding the Police Force.
4. They decided as to what items of expenditure were to be regarded as "expenditure charged upon revenues of the province." If the whole or any part of the budget was rejected, the Governors were authorised to restore the same.
5. In the event of emergency, the Governors were given the authority to suspend the Consititution and take over the administration in their own hands.

Provincial Ministers

The position of the Provincial Ministers under the Act of 1935 was certainly superior to those of the Ministers under the Act of 1919. All the Departments were to be under the charge of the Ministers. The Governor was expected to carry on the administration of the province according to the advice of the Ministers. It was laid down in the Instrument of Instructions that the Governor was to summon that person to form the Ministry who could be expected to command majority in the Provincial Legislature. The other Ministers were to be appointed by the Governor on the advice of the Premier. It was the duty of the Governor to see that minorities were given representation in the Ministry. If a person was not a member of the Legislature at the time of his appointment, he was to get himself elected within six months of his appointment. The Governors were instructed to encourage collective responsibility amongst the Ministers. They were allowed to preside over the meetings of the Council of Ministers.

However, it is to be noted that the powers of the Ministers were limited. They did not enjoy complete autonomy in the provincial field. The enormous powers of the Governor were responsible for weakening the position of the Ministers. The Governor had legislative powers which restricted the authority of the Ministers.

Provincial Legislatures

The Government of India Act, 1935, did not set up provincial legislatures of a uniform pattern. The six provinces of Assam, Bengal, Bihar, U.P., Madras and Bombay were given two Chambers each while the legislatures of the Punjab, Sind, North-Western Frontier Province, Orissa and C.P. had only one Chamber. Where there were two Houses, their names were the Provincial Legislative Assembly and the Provincial Legislative Council. Where there was only one House, it was merely the Provincial Legislative Assembly. While all the members of the Assembly were elected, some of the members of the Legislative Council were nominated.

The size of the Provincial Assemblies varied from province to province. It was 215 for Madras, 175 for Bombay and Punjab, 250 for Bengal, 228 for U.P., 152 for Bihar, 112 for C.P. and Berar, 108 for Assam, 50 for North-Western Frontier Province and 60 each for Orissa and Sind. The seats in the various provinces were distributed according to the Communal Award as amended by the Poona Pact. Some seats were known as general seats out of which some were reserved for the scheduled castes. Separate representation on communal lines was given to the Muslims, Sikhs, Anglo-Indians, Europeans and Indian Christians. Some seats were reserved for commerce, industry, mining and planting, land-holders, labour and universities. Out of the seats exclusively reserved for women, some were given to Hindus and the others to the Muslims, Sikhs, Anglo-Indians and Indian Christians.

The Legislative Councils were provided for six provinces. The maximum number of seats for a Provincial Legislative Council was 56 in Madras, 30 in Bombay, 65 in Bengal, 60 in U.P., 30 in Bihar and 22 in Assam. Out of a total of 56 seats in Madras, 10 seats were filled by the Governor through nomination. The general seats for Madras, Bombay, Bengal, U.P., Bihar and Assam were 35, 20, 10, 34, 9 and 10 respectively. Mohammedans had 17 seats each in Bihar and U.P.; 27 and 12 seats respectively in Bengal and Bihar Legislative Councils were filled by the Legislative Assemblies of those provinces. Some seats were reserved for Europeans and Indian

Christians, e.g., three for Europeans in Bengal and three for Indian Christians in Madras. The Provincial Legislative Council was a permanent body. The tenure of the members was of nine years, but one-third of them had to retire after every three years.

The age qualification for membership of the Provincial Legislative Assembly was fixed at 25 and 30 for the Provincial Legislative Council. No person could become a member of both the Houses of the Legislature at the same time. Residence in the constituency for a certain number of days, usually 180 or 120, was necessary for franchise.

The Provincial Legislatures were authorised to make laws on the subjects given in the Provincial List and Concurrent List. In the latter case, their powers were concurrent with the Federal Legislature. In case the Federal Legislature made a law on a subject included in the Concurrent List, the Federal law had precedence over the Provincial law. The powers of the Legislature also extended to those residuary subjects which were assigned to it by the Governor-General in his discretion. The Provincial List included subjects such as public order, administration of justice, constitution and organization of all courts except the Federal Court of India, preventive detention, police, prisons, reformatories, borstal institutions, public debt of the province, Provincial Public Services and Provincial Service Commissions, Provincial pensions, compulsory acquisition of land, election to the Provincial Legislature, salaries, allowances and privileges of the members of the Provincial Legislature, local self-government, public health and sanitation, hospitals and dispensaries, education, roads, bridges, ferries, water-supply, irrigation and canals, agriculture, forests, taxes on agricultural income, etc.

The Concurrent List included subjects like criminal law and criminal procedure, civil procedure, marriage and divorce, wills, intestacy and succession, registration of deeds and documents, trusts and trustees, contracts, bankruptcy and insolvency, legal, medical, and other professions, newspapers, books and printing presses, boilers, criminal tribes, factories, welfare of labour, unemployment, insurance, old age pensions, trade unions, industrial and labour disputes, electricity, etc.

It might appear from the above that the powers of the Provincial Legislature were extensive. However, a critical study of this Act, shows that innumerable restrictions were put on them. The Legislatures did not enjoy complete control over legislation. The previous sanction not only of the Governor but also of the Governor-General was required in certain cases even to introduce a bill in the Provincial Legislature. Even if that hurdle was crossed, the Governor could stop the discussion on a bill at any stage. Even if the bill was passed by the legislature, the Governor could veto it in his discretion or reserve the same for the assent of the Governor-General. The Governor was also given the power of issuing ordinances and enacting what were known as the Governor's Acts. Even in the financial field the powers of the Provincial Legislatures were limited. About 40% of the provincial budget was not under their control. That was a charge on the revenues of the province. This clearly points out the limitations of Provincial Legislature. It is obvious that the limitations imposed on the Provincial Legislatures impaired considerably the nature of provincial autonomy.

Provincial Autonomy

It cannot be denied that Provincial Autonomy as set up by the Act of 1935 was a definite improvement on the system of dyarchy introduced under the Act of 1919.[4] According to the Joint Select Committee, Provincial autonomy is a scheme "whereby each of the Governors' Provinces will possess an Executive and a Legislature... broadly free from control by the Central Government. This we conceive to be the essence of Provincial Autonomy, though no doubt there is room for wide differences of opinion with regard to the manner in which that exclusive authority is to be exercised...the Central Government and Legislature would, generally speaking, cease to possess in the Governor's Provinces any legal power or authority with respect to any matter falling within the exclusive provincial sphere, though, the Governor's authority to secure compliance in certain respects with directions which he may find it necessary to give."

As there was a lot of delay in the establishment of the All-India Federation, it was decided by the British Government to enforce

---

4. It was a system of government wherein the provinces had substantial freedom to perform the functions given to them under the Act without interference from above." M.V. Pylee: *Constitutional History of India, 1600-1950*, p. 88.

that part of the Act of 1935 which was related to the provinces. Consequently, elections were held in the provinces in January 1937. Jawaharlal Nehru, who was the President of the Congress at that time, made a whirl-wind tour and carried the message of the Congress to every nook and corner of the country. The people also responded to the national call and the Congress was able to secure clear majority in six provinces, viz., U.P., Bihar, Orissa, Bombay, Madras and C.P. It emerged as the largest party in Assam and the North-Western Frontier Province.

It is true that the Congress won elections, but there was no unanimity of opinion among the Congressmen with regard to the future. There were two distinct schools of thought among the Congressmen. One school (led by Sardar Patel, Dr. Rajendra Prasad and C. Rajagopalachariar) was of the view that offices should be accepted under the new Constitution with the object of strengthening the hands of the Congress in its struggle for complete freedom. The other school (led by Jawaharlal Nehru, J.P. Narayan and Subhash Chandra Bose) was of the view that the acceptance of office was likely to lessen the zeal of the Congress for fight for India's freedom. Mahatma Gandhi intervened and he was able to bring both the groups together. The result was that a resolution was passed by the All-India Congress Committee on 30th March, 1937 which authorised and permitted the "acceptance of office in the provinces where Congress commands majority in the legislature, provided that ministerships should not be accepted unless the leader of the Congress Party in the legislature is satisfied and able to state publicly that the Governor will not use his special powers of interference or set aside the advice of ministers in regard to their constitutional activities."

The Governors of the provinces were not prepared to act like constitutional heads and consequently refused to give the assurance demanded by the leaders of the Congress in the Congress-majority provinces. As both the parties were adamant, the Governors of the Congress-majority provinces set up interim ministries to carry on the administration. Such ministries could not hope to last long as they could not face the Provincial Legislative Assemblies on account of their minorities. In the non-Congress Provinces, popular ministries began to function from 1st April, 1937. The leaders of the parties like Unionist Party in Punjab and Krishak-Praja Party in Bengal did not demand any assurance from the Governors and consequently there was no difficulty in the formation of the ministries there.

The deadlock in the Congress-majority provinces did not last long. Lord Linlithgow, Governor-General of India, declared in a broadcast speech on 22 June, 1937 that "there is no foundation for any suggestion that a Governor is free, or is entitled or would have the power to interfere with the day-to-day administration of a province outside the limited range of the responsibilities resting on him. These special responsibilities are restricted in scope to the narrowest limits possible. Even so limited as they are, the Governor will at all times be concerned to carry his ministers with him, while in other spheres in the field of their ministerial responsibility, it is mandatory on a Governor to be guided by the advice of his ministers, even though for whatever reasons he may not himself be wholly satisfied that the advice is in the circumstances necessarily and decisively the right advice." The Congress circles welcomed the conciliatory speech of the Governor-General and consequently the Working Committee of the Congress passed a resolution on 7th July, 1937 at Wardha in favour of office acceptance.

In the Congress majority provinces some healthy conventions were set up. The ministers acted on the principle of collective responsibility. The Congress Ministry in Assam set up the convention that the government should resign if a Bill introduced by it was rejected by the legislature. Except in the case of Orissa, the Congress Ministries included members of the minority communities. The Governors continued to preside over the meetings of the provincial ministries. That was not liked by the Congress Ministries. The result was that before going to the meetings to be presided over by the Governors, the Congress Ministries met separately and arrived at their own conclusions. Then the same matter was put before the Governor and if he insisted on interfering, he was threatened with the resignation of the ministry. It is stated that the Congress ministers went to the meetings presided over by the Governor with their resignations in their pockets. It was in this way that the possibility of the Governor influencing the decisions of the ministers was eliminated in the Congress-majority provinces.

As regards the part played by the services under Provincial Autonomy, there were three kinds of civil servants in the country.

Some of them resigned on the eve of the introduction of provincial autonomy as they felt that they could not work under the new set-up. To the second category belonged those civil servants who were prepared to change themselves with the changed circumstances and carry out the orders of the new ministers. To the third category belonged those public servants who wanted to continue for the sake of mischief. In the case of U.P., the Chief Secretary issued a circular to the administrative officers under him that no order was to be executed by them unless the same was countersigned by one of the Secretaries. G.B. Pant, the Premier of U.P., protested and asked for an explanation from the Chief Secretary. He described the act of the Chief Secretary as one of "insubordination or incompetency". The result was that the circular was withdrawn, but it had a wholesome effect on other civil servants in the country.

As regards the beneficial effects of the working of Provincial Autonomy, the Congress ministries were able to do a lot of constructive work. A large number of laws dealing with prohibition, education, agricultural indebtedness, cottage industries, rural development, relations between tenants and landlords, etc., were passed. The Bombay Ministry passed a law by which the lands confiscated by the British Government on political grounds, were restored. The Ministry of Madras removed the statue of General Neil from its prominent place in Madras. The political prisoners were released. Jawaharlal Nehru described the effect of the Congress Ministries on the masses in these words: "But the psychological change was enormous and the electric current seemed to run through the country-side. The change was noticeable more in the rural areas than in the cities, though in the industrial centres the industrial workers reacted in the same way. There was a sense of immense relief as of the lifting of a weight which had been oppressing the people; there was a release of long suppressed mass energy which was evident everywhere. The fear of the police and secret service agent vanished for a while at least and even the poorest peasant added to his feeling of self-respect and self-reliance. For the first time he felt that he counted and could not be ignored."[5]

Cirticism of the Act

It seems desirable to state the important points of criticism levelled against the Act of 1935.

---

5. Nehru, *op. cit.*, pp. 391-92.

1. It was a "machine with strong brakes and no engine." According to a critic, the India Act of 1935 "tests to the full Indian capacity for administration and government exactly as a man's capacity for swimming is tested to the full by throwing him into a river with his hands and feet tied."
2. The Indians were not given control over the government of their country. They could not change or amend their constitution. They detested the dyarchical form of Government at the Centre. They protested against the control which was to be exercised by the Secretary of State for India over the Indian Civil Service, the Indian Police Service and other All-India Services, including provincial governments.
3. The Indian States were given a privileged position under the constitution. The representation given to them both in the Council of State and the Federal Assembly was more than what was due to them on the basis of their territory, population or the contributions to be made by them to the revenues of the Federal Government. While the members from British India were to be elected by the people, the Indian princes were empowered to nominate their representatives.
4. The seats in the Legislatures were to be filled on the basis of the Communal Award. The result was that the constitution was communalism-ridden. The Communal Award cut at the very root of Indian nationalism.
5. It was indeed a far cry between the Government Act and Dominion Status. The principle of Dominion Status asserts that the Dominion should have the right to the same measure of autonomy in external affairs as in internal matters and that it was the duty of the British Government to give effect to the accepted doctrine. But India had neither control in the internal nor in the external affairs. The internal administration remained under the control of the Governor-General and the Governors who were vested with tremendous powers.
6. The rulers of the Indian States criticised the Federal Scheme on the ground that it did not give them power to leave the Federation if once they joined it. The Federation had great power of coercing them. The representatives from British India were bound to predominate the Federal Legislature and

Federal Executive and thereby influence the Viceroy to take steps which might impair their authority.

7. The discretionary powers of the governors reduced provincial autonomy to a farce. Those powers and responsibilities "combine, crib and confine" the powers of the Provincial Legislature and executive. Some of these powers and responsibilities were so vaguely defined that those could be interpreted to mean anything according to the exigencies of the moment. The Governor was made the sole judge to decide whether any particular matter fell within his discretionary power or affected any of his special responsibilities. The Governor could become a virtual dictator of the province within the letter of the law.

Jawaharlal Nehru says: "This (Government of India Act. 1935) provided for some kind of provincial autonomy and a federal structure, but there were so many reservations and checks that both political and economic power continued to be concentrated in the hands of the British government. Indeed in some ways it confirmed and enlarged the powers of an executive responsible solely to that government. The federal structure was so envisaged as to make any real advance impossible, and no loophole was left for the representatives of the India people to interfere with or modify the system of British-controlled administration. The Act strengthened the alliance between the British government and the princes, landlords, and other reactionary elements in India... The whole complicated structure of government remained as it was."[6]

When the World War II broke out in September, 1939, India was immediately declared a belligerent country by the British Government without consulting the people of India. The Congress Working Committee strongly protested against this action of the British Government. They called upon the British Government to declare their war aims in clear-cut terms. The British Government refused to give the assurance demanded by the Congress. The result was that the Congress decided to non-co-operate with the British Government. The Congress High Command called the Congress Ministries in eight provinces to resign and they did accordingly in October, 1939. The administration of those eight provinces was

6. Nehru: *op.cit.*, pp. 368-69.

taken over by the Governors. Only the three non-Congress Ministries of Sind, Punjab and Bengal remained in office. V.P. Menon has criticised this action of the Congress in these words: "Had it (the Congress) not resigned from its position of vantage in the provinces, the course of Indian history might have been very different. By resigning, it showed a lamentable lack of foresight and political wisdom. There was little chance of its being put out of office; the British Government would surely have hesitated to incur the odium of dismissing ministries which had the overwhelming support of the people. Nor could it have resisted a unanimous demand for a change at the Centre, a demand which would have been all the more irresistible after the entry of Japan into the war. In any case, it is clear that, but for the resignation of the Congress, Jinnah and the Muslim League would never have attained the position they did."[7]

The August Offer (1940)

There was a lot of discontentment in the country. To meet that situation, Lord Linlithgow declared in January, 1940 that "Dominion Status of the Westminster variety as soon as possible after the war was the goal of British policy in India." However, there was no response from the side of the Congress.

Published on 8 August, 1940, it was in the form of a statement made by the Viceroy on behalf of the British Government with these terms:

1. Though the differences which prevented national unity remained unbridged in India, the expansion of the Executive Council of the Governor-General and the establishment of an Advisory War Council should no longer be postponed.
2. In view of the doubts as to whether the position of minorities would be sufficiently safeguarded in any future constitutional change, the British Government reaffirms its desire that full weight should be given to minority opinion.
3. Subject to the fulfilment of their obligations–an allusion to such questions as defence, minority rights, the treaties with the States, and the position of the Secretary of State Services-

7. Menon: *The Transfer of Power in India*, p. 152

the British Government concurs in the Indian desire that the framing of the new constitution should be primarily the responsibility of Indians themselves, and should originate from Indian conceptions of the social, economic and political structure of the Indian life.

4. After the War a representative Indian body should be set up to formulate a new constitution, and meantime the British Government would welcome and assist any efforts to reach agreement as to the form and operation of this constitution-making body and as to the principles of the constitution.
5. In the interval, the British Government hoped that all parties and communities in India would co-operate in India's war-effort, and by thus working together pave the way for India's attainment of free and equal partnership in the British Commonwealth of Nations.

It was declared that the establishment of Dominion Status in India was the goal of the British Government. It was pointed out by the critics of the August Offer that the British Government missed the last chance of bringing the Congress into the war. Although the Congress Working Committee had shown its willingness to repudiate the stand of Mahatma Gandhi on the question of war, the British Government did not respond whole-heartedly. Nehru declared that the whole conception of Dominion Status of India was "as dead as a door-nail." The Congress Working Committee passed a Resolution rejecting the British Offer.

The response of the Muslim League to the August Offer was different. Its Working Committee welcomed that part of the Offer which was condemned by the Congress. According to them, the Offer met the League's demand "for a clear assurance to the effect that no future constitution, interim or final, should be adopted by the British Government without their approval and consent." It was declared that "the partition of India was the only solution of the most difficult problem of India's future constitution." But in spite of this, the Muslim League neither accepted nor rejected the Offer. Gandhiji regretted that the Viceroy had made "a profound mistake."[8]

---

8. Menon, *op. cit.*, p. 94.

Cripps Mission (1942)

The Cripps Mission took place due to some causes. The first cause was the threat of Japan to India. By 7th March, 1942, when Rangoon fell, Japan had occupied the whole of South-East Asia. Churchill made his famous announcement only four days after the fall of Rangoon. The second cause was the pressure of President Roosevelt and Marshall Chiang Kai-Shek. Hull tells us in his memoirs: "The President and I, both before and after Pearl Harbour, were convinced that the Indians would cooperate better with the British if they were assured of independence, at least after the war." Chiang Kai-Shek (President of China) asked the British Government to give India "as speedily as possible" "real political power" in order to secure her moral and material support. Another cause was the growing frustration in India.The Indians felt happy over the reverses of the British and seemed to take pleasure in the victories of the Axis Powers. They listened to the broadcasts of Subhas Chandra Bose from Berlin and did not trust the British. Something had to be done to meet this menace.

The public opinion in England was also in favour of reconciling India. There was a debate in the House of Commons on 24th and 25th February, 1942 on war situation and fifteen speakers made references to the Indian problem and impressed upon the Government the necessity of tackling the same.

The following is the text of the Draft Declaration of the British Government brought by Cripps to India:

"(a) Immediately upon cessation of hostilities, steps shall be taken to set up in India, in the manner described hereafter, an elected body charged with the task of framing a new constitution for India.

"(b) Provision shall be made, as set out below, for participation of Indian States in the constitution-making body.

"(c) His Majesty's Government undertake to accept and implement forthwith the constitution so framed subject only to:

(i) The right of any province of British India that is not prepared to accept the new constitution to retain its present constitutional position, provision being made for its subsequent accession if it so decides.

"With such non-acceding provinces, should they so desire, His Majesty's Government will be prepared to agree upon a new constitution giving them the same full status as the Indian Union and arrived at by a procedure analogous to that here laid down.

(ii) The signing of a treaty which shall be negotiated between His Majesty's Government and the constitution-making body. This treaty will cover all necessary matters arising out of the complete transfer of responsibility from British to Indian hands; it will make provision, in accordance with undertaking given by His Majesty's Government, for the protection of racial and religious minorities, but will not impose any restriction on the power of the Indian Union to decide in future its relationship to other member States of the British Commonwealth.

"Whether or not an Indian State elects to adhere to the constitution, it will be necessary to negotiate a revision of its treaty arrangements so far as this may be required in the new situation.

"(d) The constitution-making body shall be composed as follows unless the leaders of Indian opinion in the principal communities agree upon some other form before the end of hostilities.

"Immediately upon the result being known of provincial elections which will be necessary at the end of hostilities, the entire membership of the Lower House of Provincial Legislatures shall as a single electoral college proceed to the election of the constitution-making body by the system of proportional representation. This new body shall be in number about 1/10th of the number of the electoral college.

"Indian States shall be invited to appoint representatives in the same proportion to their total population as in the case of representatives of British India as a whole and with the same powers as British Indian members.

"(e) During the critical period which now faces India and until the new constitution can be framed, His Majesty's Government must inevitably bear the responsibility for and retain the control and direction of the defence of India as part of their world war effort but the task of organizing to the full the military, moral and material resources of India must be the responsibility of the Government of

India with the cooperation of the people of India. His Majesty's Government desire and invite the immediate and effective participation of the leaders of the principal sections of the Indian people in the counsels of their country, of the Commonwealth and of the United Nations. Thus they will be enabled to give their active and constructive help in the discharge of a task which is vital and essential for the future freedom of India."

Each party criticized the proposals of Cripps from its own point of view.

1. The objection of the Congress was not so much to the long-term arrangement as to the interim arrangement. The Congress acted on the principle that one bird in hand was better than two in the bush. Cripps had given an understanding to the Congress that with the exception of the Defence Department, other Departments would be completely in the hands of Indians and the Governor-General would act as a constitutional head. However, at a later stage, he withdrew that offer. That made the Congress suspicious regarding the honesty of the British Government. The Congress wanted the Executive Council of the Governor-General to work as a cabinet, but the British Government was not prepared to make such a concession. The Congress also objected to the veto power of the Viceroy. It was also opposed to the acceptance of the novel principle of the non-accession of the provinces. It appeared to them that this provision brought in Pakistan by the back-door. According to Nehru, it opened out "a vista of an indefinite number of partitions both of provinces and states." The Congress also opposed it on the ground that ninety million of people in the Indian States were to have no voice in framing the Constitution and that was a "negation of democracy and self-determination."
2. The Hindu Mahasabha opposed the Cripps proposals on two grounds. It was opposed to the freedom given to the provinces to leave the Indian Union and set up separate governments of their own. It also objected to the elections on the basis of the Communal Award which was anti-national and un-democratic. The Sikhs also opposed the provisions relating to the non-accession of the provinces.
3. The response of the Muslim League was a mixed one. Its members were happy at the prospect of realizing their ambition of Pakistan. However, Jinnah was a politician and his

diplomacy led him to contend that the Pakistan idea as embodied in the Cripps proposals was nebulous and very serious impediments were placed in the way of its realization

So Cripps proposals failed, no matter they "embodied different items palatable to different tastes."[9]

Rajagopalachariar Formula (1944)

In March 1944, C. Rajagopalachariar put forward his formula to solve the deadlock prevailing in the country. The following was the basis for terms of settlement between the Congress and the Muslim League:

1. Subject to the terms set out below as regards the constitution for Free India, the Muslim League endorses the Indian demand for independence and will co-operate with the Congress in the formation of a provisional Interim Government for the transitional period.
2. After the termination of the war, a commission shall be appointed for demarcating contiguous districts in the north west and east of India wherein the Muslim population is in absolute majority. In the areas thus demarcated, a plebiscite of all the inhabitants held on the basis of adult suffrage or other practicable franchise shall ultimately decide the issue of separation from Hindustan. If the majority decide in favour of forming a sovereign state separate from Hindustan, such decision shall be given effect to, without prejudice to the right of districts on the border to choose to join either state.
3. It will be open to all parties to advocate their points of view before the plebiscite is held.
4. In the event of separation, mutual agreement shall be entered into for safeguarding defence, commerce and communication and for other essential purposes.
5. Any transfer of population shall be on an absolutely voluntary basis.
6. These terms shall be binding only in case of transfer by Britain of full power and responsibility of the governance of India.

---

9. P.B. Sitaramayya: *The History of the Indian National Congress*, Vol II, p. 315

The negotiations were bound to fail. There was a fundamental difference of approach towards the main question. The main object of the Congress was to win over the League with a view to achieving the independence of the country, and for that purpose it was prepared to pay some reasonable price. The Congress was not prepared to accept all the demands of the League. On the other hand, the League was not bothered about the independence of the country. It was anxious to secure the assent of the Congress to the establishment of Pakistan. Moreover, the League was not prepared to ignore its patron, the British bureaucracy in India, who had consistently helped it in all difficult situations.

Abul Kalam Azad says: "Gandhi's approach to Mr. Jinnah on this occasion was a great political blunder. It gave a new and added importance to Mr. Jinnah which the latter exploited to the full...Mr. Jinnah had lost much of the importance after he left the Congress in the twenties. It was largely due to Gandhi's acts of commission and omission that Mr. Jinnah regained his importance in Indian political life. As a consequence of Gandhi's attitude of running after him and entreating him, many of the Muslims who were doubtful about Mr. Jinnah and his policy developed a new respect for Jinnah. Moreover, it was Gandhi who first gave currency to the title Quaid-e-Azam or great leader, as applied to Mr. Jinnah. By addressing him in his letter as a Quaid-e-Azam, he recognized him as a great leader and strengthened his position in the eyes of the Indian Muslims."[10]

Desai-Liaquat Formula (1945)

Although the negotiations between Mahatma Gandhi and M.A. Jinnah failed on the basis of the Rajagopalachariar formula, efforts were made by Bhulabhai Desai, Leader of the Congress Party in the Central Legislative Assembly, to solve the deadlock. This ultimately resulted in the Desai-Liaquat formula of January, 1945 with these points:

"The Congress and League agree that they will join in forming an Interim Government at the Centre. The composition of such Government will be on the following lines:

10. Maulana A.K. Azad: *India Wins Freedom*, p. 93.

(a) "Equal number of persons nominated by the Congress and the League in the Central Executive. Persons nominated need not be members of the Central Legislature.

(b) "Representatives of minorities (in particular Scheduled Castes and the Sikhs).

(c) "The Commander-in-Chief.

"The Government will be formed and function within the framework of the existing Government of India Act. It is however, understood that if the Cabinet cannot get a particular measure passed by the Legislative Assembly, they will not enforce the same by resort to any of the powers of the Governor-General or the Viceroy. This will make them sufficiently independent of the Governor-General.

"It is agreed between the Congress and the League that if such Interim Government is formed, their first step would be to release the Working Committee members of the Congress.

"The steps by which efforts would be made to achieve this end are at present indicated to take the following course. On the basis of the above understanding, some way should be found to get the Governor-General to make a proposal or a suggestion that he desires an Interim Government to be formed at the Centre on the agreement between the Congress and the League and when the Governor-General invites Mr. Jinnah, and Mr. Desai either jointly or separately, the above proposals would be made, desiring that they are prepared to join in the forming of the Government.

"The next step would be to get the withdrawal of section 93 in the Provinces and to form as soon as possible Provincial Governments on the lines of a Coalition."

In spite of the honest efforts of Desai and Liaquat Ali, no settlement could be secured between the Congress and the League. Surprisingly, Liaquat Ali Khan disowned it after he was admonished by Jinnah.

Wavell Plan (1945)

On 14 June, Lord Wavell, Governor-General and Viceroy of India, gave a broadcast to the people of India. On the same day, L.S. Amery, Secretary of State for India, made a similar statement in the House of Commons. The thoughts and sentiments in both were practically the same. The modus operandi consisted in calling a conference of representatives chosen by the Viceroy for the purpose of obtaining from the leaders of various parties a joint list or separate lists of worthy persons in order to constitute a new Executive Council of the Viceroy. Lord Wavell pleaded for "Men of influence and ability to be recommended by the various parties who would be prepared to take decision and responsibility of administration of all the portfolios including External Affairs," except the conduct of war which was to be under the Commander-in-Chief. There was to be an equal number of Muslims and Hindus other than the Scheduled Castes. The control of the Secretary of State for India and the Governor-General was to continue as provided under the Act of 1919. The veto of the Viceroy was to continue, although the same was not to be used unreasonably. It was to be used not in the interest of England but in the interest of India. The proposals were to effect only British India and not the Indian States.

The members of the Working Committee of the Congress were released from jails and high hopes were raised on all sides. Invitations were issued to the leaders including Mahatma Gandhi and Jinnah for the proposed Conference to be held at Simla. The Conference met on 25 June, 1945.

Maulana Abul Kalam Azad, as the President of the Congress, took pains to explain the position of the Congress. He made it clear that the British plan dealt with purely temporary and interim arrangements and it should not be regarded as a precedent for the permanent arrangement in future. He also attached considerable importance to the declaration that the provisional plan was intended as a preliminary step towards the achievement of the goal of India's independence. He also made it clear that although the Congress Working Committee was taking part in the Conference, its decision had to be ratified by All India Congress Committee many of whose members were still in jails. Maulana Azad also sought certain clarifications from the Government.

On 26 June, 1945. the Conference discussed the scope, functions and responsibilities of the Executive Council of the Governor-General. After about one hour session on 27 June, the Conference adjourned till 29 June to enable the delegates to continue their private discussions. On 28 June, the private deliberations of the Conference reached a stage of impasse between the Muslim League and the Congress. On 29 June, the Conference met as scheduled, but was adjourned after about an hour "to enable the delegates to carry on further consultations" to submit lists of names for the Executive Council. It was agreed to reassemble on 14 July, 1945 at Simla.

In the meanwhile, the Secretary to the Governor-General wrote a letter to Jinnah on 29 June requesting him "to prepare and send him a list giving the names of members of the Muslim League who, in your opinion, could suitably be included in the proposed Executive Council. The number of names in this list should be not less than eight or more than twelve." Jinnah was given the choice to suggest "the names of persons of any community who are not members of the Muslim League."

On 7 July, 1945, Maulana Azad forwarded a panel of 15 names of whom five were caste Hindus, five Muslims, two non-caste Hindus, one Indian Christian, one Parsi and one Sikh." Jinnah sent a reply to the Viceroy on 7 July, 1945 in which he maintained "that all the Muslim members of the proposed Executive Council should be chosen from the Muslim League, subject to a confidential discussion between Your Excellency and the President of the Muslim League", before they were finally recommended by the Viceroy to His Majesty's Government for appointment. On 9 July, 1945, Jinnah informed Lord Wavell: "I regret I am not in a position to send the names on behalf of the Muslim League for inclusion in the proposed Executive Council as desired by you." The Conference met at on 14 July, 1945 and Lord Wavell made an official announcement of its failure.

There is a close analogy between the Cripps Mission and the Wavell Plan. Cripps came to India in the midst of beating of drums and fanfare of trumpets. He raised high hopes and made extravagant off-the-record promises to the Congress President and later denied the same. In the case of the Wavell Plan, the Viceroy definitely stated at Simla that there was no question of his veto being eliminated. To that extent, he was frank unlike Cripps.

The failure of the Simla Conference convinced the Congress that nothing could be expected from the British Government so long as the Conservative Party remained in office. The British bureaucracy in India had allowed Jinnah to have his own way. "The Simla Conference afforded a last-opportunity to the forces of nationalism to fight a rear-guard action to preserve the integrity of the country, and when the battle was lost, the waves of communalism quickly engulfed it. Only the Hobbson's choice of partition was left."[11]

Cabinet Mission Plan (1946)

On 19th February, 1946, Lord Pethick Lawrence (Secretary of State for India) made a declaration in the House of Lords in which he announced the decision of the British Government to send a special team of Cabinet Ministers to resolve the constitutional deadlock in our country. The members of the Mission were Lord Pethick Lawrence himself, Sir Stafford Cripps, President of the Board of Trade, and Mrs. A.V. Alexander, First Lord of Admiralty.

The Mission reached Delhi on March 24, 1946, Prolonged discussions took place between the members of the Mission and the leaders of the Congress and the Muslim League. It announced its plan on 16 May, 1946. After pointing out the impracticability of the Pakistan scheme, it recommended that the new constitution of India should take the following basic form:

1. There should be a Union of India, embracing both British India and the States, which should deal with the following subjects: Foreign Affairs, Defence, and Communications; and should have the powers necessary to raise the finances required for the above subjects.
2. The Union should have an Executive and a Legislature constituted from British Indian and States' representatives.
3. Any question raising a major communal issue in the Legislature should require for its decision a majority of the representatives present and voting of each of the two major communities as well as a majority of all the members present and voting.
4. All subjects other than the Union subjects and all residuary powers should vest in the Provinces.

---

11. V.P. Menon: *op.cit.*, p. 215. Larry Collins and Dominique Lapierre comment that Attlee "had come to office publicly ©committed to begin the dismemberment of the Empire." *Freedom at Midnight*, p. 5.

5. The States will retain all subjects and powers other than those ceded to the Union.
6. Provinces should be free to form Groups with executives and legislatures, and each Group could determine the Provincial subjects to be taken in common.
7. The constitutions of the Union and of the Groups should contain a provision whereby any Province could, by a majority vote of its Legislative Assembly call for a reconsideration of the terms of the constitution after an initial period of 10 years and at 10 yearly intervals thereafter.
8. The Provinces of India were given the power to opt out of the Groups by a decision of their Legislatures after the general elections under the new Constitution.
9. The Resolution of the Union Constituent Assembly regarding major communal issues were to require a majority of the representatives present and voting of each of the two major communities. The Chairman of the Constituent Assembly was to decide which resolution raised major communal issues and was to consult the Federal Court before giving his decision.
10. A plan for the Interim Government consisting of all political parties and communities was also envisaged in the Scheme.

As regards the constitution-making machinery, it was provided that the Legislative Assemblies of the Provinces would elect the members of the body on the basis of one representative for one million of the population. The Sikh and Muslim legislators were to elect the quota of their communities determined on the population basis. Others were to elect the representatives for the rest of the population. The representatives from the provinces were to divide themselves into three sections A, B and C. Section C was to consist of the representatives of Bengal and Assam, Section B of the Punjab, Sind and North-West Frontier Province and Section A of the rest of the provinces of India. "These Sections shall proceed to settle the Provincial Constitution for the Provinces included in each Section, and shall also decide whether any Group Constitution shall be set up for these provinces and, if so, with what provincial subjects the Group should deal." The representatives of the Sections of the Indian States were then to re-assemble and settle the Union constitution.

Table of Representation

Provinces	Groups	General	Muslim	Sikhs	Total
Madras	A	45	4	–	49
Bombay	A	19	2	–	21
United Provinces	A	47	8	–	55
Bihar	A	31	5	–	36
Central Provinces	A	16	1	–	17
Orissa	A	9	0	–	9
Total:		167	20		187
Punjab	B	8	16	4	28
N.W. Frontier Province	B	0	3	0	3
Sind	B	1	3	0	4
Total:		9	22	4	35
Bengal	C	27	33		60
Assam	C	7	3		10
Total:		34	36		70
Total for British India					292
Maximum for States					93
	Grand Total:				385

Formation of Interim Government

On 22 July, 1946, Lord Wavell wrote a personal and confidential letter to Jinnah with proposals to form an Interim Government. It was stated therein that the Interim Government would consist of fourteen members. Six members, including one Scheduled Caste representative, would be nominated by the Congress, five members would be nominated by the Muslim League. Three representatives of the minorities would be nominated by Viceroy. One of the three seats would be kept for Sikhs. It was not open to either the Congress or the Muslim League to object to the names submitted by the other party, provided those were accepted by the Viceroy. Distribution of portfolios was to be decided after the parties had agreed to enter the Government and had submitted their names. The Congress and the Muslim League were each to have an equitable share of the most important portfolios. It is clear from this letter that the Muslim League was not to have the right to object to the Congress nominating a Muslim in its quota of six.

The Muslim League Council had passed a resolution on 29 July, 1946 withdrawing its earlier acceptance of the Cabinet Mission Scheme. In that resolution, it was declared that "now the time has come for the Muslim Nation to resort to Direct Action to achieve Pakistan, to assert their just rights, to vindicate their honour and to get rid of the present British slavery and the contemplated future caste-Hindu domination." Jinnah called upon the Muslims throughout India to observe 16 August, 1946 as Direct Action Day. He declared, "This day we bid good-bye to constitutional methods....today we have also forged a pistol and are in a position to use it".[12] On 13 August, 1946, Jawaharalal Nehru wrote a letter to Jinnah from Wardha informing him about the Viceroy's invitation to him as Congress President to form the Interim Government. In the same letter, Nehru wrote: "I have accepted his invitation. I feel that my first step should be to approach you and seek your co-operation in the formation of a coalition provisional Government. It is naturally our desire to have as representative a Government as possible.....". Nehru met Jinnah on 16 August at Bombay and after the meeting, Nehru announced: "Co-operation in the formation of the Provisional Government is being offered to the Congress by all elements excepting the Muslim League for the moment.... We shall always look for the larger measure of co-operation...."

When all this was going on outside, Lord Wavell and Nehru had their preliminary conversations regarding the formation of the Interim Government on 17 and 18 August, 1946. On 24 August, Lord Wavell officially announced the resignation of the care-taker Government which had been appointed by the Viceroy in June 1946. He also approved of the appointment of an Interim Government proposed by the Congress Party. It was announced that the Interim Government would take office on 2 September, 1946, and would consist of six Congressmen, five Muslims and three Minority members. Nehru formed the Interim Government on 2 September, 1946.

Lord Wavell was not satisfied with having secured co-operation from the Congress. He also wanted the Muslim League to join the Interim Government. Jinnah was also anxious to join the Interim

12. Leonard Mosley: *The Last Days of the British Raj*, p. 29.

Government so that the Muslim League might be able to fight the battle of Pakistan from a position of strength. The names sent by Jinnah were Liaquat Ali Khan, I.I. Chundrigar, A.R. Nishtar, Ghazanfar Ali Khan and Jogendra Nath Mandal. He carefully selected such persons who were likely to put up fight for the Muslim League and Pakistan in the Interim Government.

Outside the Government, there were serious differences between the Congress and the Muslim League with regard to the interpretation of the Cabinet Mission Scheme on the question of the grouping of the Provinces. The contention of the Muslim League was that the grouping was compulsory. Mahatma Gandhi expressed the view that grouping was optional. A similar view was held by Jawaharlal Nehru, K.M. Munshi and other constitutional experts of India. The situation became so serious that the British Government invited the Congress and Muslim League leaders to London. The London meeting was attended by Jawaharlal Nehru, Baldev Singh, Jinnah and Liaquat Ali Khan. The final decision of the British Government was in favour of the Muslim League.

Attlee's Statement

On February 20, 1947 Prime Minister Attlee, made his famous declaration. He referred to the differences among the Indian parties which were preventing the Constituent Assembly from functioning as it was intended. He said: "His Majesty's Government desire to hand over their responsibility to authorities established by a constitution approved by all parties in India in accordance with the Cabinet Mission's Plan. But unfortunately there is at present no clear prospect that such a constitution and such authorities will emerge. The present state of uncertainty is fraught with danger and cannot be indefinitely prolonged. His Majesty's Government wish to make it clear that it is their definite intention to take necessary steps to effect the transference of power to responsible Indian hands by a date not later than June 1948.

Mountbatten Plans

The fact is that when Lord Mountbatten reached India on 23 March, the situation in the country was drifting towards a civil war. There was no security of life or property. People were disposing of properties in areas inhabited by the other community. The whole situation was volcanic. The Government officials were taking sides.

The first plan of Lord Mountbatten (also known as Plan Balkan or Dicky Birds Plan) was to hand over power to the Provinces or to such confederations of Provinces as the latter might decide to form. He was also in favour of partitioning the Provinces of Bengal and Punjab with a view to separate the predominantly Muslim areas from the predominantly non-Muslim areas. He was also in favour of allowing the Muslim district of Sylhet the option of joining the Muslim Province of Bengal. In the case of North-Western Frontier Province, fresh elections were to be held to ascertain the wishes of the people. There was opposition to his proposals. Sir Evan Jenkins, Governor of the Punjab, opposed the partition on the ground that the divided Provinces would still be having minorities. The contention of the Governor of Bengal was that the division of Bengal would make East Bengal a rural slum. Jinnah contended that the division of the Punjab and Bengal would destroy the administrative and economic fabric of the Provinces which had been built up during the last century. He contended that ultimately there would be exchange of populations between India and Pakistan and the problem of the minorities would be automatically solved in that manner. Jinnah's argument was that if the Punjab and Bengal were to be partitioned, then the other Provinces where the Muslims lived in large numbers must also be partitioned. The Congress rejected it.

Then came the Plan of 3 June 1947 with these points:

1. It has always been the desire of His Majesty's Government that power should be transferred in accordance with the wishes of the Indian people themselves.
2. His Majesty's Government wish to make it clear that they have no intention of attempting to frame any ultimate constitution of India. This is a matter of the Indians themselves. Nor is there anything in this Plan to preclude negotiations between communities for a United India.
3. It is not the intention of His Majesty's Government to interrupt the work of the existing Constituent Assembly.
4. It is clear that any constitution framed by this Assembly cannot apply to those parts of the country which are unwilling to accept it. His Majesty's Government are satisfied that the procedure below embodies the best practical method of ascertaining the wishes of the people of such areas on the issue whether their constitution is to be framed (a) in the existing Constituent

Assembly; or (b) in a new and separate Constituent Assembly consisting of the representatives of those areas which decide not to participate in the existing Constituent Assembly.

5. The Provincial Legislative Assemblies of Bengal and Punjab would meet in two parts, one representing the Muslim majority districts and the other the rest of Province. "The members of two parts of each Legislative Assembly sitting separately will be empowered to vote whether or not the provinces should be partitioned. If a simple majority of either part decide in favour of partition, partition will take place and arrangements would be made accordingly.

6. The Legislative Assembly of Sind would take its own decision at a special meeting.

7. A decision by referendum was provided for in the case of the North-Western Frontier Province. The Muslim-majority district of Sylhet would decide by a referendum whether it would join East Bengal or remain in Assam.

8. A Boundary Commission would be set up to settle the details of the boundaries in case partition was decided upon.

On 10 June, 1947, the Council of the All-India Muslim League met in New Delhi and passed a resolution accepting the 3 June Plan. On the same day, the National Executive of the Socialist Party of India met in New Delhi and resolved that it "expresses its disapproval of and grief at the proposed division of the country." A joint conference of the Sikhs was held at Lahore and it passed a resolution on 12 June stating: "This joint conference disapproves of the scheme for the division of India into two sovereign States. In its opinion, the only redeeming feature of the plan is the acceptance of the principle of partition of the Punjab....while the plan is designed to carve out a sovereign Muslim State to satisfy Muslim demands, it fails to provide for the Sikhs any position of power or status or any means for the protection of their interests in the constitution-making machinery..."

The Working Committee of the All-India Majlis-Ahrar passed a resolution on 13 June, 1947, declaring that the Plan would result in the "political subjugation of Pakistan in the shape of economic and defence alliances. Ahrars have always stood for complete independence and as such the Majlis cannot lend its support to it."

An emergency meeting of the All-India Congress Committee was held in New Delhi in the Constitution House to consider the Plan under the presidentship of Acharya Kripalani. On 15 June, it passed a resolution by 157 votes to 29 votes. The resolution read: "The All-India Congress Committee accept the proposals embodied in the announcement of June 3 which have laid down a procedure for ascertaining the will of the people concerned...The proposals of June 3, 1947, are likely to lead to the secession of some parts of the country from India. However much this may be regretted, the All-India Congress Committee accepts this possibility in the circumstances now prevailing."

Indian Independence Act of 1947

The object of this Act was to give effect to the June 3 Plan of Lord Mountbatten. It had these important provisions:

1. It provided for the partition of India and the establishment of the Dominions of India and Pakistan from the appointed day – 15th August 1947. The Legislatures of the two Dominions would have full power to make laws having extra-territorial jurisdiction. The British Government would have no control over the affairs of the Dominions, Provinces, or any part of the Dominions after 15th August, 1947.

2. Until a new constitution was framed for each Dominion, the Act made the existing Constituent Assemblies the Dominion Legislatures for the time being. The Assemblies were to exercise all the powers which were formerly exercised by the Central Legislature, in addition to its power regarding the framing of a new constitution.

3. Pending the framing of a new constitution, each Dominion and all the Provinces would be governed in accordance with the Government of India Act. 1935. Each Dominion was authorised to make modifications in the Government of India Act, 1935 in the light of the Indian Independence Act.

4. The Governor-General was given the power to modify or adapt the Government of India Act. 1935 as might be considered

necessary till 31st March,1948. After that day it would be open to the Constituent Assembly to modify or adapt the same Act.

5. The Act provided for the termination of the suzerainty of the Crown over the Indian States. All treaties, agreements and functions exercisable by His Majesty with regard to States and their rulers would lapse from 15th August, 1947. It was also provided that the existing arrangements between the Government of India and the Indian States would continue pending the detailed negotiations between the Indian States and the new Dominions.

6. It was provided that for each of the new Dominions there shall be a Governor-General appointed by His Majesty who shall represent His Majesty for the purpose of the Government of the Dominions.

7. It was also provided that every person who having been appointed by the Secretary of State or Secretary of State-in-Council to a Civil Service of the Crown in India shall continue on and after 15th August, 1947, to serve under the Government of either of the new Dominions or of any province or part thereof, or having been appointed by His Majesty before 15th August, 1947, to be a judge of the Federal Court or any High Court.

Thus the British colonial rule came to an end. It marked the culmination of the policy of 'divide and rule' converted into the policy of 'divide and quit'. It signified the triumph of Indian nationalism in the form of advent of independence, it also signified its tragedy in the form of partition of the country. The national leaders accepted the division of the country with a heavy heart, but with the hope that this unfortunate event would be undone in time to come after the exit of the 'third party'. Realists like Nehru and Patel hoped that the creation of a separate Muslim state "would finally settle the communal problem which had so far long bedevilled Indian politics and thwarted all progressive aspirations, that India and Pakistan would thereafter live in peaceful relations with each other, and that all men of good will on either side would be free to concentrate on improving the economic conditions of the common people."[13]

13. Menon, *op. cit.*, p. 440.

4

Towards Swaraj

What we have said in the preceding two chapters about India's constitutional development needs to be supplemented with an account of many events, big and small, so as to plug the loopholes in the narration of the story of our freedom movement. In course of time, the base of the struggle grew wider and wider that converted a 'class movement' into a 'mass movement'. Three distinct stages of this movement may be marked out to show as to how the implications of Swaraj gradually changed from a loose and vague to a precise and clear-cut form. Victory came to the clarion calls of great national leaders as Tilak's claim for Swaraj as our birth-right, Bhagat Singh's slogan of Inquilab Zindabad (Long Live Revolution) and Bose's exhortation for Chalo Dilli (On to Delhi). It all signified, in the words of Nehru, our 'tryst with destiny'. Curzon's proud contention that 'from Peshawer to Calcutta a sparrow could not twitter its tail without his permission', saw its replacement by these solemn words uttered by Mountbatten: "From today I am your constitutional Governor-General and I would ask you to regard me as one of yourselves, devoted wholly to the furtherance of India's interests."[1]

Struggle for Self-Rule Within the Empire

The history of the struggle for Swaraj begins with the partition of Bengal in 1905. Though Tilak had raised the slogan of Swaraj as our birth right almost a decade earlier, it is the partition of Bengal that sharpened the process and forced the moderate leaders of the Indian National Congress to adopt a resolution in favour of Swaraj at the Calcutta session of 1906. Henceforth, Swaraj became a

1. H.V. Hodson: *The Great Divide,* p. 394.

favourite word for every nationalist in spite of the fact that nobody bothered for its implications until Mrs. Annie Besant came on the scene in 1916 to identify it with 'home-rule'. Gandhiji made a fundamental change in its implications in 1920 by defining it as 'self rule within the Empire if possible, without the Empire if necessary'. But credit goes to the 'heroes' of the new generation like Jawaharlal Nehru and Subhas Chandra Bose who defined it as nothing short of complete independence and the Lahore Congress of 1929 adopted a comprehensive resolution in this regard. The apparently-looking prophetic expression of Minto proved untrue that the "Raj will not disappear in India as long as the British race remains what it is, because we shall fight for the Raj as hard as we have ever fought.... and we shall win as we have always won."[2]

Partition of Bengal and its Effects: Words come into currency, but their implications change with the passage of time and with the change in the prevailing conditions and circumstances. The early leaders of the Congress appreciated the British rule as 'a divine dispensation' and they digested the comments of the English leaders that India was not a nation but a mosaic of numerous races and nationalities. But all English leaders did not contribute to what was said by Wood and Morley in England and by Lytton and Curzon in India. Hume, Wedderburn and Cotton were Englishmen who had a better sense. In his confidential letter to Pandit Ajodhya Nath, Hume had warned of a bloody revolution in the country in case the British administration did not respond well to the needs and urges of the Indian people[3]. Similar words of advice were given by Wedderburn in his presidential address at the Bombay session of the Congress held in 1889. When the news of the partition of Bengal was very much in the air, Sir Henry Cotton in his presidential address at the session of the Indian National Congress held at Bombay in December, 1904 expressed his fears and defined the goal of India in these words: "The ideal of an Indian patriot is the establishment of a federation of free and separate States, the United States of India, placed on a fraternal footing with the self-governing

2. Minto's letter to Morley, 27 May 1908 in S. Wolpert: *Morley and India*, p. 46.

3. Known as the Hume Circular, it was circulated among the delegates assembled at the Allahabad session of the Indian National Congress held in December, 1888.

colonies, each with its own autonomy, cemented together under the aegis of Great Britain."[4] He continued that the proposal "to break up Bengal against the wishes and sentiments of the Bengali people can only be described as the most arbitrary and unsympathetic evidence of irresponsible and autocratic statesmanship."[5]

But Viceroy Curzon was determined to 'dethrone Calcutta'. Bureaucrats like Risley and the Secretary of State Morley fell in line as they all had the fears of growing strength of national movement.[6] The way out was discovered in the partition of Bengal as a result of which the province of East Bengal with its capital at Dacca was created under a Lt. Governor. On 16 October, Bampfylde Fuller took the charge and immediately thereafter he issued a circular calling upon district authorities to furnish names of prominent residents taking a leading part in the agitation. A little earlier, Carlyle (officiating Chief Secretary of Bengal) had issued a circular to all district magistrates to stop the enrolment of teachers and the grants-in-aid and to disaffiliate any school or college whose students, teachers and staff took part in anti-partition agitation. Military contingents were taken around the sensitive areas so as to terrorise the people. Singing of Bande Matram and taking out of procession in the streets was also prohibited.

Obviously, the partition of Bengal was the first act of provocation which affected even the moderate sections of the Indian nationalists. Ambika Charan Mazumdar declared that with this act, "political agitation in this country enters upon a new phase. It has unmistakably demonstrated two things; first, the resolute despotism of the Government, and secondly, the utter futility of the kind of agitation to which we have grown accustomed. Hence, we must now transform our ideas from the sphere of thought to the

---

4. See Tara Chand: *History of the Freedom Movement in India*, Vol. III, pp. 325-26.

5. *Ibid.*

6. For instance, the then Home Secretary (Risley) in his note of 13 September, 1904 said : "Bengal united is a power, Bengal divided will pull in several different ways. That is what the Congress leaders feel; their apprehensions are perfectly correct and they form one of the greatest merits of the scheme....one of our main objects is to split up and thereby weaken a solid body of opponents to our rule." *Ibid*, p. 313.

sphere of action."[7] Aurobindo Ghose termed it 'the pettiest and narrowest of all political objects'. The Swadeshi movement took a broader form. With the *Swadeshi Samaj* Aurobindo, Tagore and B.C. Pal were associated. The *Dawn Society* banking on the support of Nilratan Sircar and Satish Chandra Mukherji played a seminal role in national educational movement. The *Swadeshi Bandhav Samiti* of Babu Aswini Kumar Datta did constructive work in the villages. Many papers as *New India* of Pal, *Bande Matram* of Aurobindo and *Sandhya* and *Yugantar* of Brahmbandab Upadhyaya openly and boldy called for a struggle for *Swaraj*. It all appeared like "a mere stepping stone in a struggle for Swaraj or complete independence."[8]

Swadeshi and Boycott Movement: While the history of Indian nationalist movement begins from the later part of the nineteenth century when a section of the far-sighted and enlightened English leaders thought in terms of having an organisation of the 'sane' and 'loyal' nationalists in India and thus they succeeded in establishing the Indian National Congress in order to implement their 'Save the British Empire' theory, the history of anti-colonial movements begins from 1905 when, for the first time, a section of the 'new nationalist leaders' rose in revolt against the philosophy of those who had full faith in British sense of justice and fairplay and, who for this reason, were the defenders of the idea of keeping India as a loyal partner of the British Empire. The new line, called the trend of extremism, appeared in the Swadeshi and Boycott Movement. It boldly revealed that while the motto of the Moderates was 'reform', the motto of their opponents was 'revolution'.

This movement was prosecuted by a section of the Indian leaders who drew inspiration from religious and social orthodoxy; who belonged to the middle class, and for that reason, understood the meaning of prevailing economic discontent; who had no faith in British sense of justice and fairplay and, for that reason, believed in the methods distinctly opposed to the tactics of prayer-making and petition-mongering; and, above all, who stood for the boycott of everything 'foreign' and instead adoption of everything *swadeshi* or home-made. While this movement prevailed in many parts of the

7. *Ibid.*, p. 320.

8. Sumit Sarkar: *Modern India*, p. 112.

country, it had its special manifestation in Bengal where the boycott of foreign goods was described as a special weapon of protest.

This movement had a politico-economic character and was based on the inspiration that its leaders drew from the canons of religious revivalism. In Bengal, the chief exponents of this movement like Brahma Bandhab Upadhyaya, Bipin Chandra Pal and Aurobindo Ghose drew inspiration from the writings of Bankim Chandra Chatterji and the messages of Swami Vivekanand. The names of Tilak in Maharashtra, of B.C. Pal in Bengal and of Lala Lajpat Rai in Punjab became very prominent that led to the formation of the trio of Lal, Bal, Pal who preached the gospel of using home-made goods and boycotting the use of everything foreign. The Swadeshi vow ran: "Invoking God Almighty to be our witness, and standing in the presence of after generations, we take this solemn vow that, as far as practicable, we shall use home-made articles and abstain from the use of foreign articles. So God help us."

The idea of boycott was to put the British imperial rulers in a state of disadvantage, because the use of home-made goods would eventually make it impossible for them to stay on in India. Understanding this point, Lalaji once said: 'The logic' of losing business is more likely to impress this nation of shopkeepers than any arguments based on the ethics of justice." In more clear terms, Aurobindo Ghose said that the aim of boycott was "to propose to render the further exploitation of the country impossible. We refuse to send our boys to government schools or to schools aided and controlled by the government, propose to make the bureaucratic administration of justice impossible while these conditions continued, propose to reduce executive control and interference to a mere skeleton of its former self."[9]

The swadeshi and boycott movement had its official endorsement at the twenty-second Congress held at Calcutta under the presidentship of Dadabhai Naoroji. While the moderates under the leadership of Gokhale had managed to defeat the extremists at the twenty-first Congress held at Kashi or Benares in 1905, they had their day at the Congress session of 1906 when four important resolutions on Swadeshi, Boycott, Swaraj and National Education were adopted. The resolution on the Boycott said: "Having regard

9. Aurobindo Ghose: *The Doctrine of Passive Resistance*, pp. 35-38.

to the fact that the people of this country have little or no voice in the administration and that their representations to the Government do not receive due considerations, the Congress is of opinion that the Boycott Movement inaugurated in Bengal by way of protest against the partition of that province, was and is legitimate."[10] The resolution on Swadeshi said: "Congres accords its most cordial support to the Swadeshi movement and calls upon the people of the country to labour for its success by making earnest and sustained efforts to promote the growth of indigenous industries and to stimulate the production of indigenous articles by giving them preference over imported commodities, even at some sacrifice."[11]

While the Calcutta Congress of 1906 could pass resolutions on important subjects like Swadeshi and Boycott, its resolution on 'Swaraj', though a quite novel step, was not free from certain ambiguities. The word Swaraj, though used for the first time in the programme of the Congress, included a clear-cut reference to self-government 'like that of the United Kingdom or the Colonies'. Thus, it became a matter of serious controversy. While the moderates like Dadabhai Naoroji, Pherozeshah Mehta, Surendranath Banerjea and Gopal Krishna Gokhale defined Swaraj as 'self-government within the Empire', others like Lala Lajpat Rai and B.C Pal took an entirely different position with Tilak oscillating between the two poles though leaning on the side of the latter. Thus, leaders belonging to the extremist school dismissed the path of making prayers and appeals to the British Government as 'useless mendicancy'. Lala Lajpat Rai in very clear terms emphasised that the Government of India would hand over its powers when the "force of circumstances compelled it to do so in spite of itself."[12]

Implicit in the rejection of the path of prayer-making and petition-mongering to the British Government, as Daniel Argov says, "was an underlying rejection of Western values and ideals."[13] Thus, Bipin Chandra Pal said: "We loved the abstraction we called India, but we

---

10. See Daniel Agrov: *Moderates and Extremists in Indian Nationalist Movement*, p. 120.

11. *Ibid.*

12. *Ibid.*, p. 118.

13. *Ibid.*, p. 122.

hated the things that it actually was. Our patriotism was not composed of our love for our own history, literature, arts and industries, culture and institutions but as a prototype of England, which we wished her to be. The new spirit cured us on an imaginary and abstract patriotism. Love of India means love for its rivers and mountains, for its paddy fields and its arid sandy lands, its towns and villages and poor people for its languages, literature, philosophies, religion, culture and civilisation."[14] The term 'Swadeshi' was a quite comprehensive one and its meaning was described by Aurobindo Ghose who 'urged boycott of British goods and the sole use of swadeshi, boycott of government-controlled schools and the establishment of independent schools teaching 'national education', boycott of the courts of law and the administration of justice through popular arbitration, and, lastly boycott of Government offices, police and the army and the establishment of a national league of defence."[15]

The swadeshi and boycott movement had a political as well as an economic character. While its political character could be traced in its aim to paralyse the executive functions of the alien rule and to foster a self-sustained popular system of administration, its economic character could very well be discerned in its aim to boycott the use of foreign goods and thus give promotion to indigenous industries. The leaders staged bonfires of foreign stuff and picketing of shops. To resolve to abstain from the use of foreign-made goods became a solemn religious vow. A National Education Council was set up with leading persons like Gurudas Bannerji, Rash Behari Ghose, Rabindranath Tagore, B.C. Pal and C.R. Das for starting national schools and colleges. Thus as the 'new nationalists emphatically asserted. Swadeshi" was a weapon forged by the people to achieve the industrial and general economic regeneration and advance of India. Its implementing demanded great sacrifice especially, as Tilak remarked, from the middle classes who were the greatest consumers of the foreign goods."[16]

This movement failed to have a long life as the foreign government adopted a highly repressive policy to crush it in order

14. *Ibid.*, pp. 122-23.

15. *Ibid.*, pp. 123-24.

16. A.R. Desai: *Social Background of Indian Nationalism.* p. 331.

to safeguard its political and economic interests; it also failed to make much headway as the entrenched leadership of the Congress in the hands of bourgeois and upper-middle classes opposed it on account of its own political and economic interests that had their natural connection with the maintenance of the British Empire. The movement, however, proved successful in bringing about a change in the course of our nationalist struggle, since it could rouse "among the people a militant determination to win swaraj."[17] It definitely "marked the birth of a new era in Indian political life. The nation learnt that the only effective guarantee against misrule is the vigorous assertion of its will. It was also the fore-runner of non-co-operation movement of the later period."[18]

It is true that the extremists had a different perception of Swaraj, but there was hardly any real distinction between the perceptions of the moderates and the extremists on this point. Both desired 'self-rule within the Empire' that, after some time, got the refined name of 'Dominion Status' and became a favourite instrument in the hands of old stalwarts like Jinnah, Motilal Nehru and Annie Besant. Not the implication but the tone of expression marked the line of distinction between the two. When Tilak came back to India in 1914 after passing the period of internment in the jail of Mandalay, he supported the case of self-rule within the Empire. He played instrumental in the making of the Lucknow Pact whereby both the Congress and the League adopted a similar goal. Now the Congress was a united body; what happened at Surat in 1907 was undone. With one voice, it told the Government that the time had come for the British government to confer self-government on India. Since Annie Besant preached the same thing in her call for Home Rule, Tilak and Jinnah rendered their full cooperation to her movement. Her internment in June 1917 was condemned by all sections of the Indian public opinion and so her release after a couple of months was widely hailed. Her movement made explicit what was so far implicit in the meaning of Swaraj. It is evident from the comment of Tej Bahadur Sapru, "We were talking of reforms and expansion of Councils, and swore by Swaraj, but our ideas were nebulous.

---

17. *Ibid.*

18. V.P.S. Raghuvanshi: *Indian Nationalist Movement and Thought*, p. 91.

Her clear thinking gave concrete shape to our undefined and indefinite ideas, resulting in an organised movement for Home Rule for India."[19]

Revolutionary Activities: The pace of revolutionary activities became quicker after World War I broke out in July, 1914. Rash Behari Bose and Sachin Sanyal hatched conspiracies to kill notorious English military officers and for this purpose they threw bombs in the cantonment area of Lahore. After the departure of Bose to Japan in1915 Sachin continued such activities in the cantonment areas of Lucknow, Benares and Danapur. He was caught in the Benares Conspiracy Case and given the sentence of transportation for life in 1915. On 29 September, 1914 a riot occurred in Calcutta when the police mercilessly beat the Sikhs and forcible entrained them to Punjab after they had returned from the unsuccessful trip to Canada by a Japanese steamer **Komagata Maru.** The Canadian authorities had refused them permission to land and the ship had to return from Vancouver. In the riot 22 men were killed, but the leader of this Jatha (Baba Gurdutt Singh) managed to escape.

Since Germany was against Britain in this war, Berlin became the centre of revolutionary activities. Virendranath Chattopadhyaya. Bhupen Datta, Obeidullah Sindhi and Barkatullah formed Indian Independence Committee there. Har Dayal who had set up the Ghadar Party in San Francisco by converting the Hindu Association into this Party in 1913 and then had founded the Yugantar Ashram came to Berlin, while Champak Raman Pillai came here from Geneva. Sindhi was sent to Kabul where he tried to win over the Amir of Afghanistan. Mahmud-al Hasan and Husain Ahmed Madni went to Arabia and met the Turkish officers there like Ghalib and Enver Pasha. Silk letters were secretly distributed in India and outside. In December, 1915 the Zimmerman Plan was hatched whereby the Indian revolutionaries would get German military aid and move to Afghanistan with the help of Turkey to create tribal uprisings in the Frontier area so as to eventually enter India. An Indo-German-Turkish mission tried to stir up anti-British feelings among the tribes near Indo-Iranian border. So a band of Indian revolutionaries could reach Kabul and set up there provisional Government of Free India with Raja Mahendra Pratap as its President

19. See Kanji Dwarkadas: *India's Fight for Freedom*, p. 36.

and Barkatullah as its Prime Minister with some backing from Crown Prince Amanullah. However, all such efforts failed and they had their end after the War as Germany had been defeated.[20]

Change in Muslim League's Objects: The nasty elements behind the partition of Bengal sharpened the wave of Muslim separatism, though all sections of the Muslims could not be entrapped into it. The wave of resentment continued to blow in spite of the new policy of 'repression-cum-concession' adopted by Secretary of State Morley and willy-nilly accepted by Viceroy Minto. Fuller expressed his differences with the new policy and in 1907 he tendered his resignation. While Morley hailed the creation of the Muslim League as 'a native opposition' to the Congress, he sought to allow some concessions to the Congress to assuage its resentment. It is for this reason that he once thought about not giving separate electorates to the Muslims, but he yielded to the pressure exercised on him by Syed Ameer Ali, a member of the India Council as well as the in-charge of the British Committee of the Indian Muslim League in London. In his letter to Minto dated 7 April, 1909, Morley said: "Mohammedan electorates are absolutely necessary if we treat at all from that view, we shall have an infinite worse trouble than anything that can arise from the Hindu opposition."

However, the implementation of the policy of repression-cum-concession went on as a result of which the partition of Bengal was annulled in December, 1911. A noticeable change took place in the objects of the League when the Balkan wars broke out in 1912 and the fate of the Turkish Caliphate became a matter of anxiety. The League was 'founded on the safe and sure rock of loyalty to the British Raj' and the English rulers had hoped that it 'would provide an effective answer to the Congress."[21] But now situation had changed. The League resented annulment of the partition of Bengal. At its session held at Lucknow in March 1913, under the

20. After the departure of Har Dayal from America, Ramchandra continued to do the work of the Ghadar Party with the association of Chandra Chakrabarti. They received funds from Germany. But they were caught in the Hindu-German Conspiracy Case and so the role of the Ghadar Party ended. The trial took place (1917-18) in San Franciso.

21. S.R. Wasti: *Lord Minto and the Indian National Movement*, p. 87.

presidentship of Muhammed Shafi, its object was changed and in the place of loyalty towards British Government, 'attainment under the aegis of the British Crown, of self-government through constitutional means suited to India was substituted. Then at its Bombay session held in December, 1915 under the Presidentship of Mazharul Haq, it desired to move closer to the Congress. Surprisingly, Gandhiji, Malviya, B.N. Dhar and Sarojini Naidu attended this session of the League. The idea of supporting Turkey against Britain was not liked by some stalwarts like the Agha Khan and Salimullah Khan and so they left the organisation.[21] Now it "appeared as if Sir Syed had been defeated and Shibli vidicated."[22]

The 'sphere of loyalty' that was the basic touchstone of League's ideology was widened in view of the fact that in stead of infusing a sense of loyalty for the British Raj among the Muslims alone, it now wished to cultivate it among the people of the country as a whole. It said about the promotion of friendship and union between the Muslims and other communities of India. It desired protection and promotion of the political and other rights of the Indian Muslims. The ambition to attain suitable self-government for the country was laudable in so far as it "introduced a serious innovation in the traditional policies and practices of the League and constituted a very important departure from its early attitude to all national sentiments. It also opened a wide door to further negotiations and amicable settlement between the two communities, which materialised in the Lucknow Pact of 1916."[23]

Home Rule Movement: Another important event is the Home Rule Movement of 1916-17 that was launched by Mrs. Annie Besant–an Irish Christian lady–who had embraced Hindu religion and joined the Congress with a mission to serve as 'an Indian tom–tom waking

21. The diehard elements desired all support to Turkey in the Balkan wars. Maulana Abdul Bari of Lucknow and his disciple Maulana Mohammed Ali formed a body named Anjuman-i-Khuddam-i-Kaaba to raise funds for the help of Turkey. These leaders frankly criticised the British leaders for directly or indirectly helping Italy against Turkey in the Balkan wars. Naturally, it could not be acceptable to the Agha Khan and his followers who preferred to leave this body.

22. Tara Chand, *op.cit.*, p. 414.

23. Lal Bahadur: *Struggle for Pakistan,* pp. 75-76.

up all the sleepers so that they may awake and work for their motherland."[24] A well-known leader of the Theosophical Society having its headquarters at Madras, she had stayed in England from 1908 to 1914, where she was immensely impressed with the Home Rule Movement of Redmond. While in England, she set up a Home Rule League and convened its first meeting in Queen's Hall, London, with Earl Brassey in the chair. On her return to India in 1914, she started the same movement and in no time won the support of leading Indian nationalists like M.A. Jinnah and Lala Lajpat Rai. For the sake of propagating her views, she started periodicals with the title of 'Commonweal' and 'New India' that "formed the battery of the Home Rule Movement."[25]

The motivating force behind this movement was the political philosophy of the arch-leader of the Theosophical Society which was, however, sharpened by the obtaining conditions. While Mrs. Besant wanted to serve this country that, in her view, was 'a tremendous reservoir of man power', she was equally concerned with the rise and growth of extremism in the Indian national movement and the rise of German militarism in Europe in as much as both were posing formidable threats to the interests of the English empire. At one stage, she herself declared: "One thing that lies very near to our hearts is to draw Great Britain and India nearer to each other by making known in Great Britain something of Indian movements, and of the men who will influence from here the destinies of the Empire."[26] It was, thus, aptly commented that the plan of Mrs. Besant "was to disentangle the nationalist extremists from their compromising alliance with the revolutionaries and to reconcile them to a position within the British Empire, and to bring them with the Moderates into line in a reunited Congress."[27]

The aim of the Home Rule Movement, in this way, was both apparent and real. Its apparent aim, as so often stressed by Mrs. Besant and also repeated by others like Lala Lajpat Rai and Tilak,

24. V. Levett: *A History of Indian Nationalist Movement*, p. 7

25. V.P.S. Raghuvanshi, *op. cit.*, p.137.

26. *Ibid.*

27. *Ibid.*

was to have a sort of self-rule on the Irish lines. As Mrs. Besant said: "In Political Reforms we aim at the building up of the complete self-government from village councils through District and Municipal Boards and Provincial Legislative Assemblies to a National Parliament, equal in its powers to the legislative bodies of Self-Governing Colonies, by whatever names they may be called; also at the direct representation of Imperial Parliament, when that body will contain representatives of the self-governing States of Europe."[28] Tilak, who had recently come from Mandalay after completing his period of internment, at the Lucknow Congress of 1916, called for action and voiced the demand of the Congress for Home Rule, *i.e.*, India to be a self-governing Dominion in which Indians would have control over the Central Legislative Council with the exception of military matters and foreign affairs, and complete Indian control over all matters in provincial government."[29]

The Home Rule Movement of Mrs. Besant could not make any noticeable headway until a great figure like Tilak supported it. The Irish lady failed to impress the Bombay Congress of 1915 with her programme and outlook in this regard. A great moderate leader like Surendranath Banerjea defeated the proposals of Mrs. Besant by saying that an organisation like that of the Home Rule would serve to overlap and perhaps weaken the Congress. Situation, however, underwent a transformation when a great national leader like Tilak supported the move and Lala Lajpat Rai also fell in line though with a slightly different version of his own. The Home Rule Movement thus witnessed its success at the Lucknow Congress of 1916 where Tilak forcefully stressed the need for a change. Said he: "The Congress had done its work as a deliberative body."[30] Thus, the way was cleared for carrying on the nationalist movement in a direction desired by Mrs. Besant and Tilak.

The Home Rule Movement gained India-wide importance when home rule societies were set up in different parts of the country. In no time, it became a source of concern to the English administration

---

28. *Ibid.*

29. See Daniel Argov, *op. cit.*, p.159.

30. *Ibid.*

so much so that Lord Pentland, the then Governor of Madras, issued orders for the internment of Mrs. Besant along with her two trusted lieutenants–Wadia and Arundale. The arrest of Mrs. Besant on 16 June, 1917 contributed to her popularity and gave strength to this movement, for her internment was widely resented. Jawaharlal Nehru says that the political atmosphere "became electric and most of us youngmen felt exhilarated and expected big things in the near future."[31] In view of the mounting national resentment, the British administration freed Mrs. Besant after a couple of months. It thus set in motion a powerful impulse that placed her on the chair of the Congress president in 1917. This event marked the culmination of the Home Rule Movement.

This movement is known for two great contributions. First, it brought about unity in the ranks of the Congress. Mrs. Besant took much of the moderates and something of the extremists and fused them in such a way that the two wings of the Congress came closer. Thus, she could undo what had happened at Surat in 1907. Emphasis on the use of purely peaceful and constitutional means and achievement of self-rule within the British empire were such stances of this movement that the moderates found herein what they had really wanted. The leadership of Tilak was the source of attraction as well satisfaction for the extremists. Moreover, the death of great moderates like Gokhale and Pherozeshah Mehta in 1915 also convinced the extremists with the fact that the Congress at the hands of the moderates with 'caution as the watchword' was no longer in existence; it had become the national forum and constituted the vanguard of militant nationalism. This change was very well appreciated by Lala Lajpat Rai when he said: "India of 1917 was different from India of 1907. In 1907 we were fighting for crumbs. In 1917 we no longer pray for concessions but are demanding rights."[32]

It may, however, be pointed out that the Home Rule Movement came as a refined version of agitation launched by early moderate leaders of the Congress. It sought to give a new life to what the 'loyal' nationalists had desired. The emphasis on the 'rights of the

31. Nehru: *An Autobiography*, p.31.

32. Agrov, *op. cit.*, 159-60.

Indian people' was couched in a very sophisticated language that was designed for renewing the mission of Hume.[33] The real motivating force was the fear of German militarism and the menace created by the movements of the extremist and the terrorist sections of the Indian nationalists. Thus came another version of 'Save the British Empire' theory. One may ask as to why great extremist leaders like Tilak and Lajpat Rai joined this movement when the declarations of the Irish lady were so frank and outspoken. An answer to such a question should be discovered in the statement that they found much to their satisfaction in her 'emphasis on the rights of the Indian people' and also in their hopes to control the Congress at a time when the moderates had no great leader except Surendranath Benerjea. If studied from such a critical standpoint, it may be commented that the founder of this movement (Mrs. Besant) "sought to guide the national movement in channels of 'loyalty' to the Empire and was later to take an active part in the fight against non-co-operation."[34]

Khilafat Movement: The Khilafat agitation of 1918-20 has a place of its own where the progress of freedom movement of India came to have a strange synchronization with pan-Islamic sentiments. It arose as a stern resentment against serious injustice done to Turkey by the Allied Powers, particularly Britain, after the conclusion of the first World War in the name of peace settlement.[35] The obdurate role of British government in applying the principle of national self-determination to all peoples, whether Christians or Muslims, alike and treating Turkey as a defeated power like

33. As Mrs Besant said "India does not chaffer with the blood of her sons and the proud tears of her daughters in exchange for so much liberty, so much right. India claims the right, as a Nation, to justice among the people of the Empire. India asked for this before the War, India will ask for it after the War, not as a reward but as a right does ask for it. On that there must be no mistake." *How India Wrought for Freedom*, pp. 574-75.

34. R.P. Dutt: *India Today*, p.334.

35. During the period of war, but particularly after Turkey joined it with Germany, the British statesmen and some other important leaders of the Allied powers had assured the Indian Muslims that a fair treatment would be accorded to Turkey after the termination of hostilities. On January, 5, 1918, Prime Minister Lloyd George said:

Germany could not carry conviction with the Indian Muslims. Thus, in the ruin of Turkey or in the dismemberment of the Ottoman Empire leading to the giving away of their holy places to the 'infidels', they "saw a death-blow to her life, and rallied round the Khailfat to save itself." Besides, since the Hindus realized it all necessary for maintaining unity to prosecute national struggle with more vigour, they "made its cause their own."[36]

This agitation started in India with the observance of the Khilafat Day throughout the country on October, 17, 1919 as a vigorous protest against the dismemberment of the Turkish empire. As a result of this, most of the prominent Muslim leaders like Muhammed Ali and Shaukat Ali (known as the Ali Brothers) were interned. However, in consultation with some friends, Abdul Bari decided to hold an All-India Muslim Conference with the co-operation of Hakim Ajmal Khan, Dr. M.A Ansari and others. The proposed conference was held at Lucknow where a decision was taken to set up in Bombay an All-India Khilafat Committee with branches in different parts of the country.[37] Then, at a meeting held on November 11, 1919, this Khilafat Committee changed its title to the Central Khilafat Committee of India with three objectives:

(*i*) to secure for Turkey a just and honourable peace;

(*ii*) to secure the fulfilment of pledges given by British Prime Minister to preserve the integrity of the Turkish empire, and

(*iii*) to memorialize the British Prime Minister, American President and Indian Viceroy as a token of gratitude for securing these objectives.

The meeting of the All-India Khilafat Conference took place in Delhi on November 23 and 24, 1919 where resolutions were passed calling the people of the country to boycott British goods and desist

---

"Nor are we fighting to deprive Turkey of its capital or of the rich and renowned lands of Asia Minor and Thrace which are predominantly Turkish in race." Likewise, President Wilson of the United States assured them in his statement of July 8, 1918. See A.R. Leonard: *War Addresses of Woodrow Wilson*, p. 99.

36. N.V. Thadani: *The Historic Trial of Ali Brothers*, pp. iii-iv.

37. M. Husain. I.H. Qureshi and others: *History of the Freedom Movement*, pp. 215-16.

from participating in the forthcoming peace celebrations. It was also decided not to cooperate with the Government of India. While addressing this conference, Gandhiji said: "We talk of Hindu-Muslim unity. It would be an empty phrase if the Hindus held aloof from the Mohammedans when the vital interest of the latter were at stake."[38]

The resentment against the British Government became very strong after the release of the Ali Brothers. Both the Muslim League and the Indian National Congress held their annual sessions in the city of Amritsar in December, 1919. On this occasion, the Congress passed a resolution urging the British rulers "to settle Turkish question in accordance with the just and legitimate sentiments of Indian Mussalamans and the solemn pledges of the Prime Minister without which there will be no content among the people of India."[39]

In the same month Khilafat Conference was held under the presidentship of Shaukat Ali where a decision was taken to dispatch a deputation to meet the Viceroy of India and then hold parleys with the authorities of British and Allied governments. Thus, on January 19, 1920 a deputation consisting of prominent persons (like Muhammed Ali, Shaukat Ali, Hakim Ajmal Khan, Dr. M.A. Ansari, Abdul Bari, Maulana Azad, Seth Chhotani, Hasrat Mohani, Dr. S.U. Kitchlew, Gandhiji and Swami Shradhanand) waited on the Viceroy (Lord Chelmsford) in New Delhi. It presented a memorandum highlighting these important demands.[40]

1. It was not merely to be a settlement between Turkey and Allies, rather it was to be a settlement in which the Muslims of India had an equal share. Khilafat was the embodiment of a common Muslim parentage, culture and outlook on life having two centres–personal in the Khalifa and local in Arabia. The Khilafat must be preserved with adequate temporal power.

---

38. Cited in N.M.P. Srivastava: *Growth of Nationalism in India (Effects of International Events)*, p. 141.
39. *Ibid.*, p. 142.
40. Shan Muhammed: *Freedom Movement in India: The Role of Ali Brothers*, pp.112-13.

2. Jazirat-ul-Arab (entire Arabian peninsula including Syria, Palestine and Mesopotamia) should remain under exclusive Muslim control within the scheme of Ottoman sovereignty.

3. Holy places (the three sacred places of Mecca, Madina and Jerusalem) and holy shrines of Mesopotamia should be under the control of the Khalifa himself.

Nothing fruitful could happen as the Viceroy regretted his inability to do anything that was already decided by His Majesty's Government and the Allied Powers in recognising the principle of national self-determination irrespective of the religion of the concerned peoples. Naturally, it "convinced the Muslims that their constitutional policy was futile and only with agitation they could get their demand fulfilled. Muhammed Ali came to the conclusion that freedom of India was absolutely necessary for the freedom of Islam."[41]

The third session of the Khilafat Congress took place in the city of Bombay on February 15, 1920 in which the leaders refuted the plea of British Prime Minister that the treatment with Turkish empire was a matter concerned with Allied Powers as a whole and thus his hands were restricted. Then, at another Khilafat Conference held at Calcutta on February 29, 1920 a decision was taken that in the event of any decision at the religious duty of every Muslim "to have recourse to every possible means to keep the Khilafat intact and maintain the position and dignity of the Khalifa."

At the same time, a Khilafat delegation was sent to Europe under Muhammed Ali that included prominent figures like Syed Sulaiman Nadvi, Syed Husain and Hayat Mohammed Khan. In his meeting with the English Prime Minister, Muhammed Ali pleaded:

(*i*) That the Khalifa must possess adequate territories, naval and military forces as well as financial sinews, for he was the Commander of the Faithful.

(*ii*) That the islands of Arabia should remain under the Muslim control.

(*iii*) That the Khalifa should be the warden of the three sacred harems of Mecca, Madina and Jerusalem as well as of the holy shrines of Najaf, Karbala, Kazmain, Samara and Baghdad.

41. *Ibid.*, p. 114.

But it all proved of no avail, because the English Prime Minister adhered to his decision of implementing the principle of national self-determination whereby Turkish claim to non-Turkish possessions could not be conceded.[42] The reply of Lloyd George greatly disappointed the Muslims. Gandhiji was also shocked at this and he gave a statement: 'Khilafat question has now become a question of questions.' March 19, 1920 was observed as a day of national mourning. And yet the British rulers went ahead with their plan. The Allied Powers offered peace terms to Turkey amounting to the dismemberment of the Ottoman empire which she had to accept and then the Treaty of Sevres was presented. In November 1922, the government of Mustafa Kemal Ataturk abolished monarchy (Sultanate) and declared this country a 'republic'. It appointed Abdul Majid as the Khalifa with no temporal power and removed him on March 3, 1924. As per the decision of the Angora Assembly, even the puppet Khalifa, his wives and children were expelled from Turkey. Thus, the Khilafat agitation came to an end showing that "while Indian Muslims were struggling for the restoration of the Khilafat, the aims and aspirations of the Turkish government were more national than religious in character."[43]

In this way, the Khilafat movement ended in a bitter failure. Its importance, in the history of our freedom struggle, is owing to remarkable change in the attitude of the diehard Muslims whose anti-British postures intensified the pace of freedom struggle under the leadership of Gandhiji. Its definite contribution must be seen in quickening the pace of Gandhi's leadership. However, its negative effect could be seen in sharpening the force of Muslim communalism. Evaluating it all, an English writer says: "The dependence of the Khilafat movement on circumstances outside India necessarily limited its long-term importance. But it was not without significance for political developments inside India. Firstly, it did have a bearing on the constitutional situation. Both before the first World War in co-operation with the constitutionalists and afterwards in co-operation with Gandhi, the pan-Islamists played an important role as the shock-troops of Reformist politics. Secondly, the religio-

42. Rushbrook Williams: *India in 1920*, p.37.

43. Srivastava, *op. cit.*, p. 159.

political alliance formed at this time in some respects foreshadowed the Pakistan movement itself. The Khilafat movement was the most significant mass movement among the Muslims before the 1940s and many of the politicians involved in it were later to figure in the Muslim League platform."[44]

Struggle for Swaraj Within the Empire if Possible, Outside the Empire if Necessary

Before the advent of Annie Besant, the implications of Swaraj were vague, she made them clear and understandable. Her successors refined them so that they became like a chiselled diamond. The British rulers failed to read the bold writing on the wall and yet they had to succumb to the weight of public opinion. They dilly-dallied as is evident from the Montagu Declaration of August, 1917, Irwin's offer of October, 1929 and Cripps proposals of March,1942. The pace of the movement could not be checked so much so that eventually the case of *Swaraj* within the Empire saw its replacement by the case of *Swaraj* without the Empire, popularly known as *Purna Swaraj*. Credit for first harmonising the two implications of the Swaraj and then discarding the first at the cost of the second goes to Gandhiji. No doubt, his advent into Indian politics "was the opening of a new chapter in its history."[45]

Satyagraha in Champaran, Ahmedabad and Kheda: Gandhiji invented and experimented his weapon of Satyagraha in South Africa where he stayed from 1893 to 1914. In early 1915 he came to India and had a meeting with Gokhale and Tagore. Then he sailed for England to render his voluntary services to the British. He raised an ambulance corps there and attended to the wounded soldiers in the military hospitals. His services were greatly appreciated and for this he was awarded a gold medal and the title of Kaiser-i-Hind. In December, 1916 he came back to India and attended the session of the Indian National Congress held at Lucknow. Here Raj Kumar Shukla apprised him of the harrowing tales of the indigo cultivators and requested him to visit the area of Trihut division. At his insistence Gandhiji reached there in March, 1917 and did his first Satyagraha in Champaran.

---

44. David Page: *Prelude to Partition,* pp.21-22.

45. Tara Chand, *op. cit.*, p. 475.

The cause of the exploitation and torture of the cultivators was the *tinkathia* system sanctioned by the Bihar Agrarian Act of 1861 whereby a landholder was required to cultivate indigo on at least 3/20 part of his land. The landholders had leased out their lands to the English planters who had started the practice of share-cropping and they charged some excess amount known as *Sharabheshi*. Gandhiji could see that the system was extremely unjust. Some influential persons of Bihar like Rajendra Prasad, Brajkishore Prasad and Prof. J.B. Kripalani also took part in the Satyagraha. The cultivators took out processions and staged *dharnas*. When the matter was brought to the notice of the Governor of Bihar (Edward Gait), he asked the Commissioner of the Trihut Division (Frank Sly) to submit his report. The Sly Report did plain-speaking and the Governor accepted it. The result was the termination of the notorious *tinkathia* system in April, 1917.[46]

In April, 1918 Gandhiji made second experiment of Satyagraha in Ahmedabad. Here the textile mill workers had gone on a strike. Their demand was enhancement of the wages by 50 per cent in view of the rise in prices due to war conditions. Indulal Yajnik and Ansuyia Behn joined the Satyagraha. Here Gandhiji observed hunger strike, for the first time, in support of the workers. It lasted for three days (15 to 17 April, 1918) and then a settlement was arrived at. The president of the Textile Owners Mills Association (Ambalal Sarabhai) yielded to enhance the wages of the workers by 35 per cent.

Shortly after this, Gandhiji took part in the Kheda peasant agitation. A condition approaching famine had arisen in this district of Gujarat owing to widespread failure of crops and so the Patidars had demanded suspension of the payment of revenue for the year. The authorities of the revenue department had falsely reported that the crops were not damaged to an extent that the payment of the revenue could be suspended. Here Vallabhbhai Patel and Mahadev Desai became the followers of Gandhiji. The Governor of

---

46. About the marvellous success of the Champaran Satyagraha, Gandhiji says: "The country had its first direct object-lesson in Civil Disobedience.... The Champaran struggle was a proof of the fact that disinterested service of the people in any sphere ultimately helps the country politically." *An Autobiography*, p. 346.

Bombay could realise the truth of the situation. He did not endorse what was given in the reports of the revenue department. He issued confidential orders that revenue should be recovered from those pesants who could pay. So the agitation came to an end. Gandhiji says: "The campaign was not, however, without its indirect results which we can see today and the benefit of which we are reaping. The Kheda Satyagraha marks the beginning of an awakening among the peasants of Gujarat, the beginning of their true political education."[47]

The success achieved in all the three events stands out as the proof of Gandhi's initial activism and his endeavour for creating mass nationalism in India. A large number of local figures joined his Satyagraha and thereby became his loyal lieutenants whom Judith Brown has misnamed as his 'subcontractors'. His new style of agitation won laurels and enabled him to carve out a place for himself in the heart of the countrymen. It is well said: "Champaran, Ahmedabad and Kheda served as demonstrations of Gandhiji's style and method of politics of the country at large. They also helped him find his feet among the people of India and study their problems at close quarters. He came to possess as a result of these struggles, a surer understanding of the strength and weakness of the masses, as well as the viability of his own political style."[48]

Anti-Rowlatt Act Agitation and Amritsar Tragedy: The incidents of Champaran, Ahmedabad and Kheda "were like the flappings of the wings before the start of his flights into the high empyrean."[49] The recommendations of the Rowlatt Committee (also known as Sedition Committee)[50] startled him and created a new

---

47. *Ibid.*, p. 366.

48. Bipan Chandra and others, *India's Struggle for Independence*, p. 181.

49. Tara Chand, *op.cit.*, p. 476.

50. On 10 December, 1917 the Government of India appointed a committee "to investigate and report on the nature and extent of criminal conspiracies connected with the revolutionary movement in India and to advise as to the legislation necessary to deal effectively with them." Rowlatt, a Judge of the High Court of Justice in England, was its chairman. It had two judges of the Indian High Court (one Englishman and the other an Indian) and two officials.

wave in his mind which, after the Amritsar tragedy, converted him from a loyal servant to that of a friendliest foe of the Empire. "This was the beginning of the transformation from a loyal citizen of the Empire who had so far believed that the 'Empire has been on the whole a power for good', to an extreme rebel whose new creed was: 'The British Empire today represents Satanism, and they who love God can afford to have no love for Satan'. The change in such a high-sounded, scrupulously truth-loving person marked the final stage in the destruction of the moral foundation of the British Empire in India. Gandhiji represented the conscience of India and the revolt in his mind was the starting point of the revolution which culminated in the end of the Empire."

On the basis of the recommendations of the Rowlatt Committee, two official bills were moved in the Central Legislative Council and while one of them was withdrawn, the other one was passed and became an Act on 21 March, 1919.[51] Jinnah, Malaviya and Mazharul Huq not only opposed this Draconian measure, they tendered their resignations from the Council. Gandhiji issued the call of Satyagraha campaign so as to revolutionise politics and restore moral force to its original position. 'Black Day' was observed in Delhi and Punjab on 30 March, 1919. The whole country was under an electric effect. Gandhiji called it 'a wonderful spectacle'. After a week, on Sunday, 6th April, the agitation covered places in the South as well. Unfortunately some events of violence took place in Delhi, Bombay and Ahmedabad. The people by now had not learnt the lesson of organising Satyagraha campaigns; so Gandhi confessed his fault and called it as his 'Himalayan miscalculation'.

In Punjab the situation became very tense. Many prominent leaders like Satya Pal and Saifuddin Kitchlew were detained and sent to unknown places. The Governor (Michael O'Dwyer) handed over the administration of the province to the military. Gen. N. Dyer issued orders so as to terrorise the people. The festival of

---

51. The Rowlatt Act had very stringent provisions. It empowered the provinical government to arrest any person on the suspicion of being a terrorist and to keep him under detention for any length of time. It also conferred extraordinary powers of search, arrest, demand of security etc. It provided for trial in camera by a special court whose judgment could not be taken in appeal to any higher court. Motilal Nehru commented: 'No Vakil, No Dalil (Argument), and No Appeal'.

Baisakhi was being celebrated on 13th April, 1919. It was not a public meeting but a mela (fair). The power-drunk Gen. Dyer took it as a violation of his order banning public meetings and reached the Jallianwala Bagh in the afternoon hours with a contingent of 40 soldiers. Without issuing any warning, he ordered firing in which hundreds of innocent people were killed. Two days after, he promulgated the martial law that continued till 29 May. Well-known leaders of Punjab like Rambhuj Dutt Chowdhury, Lala Har Kishen Lal and Duni Chand were put behind the bars. By all means, Punjab "was isolated or cut off from the rest of India; a thick veil seemed to cover it and hid it from the outside eyes."[52]

The massacre of the innocent people was widely and strongly condemned. Tagore renounced his Knighthood and Gandhiji returned his gold medal and the title of Kaiser-i-Hind in protest. The people demanded recall of the Governor and dismissal of Gen. Dyer. In order to assuage the feelings of the people, the Governor-General appointed a committee of inquiry (Disorders Inquiry Committee) under the chairmanship of Hunter with four Englishmen and four Indians (C.L. Setalvad, Sankaran Nair, Sahibzada Sultan Ahmed Khan (as Jinnah had declined the assignment) and Lala Jagat Narain) on 14 October, 1919. The European members wrote a report in which they held the Government of India 'blameless' and said that 'the disturbances were of the nature of a rebellion which might have developed into a revolution'. But the Indian members did not endorse these points. At the instance of Gandhiji, the President of the Indian National Congress (M.M. Malaviya) set up a committee of inquiry. It had Motilal Nehru, C.R. Das, Abbas Tyabji, M.R. Jayakar (in place of Fazlul Haq) and Gandhiji. When the bar of 3 months on the entry of these leaders into Punjab was removed, Gandhiji visited the area. This committee submitted its report on 20 February, 1920 which passed severe strictures against the Governor of Punjab (Michael O' Dwyer) and Gen. Dyer and demanded suitable punishment for them.[53]

---

52. Jawaharlal Nehru: *An Autobiography*, p. 42.

53. The Hunter Committee Report said about 150 casualties in this massacre, but the Congress Inquiry Committee Report had the figure of about 400 deaths and called it as "a calculated piece of inhumanity towards utterly innocent and unarmed men, and unparalleled for its ferocity in the history of modern British administration."

Effort for Hindu-Muslim Unity and Call for Non-Cooperation: The Amritsar tragedy "kindled a conflagration throughout India."[54] Gandhi's severe indictment of the Rowlatt Act and his call for Satyagraha campaigns made him immensely popular among the Hindus and the Muslims alike. The wave of Hindu-Muslim unity blew so fast that Swami Shradhanand was invited to address the meetings of the Muslims in the Jama Masjid of Delhi and Gandhiji and Sarojini Naidu addressed such meetings in the mosques of Bombay. The issue of the Khilafat stood like 'a question of the questions' and Gandhiji's support for the cause made him popular among the Muslims as well. So he was invited at a joint conference of the Hindus and the Muslims to deliberate on the Khilafat question. This meet took place on the 22, 23 and 24 November, 1919 in Delhi and here Gandhiji had to be face to face with a number of prominent Muslims like Hakim Ajmal Khan, Asaf Ali, Dr. M.A. Ansari, Maulana Abdul Bari and Hasrat Mohani. A little earlier, he had said something in broken Urdu at the meeting of the Muslim League held at Calcutta, but now he had to deliver a sort of argumentative speech in many words that could impress the audience with what he really desired to convey. It is here that he thought about making a hybrid of Hindi and Urdu languages known by the name of Hindustani as the *lingua franca* of the country.

At this conference, a number of Muslim leaders expressed their readiness to stop cow slaughter as it was a serious roadblack in the way of communal amity. And it is here that Gandhiji publicly revealed his idea of no cooperation to the British raj in case the demand of the Muslims for 'Justice to the Khilafat' was not honoured. In a very sharp tone, he said: "It is an inalienable right of the people thus to withhold cooperation. We are not bound to retain Government titles and honours, or to continue in Government service. If Government should betray us in a great cause like the Khilafat, we could not do otherwise than non-cooperate. We are, therefore, entitled to non-cooperate with Government in case of betrayal."[55]

After a month, the session of the Indian National Congress was held at Amritsar under the Presidentship of Motilal Nehru. For the first time, Gandhi took active part in the deliberations and he described it as 'his real initiation or entrance into the Congress

---

54. Surendranath Banerjea: *A Nation in Making*, p. 304.

55. Gandhi: *An Autobiography*, p. 402.

politics'. But his idea of non-cooperation was so revolutionary that it could not be acceptable to the galaxy of the great Congress leaders like Annie Besant, Jinnah and Tilak. Tilak's plea of responsive cooperation held the field which amounted to the rejection of Gandhi's thesis, though it partly accommodated to some extent what he had desired. But the Mahatma remained steadfast. On 10 March 1920 he issued a manifesto advocating the start of a non-violent non-cooperation movement. On 15 May 1920 the terms of the Treaty of Sevres were released whereby the Ottoman Empire was to be dismembered. Now the Khilafat issue was at its zenith. In his paper Gandhiji wrote: "If I deem a Mohammedan to be my brother, it is my duty to help him in this hour of trial to the best of my ability, if his cause commends itself to me as just." [56] The Khilafat Committee had its meeting at Allahabad on 9 June, 1920. 'It adopted a resolution enunciating four stages of non-cooperation—(i) renunciation of titles and resignation of honorary posts, (ii) leaving services of the Government including police and military services, and (iii) refusal to pay taxes.[57]

What Gandhiji could not achieve at the Amritsar Congress, he could have it in the following year. Shortly after the meeting of the Khilafat Committee at Allahabad, the Gujarat political conference was held at Ahmedabad under the Presidentship of Abbas Tyabji where Gandhi's motion of non-cooperation was adopted by an overwhelming majority. It was confirmed at the Special Calcutta Congress held on 4 September, 1920 with a majority of votes. Happily, it was finally endorsed at the Nagpur session with a unanimous vote in December, 1920. The declaration of non-cooperation with the Government was, in fact, a revolutionary step tantamount to the proclamation of war, with this difference that the war was non-violent. It inflicted neither pain nor injury upon the opponent, reserving all suffering for the non-cooperation.[58]

---

56. *Young India*, 2 June, 1920.

57. Tara Chand, *op.cit.*, p.490. The Jamiatul Ulema-i-Hind issued a fatwa (religious decree) calling upon the Muslims to boycott elections, government schools and colleges and law courts and to renounce titles and ranks conferred by the British Government.

58. Gandhiji made it clear in these words: "Complete civil disobedience is a state of peaceful rebellion-a refusal to obey every single state-made law. It is certainly more dangerous than an armed rebellion." D.G. Tendulkar: *Mahatma*, Vol. II, p. 71.

Non-Violent Non-Co-Operation Movement: The course of our anti-colonial struggle had a basically different turn when Mahatma Gandhi took over the leadership of the Congress and declared at the Special Session of the Congress held at Calcutta in September 1920 under the presidentship of Lala Lajpat Rai that the British Government was a 'Satan' with whom no co-operation was possible. It showed that what the Mahatma could not achieve at the Amritsar Congress of 1919 on account of the opposition of the rump section of the liberals like Jinnah, Malaviya and Mrs. Annie Besant (who had described his thesis of non-co-operation 'as the greatest setback to India's freedom') and also of some extremists like Tilak (who had said that 'saintliness was no match to imperialism' and who thus adhered to the thesis of responsive co-operation implying constitutional co-operation or constitutional opposition whichever was expedient') could now hold the field the reason of which should be seen in the parting away of the liberals as well as in the death of Tilak coupled with the presidentship of the Special Congress session at Calcutta in the hands of one who was an extremist in the true sense of the term.[59]

The novelty of the Special Calcutta Congress thus lies in its honouring Gandhiji's revolutionary proposal of non-violent non-co-operation movement. Not 'reform' but 'revolution' became the watchword. It became fully evident from the presidential address of the Lalaji when he said: "It is no use blinking the fact that we are passing through a revolutionary period.. We are by instinct and tradition averse to revolutions. Traditionally, we are a slow-going people; but when we decide to move, we do move quickly and by rapid strides. No living organism can altogether escape revolutions in the course of its existence."[60] While the president laid clear-cut emphasis on the need for a revolution, Gandhiji bracketed with it the condition of using truthful and non-violent methods. Thus, the way was cleared for the ushering in of a new era of the revolutionary movement of the masses following the path of truth and non-

59. In his message to Punjabis on August 15, 1919, Lalaji had said: "We are neither fit nor ripe for a militant revolutionary struggle. We want a revolution but not force or violence.....organise the middle class, the peasants, the workers. Follow Gandhi." Cited in Argov, *op. cit.*, p.165.

60. See R.P. Dutt, *op. cit.*, p.339.

violence. In this way, the creed of the Congress "was changed from the previous proclamation of the aim of colonial self-government within the Empire to be attained by constitutional means to the new aim of the attainment of Swaraj by peaceful and legitimate means."[61]

That the Congress under Mahatma Gandhi now overthrew the 'reforms' and executed a decisive change of front with a determination to take the leadership of the rising masses committed to the path of non-violent non-co-operation became quite obvious at the regular session of the Congress held at Nagpur in December, 1920. The resolution of non-violent non-co-operation passed at the Special Calcutta Congress with 1886 votes to 884 was confirmed here with a unanimous vote boldly showing that even some dissidents led by C.R. Das had by this time fallen in line leaving others like Madan Mohan Malaviya, Mrs. Besant and Jinnah grumbling. Not only this, at this stage, Gandhiji produced the new constitution of the Congress in which swaraj was declared as the goal 'within the British Empire, if possible, and without it, if necessary' and in which the emphasis on 'by constitutional means' was changed to 'by all peaceful and legitimate means'. It marked an important stage in the development of our national movement showing that "with the baptism of the non-co-operation, the old Congress was virtually dead."[62]

Mahatma Gandhi's resolution on non-violent non-co-operation first passed at the special session of the Calcutta Congress and then confirmed at the Nagpur session in 1920 emphasised these important points:

(*a*) Surrender of titles and honorary offices and resignation from nominated seats in local bodies,

(*b*) Refusal to attend Government levees, durbars and official and semi-official functions held by the Government officials in their honour,

(*c*) Gradual withdrawal of children from schools and colleges owned, aided or controlled by the Government and establishment of national schools and colleges in the various provinces,

61. *Ibid*, p. 341.

62. Raghuvanshi, *op. cit.*, p. 166.

(*d*) Gradual boycott of British courts by lawyers and litigants and establishment of private arbitration courts for the settlement of disputes with the aid of lawyers,

(*e*) Refusal on the part of military, clerical and labouring classes to offer themselves as recruits for service in Mesopotamia,

(*f*) Withrawal by candidates of their candidature for election to the Reformed Councils and refusal on the part of the voters for any candidate offering himself for election; and

(*g*) Adoption of Swadeshi in piece-goods on a vast scale and revival of hand-spinning on the part of the weavers who had abandoned the calling.

The non-violent non-co-operation movement was at its highest pitch in 1921. Many distinguished Congressmen like Motilal Nehru, C.R. Das, Vallabhbhai Patel, Rajendra Prasad and Vithalbhai Patel left their lucrative legal practice to join this movement. Prominent Muslim figures like Muhammed Ali and Shaukat Ali (known as Ali Brothers), Hakim Ajmal Khan, Maulana Abul Kalam Azad and Dr. Ansari took part in the movement. National educational institutions like Gujarat Vidyapeeth, Bihar National University, Jamia Millia in Delhi, National Muslim University of Aligarh and National College of Lahore came into being. About 40 lakh volunteers were enrolled and 20,000 charkhas manufactured. The visit of His Royal Highness the Duke of Connaught to Delhi was boycotted. Gandhi established Tilak Memorial Swaraj Fund. Seth Jamnalal Bajaj, Chairman of the Reception Committee to the Congress at Nagpur, donated a lakh of rupees for the assistance of the persons participating in this movement. Strikes took place in different parts of the country. In this situation, the Ahmedabad session of the Congress was held towards the end of 1921 "with Gandhi now almost alone in the leadership."[63]

It was on account of the astounding success of the movement that the Congress had happily agreed to designate Gandhi as the 'dictator' or the chief executive authority. Amid full enthusiasm, the Ahmedabad Congress held under the presidentship of Hakim Ajmal Khan passed a resolution proclaiming the firm determination of the Congress "to continue the campaign of non-violent non-co-operation with greater vigour...till Swaraj is established and the

63. R.P. Dutt, *op. cit.*, p. 45.

control of the Government of India passes into the hands of the people", calling all over eighteen years of age to join the illegal National Volunteers pledging the aim "to concentrate attention upon the Civil Disobedience, whether mass or individual, whether of an offensive or defensive character", and "placing full dictatorial powers for this purpose in the hands of Mahatma Gandhi as the sole Executive authority of the Congress."[64]

Though the year 1921 witnessed the triumphant results of Gandhi's non-violent non-co-operation movement, it also saw some incidents of violence. Gandhi very anxiously looked at the growing tide of violence raising its ugly head. Thus, he, in very clear-cut terms, denounced the rising trend of violence and resolved to meet the repressive policy of the British Government by means of individual mass civil disobedience. Said he: "We must draw the gun powder on our heads and that too at the earliest possible opportunity." He himself knew that the people of India had not yet fully understood the meaning of Swaraj. The violent incident at Chauri Chaura (a place in Gorakhpur in U.P. where the people had set fire on a police station that resulted in the death of a Police Inspector and some policemen) on 5 February, 1922 came to him as the 'last straw' that forced him to suspend this movement with immediate effect.

As a result of this and a little later on account of his internment in the Yervada jail, Gandhi's first experiment in the direction of an anti-colonial struggle came to an end that left some nationalist leaders criticising him for different reasons. Leading Congressmen like Motilal Nehru, C.R. Das and Lajpat Rai reproached Gandhi from behind the prison bars. Later on, Jawaharlal Nehru wrote: "We were angry when we learnt of this stoppage of our struggle at a time when we seemed to be consolidating our position and advancing on all fronts."[65] The most vehement denunciation came from Subhas Bose who criticised Gandhiji's action in the name of a 'dictator's decree' and dubbed Gandhi's promise of 'Swaraj within a year' as 'unwise and childish.' Said he: "To sound the order of retreat just when public enthusiasm was reaching the boiling point was nothing short of a national calamity."[66]

---

64. *Ibid*.

65. Nehru: *An Autobiography*, p. 81.

66. Subhas Chandra Bose: *The Indian Struggle*, p. 108.

The sudden suspension of the first mass movement by Gandhiji was grossly misunderstood by the leaders and writers belonging to the Marxist school who looked at it through the spectacles of the class war and thus dubbed Gandhi as a religious revivalist championing the cause of the Indian bourgeoisie.An orthodox communist like M.N. Roy (as he then was) while living in the Soviet Union and thinking in terms of radicalising the politics of India therefrom, wrote a pamphlet titled 'One Year of Non-Co-operation' wherein he criticised the withdrawal of this movement as a compromise with the bourgeois class. He described the action of the 'Supreme Executive Authority of the Congress' as an instance of "rank betrayal of the revolutionary forces." Rajni Palme Dutt says: "The battle was over. The whole campaign was over. The mountain had indeed borne a mouse."[67] Again: "Not the question of violence or non-violence, but the question of class interest in opposition to the mass movement, was the breaking point of the national struggle in 1922. This was the rock on which the movement broke. This was the real meaning of non violence."[68]

Congress at the Cross-Roads: The Chauri Chaura violence entailed the end of the first unarmed revolt of Gandhi and his decision to stop it abruptly was endorsed by the Congress Working Committee at its Bardoli meeting on 12 February, 1922. On 10th March, Gandhiji was arrested and awarded six years imprisonment, though he was released on 5 February, 1924 owing to serious illness. The action of Gandhiji became the subject of critical appreciation.[69] Civil Disobedience Enquiry Committee was set up to take stock of the situation and to assess the attitude of the people. It presented its report in August, 1922. While it accepted that Gandhi's pledge of getting Swaraj within a year could not be fulfilled, the whole exercise could not fail to have its dividends. It stressed that the movement

67. R.P. Dutt, *op. cit.*, p. 348.

68. *Ibid.*, p. 353.

69. Even English leaders had different views on this point. For instance, while the Governor-General Chelmsford called Gandhi's programme of non-cooperation as 'the foolishest of all foolish activities', the Governor of Madras (Willingdon) said that "this movement, whatever may be its other achievements, has spread political ideas among the masses of the people and their placid content has been disturbed." Tara Chand, *op.cit.*, pp. 501 and 509.

yielded these gains–general awakening of the masses to their political rights and privileges, total loss of faith in the present system of government, the belief that it was only through their own efforts that India could hope to be free, the faith in the Congress as the only organisation which could properly direct national efforts to gain freedom, and the utter failure of repression to cow down the people[70]. According to Tara Chand, "the gain was two-fold–moral and political. It strengthened the traits of character essential for a free society and removed the illusion that the freedom-loving people of England intended to educate the backward Indian people in the ways of self-government, though necessarily the process had to be slow and gradual."[71]

When Gandhiji was behind the bars, C.R. Das and Motilal Nehru formed the Swaraj Party with its programme patently different from the programme of non-cooperation. But the problem could be sorted out at the special session of the Indian National Congress held at Delhi under the presidentship of Maulana Azad on 15 September, 1923. The Delhi resolution was confirmed at the regular session of the Congress held in December 1923 at Cocanada under the presidentship of Maulana Muhammed Ali. As a result of this, "the umblical cord which bound the Swaraj Party to the mother organisation was not cut."[72] In April, 1924 Das and Motilal Nehru had a meeting with Gandhiji at his Juhu resort in Bombay, but the 'Juhu conversations' failed to convince him with the ideology of the Council-entry.[73] He attended the meeting of the AICC held at Ahmedabad in June, 1924 with a determination to conquer the Swarajists, but he came back 'defeated and humbled.'[74] However, as a moderate leader, he did not want to put any obstacles in their way or to commence any progaganda against them. In fact, later in the year when the government of Bengal started a campaign against

70. *Ibid.*, pp. 508-09

71. *Ibid.*, pp. 500.

72. *Ibid.*, p. 501.

73. P.B. Sitaramayya: *The History of the Indian National Congress*, Vol. I. p. 452.

74. *The Indian Quarterly Register*, Vol.II (July-December, 1924), Numbers III and IV, p.132 (b).

Das and the Swarajists and promulgated an ordinance on 25 October, 1924 sanctioning house searches and arrests on a large scale, he rushed to Calcutta and issued a statement in support of the Swarajists. With Das and Motilal Nehru, he issued a statement which recommended that the "Swaraj Party should carry on work in connection with the Central and Provincial legislatures on behalf of and as an integral part of the Congress."[75] In December, 1924 the session of the Congress was held at Belgaum under the presidentship of Gandhiji and there the seal of approval was put on this statement.

Swaraj Party: The sudden suspension of the non-cooperation movement showing non-fulfilment of Gandhi's promises of Swaraj within a year caused a setback to his leadership and instead re-emergence of those subscribing to the moderate tradition who had already expressed their misgivings at the Amritsar Congress of 1919 with regard to the feasibility of the programme of non-co-operation.[76] Thus, there occurred the revival of old liberal politics, though in a different complexion. While leaders like C.R. Das, Motilal Nehru, Hakim Ajmal Khan, Vithalbhai Patel and Madan Mohan Malaviya desired to take to the path of parliamentarism as

---

75. Tara Chand, *op. cit.*, Vol. IV, p.1. Although Gandhiji disfavoured the idea of Council-entry of the Swarajists, he tried to reconcile himself with what Das and Motilal so keenly desired. He called it as his 'surrender' to an extent he and his friends had never expected. *Young India,* 13 November, 1924.

76. It is a fact that leading Congressmen, though crying for the Swaraj, were not very clear about the real meaning of this term. While supporting the resolution for the achievement of Swaraj by the people of India by all legitimate and peaceful means, Lala Lajpat Rai at the Special Calcutta Congress of 1920 explained that this word "was deliberately chosen for its ambiguity in order to enable Indians to remain within the projected commonwealth or to leave it, according to their own preference." See Argov, *op.cit.*, p.168. Nehru recorded his impression about the time of non-co-operation thus: "It was obvious that to most of our leaders Swaraj meant something much less than independence. Gandhiji was delightfully vague on the subject and he did not encourage clear thinking about it either." *Op.cit.*, p.76. It is discernible in his statement that 'Swaraj' means a state in which we can maintain our separate existence without the presence of the English. If it is to be a partnership, it must be a partnership at will."

the country was not prepared to embark upon general mass civil disobedience and thus they were known as 'pro-changers', others like Rajendra Prasad, Dr. M.A. Ansari, Kasturi Ranga Iyenger and C. Rajagopalachari adhered to the line of Gandhi's non-co-operation and were thus known as the 'no-changers'. A a result of this, the meeting of the All-India Congress Committee held at Calcutta in November, 1922 was described by Pattabhi as 'a tournament between these two sections of the leading Congressmen.'[77]

On account of Gandhi's still being behind the bars and also on account of their capitalising on the failure of the Gandhian leadership, the 'pro-changers' managed to influence the Gaya Congress of 1922 (held under the presidentship of C.R. Das) at which the proposal of the Council-entry was discussed with a forceful opinion in their favour. This decision was ratified at the special session of the Congress held at Delhi in September, 1923 under the presidentship of Maulana Azad and thereafter at its regular annual session held at Cocanada under the presidentship of Mohammed Ali. The proponents of the idea of Council-entry emphasised the point that non-co-operation could be effected from inside the Councils also. Thus in 1923 came into being a new organisation of the 'pro-changers' with the name of the Swaraj Party under the leadership of C.R. Das. The victory of the Swarajists in the elections of 1923 enthused them so much that even Gandhi, after his release from the jail in 1924, thought it difficult to bring the Congress back on the track of civil disobedience movement and, as a wise physician of the nation, he advised his staunch followers–the 'no-changers'–at the Belgaum Congress of December 1924 (held under his presidentship) to reconcile with the Swarajists.

The special session of the Indian National Congress held at Delhi in September, 1923 under the presidentship of Maulana Azad adopted the Swarajist plan of council-entry and thereafter Swarajist party "became the legislative wing of the Congress. Swaraj party leaders justified entry into the legislatures saying that under the contemporary situation, it was the best course to make the

77. Pattabhi Sitaramayya: *The History of the Indian National Congress*, Part I, p. 249

administrative system hollow and ineffective."[78] The prgramme of the Swarajist had these importan items:[79]

1. To throw out budget unless and until the system of administration was altered in recognition of our rights or as a matter of settlement between the Parliament and the people of this country:
2. To throw out all proposals for legislative enactments by which the bureaucracy proposed to consolidate its power;
3. To introduce resolutions etc., for the healthy growth of our national life; and
4. To follow an economic policy based on the same principles so as to prevent drainage of public wealth from India by checking all activities leading to exploitation.

That the Swarajists did not discard the line of Gandhi in toto is evident from the fact that they expressed their willingness to tread the path of civil disobedience in case their experiment of 'Council-entry to smash Reforms' proved a failure. Thus, it is well observed: "Outside the legislatures, the Swarajists were to render support to the constructive programme and, finally, there was an assurance that the moment we find that it is impossible to meet the selfish obstinacy of the bureaucracy without Civil Disobedience, we will retire from the Legislative bodies and help him (Gandhi) to prepare the country for Civil Disobedience."[80]

The Swarajits began their political agitation with the policy of entering the Legislative Councils to wreck the reforms. They borrowed the strategy of 'smashing councils, wrecking reforms' from Michael O' Dwyer who in his book *India As I Knew It* had written about the sabotage as 'being more difficult to deal with than an open rebellion.' Thus, the real aim of the Swarajists was to contest elections in order to secure the membership of the Legislative Councils and then to enter there with a mind to sabotage the

78. S.C. Kashyap: *Our Parliament*, p.11.
79. Bisheshwar Prasad: *Changing Modes of Indian National Movement*, p. 103.
80. *Ibid.*

programmes of the English bureaucracy. For this reason, it was said by their critics that they wanted nothing else than to destroy. Giving a befitting reply to such a distorted version of their aims, C.R. Das said in the Bengal Legislative Council in 1925: "We want to destroy and get rid of a system which does no good and can do no good. We want to destroy it, because we want to construct a system which can be worked with success and will enable us to do good to the masses."[81]

As a matter of fact, the aims of the Swarajists were twofold– destructive as well as constructive. Their methods, on the destructive side, emphasised attack on the votable part of the budget and rejection of proposals emanating from the bureaucracy. On the constructive side, they sought to move resolutions necessary for the healthy growth of national life and displacement of bureaucracy. To make their policy effective, they intended to occupy every place open to the members of the Central and Provincial Legislatures by election, and serve on committees where it was possible to carry out the policy of obstruction. Outside the Councils, they were to give whole-hearted support to the constructive programme of Mahatma Gandhi. Civil disobedience was to be the last resort against bureaucratic truculence. The Swarajists "hoped to win Swaraj in the legislatures when the battle outside had turned out to be a fiasco."[82]

Not only this that the Swarajists showed a brilliant success in the elections of 1923, they also made their mark on the working of the Central Legislative Assembly under the leadership of Motilal Nehru and in the Legislative Council of Bengal under the leadership of C.R. Das. They had a contingent of 45 out of 145 members in the Central Legislative Assembly under Motilal Nehru who could manage to requisition the help of some Independents also. Thus, on February 18, 1924 he could have his resolution passed by the House wherein it was recommended that a Round Table Conference be held for making a new constitution with a view to establish full responsible government in the country. The Swarajists succeeded in throwing out the budget of 1924-25 and thereby compelling the Government of India to lean on its power of 'certification.' A

81. See P.C. Ray: *Life and Times of C.R. Das.*, p. 201.

82. Raghuvanshi, *op. cit.*, p. 181.

resolution moved by C.D. Iyenger was passed by 58 votes to 45 that urged the suppression of the Bengal Ordinance by an Act of the Legislature. In February, 1925 the House passed bills moved by Vithalbhai J. Patel for the repeal of the State Prisoners' Act and the Prevention of Seditious Meetings Act. The Swarajists had a creditable record in the Bengal Legislative Council where C.R. Das led a contingent of 36 members and he refused to form the ministry having charge of the 'transferred' departments in spite of several requests made by the Governor. Rather, he made a coalition with a group of the Independents (called Nationalist Party) and could defeat the official proposals in 1924 and 1925 with regard to the payment of salaries to the ministers. It compelled the ministers to resign as a result of which their work was shared by the Governor and his Executive Councillors. In this way, C.R. Das, as his biographer says, "became an awful portent of danger and a lion in the path of the Indian bureaucracy."[83] The Swarajists had some success in the Central Provinces also under the leadership of N.C. Kelkar.

Provincial Legislative Councils (1923)

Provinces	Seats secured by other parties	Seats secured by the Swarajists
1. Madras	98	7
2. Bengal	111	36
3. Bombay	86	32
4. U.P.	101	31
5. Punjab	71	9
6. Bihar and Orissa	73	13
7. C.P. and Berar	54	40
8. Assam	39	1
	Total 633	Total 181

The Swarajists could not pursue their policy of 'uniform, continuous and consistent obstruction' for a sufficiently long time. A definite change in their attitude became visible in 1925 both on account of their own awareness of the inadequacy of their policy of 'sabotage' as well as owing to the declining health of the real

83. P.C. Ray. *op. cit.*, p. 202.

Swarajist–C.R. Das. In the first instance, the Swarajists took to the line of 'walk-in, walk-out' to express their resentment if an official measure was not appreciated by them; in the second instance, it was converted into the form of 'responsive co-operation.' Thus, there started a sort of demoralisation of the Council Front. Even C.R. Das at the Faridpur Provincial Congress of 1925 announced his terms of settlement if certain concessions were made by the British Government as transfer of some real responsibility to the people, granting of Swaraj in the near future, creation of an atmosphere of trust showing a change of heart on the part of the rulers, granting of general amnesty to all prisoners and immediate recognition of the Dominion Status signifying self-government in India having a free and voluntary association with the British Empire. The result was that there occurred a split in the ranks of the Swarajists whereby the sections of the Responsivists and Non-Co-operators came into being. Madan Mohan Malaviya and Lala Lajpat Rai looked at the pace of communal riots with concern and organised their own group (called Congress Independents) to protect the interests of the Hindus. Thus, the Swarajists failed to retain their glamour in the elections of 1926. The movement failed with the death of C.R. Das on 16 June, 1925 and even Motilal Nehru's threat that 'the diseased limb of the Swaraj Party must be amputated' failed to save the Party from extinction at the hands of those who were cultivating an increasing faith in the cult of responsivism.

The movement of the Swarajists–'peripetetic patriots' or men of 'patriotism in locomotion' (as described by Sir Tej Bahadur Sapru) –failed to achieve anything more than to demonstrate that the constitutional reforms of 1919 "were a charter of irresponsibility of the Executive heads and a denial of even elementary priciples of democracy."[84] While the Government asserted 'no anarchy but autocracy', the Swarajists declared 'no dyarchy but Swaraj'. However, the walk-in, walk-out policy of the Swarajists became a source of confusion and, for this reason, most of them found in the elections of 1926 that "the gilt was off the ginger bread."[85] The result was that the leadership of Gandhi had its re-emergence and the way was cleared for the second experiment under Mahatma's

84. Raghuvanshi, *op. cit.*, p.186.

85. C.Y. Chintamani: *Indian Politics Since the Mutiny,* p. 107.

leadership that ensued in the form of the civil disobedience movement of 1930-31. In fine, the Swarajists could not do any great thing than making a brief attempt in the direction of parliamentarism and that too of a type that could satisfy neither the liberals who were wiped off their leadership[86], nor could they satisfy the progressive section of the Congress that was really interested in giving a revolutionary character to the anti-colonial struggle and thus treated their movement as an inept exercise of bourgeois politics.[87]

Efforts for Communal Unity: The need for communal amity engaged the attention of all nationalists like Ghulam Muhammed Bhurguri and Dr. M.A. Ansari of the Muslim League, Das and Motilal Nehru of the Swaraj Party, and Gandhi and Lajpat Rai of the Congress. The Congress appointed a committee consisting of Lajpat Rai, Dr. Ansari and Sardar Mahtab Singh (who was replaced by Sardar Amar Singh after his arrest) that drew up an agreement known as the Solan Pact. In a fit of zeal, Das drew up the Bengal Pact which was too lenient in favour of the Muslims. So it was discarded by the Congress at its Cocanada meet.

Communal riots in different parts of the country, particularly at Kohat in the N.W.F.P., uneased the Mahatma to an extent that he went on a fast of 21 days (18 September to 8 October, 1924) so as to prevent Hindus and Muslims from the suicidal courses which they were following. A Unity Conference was held at Delhi on 26 September under the presidentship of Motilal Nehru. It adopted a resolution condemning religious conversions by force and desecration of the places of worship and laid stress on the freedom

---

86. For instance, Surendranath Banerjea remarked: "The obstructionists may temporarily pose as heroes who have defied autocratic Government, but they will leave behind them for the countrymen the bitter harvest of their sinister activities." *A Nation in Making.*, p. 381.

87. As Palme Dutt says: "But in practice, the Swaraj Party was the party of the progressive upper bourgeoisie: its existence depended on the support of these elements just as its main leaders came from among them; and however much they might talk sentimentally of the workers and peasants to win the support of the upper class elements, they had to make it perfectly clear that their party was sound on the essential basis of landlordism and capitalism." *op. cit.*, pp. 354-55.

of conscience. It also appealed to Gandhiji to break his fast. Shortly after, on 21 November, an All-Parties Conference had its session at Bombay at the instance of Maulana Muhammed Ali. Most of the members expressed their opposition to the claims of Muhammed Ali that the Muslim representatives should not be in minority in the Legislative Councils of Punjab and Bengal and that the Muslims' share in the public services should be separately decided. Gandhiji attended this meet and he came to the conclusion that under such conditions, any scheme of unity could not be possible. In the following month, Jinnah called a meet of the Muslim League at Bombay and, as the Chairman of the Reception Committee, he thundered: "No power on earth can dare obstruct our demand for Swaraj provided the Hindus and the Muslims become sincerely united."[88]

The Hindu Maha Sabha had its session at Calcutta on 11 April 1925 under the presidentship of Lala Lajpat Rai who advocated "a democratic Raj in which the Hindus, Muslims and all other communities of India may participate as Indians and not as followers of any particular religion."[89] But in his presidential address at the Kanpur meet of December, 1925, Kelkar laid stress on the *sangathan* (organisation) and *shuddhi* (conversion to Hinduism) in defence of making a strong Hindu society. In retaliation the Muslim League at its Aligarh meet in December, 1925 under the presidentship of Abdur Rahim laid all blame on the Hindu communalists. As a result, the unity efforts could not make much headway, though such efforts continued to linger on as we see in the deliberations of the All-Parties Conference held at Delhi in February and May, 1928 and in the provisions of the Nehru Report (1928) that unfortunately foundered on the rock of communalism.[90]

Call for Complete Independence: The Nagpur Congress of December, 1920 had adopted a resolution moved by Gandhiji which clarified the goal of the Indian National Congress as 'the achievement of Swaraj by peaceful and legitimate means within the Empire if possible, without the Empire if necessary'. It was inserted into the

---

88. Tara Chand, *op. cit.*, Vol. IV, p. 21.

89. *Ibid.*, p. 22.

Ibid., pp. 22-23.

constitution of the Congress. In its strict sense, it desired Dominion Status in ideal terms that could not be acceptable to the British rulers as they would not recognise the status of equality of the Indians with them on the pattern of the Dominions like Canada and Australia. At the same time, it made an opening for those who would desire nothing short of complete independence. The phrase was so flexible that it could satisfy the 'old guards' like Motilal Nehru and C.R. Das as well as the 'new heroes' like Jawaharlal Nehru and Subhas Chandra Bose. Above all, it allowed full option to the English rulers to satisfy the demand of the Indians for Swaraj in an honourable way. But the English masters failed to appreciate its short-term and long-term implications and they continued to adhere to their policy of *suppressio veri* and *suggestio falsi*' (misrepresentation of truth or facts). It implied that the Indians were unfit for responsible government, let alone self-government, of the Dominion Status type.[91]

It is owing to this that a resolution moved in the Central Legislative Assembly on 5 February, 1924 urging an early revision of the Government of India Act of 1919 so as to accord India the status of self-governing Dominion could not be acceptable to the Government, as it took the view that 'the conception of the full responsible government with Dominion Status meant entrusting the interest of the minorities in the hands of the majority.[92] On 18 February, Motilal Nehru moved a resolution in the Assembly that was passed by 76 votes in favour, with 48 against. It recommended the Governor-General-in-Council to take steps to establish full Responsible Government in India and for the said purpose: (a) to summon at an early date a representative Round Table Conference to recommend with due regard to the protection of the rights and interests of important minorities the scheme of a constitution for India, and (b) after dissolving the Central Legislature to place the said scheme for approval and submit the same to the British Parliament to be embodied in a statute.[93]

---

91. *Ibid.*, p. 30.
92. *Ibid.*
93. *Ibid.*

But the obstinate stand of the Government forced the zealous fighters for freedom to come forward with the demand for complete independence. Jawaharlal Nehru, Srinivas Iyengar and Subhas Chandra Bose formed a group for this purpose with the name of Independence of India League. A long resolution was moved in the session of the Indian National Congress held at Madras in December, 1927 under the presidentship of Dr. M.A. Ansari. It was stoutly opposed by the advocates of 'Swaraj within the Empire', but it could be passed in a snap form at the instance of Gandhiji[94]. Gandhiji's suggestion that the controversial resolution should be boiled down to a single sentence resolved the situation for the time being, as the demand for complete independence had by this time grown into a powerful claim that carved out a bold place in the resolution moved by Gandhi at the Lahore Congress of 1929.

Belatedly came the offer of Viceroy Irwin on 31 October, 1929 in which he declared Dominion Status to be the 'natural issue' of India's constitutional progress and promised a Round Table Conference after the report of the Simon Commission had been published.[95] Just two days after, Gandhiji, Motilal Nehru and Malaviya accepted the offer with conditions: (*i*) That the Round Table Conference should discuss the details of the Dominion Status, not the basic principles which the British should accept immediately, (*ii*) that the Congress must have majority representation in the Conference, and (*iii*) that there should be an amnesty and a policy of general conciliation. Known as the Delhi Statement, it was signed by Gandhiji, Motilal and Malaviya. Bose refused to sign it. Jawaharlal signed it, but he showed his reservations afterwards. Accordingly, Gandhiji saw the Viceroy on 23 December, 1929, but negotiations came to nothing as the latter rejected the Congress conditions. The fiery advocate of 'Swaraj within the Empire' if possible' now became an equally fiery

94. Gandhi had made his mind clear on this subject by saying: "I can wait for the Dominion Status in action, if, that is to say, there is a real change of heart, a real desire on the part of the British people to see India a free and self-respecting nation, and on the part of the officials in India a true spirit of service. But that means substitution of the steel bayonet by that of the goodwill of the people." *Young India*, 14 November, 1929.

95. It was like a gambit and the Viceroy had been privately urging it in the context of the strength of the boycott of the Simon Commission during its second visit to India.

advocate of Swaraj without the Empire.' The Lahore Congress endorsed it. "At last, the hesitations and uncertainties were over. The goal was clear and though the path might be strewn with pits and snares, the direction was no longer in doubt."[96]

Fight to the Finish for Purna Swaraj (Complete Independence)

After the Lahore Congress, our freedom movement entered into its last stage. The call for Purna Swaraj replaced for ever the call for Dominion Status, though some ups and downs continued to linger on. Gandhiji's 11-Point Ultimatum given to Viceroy Irwin in his letter of 31 January, 1929 [97] "seemed to many a sad climbdown from the Purna Swaraj resolution, since no demand was made for any change in the political structure, not even Dominion Status."[98] The reason behind the presentation of this ultimatum was that Gandhiji had taken Irwin at his word and in stead of demanding full Dominion Status, he entreated him to concede what was given in his 11-points.[99] But it had its serious effect. "Friends were surprised and protested in consternation. The British press reacted violently against them, and Malcolm Hailey repudiated them indignantly. The episode was closed."[100]

---

96. Tara Chand, *op. cit.*, Vol. IV, p. 97.

97. The 11-Points were—total prohibition, reduction of rupee-sterling ratio, reduction of land revenue by at least 50 per cent, abolition of the salt tax, reduction of military expenditure by at least 50 per cent, reduction of the salaries of the highest grade services by half so as to suit the reduced scheme, protective tariff on foreign cloth, passage of the Coastal Traffic Reservation Bill (then known as the Haji Bill according to the name of its sponsor), release of political prisoners, abolition of Criminal Investigation Department or its popular control, and use of licences for fire arms for self-defence.

98. Sumit Sarkar, *op. cit.*, p.284.

99. On 25 January. 1930 Viceroy Irwin in his address before the Central Legislative Assembly adhered to his favourite theory : "The assertion of a goal is of necessity a different thing from the goal's attainment. And no sensible traveller could feel that a clear definition of his destination was the same thing as the completion of the journey."

100. Tara Chand, *op. cit.*, Vol. IV, p. 124.

Civil Disobedience Movement: A clear preparation and fight for Swaraj appeared in 1928 what Nehru called "a full year with plenty of activity all over the country."[101] The fact that the mercury of political barometer had risen became evident when the country boycotted the Simon Commission and Motilal Nehru, who had an occasion to preside over the Calcutta Congress of the same year, in a quite forceful and unequivocal voice, thundered that "the Parliament and the British public and the British Government have no shadow of a right to force a constitution upon us against our own will."

It was the year in which the Nehru Report (prepared by a committee consisting of Sir Tej Bahadur Sapru, Sir Ali Imam, Subhas Chandra Bose etc. under the chairmanship of Motilal Nehru) was written to meet the challenge of the then Secretary of State (Lord Birkenhead) who had said that even Indian leaders themselves could not make a constitution acceptable to all sections of the people. The following year saw, for the first time, that the Congress session held at Lahore under the presidentship of Jawaharlal Nehru had taken a basically different turn by declaring the demand for complete independence. It was here that the Congress decided for observing the 26th of January, 1930 as the day of 'Purna Swaraj'. Thus, the meaning of the term Swaraj became quite clear and now it became above board that the Congress under the leadership of Mahatma Gandhi and Jawaharlal Nehru wanted to achieve complete independence for the country by truthful and non-violent means.[102]

---

101. Nehru, *op. cit.*, p. 170.

102. It is evident from the declaration of Purna Swaraj that began thus: "We believe that it is the inalienable right of the Indian people, as of any other people, to have freedom and to enjoy the fruits of their toil and have the necessities of life so that they may have full opportunities of growth. We believe also that if any Government deprives the people of these rights and oppresses them, the people have a further right to alter it or to abolish it. The British Government in India has not only deprived the Indian people of their freedom but has based itself on the exploitation of the masses, and has ruined India economically, politically, culturally and spiritually. We believe, therefore, that India must sever the British connection and attain Purna Swaraj or complete independence."

It was in this context the Gandhiji launched his civil disobedience movement that witnessed a peculiar amalgamation of the keynotes of the Swadeshi and Non-Co-operation movements at a mature stage of his experiments with political truths. It may be pointed out here that one thing that especially enjoined upon Gandhiji to launch such a movement was his concern at the rising tide of violence in the country. Thus concerned, the Mahatma wrote to the Viceroy on March 2, 1930 "The party of violence is gaining ground and making itself felt. It is my purpose to set in motion that force (non-violence) well against the organised violent force of the British rule and the unorganised violent force of the growing party in violence. To sit still would be to give rein to both the forces above mentioned."[103]

The celebration of the first Purna Swaraj Day virtually opened the way for the civil disobedience movement that the Mahatma launched to counter the force of violence unleashed in an unorganised form by a section of his own over-enthusiastic youngmen and in an organised form by the foreign rule. The wave of non-co-operation had its second blow when many members of the Legislative Assemblies tendered their resignations. The All-India Congress Committee at its meeting held at Wardha on 14-16 Feb. 1930 entrusted Gandhiji with full powers to launch his contemplated civil disobedience movement. Thus, he sought to contact the Viceroy so as to advise him to abandon the repressive policy that had caused India's ruination. However, after getting nothing but sheer disappointment, he wrote to the Viceroy on 2 March, 1930: "On bended knees, I asked for bread and received a stone instead .... Civil disobedience alone can save the country from impending lawlessness and secret crime, since there is a party of violence in the country which will not listen to speeches, resolutions or conferences, but believes only in direct action."[104]

---

103. Cited in A.R. Desai, *op. cit.*, p.363. Agreeing with this fact Zacharias says: "The only thing that the Mahatma felt he could do was to prevent it from becoming a butchery by placing himself at the head of the revolution and making it a non-violent one of satyagraha." *Renascent India*, p. 261.

104. Viewing thus, one may differ from the observation of R.P. Dutt who says that Gandhian non-violence "was a one-way non-violence It was a non-violence to his Indian masses, but not for imperialism —which practised violence for the heart's content—won the battle" *India Today*, p. 365.

Though Gandhi launched his civil disobedience movement on 12 March, 1930 (when he started his historic Dandi March), he made his conception of the agitation clear in a note of instructions issued on 9 April that said: "Our path has already been chalked out for us. Let every village fetch or manufacture contraband salt; sisters should picket liquor shops, opium dens and foreign cloth dealers' shops. The young and the old in every home should ply the *takli* and spin and get woven heaps of yarn every day. Foreign cloth should be burnt. Hindus should eschew untouchability. Hindus, Muslims, Sikhs, Parsis and Christians should all achieve heart unity. Let the majority rest content with what remains after the minorities have been satisfied. Let students leave Government schools and colleges, and Government servants resign their service and devote themselves in the service of the people, and we shall soon find that Purna Swaraj will come knocking at our door."[105]

The civil disobedience movement meant a call of the Mahatma for the non-payment of all black taxes, though salt tax was chosen by the supreme leader as the test case on the ground of his conviction that this was a commodity used by each and every countryman and even this essential item was not spared by the foreign rulers from taxation. Accompained by a contingent of 78 followers, he started his famous Dandi March from Sabarmati Ashram in Ahmedabad. On 5 April, he reached Dandi, a sea-side village in Gujarat, after covering a distance of some 250 miles. The compaign against salt tax started the next day. It was a symbolic resistance to stir the dormant energies of the nation based on his call for 'a fight to the finish', no matter he himself was thrown behind the bars. The Congress Working Committee called upon the students, workers, peasants, merchants, lawyers, and Government servants to withdraw co-operation from the British rule and join the movement by stopping payment of all taxes, picketing liquor shops, and boycotting foreign cloth. The Congress committees organised meetings in defiance of the ban and the police resorted to lathi charge and firing to break up the banned rallies. This movement had its special manifestation in Peshawar where Indian soldiers belonging to the 18th Royal Garhwal Rifles, when ordered to fire on the crowd, refused to do so.

---

105. *Ibid.*

The Government adopted severest possible measures to suppress it. The Press Act of 1910 was revived. Satyagrahis were arrested on a large scale; public meetings were banned; lathi charges and firing by the police became the order of the day. Jawaharlal Nehru in Allahabad and Khan Abdul Ghaffar Khan in Peshawar were arrested. Vitthalbhai Patel (the President of the Central Legislative Assembly) and Malviyaji, (the leader of the Nationalist Party) resigned on 25 April from the Assembly. When Gandhi issued the threat of taking possession of the Dharsana Salt Works in Surat, he was arrested and sent to the Yervada jail of Poona on 5 May. And yet Dharsana Satyagraha took place in which Sarojini Naidu, Pyarelal, Manilal Gandhi and Imam Saheb took the leading part. Police resorted to lathi-charge in which 320 men were injured and 2 died. At this Gandhiji commented: "Even Dyerism pales into insignificane."[106]

But what happened at Chittagong in April, 1930 makes a tragic part of this thoroughly non-violent movement. A group of revolutionaries led by Surjya Sen seized the local armoury and cried 'Gandhi Raj has come'. On 18 April they issued a Proclamation of Independence in the name of the 'Indian Republican Army'. Additional troops rushed from Calcutta which quelled the revolt on 22 April, but 12 persons were killed in a fight at the Jalalabad hill. It is known as the Chittagong Armoury Case. In retaliation about 56 skirmishes between the revolutionaries and the army took place in different parts of Bengal. In appreciation of it, a noted writer says that it "brought off the most spectacular coup in the entire history of terrorism."[107] However, what happened throughout the country boldly demonstrated that truth and non-violence had been tested in the crucible of suffering with success. "The British beat the Indians with batons and the rifle butts. The Indians neither cringed nor retreated. That made England powerless and India invincible."[108]

Since all great leaders were behind the bars, the participation of Congress in the first Round Table Conference could not be possible. So Irwin deputed Sapru and Jayakar to confer with Gandhiji and

---

106. Tara Chand, *op. cit.*, p. 126.

107. Sumit Sarkar, *op. cit.*, p. 287.

108. Louis Fischer: *The Life of Mahatma Gandhi*, p. 300.

other detained leaders so as to find a way out of the impasse. The two emissaries met Motilal Nehru and Jawaharlal Nehru in the Naini Jail and brought them to the Yervada jail where a meeting with Gandhiji took place. It was attended by Sardar Patel and Mrs. Sarojini Naidu as well. Now Gandhiji made it quite clear that the Congress would not take part in the proposed RTC without an assurance that the discussion would proceed on the basis of full responsible government, *i.e.*, Purna Swaraj. As Irwin was not prepared to concede the demand, Sapru-Jayakar parleys failed. The First RTC had no Congress representative and so 'it met in an atmosphere of unreality."[109] The second experiment of civil disobedience ended on 5 March 1931 when Delhi Pact or Truce was signed by Gandhiji and Irwin. It was neither a climb-down nor a defeat, but another enactment of the struggle-truce-struggle strategy of Gandhiji. As he counselled: "Suffering has its well defined limits. Suffering can be both wise and unwise; and when the limit is reached, to prolong it would not be wise but the height of folly."[110]

Gandhi was released on January 25, 1931 with 19 members of the Congress Working Committee so that they could hold discussions among themselves before having a dialogue with the Viceroy with regard to the participation of the Congress in the Second Round Table Conference entrusted with the task of evolving an agreed plan for a new constitutional set up for India. Gandhiji's conference with the Viceroy began on 17 Feb. and ended on 5 March, 1931 that culminated in his signing a pact known as the Delhi Truce or Gandhi-Irwin Pact. The Pact became a subject of controversy that made the matter of Mahatma's leadership a serious subject of criticism. The radical elements interpreted it as a tame surrender of Indian nationalism to British imperialism. The Mahatma was criticised for side-tracking a vigorous movement and abandoning the fight for Swaraj abruptly. It was also said that he "recanted from the struggle as a concession to Indian capitalism."[111] It was also said that this agreement "secured not a single aim of the Congress struggle (not even the repeal of the salt tax). Not a single concrete

---

109. Tara Chand, *op. cit.*, p. 142

110. Sitaramayya, *op. cit.*, p. 748.

111. Raghuvanshi, *op. cit.*, p. 214.

step of self-government was granted."[112] Gandhi, however, dispelled all such allegations of his critics at the Karachi Congress of March, 1931 and carried the Congress with him by emphasising that the movement demonstrated the great power of non-violence and the Swaraj could never be achieved by means of violence.[113]

Gandhi, as per his agreement with Viceroy Irwin, took part in the Second Round Table Conference held in London from Sept. to Dec., 1931. This occasion proved an utter failure. The Conference failed to solve the communal tangle hinging on the issue of representation of various communities in the legislative bodies. Thus, Gandhi returned from England without getting anything. More than this, the moment he landed at the Bombay port on Dec. 28. 1931, he was arrested and taken to the Yervada jail on a false charge that he had given a press statement at Rome saying that he was going to renew his civil disobedience movement in as much as the relations between India and England had totally ruptured. Under these conditions, the Mahatma had to re-start his civil disobedience movement that led to the reopening of the repressive machinery of the English rule. The Congress organisation was proscribed and its funds, papers, buildings etc. were confiscated. New ordinances were promulgated to arrest anybody on the charge of mere suspicion. Freedom of the press was drastically curtailed. All this showed that the British Government "was determined to break the spirit of the nation by its policy of frighfulness."[114]

The failure of the Second Round Table Conference engaged the attention of Gandhi in a different direction. It was to find out a solution to the communal problem with its particular relationship to the cause of the Harijans. On his release from the jail on May 8, 1933, he issued a call for the suspension of the mass civil disobedience movement and instead taking to the individual satyagraha to carry on the declared 'fight to the finish'. As in 1922, so now Gandhi's action was vehemently criticised by leading Congressmen who charged that he had been cowed down by the British repressions. In his message from Vienna, Subhas Bose charged him with the failure

112. R.P. Dutt, *op. cit.*, p. 273.

113. See Pattabhi Sitaramayya, *op. cit.*, pp. 444-48.

114. Raghuvanshi, *op. cit.*, p. 219.

of leadership. Looking at the fact of increasing demoralisation in the ranks of the Congress, Gandhi refrained from preventing, or even discouraging, those like Dr. Ansari who started thinking in terms of reviving the lines of the Swarajist politics. It is a fact that Gandhi even blessed such a move. After some time, he announced total withdrawal of the movement and his retirement from the Congress. In a word, the civil disobedience movement came to an end with facts showing, as Rev. Verrier Elwin says, "the determination of the Indian masses to win freedom: they also illustrate, all too tragically, the repression which is an inevitable result of the domination of one nation by another."[115]

Congress Right Versus Left: A section of the Congress leaders had been critical of Gandhi's idea of non-cooperation right from its beginning in 1920 and they had formed their Swaraj Party in 1923. In course of time, some other members sought to revive the course of Council-entry. But when the Congress remained a banned organization (1932-34) and a volatile section formed the Congress Socialist Party in 1933, all such forces organized themselves into the form of 'Congress Right' and they advocated the path of making an experiment with the Act of 1935. The idea of Council-entry mooted by Satyamurthy in October 1933 was ardently supported by C. Rajagopalachari, Bhulabhai Desai, Dr. M.A. Ansari and Dr. B.C. Roy. A little after, Rajendra Prasad and Sardar Patel also fell in this line. Since Gandhi had a patent disliking for the Congress socialists due to their sinister ideology, he desired that the reins of the Congress should be in the hands of the Rightist group, as there "will always be a party within the Congress wedded to the idea of Council-entry."[116]

As Jawaharlal Nehru declined to join the CSP, it was thought expedient to keep the leadership of the movement in the hands of the Congress Right, but the post of the highest office of the organization should be with Nehru whose radical expressions would be of immense use at the time of elections under Act of 1935. It is due to this that while the Congress left led by Jayaprakash Narayan,

---

115. See Zacharias, *op. cit.*, p. 271.

116. G.D. Birla: *In the Shadow of the Mahatma: A Personal Memoir*, p. 138.

fought tooth and nail for discarding the Act of 1935, the Congress Right appreciated the course of Council-entry so as to make an experiment with the provincial autonomy that had replaced the notorious system of dyarchy. The architect of this Act (Linlithgow) made implementation of the Act of 1935 a point of his prestige and through G.D. Birla, he could win Gandhi over to his side. Nehru, who had declared the Act of 1935 as the 'charter of slavery', cast off his hesitation and sided with the Congress Right as a result of which the Congress under his leadership took part in the provincial elections of January, 1937 and after a lapse of six months formed its government in 8 provinces. The cry of the Congress Left that such an action would amount to cooperation with the British Raj and thereby impede the fight for complete independence went into wilderness. "The consolidation of a Right-wing within the Congress based on a rapprochement between the advocates of conventional Assembly-politics and Gandhian constructive workers, and backed by considerable business pressures and patronage from 1934 onwards was really an important development."[117]

In the fight between the Right and the Left, Nehru cautiously as well as confidently played the role of a balancer. In his presidential address delivered at the session of the Congress at Lucknow in April 1936, he made it above board: "We go to the Legislatures not to cooperate with the apparatus of British imperialism, but to combat the Act and to seek to end it, and to resist in every way British imperialism in its attempt to strengthen its hold on India and its exploitation of the Indian people......We are not going to the Legislatures to pursue the path of constitutionalism or barren reformism. We must think in terms of deadlocks and not in terms of carrying on with the office."[118] The Congress fought elections under Nehru's leadership. It preferred the course of ministry-making in July, 1937 when he was the president of the organization, though in his private utterances he expressed his misgivings about the working of Congress ministries. For instance, in his letter to G.B. Pant dated 25 November, 1937 he debunked the Congress ministries as 'counterrevolutionary' and 'merely carrying on the tradition of the previous governments."[119]

---

117. Sumit Sarkar, *op. cit.*, p.345.

118. *The Indian Annual Register*, 1936, Vol. II, p.227.

119. Nehru: *A Bunch of Letters*, p. 263.

Quit India Movement: Though Gandhi had left Congress in 1934 he, as R.P. Dutt holds, remained the most powerful guiding influence behind the scene, ready in case of need to assume direct leadership anew. In the crisis of 1939-40 and again in 1942 he "assumed direct leadership."[120] Gandhi looked with great concern at the way the Congress was drifting under the influence of those who believed in direct action. Thus, he advised M.N. Roy (who had joined the Congress in 1936 after his release from the jail with a mind to radicalise Indian politics) to render his 'mute services' to the nation. He, however, picked up a scuffle with Subhas Bose and had his victory when the Subjects Committee passed a resolution moved by Gobind Vallabh Pant at the Tripuri session in March, 1939 saying: "In view of the critical situation that may develop during the coming years and in view of the fact that Mahatma Gandhi alone can lead the Congress and the country to victory during such a crisis, the Congress regards it as imperative that the Executive authority of the Congress should command his implicit confidence and requests the President to nominate the Working Committee for the ensuing year with the wishes of Gandhi."[121]

It entailed the exit of all those who had sharp differences with Gandhi as a result of which he once again became the generalissimo of the Indian National Congress. The Congress under Mahatma's leadership resented the action of the British Government in declaring India as a party to the Second World War on behalf of the Allied Powers without consulting the national leaders. At the Ramgarh session of 1940, the Congress declared that 'nothing short of complete independence can be accepted by the people of India.' It demanded a constituent assembly to frame a constitution of India on the basis of democracy, independence and national unity. It also issued an appeal to all classes and communities of the country to take part in the civil disobedience struggle that was 'for the freedom of the whole nation.' Satyagraha committees were formed and they started individual civil disobedience movement in 1940.

A point of difference between Gandhi and his trusted lieutenants like Jawaharlal Nehru and Azad developed at this stage on the matter of rendering co-operation to the British Government. As Gandhi

120. R.P. Dutt, *op. cit.*, p. 381.

121. *The Indian Annual Register*, 1939, Vol. 1, p. 382.

still cultivated hopes in the good sense of the British statesmen, he stressed the point that the Congress should give its co-operation to the British Government as 'non-violence requires rendering assistance to the enemy when he is in difficulty'. He was, however, disillusioned when Prime Minister Churchill made it very clear that he had not assumed his office to preside over the liquidation of the British Empire and thereafter the Cripps Mission proved a failure. In 1942, conditions deteriorated further when Japan started invading the countries of South-East Asia that entailed serious danger to the security and territorial integrity of our country. It all left no other option before the leaders of the Congress than to demand the exit of the English rule that was the sole source of all trouble. In this situation Gandhi plainly asked the British to walk out of India leaving the country in a state of anarchy'. Thus, the Congress under the leadership of Gandhi came out with its 'Quit India' demand that manifested the paradox of Gandhism. "It asked the British to lose the Empire and win the War, to leave India and gain India."[122]

The historic 'Quit India Resolution', was passed by the All-India Congress Committee at its meeting held at Bombay on Aug. 8, 1942. It stated: "Immediate ending of the British rule in India is an urgent necessity both for the sake of India and for the success of the United Nations. The constitution of that rule is degrading and enfeebling India and making her progressively less capable of defending herself and of contributing to the cause of the world freedom. The possession of Empire (by the British) instead of adding to the strength of the ruling power has become a burden and a curse. India, the classic land of modern imperialism, has become the crux of the question, for by freedom of India will Britain and the United Nations be judged and the people of Asia and Africa be filled with hope and enthusiasm.. No future promises or guarantees can affect the present situation to meet that peril. They cannot produce the needed psychological effect on the mind of masses. Only the glow of freedom can now release that energy and enthusiasm of millions of people, which will immediately transform the nature of War."

It further said that if "India were made free, a Provisional Government will be formed and free India will become an ally of the United Nations. Such a Government can only be formed by the co-operation of the principal parties and groups in the country. It will

---

122. Raghuvanshi, *op. cit.*, p. 236.

thus be a composite Government representative of all important sections of the people of India. Its primary function must be to defend India and resist aggression with all armed as well as non-violent forces at its command. The Provisional Government will evolve a scheme for a Constituent Assembly which will prepare a Constitution for the Government of India acceptable to all sections of the people." It "resolved the sanction for the vindication of India's inalienable right to freedom and independence, the starting of a mass struggle on non-violent lines, on the widest possible scale so that the country might utilise all the non-violent strength gathered during the last 22 years of peaceful struggle." It also appealed to the people of India "to hold together under the leadership of Gandhiji and carry out his instructions as disciplined soldiers of the Indian freedom struggle."[123]

Frightened by the historic decision of the Congress, the Government applied brakes at the law breakers at the daybreak. All prominent leaders were arrested early in the morning of Aug. 9, 1942. The sudden arrest of the top leaders made the people mad with fury and forced them to drift into violent channels. As usual, the British Government used its machinery of repression. According to the official estimates, in a period of about three months, some 250 railway stations were damaged, 500 post offices and 150 police stations were attacked. A very large section of the workers, particularly of the Tata Iron and Steel Works of Jamshedpur went on strike. For several weeks railway communication between Bihar and eastern U.P. remained out of order. Shyama Prasad Mookerji resigned his ministership of the Bengal Government in protest against heavy collective fines imposed on the Hindus alone. The people of Bengal suffered heavily as they were feared to be in sympathy

---

123. Mahatma Gandhi thought of conducting the movement on these lines: (*i*) There should be an all-India strike. (*ii*) All freedom-loving Indians should join the struggle. (*iii*) The students should leave Government-controlled institutions. (*iv*) The people should break the salt laws and refuse to pay land taxes. (*v*) At a later stage Government employees should also participate. (*vi*) The members of Central and Provincial Assemblies and municipalities should vacate their seats. (*vii*) As a last resort every Congressman would be his own leader and a servant of the whole nation. Every satyagrahi should vow that he would be either free or would die in the attempt to make himself so. See Sandhya Chaudhri: *Gandhi and the Partition of India,* p. 96.

with the INA Government of Subhas Bose. Acting under instructions issued by the British bureaucracy, the military and the police made many excesses to crush this movement.

While in jail, Gandhiji undertook his epic fast of 21 days to refute the charge of the English bureaucracy that he had goaded the innocent people of India to indulge in the activities of violence. The fast was also undertaken to protest against the trend of violence raising its ugly head in the name of his civil disobedience movement. The fast started on 10 Feb., 1943. The condition of Gandhi went on deteriorating, but the Viceroy did not agree with the advice of his Executive Councillors to release him. The release of Gandhiji took place on May 6, 1944 after Lord Wavell took charge from Viceroy Linlithgow in view of the anxiety of the British Government at the progress of the Indian National Army under Netaji.

The British Government did it against its previous stand that no Congress leader would be released unless the 'Quit India' resolution was withdrawn. All other prominent leaders like Nehru and Patel were also released in June, 1945 as the War in Europe had virtually come to an end and general elections in England were to take place in the following month.

The Quit India Movement gave the last terrible jolt to the English rule; it had its impact upon the minds of the new rulers of England who had won the elections of 1945 on the tickets of the Labour Party. It meant that the way of India's freedom was finally opened as Britain, that had risen from the War like a shattered power, was no more capable of maintaining her rule over India, that was converted from a big asset into a massive liability, throwing her power on the debit side of an imperial adventure It also signified that the leadership of the Congress had fallen into the hands of Gandhi working as 'the chief servant of the nation' who had frankly said at the A-ICC meeting of Bombay on Aug. 8, 1942. "The voice within me tells me that I shall have to fight against the whole world and stand alone. Even if the United Nations oppose me, even if the whole of India tries to persuade me that I am wrong, even then I will go ahead, not for India's sake alone, but for the sake of the world...I cannot wait any longer for India's freedom. I can't wait until Jinnah is converted... If I wait any longer, God will punish me. This is the last struggle of my life."

An account of anti-colonial movements in India beginning from the Swadeshi and Boycott Movement of 1905 and ending in the Quit India Movement of 1942-44 shows how our struggle started by the nationalists belonging to the extremist school and hailing from the middle class intelligentsia was converted into a mass agitation under the dynamic leadership of Gandhi. It will be sheer distortion of facts to dub the Gandhian movement as an exercise in the direction of protecting or promoting the interests of the 'bourgeois' class or to interpret the three 'political experiments' of Gandhi in terms of his being 'an agent of the capitalist class'. A correct understanding of Gandhi and Gandhism refutes all such explanations. India under Gandhi's leadership waged a war for national liberation by means of *ahimsa* and *satyagraha*. The only fault of the Mahatma may be discovered in his too much optimism in the capacity of the Indian people who failed to prove loyal to the extent he desired and thus many of them drifted into channels of sporadic violence. A very plausible assessment of the nature of Gandhian leadership was thus given by Nehru in 1945: "Gandhi's influence in these various directions has pervaded India and left its mark. But it is not because of his non-violence or economic theories that he has become the foremost and most outstanding of India's leaders. To the vast majority of India's people he is the symbol of India determined to be free, of militant nationalism, of a refusal to submit to arrogant might, of never agreeing to anything involving national dishonour."[124]

INA Trial and RIN Revolt: The British could arrest a very large number of officers and soldiers of the Indian National Army. But three officers (P.K. Sehgal, Shah Nawaz Khan and G.S. Dhillon) were put in the dock. In November, 1945 the trial opened in the Red Fort of Delhi. They were charged with 'waging war against the King-Emperor' and were accused of 'doing gross brutality in the method employed to induce their fellow prisoners to join them'. The Congress took upon itself the task of defending them in the court. So Bhulabhai Desai, Tej Bahadur Sapru and Jawaharlal Nehru appeared in the court on their behalf. The burden of their argument was that taking part in the freedom struggle was the birth right of every citizen and as such the accused persons had committed no crime. The public opinion expressed itself strongly in favour of the

124. Nehru: *The Discovery of India*, p. 473.

accused persons. The trial continued for a couple of months and ended in the acquittal of all the accused persons.[125]

The failure of the Indian National Army had its certain effect on the ratings of the Royal Indian Navy who staged a strike and took over the British naval army in 1946. The strike continued from 18 to 22 February and, though it failed, it was described as the most successful strike by the naval ratings against British rule during the entire struggle for freedom after the 'mutiny' of 1857. The young fighters for freedom of the RIN under S.M. Khan, the President of the Naval Central Strike Committee, took over the entire naval command. They could establish their hold over 74 ships, 4 flotillas, and 20 shore establishments in Bombay, Karachi, Cochin, Vizag and Calcutta. Even Delhi Headquarters had come under their influence. Their list of grievances included supply of bad food and maltreatment given to the Indian ratings by a racially discriminating regime run by foul-mouthed British officers. The determination to stand up for one's honour began crystallizing only after some Indian sailors on beach signalling duty, during the British recapture of Burma, saw the remnants of the INA and felt a surge of patriotism swelling up in themselves. When they exploded in Bombay, the mutineers hoisted the tricolour (national flag) on their shipmasts together with a picture of Netaji Bose. They raised the slogan of 'Jai Hind' in their barracks. Now the list of their demands included release of all political prisoners including the soldiers of the INA and the return of the Indian soldiers deployed to help the Dutch forces engaged in re-establishing their hold over the East Indies (now Indonesia).[126] "In their final desperate

---

125. This trial evoked the sympathy of all sections of the countrymen. Maulana Azad described how the men of the army, navy and air force gathered around him wherever he went and assured them of their loyalty to the Congress. B. Shiva Rao reported that there "is the slightest feeling among them of Hindu and Muslim. A majority of the men now awaiting trial in the Red Fort is Muslim. Some of these men are bitter that Jinnah is keeping alive a controversy about Pakistan." N. Mansergh, (ed.) *The Transfer of Power in India*, Vol. VI, pp.514 and 564.

126. Japan had established its hold over the East Indies defeating the Dutch in 1941. But when she surrendered on 11 August, 1945 the national leaders declared independence of their country by calling it Indonesia and made Soekarno its President.

moments the young soldiers at their action stations even thought of blowing the British out of India."[127]

The rebel ratings of Royal Indian Navy had made the *HMIS Talwar*, a shore-based signals establishment in Bombay, as their headquarters. But the movement failed to have a life of more than a couple of days. The British government took the matter very seriously and sought to suppress the revolt at the earliest possible time. A small corvette (*HMIS Kathiawad*) raced across the Arabian Sea to go to the aid of *HMIS Hindustan* which was under attack from the British troops in Karachi harbour. But when that proved too late, it turned and tried to engage a British cruiser (*HMIS George*) which London had ordered to Bombay to quell the revolt. In this action against *HMIS Hindustan*, British forces killed at least 14 Indian sailors after the Gurkhas of the Indian army had refused to open fire. The revolt could be suppressed and in the follow-up action about 12,000 'rebels' of the RIN lost their jobs. Thus ended a short drama enacted by the fiery patriots of the RIN under the influence of the INA and its supreme leader (Subhas Bose) giving a clear warning to the British rulers that the time for Britain's withdrawal from India had come. This is a reality which the then British Prime Minister (Attlee) accepted.

However, the unfortunate part of this story is that the national leaders did not come to the defence of these gallant fighters. Mahatma Gandhi devalued it as 'a thoughtless and distressful unrest.' Jawaharlal Nehru took a diabolical stand. While he appreciated the fact that this mutiny had helped to break down the iron wall created between the Indian army and the Indian people', he publicly asserted that 'revolution through barricade was out of place and time.' Sardar Patel denounced the 'folly of disorder and violence'. Jinnah appealed to the rebels to call off their strike and went to the length of calling upon the Muslims 'to stop and create no further trouble.' But the working class of Bombay stood up in support of the naval mutineers where 228 persons lost their lives as a result of police action.

The British rulers went on the offensive after both the Congress and the Muslim League disclaimed any responsibility for the mutiny

---

127. Punyapriya Dasgupta: "Naval Mutiny 1946: Conventional National Amnesia' in the *The Hindustan Times* (New Delhi), 17 March, 1996, p.13.

and the leaders of both the national organizations assured Sir John Colville, the Governor of Bombay, that they were ready to deploy their volunteers to assist the administration in this regard. For this reason, the cause of the young fighters was defended by some 'leftist' elements and by a leading paper (*Free Press Journal*) of Bombay. It is all the more surprising that while the national leaders appreciated the role of the Indian soldiers in the war of 1857, they did otherwise now. The reason for this should be traced in the fact that the great national leaders had become conscious of the freedom of the country in near future and so they preferred to appreciate the view that armed soldiers should not rise in revolt.[128]

British Designs of Partition: The results of the elections of 1937 paved the way for country's partition. A thoroughly disgruntled Muslim League led by Jinnah came to the conclusion that the creation of a Muslim state was the only course for its survival. A British officer of the Bengal government (Filkins) mooted the idea, as early as in June 1938, of a loose federation of India with provinces having the option to withdraw from it as per their desire. While Nehru rejected it in a fit of anger, Cripps dexterously accommodated it in his scheme of 1942. A little before his coming to India in March, 1942 Cripps had advised Prime Minister Churchill to make a declaration promising Dominion Status to India after the War with the right of secession to the provinces.It is true that Churchill disfavoured this proposal, but Secretary of State Amery privately admitted it as the 'first public admission of the possibility of Pakistan.'[129]

---

128. One of the leaders of this revolt, B.C. Dutta, in his book *The Mutiny of the Innocents,* narrates the whole story in detail so as to show that no justice was done to the young fighters even after indepencence. Jinnah reinstated S.M. Khan in Pakistan. Reference may be made to his book (*Disastrous Twilight*) on this subject. One important reason of such an attitude of the great national leaders was that some agitators had hoisted flags of the Muslim League and of the Communist Party of India in addition to the tricolour flag of the Indian National Congress.

129. N. Mansergh, *op. cit.*, Vol. I, pp. 282-83. The case of India's partition was accommodated in the provision of the Cripps plan that any province, which was not prepared to accept the new constitution framed by a Constituent Assembly after the War, would have the right to sign a separate agreement with Britain regarding its future status. Nehru says that when he saw such a proposal, he "was profoundly depressed." *The Discovery of India*, p. 339.

Wavell replaced Linlithgow in 1943 and he was the first Viceroy who, boldly put forward the idea of converting the policy of 'divide and rule' into the policy of 'divide and quit'. He thought in terms of dividing India into Hindustan, Pakistan and Princestan.[130] In his talks with Churchill he desired that the British should leave India as early as possible, though in degrees, by handing over some portion of the country to the Muslim League. Known as his 'breakdown plan', Churchill rejected it and called him 'an ignoble and sordid scuttle'. Wavell repeated the same theme before the members of the Cabinet Mission in May, 1946 in the form of his proposal visualizing as a middle course between 'repression' and 'scuttle', withdrawal of the British army and officials to the Muslim provinces of the N.W.F.P. and North-East India, handing over the rest of the country to the Congress. It was not appreciated by the Cabinet Mission.[131]

After the War, the situation had really become very grim what Penderel Moon, Viceroy's Private Secretary, termed as 'edge of a volcano'. The plan of Wavell was rejected by Churchill and Attlee thought it better to shelve it. Since the author of the plan remained steadfast on this point, he had to see his dismissal on 23 March, 1947. Mountbatten was avowedly appointed to arrange the termination of British rule in India. His assignment was extra-ordinary and he had to be armed

---

130. Penderel Moon (ed.) : *Viceroy's Journal*, p. 120. In this plan Wavell desired the withdrawal of the British control from India in accordance with a planned programme of their own interests. The British shall first relinquish control in the south of India, but retain control in the northern provinces for a limited period, and so long as they do so, they would continue to try to secure agreement for a united India, but they would not allow failure to reach agreement on anything else to interfere with their programme for withdrawal from the whole of India within a short period of time. After some days of discussion, the India Committee of the British Cabinet seemed at last more or less to agree to this plan and to the fixing of 31 March, 1948 as the date for final British withdrawal. Attlee assured Wavell that he had got all he wanted. But after his return to India, Attlee changed his mind. *Ibid.*, pp.455-57

131. Wavell was so insistent on his plan that he opposed the suggestion of Secretary of State Amery to give to the present Government of India the status of a Dominion, abrogate the authority of the Parliament to legislate for India and thus concede India's demand for independence at once." Tara Chand, *op. cit.*, p. 442.

with extra-ordinary authority to execute it."[132] Soon after taking over the charge, Mountbatten felt that the framework of the Cabinet Mission had become unworkable and so he prepared his own nefarious plan envisaging transfer of power to separate provinces or to confederations, if formed before the transfer, with Bengal and Punjab Assemblies being given the option to vote for partition of their provinces. It also envisaged that the various units thus formed, along with princely states rendered independent by the lapse of paramountcy, would then have the choice of joining either India or Pakistan or remaining separate. Known as the Plan Balkan or Dicky Birds Plan, it was sternly condemned by Nehru and so its author abandoned it[133] And yet he put it in a refined form in his partition plan of 3 June known as his Second Plan that was accepted by the

---

132. Tara Chand, *op. cit.*, p. 503.: Prime Minister Attlee in his Letter of Instructions to the new Viceroy reminded him of the salient points which he had to keep in mind in dealing with the situation:

   (*a*) to aim at establishing a government in India on the basis of the Cabinet Mission Plan of 1946,

   (*b*) in case this was not achieved by 1 October, to report to Government in England the steps considered necessary for handling over power by June, 1948,

   (*c*) not to hand over power and obligations under Paramountcy to any successor Government earlier than the date of transfer of power, but to begin negotiations with individual states for adjusting their relations with the crown,

   (*d*) to treat the Interim Government with the same consultation and consideration as a Dominion Government and give it the greatest possible freedom in the day-to-day exercise of the administration of the country,

   (*e*) to maintain the closest cooperation with the Indians and the Indian leaders, and

   (*f*) to stress the importance of ensuring that the transfer of power was effected with full regard to the defence requirements of India, of avoiding any breach in the continuity or organisation of the Army, and of collaboration in the security of the Indian Ocean.

   Michael Edwardes: *Last Years of the British Raj*, pp. 145-47.

133. Sumit Sarkar, *op. cit.*, p. 448.

Congress under very trying and compelling circumstances. Surprisingly, Attlee who declined to give a long rope to Wavell acquiesced and so Mountbatten went ahead with all authority in his hand in seeing that the last Viceroy "negotiated, persuaded, decided and imposed his decisions."[134]

Facts show that while the 'first plan' of Mountbatten was a creation of his personal European staff (facetiously described as 'Dickie birds'), the 'second plan' was based on the advice of V.P. Menon, the official Constitutional Adviser and Reforms Commissioner. Nehru called the 'first plan' "an ominous one" whose inevitable consequence would be the Balkanisation of India.[135] He accepted the 'second plan' in the light of wisdom contained in what came to be known as the 'amputation theory' of Patel.[136] Though Attlee had fixed the last day of June, 1948 as the final date of the termination of the British rule, it was antedated to December, 1947 and then to 15 August 1947. It shows that the British rulers were keen to leave India as early as possible with the blame of partition laying at the forehead of the Indian leaders.[137] They "were worried that they had lost control over the Frankenstein's monster they had helped to create, but felt it was too late to tame it."[138] And yet they could contrive a situation in which morality could be sacrificed at the altar of expediency. The end result was that "the champions of nationalism, secularism and Indian solidarity had bent their knees before the gods of communalism, dogmatism and disintegration."[139]

Swaraj came of course, but not in the form as desired by our national leaders. The Radcliffe Award drew the boundary line

---

134. Tara Chand, *op. cit.*, p. 504.

135. L. Mosley : *Last Days of British Raj*, pp. 123-24.

136. Patel's argument was that the diseased limb of the body should be cut off if there was no other way to save the life of patient.

137. In his Memoirs, Attlee wrote later : "We would have preferred a United India. We could not get it, though we tried hard." Francis Williams : *A Prime Minister Remembers*, p. 212. Contrary to this, the plan prepared by the 'Dickie birds' envisaged that if "partition comes, its responsibility is to rest fairly upon the Indians themselves." Campbell-Johnson: *Mission with Mountbatten*, p. 62.

138. Bipan Chandra and others, *op.cit.*, 494.

139. Tara Chand, *op.cit.*, p. 518

between India and Pakistan and divided the assets and the liabilities between them. On 14 August, the Governor-General issued Provisional Constitution Order specifying that from tomorrow such and such sections of the Government of India Acts of 1919 and 1935 would be inoperative. Next day the national flag was unfurled. Mountbatten called it 'the most remarkable and inspiring day of his life'. Rajendra Prasad expressed his sentiments in these words : "The period of domination of the British over India ends today, and our relationship with Britain is henceforth going to rest on the basis of equality, of mutual goodwill, and mutual profit."[140]

---

140. A. Campbell-Johnson: *Mission with Mountbatten*, p. 159.

5

Communal and Class Movements

A full narration of the freedom movement of our country requires some study of the agitations, disturbances, uprisings, revolts and movements of various communities and classes belonging to different religions, regions and vocations of the country. The role of traditional elements belonging to predominantly lower social strata deserves its own place in this regard if justice is to be done to their contribution to the cause of struggle for swaraj. Focus should be thrown on big and small events, as far as possible, so as to highlight the greatness of small entities in the history of our freedom struggle. Such a role may not be neglected in view of the fact that it breaks the myth that all was done by the great leaders of India's only great party–Indian National Congress.

Role of Muslim Organisations

First of all, we take up the case of some Muslim leaders and their organisations which, with the exception of the Aligarh movement led by Syed Ahmed Khan, played an anti-British role that ultimately led to the partition of the country in 1947. All other movements were anti-British in spite of the fact that their real aim was to recapture the lost power of the Muslims, by the Muslims and for the Muslims. The Faraizis, the Wahabis, the Deobandis and the Ahrars had their common grievance against the foreign rulers who had deprived them of power that they had been enjoying for the last seven hundred years. They preached the message of being pure to the faith and to save their community from the influence of Hinduism and Christianity. In this way, they took to the path of orthodoxy and came closer to the Indian National Congress which developed its anti-British tone after the partition of Bengal in 1905. The Aligarh movement is a class by itself that desired modernisation of the Muslim community and its loyalty to the Raj.

Faraizi Movement: Launched by Haji Sheriatullah (1781-1840) of Faridpur in 1804, this movement covering the areas of East Bengal had a religio-political character. While its head preached the doctrine of purity of faith as corruption in Muslim society had caused the loss of Muslim power in Bengal, it assumed political overtones when the Faraizis took the vow of overthrowing the British rule. He branded Bengal as *Dar-ul- harb* (enemy territory) and advised his followers not to hold Friday and festive prayers on that day. Soon he attracted a large number of followers particularly the peasants who had grievances against the landlords and the idle craftsmen who had lost their work due to the development of industry there. His biggest achievement, according to James White, was that "the apathetic and careless Bengali peasant was roused into enthusiasm."[1]

After the death of Sheriatullah in 1837, his son Mohammed Mohsin alias Dudu Mian (1819-60) reorganised his followers by dividing East Bengal into circles *(halkas)* each under a controller *(Khalifa)* whose duty was to keep the sect together, make converts to Islam, and collect contributions for the furtherance of their object. He was opposed to the exploitation of the peasants by the zamindars and so he started a campaign for the non-payment of taxes. He established village courts under old and experienced peasants to settle their disputes and helped to resist the exactions of the landlords. So the landlords lodged several complaints against him. He was arrested in July 1857 and put as a State prisoner. He died on 24 September, 1860 at Bahadurpur.

Mir Nasir Ali (better known as Titu Mir or Titu Mian of Chandpur and a disciple of Syed Ahmed of Rae Bareili whom he had met at Mecca in 1822) was active at Barasat in 1827. He mixed the Wahabi tradition with this movement and thus made it more volatile. His followers marched to Purnea, killed a Brahmin priest, slaughtered two cows, sprinkled blood on Hindu temples, insulted the Muslims who did not join their ranks and committed violent outrages on the life and property of the Hindus. Thus in 1831 a contingent of the Calcutta militia under Alexander reached there to suppress the revolt. Titu was killed and his followers were taken prisoner.

This movement got some strength by the appearance and collaboration of the followers of Syed Ahmed Shahid--a disciple of

---

1. R.C. Majumdar: *The History and Culture of Indian People: British Paramountcy and Indian Ranaissance*, Vol. IX, Part I, p. 882.

Shah Waliullah of Delhi and the leader of the Mujahids in Bengal. He wanted to establish the *Tariqua-i-Muhammedia* or a purified system of faith as practised in early times of Islam. His three disciples (Mir Mithan Ali alias Titu Nizam, Vilayet Ali and Inayet Ali) worked in Bengal. As a matter of fact, after the departure of Titu Mian, this movement lost its weight and its ardent supporters ultimately amalgamated themselves with the Wahabis. It is a different matter that some bands of the Faraizis continued to fight against the landlords till indigo trouble broke out in 1859-60.[2] The Lt.—Governor of Bengal reported in 1857: "It will thus be seen that hardly a single district under the Government of Bengal has escaped either actual danger or the serious apprehensions of danger."[3]

Wahabi Movement: Started by Syed Ahmed of Rae Bareili (1786-1831) as a religious reform movement to eliminate 'corruption' in the Muslim society or to restore pristine purity or simplicity of faith of the Islamic community, it assumed political overtones when he and his ardent followers vowed to revive and restore Muslim power in India by overthrowing the rule of the Sikhs in Punjab and of the British in Bengal. He came under the influence of Abdul Aziz, son of Shah Waliullah (1702-1762), a well-known sufi of Delhi. Once a soldier in the army of Amir Khan, the Pindari who later on became the ruler of Tonk, visited Mecca around 1821 where he imbibed some of the teachings of Abdul Wahab of Nejd and, for that reason, his followers were mistakenly given the name of the Wahabis, though his movement had no connection with the Wahabis of Arabia.[4]

---

2. The activities of the Wahabis cover the period, roughly speaking, from 1820 to 1870. Although confined to East Bengal and comparatively of minor importance, the Faraizi movement requires a brief notice for three reasons. First, it occurred earlier as Shariatullah began to preach his doctrine as early as 1804. Second, he anticipated some of the important views of the later Wahabi movement. Third, there are reasons to believe that Faraizis were ultimately amalgamated with the Wahabis. See Majumdar, *op. cit.*, p. 884.

3. Tara Chand, *History of the Freedom Movement in India,* Vol. II, p. 12.

4. The followers of Syed Ahmed were wrongly called the Wahabis, for Waliullah's Islam was more comprehensive, richer and flexible laced with Sufi colouring than that of Abdul Wahab of Nejd (1703-67)

Syed Ahmed Barelvi first preached his doctrines in 1819 in the Rohilkhand area and then with his followers moved to Calcutta where he was warmly received by Vilayet Ali. After his return from the Haj in 1822, he stayed at Patna where he could have a very large number of his devout followers and he converted them into his private organisation.[5] For this sake, he appointed four deputies (*Khalifas*) or spiritual vice-regents–Vilayet Ali, Inayet Ali, Muhammed Hussain and Farhat Hussain. Soon after, the movement took a political form when, like his teacher Abdul Aziz, the Barelvi invoked the argument of describing India as the *Dar-ul-harb* (enemy territory) that should be converted into *Dar-ul-Islam*. He exhorted his followers to launch *jehad* (holy war) or to do *hijrat* (migration) to other Muslim countries. He made an unsuccessful attempt to seek the help of Raja Hindu Rai, a Maratha chief, to drive out foreigners from India. He moved to Afghanistan to enlist the support of the Frontier tribals in his holy war against the Sikhs of Punjab. In 1826 he brought out a pamphlet *Taghrib-ul-Jehad* (Incitement to Religious War) in which he branded Sikhs as the 'oppressors' who had killed thousands of Muslims. In 1830 he captured Peshawar. But then dissensions developed between his Indian and Afghan followers. The latter finished most of the former. The Sikhs recaptured Peshawar in the battle of Balakot in 1831 in which Syed Ahmed was killed. Moulvi Quasim, one of the Wahabi *Khalifas* who was at Muzaffarabad in Kashmir at that time, took refuge with the surviving members of Barelvi's family at Sittana under the protection of Syed Akbar. From there they shifted to Takhtabad in Bonair.

The death of Syed Ahmed gave a serious setback to this movement. And yet it continued. While Vilayet Ali and Inayet Ali preached in Kabul and in other Frontier areas, Shah Muhammed did the same in Bengal and Bihar. Later on, Vilayet Ali moved to

---

whose followers formed the sect of the Wahabis in Arabia. The followers of the Barelvi called them 'unitarians', but their adversaries called them 'Wahabis'. So Rajendra Prasad holds this designation as a 'misnomer'. *India Divided*, pp. 91-94.

5. No doubt, till now it was a religious reform movement in appreciation of which W.W. Hunter says.: "Much of their teaching was faultless and it has been given to them to stir up thousands of their countrymen to a purer and truer conception of the Almighty." *The Indian Mussalmans*, p. 68.

Hyderabad and could take Nawab Mubraiz-ud-Daulah (brother of the ruler of Hyderabad state) under his influence. From there he established his contacts with the rulers of Tonk, Rampur and Kurnool. So Mubraiz-ud-Daulah was arrested for waging a war against the British and was put in the Golconda Fort where he died in 1854. The Wahabi *Khalifas* chose Maulvi Nasiruddin as the commander-in-chief who was to march through Tonk and Sind so as to eventually join the Wahabis at Bonair. He moved ahead with Qasim Khan and helped Dost Muhammed of Afghanistan in his fight against the British. It could not meet with success. Now they attacked Punjab, for the power of the Sikhs had declined due to internecine fights among them after the death of Ranjit Singh in 1839. However, after the establishment of British rule in Punjab in 1847, they saw their final defeat at Haripur. Aulad Ali escaped to Sittana, while Vilayet Ali and Inayet Ali secretly came to Patna.

After the death of Vilayet Ali, Inayet Ali became the supreme leader. Under his stewardship the Wahabi preachers now became very active in the areas of Meerut, Moradabad. Bareilly and Delhi. They declared their support to Bahadur Shah Zafar, the last Mughal emperor of India. They could make some successful attempts in the Frontier area by routing the British camp at Sheikhjana and looting money. But when the mutiny broke out in 1857, their line of supply from Patna (Secretly coded as 'little godown' or *chhota godam*) was cut. The Commissioner of Patna (Tayler) invited some Wahabi leaders (Abdullah and Muhammed Hussain) for consultation and then treacherously imprisoned them. In Hyderabad a Wahabi uprising was crushed when Turrabaz Khan was shot dead, while Alauddin was deported to the Andamans. Vazir Khan surrendered himself at the Agra Fort. The Sittana camp (secretly coded as 'big godown' or *bara godam*) was dismantled by the British forces led by Sydney Cotton. Maksud Ali died and then Vilayet Ali's son (Abdullah) succeeded him as the Wahabi leader at Sittana. But British forces under Gen. Garvock could finally wipe out the Wahabi bases in 1863. Many Wahabis were caught and tried at Ambala. Mohammed Shafi, Mohammed Jaffer and Yahya Ali were given sentence of death, while 80 others were transported for life. In appeal the death sentence of the three Wahabi leaders was commuted to transportation for life.

Obviously, as a result of the harsh and vigorous measures adopted by the British rulers, the Wahabi 'movement', called 'conspiracy' by the British, was gradually stamped out of India, though its sparks continued to rise sporadically in the form of anti-British disturbances in the Frontier region. It should, however, be taken note of that in spite of its widespread character and the great enthusiasm that it evoked, it "cannot be regarded as a national movement. It was a movement of the Muslims, by the Muslims, and for the Muslims. The Wahabis were undoubtedly inspired by the motive of freeing India from the British rule, but their struggle was not for securing freedom for India but for the re-establishment of Muslim supremacy."[6] And yet the whole episode is illustrative of the policy of 'divide and rule.' "So long as the Sikhs were a thorn in the side of the British, the Musalmans were encouraged to carry *jehad* (religious war) against them. Once the Sikhs had been defeated and the Punjab conquered, the *jehadis* were declared rebels against the British and convicted and sentenced to transportation for life and their entire organisation was broken up."[7]

Aligarh Movement: Syed Ahmed Khan is regarded as the father of Muslim renaissance in modern India. He laid stress on the reconciliation of the teachings of Islam with the needs of modern age. "Holding that religious tenets were not immutable, Syed Ahmed Khan emphasised the role of religion in the progress of society; if religion did not keep pace with and meet the demands of the time, it would get fossilised as in the case of Islam in India."[8] His interpretations of Islam emphasised the validity of free inquiry (*ijtehad*) and the alleged similarities between Koranic revelation and the laws of nature discovered by modern science. It is said that he wrote a commentary on the reinterpretation of the Koran which could not be published perhaps owing to the fear of its stern opposition by the orthodox sections of the community. In 1864, he founded Scientific Society to convert the upper-class Muslims to the virtues of the benefits of English education. In 1874 he established Muhammedan Anglo-Oriental School that became a College two years after for imparting English education to the Muslims so that they could enter public services of the country. He started a Urdu journal *Tahzib-ul-Akhluq* in 1870 for disseminating

---

6. R.C. Majumdar, *op. cit.*, p. 901.
7. Rajendra Prasad, *op. cit.* p. 94.
8. Bipan Chandra and others, *India's Struggle for Independence.*, p. 85.

his views and thereby influencing his co-religionists with the need for change in their ways of thought and action. In 1886 he organised the Muhammedan (later Muslim) Educational Conference which, in fact, was a political body as it "succeeded in evolving a feeling of solidarity in the community and the consiousness of a Muslim society."[9]

The political aspect of the Aligarh movement overshadows its social or religious aspect. In 1858 Syed Ahmed Khan brought out his book *Risala-i-Asbab-i-Baghavat-i-Hind* that became *Causes of the Indian Revolt* when Auckland Colvin translated it into English. Surprisingly, he designated the war of 1857 as 'rebellion' and thereby earned the goodwill of the English masters. Then, he brought out his *Loyal Muhamedans of India* in which he counselled the Muslims to win the favour of the English rulers by expressing their loyalty towards them. Raja Ram Mohan Roy lauded the English rule as it would shower the blessings of the English system on our people, but Syed Ahmed Khan appreciated the alien rule as it could set aside the possibilities of power shifting into the hands of the Hindus after the fall of the Mughal empire. It is for this reason that he did not join the Indian National Congress formed in 1885 and labelled it as a Hindu and anti-British organisation. In 1888 he founded the **United India Patriotic Association** so as to put it as a force against the Congress. Theodore Beck, the first principal of the M.A.O. College of Aligarh, took advantage of the situation and founded **Muhammedan Defence Association** which had the blessings of Syed Ahmed Khan and his son (Syed Mahmood) was its Secretary.[10]

Thus, the awakening of the Muslim community at the hands of Syed Ahmed Khan strengthened the force of Muslim communalism that yielded its sinister results in course of time. What he occasionally preached as a secular or a nationalist leader and what he actually did radically differ from each other and this contradiction is quite amazing. As Tara Chand comments; "Aligarh failed to become the centre of renascent Islam. It did not produce a Ghazali, a Waliullah, a Jamal-al-Din, or a Rashid Raza. In the religious teachings of the College, tradition asserted its supremacy; but tradition and Western sciences, philosophies and literatures ill-

9. Sumit Sarkar, *Modern India.*, p. 76.

10. Tara Chand, *op. cit.*, p. 374.

assorted with one another. Hence, in the minds of the students, there was intellectual dichotomy. No reconciliation took place between dogma and reason."[11]

Deoband School: On the other extreme stands the Seminary or Dar-ul-ulum founded by Muhammed Qasim Nanautwi and Rashid Ahmed Gangohi in 1867 at Deoband, a place near Haridwar. The Deoband School had these objects:[12]

1. To exalt the word of God, unaffected by any temptation, patronage, pressure and favour,
2. To extend contacts with the Muslims in order to organise them for leading their lives according to the original Islamic principles,
3. To regard any cooperation with the Government of the nobility as injurious to the interest of the school,
4. To follow firmly and strictly the teachings of Shah Waliullah, and
5. To avoid aristocratic and despotic ways and to work through cooperation and mutual consultation to set an example of democratic and republican methods of administration.

Obviously, the leaders of this movement took inspiration from the message of Shah Abdul Aziz of Delhi who after the fall of the Mughal Empire had issued a *fatwa* (decree) calling India as *Dar-ul-Harb* (land of war) and thus vowed to finish the British power so as to restore the power of the Muslims. But now situation had fundamentally changed. So the leaders of the Deoband School looked towards cooperation with the Hindus for overthrowing the English rule. It is for this reason that they appreciated the creation of the Indian National Congress that would one day bring about country's independence. Later, leading figures of this movement like Syed Madni joined the Congress, while Barkatullah and Obeidullah Sindhi joined terrorist groups operating abroad. One may say that

---

11. *Ibid.*, p. 379. While addressing the London Muslim Association in 1895, Beck laid stress on the impossibility of Hindu-Muslim unity and advised them not to join the 'seditious' Indian National Congress led by Naoroji and Bengali politicians.

12. *Ibid.*, p. 383.

while the Deobandists did hardly anything for the cause of renascent Islam as they resented modernisation of the Muslim community, they certainly did much for the sake of awakening their community to play its part in the freedom struggle of the country.

The Ahrars: A small section of the Muslims of Punjab known as the Ahrars or freedom fighters, has its own place in this direction for taking an anti-British stand at the time of the fall of the Mughal rule and thereafter by espousing the cause of the Indian nationalist. "In the revolt of 1857, the leading family of the Ulema of Ludhiana threw in their lot with the revolutionaries."[13] Abdul Qadir and his sons marched to Delhi to save the last Mughal emperor. When Delhi came under the control of the British, they escaped to the jungle of Patiala and returned to Ludhiana after the proclamation of general amnesty by Queen Victoria in 1858. After the death of Abdul Qadir, his sons continued their profession of imparting religious instructions, but their anti-British sentiments remained. The followers of Qadir appreciated the formation of the Indian National Congress in 1885. They resented the role of Syed Ahmed Khan when he advised his co-religionists to keep themselves away from the national organisation. Shah Muhammed, son of Qadir issued a *fatwa* (religious edict) signed by about one thousand Maulvis of the country condemning the stand of Sir Syed and in stead advising his co-religionists to cooperate with the Hindus for political purposes.[14]

The leaders and the followers of this movement resented the disintegration of the Ottoman empire after the First World War along with the termination of the Caliphate. So they appreciated and supported Gandhi's call for non-co-operation to the 'Satanic rule' of the British. Habib-ur-Rahman, the grandson of Shah Muhammed, joined the Indian National Congress and remained true to his faith till his death in 1956. Thus, he came very close to the great national leaders like Gandhi, Jawaharlal Nehru and

13. Tara Chand: *History of the Freedom Movement in India,* Vol. III, p. 282.

14. This *fatwa* was printed in English with the title of Nusrat-al-Ahrar (Victory of the Good) and its copies were distributed at the fourth session of the Indian National Congress held at Allahabad in December, 1888. After some time, a weekly paper *Observer* was printed from Ludhiana which ceased its publication in 1919 due to the wrath of the British government. *Ibid.*

Maulana Abul Kalam Azad At the instance of Azad, he founded an association with the name of Majlis-i-Ahrar in 1929 with these aims and objects:

1. Complete independence of India,
2. Freedom of religion, culture, civilisation and education for all in independent India.
3. Autonomy of provinces with full authority in internal affairs, and the fixation of the powers of the Central government by the agreement of the provinces,
4. The Central government to be the federation of the provincial units with these provisions:
   (*a*) Central legislature to be constituted on the basis of the equality of Hindu and Muslim representatives with 10 per cent seats for other communities,
   (*b*) Bills affecting Muslim religion or culture to be withdrawn in the event of their opposition by 2/3 Muslim members,
   (*c*) A Supreme Court to be established with equal number of Hindu and Muslim judges,
   (*d*) Establishment of a Department of Muslim charitable trusts,
   (*e*) Army to be recruited from both Hindu and Muslim communities,
   (*f*) Central financial assistance to be given to backward provinces,
   (*g*) Termination of weightage on any ground in legislature and public services,
   (*h*) Non-interference of the government in religion, culture, language, education, and place of worship of all religious communities,
   (*i*) No interference with the personal law of the Muslims, and
   (*j*) Appointment of Muslim judges for trying cases involving religious laws.
5. Unyielding opposition to the establishment of a separate and independent Muslim state.

It shows that the Ahrars were nationalists to the core of their heart. "The sacrifices which they made and the sufferings which they cheerfully bore in the cause of Indian independence constitute a shining chapter of Indian history."[15]

Peasant Movements

India is an agricultural country. Most of the people live in villages and their main vocation is agriculture. The tillers of the land are called *Kisans* (farmers) who have been the victim of exploitation and oppression from ancient times. The British rulers claimed that they had established rule of law, but its benefits could not reach the landed peasantry. They were exploited and tortured by the foreign power as well as by the local landords who remained loyal supporters of the alien Raj. On occasions these kisans formed their associations and they fought against the misrule of the landlords and the contractors. On certain occasions their fight came to have some touch, near or remote, with the freedom struggle of the country. Thus, a brief narration of the role of such organisations becomes relevant in this regard.

Indigo Revolt: The most voilent and widespread revolt of the peasants of Bengal engaged in indigo cultivation, called 'Blue Mutiny' by B.B. Kling, has its own place here. The poor peasants badly suffered at the hands of the British planters, as they had to grow indigo on their best land even if they wanted to grow rice there. Those who declined to do so were harshly treated by the armed men of the planters called *lathiyals*. As Tara Chand says: "These planters were a lawless set of men. In stead of cultivating the plant themselves, they employed local peasants under a system of advances. The cultivator who accepted the advance became, to all intents and purposes, a serf. The planter was a slave driver who used force and fraud to obtain the crop."[16] The resentment of the peasants grew more when in 1857 the Bengal government appointed

15. *Ibid.*, p. 283. In May 1937 a conference of the Ahrars denounced Jinnah as 'an out of date politician... making a fetish of constitutionalism' and the League as 'a coterie of a few knights, Khan Bahadurs and Nawabs'. Sumit Sarkar, *op. cit.*, p. 354.

16. Tara Chand, *op. cit.*, p. 533.

29 planters as Honorary Magistrates to settle legal claims in such a matter and then they raised the slogan *je rakhak se bhakak* meaning 'our protectors are our devourers.'

The attitude of the government was not outspokenly hostile towards the indigo cultivators. Macaulay called for the punishment of the dishonest planters.[17] J.P. Grant, the Lt. Governor of Bengal, admitted that "the root of the whole question is the struggle to make the ryots grow indigo plant without paying them the price of it." Hem Chandra Kar, the Deputy Magistrate of Kalaroa, issued a directive to the police not to deprive the cultivators of their possessions over their land in the event of any riot. While Kar did so in excess of his authority, the ryots found more meaning in it and they interpreted it as their right to grow indigo or not. Under the leadership of the Biswas brothers (Digamber and Vishnu), the peasants of Govindpur village in Nadia district rose their heads. They abandoned indigo cultivation and countered the armed forces of the planters in September, 1859.

In not much time the disturbances spread out in all areas of indigo cultivation of Bengal. The ryots attacked indigo factories. In order to harass the peasants, the planters enhanced rent. The ryots refused to pay the enhanced rent and they physically resisted their eviction. Ultimately they had their victory due to their concerted efforts and sustained fight as well as due to the sympathy and support of the Hindu landlords and the leading intellectuals of Bengal. Harish Chandra Mukherji wrote notes in favour of the ryots in the *Hindoo Patriot* and Din Bandhu Mitra's play *Nildarpan* presented its vivid portrayal.[18] A Muslim organisation (Wahabi Rafique Mandal) supported the cause of the ryots.

---

17. Macaulay's observation on the situation was that "the great evils exist, that great injustice is frequently committed, that many ryots have been brought partly by the operation of the laws and partly by acts committed in defiance of the law, into a state not very far removed from that of predial slavery". L.C. Mitra: *History of Indigo Disturbances in Bengal* (1906), p. 3. While appearing before the Indigo Commission W.E. de Latour, the Magistrate of Faridpur, as a witness called it 'system of bloodshed.'

18. It was translated into English by Michael Madhusudan Datta (under the supervision of Revered Long) against whom a suit was filed by the planters. He was given the sentence of one month

In November, 1860 the government of Bengal issued a notification that the ryots could not be forced to grow indigo. At the same time, it provided for the fulfilment of indigo contracts. Under this act, an inquiry commission under the chairmanship of W.S. Seton-Karr (called Indigo Commission) was set up that submitted its report on 27 August, 1860. It found that the cultivation of indigo was not profitable to the ryot on the terms offered to him. The ryot was deprived of his free will as he was bound to continue a cultivation which did not give him adequate remuneration. It came to the conclusion that the complaints urged by the ryots against the unprofitable nature of cultivation of indigo and the oppressive system of advances were true and so the oppression of the planters should be stopped. The Government accepted it.[19] Thus the "outrages perpetrated by the British indigo planters constituting one of the blackest chapters in the history of British rule in India" came to an end.[20]

Deccan Riots: The peasants of Poona and Ahmednagar protested against heavy assessment of land revenue in Bombay and consequent poverty and indebtedness of the cultivators. The agitators made the money-lenders their target of attack as they charged a high amount of interest on loans by which the peasants could pay enhanced land revenue. In May 1875 the peasants of Poona started this agitation and therefrom it spread to Ahmednagar. A leader calling himself Shivaji II challenged the authority of the Government, offered a reward of Rs. 500 for the head of the Governor of Bombay (Sir Richard Temple), and claimed to lead a national revolt on the lines on which the Maratha power

imprisonment and a fine of one thousand rupees. In his book *Remarks on the Black Acts,* Ram Gopal Ghose presented a vivid account of what he had himself seen during the course of his travel. Sisir Kumar Ghose, the founder-editor of *Amrita Bazar Patrika,* devoted himself heart and soul to the cause of the indigo cultivators.

19. Even Viceroy Canning said that the indigo problem had caused him more anxiety than he had felt since the days of Delhi. He himself saw the peaceful demonstration of the ryots crying for justice. And so in his letter to the Secretary of State (Sir Charles Wood) dated 30 October, 1860 he said that "the people who can do this so intelligently cannot be dealt with so carefully."

20. Majumdar, *op. cit.,* p. 914.

had originally been founded. The Government of Bombay set up a Commission on the Riots in Poona and Ahmednagar whose report (1876) failed to realise the gravity of the situation.

No Revenue Movement in Assam: The peasants of Assam resented the enhancement of land revenue by 70 to 80 per cent and their movement was surprisingly supported by the local notability and the intelligentsia. The rural protesters organised mass assemblies (*raij mels*) particularly in the districts of Kamrup and Darrang in 1893. They enforced the norms of caste solidarity and threatened to ex-communicate those who would pay revenue to the government. Not only this, some violent elements inspired by Pusparam Kanhar looted markets and police had to do firing in Rnagaiya and Patharughat in January, 1894. The Jorhat Sarvajanik Sabha supported the movement and Rashbehari Ghose raised this issue in the Central Legislative Council. The movement subsided as eventually some concessions were allowed. The disturbances that occurred in various parts of Assam during the second half of the nineteenth century showed that the tribals loved freedom above everything else and they resented imposition of different kinds of taxes to which they were unaccustomed. In a long review of the whole situation Deputy Commissioner of Assam McCabe observed that the question of the day was as to 'who was the paramount authority—the mels or the Sarkar?'

Pabna League: Anti-landlord riots occurred in many parts of the country during the British rule, but the case of Pabna disturbances has its peculiar significance. Here more than 50 per cent of the cultivators had occupancy rights (giving them immunity from eviction and some restraints on enhancement of rent) under Act X of 1859. But the landlords of Bengal had enhanced rents through many other devices as *abwabs* (cesses) and physical coercion. Just to save themselves from such injustices, the tenants of the Yusufshahi Pargana of Pabna district organised an agrarian league in 1873 which raised funds to meet litigation expenses, held mass meetings to which villagers were called by the sounding of buffalo horns, drums and night cries passing from hamlet to hamlet, and also occasionally withheld rent. Soon the agitation spread to other districts of Bengal as Dacca, Mymensingh, Tripura, Backergunj, Faridpur. Bogura and Rajshahi. Surprisingly, the agitation was anti-zamindars, but it was not patently anti-British in view of the fact that the peasants proclaimed themselves to be 'the ryots of Her Majesty the Queen, and of Her alone.'

The association of the zamindars (British Indian Association) condemned the agitation of the Pabna League and its mouthpiece *Hindoo Patriot* sought to portray it as a communal agitation of the Muslim peasants against Hindu landlords. It was a mispropaganda.[21] The fact stood out that while the peasants committed some acts of looting the houses of the zamindars, they did not kill anyone and, by and large, they showed that they had developed a strong sense of law. Though their activities simmered till 1885, most of the disputes could be settled under the weight of official pressures and persuasions. Those who had indulged in acts of violence were awarded punishment. A big landlord Dwijendranath Tagore urged the Government to take strong action against the agitators. But it assumed "a position of neutrality as far as legal battles or peaceful agitations were concerned."[22] The Bengal Tenancy Act of 1885 could satisfy the demand of the agitators to a considerable extent. In appreciation of this, it is obvserved: "Once again the Bengal peasants showed complete Hindu-Muslim solidarity, even though the majority of the ryots were Muslim and the majority of the zamindars Hindu. There was also no effort to create peasant solidarity on the grounds of religion or caste."[23]

Bijolia and Bardoli Peasant Satyagrahas: The agitation of the peasants of Bijolia of Udaipur State acquired great significance on account of its timing and leadership.[24] It broke out in 1916 and ended in 1922 and thus coincided with the Gandhian experiments in Champaran and Kheda and, above all, with his non-cooperation movement. The agitation initiated by Swami Sitaram, became more volatile when it was led by Bhoop Singh alias Vijai Singh Pathik who could persuade Manik Lal Verma (an employee of the State of Udaipur) to join his movement. The peasants refused to pay land

---

21. The Pabna League had Hindu leaders like Ishan Chandra Roy and Shambhu Pal and a Muslim Jotedar named Khoodo Mullah. Leaders like Surendranath Banerjea, Dwarkanath Ganguly and Anand Mohan Bose supported the peasants. Intellectuals like Bankim Chandra Chatterjee and R.C. Dutt sympathised with this movement.

22. Bipan Chandra and others, *op. cit.*, p. 55.

23. Sumit Sarkar, *op. cit.*, p. 48.

24. M.S. Jain; *Concise History of Rajasthan.*, p. 137.

revenue unduly enhanced by the *jagirdars* and the *thikanedars* and they also refused to contribute to war loans. The Maharana shielded the *jagirdars* and *thikanedars* and though he set up two inquiry commissions, he did not act upon their reports. On 11 June 1922 an agreement was made with the *jagirdars* and State officials which stipulated reduction of various taxes including abolition of some *lagats* (cesses), no payment of revenue in case there was no cultivation, and greater facilities for grazing areas, cutting wood and suspension of the realisation of court decrees. It also provided that personal belongings were not to be sold in the execution of the decrees. The whole episode showed that "now the peasantry had acquired a new sense of confidence about their power and they would not hesitate to restart the conflict if the Durbar or the *thikanedars* behaved unjustly or oppressively."[25]

However, the Bardoli Satyagraha provides a better account of the success of the Gandhian techniques. When the Bombay Government announced a revenue hike of 22 per cent, in Bardoli in 1927 Kunvarji Mehta and Kalyanji Mehta of the Patidar Yuvak Mandal persuaded Vallabhbhai Patel to lead the agitation. So a no-revenue campaign was organised. The peasants could not be cowed down by the attachments of their land and cattle on such a large scale, while the people of the Dubla tribals (known as Kalipraja) rejected the bait of the land on easy terms being offered by government officials. The movement attracted wide attention. The workers of Ahmedabad collected Rs. 13,000 for the help of the agitators and Lalji Naranji resigned from the Legislative Council in protest. The Maxwell-Broomfield Enquiry Committee admitted that the enhancement of land revenue was undue. Victory came to the Bombay Presidency Land League led by Patel when on 16 July 1929 the Bombay Government abandoned revenue revisions till the completion of the current round of constitutional reforms.

Tebhaga Agitation: The peasant agitations of Bijolia and Bardoli are known for the adoption of the Gandhian tactics, but the uprising of Tebhaga in Bengal has a different character. It was organised and led by the Communists who took recourse to the methods of mass violence. In September, 1946 the Bengal Provincial Kisan Sabha gave a call to implement through mass struggle the

25. *Ibid.*, p. 140.

recommendation of the Floud Commission. They declared that they would pay not half but one-third of their crop to the share-cropper. In the month of November, agitation became hot in the areas of North Bengal. The agitators used *lathis* and guns in defence of their claim as a result of which they clashed with the police. In the fight about 49 peasants lost their lives. The Muslim League Ministry led by Suhrawardy sought to move a bill (Bargardars Temporary Regulation Bill) which could not make any headway. But it encouraged the peasants to intensify their struggle. Encouraged with the fact that the demand for *tebhaga* could not be termed illegal, they tried to remove the paddy already stored in the jotedars *khamars* to their own and this resulted in innumerable clashes. The movement gradually declined, but the Congress government passed the Bargardar Bill in 1950.

Sikh Movements

The Sikhs are a community by themselves. They are Hindu by religion, but a distinct sect by their faith in the panth and also by their tradition. The hard elements regard Sikhism as a religion, while the moderate ones have no objection to their being regarded as a part of the wider Hindu society. Most of the Sikhs live in Punjab and manage their holy shrines called Gurudwaras. The nineteenth century renaissance had its effect on Punjab as a result of which reform movement broke out. The Sikh leaders laid stress on maintaining purity of faith and immunising the management of their gurudwaras from corruption. Thus, Singh Sabha movement had its start as a religious or social reform campaign. At the hands of Guru Ram Singh it assumed political overtones.

Singh Sabha Movement: In 1873 this movement was founded at Amritsar with the object of maintaining purity of the faith and to enlighten the community with the benefits of Western learning. It also countered the proselytising activities of the Christian missionaries as well as of the Hindu revivalists. The Sabha opened many schools and colleges in Punjab so as to impart education to the Sikhs. It had its offshoot in the form of Akali movement that for its object sought to liberate the gurudwaras from the control of the corrupt *mahants* banking on the support of the government. The picture of the Hindu gods and goddesses were removed from the gurudwaras. Schism occurred in the ranks of the Sikhs. While the followers of Baba Ram Singh adopted sternly anti-British postures and played their role in the Kuka movement, the moderates became loyalists to the British rule.

Kuka Revolt: The Sikh reform movement started in Western Punjab in the 1840s by Bhagat Jawahar Mal, known as the 'Sian Saheb', shortly before the British conquest of Punjab in 1849. Its original aim was to purify the Sikh religion by removing the evils that had crept into it. Sian Saheb and his disciple Baba Balak Singh, collected their followers and established their centre at Hazru in the Frontier province. They proclaimed Gobind Singh as their only 'true guru' and their tenets included abolition of restriction on inter-caste marriage, abstinence from meat and intoxicants, and comparatively free intercourse between the sexes.

However, after the conquest of Punjab by the British in 1849, their activities in the form of a religious movement declined and they gradually assumed political overtones. After the death of Balak Singh in 1863, Baba Ram Singh became their leader. He declared himself as the incarnation of Guru Gobind Singh and preached the revival of the *Khalsa* and the overthrow of the British rule. He exhorted his followers not to accept any government job, not to send their children to government schools, not to go to the courts of law but to settle their disputes through panchayats, not to use foreign goods, and not to use government's postal services. Baba Ram Singh settled down at Bhain Ala (Bhaini), a place near Ludhiana, and imparted military training to his followers. It was reported that he was carrying on secret intrigues with the Maharaja of Nepal and with his help a Kuka regiment was organised in Jammu in 1870.[26]

---

26. 'Kuk' is a Punjabi word meaning 'cry'. Hence Kuka is a person who raises a cry. Here it means a person crying for freedom. The credit for starting this movement goes to Baba Ram Singh who after the suppression of the revolt of 1857 thought of some type of concerted action against the British government. He looked towards Raja Ranbir Singh of Kashmir and Rana Jang Bahadur of Nepal for help in his cause. The British government could gather information about the designs of this movement and so Kuka assemblies were banned. The Commissioner of the Ambala Division (R.G. Taylor) wrote to the Lt.-Governor of Punjab on 16 June, 1867 that the time "has come for taking serious notice of the proceedings of the Kukas alleging their large-scale infiltrations in the armed constabulary of the police both in Punjab and outside." See M.L. Ahluwalia: *Landmarks in Sikh History*, Chapter 14.

The Kukas joined the native forces of the princely States; they destroyed the idols and the shrines of the Hindus and killed many butchers who were suspected of being cow killers. So some Kukas were arrested, a few were hanged, and some were given the sentence of transportation for life. A section of the Kukas broke away and took to the path of fierce fighting. They did a lot of destruction in the States of Patiala and Malerkotla in 1872. Though Ram Singh had no hand in such activities, he was put under strict surveillance and then deported to Rangoon. There he lived like a state prisoner till his death in 1885 Thus ended the Kuka movement. "There is hardly any doubt that the rash action of a small group of fanatics among the Kukas, undertaken in direct defiance of their leader, was principally responsible for the unexpected and speedy end of the movement."[27]

Tribal Agitations

The movements of the tribals living mostly in Bihar, Orissa and the north-eastern parts of the country have their own place in this regard. From ancient times they have been victim of exploitation and oppression by the rich landlords, the contractors and other such elements having their alliance with the ruling power. Whenever they raised their voice against the local exploiters, they had to face the wrath of the British masters. Hence, some place should be given to their 'disturbances' in this study.

Birsa Movement: Among the tribal and agrarian disturbances of the nineteenth century, the most serious one was of the Mundas led by Birsa who was reverentially addressed by his followers as 'Birsa Bhagwan'. Known as the *Ulgulan* (Great Tumult) in the region of Ranchi in Bihar, it drew its sustenance from the grievances of the tribal people who resented their traditional *khuntkatti* land system (joint holdings by *khunts* or tribal lineages) being eroded by the *jagirdars* (big landlords) and *thekedars* (contractors) coming from the northern plains as merchants and money-lenders. The outsiders, whom they called *dikus*, exploited the indentured labour and imposed *beth begari* (forced labour). The exploited tribal people raised their voice against it; they tried to bank upon the support of Christian missions; they also sought the help of the courts, but to no avail. So the Munda saviour came in the form of Birsa

27. Majumdar, *op. cit.*, p. 904.

(1874-1900), son of a share-cropper, who preached the message of internal purification and along with it he gave the call to remove the alien government with its henchmen in the form of *jagirdars* and *thekedars*.

Educated at Chaibasa with some knowledge of English, he became a convert to German Christian mission, but he returned to his old faith after some time. In 1896 he claimed that he had the vision of God (Sing Bonga). As Birsa Bhagwan, he exhorted his followers to cultivate higher ethical virtues for self-purification. He urged upon them not to make animal sacrifice before any deity (Bonga) and to worship God alone. His followers, including the Christian converts, addressed him as *Dharti Aba* (Father of the World). The British rulers considered his tenets as 'dangerous' and scented political designs in his movement aiming at the overthrow of their Raj. On the eve of Christmas in 1899, he and his followers shot arrows and tried to burn down churches over an area covering six police stations in the districts of Ranchi and Singhbhum. Even police stations were not spared. Thus. Meares, the Police Superintendent posted at Ranchi, secretly moved to Chalkad village and arrested Birsa with 15 of his strong followers. They were prosecuted and sentenced for two years imprisonment with some fine.

However, after his release from jail, Birsa became a firebrand, a more dangerous agitator. He organised an army of his own under the command of Gaya Munda. Khunti became the centre of his revolutionary activities, while training centres were opened at Ranchi, Bundu, Chandradharpur and other places. Thereafter, sporadic raids took place, the most significant of which was the attack on Khunti police station on 7 January 1900 with bows, arrows, sticks and spears. The agitators killed one police constable and set fire to some houses. Then, the Deputy Commissioner of Police reached Dumari hill with 200 Munda soldiers. Many casualties took place. Gaya Munda was killed, but Birsa was arrested on 3 February 1900. Nearly 300 Mundas were prosecuted, 3 were hanged, and 44 were transported for life. Birsa died of cholera in the jail of Hazaribagh on 2 June 1900. No doubt, the movement was stamped out, but it had a positive result. In 1908 an important amendment was made in the Chhota Nagpur Tenancy Act whereby the *Khuntkatti* land system was recognised and *beth begari* was prohibited. Birsa is regarded by his tribals as a full-fledged nationalist and a prophet of the Jharkhand Movement that had its appearance after a couple of decades. He was certainly a local nationalist, though not a nationalist in the strict sense of the term as his vision "could not have embraced anything broader than a heroic defence of his tribal homeland against all intruders."[28]

Tribal Outbursts in other Areas: The outbursts of the tribals in different parts of the country were informed not only by the factor of religious, social or cultural reform but also by the challenge coming from the side of the Christian missionaries and orthodox Hindus. The elements of dissatisfaction had their confluence with anything like resentment against payment of enhanced land revenue and other taxes or redemption from the cruel hold of the landlords, *thekedars* and money-lenders. However, the surprising feature of all such movements was the belief of the people created by some charismatic leader in the advent of a 'golden period' (milleniarism) under their 'divine' leadership. They claimed themselves as the possessor of divine powers and thus their images became the objects of worship by their followers.

The Naikda forest tribes of Gujarat attacked government offices and police posts with a view to establish Dharam Raj. The Kacha Nagas of Kachar attacked the whites at the instance of Shambhudan under the illusion that by his miracle-power he would convert the guns of the enemy into sticks. In the agency of Vizagapatnam a Konda Dorra named Kora Mallaya pretended himself as a Pandava and declared his son as the incarnation of Lord Krishna and thereby exhorted his followers to drive the English out of the country. In the skirmish a number of innocent tribals were killed. In 1879-80 a rebellion arose in the Godavari agency (whose heart lay in the 'Rampa' country of Chodavaram) where triabls rose against the *mansabdars,* who had aligned with the British. In 1886 a group of rebels who called themselves *Rama Dandu* (Rama's Army) under the leadership of Rajana Anantayya appealed to the Maharaja of Jeypore to help him in driving the English out of the country.

Disturbances in Some Protected States: On the death of the Raja of Keonjhar in 1860, his son Dhananjay Bhanja was recognised by the British government and as he came of age in 1867, it was decided to permit him to take over the management of the estate. But his step mother supported the case of Brindaban

28. Sumit Sarkar, *op. cit.*, p. 48.

Chandra Bhanja and the tribals (Bhuias) led by Ratna Naik supported her. About 20,000 insurgents disarmed the police at the Garh and dismounted the guns. The entire country was disorganised and plundering was rife. Some wild clans (as the Juangas and the Kols) also joined hands with the Bhuias. Situation could be controlled when Dr. Hayes reached Garh with his military contingent and he suppressed the armed resistances. In the State of Sambalpur the mutineers released Surendra Sai. He and his brother (Udwant Singh) collected about 1600 followers and established a parallel government. The local people supported them, but Sir Richard Temple could suppress this agitation.

A cursory survey of such activities shows that most of them were directed against the foreign planters, landlords and the money-lenders who, in their view, were their immediate enemies. Moreover, their struggles were directed towards specific and limited objectives and aimed at the redressal of their specific grievances. They did not make British rule their target, but the agitations of the Faraizis, the Wahabis and the Kukas stand like bold exceptions in this regard. A faint reflection of anti-British orientation may be traced in the exercises of Birsa Munda. Moreover, all such activities were of a very limited nature. Their territorial reach was limited and they had no links with similar activities going on in other parts of the country. Since the feudal lords had been crushed or coopted by the British rulers, and since the local exploiters like the planters, petty zamindars and the money-lenders were on the side of the alien rulers, only the exploited classes like the tribals and the peasants took upon themselves the mantle of creating uprisings and insurrections. Since all such activities were disorganised, they could be easily suppressed by the police and the military forces of the British Government. As a result of this, "at no stage did these movements threaten British supremacy or even undermine it."[29]

Zeliangrong Movement: Reference should be made to two tribal movements which were inspired by the idea of inter-tribal unity and had anti-British overtones to some extent. The movement of the three tribes of Manipur, namely Zemeis, Liangmeis and Rongmeis (the first two also known as the Kacha Nagas and the last one as

29. Bipan Chandra and others, *op. cit.*, p. 58.

Kabuis) was a counterproduct of British colonial rule.[30] In 1891 the British conquered Manipur in the First Burmese War and then they compelled the tribes to pay house tax direct to the Government (a tax which they had never paid to the ruler of Manipur), supply forced labour and provide travelling allowances in the form of cash and food for the touring officials. And yet the British could not protect them against the attacks of the Kukis who came here and occupied their lands. Jadonang came forward to speak against the apathy of the British Government and he raised the voice of freeing his tribals from the oppressive hold of the British and the Kukis as both were labelled by him as the 'outsiders'. He launched the movement for creating social unity among the three tribes and advised his people to abandon irrational social and religious customs by taking them as 'impure'. It came to be known as *Haraka* cult. With the object of creating a Naga Raj, he organised his people and committed raids on the offices and treasuries. He was caught and given the sentence of death in 1931. Then, his sister Gaidinlieu took over the charge. Her movement was crushed by the Assam Rifles in 1932 and she was given the sentence of transportation for life. Accidentally, this movement coincided with the civil disobedience movement of Mahatma Gandhi and so the leaders of the Indian National Congress tried to contact Gaidinlieu who was reverentially addressed as the 'Rani'. Jawaharlal Nehru tried to see the release of the Rani, but his effort could succeed after the advent of independence in 1947.

Even after its violent suppression, the movement continued in a peaceful form. At the suggestion of the Raja of Manipur, the Kabui Samiti was formed in 1934 and the Kabui Naga Association came into being in 1946. The Zeliangrong Council and the Manipur Zeliangrong Council came into being in 1947 and their endeavours constituted the genesis of the movement for Nagaland. However, in view of its programme and apparent influence on it of contemporary national movement for independence as also the fact that it caused considerable anxiety to the British Government, it "can definitely be said to have formed part of our national freedom struggle."[31]

---

30. A combination of the initial letters of the names of these three tribes makes the word 'Zeliangrong' that came into currency in 1947. Gangmumei Kabui: "The Zeliangrong Movement: An Historical Study" in K.S. Singh (ed.): *Tribal Movements in India*, Vol. I, pp. 53-66.

31. D.P. Mukherjee, P. Gupta and N.K. Das: "The Zeliangrong or Haomei Movement", *Ibid.*, p. 86.

Nebula Movement: But the story of the Nebula movement has a different character.[32] The British established their control over the Darjeeling area in 1835 and after that began immigration of the Nepalis from Nepal and of the Bhutias from Sikkim. The number of the Nepalis went on increasing so much so that in 1941 they constituted 87 per cent of the population of the three hill sub-divisions of the Darjeeling area. Naturally, it was not appreciated by the local populace of the Lepchas who became a minority in course of time. The British kept it as a Partially Excluded Area and played their policy of divide and rule. In 1869 Macfarlane noted that since the Lepchas could converse in Hindi, so English and Hindi could be the medium of instruction. Later on, Hindi was replaced by the Nepali language. So Bhutia leader Laden La and Lepcha leader Yen Singh opposed the view that Nepali should be the medium of instruction and yet the British Government accepted the recommendation of the Griffifth Committee in 1927.

Mahatma Gandhi visited Darjeeling in 1921. Then, Dal Bahadur Giri of Darjeeling, Jangbir Sapkota of Kalimpong and Prithiman Lama of Kurseong came under his influence. The Hill People's Social Union came into being on 22 December, 1934 at Darjeeling under the leadership of Laden La with the object of fostering brotherhood and unity among different tribes. This body had the ideology of regional integration as it was opposed to the idea of ethnocentrism in spite of the fact that the Nepalese dominated the Union by having 12 seats out of 20. After the death of Laden La in 1936, the Nepalese became more vocal in their domination. Gurung was elected to the Legislative Council of Bengal in 1937 and he set up District Gurkha League in 1943. It constituted the genesis of the movement for Gorkhaland in the post-independence period. It is clear that not this movement but the Zeliangrong movement "could establish linkages with the national freedom struggle."[33]

Dalit Movements

In the end, we may make a passing reference to the movements of the Dalits or the persons belonging to the Depressed Classes called

---

32. 'Nebula' is a combination of the initial letters of the names of three tribes, namely, Nepali, Bhutia and Lepcha. S.R. Baghai and A.K. Dandia: "Ne-Bu-La--A Movement for Regional Solidarity", *Ibid.*, pp. 339-48.

33. K.S. Singh: "Introduction": *Tribal Movements in India,* Vol. I, p. *xiii*.

the untouchables. These may be described as agitations launched "by and large by inward looking groups with a rather too narrow focus of interest."[34] Credit goes to Mahatma Gobind Phule of Poona who set up an association (Satya Shodhak Samaj) in the province of Bombay (now Maharashtra) and whose task was taken over by Gopal Baba Walangkar, S.J. Kamble and B.R. Ambedkar. Men like T.M. Nair and G.N. Mudaliar deserve the same credit for launching such a movement in the province of Madras (now Tamilnadu) that was given a potential form by E.V. Ramaswamy Naicker (Periyar) who launched Self-Respect Movement in 1925.

Satya Shodhak Samaj: To save the people of the Depressed Castes or classes from exploitation and torture at the hands of Brahmins in particular, Mahatma Jyotiba Govind Phule founded this body on 24 September, 1873. He preached his ideas through his books—*Sarvajanik Satyadharma Pustak* and *Goolamgiri* (written in Marathi) and appreciated the British Raj for establishing rule of law that could save the Dalits from the social injustice perpetrated by the *Shetji* (money-lenders) and *Bhatji* (Brahmins). As he said: "For thousands of years with the help of their books, the Brahmins have declared the masses as low-born and are exploiting them. To liberate them from the thraldom of the sacerdotal authority and make them conscious of their rights by educating them is the function of the Samaj." Gopal Baba Walangkar, an ex-serviceman, organised the Dalits and converted this social reform movement into a political movement by setting up an organisation with the name of **Bahujan Samaj.**

Movement in Bombay: Phule exhorted his followers not to do servitude to the people of the upper classes and in stead improve their lot, but Walangkar infused in them the sense of demanding reservations in army and public services. In 1894 he submitted a petition to the Bombay Government on behalf of the Ratnagiri-based Mahar groups claiming Kshattriya origin of the Dalits. A similar petition was submitted by Shivram Janbi Kamble on behalf of the Mahar groups of the Deccan region highlighting the services of such people to the state. Ambedkar's role begins from 1919 when he appeared before the Southborough Committee (Franchise Committee set up to consider the case of reservation of seats for

34. Debi Chatterjee: *Up Against Caste; Comparative Study of Ambedkar and Preriyar*, p. 6.

the Depressed Classes in the Legislative Councils) and demanded that 9 seats be reserved for them with the provision that one of them would represent the Depressed Classes in the Central Legislative Council. As a result of such efforts, the Government of India Act of 1919 provided one reserved (nominated) seat to the Depressed Classes in the Bombay Legislative Council. It was, indeed, too inadequate. He repeated his demand before the Simon Commission in 1928-29 and now demanded 22 seats to be reserved for the Depressed Classes in the Bombay Legislative Council. Nothing could occur to the satisfaction of the Dalit leaders.

Under Ambedkar's leadership the social aspect of the movement "against caste, casteism and the Brahminical order reached its peak."[35] The Bahishkrit Hitkarni Sabha (Association for the Welfare of the Outcastes) set up in 1924 with the motto 'Educate, Agitate and Organise' the Dalits could make its mark in not much time. The Mahad Municipality had taken a decision to open Chowdar Tank to the untouchables so that they could use and take its water. It remained unimplemented. So on 25th December, 1927 a satyagraha was staged there to allow the Dalits to use its water. Then followed the Parwati temple entry movement in the city of Poona in 1929 and entry into Kala Ram Temple in Nasik in 1930. Such attempts could not have the desired success and so Ambedkar expressed his anguish in these words: "The superman is the Brahmin and the common man is the Shudra." The Mahad Tank struggle "widely acclaimed as the first untouchable liberation movement did not succeed in getting water, but it did succeed in the public burning of the *Manusmriti*."[36]

In pursuance of a resolution moved by Dr. P.G. Solanki, the Bombay Legislative Council set up a committee under the chairmanship of Starte in 1929 with Ambedkar, Kamble, Solanki and A.V. Thakkar as its members. It recommended that the students of the Depressed Classes be given scholarship and hostel facilities and jobs should be reserved for them in the mills and railway workshops. In December, 1930 and again in September 1931 Ambedkar represented his case at the Round Table Conferences held in London. It came as "a recognition of his importance as a representative of the Depressed Classes as also a recognition of the

35. *Ibid.*, p. 14.

36. Gail Omvedt: *Dalit Visions*, p. 44.

national importance of the Depressed Classes issue." The terms of the Communal Award of 1932 followed by the Poona Pact could satisfy Ambedkar to a considerable extent. But his grievances against the injustices of a caste-ridden Hindu society remained. On 25th November, 1949 he said these words: "Political democracy cannot last unless there lies at the base of it social democracy."[37]

Movement in Madras: The earliest organised socio-political protest in South India appeared in 1912 with the creation of the Dravidian Association under the leadership of the Raja of Panagal with T.M. Nair as its vice-president and G.N. Mudaliar as its secretary. In 1916 South Indian People's Association was formed. It issued 'Non-Brahminical Manifesto' highlighting serious grievances of the non-Brahmins and urging them to fight for their rights. In the same year some leading figures like S.R.P. Thyragarayar formed the South Indian Liberal Federation which soon after was known as the Justice Party of Madras. E.V. Ramaswamy Naicker (once a Congressman and the president of the Tamilnadu Congress in 1923-24 and a follower of Gandhiji) became the hero of this movement with a powerful attack on the Congress and its leaders like Gandhi. He launched an anti-Brahminical agitation called Self-respect Movement in 1925. He is admired "for developing a theory of rights, powers and justice and a definition of the community which brought a new subject of history: rational, committed to reciprocity, equality, yet desirous of fraternity and above all free, bound up by the ideals of self-respect."[38]

The Self-respect Movement aimed at the abolition of God, Religion, Congress, Gandhism and Brahminism. Its first conference was held at Chenglapattu in 1929 where about six thousand people took the pledge to abolish caste system and to derecognise the role of the temple priests. The second conference held at Erode in 1930 under the chairmanship of M.R. Jayakar condemned idol worship in the temples. At the Virudhnagar conference held in 1931 a resolution was adopted to propagate the system of inter-caste marriages. Naicker preached the idea of gender equality. He supported some progressive ideas like education for women, widow

---

37. *Constituent Assembly Debates*, Vol. XI. p. 979.

38. V. Geetha and S.V. Rajadurai: *Towards a Non-Brahminical Millenium from Jyothee Thass to Periyar*, p. 514.

re-marriage, daughter's share in father's property, wife's right to seek divorce and employment of women in public services. In his paper *Kudi Arasu* he strongly condemned Hindu religion and scriptures and spoke of the emerging identity of the Dravidians. Syed Ahmed Khan spoke of the exclusive and distinctive identity of the Muslims, Naicker said the same thing about the Dravidians. Jinnah came forward with theory of two nations—Hindus and Muslims and on that basis demanded a separate state of Pakistan, Naicker came forward with his theory of three nations–Hindus, Muslims and Dravidians–and demanded Dravidisthan.

After the victory of the Congress in the provincial elections of 1937, Naicker became more furious in his assertions. He frankly advocated the use of constitutional and extra-constitutional methods for the achievement of his aims. He was highly critical of the Congress government under the premiership of Rajagopalachari. He opposed teaching of Hindi in the schools of Madras, demanded reservation of seats in admissions to educational institutions and recruitment to public services in proportion to their population in the province of Madras. It is strange that a person, who as a follower of Gandhi had launched the successful satyagraha in Vaikkom in 1924 and had earned the title of 'Vaikkom Veerar', became a fiery advocate of the three nation theory and branded Hindu religion, Hindi language and Hindustan as the three enemies of the Dravidians.[39]

Naicker's influence did not remain confined to the province of Madras. In 1923 the Backward Classes in U.P. organised the Hindu Backward Classes League at Lucknow under the chairmanship of Rai Saheb Ram Charan. A Backward Classes Conference was held at Kanpur in 1944 which was addressed by Naicker.[40] It was a result of the efforts of its secretary Gouri Shanker who became a member of the First Backward Classes Commission headed by Kaka Saheb Kaelkar set up in 1955. Happily, in 1949 the moderate elements in Naicker's Dravida Kazhgam led by C. Annadurai abandoned the lines of extremism, militancy and secessionism and his Dravida Munnetra Kazhgam joined the national mainstream.

---

39. Debi Chatterjee, *op. cit.*, pp. 154–55.

40. *Ibid.*, p. 155.

6

A Miscellaneous Study

Much has been said about India's constitutional development and national movement in the preceding chapters. Some topics, however, have remained to be discussed as they have their own significance. The new awakening (renaissance) of the nineteenth century appearing in the form of social and religious reform movements prepared ground for the rise of nationalism. Different trends appeared during the course of our freedom struggle ranging from moderatism of the first generation and the extremism of the second generation of the national leaders to the Muslim communalism of the separatists and the exclusivists that culminated in the unfortunate division of the country. The Gandhian trend by assimilating the virtues of the trends of moderatism and extremism dominated the scene from 1917 to 1947. The trend of revolutionary and aggressive nationalism could give a setback to the foreign rule in its own way. Some reference to the trials of freedom fighters deserves its own place in such a study.

Renaissance in Bengal, Maharashtra and Madras

The story of nineteenth-century renaissance begins from Bengal where pioneering work was done by Raja Ram Mohan Roy and, for that reason, he is known as the 'father of modern Indian renaissance'. Among others are Keshab Chandra Sen, Debendranath Tagore, Pandit Sivnath Sastri, Anand Mohan Bose, Raj Narain Bose, Swami Vivekanand etc. The messages of the great Bengali leaders reached other parts of the country and mingled with the messages of their counterparts living there. Since Bengal became the most important province of India under the Company rule after the enforcement of the Regulating Act of 1773, it was natural that it should have taken the lead in this direction. The new awakening in this part of the country covered not only social, religious and cultural spheres, it also influenced the domains of literature, art and politics.

Perhaps keeping it all in his view, Gokhale once gave his tribute in these words : "While the whole country thinks of today, Bengal thinks of tomorrow."

Brahmo Samaj: In 1816 Raja Ram Mohan Roy founded Atmiya Sabha that became Brahmo Samaj in 1828. He preached the message of monotheism or 'oneness of God' (Tauhid) and thereby he denounced all distinctions created by religions and castes. The manner of worship consisted in congregational study, contemplation and meditation without any colourful appurtenance usual in the rituals of the religious prayers. As he was much impressed with the 'Wind of the West', he appreciated the system of English rule. When in 1823 Governor-General Adam imposed press censorship,[1] he fought a case in the Supreme Court of Judicature at Calcutta and lost it. Then he sent a petition to the King-in-Council that had the same fate.[2] He also stressed need for the independence of judiciary and the Indianisation of judicial services. But his most important contribution is the abolition of *sati* system which could be effected by a regulation of Governor-General William Bentinck in 1829.[3]

The progress of the movement of Brahmo Samaj retarded after the death of the Raja in 1833. Situation changed after Keshab Chandra Sen joined it in 1857. In a way, he humanised the trend set by the Raja.The ideas of prayer and communion with God, of consecration of life, of loving devotion to God and service of man according to His will, and of search for His light, inspiration and blessing, became parts of the faith and imparted to it the emotional content which it had lacked. In 1860 he founded the Sangat Sabha where inquiries were held into the validity of the Hindu rites like Durga Puja and the caste orders. In 1861 Calcutta College was established to impart English education and a paper (*Indian Mirror*)

---

1. Raja Ram Mohan Roy published three periodical papers-*Mirat-ul-Akhbar* in Persian, *Sambad Kaumudi* in Bengali (the official organ of his Brahmo Samaj) and *Brahmanical Magazine* in English. An order of the government stopped their publication and, for this reason, the Raja fought for the freedom of the press.
2. This petition was given the name of 'Indian Areopagitica' by Sophia Dobson Collet. John Milton's *Areopagitica* written in 1644 is regarded as the monumental work on the freedom of the press.
3. It was a cruel practice whereby the widow was burnt alive with the body of her dead husband.

was started to give publicity to the activities of the mission. After this, Sen toured the provinces of South India and mooted the idea of converting the Brahmo Samaj into 'Bharatvarshiya Brahmo Samaj' or Brahmo Samaj of India so as to admit all the 'Brahmos' of the country into one body and to establish the principles of Brahmo religion on a universal basis, gleaned from the teachings of all religions. Since this proposal was strongly opposed by Debendranath Tagore and other members of the Brahmo Samaj, Sen left this organisation in 1865 and founded his Brahmo Samaj of India after a year that was also known as his 'Naya Vidhan' or 'New Convention' or 'New Dispensation'.

As a result of this schism, the original Brahmo Samaj came to be known as the 'Calcutta Brahmo Samaj' or the 'Adi Brahmo Samaj' under the leadership of Raj Narayan Bose committed to its belief in the following tenets:

1. God is a personal being with sublime moral attributes.
2. God has never become incarnate.
3. God hears and answers prayers.
4. God is to be worshipped only in spiritual ways. Religious injunctions make no sense.
5. Repentance and cessation from sin is the only way to forgiveness and salvation.
6. Nature and Intuition are the sources of knowledge of God. No book is final.

Different from this, Sen's New Dispensation expressed its belief in the following tenets:

1. God is one, Creator, Father, Mother, Friend, Guide, Judge and Saviour.
2. Soul is immortal and eternally progressive.
3. Have faith in natural inspiration, general and special.
4. Have faith in God's moral law as revealed through the commandments of conscience and be accountable to God for the faithful discharge of manifold duties.
5. Accept and revere the scriptures and also revere the saints and prophets of the world.

6. Have faith in the Universal Church, the Kingdom of God.
7. Our creed is the science of God which enlightens all.

Sivnath Sastri and Anand Mohan Bose left this body in 1878 and formed a new organisation with the name of Sadharan Brahmo Samaj whose membership was open to those who completely refrained from idolatrous practices and caste system of the traditional Hindu society. They expressed their faith in the following tenets:

1. There is only one God, Creator, Preserver and Saviour of this world.
2. Human soul is immortal and responsible to God for all doings.
3. God is to be worshipped in spirit and truth.
4. No created object is to be worshipped as God.
5. God rewards virtue and punishes sin.
6. Fatherhood of God and brotherhood of man is the essence of all religions.
7. Union with God is the true salvation.

After the death of Sen in 1884, no other leader of stature could emerge and so the Brahmo Samaj movement gradually declined. Indisputable is the fact that "in rousing the sentiment of patriotism, the Samaj played a prominent role."[4]

Tattvabodhini Sabha: It was a small body formed by Debendranath Tagore in 1838 which published Tattvabodhini *Patrika* under the editorship of A.K. Dutt. Debendranath Tagore was much impressed with the ideas of Raja Ram Mohan Roy and so this body was like an adjunct of the Brahmo Samaj. He established Tattvabodhini school to train Brahmo missionaries and to prepare them for religious and philosophical discussions. In 1859 he had this body amalgamated with the Brahmo Samaj.

Neo-Hinduism or Revivalist Movement : While Raja Ram Mohan Roy took inspiration from the West and infused the spirit of rationalism, the conservative elements sought to overshadow it by

---

4. Tara Chand, *History of the Freedom Movement in India*, Vol. II, p. 394.

the dogmatic force of assertive Hinduism. Such leaders opposed the abolition of the *sati* system and spoke against official intervention in the affairs of Hindu religion. For this sake, Radha Kant Deb founded Dharam Sabha in 1830. While his earlier association called Gaudiya Samaj founded in 1823 had its aim at the propagation of education and knowledge, this body had its aim at opposition to the law that had abolished *sati* system. A petition signed by Maharaja Girish Chandra, Radha Madhab Bonnerji, Kashinath Bonnerji and others was presented to the Governor-General in January, 1830 protesting against official interference in the religious customs of the Hindus. When the Governor-General rejected it, it was sent to the King-in-Council which had the same fate.

New or Young Bengal Movement: A section of the ex-students of Hindu College of Culcutta inspired by the ideas of their teacher (Henry Derozio) imbibed rationalist thought of Europe. On the father's side a Protuguese and on the mother's side an Indian, Derozio taught English Literature and History at the Hindu College, Calcutta, preached the message of patriotism and infused the spirit of free inquiry and free thinking in his students. The result was a revolution of thought. Krishna Mohan Bandopadhyaya, Rasik Krishna Mallik, Radha Nath Shikdar, Dakshina Ranjan Mukhopadhyaya, Pearey Chand Mittra and Ramtanu Lahiri were the leading figures of this new trend. They recalled India's glorious past and lamented its ignominous present. They rendered their services through writing in the papers or books as well as by doing social work. While Tara Chandra Chakravarty established Society for the Acquisition of General Knowledge in 1838, Kishori Chandra Mitra founded the Theophilanthropic Society in 1843. "They were men of honour in whom the nationalist sentiment-the love of India-first manifested itself."[5]

Ramakrishna Mission: It was set up by Swami Vivekanand in the memory of his teacher Ramakrishna Paramhamsa in May, 1897 at Dakshineswar, near Calcutta. He gave a new meaning to religion by identifying it with the service of the poor and the downtrodden. Poor people are God and their service is the service of the Lord. So he chided that the rich and the upper classes of the society were physically as well as morally dead. He accused the Indian National Congress (formed in 1885) of being useless as it had done nothing

5. *Ibid.*, p. 246.

for the welfare of the wretched masses of the country. He opposed casteism, sectarianism, untouchability and all kinds of social inequalities. At the same time, he exhorted his people to be bold, not to imitate the West blindly, and win the whole world by soul force. His message had its electric effect on a section of the young nationalists who swelled the ranks of the 'extremist school'.[6] It is rightly said that he "is the first Indian who had questioned the superiority of the West and in stead of apologising for his religion and defending it against the attacks of his critics, boldly asserted its spiritual pre-eminence and incomparable greatness. He was the hero who had faced the critics and the detractors in their own homeland and elicited from them admiration, even their homage. India felt greatly elated by this achievement and it helped in changing its mood from one of self-abasement to that of self-esteem."[7]

The Mission believes in the truth of all religions. It stands for social and religious reform, but takes inspiration from the ancient culture of India. It holds up the pure Vedantic doctrine as its ideal and aims at the development of the highest spirituality inherent in man. At the same time, it recognises the value and utility of later developments in Hinduism such as the worship of the images, and modern developments in natural sciences and technology. But its greatest emphasis is on rendering social service to the poor, the weak and the downtrodden sections of the society. Credit for all this goes to Swami Vivekanand whose utterances "made him an embodiment of the highest ideas of the renascent Indian nation."[8]

Political Associations: In 1837 some zamindars of Bengal founded Bengal Landholders Society under the leadership of Joyakrishna Mukerji that became British Indian Association in 1851 when the group led by Sisir Kumar Ghosh formed Indian League with the aim of fighting for the cause of the tenants as well. In 1876 Surendranath Banerjea formed Indian Association and the Indian League of Ghosh was merged with it. In 1886 Banerjea had his Indian Association merged with the Indian National Congress formed in 1885.

Maharashtra occupies the second place in terms of a chronological

6. Romain Rolland: *Vivekanand,* pp. 165-66.
7. Tara Chand, *op. cit.*, p. 416
8. R.C. Majumdar, H.C. Raichoudhury and K. Datta: *An Advanced History of India*, p. 876.

account, while it deserves to have the first place in terms of the diversity of new awakening that covered almost all sections of the people. The Pandurang brothers spread the message of Brahmo Samaj; Phule took up the cause of the depressed castes; Dayanand launched Arya Samaj movement; Joshi, Bhandarkar and Agarkar worked for social and educational reform; Fardonji, Malabari and Naoroji worked for the reform of the Parsee community; P.M. Mehta founded the Bombay Presidency Association. But the name of M.G. Ranade stands out that entitles him for being the father of renaissance in Maharashtra.

Prarthana Samaj: The message of the Brahmo Samaj reached other parts of the country, but nowhere did it take deep root except in Maharashtra where Keshab Chandra Sen established Prarthana Samaj in 1867. But the typical character of the people of this province had its own role as a result of which some points of distinction between the two could be noted. In Bombay the followers of the Prarthana Samaj 'never looked upon themselves as adherents of a new religion or a new sect, outside and alongside of the general Hindu body, but simply as a movement within it."[9] Like the Brahmo Samaj, rational worship of one God and social reform formed its ideals. "It has been truly remarked, however that differences between the emotional character of the Bengalis and the practical shrewd commonsense of the Marathas are clearly reflected in the two institutions which sprang up under similar conditions."[10]

Daduba Pandurang and Atma Ram Pandurang founded the Paramhamsa Sabha or Mandali in Bombay in 1849 to preach the concept of the unity of God and brotherhood of man. This body was interested in the moral improvement of the individual and condemned outworn customs and rites; it insisted on charity, love of truth, righteousness and toleration as the guiding principles of conduct. It had its end some ten years after, but it was revived by Keshab Chandra Sen when he visited Maharashtra. It expressed its faith in the following tenets:

1. God is the creator of this universe. He is the only true God.

---

9. H.C.E. Zacharias: *Renascent India*, p. 43.

10. Majumdar and others, *op. cit.*, p. 871.

2. His worship alone leads to happiness in this world and the next.
3. Love and reverence for him, an exclusive faith in Him, praying and singing to Him spiritually with these feelings and doing the things pleasing to Him constitute His true worship.
4. God does not incarnate Himself and there is no revealed book.
5. To worship and pray to images and other created objects is not a true mode of divine adoration.
6. All persons are His children.

The Samaj became very popular as it was joined by eminent figures like M.G. Ranade and R.G. Bhandarkar. It started a paper *Subodh Patrika* to preach its message and a night school was started to impart education for the working classes. Pandita Ramabai established Arya Mahila Samaj. Ranade laid stress on the equality of all persons that involved eradication of caste system and introduction of inter-caste marriage. He also insisted on the banning of child marriage and legalisation of widow remarriage. For this sake, he formed an association of his own with the name of Social Conference that had its session in the evening hours when the session of the Indian National Congress was over.

Arya Samaj: Established by Swami Dayanand Saraswati in Bombay on 10 April, 1875 this movement spread to other parts of the country. The Swami gave the call of 'Back to the Vedas' and so he renamed Hindu religion as Vedic Dharam. He deprecated all that is given in the *Puranas* and on that basis denounced case system as well as idol worship. He laid stress on the regeneration of Hindu society. For this sake, he attacked the premises of Islam and Christianity and preached the supremacyof Hindu faith in his book *Satyartha Prakash* written in Hindi. He started *shuddhi* campaign i.e., conversion of non-Hindus to Hinduism. Abolition of child marriage, introduction of women education and widow remarriage, renunciation of alcoholic drinks etc. were other points which he emphasised. In 1882 he set up a Society for the Protection of the Cow.

The official creed of the Arya Samaj includes these tenets:

1. God is the primary cause of all true knowledge and of everything known by his name.

2. God is all Truth, all Knowledge, all Beautitude, Incorporeal, Almighty, Just, Merciful, Un-begotten, Infinite, Unchangeable, Incomparable, All-pervading, Omniscient, Imperishable, Immortal, Eternal, Holy and the Cause of the Universe.
3. The Vedas are the books of true knowledge.
4. One shold always be ready to accept truth and renounce untruth.
5. All actions ought to be done conformably to virtue.
6. The primary object of the Samaj is to do good to the world by improving physical, spiritual and social conditions of mankind.
7. All ought to be treated with love, justice and due regard to their merits.
8. Ignorance ought to be dispelled and knowledge diffused.
9. No one ought to be contented with his own good alone.
10. In matters which affect the general social well being of the whole society, one ought to discard all differences and not allow one's individuality to interfere.

The distinctive feature of this movement is that it not only elevated Hindu religion by looking to its glorious past, it also synthesised it with the achievements of the present. It was a new trend that sought to awaken the sense of national identity among the people of the country. It is evident from the tribute of Dr. Griswold who said that Dayanand "had a vision of India purged of her superstitions, filled with the fruits of Science, worshipping one God, fitted for self-rule, having a place in the sisterhood of nations and restored to her ancient glory."[11]

Lokahitwadi: Gopal Hari Deshmukh of Poona has a place of his own in this direction. While associated with Prarthana Samaj of Ranade, the Arya Samaj Movement of Dayanand and the Theosophical Movement of Olcott, he had his own line of doing social service by adopting the pseudonym of 'Lokahitawadi'. In 1877 he wrote *Jatibheda* in which he denounced Hindu caste system and thus came close to what Phule was preachng. He brought out two more books (*Gitattatva* and *Subhashita*) to popularise the teachings

11. J.N. Farquhar: *Modern Religious Movements in India*, p. 112.

of the *Bhagwad Gita*. In 1880 he published *Swadhyaya* and *Ashvalyana Grihya-Sutra* to explain the rites of the Hindu society in a critical tone. His book *Gramarachna* had a discussion of the condition of the villages. He wrote monumental volumes on the history of Rajasthan, Gujarat, Saurashtra and Ceylon (now Sri Lanka). Like Ram Mohan Roy, he appreciated British rule as it was based on the norms of a democratic government. But what is peculiarly important about him is that he was not only a social reformer, he also looked at the economic condition of the country. He studied the problem of poverty and the fact of the ruin of commerce and industry. In this way, he became the precursor of Ranade and Joshi who started Swadeshi movement in Maharashtra. In one of his writings, he set down his creed as follows:

1. All should devoutly worship God.
2. All ceremonies except those connected with initiation, marriages and death should be abolished. Ceremonials and prayers should be performed in one's own language.
3. Every person should have liberty to act, speak and write according to what he thinks.
4. Men and women should have equal rights in social and religious functions.
5. Morality is higher than performance of rituals.
6. No person is to be treated with contempt. Pride of caste is unbecoming. Do good to all.
7. Love of the motherland and good of the country should always be borne in mind.
8. The rights of the people are higher than those of the Government.
9. The rules laid down by the Government and rules suggested by reason should be observed.
10. Everybody should strive for the growth of learning.
11. Truth should be the abiding principle of conduct.

In short, this man of many parts did a lot for the sake of social reform and also touched political and economic issues despite being a high government servant like a judge posted at Nasik and Ahmedabad, then a nominated member of the Legislative Council of Bombay and finally, as the Dewan of Ratlam state.

Parsee Community Reforms: The credit for launching social reform in the community of the Parsees goes to some prominent figures like Nauroz Fardunji, Dadabhai Naoroji, B.M. Malalbari and Pherozeshaha Mehta. The first newspaper started in Bombay with the name of *Bombay Samachar* was a Parsee venture. Under the chairmanship of Naoroji was started the Students Literary and Scientific Society. The Rahnumai Mazdayasnan Sabha founded in 1851 had for its object the restoration of Zoroastrian religion to its pristine purity. Naoroji published a paper in Persian with the name of *Rast Goftar*. Malabari laid stress on the education of the women and widow remarriage.

Poona Sarvajanik Sabha: Prominent figures like Ranade, Joshi and Agarkar played their part in founding this association in 1870. It published a paper *Sudharak* whose Marathi edition was edited by Agarkar and its English edition by Gokhale. Agarkar started *Kesari* (Marathi) and *Mahratta* (English) papers which, later on, were taken over by Tilak. The leaders of this movement laid special stress on imparting English education to the young students. For this sake, Deccan Education Society was set up which established Fergusson College at Poona in 1885. It had political character as well in view of the fact that it was formed to represent to the Government the wishes and needs of the people and its membership included landlords, merchants, bankers, retired public servants, lawyers, teachers and some ruling chiefs of the princely states of Maharashtra. Ranade was its guide, philosopher and teacher. Its main aim was to educate public opinion, though it devoted much of its attention to study the problems of Indian economy and drew attention of the Government towards economic hardships of the people. It sent a petition to the Queen for reforming the Legislative Councils set up under the Indian Councils Act of 1861. In 1884 P.M. Mehta, K.T. Telang and Badruddin Tyabji formed Bombay Presidency Association that had its merger with the Indian National Congress in the following year.

The wave of new awakening touched the presidency of Madras as well, though here the work of the social and religious reformers could not be of that magnitude as we see in the cases of Bengal and Maharashtra. Keshab Chandra Sen visited this province and set up a branch of his Brahmo Samaj with the name of Veda Samaj. Col Olcott and Madam Blavatasky opened a branch of the Theosophical Society at Madras in 1882 which became very active after it was taken over by Mrs. Annie Besant. Prominent figures like Pandit Anand Charlu and Vijairaghavachari established Madras Mahajan Sabha. A brief description of these associations may be put as under.

Veda Samaj: Keshab Chandra Sen took the message of Brahmo Samaj to the South as a result of which Veda Samaj came into being under his stewardship in Madras in 1864. Prominent people of Madras province like V. Rajagopal Charlu, P. Subrayala Chetty and Visvanath Mudaliar joined it. But the leading part was played by a Tamil Brahmo Samajist and an ardent follower of Sen, K. Sridharalu Naidu, who changed the name of this association as Brahmo Samaj of Southern India in 1871. He translated the books of the Brahmo Dharma from Bengali into Tamil and Telugu languages and undertook missionary tours to propagate the new faith. After his death in 1874, dissensions developed. A major section joined the Sadaharan Brahmo Samaj. Due to this, the movement of Naidu grew weak and it lost its popularity.

Theosophical Society: A movement that was more conservative and more mystical than the Arya Samaj of Dayanand Saraswati was launched in India by Col. Olcott and Madam Blavatsky who had founded. Theosophical Society in New York in 1875 and had established its headquarters at Adyar (near Madras) in December, 1882. The theosophy as a system of religion, science and practical life attracted a section of the educated people who believed in the freedom of thought and expression. The religious principles of this Society were (i) Unity of God, (ii) threefold emanation of God, (iii) hierarchy of beings consisting of spiritual intelligences of gods and angels, human spirits and sub-human intelligence, and (iv) universal brotherhood subject to the recognition of varying degrees of man's development. Its tenets are:[12]

1. Philosophically, the Society supports the school of idealism, asserts the primacy of consciousness, and believes that human thought is of the same nature as divine thought. Thought is capable of mustering man's lower nature and his physical surroundings. The spirit is eternal and immortal and reincarnates from one body to another, gathering life-experience, climbing upwards until it masters all that the world has to teach and nothing more is left to learn. Then, it is beyond birth and death, 'fitted for immortality'.

---

12. Tara Chand, *op. cit.*, p. 425.

2. Theosophy is 'occult science', which comprises a body of facts discovered by recognised experts. These facts include the constitution of the universe and of man and the laws of action and reaction, evolution and human perfection. This occult science, unlike the ordinary science, is not based upon hypothesis, experiment and inferences but on intuitions of clairvoyant adepts by mediumistic methods which constitute the infra-structure of theosophy.

The branches of the Society were opened at Bombay under the charge of P.M. Mehta and at Simla under the charge of A.O. Hume. But only its Madras branch could work well particularly after the coming of Annie Besant in 1893, who had already joined it in England five years earlier. She laid stress on the education of the young people and for this established Central Hindu College at Benares in 1898. In many places of the country the Society opened schools for boys and girls. It opposed child marriage, advocated abolition of caste and amelioration of the condition of the widows, and desired upliftment of the depressed classes. Most of the members of the Society joined the Indian National Congress when it had its third session at Madras in 1887. Most outstanding is the role of Annie Besant who defined the word Swaraj in terms of Home Rule and avowed her faith in these words: "India must be governed on the basis of Indian feelings, Indian traditions, Indian thoughts and Indian ideas."[13]

Madras Mahajan Sabha: Prominent figures of the city like Vijayraghavachari and Pandit Anand Charlu started a paper *The Hindu* in 1878 and founded this body in 1884. It had its first conference in December, 1884 that discussed the problem of reform of the Legislative Councils, separation of the judiciary from revenue functions, civil services and military expenditure. Memorials were drafted and presented to the Government. It was merged with the Indian National Congress in 1887.

Different Trends of Freedom Movement

The story of the rise and growth of Indian nationalism leaves an unmistakable impression that our freedom movement passed through several crucial stages in which different political trends came to have their sway beginning from the moderate trend set by

13. *Ibid.*, p. 426.

the early Congress leaders. then the extremist trend adopted by their successors belonging to the second generation, thereon to the Gandhian trend assimilating as well as superseding both and thereby having a predominant position of its own for a period of the last thirty years or so. While the trend of the moderates prevailed for a period of first twenty years of the Congress and came to have some of its essential ingredients like those of agitation on peaceful lines assimilated in the trend of Gandhi, the trend of the extremists could have a life of about a decade and had its final assimilation in the Gandhian trend that can be traced in the Mahatma's aim of Swaraj, *i.e.*, liquidation of the British rule by means of a militant agitation based on the dynamic principles of *ahimsa* and *satyagraha*. Different from all, the trend of Muslim communalism adhered to the line of separatism and exclusiveness that entailed the partition of the country.

Moderatism: The nationalist movement witnessed its first political trend in moderatism on account of the very fact that it emerged as the 'foster child' of the alien imperial genius. The Indian National Congress was founded by the far-sighted and enlightened English intellectuals who had become convinced, towards the later part of the nineteenth century, with this point that some definite action was called for to counteract the growing unrest of the Indian people. In this atmosphere Hume emerged on the scene.

The early Indian nationalist leaders thus began their career with three cardinal principles that ascribed to them the title of 'moderates'-admiration of India's connection with English empire on account of their faith in British sense of justice and fairplay, demands for gradual constitutional reforms, and application of purely constitutional means. Leaders like W.C. Bonnerjee, Dadabhai Naoroji, Pherozeshah Mehta, Dinshaw Wacha, Anand Mohan Bose, Lal Mohan Ghosh, Anand Charlu, Rash Behari Ghose, Surendranath Banerjea and, above all, Gopal Krishna Gokhale were a product of the westernised environment and belonged to the bourgeois and upper middle classes of the Indian society. On account of their background of western education and their full faith in British sense of justice and fairplay, these leaders were said to have drunk the 'new wine of western learning' or been a class of citizens 'Indians in blood and colour, but English in taste, opinions, morals and intellect. It was remarked that they "plucked with both hands the fruits of the trees of Western knowledge" as they were 'humble students of Kant and Spencer, Burke and Mill."[14]

Thus, the history of the Indian nationalist movement at the hands of the liberal Congress leaders begins with forceful words in the praise of English education, British style of administration and appeals for 'reasonable' constitutional reforms and an expression of their full faith in the efficacy of peaceful and constitutional methods. While delivering his first presidential address at the Bombay session in December in 1885, W.C. Bonnerjee described the Congress as 'National Assembly of India' and explained that it would promote Indian national unity by projecting from a single platform the common interests of the people throughout India. He concluded by emphasising that Congressmen desired the permanence of British rule in India and that their ultimate aim was only to gain a share in the administration of its government. While delivering his presidential address at the second Congress held at Calcutta in December 1886, Dadabhai Naoroji said: "We are British subjects, we can demand what we are entitled to...if we are denied Britain's best institutions what good is it to India to be under British sway? It will simply be another Asiatic despotism."

This trend continued in time to come. The fourth Congress held at Allahabad in 1888 deliberately chose George Yule-an Englishman -to act as its president in order to curry favour with the English critics of the Congress. The fifth Congress held at Bombay elected William Wedderburn in order to further disarm its critics. It also appointed leading moderates like Phcrozeshah Mehta, Surendranath Banerjea, Manmohan Ghose and W.C. Bonnerjee to propagate the programme of the Congress in England. The Congress leaders tried to choose an Englishman as the president for the sixth session and preferred Pherozeshah Mehta after Herbert Gladstone and W. Gantz had declined the offer. Mehta repeated the slogan: "Our motto is reform, not revolution." The seventh Congress session held at Nagpur in 1891 had the same theme. This trend had its equally emphatic endorsement in the presidential address of Surendranath Banerjea at the Poona Congress in 1985 when he summed up the whole ideology in these words: "We Congressmen know that we are about,

14. Valentine Chirol: *Indian Unrest*, p. 24.

we know our minds, we know our methods, we stick to them with resolute tenacity of purpose and faith....We are advocates of reform and not of revolution. Above all, we rely with unbounded confidence on the justice and generosity of the British people and their representatives in Parliament."[15]

A critical study of the role of the moderates, however, shows that they cannot be accused of being anti-nationalist, though they may not be free from the charge of being pro-British. Facts illustrate the point that they were so much obsessed with their faith in the British sense of justice and fairplay that they never desired to speak strongly in anti-British terms. It does not imply that they desisted from criticising the alien rule. Like enlightened nationalists and also like persons well aware of the limitations of the obtaining situations, they adopted an attitude of cautious and loyal critics of the foreign administration. A great moderate leader like Surendranath Banerjea accused the British Government in the name of its having rule of law that it denied to its subject peoples. Another leading figure of this school like Gokhale condemned the English administration from a moral point of view. He gave his evidence before the Welby Commission (1897) when he frankly said: "The excessive costliness of the foreign agency is not, however, its only evil. There is a moral evil which, if anything, is even greater. A kind of dwarfing or stunting of the Indian race is going on under the present system... The full height to which our manhood is capable of rising can never be reached by us under the present system. The moral elevation which every self-governing people feel cannot be felt by us. Our administrative and military talents must gradually disappear, owing to sheer disuse, till at last our lot as hewers of wood and drawers of water in our own country is stereotyped."[16]

It may, however, be added at this stage that, despite being a great moderate leader, Gokhale could not remain thoroughly oblivious to the force of arguments advanced by the extremists. He believed in Justice Ranade's theory that the British empire was in the scheme of a divine dispensation and was meant to be of immense benefit to our country. At the same time, he appreciated the call for

15. Cited in Daniel Argov: *Moderates and Extremists in the Indian National Movement*, p. 57.

16. Cited in Tara Chand, *op. cit.*, pp. 572-72.

Swadeshi, though he opposed the course of boycott of foreign goods. In very emphatic terms, he denounced the rule of Lord Curzon and, in the zeal of his love for the country, spoke like an extremist in bidding good-bye to all hope of cooperating in any way with the bureaucracy in the interest of the people.[17] He set out a charter of nine demands in his Presidential address at the Kashi Congress of 1905 enumerating.

1. A reform of the Legislative Councils by raising the proportion of the elected members to one-half. and by requiring that the budgets be passed by them;
2. Appointment of at least three Indians to the India Council of the Secretary of State for India:
3. Creation of advisory boards in all districts throughout the country; the district magistrates should consult these boards compulsorily in all important matters of administration;
4. Recruitment of the judicial branch of the Indian Civil Service from the ranks of the legal profession;
5. Separation of judicial and executive administration;
6. Reduction of heavy military expenditure;
7. Expansion of primary education;
8. Growth and extension of industrial and technical education; and
9. Alleviation of rural indebtedness.

These demands "represent in a summarised form the political philosophy of the Indian Moderates"[18]

The moderate or liberal leaders of the Indian National Congress cannot be accused of being purely reactionary or anti-nationalist irrespective of the fact that they were rank admirers of the British system of government and during the first phase of 1885-1895 the only progress that the Congress could make "was in proving that it

---

17. See Stanley A. Wolpert: *Tilak and Gokhale: Revolution and Reform in the Making of Modern India*, p. 176.

18. V.P. Varma: *Modern Indian Political Thought*, VII Ed., 1980, p. 193.

was not a seditious organisation."[19] The trend of rank moderatism continued even during the second phase of 1895-1905 with the only difference that some moderate leaders did not refrain from criticising the foreign rule, though in a mild manner, no matter their words were noted with concern even by those whom they wanted to admire and emulate. The assessment of an extremist leader like Lala Lajpat Rai was, therefore, too rash when he remarked that the Congress lacked the essentials of a national movement', though this part of his observation cannot be refuted that the movement was neither inspired by the people nor devised or planned by them.[20] What a fine evaluation is that of Rajni Palme Dutt: "It should not be assumed from the tone of these declarations that these early Congress leaders were reactionary anti-national servants of the alien rule. On the contrary, they represented at that time the most progressive force in the Indian society. So long as the nascent working class was still completely without expression to organisation, and the peasants were still the dumb millions, the Indian bourgeoisie was the most progressive and objectively revolutionary force in India."[21]

Extremism: From 1905 begins the era of extremism and radical nationalism that has its genesis in the phase of the preceding ten years in which the Indian leaders had started criticising the British administration for its lapses, political as well as moral. The new thing about this period is that a different school developed to challenge the hold of the moderates and to prosecute the struggle for freedom on extremist lines. Thus, it appeared that the nationalist agitation had acquired a new energy and consciousness in decrying adulation of the West as well as efficacy of purely peaceful and constitutional methods. The novel feature of this trend was that the leaders of the movement hailed from the middle class who drew inspiration from religious and social orthodoxy and laid stress on the use of extremist means to pursue a policy which would represent a definite breaking of the ties with imperialism. The starting point of the leaders of this school was not only to criticise the 'Old Guards' but was undoubtedly the desire "to make a break with compromising policies

19. Daniel Argov., *op. cit.*, p. 47.
20. See Lajpat Rai: *Young India*, pp. 145-47.
21. R.P. Dutt: *India Today*, p. 322.

of conciliation with imperialism, and to enter on a path of decisive and uncompromising struggle against imperialism."[22]

The rise of the trend of extremism was a result of certain factors. which may be put as under:

1. The 'Tory Misrule' gave a rude setback to the faith of the Indian leaders in the British sense of justice and fairplay. The English government did not abandon its reactionary policies towards higher education and recruitment of the Indians in the highest public services of the country, running of local self-governing institution and liberalising the law and order machinery that was a potential check on the rise and growth of the national movement. The prosecution of Tilak and the detention of the Natu Brothers were clear examples of the repressive policy. The most conspicuous examples of the arbitrary and reactionary character of the British rule occurred during the period of Lord Curzon (1898-1905) when Official Secrets Act, Indian Universities Act and Calcutta Corporation Act were put into effect. The most notorious case was furnished by the partition of Bengal into Muslim-dominated eastern and Hindu-dominated western parts in the name of administrative convenience and efficiency.

2. The religious revivalism imparted a great impetus to the feelings of extremism. Bankim's Vande Matram' became the source of inspiration for fiery patriotism. The messages of great leaders like Swami Vivekanand inspired hopes and enthusiasm in India's genius. The Indian people thought in terms of giving a befitting reply to the claim of racial superiority as made by the English people. The Hindu mind sought relief in religious nationalism and drew inspiration therefrom "in the thought that at least in the sphere of religion and philosophy we were second to no other people."[23]

3. The factor of economic discontent had its own part to play. The conditions of all-round depression, famine, epidemics and unemployment hit hard the Indian people particularly the middle class and poor sections of the Indian people. Owing to the pressure of population on land, land tenure also became a

---

22. *Ibid.*, p. 324.

23. Nehru: *An Autobiography,* p. 426.

costly affair. While the country was caught in a grip of economic discontent, the British people were leading a life of affluence and imperial durbars were held like gigantic pompous exercises. The writings of great figures like Dadabhai Naoroji and Romesh Chander Dutt played a revolutionary part in creating economic thought in India. It made the people aware of the real causes of Indian poverty and economic degradation. These writers "contended that India's village industries, spinning and weaving, had been extinguished because of unprotected competition with industrial England, that the peasants were thus left dependent entirely on land cultivation and that the over-assessment of land revenue and its rigid exaction prevented the peasants from saving any reserves to meet failure of harvest."[24]

4. Some foreign events like those of defeat of the Italians at the hands of the Abyssinians in 1896 and of the Russians at the hands of the Japanese in 1904 gave a great stimulus. These events shattered the myth of the superiority of the white races of Europe over the black races of Asia and Africa and thus imparted a militant and aggressive outlook to the nationalism of these peoples. Thus, these two great foreign events 'thrilled the entire Orient with a new hope and ambition', it proved 'a tonic to the Oriental pride' and the "most potent source of stimulus to Indian nationalism, following as it did the seven years of smarting under Lord Curzon's regime."[25]

The rise of the extremist movement had its first noticeable manifestation at the twenty-first Congress held at Kashi in 1905 under the presidentship of Gokhale. The extremists came out with a demand for swadeshi and boycott. It was a big challenge to the hold of the moderates. What the extremist leaders like Tilak, B.C. Pal and Lajpat Rai failed to have at this session, they got it at the twenty-second session of the Congress held at Calcutta under the presidentship of Naoroji when resolutions on Swaraj, Swadeshi, Boycott, and National Education were passed. The extremist leaders frankly condemned the moderates for their denationalisation programmes contained in their adherence to the course of 'Western reformism.' For this, they offered the courses of swadeshi and boycott.

---

24. Agrov, *op. cit.*, p. 97.

25. F.B. Fisher: *India's Silent Revolution*, p. 27.

For some time, the trend of moderatism lingered on. It, however, had its days. What gave weight and dominance to this trend was the British support that came to it in an indirect way. The repressive policy of the British government entailed detention of several extremist leaders like B.C. Pal and Aurobindo Ghose and deportation of others like Tilak and Lala Lajpat Rai. It indirectly strengthened the position of the moderates for the time being. On account of the death of great moderate leaders like Pherozeshah Mehta and Gokhale in 1915 and the release of other extremist leaders like Pal and Tilak, the trend of extremism emerged once again though in a considerably modified and liberalised form. With Bipin Chandra Pal and Aurobindo Ghose having retraced their extremist steps and Lala Lajpat Rai living in the United States, Tilak alone failed to revive the trend in a manner he had left it some seven years ago. The efforts of Mrs. Annie Besant succeeded in bringing unity in the Congress with the result that at the Lucknow Congress of 1916 the two wings of the Congress became one and the prophecy of Tilak made in 1907 proved true: "The Extremists of today will be Moderates of tomorrow, just as the Moderates of today were the Extremists of yesterday."

No doubt, the extremist trend changed the course of Indian nationalist movement. It signified the emergence of the middle class and thus broadened the base of the anti-colonial nationalism. It definitely gave a setback to the philosophy of moderatism that had faith in British sense of justice and fairplay and in the achievement of self-rule within the British empire. It created a different sort of political consciousness that, as Lala Lajpat Rai said, "could not have been created by the moderates in half a century."[26] However, it had its weaknesses. It was not wholly free from the bond of social reaction. The fact that the extremists drew inspiration from religious revivalism and antiquated creeds had its own adverse effect on the progress of the movement. Nehru says: "Socially speaking, the revival of Indian nationalism in 1907 was definitely reactionary."[27] It is, likewise, said that this trend 'not only inevitably weakened the advance of the political consciousness and clarity of the movement (nearly all the best-known leaders of the extremism

---

26. See Argov, *op. cit.*, pp.155-56

27. Nehru, *op. cit.*, p. 24.

moved later in varying degrees of co-operation with imperialism, or to speculative abstraction from politics, and found themselves out of sympathy with the subsequent advance of movement), but also divided the advancing forces. The programme of social reaction alienated many who could have been ready to accept the reactionary and metaphysical rubbish which was being offered as a substitute for left-wing movement."[28]

Revolutionary and Aggressive Nationalism: This trend should be described as an extension of the extremist trend that came into being on account of the increasingly repressive and reactionary policy of the alien administration. The exit, rather the termination, of the extremists from the Congress owing to the obdurate approach of the moderates coupled with the policy of repression exercised by the alien administration forced a zealous section of the patriots to take to the course of terrorism. "The disillusionment about the efficacy of the programmes and methods of the Liberals together with the study of the revolutionary movement of European nations for freedom and the methods of conspiratorial terrorism adopted by the Russian Nihilists as well as other European underground groups, influenced a section of the Indians to build up and operate like organisations and adopt like methods in India. The political measures of the government during Curzon's rule and subsequent repression directed against the nationalist movement, which drove even the Liberals to support the militant Boycott Movement, exasperated this section into adopting the methods of political terrorism."[29]

The terrorists had three main objectives--political assassinations generally of unpopular English officials to strike terror in the ranks of the white bureaucracy with a hope to create an atmosphere favourable for the rise of an armed insurrection, organising armed dacoities with a view to secure money from a foreign government as well as from wealthy sections having a pro-British attitude for the prosecution of an armed struggle against foreign rule, and fomenting mutinies in the ranks of the armed forces. The terrorists thus hatched plans and tried to prosecute them with the fiery zeal

28. R.P. Dutt, *op. cit.*, p. 328.

29. A.R. Desai: *Social Background of Indian Nationalism*, p. 339.

of revolutionary patriots. Not only that, they issued papers extolling the activities of political assassinations and organised dacoities, what they called 'actions', to overthrow the oppressive alien rule.[30] The most important thing about the movement was that it had its prominent development in the areas of Bengal, Maharashtra and Punjab and, in addition to that, it had its flow abroad in which London, San Francisco and Berlin became the well-known centres. A section of the terrorist leaders also sought to requisition German help for smuggling a revolution in the country. Thus, the terrorists were said to have taken to the cult of the pistol and the bomb.

First, we take up the case of this movement in India. It had its most conspicous manifestation in Bengal where Aurobindo Ghose, Barindra Ghose and Bhupendranath Datta were associated with this militant movement. Three papers 'Yugantar', 'Nava-Sakti' and 'Sandhya' openly preached the gospel of a revolution by means of an armed insurrection. A zealous patriot Hem Chandra Das went to France to learn the art of manufacturing explosives. Anusilan Samiti was organised to train young men in the art of carrying on a revolutionary struggle with men like Babu Aswini Kumar Datta, Jatindranath Mukerji (later known as Bagha Jatinda) and Narendranath Datta (later known as M.N. Roy) that established its headquarters in leading towns and cities of Bengal. On December 6, 1907 a train in which Lt. Governor was travelling was blown up by a bomb near Midnapore. On December 23, Allan, ex-District Magistrate of Dacca, was shot in the back at a railway station in Faridpur. On April 30, 1908 an attempt was made to kill Kingsford, the judge of Muzaffarpur (ex-presidency magistrate of Calcutta) that instead resulted in the murder of Mrs. Kennedy and Miss Kennedy. On Jan 24, 1910, a Deputy Superintendent of Police was shot dead while leaving the High Court in connection with the Alipore Conspiracy Case.

In Maharashtra the movement gained momentum owing to the

---

30. Damodar Chafekar and his brother Balkrishan Chafekar formed a Society for the Protection of Hindu Religion in 1894 and on June 22, 1897, they murdered Rand and Ayerst. This "is regarded as the first example of terrorist violence in Indian politics, although it is the view of some historians that the activities of Vasudev Balvant Phadke in 1876 should be regarded as the first instance of political violence." See Varma, *op. cit.*, p. 328.

patronage of Tilak and the association of the Savarkar brothers. In his paper 'Kesari', Tialk extolled the Russian methods of agitation. At Nasik a revolutionary committee called 'Abhinav Bharat' was set up to work on the lines of the Russian Nihilists. On 21 Dec. 1909 Jackson, the District Magistrate of Nasik, was shot dead, for he had given a sentence of transportation for life to Ganesh Savarkar. An unsuccessful attempt was made on the life of Lord Minto and Lady Minto in Nov., 1909 when they were driving in a carriage in Ahmedabad. This trend had its manifestation in Punjab also where the people under the leadership of Lala Lajpat Rai protested against the Punjab Colonisation Bill that aimed at discouraging further fragmentation of land in the Chenab Colony by introducing the provision of primogeniture. The people resented as it interfered with the traditional rights of succession. After the deportation of Lala Lajpat Rai, the work was carried on by a group of Arya Samajists like Lala Amir Chand and Lala Har Dayal. An abortive attempt was made to kill Viceroy Hardinge in Delhi in 1912.[31]

The Naujawan Hindustan Sabha founded in 1925 with Bhagat Singh as its Secretary became the most important organisation of Punjab. It changed its name to become Hindustan Republican Association or Army (HRA) and then Hindustan Socialist Republican Association. The arch-leader (Bhagat Singh) thus justified the 'philosophy of the bomb': "Terrorism is a phase, a necessary inevitable phase in the revolution is not complete without terrorism. This thesis can be supported by an analysis of any and every revolution in history. Terrorism shatters the spell of superiority of the ruling class and raises the status of the subject race in the eyes of the world, because it is the most convincing proof of a nation's hunger for freedom. Here in India, as in other countries in the past, terrorism will develop into revolution and the revolution into independence-social, economic, political."[32]

The terrorist movement spread abroad also and had its two important centres—at London in the United Kingdom and at San Francisco in the United States. Shyamji Krishna Verma set up the Indian Home Rule Society at London in 1905 and then at Indi

31. The Hardinge Bomb Case occurred on 23 December, 1912. Bha Balmukand, Lala Amir Chand, Awadh Behari and Basant Kuma Biswas were caught and hanged in May, 1915.

32. Gopal Thakur: *Bhagat Singh*, p. 41.

House and High Gate soon after. One of the associates of this Society, Madan Lal Dhingra, assassinated William Curzon Wyllie, Political A.D.C. at the India office, at the Imperial Institute of London, on July 1, 1909. He explained his aim in these words: "Terrorise the officials, English and Indian, and the collapse of the whole machinery is not very far."[33] The movement had, however, its most significant expression in the United States. It began with the organisation of the Ghadar Party by Lala Har Dayal at San Francisco in California in 1913.[34] This organisation ran two important papers, one in Punjabi and the other in English, titled *Hindustan Ghadar* to advocate the cause of organising Indian people in a rebellion against the foreign government. Through this paper a persistent and relentless campaign was launched to attain the desired goal. The party produced rugged, selfless and faithful disciples who spearheaded revolt against British authorities.

The formation of the Ghadar Party with its mouthpiece in the *Hindustan Ghadar* was a result of the successful efforts made by Lala Har Dayal in an atmosphere already created by leading Indians in America like Taraknath Das, Ram Nath Puri, Sant Teja Singh and Bhai Parmanand. The party prepared a constitution highlighting its aims and objects as "to encourage the establishment and maintenance of a system of government in India which shall be free from all foreign control and which shall have as its aim the greatest good of the greatest number." Moreover, it "shall guarantee freedom of thought, speech, press, organisation and ensure the minimum necessities of life to all." The party "shall adopt in India any and all means that it approves to attain its objectives. In foreign countries, however, the activities shall be conducted within the laws of these countries." It was clearly said that the means to attain the end

---

33. W. Roy Smith: *Nationalism and Reforms in India*, pp. 63-64.

34. Har Dayal announced the existence of Ghadar Party on 1 November, 1913 with Baba Sohan Singh as its elected President and himself as its elected Secretary. The constitution of the party had 17 rules. A person could be its member if his name was recommended by one or two members of the staff of the Ashram; he could not have access to the secrets of the ashram unless he completed a term of at least 6 months; if anyone exposed these secrets or grafted money, he must be killed. E.C. Brown: *Har Dayal: Hindu Revolutionary and Rationalist*, pp. 142-43.

were to be nothing short of an armed revolt, an inspiration from the 1857 mutiny. The leaders of this movement "were firm believers in using violence and any negotiation to attain the desired goal was considered a weakness. As the bulk of its activities were to be secret, the constitution was framed in such a way as to ensure secrecy, promptness in action and control by an elite. That is why, it provided for 'inner' and 'outer' membership."

The members of the Ghadar Party thus threw themselves into the mission of fomenting rebellion in the ranks of the police and armed forces and also looked towards Germany for material assistance. Persons like Kartar Singh Sarabha, Satyendranath Sen, V.G. Pingale, Pt. Jagat Ram, Prithvi Singh and Jagat Singh successfully infiltrated into military cantonments and persuaded the army units to revolt at the appropriate time. Contacts were established with Brincken, Bopp and Pappen of the German Embassy in the United States for collecting material assistance. Tons of propaganda literature were sent to India and efforts were made to collect arms and ammunition for smuggling them into the Indian territory. An elaborate plan was hatched to revolt against the British Government in India on Feb. 21, 1915 that was, however, nipped in the bud owing to the treacherous action of Kirpal Singh. Afraid of the growing trend of this movement the British Government put a heavy hand on the leaders of the movement. This movement had a natural setback when the American Government rendered its co-operation to the officers of the British Government in arresting the growth of this movement in the United States. Thus this trend of violence could not have a longer life. It "was ruthlessly suppressed. Sardar Kartar Singh Sarabha and a score of his colleagues were sent to the gallows. Many others were sentenced to life imprisonment and they spent a greater part of their lives in the Andamans and other similar jails. The movement failed because of the betrayal by some Ghadar members, the antipathy of the nationalist leaders to the violent character of the movement, and because of the lack of mass following."(J.S. Bains)

True that the terrorist movement lost its ground after the emergence of Gandhi both on account of the ruthless repression at the hands of the alien administration and its frank disavowal by the leading Indian nationalists now gathered under the leadership of the Mahatma. It had its resurgence shortly after for the same reason-increasingly repressive policy of the imperial power. The Jallianwala

Bagh tragedy of 1919 revived the same spirit. The martyrdom of Lala Lajpat Rai in 1928 on account of brutal police attack on him added fuel to fire as a result of which young leaders like Bhagat Singh, Sukhdev and Rajguru took to the path of terrorism. Thus, on December 17, 1928, J.P. Saunders, Deputy Superintendent of Police, was shot dead after he left his office near the DAV College, Lahore, to avenge the loss of Lalaji. The following day it was announced by the association of these revolutionary leaders (Hindustan Socialist Republic Association): "The murder of a leader respected by millions of the people at the unworthy hands of an ordinary police official like J.P. Saunders was an insult to the nation and it was the bounden duty of the youngmen of India to efface it... We regret we had to kill a person, but Saunders was part and parcel of that inhuman unjust order which has to be destroyed...The shedding of human blood grieves us, but there comes a time when it becomes unavoidable in the quest for freedom."

Afterwards, while justifying his action of throwing a bomb in the Central Legislative Assembly (on April 8, 1929) in the light of the philosophy of the revolutionary movement, Bhagat Singh said: "We hold human beings to be sacred beyond words and would sooner lay down our lives in the service of the humanity than injure anyone else. Unlike mercenary soldiers who are disciplined to kill without compunction, we respect human life. And still we admit having deliberately thrown bombs into the Assembly Hall. However, facts speak for themselves and intention should be judged from the result of the action without drawing conclusions based on presumptions."

The terrorist trend had its manifestation in U.P. also where the names of youngmen like Chandra Shekhar Azad were on the finger tips. Ram Prasad Bismil, Lahiri and Ashfaqullah were arrested and tried in connection with the Kakori Dacoity Case of August, 1925. Bismil, Lahiri, Ashfaquallah, Bhagat Singh, Sukhdev and Rajguru, paid with their lives and thus became martyrs showing that "the guns they had fired had more than human targets, the shots reverberated all over the world calling attention to India's plight under the Raj." (K. Sunder Rajan)

Muslim Communalism: The rise and growth of the trend of Muslim communalism should be attributed to the single-most important factor of the successful implementation of the pernicious colonial policy of 'divide and rule'. How the English rulers rejoiced at the so-called traditional communal discord and how by their policies and actions, deliberate or otherwise, they helped to inflame anti-national and anti-secular feelings is amply borne out by facts. For instance, Sir Charles Wood wrote to Elgin on March 3, 1862: "We have maintained our power by playing off one part against the other, and we must continue to do so... Do what you can, therefore, to prevent all having a common feeling."[35] As the English rulers were more afraid of the sentiments of hostility harboured by the Muslims than by the Hindus for the reason they had wrested power from them, they looked towards the Muslim community with a sense of particular concern. It could be seen in the warning that Lytton gave to Salisbury on June 23, 1877 saying that "there is no getting over the fact that the British empire of India is a Mohammedan Power; and that it entirely depends upon the policy of Her Majesty's Government whether sentiment of our Mohammedan subjects is to be an immense security or an immense danger to us."[36]

Thus, in the first instance, the British rulers sought to patronise the Hindu community for the sake of making a successful implementation their mischievous policy of divide and rule; they looked towards the Muslims after they failed in the desired direction. The launching of political agitation by Surendranath Banerjea through his Indian Association and progress in the direction of making the Indian National Congress "created a flutter in the official dovecotes."[37] Lord Reay, while forwarding a memorial from the Anjuman-e-Islami to Dufferin, remarked that "the Mohammedans are undoubtedly handicapped in their competition with the Hindus; and I am anxious to see what can be done for them, though any increase of number of applicants for Government offices is not pleasant to contemplate." Sir Rivers Thompson, Lt. Governor of Bengal, welcomed the change in the policy of the Government extending a helping hand to the Mohammedans in securing appointments."[38]

The formation of the Indian National Congress, though accomplished with the blessings of the enlightened and far-sighted Englishmen, forced the rulers to think in terms of keeping the

---

35. Tara Chand, *op. cit.*, p. 514.

36. *Ibid.*, p. 515.

37. *Ibid.*

38. *Ibid.*

nationalist organisation weak both by securing the co-operation of, what they called, 'sane and constructive nationalists' and by creating another agency to act as a counterblast to it in case it (Congress) took to a different line. The Mohammedan Anglo-Oriental College established at Aligarh with English Principals like Theodore Beck, Morrison and Archbold thus played the game of keeping the Muslims away from the mainstream and instead inculcating in them the feelings of separatism through the provision of their education. Sir W.H. Gregory, while appreciating the Resolution of the Government of India on Mohammedan Education, wrote to Dufferin on February 24, 1886 : "I am confident that it will bear good fruits; indeed, it seems to have done so already by the complete abstention of the Mohammedans from Brahmin and Baboo agitation. It will be a great matter to sweeten our relations with this portion of the Indian population, the bravest and at one time the most dangerous."

The changed British policy thus found in a great Indian Muslim like Syed Ahmed Khan a good instrument to discourage leading co-religionists who looked towards the Congress as a nationalist organisation. It was on account of the good offices of Archbold that a deputation of the Muslims under His Highness Sir Agha Khan had a meeting with Viceroy Minto at Simla on October 1, 1906 that soon led to the formation of the Muslim League with the Nawab of Dacca, Salimullah Khan, as its founder-president on 30 Dec. 1906 with three principal aims and objects-" (a) infusing the sense of loyalty in the heart of Indian Mussalmans for British Government and removing any misunderstanding that might creep in the community regarding any measure of Government, (b) safeguarding the political rights and welfare of the Indian Mussalmans and presenting their demands and requirements in a respectful manner before the Government, and (c) without prejudice to the aforesaid objects of the League, preventing the growth among Indian Mohammedans of ideas prejudicial to other communities of the country."[39]

The formation of the League with obvious blessings and as a result of the concerted efforts of the shrewd English rulers showed that they had now sharpened their policy of 'divide and rule' with their strategy of conciliation and counterpoise of the natives against the natives. It had its first dividend in the Morley-Minto Reforms of

---

39. Lal Bahadur: *Struggle for Pakistan*, p. 75.

1909 that introduced the system of communal electorates. Thus, at the Lahore session of 1909, the Congress expressed its resentment at the Act of 1909 in the name of 'excessive representation given to the Muslims' and "the unjust, invidious and humiliating distinction made between Muslim subjects...in the matter of electorates, the franchise and the qualifications of the candidates." A great moderate leader like Surendranath Banerjea pointed out that the white bureaucracy had taken its revenge upon us for the part we have played in these concessions."[40]

Though the Muslim League at its third session held at Delhi on Jan. 29, 1910 welcomed the Reforms of 1909, circumstances, like unblushing brutality with which Russia was treating Persia, the apparently unprovoked assault of Italy upon the Turkish position in Tripoli, and the disappointment of the Indian Muslims over delay in the establishment of Muslim University "drove the Muslim leaders to the side of the Congress and a consciousness dawned on them for the cultivation of a speedy friendliness with it."[41] Thus, there occurred a noticeable change in the aims of the Muslim League. At a meeting of its Council held at Lucknow on December 31, 1912, it was resolved that, apart from its aims and objectives already announced, it would demand a system of self-government suitable to India by bringing about through constitutional means a steady reform of the existing system of administration by promoting national unity and fostering public spirit among the people of India; and by co-operating with other communities for the said purpose."[42] It made the way clear for the Congress-League Concordat concluded at Lucknow in 1916 that came as an impressive demonstration of the willingness on the part of the Hindus and the Muslims to sink their differences for a common end-attainment of self-government."[43]

However, what brought the League closer to the Congress was the Khilafat agitation started in 1919. This movement, arose on account of the Treaty of Sevres signed between the Allied Powers, including Britain, and Turkey whereby Ottoman Empire was to be dismembered and many holy places of the Muslims, hitherto under

40. See Annie Besant: *How India Wrought for Freedom*, p. 495

41. Lal Bahadur, *op. cit.*, p. 74.

42. *Ibid.*, p.75.

43. See H.C.E. Zacharias: *Renascent India*, p. 188.

the protection of the Caliph (Khalifa), were to be taken over by the 'infidels'. It infuriated the Muslims, since the Khilafat (Caliphate) was humiliated and the holy lands were placed under the occupation of the 'infidels'. Thus, the aim of movement was the restoration of the temporal as well as spiritual jurisdiction of the Sultan of Turkey, the Caliph of Islam. Mahatma Gandhi, who had now taken reins of the Congress leadership, decided to make the Khilafat grievances an all-India issue that naturally brought the two communities together in as much as it, as Gandhiji said, "provided such an opportunity of uniting the Hindus and the Muhammedans as would not arise in a hundred years."[44] It helped in channelising the wave of Hindu-Muslim unity in his non-violent non-co-operation movement of 1920-22 that showed how the policy of conciliation and counterpoise of the natives against the natives, as so assiduously pursued by the British rulers, was defeated.

The unity in the ranks of the Hindus and the Muslims became a source of acute concern to the British who could discover its setback in the Moplah riots of 1921 in the Malabar region of extreme south India the reason of which was mischievously ascribed to the 'failure' of Gandhiji's non-co-operation movement. The role of the callous and shrewd white bureaucracy could be discovered behind this communal holocaust that, within a period of some next five years, took about 450 lives. Henceforth, the attitude of the League became not only hard and uncompromising but deliberately hostile to what the Congress demanded. As such, in 1928 it welcomed the appointment of the Simon Commission and rejected the Nehru Report that had been prepared as a result of the agreement at the all-parties conference. At the Delhi session of the League held in 1929, M.A. Jinnah presented his 14-Points. Thus, the League debated the issue of Indian constitutionalism at the London Round Table Conferences of 1930, 1931 and 1932 on the basis of the Jinnah Plan and thereafter did much in opposition to the Congress in matters of reacting to the Act of 1935 and in the formation of provincial ministries in 1937.

What gave a measure of radical transformation to the trend of Muslim communalism was the leadership of Jinnah. After leaving the Congress in 1920 in retaliation to what he called the adulation

---

44. Cited in R. Coupland: *The Constitutional Problem in India*, Part I, p. 73.

of Gandhi in the form of his 'Mahatmahood', he assumed the leadership of the League after some time and his 14-Points became the sheet-anchor of its policy. However, what gave a terrible astonishment was his 'theory of two nations' that he enunciated at the session of the League held at Lahore in March, 1940. In his presidential address delivered at the 27th session of the League, he said: "The problem in India is not of an inter-communal character, but manifestly of an inter-national one, and it must be treated as such...It is extremely difficult to appreciate why our Hindu friends fail to understand the real nature of Islam and Hinduism. They are not religions in the strict sense of the word, but are, in fact, different and distinct social orders, and it is only a dream that Hindus and Muslims can ever evolve a common nationality." Herein was given a clear-cut demand for Pakistan when he said : "To yoke together two such nations under a single state, one as a numerical minority and the other as a majority, must lead to growing discontent and final destruction of any fabric that may be so built up for the government of such a state."

Henceforth, the principal aim of the League became the achievement of a separate and sovereign Muslim state of Pakistan. Thus, the idea that was faintly mooted by poet Iqbal at the Allahabad session of the League in 1930[45] and thereafter advanced by some Muslim students of the Cambridge University, that was labelled as "students' dream" and also as 'chimerical and impracticable', became an instrument of struggle into the hands of the League.[46] It well

45. For instance, in his presidential address at the annual session of the Muslim League held at Allahabad on December 29, 1930, Iqbal said: "I would like to see the Punjab, the North-West Frontier Province, Sind and Baluchistan, amalgamated into a single state. Self-government within the British Empire or without the British Empire, the formation of a consolidated North-West Indian Muslim State appears to me to be the final destiny of the Muslims, at least of North-West India."

46. Chaudhry Rahmat Ali in a pamphlet titled 'Now or Never' is credited with having coined the word 'Pakistan' as an acronym created from the names of the territories proposed to be included in it-P for Punjab, A for Afghani Suba (NWFP), K for Kashmir, I for Iran, S for Sind, T for Tukharistan, A for Afghanistan, and N for Baluchistan. See K.B. Sayeed: *Pakistan : The Formative Phase*, p. 104.

signified that the demand for an 'Ulster' in the country was transformed into the struggle for a separate and sovereign state consisting of the Muslim-majority provinces of India. The obduracy of the League in this regard went on increasing owing to the clandestine support of the British bureaucracy and the appeasement policy of the Congress leaders. The League thus rejected the Cripps Scheme of 1942, the Rajaji Formula of 1944, and the Cabinet Mission Plan of 1946, since all had set aside the case of Pakistan as desired by it. Instead, it took to the strategy of 'direct action' in 1946 as a result of which communal massacres took place in different parts of the country that created conditions for the realist leaders of the Congress to accept the Mountbatten Plan of June 1947. The final result was the success of the trend of sectarianism, separatism and anti-nationalism leaving Gandhi grumbling that it all occurred owing to the part of the "third power"—the role of the English power that the Muslims and the Hindus were to be kept apart in order to maintain the domination of India.

It may, therefore, be understood without any difficulty that the rise and growth of Muslim communalism in India, that ultimately resulted in the unfortunate event of the vivisection of the country, was a special product of the British rule and, in particular, of the latest period of the British rule, or of the declining imperialist ascendancy. It was all on account of that policy about which Sir John Strachey in his work 'India of 1888' said: "The truth plainly is that the existence side by side of these hostile creeds is one of the strong points in our political position in India." Though he presented a slightly modified version of this statement in the next edition of his work in 1894, he still adhered to this point: "The better classes of Mohammedans are a source of strength to us and not of weakness. They constitute a comparatively small but energetic minority of the population, whose political interests are identical with ours and who under no conceivable circumstances, would prefer Hindu domination to our own." However, what added weight to the success of this policy was the role of the vested interests belonging to both the Hindu and Muslim communities that "looked towards the prospects of their material benefits in a situation of communal strife."[47]

---

47. Desai, *op. cit.*, p. 407.

Trials of Freedom Fighters

The British rulers arrested and prosecuted some leading figures of our country ranging from the last Mughal Emperor (Bahadur Shah Zafar) and great political leaders to the officers of the Indian National Army. A brief study of the trials of such freedom fighters has its own place in the history of our freedom struggle which shows the patriotic boldness of the Indian leaders on the one side and the Machiavellian methods of the alien masters on the other. The names of Surendranath Banerjea, Tilak, Sri Aurobindo and Gandhiji deserve their place in this regard. A number of communist leaders were implicated in the Meerut Conspiracy Case which was the example of a false prosecution and so it shatters the myth that the British rulers had a sense of justice and fairplay.

Trial of Bahadur Shah Zafar: The great uprising broke out on 10 May and had its final suppression by the end of September, 1857. At that time, Bahadur Shah Zafar was the Mughal Emperor. He was a pensioner of the East India Company who allowed shelter in the Red Fort for the people who had escaped from the Meerut jail. His eldest son Mirza Mughal caused massacre of the English people in the city of Delhi. Zafar was arrested by Lt. Gen. William Hodson. For some time he was put as a prisoner in the Holkar Fort at Mandu and then brought back to Delhi. Sir John Lawrence, the Chief Commissioner of Punjab, instructed Maj. Gen. Penny to appoint a Military Commission for the trial of the deposed Emperor. He was charged with the act of encouraging, aiding and abetting Mirza Mughal, Subedar Bakht Khan and a number of other persons to rebel and wage war against the state so as to overthrow and destroy the British government in India. The revolt caused the murder of 49 persons of the European descent.

The trial opened in the Red Fort on 27th January, 1858. Bahadur Shah pleaded that he was not guilty. Whatever was done by the people during the days of the revolt was a result of their own act as he had not issued any order or firman for such a cause. But his plea was not accepted by the military court. On 29th March, 1858 the Court delivered its verdict holding him guilty of all the charges and awarding him life imprisonment with exile to Rangoon. This was the first trial by the Britishers, which established British supremacy in our country. It marked the end of the Mughal rule in India.

Trial of Surendranath Banerjea: Also known as the 'Indian Gladstone' and 'a silver-tongued orator of India', Banerjea was the editor of an English newspaper (*Bengalee*) in which he published an article on 28th April 1883. It was based on a report published in *Brahmo Public Opinion* stating that one of the judges of the Calcutta High Court (Norris) had ordered a Hindu litigant to bring his household deity (Saligram) for identification in the court. In his article Banerjea criticised the action of the English judge. So he was given the notice of contempt of court and awarded a sentence of two months. It was a case of court's over-acting. The European judges of the Calcutta High Court paid no heed to the sentiments of the Hindus that their deities could not be brought to the court for identification. Since Banerjea was associated with a political party (Indian Association), the verdict of the court came to have a political significance. What happened to Tilak and Gandhi afterwards has its genesis here.

Trial of Tilak: Tilak was a fiery writer and speaker. He was the editor of a daily paper (*Kesari*) in Marathi and of a weekly paper (*Maratha*) in English. He published some articles in his papers which were taken as 'seditious' by the British government under the Indian Press Act of 1908. His two articles under the caption 'The Country's Misfortune' and 'These Remedies are not Enough' constituted the material on the basis of which a charge was framed that he brought or attempted to bring into hatred or contempt or excited or attempted to excite feelings of disaffection towards the government established by law in India. He was awarded a sentence of six years by the Bombay High Court and then taken to the Mandalay jail in Burma. This conviction shocked the lovers of liberty of thought and expression and carved out a place of its own in the annals of the freedom of the press in our country.

Trial of Sri Aurobindo: The partition of Bengal in October, 1905 created a very hot atmosphere in the country. The wave of extremism had its manifestation in the form of swadeshi and boycott movement. The zealous nationalists took to the course of terrorism. A number of people were arrested in the Alipore Bomb Case (1908) and were charged with wrecking a train by a bomb in which the Lt-Governor was travelling. It was an act of waging war against His Majesty the King-Emperor of India. In this case Aurobindo was awarded a sentence of two years and then put in the Alipore jail. C.R. Das defended his case in the court and went to the extent of calling him 'the prophet of Indian nationalism'. In the jail he had the vision of Lord Krishna. So he became a saint. He changed the way of his life and established an ashram at Pondicherry.

Trial of Mahatma Gandhi: Gandhiji was tried and convicted in March 1922 for writing four inflammatory articles against the British rule. These were published in *Young India* and captioned as 'Disaffection... A Virtue', 'Tampering with Loyalty', 'A Puzzle and Its Solution' and 'Shaking the Manes'. He was charged with creating a peaceful rebellion in the country by inciting the people not to remain loyal to the Satanic British Raj. Gandhiji offered no defence, he engaged no lawyer to plead his case, and he happily accepted the verdict of the court that awarded him the sentence of four years. The Hon'ble Chief Justice of the Gujarat High Court (J.M. Shelat) later commented: "Barring the trial of Socrates, there is perhaps no trial in the history of mankind comparable to that of Gandhiji which stimulated so much interest and whose influence on the life of humanity has been so profound."

Meerut Conspiracy Case: In 1929, a number of communist leaders were charged with hatching a conspiracy to overthrow the rule of His Majesty the King-Emperor of India by insurrectionary means. It included prominent leaders like S.A. Dange, Muzaffar Ahmed, P.C. Joshi, M.N. Roy etc. The trial ran for about four years and some of the accused persons were convicted. It is a very notorious case in view of the fact that the court acted on the basis of false evidence. Gandhiji took note of it and he constituted a panel of lawyers to plead the case of the detained people in the court.

INA Trial: Three captains of the Indian National Army (Shah Nawaz Khan, P.K. Sehgal and G.S. Dhillon) were arrested in 1945 and charged with the act of treason. They were accused of committing acts of murder and joining the Indian National Army of Subhash Chandra Bose who had formed the Provisional Government of Free India in Singapore in 1943. Bhulabhai Desai defended their case before a military court in the Red Fort of Delhi on the ground that service to the motherland could never be an act of treason. The trial ended in March 1946. In view of the prevailing conditions in the country all the three accused persons were acquitted, but their arrears of pay and allowances were cashiered. It created a new awareness towards independence throughout the country. On its significance, a learned jurist M.C Setalvad commented: "This trial has perhaps been the most notable trial in the history of British

India; indeed, in some respects it may rank as one of the most notable trials in history. It had a double aspect. It was the occasion of a debate of far-reaching and, in some respects, altogether novel propositions of International Law, a subject of lasting interest of lawyers and those interested in law. To the ordinary citizen it was the fascinating and inspiring story of a heroic effort the most famous in Indian history-of a great India patriot, supported by thousands of his countrymen to liberate their country."

The story of such trials hovers between the trials of Bahadur Shah Zafar and of the INA officers held in the Red Fort of Delhi. The former signified the end of the Mughal empire, the latter entailed the termination of the British rule. The trials of Banerjea, Tilak and Gandhi have their place in the history of the freedom of the press in our country. The Meerut Conspiracy Case revealed the fact that the foreign rulers could go to such an extent in suppressing a leftist movement with the use of false and concocted evidence. The trial of Bahadur Shah confirmed the dictum of Thrasymachus that 'justice is the interest of the stronger', the trial of the INA officers revealed the fact that the British had the sense of statesmanship.[48]

---

48. B.R. Agarwala: *Trials of Independence*, p. 170.

7

Constitution-Making

Modern state is a nation-state. As such, it has the attributes of nationalism, sovereignty and secularism. It has its own Constitution that is known by various names as 'organic law', 'basic law', 'fundamental law of the land' and the like. It is also labelled as the 'cornerstone of a nation'. Hence, to the students of contemporary Indian history, politics and constitutional law, the most important event of the past century is the framing of our Fundamental Law by a grand assembly that worked for a period of about three years for this purpose. It was by all means the most stupendous task before our founding fathers who, after a lot of political wrangling, managed to start their monumental work on 9th December, 1946 in the midst of many gigantic constraints and difficulties and completed it on 26th November, 1949.

Making of the Constitution

A historical survey of our freedom struggle bears testimony to the fact that a move that India's political destiny should be determined by the Indians themselves had been put forward by Mahatma Gandhi as early as in 1922. The demand for the setting up of a Constituent Assembly in very clear terms, however, assumed a shape of its own after the failure of the Indian Statutory (Simon) Commission (1928–29) and the three Round Table Conferences held at London (1930, 1931, 1932) that led Jawaharlal Nehru to say in early 1934: "Politically and nationally, if it is granted, as it must be that the people of India are to be the sole arbiters of India's fate and must, therefore, have full freedom to draw up their Constitution, it follows that this can be done by means of a Constituent Assembly elected on the widest franchise. Those who believe in independence have no other choice."

However, the way for the creation of the grand Con'sembly was cleared by the recommendations of the Cabinet Mission Plan released on 16 May, 1946, that provided:

1. Each Province and each Indian State or a group of States were to have a total number of seats proportional to their respective population roughly in the ratio of one to a million. As a result, the then Provinces were to elect 292 members, while the Princely States were allotted a maximum of 93 seats.

2. Seats in each Province were distributed among three main communities—Muslims, Sikhs and General—in proportion to their respective population.

3. The members of each community in the Provincial Legislative Assemblies were to elect their own representatives by the method of proportional representation with single transferable vote.

4. The method of selection in the case of the representatives of the Princely States was to be determined by consultation.

Thus, the Con'sembly had 292 members elected by the Legislative Assemblies of the then 11 British Indian Provinces: 93 members were nominated by the rulers of Princely States; while 4 members represented the Chief Commissioners' Provinces of Delhi, Coorg, Ajmer-Merwara, and Andaman and Nicobar Islands.

As a result of the partition according to the Mountbatten Plan of 3rd June, 1947, a separate Constituent Assembly was set up for Pakistan. The representatives of East Bengal, West Punjab, Sind and Baluchistan, North-West Frontier Province and the Sylhet District of Assam, which joined Pakistan, ceased to be the members of the Con'sembly after the advent of independence. Fresh elections were held for the vacant seats in the new Provinces of East Punjab and West Bengal. Consequently, when the Con'sembly reassembled on 31st October, 1947, its membership was reduced to 299 of which 284 appended their signatures to the Constitution as finally adopted on 26th November, 1949. On 29th August, 1947 it set up the Drafting Committee under the chairmanship of Dr. B.R. Ambedkar. It embodied the decisions of the Assembly with alternative and additional proposals in the form of the Draft Constitution of India that was published in February, 1948.

The Con'sembly next met in November, 1948 to consider the provisions of the Draft Constitution clause by clause. The whole work was over on 17th October, 1949 and the coping stone was placed on 26th November, 1949 when the Preamble was adopted to complete the structure of the edifice of the Basic Law of the land. The President of the Con'sembly (Dr. Rajendra Prasad) placed his signatures and declared it as finally passed. The Con'sembly had its 11 sessions. It worked for 2 years, 11 months and 18 days. As many as 7,635 amendments were proposed and 2,473 were actually taken up for discussion. The making of the Constitution incurred an expenditure of about 64 lakhs of rupees. An American writer comments that with the adoption of this Constitution, India "became the largest democracy in the world. By this act of strength and will, Assembly members began what was perhaps the greatest political venture since that originated in Philadelphia in 1787."[1]

Some of the provisions of this Constitution (as those relating to citizenship, election, provisional Parliament, temporary and transitional measures) were given immediate effect. But the rest of the provisions came into effect on 26th January, 1950 to perpetuate the memory of the First Complete Independence Day observed in 1930. No doubt, the grand Con'sembly did an immortal work by giving to us a Constitution in the form of as good and as workable a document that could have been made and that too as much democratically as possible under the prevailing conditions. It is nothing like 'imposed'; it is everything like 'adopted, enacted, and given to ourselves' by 'We. the People of India' for 'We, the People of India'. It is well observed: "It is as much democratically made as circumstances permitted."[2]

Philosophy of the Constitution

Every Constitution is based on certain definite principles of social, political and economic relevance which constitute its philosophy that may also be termed as its 'ideology'. For this, we must, first of all, look into the contents of the Objectives Resolution moved by Nehru on 13 December, 1946 and adopted by the Con'sembly on 22nd January, 1947. It said:

"This Constituent Assembly declares its final and firm resolve to proclaim India as Independent Sovereign Republic and to draw up for her future governance a Constitution;

---

1. Cranville Austin: *The Indian Constitution: Cornerstone of a Nation*, p. 308.
2. K.V. Rao: *Parliamentary Democracy of India*, p. 26.

Main Sessions and Activities of the Constituent Assembly

Sessions	Duration	Activities
First	9 to 23 Dec. 1946	Introduction of the Objectives Resolution by Nehru and discussion over it.
Second	20 to 25 Jan. 1947	Adoption of the Objectives Resolution.
Third	22 April to 2 May 1947	Setting up of Union Constitution Committee under the chairmanship of Nehru and the Provincial Constitution Committee under the chairmanship of Patel.
Fourth	14 to 31 July, 1947	(*i*) Presentation of the report of the Union Constitution Committee by Nehru recommen- ding the pattern of a weak centre as recommended in the Cabinet Mission Plan. (*ii*) Presentation of the reports of the Com- mittees on Minorities, Fundamental Rights, and Tribal and Excluded Areas. (*iii*) Commencement of general discussion on these reports. (*iv*) Adoption of the National Flag on 22 July. (*v*) Setting up of Committees on Chief Commissioners Pro- vinces and Expert Committee on Financial Relations.

Fifth	14 Aug. 1947 to 21 Feb. 1948.	(*i*) Appointment of Mountbatten as the Governor-General of free India and of Nehru as the Prime Minister. (*ii*) Constituent Assembly became the supreme legislature of the country. (*iii*) Discussion over the revised report of the Union Powers Committee recommending strong Centre as now the Assembly became a sovereign body. (*iv*) Discussion over reports of Advisory Committee on Minorities and on Fundamental Rights.
Sixth to Tenth	4 Nov. 1948 to 26 Nov. 1949	(*v*) Setting up of the Drafting Committee on 29 Aug. under the chairmanship of B.R. Ambedkar with 6 members. (*vi*) Submission of the Draft Constitution, general discussion on draft provisions and adoption of the Constitution.
Eleventh	24 to 26 Jan. 1950	(*i*) Election of Dr. Rajendra Prasad as the first President of the Republic. (*ii*) Inauguration of the Constitution.

(2) Wherein the territories that now comprise British India, the territories that now form the Indian States, and such other parts of India as are outside British India and the States as well as such other territories as are willing to be constituted into the Independent Sovereign India, shall be a Union of them all.

(3) Wherein the said territories, whether with their present boundaries or with such others as may be determined by the

Constituent Assembly and thereafter according to the law of the Constitution, shall possess and retain the status of autonomous units, together with residuary powers, and exercise all powers and functions of Government and administration, save and except such powers and functions as are vested in or assigned to the Union, or as are inherent or implied in the Union or resulting therefrom; and

(4) Wherein all powers and authority of the Sovereign Independent India, its constituent parts and organs of Government are derived from the people; and

(5) Wherein shall be guaranteed and secured to all people of India justice-social, economic and political; equality of status, of opportunity, and before the law; freedom of thought, expression, belief, faith, worship, vocation, association and action, subject to law and public morality; and

(6) Wherein adequate safeguards shall be provided for minorities, backward and tribal areas, and depressed and other backward classes; and

(7) Wherein shall be maintained the integrity of the territory of the republic and its sovereign rights on land, sea and air according to justice and the law of civilised nations; and

(8) This ancient land attain its rightful and honoured place in the world and make its full and willing contribution to the promotion of world peace and the welfare of mankind."

These glorious words inspired the shaping of the Basic Law of our land through all subsequent stages and got into the contents of the Preamble that reads:[3]

WE THE PEOPLE OF INDIA, having solemnly resolved to constitute India into a SOVEREIGN *SOCIALIST SECULAR* DEMOCRATIC REPUBLIC and to secure to all its citizens;

JUSTICE social, economic and political:

LIBERTY of thought, expression, belief, faith and worship;

EQUALITY of status and of opportunity:

---

3. The italicised portions were added vide 42nd Constitution Amendment Act of 1976.

And to promote among them all FRATERNITY assuring the dignity of the individual and the unity *and integrity* of the Nation.

IN OUR CONSTITUENT ASSEMBLY, this twenty-sixth day of November, 1949, do HEREBY ADOPT, ENACT AND GIVE TO OURSELVES THIS CONSTITUTION. The judiciously chosen words contained in the text of the Preamble and written in capital letters have a significance of their own. Their implications must be understood in a correct perspective. These are:

1. **We, the People of India:** It indicates that the architects of this great document are the people of the country themselves. It is not the gift of British Parliament as the Canadian Constitution of 1867 and the Australian Constitution of 1900, nor is it something imposed upon us by the alien conquerors the example of which may be seen in the Japanese Constitution of 1946. It embodies three cardinal points—that the ultimate sovereignty is with the people of the country; that the founding fathers are the real representatives of the people; and that it is based on the acquiescence of the people of India.

2. **Sovereign:** We are a free people under this Constitution. India does not pay final allegiance to any external power like the British Crown and no other country can impose its will upon us. India's membership of any international body like the United Nations, Commonwealth of Nations, World Trade Organisation etc, does not affect her sovereign character for the simple reason that it is all a voluntary affair.

3. **Socialist:** It means that the State has taken upon itself the responsibility for wiping off poverty, for initiating steps to increase employment, for modernizing national economy, for enforcing social purpose in all economic activities, for reducing disparities and setting right the historic inequalities between different sections and parts of the country and, in particular, for checking the growth of monopoly or concentration of national wealth into the hands of few persons. It resembles the Fabian Socialism of England and thus may be labelled as 'democratic socialism'.

4. **Secularism:** It means that the State has no religion of its own. It ensures equal respect for all religions. Discrimination among the people on the basis of religion is prohibited. It is not to be identified with atheism or irreligiousity. As Dr. Radhakrishnan says: "When

India is said to be a secular state, it does not mean that we reject the reality of an unseen spirit or the relevance of religion in life, or that we exalt irreligion. It does not mean that secularism itself becomes a positive religion or that the State assumes divine prerogatives...We hold that no one religion should be given preferential status...The view of religious impartiality or comprehension and furtherance has a prophetic role to play within national and international life."

5. **Democratic:** The Constitution establishes representative government at the Centre, in the States, and also at the local levels. It guarantees universal adult franchise and free and fair periodic elections. Power is vested in the people and it is exercised by their representatives who are accountable to them for their acts of commission and omission. It has provisions for the independence of the press and the judiciary. It all enables India to become the 'largest democracy' in the world.

6. **Republic:** A republican system is invariably democratic in view of the fact that power resides in the people and it is exercised by their chosen representatives. It also requires that the head of the State should be elected directly or indirectly for a specific period and that he must be accountable for his acts of commission and omission. Hence, the office of the head of the state should not be hereditary or non-elective. As President Narayanan observed in his message to the nation given on the eve of the Republic Day in 2000: "The word 'Republic' is no ordinary word. It is a commitment to the effect that in our State supreme power is exercised not by some remote monarch but by the people."

7. **Justice:** The essence of justice is the attainment of the common good as distinguished from the good of the individuals or even of the majority of them. It has three dimensions. Social justice desires equality among the people and, as such, it seeks eradication of those barriers and discriminations which make some people high or low. The worth and dignity of each individual should be recognized irrespective of his religion, race, caste, descent and the like. Economic justice desires equitable distribution of national wealth so as to remove the evils of poverty, unemployment, disease, starvation, squalor and the like. Political justice desires free and fair participation of the people in their public affairs. It stands for a liberal-democratic order in which people enjoy their liberties within the framework of reasonable restrictions.

8. **Liberty:** Liberty lies in the existence of healthy conditions for the development of human personality. A man without liberty is no man at all, he is like a dead weight. Our Constitution ensures liberty of thought, expression, faith, belief and worship. Part III of the Constitution has a catalogue of fundamental rights relating to equality and liberty and it is so important that Jawaharlal Nehru called it 'conscience of the Constitution'.

9. **Equality:** Liberty and equality live together, they supplement each other. Hence, our Constitution guarantees equality in respects of status and opportunity. It implies that all citizens, being equal in the eye of law are equally eligible to all public dignities, places and employment, according to their capacities and without discrimination of their religion, race, caste, descent, sex, place of birth etc.

10. **Fraternity:** Finally, the Preamble desires unity and integrity of the nation. It aims at the fulfilment of the idea of 'unity in diversity'. Irrespective of their social and cultural differences, all people should regard themselves, in the words of Nehru, as Indians first and Indians last.

It may be seen that the ideals embodied in the Objectives Resolution "are faithfully reflected in the Preamble to the Constitution."[4] Nehru termed his Objectives Resolution as "a declaration, a firm resolve, a pledge, an undertaking and for all of us a dedication." K.M. Munshi, a member of the Drafting Committee of the Con'sembly, proudly described the Preamble as 'political horoscope' and Acharya J.B. Kripalani, in a more philosophical vein, lauded it as 'mystic principles of a welfare state'.

The Preamble is certainly a very important piece of our Constitution. In the *Berubari Reference Case* (1960), the Supreme Court observed that it "is the key to open the mind of the makers and shows the general purpose for which they made the several provisions of the Constitution. It contains the ideals and the aspirations of the people of India." Repeating the remark of Prof. E. Barker, an Indian writer comments that it "is one of the best of the kind ever drafted. A glance over the Preambles of the Constitutions all over the world will show that both in ideas and ideals and in expression, ours is unrivalled. It embodies the spirit of the

---

4. D.D. Basu: *Introduction to the Constitution of India*, Ed XII of 1989, p. 20.

Constitution, the determination of the Indian people to unite themselves in a common adventure of building up a new socialist and secular nation which will ensure the triumph of justice, liberty, equality and fraternity."[5]

The making of our Constitution by the grand Con'sembly signifies the triumph of a revolution by the consent of the people of the country. The Assembly was a symbol of freedom (political) to achieve freedoms (social and economic). By all means, it was a people's body chosen by their representatives sitting in the Provincial Legislative Assemblies. Its sovereign character became a patent fact the day it framed its Rules of Procedure wherein it was laid down: "It shall not be dissolved except by a resolution assented to by at least two-thirds of the whole number of the members of the Assembly." And, yet a critic may say that the Con'sembly was not a really popular body and it was a body of prominent figures like Rajendra Prasad, Jawaharlal Nehru, Sardar Patel, Ambedkar, Munshi, Sir Alladi etc. who were men of law by their profession and so had the character of a lawyer-politician. Its provisions are unnecessarily lengthy and it provides for several areas (as citizenship, public services, elections and official language etc.) which could and should have been covered by ordinary legislation or administrative action or both. Moreover, on many important points it is either vague or so brief that it leaves much scope for litigation. Hence, Sir Ivor Jennings called it a "lawyer's paradise."

It is also said that the Indian Constitution lacks ideological clarity. It may be termed liberal as well as socialist. Prof K.T. Shah's suggestion was not appreciated by the Con'sembly that India should be declared a 'socialist state'. And though the word 'socialist' has now been incorporated into the Preamble, its implications are so loose that it may mean anything to anybody ranging from a liberal to a socialist of any hue. So is the case with secularism. A critic may say that unforeseen complications have been introduced into the Constitution by the insertion of the words 'socialist' and 'secular' into the Preamble. Whatever meaning might have been intended by the authors of the 42nd Amendment to be imputed to these two words, it is obvious that both these words are vauge. It may, however, be added that the founding fathers were great nationalists and they preferred to draw upon "a rich fund of human experience,

---

5. M.V. Pylee: *Constitutional Government in India*, p. 73.

wisdom, heritage and traditions in the area of government process in order to fashion a system suited to the political, social and economic conditions of India."[6]

Salient Features of the Constitution

The salient or basic features of this Constitution may be enumerated as under:

1. **An Enacted, Written and Partly Rigid Constitution:** It is the creation of Constituent Assembly that worked for a period of about three years. It is known as the lengthiest Constitution of the world. It has 395 articles grouped into XXII Parts followed by 12 Schedules (originally 8 Schedules). Many articles are loaded with clauses and sub-clauses which make it a quite lengthy document. Its process of amendment is partly flexible and partly rigid. While most of its provisions are amendable by the unilateral action of the Parliament, some provisions relating to federal set up can be amended by the Parliament with the concurrence of at least half of the States. Most of the provisions can be amended if a bill to this effect is passed by both the Houses of Parliament by simple majority of the members present and voting and then assented to by the President. Some important provisions (like Fundamental Rights and Directive Principles of State Policy) are amendable if a bill to this effect is passed by both the Houses of Parliament by special majority (absolute majority of the whole House coupled with two-thirds majority of the members present and voting) and then assented to by the President. However, some provisions affecting our federal set up are amendable if a bill to this effect is passed by both the Houses of Parliament by special majority and then ratified by the legislatures of at least half of the States and then assented to by the President. The procedure is really unique on account of being a mixture of flexibility and rigidity.

2. **Derivations:** The framers of the Constitution intelligently borrowed material for their purpose from diverse sources as the Nehru Report of 1928 and the Government of India Act of 1935. They preferred the British parliamentary system in view of its experiment in our country since the inauguration of the Montford

---

6. M.P. Jain: *Indian Constitutional Law*, III ed., 1978. p. 2.

Reforms in 1920. They borrowed the system of judicial review from the American Constitution. The idea of incorporating Directive Principles of State Policy was taken from the Irish Constitution. The inclusion of Concurrent List was informed by the Constitution of Australia. From the Japanese Constitution they borrowed the phrase 'procedure established by law' and commitment to the cause of international peace and security. It shows that our Constitution is like a splendid mixture of diverse institutional arrangements. It should not be debunked as 'a rag bag of borrowings'. The makers preferred to borrow material from diverse sources keeping in view the requirements of the time and their suitability to the country. Despite derivations from diverse sources, the design framed by the architects has its originality that cannot be found in any other Constitution of the world.

3. **Sovereign, Socialist, Secular, Democratic Republic:** The Constitution in its original form declared India a Sovereign Democratic Republic. But the forty-second amendment of 1976 inserted the words Socialist and Secular into the text of the Preamble. India is a sovereign country. It implies that she is not under the domination or control of any alien power. India is a socialist country. The word 'socialism' should not be taken in a rigid sense. It may be identified with a flexible variety of socialism that is called 'democratic socialism'. India is a secular country. It means that there is no state religion All religions have equal respect and discrimination cannot be made among the people on the basis of religion. No religion can interfere in the affairs of the state, but the state may control and regulate the affairs of any religion for the sake of social reform. India has a democratic set up. It means that power is vested in the people which is delegated to their chosen representatives who are accountable to their electors. The rule of law prevails in the country that makes the government limited and responsible. Finally, India is a republic. It means that the head of the state (President) is elected for a definite period and he can be removed by the process of impeachment on the charge of violation of the Constitution. He does not hold his office by the rule of hereditary succession

4. **Parliamentary Form of Government:** At the Centre as well as in the States, parliamentary model of government has been established. At the Centre, the President is the nominal head who acts on the aid and advice of the Council of Ministers, headed by the

Prime Minister, that is collectively responsible to the Lok Sabha. At the State level, the Governor is the head who acts on the aid and advice of his Council of Ministers, headed by the Chief Minister, that is collectively responsible to the Vidhan Sabha. Similar pattern prevails in a Union Territory if the Parliament by its law provides for a Legislative Assembly and a Council of Ministers there as we have in Pondicherry and Delhi.

5. **Federal System:** The Constitution establishes federal polity in the country. It is the supreme law of the land and the Central and State governments derive their powers from it. It is written. It is partly rigid as well in view of the fact that provisions relating to federal set up can be amended by the Parliament with the concurrence of at least half of the States. Powers have been distributed between the Centre and the States. The items of local importance (contained in the State List) have been assigned to the States. Both the governments are coordinate and autonomous in their allotted spheres. Items of common importance (contained in the Concurrent List) have been assigned to both with this provision that in the event of any conflict the Centre has the over-riding authority. Last, there is the Supreme Court to interpret the provisions of the Constitution and to settle any legal dispute between the Centre and the States. Its decision or interpretation is final.

6. **Judicial Review:** The Supreme Court and the High Courts have the power to examine the constitutional validity of any law, regulation, or order of the state. The aggrieved party, or any public-spirited person on its behalf, may challenge the law, regulation or order of the state. The Court examines the case and then may declare the law or regulation or order of the state constitutionally valid, or it may declare it void and therefore unenforceable to the extent it is repugnant to the provisions of the Constitution. The forty-second amendment of 1976 had a provision that an act of Constitutional amendment could not be struck down by the Courts, but the Supreme Court in the *Minerva Textile Mills Case* (1980) struck it down. In the *Waman Rao Case* (1981) the Court ruled that it could strike down a law or regulation or order of the state even though it was incorporated into the Ninth Schedule, if it altered or destroyed the basic structure of the Constitution. The Court reiterated its view in the *Ninth Schedule Case* (2007) with this clarification that it could look into the constitutional validity of an impugned law or regulation or order of the state incorporated into the Ninth Schedule

after the delivery of its verdict in the *Kesavanand Bharati Case* on 24th April, 1973.

7. **Fundamental Rights:** Part III of the Constitution has a long list of fundamental rights guaranteed to the people living in the country, while some of them are available only to the citizens of India. These rights cover the spheres of Equality, Freedom, Non-exploitation, Religion, Culture and Education, and Constitutional Remedies. Art. 14 guarantees equality before law and its equal protection. Art. 15 prohibits discrimination on the grounds of religion, race, caste, sex and place of birth. It also empowers the state to make discrimination in favour of Women, Children, Scheduled Castes, Scheduled Tribes, and other socially and educationally backward castes or classes. Art. 16 prohibits discrimination in public services. It also makes provision for adequate representation of the Scheduled Castes, Scheduled Tribes and Other Backward Castes or Classes in public services for the sake of social justice. Art. 19 guarantees essential freedoms of the citizens relating to speech and expression, peaceful assembly, formation of unions, free movement throughout the country, residence or settlement in any part of the country, and doing of any trade or vocation. Art. 20 prohibits making of *ex-post facto* laws and double jeopardy. Art. 21 secures right to life and personal liberty. Art. 22 prohibits arbitrary arrest or detention of a person. Art 23 prohibits traffic in human beings and taking of forced labour. Art 25 ensures freedom of conscience or religion. Art. 29 guarantees right to conserve and preserve distinct language, script and culture. Above all, Art 32 guarantees right to move the Courts for the protection and enforcement of these rights. This part is so important that Prime Minister Nehru called it the 'conscience of the Constitution'.

8. **Directive Principles of State Policy:** Part IV of the Constitution has a long list of principles whose aim is to establish social welfare state in the country. Art. 38 enjoins that the state shall create, as effectively as possible, a social order in which justice—social, economic and political—shall inform all institutions of national life. Hence, the state should undertake steps to create adequate means of livelihood for all, prevent concentration of wealth in the hands of few people, ensure equal pay for equal work for men and women, establish village panchayats to make them units of rural self-government, create humane conditions of work, provide

social security and improve cottage industries, implement uniform civil code throughout the country, adopt measures for the welfare of Scheduled Castes, Scheduled Tribes and other weaker sections of the society, prohibit cow slaughter, modernise system of agriculture, protect national monuments, separate judiciary from the executive and follow policy of international peace and security. These principles are not judicially enforceable, but it is expected that the state shall take them as nevertheless fundamental in the governance of the country. According to Dr. B.R. Ambedkar, these principles constitute the charter of social and economic democracy in our country.

9. **Fundamental Duties:** The forty-second amendment of 1976 has inserted Part IV A with Art. 51A that contains a long list of the fundamental duties of the citizens. It is enjoined that they should respect national flag, national anthem and abide by the provisions of the Constitution; they should cherish and follow the ideals of the leaders of the freedom movement; they should defend the motherland and protect the sovereignty, unity and integrity of the country; they should promote harmony and spirit of common brotherhood and not to do anything derogatory to the dignity of women; they should value and preserve our composite culture; they should protect and improve environmental conditions; they should safeguard public property and abjure violence; they should strive to achieve excellence in all walks of like; and the parents and the guardians should provide education to their children from 6 to 14 years of age. It is true that, like Directive Principles of State Policy, these duties do not form part of the justiciable provisions of the Constitution, yet it is expected that, as conscientious and enlightened citizens of the country, they should observe them in their daily life.

10. **Democratic Decentralisation:** In a democratic system, power should be decentralised so that people living at the lower level may manage their affairs themselves. Local people may understand their problems and they may solve them in their own way. The seventy-third amendment of 1993 makes provisions for village panchayats whose 29 functions are specified in the Eleventh Schedule. The seventy-fourth amendment of 1993 has similar provisions for the municipalities whose 18 functions are specified in the Twelfth Schedule of the Constitution. It is really appreciable

that the provisions of local self-government have constitutional sanction in our country.

Our Constitution is the cornerstone of our nation. It has been in existence since its inauguration in 1950. Unfortunately, its working has now seen the trend of deterioration. President Narayanan was right when he said: "The Constitution has not failed us, rather we have failed the Constitution." On the basis of such an observation, he gave a hint of the futility of setting up a National Constitution Review Commission in 2000. We should remember the glorious words of Ambedkar: "However good a Constitution may be, it is sure to turn out bad, because those who are called to work out it, happen to be a bad lot. However bad a Constitution may be, it may turn out to be good if those who are called to work it, happen to be a good lot."[7]

So the President of the Assembly (Rajendra Prasad) observed in his valedictory address delivered on 25th November, 1949: "Whatever the Constitution may or may not provide, the welfare of the country will depend upon the men who administer it. It is a trite saying that a country can have only the Government it deserves. Our Constitution has provisions in it which appear to some to be objectionable from one point or another. We must admit that the defects are inherent in the situation in the country and in the people at large. If the people who are elected are capable and men of character and integrity, they would be able to make the best even of a defective Constitution. If they are lacking in these, the Constitution cannot help the country. After all, a Constitution like a machine is a lifeless thing. It acquires life because of the men who control it and operate it, and India needs today nothing more than a set of honest men who will have the interest of the country before them."[8]

---

7. *Constitution Assembly Debates*, Vol, XI, p. 975.

8. *Ibid.*, p. 993.

8

Fundamental Rights and Directive Principles

A state is known by the system of rights it maintains.[1] A man without rights is like a bird shut in a cage. A slave leads the life of a deaf and dumb-driven cattle, because he has no rights at all. Rights constitute the necessary conditions in which a man may have the best possible development of his personality. Since liberty is a bundle of rights, the more are the rights, the more is the scope of liberty. F.A. von Hayek takes freedom as the absence of coercion of any sort and identifies it with the availability of options or choices. A mountain trekker may feel that he is free, virtually he is not free as he has no option before him. Thus, a line of difference may be drawn between feeling free and being free. So significant is the place of rights, collectively known as freedom or liberty, in the life of a person that the great American leader (Thomas Jefferson) says: 'Give me liberty or give me death.'

Fundamental Rights

All rights are not of equal importance. Some rights are very important as those related to life, thought and expression, employment or vocation, privacy, education, profession of faith etc. The early liberal thinkers defined most important rights of a person as 'natural rights.' To Hobbes, it is right to life; to Locke, these are related to life, liberty and property. Since these rights are available to a person just after his birth, they cannot be restricted or abolished by the state, nor can they be subjected to regulation and control in the name of anything like public interest or common good. The concept of natural rights was rejected by Bentham as 'rhetorical nonsense upon stilts.' The new awareness developed according to

---

1. Laski: *A Grammar of Politics*, p. 89.

which no right of a person is beyond social and political control. Even right to life or right to liberty and property may be regulated or restricted by the state in the public interest.

In the twentieth century the concept, rather the dogma, of natural rights, or rights having a transcendental character, lost its relevance, but the concept of 'fundamental rights' came to have its own significance. Some rights of the people are so important that they should be incorporated into the provisions of the Constitution and their amendment may be done by following a special procedure. Besides, judicial protection should also be ensured so as to prevent their violation by any person, institution, or the state. However, it depends upon the social and political philosophy of the constitution framers to make such a catalogue of rights. The Constitution of a socialist country may include right to work and social security in the category of fundamental rights, but the Constitution of a liberal-democratic country would not make such an arrangement in view of the limitations of the state. Such a constitution attaches prime importance to certain rights as equality before law and its equal protection, freedom of thought and expression, doing of any trade or occupation, professing faith in any religion or creed and the like.

Since our Constitution is a liberal document by nature, we have not followed the tradition of a socialist country like erstwhile USSR or present China where the list of fundamental rights includes rights relating to work, rest and leisure and social insurance. The original Constitution had included right to property, but it was deleted in 1978 by the forty-fourth amendment. The eighty-sixth amendment of 2003 has inserted right to free and compulsory education for children from 6 to 14 years of age. But the Supreme Court has evolved the concept of 'deemed fundamental rights'. It implies that certain rights are so important that they should be protected by the Court like fundamental rights in spite of the fact that they have no mention in Part III of the Constitution. A look at the decisions of the Court in a number of cases shows that in this category some important rights may be included as freedom of the press, right to information, right to travel abroad, right to privacy, right to have clean and healthy environment, right to fight against torture and inhuman behaviour and the like.

Our Constitution has a number of rights contained in Part III titled 'Fundamental Rights'. It is the most important part of the fundamental law of the land so much so that Prime Minister Nehru called it 'the conscience of the Constitution'. Some rights are contained elsewhere also, but they may or may not have the status of a fundamental right. For instance, right to vote is contained in Art. 326 (Part XV) of the Constitution. As such, it is not a fundamental right, but the Supreme Court has treated it like that in view of its great importance. Right to property is no longer contained in Part III, it has been shifted to part XII-A (Art. 300-A) and so it has the status of a legal right. It can be amended by the Parliament by passing a bill by its simple majority and then assented to by the President and, more than that, it cannot enjoy the protection given to fundamental rights under Articles 32 and 226 of the Constitution whereby the Supreme Court and the High Courts may respectively entertain a petition and then issue a prerogative writ for the enforcement of such a right.

An exhaustive definition of the term 'fundamental rights' with its reference to our Constitution is thus furnished by Basu: "A legal right is an interest which is protected by law and is enforceable in the courts of law. While an ordinary legal right is protected and enforced by the ordinary law of the land, a fundamental right is one which is protected and guaranteed by the written Constitution of the State. These are called 'fundamental', because while ordinary rights may be changed by the legislature in its ordinary process of legislation, a fundamental right, being guaranteed by the Constitution, cannot be altered by any process shorter than that required for amending the Constitution itself. Nor can it be suspended or abridged except in the manner laid down in the Constitution itself. On the other hand, the fundamental rights being guaranteed by the fundamental law of the land, no organ of the state—executive, legislative or judicial–can act in contravention of such rights, and any act which is repugnant to such rights must be void."[2]

Nature and Categorisation

From the above, it is clear that a fundamental right has its own significance. As such, every right cannot be taken as a fundamental right. Such a right enables a person to have the best possible

2. D.D. Basu: *Commentary on the Constitution of India*, Vol. I, pp. 126-27.

development of his personality in a way that the higher interest of the society and the state is not adversely affected. "Fundamental rights are those rights of liberty and property which are essential to the development of a man as an individual. A fundamental right does not, therefore, merely mean a right to liberty permissible under the law, it must necessarily mean a right to liberty which enables an individual to develop his faculties in his interest and in the interest of the community as a whole."[3]

A deeper study of the fundamental rights, as contained in our Constitution, informs us that they have certain characteristics of their own. First, the list of such rights may be revised by the state in the public interest. The ruling of the *Golak Nath Case* (1967) that no law of the state could effect their abridgement has been superseded by the 24th Amendment of 1971. It is due to this that while the 44th Amendment of 1978 deleted right to property, the 86th Amendment of 2002 has inserted right to free and compulsory education for children from 6 to 14 years of age as determined by a law of state. Second, some rights are available to the citizens, while some are available to all persons living in the country. For instance, right to equality before law or right to profess any religion according to conscience is available to all, but right to have a public employment or right to move and reside in any part of the country or right to do any trade or profession is available to only to the citizens. Last, by an order of the President the enforcement of fundamental rights may be suspended during emergency, but such an order cannot cover protection in respect of conviction for offences and right to life and personal liberty contained in Articles 20 and 21 of the Constitution.

Part III of the Constitution incorporating fundamental rights constitutes the Magna Carta of the Indian people. It contains a very comprehensive list of the rights that have a justiciable character in spite of the fact the State may impose 'reasonable restrictions' on certain grounds on their use and enjoyment and that their enforcement can be suspended by the President during the days of emergency excluding those relating to life and personal liberty enshrined in Articles 20 and 21. As Chief Justice S.M. Sikri in the

---

3. D.K. Sen: *A Comparative Study of the Indian Constitution*, Vol. II, p. 188.

Kesavanand Bharati Case (1973) observed: "Applied to Fundamental Rights it would mean that while fundamental rights could be abrogated, reasonable abridgement of fundamental rights can be effected in the public interest." This Part mentions six categories of fundamental rights along with qualifying provisions hedged around them with the more formidable provisions enabling the Parliament to make necessary amendments in the Constitution in the name of placing 'reasonable restrictions' on the use and enjoyment of these rights. These are:

Right to Equality: First of all, we have *right to equality*. Art 14 says that the State shall not deny to any person equality before law or equal protection of laws within its territory. Art. 15 prohibits discrimination on the grounds of religion, race, caste, sex, and place of birth; nor can any citizen on any of these grounds be held able or unable for access to shops, hotels, public restaurants and places of public entertainment, use of wells, tanks, *bathing ghats,* roads and places of public resort maintained wholly or partly by the State funds or dedicated to the use of general public. Art. 16 says about the equality of opportunity in matters of public employment. It is further provided that in respect of public employment, the State can make no discrimination on the grounds of religion, race, caste, sex, descent, and place of birth or residence Vide Art. 16 (5) appointment in religious or denominational institutions may be made in favour of a member professing same faith if it is provided by a law for the post of any incumbent or for a member of its governing body. Art. 17 declares abolition of untouchability and forbids its practice in any form. Finally, Art. 18 says that the State shall confer no title on any person save that of a military or academic distinction.

The Constitution also specifies that these rights are subject to certain restraints. Thus, Article 15 (3) and (4) lays down that though there can be no discrimination against persons on several grounds, it shall be open for the State to make any provision for the welfare of the women and children, or for the advancement of socially and educationally backward classes of the society, or for the Scheduled Castes and Scheduled Tribes. Similarly, in the case of Art. 16 providing for non-discrimination in matters of public employment, it is further given that it shall be open for the State to lay down qualifications of residence (domicile) in respect of public employment in any part of the country. (cl.3) that the State can make adequate reservations for the representation of the weaker sections of the society in public services (cl.4), Likewise, Art. 18 dealing with the abolition of titles, save those of military and academic distinction, further says that no citizen shall receive a title from a foreign State without the permission of the President of India. It follows that while our Constitution ensures fundamental right to equality, it also sanctions protective or compensatory discrimination in favour of certain castes or classes of society. The State enjoys broad discretion in determining the extent and method of the operation of such schemes leaving little scope for judicial review.

Not only this, amendments have been made from time to time to reinforce such provisions in a more effective manner. For instance, the 77th Amendment of 1995 inserts Art. 16 (4A) which empowers the State to provide reservation in public services for the members of the Scheduled Castes and Scheduled Tribes at the time of promotion of any class or classes of posts so as to give them adequate representation. The 81st Amendment of 2000 inserts Art. 16 (4B) which provides that the vacancies in public services for the Scheduled Castes and Scheduled Tribes, if carried over to the next year, shall not be aggregated with the new vacancies in determining the ceiling of 50 per cent as laid down by the Supreme Court in various important decisions. Then, the 82nd Amendment of 2000 adds a proviso to Art. 335 which says that for the members of the Scheduled Castes and Scheduled Tribes the State may, to any extent, allow relaxation in the qualifying marks in any examination or lower the standards of evaluation for reservation in matters of promotion to any class or classes of services or posts in connection with the affairs of the Union or of a State. The 85th Amendment of 2001 revises the text of Art. 16 (4A). It inserts the words "in matters of promotion with consequential seniority to any class or classes of posts." The 93rd Amendment of 2006 empowers the State to make reservation of seats for the Scheduled Castes, Scheduled Tribes and other backward classes in private and unaided educational institutions. Such a law shall not cover minority institutions.

These amendments have taken much out of what is contained in the provision relating to equality before law. The argument of 'social justice' is cleverly invoked to justify it all. The scope of judicial review is possible only to the extent that these provisions are not administered so as to prejudice others in an undue or unreasonable manner.

Right to Freedom: Art. 19 guarantees six kinds of essential freedoms to the citizens of India relating to speech and expression, peaceful assembly without arms, forming associations or unions, free movement throughout the territory of India, residence and settlement in any part of the territory of India, and practice of any profession, trade or business. Art. 20 provides for protection in respect of conviction for certain offences. It prohibits the promulgation of *ex-post facto* laws or laws with retrospective effect going to the disadvantage of the accused. It says that no person shall be convicted for any offence except for the violation of law in force at the time of the commission of the act charged as an offence, nor be subjected to a penalty greater than that which might have been inflicted under the law in force at the time of the commission of the offence; that no person shall be prosecuted and punished for the same offence more than once; and that no person accused of any offence shall be compelled to be a witness against himself. Art. 21 says that no person shall be deprived of his life or personal liberty except according to the procedure established by law. Art. 21 A inserted by the 86th Amendment of 2002 says that the State shall provide free and compulsory education to all children from 6 to 14 years of age in such a manner as determined by its law. Finally, Art. 22 guarantees protection against arbitrary arrest and detention. The man in custody will be informed, as soon as possible, of the grounds of such arrest. Moreover, an arrested person shall not be denied the right to engage or consult a legal practitioner of his choice for the sake of making his defence. It is also provided that a person who is arrested and placed under police custody shall be produced before the nearest magistrate within a period of 24 hours of such arrest (excluding the time necessary for the journey from the place of his arrest to the court of the magistrate) and that no such person shall be kept in custody beyond the said period without the order of the magistrate.

All these rights are subject to reasonable restrictions. Art. 19 ensuring six kinds of essential freedoms has qualifying provisions that enable the State to lay down reasonable restrictions in the interest of the sovereignty and territorial integrity of India, security of the State, friendly relations with foreign States, public order, decency, morality, contempt of court, defamation, incitement to an offence etc. The State may also lay down special rules for technical and professional services, or for carrying on any trade or profession in general public interest; similar arrangements can be made for the protection of the interest of the weaker sections of the community. Then, Art. 22 provides for preventive detention that makes a distinction between a citizen and an alien, particularly one belonging to an enemy country, and it also provides for a special procedure in case of persons rounded up under the law of preventive detention as made by the government of the Centre or of any State.

Rights Against Exploitation: Art. 23 prohibits traffic in human beings and taking of forced labour like *begar*. A qualifying clause says that nothing shall prevent the State from imposing compulsory service for a public purpose, and in imposing such a service, the State shall not make any discrimination on various grounds like those of religion, race, caste, class and the like. This provision specifically prohibits slavery or 'bonded labour' and traffic of human beings for immoral purposes. Art. 24 prohibits employment of children below 14 years of age in hazardous jobs.

Right to Religion: The right to religion constitutes the sheet anchor of our secular state. Art. 25 ensures freedom of conscience and free profession, practice and propagation of any faith or religion. Art. 26 guarantees freedom to every religious denomination or to any section thereof to establish and maintain institutions for religious and charitable purposes, to manage its own affairs in matters of religion, to own and acquire movable and immovable property, and to administer such property in accordance with law. Art. 27 says that no person shall be compelled to pay any tax the proceeds of which are specifically appropriated in payment of expenses for the promotion or maintenance of any particular religion or religious denomination. Finally, Art. 28 prohibits compulsory attendance at religious instructions imparted in an institution wholly or partly maintained by the State.

Like other fundamental rights, this right is also subject to certain qualifying restrictions as norms of public order, morality and health. It is also provided that the State shall have the right to regulate or restrict any economic, financial, political or other activity that may be associated with a religious practice, or to provide for social welfare and reform, or the throwing open of Hindu religious institutions of public character to all classes and sections of the Hindus. While defining the world 'Hindu', it is said that it shall be construed to

Fundamental Rights

Equality	*Freedom*	*Non-Exploitation*	*Religion*	*Culture and Education*	*Constitutional Remedies*
1. Equality before law and its equal protection within the territory of India 2. Prohibition of discrimination on various grounds-religion, race, caste, sex, place of birth etc., for the use of or access to public places 3. Equality of opportunity in matters of public employments 4. Abolition of untouchability and prohibition of its practice in any form 5. Abolition of titles except those of military and academic distinctions	1. Guarantee of six freedoms–speech and expression, assembly without arms, forming assciations and unions, free movement throughout the country, residence or settlement in any part of India, and carrying on any trade, profession, or occupation 2. Protection in respect of conviction for certain offences 3. Protection of life and personal liberty 4. Free and compulsory education for all children from 6 to 14 years of age as determined by a law of the state 5. Protection against arbitrary arrest and detention	1. Prohibition of traffic in human beings and taking of forced labour 2. Prohibition of employment of children below 14 years of age in hazardous jobs	1. Freedom of conscience and profession of any faith and propagation of any religion by peaceful means 2. Freedom to manage religious affairs 3. Freedom as to payment of taxes for promotion of any particular religion 4 Freedom as to attendance at religious instruction or religious worship in recognised educational institutions	1. Protection of the interests of the people relating to their language, script and culture 2. Rights of the minorities to establish and administer educational institutions of their choice	1. Enforcement and protection of these rights through the Supreme Court and High Courts which may issue writs in the nature of (a) Habeas Corpus (b) Mandamus (c) Prohibition (d) Quo Warranto (e) Certiorari

cover the Sikhs, Buddhists and Jains, and the wearing and carrying of *kirpans* shall be deemed to be included in the profession of Sikh religion. The provision of attendance at religious instruction in educational institutions, either wholly or partly maintained by the State, shall not apply to an institution which is administered by the State but has been established under some endowment or trust enjoining that religious instruction of that variety be imparted in the institution.

Cultural and Educational Rights: Art. 29 lays down that any section of the citizens residing in the territory of India having its distinct language, script or culture shall have the right to conserve the same. No citizen shall be denied admission to an educational institution maintained by the State or receiving aid out of the State funds on the grounds of religion, race, caste, language or any of them. Art. 30 says that all minorities, whether based on religion or language, shall have the right to establish and administer educational institution of their choice. The State shall not, while granting aid to educational institutions, discriminate against any educational institution on the ground that it is under the management of a minority, whether based on religion or language. In making a law providing for compulsory acquisition of any property of an educational institution established and administered by a minority, the State shall ensure that the amount fixed by or determined under such law for the acquisition of such property is such as would not restrict or abrogate the right guaranteed under that clause.

Right to Constitutional Remedies: Since Part III of the Constitution is justiciable, an aggrieved person may move the High Courts (under Art. 226) or the Supreme Court (under Art. 32) for the protection of his fundamental rights. Art 13 (2) clearly lays down that no law (including executive action) of the Centre, or of the States, or of any subordinate government can prevail that is inconsistent with Part III of the Constitution. Thus, the Courts may look into the matter and then hold that law invalid, either fully or in part, so as to enforce the provision of this part of the Constitution. For this sake, they may issue prerogative writs in the nature of *habeas corpus, mandamus, prohibition, quo warranto* and *certiorari*. In the words of a former Chief Justice of India, this provision is 'a very distinguishing feature of the Indian Constitution' and 'a cornerstone of the democratic edifice raised by the Constitution.'[4]

The Constitution empowers the Supreme Court and the High Courts to issue five kinds of writs for the protection and enforcement of fundamental rights. These are:

1. **Writ of Habeas Corpus:** The Court may direct the detaining authority to produce the person before it and justify the cause of his detention there.

2. **Writ of Mandamus:** The Court may order any inferior authority to perform some public or quasi-public legal duty which it has refused to perform and the performance of which cannot be enforced by any other adequate legal remedy.

3. **Writ of Prohibition:** The Court may order any inferior authority not to do what is not within its jurisdiction. It is different from *mandamus* in the sense that while the latter commands activity, it commands inactivity.

4. **Writ of Certiorari:** While the writ of prohibition is available at an earlier stage, the writ of *certiorari* is available at a later stage only. The two resemble as well as differ. The object of both is to secure that the jurisdiction of an inferior court or tribunal is properly exercised and that it does not usurp the jurisdiction which it does not possess. Thus, the Court may ask any inferior court or tribunal not to proceed ahead with the case before it but to transfer it to some other court or tribunal.

5. **Writ of Quo Warranto:** The Court may inquire into the legality of the claim which a person asserts to a public office and to oust him from its exercise if the claim be not well founded. Thus the Court may quash a wrong appointment. But here three conditions must be satisfied. First, the office must be public and it must be created by a statute or by the Constitution itself. Second, the office must be a substantive one and not merely the function or employment of a servant at the will and during the pleasure of another. Last, there must be a contravention of the Constitution or of a statute or of a statutory instrument in appointing such person to that office.

---

4. P.B. Gajendragadkar: *The Constitution of India: Its Philosophy and Basic Postulates*, pp. 60 and 62.

Fundamental Rights, as enshrined in Part III of our Constitution, have been lauded as the 'bedrock of Indian democracy.' On the other hand, they have been attacked on the ground of being given by one hand and taken away by another due to the qualifying provisions that highly circumscribe the scope of their exercise and enjoyment. We may enumerate some of the points of criticism as under:

1. Part III of the Constitution has a number of key terms without offering their precise or standard definition. In particular, we may refer to such terms as 'weaker sections of the community', 'socially and educationally backward classes of citizens', 'minorities', 'hazardous jobs', 'public purpose', etc. as a result of which scope for litigation is widened more and more. More perplexing is the fact that the Courts give different meanings to the same terms from time to time with the result that the problem remains unsolved.

2. The beautiful picture of our fundamental rights, as given in the original Constitution, has been vitiated by a series of amendments made by the rulers of the country just for political considerations. The First Amendment inserted clause (4) into Art. 15 and thereby introduced the system of reservation in favour of Scheduled Castes and Scheduled Tribes and other socially and educationally backward classes of citizens in clear violation of the principle of equality. The Fourth Amendment of 1955 deleted the requirement of compensation's being just or adequate or reasonable. The Twenty-fifth Amendment of 1971 put the word 'amount' in place of 'compensation' in Art. 31 (2) and also introduced Art. 31 C so as to keep a law of the Union or of the States immune from judicial scrutiny if it was made to implement a directive principle contained in Art. 39 (b) or (c). The Forty-fourth Amendment of 1978 deleted right to property from Part III and inserted it into Part XII A in the form of Art. 300A and thus created a confusion worst confounded in matters of a right relating to property.

3. The enforcement of our fundamental rights may be suspended during emergency declared by the President. In such a situation the President would have the power to suspend the right to move the Courts for the enforcement of fundamental rights. Thus a very critical member of these provision like H.V. Kamath said in the Con'sembly: "I fear that by this single chapter we are seeking to lay the foundations of a totalitarian

state ... where the rights and liberties of the millions of innocent men and women will be in continuous jeopardy."[5] The Forty-fourth Amendment of 1978 has made a little change that only two fundamental rights relating to protection in respects of conviction for offences (Art.20) and protection of life and personal liberty (Art. 21) cannot be suspended. The fear remains that as soon as the proclamation of emergency is made by the President, the State "shall be freed from the limitations imposed by Art. 19. This means that the Legislature shall be competent to make any law and the Executive shall be at liberty to take any action, even though it contravenes or restricts the right to freedom of speech and expression, assembly, association, movement, residence, profession or occupation."[6]

However, such points of criticism cannot efface the real significance of fundamental rights. "Despite the fact that some of the rights have been substantially modified in scope as a result of constitutional amendments, the chapter on fundamental rights taken as a whole remains a formidable bulwark of individual liberty, a code of public conduct and a strong and sustaining basis of Indian democracy."[7]

Directive Principles of State Policy

The Directive Principles of State Policy, contained in Part IV of the Constitution, covering Articles from 36 to 51, underline the philosophy of democratic socialism with a touch of Gandhian idealism as incorporated into the fundamental law of our country. Though the direct source of inspiration is not the Instrument of Instructions issued under the Government of India Act of 1935 but the Irish Constitution of 1937 that has placed the two-Fundamental Rights and Directive Principles-as distinct entities by making the former enforceable and the latter non-enforceable through the Courts, this Part of our Constitution has assumed the form of a very novel as well as a very controversial feature. But the fact stands out that

5. *Constituent Assembly Debates*, Vol. IX, p. 539.
6. D.D. Basu: *Introduction to the Constitution of India*, XII ed., 1989, p.130.
7. M.V. Pylee: *Constitutional Government in India*, p. 235.

this part of the Constitution "constitutes a very comprehensive political, social and economic programme for a modern democratic State."[8]

What strikes us at the very outset is the provision of Art. 37 that makes these principles judicially non-enforceable. It says that, inspite of their being of a non-justiciable character, the State shall nevertheless regard them as fundamental in the governance of the country and, hence, it shall be its duty to apply these principles in making laws. Art. 38 makes India a social welfare state. It says: "(1) That the State shall strive to promote the welfare of the people by securing and protecting as effectively as it may, a social order in which justice-social, economic and political-shall inform all the institutions of the national life. (2) The State shall, in particular strive to minimise the inequalities in income and endeavour to eliminate inequalities in status, facilities and opportunities, not only amongst individuals but also amongst groups of people residing in different areas or engaged in different vocations."

The Directive Principles may be enumerated as under:

1. The most important item of this chapter is contained in Art. 39 that imbibes the content of democratic socialism. It lays down that the State shall, in particular, direct its policy towards securing:

   (*a*) that the citizens, men and women equally, have the right to an adequate means of livelihood;

   (*b*) that the ownership and control of the material resources of the community are so distributed as best to subserve the common good;

   (*c*) that the operation of the economic system does not result in the concentration of wealth to the common detriment;

   (*d*) that there is equal pay for equal work for both men and women.

   (*e*) that the health and strength of workers, men and women, and the tender age of children are not abused and that the citizens are not forced by economic necessity to enter a vocation unsuited to their age or strength;

---

8. G.N. Joshi: *The Constitution of India*, p. 112.

(*f*) that children are given opportunities and facilities to develop in a healthy manner and in conditions of freedom and dignity and that childhood and youth are protected against exploitation and against moral and material abandonment.

2. The State shall secure that the operation of the legal system promotes justice on the basis of equal opportunity, and shall in particular, provide free legal aid, by suitable legislation or schemes or in any other way, to ensure that opportunities for securing justice are not denied to any citizen by reason of economic or other disabilities. (Art. 39A)
3. The State shall take steps to organise village panchayats and endow them with such power .and authority as may be necessary to enable them to function as units of self-government. (Art. 40)
4. The State shall, within the limits of its economic capacity and development, make effective provision for securing the right to work, to education and to public assistance in cases of unemployment, old age, sickness and disablement, and in other cases of undeserved want. (Art. 41)
5. The State shall make provision for securing just and humane conditions of work and for maternity relief. (Art. 42)
6. The State shall endeavour to· secure, by suitable legislation or economic organisation or in any other way, to all workers, agricultural, industrial or otherwise, work, a living wage, conditions of work ensuring a decent standard of life and full enjoyment of leisure and social and cultural opportunities and, in particular, the State shall endeavour to promote cottage industries on an individual or cooperative basis in rural areas. (Art. 43)
7. The State shall take steps, by suitable legislation or in any other way, to secure the participation of workers in the management of undertakings, establishments or other organisations engaged in any industry. (Art 43A)
8. The State shall endeavour to secure for the citizens a uniform civil code throughout the territory of India. (Art. 44)
9. The State shall endeavour to provide early childhood care and education for all children until they complete the age of six years. (Art. 45)

10. The State shall promote with special care the educational and economic interests of the weaker sections of the people and, in particular, of the Scheduled Castes and the Scheduled Tribes, and shall protect them from social injustice and all forms of exploitation. (Art. 46)
11. The State shall regulate the raising of the level of nutrition and the standard of living of its people and the improvement of public health as among its primary duties and, in particular, the State shall endeavour to bring about prohibition of the consumption, except for medicinal purpose, of intoxicating drinks and of drugs which are injurious to health. (Art. 47)
12. The State shall endeavour to organise agriculture and animal husbandry on modern and scientific lines and shall, in particular, take steps for preserving and improving the breeds, and prohibiting the slaughter of cows, calves and other milch and drought cattle. (Art. 48)
13. The State shall endeavour to protect and improve the environment and to safeguard the forests and wild life of the country. (Art. 48A)
14. It shall be the obligation of the State to protect every monument or place or object of artistic interest declared by or under a law made by the Parliament to be of national importance, from spoliation, disfigurement, destruction, removal, disposal or export as the case may be. (Art. 49)
15. The State shall take steps to separate the judiciary from the executive in the public services of the State. (Art. 50)
16. The State shall endeavour to (*a*) promote international peace and security, (*b*) maintain just and honourable relations between nations, (*c*) foster respect for international law and treaty obligations in the dealings of organised people with one another; and (*d*) encourage settlement of international disputes by arbitration. (Art. 51)

Though the list of the Directive Principles well indicates that these are like the ideals, particularly of a socio-economic character, that the State should strive for, or these are like directions which the legislature and the executive should follow while making laws or issuing orders, the fact remains to be stressed that their underlying spirit "is to make India not a Police State but a Welfare State. Herein lies a standard presentation of what may be called a 'plastic state' in the sense that it can serve any party with any ideology unlike the fixed Constitutions of America and Russia."[9]

The difference between Fundamental Rights and Directive Principles of State Policy may be highlighted with the help of these points:

1. While Fundamental Rights are like negative injunctions asking the State not to do this or that, the Directive Principles are like positive directions that the State must follow in order to establish social and economic democracy in the country. An English writer well observes that while Fundamental Rights "are injunctions - to prohibit the Government from doing certain things, the Directive Principles are affirmative instructions to the Government to do certain other things."[10]
2. While the Fundamental Rights are of a justiciable nature, the Directive Principles are not. That is, while the Courts may enforce and protect Fundamental Rights, they cannot do so in the case of Directive Principles.
3. Last, and it seems to follow from the above, the Directive Principles, unless otherwise determined by a law of the State, are subsidiary to the Fundamental Rights, the latter being primary parts of the Constitution in relation to the former. There should be no conflict between the two and in case there is any controversy, it is the Rights that prevail over the Principles. As early as in 1951 the Supreme Court in the *Champakam Case* ruled: "The Chapter of Fundamental Rights is sacrosanct and not liable to be abridged by any legislative or executive act or order, except provided in the appropriate Art. in Part III. The Directive Principles of State Policy have to conform and run subsidiary to the Chapter on Fundamental Rights." As an Indian writer comments: "The Fundamental Rights would be reduced to a mere rope of sand if they were to be overridden by the Directive Principles."[11]

---

9. K.V. Rao: *Parliamentary Democracy of India*, p. 353.
10. Allen Gledhill: *The Republic of India*, p.161.
11. M.P. Jain: *Indian Constitutional Law*, III ed, 1978. p. 596.

Committed to realise the idea of social and economic justice, the government of Indira Gandhi made the 25th Constitution Amendment Act in 1971 which inserted Art. 31 C. It laid down that any law made by a Legislature could not be called in question in any Court if it was made to implement Directive Principles contained in Art. 39 (b) and (c) despite being inconsistent with Articles 14, 19 and 31 of the Constitution. This was an innovatory measure and the Supreme Court in the *Kesavanand Bharati Case* struck it down in 1973. But the Forty-second Constitution Amendment Act of 1976 revived this clause by making the Legislature capable of making any law to implement any Directive Principle of Part IV that could not be questioned in the Courts on the ground of being inconsistent with the provisions of Part III of the Constitution. The Supreme Court invalidated it again in the *Minerva Mills Case* in 1980.

Since the Directive Principles are of a non-justiciable nature, they have been identified with ideal aspirations or 'pious superfluities' or something comparable with a cheque payable by a concerned bank as per its convenience, as said by Prof. K.T. Shah.[12] An English writer says that the ghosts of the Fabians 'stalk through the pages of the text.[13] The main point of attack is that these Principles are nothing more than a manifesto of high aims and aspirations. However, such a view looks cynical and pessimistic. The critics have certainly failed to understand the organic nature of relationship between Parts III and IV of the Constitution. A long list of the measures taken by the Governments at the Centre as well as in the States shows that these principles have been well honoured over the years since the inauguration of the Constitution in 1950. Reference in this connection may be made to land reform laws relating to the abolition of the system of landlordism. These statutory measures have given to the tillers of the soil security of tenure and prevented concentration of land holdings by imposing ceiling on land that a person may keep under his own cultivation. Several States have made laws to implement the system of democratic decentralisation and to provide free and compulsory education for the children. While pursuing the policy of prohibition, according to the recommendations of the National Prohibition Enquiry

---

12. *Constituent Assembly Debates*, Vol. VIII, p. 470.

13. Ivor Jennings: *Some Characteristics of the Indian Constitution*, p. 31.

Committee set up by the Planning Commission, severe restrictions have been imposed on the production and consumption of intoxicating goods. The Criminal Procedure Amendment Act of 1973 has gone a long way in realising the aim of separating judiciary from the executive.

The most appreciable point of discussion, in this direction, is that the judiciary has judiciously interpreted the real value of the Directive Principles particularly in cases involving their constitutional relationship with the Fundamental Rights. Chief Justice H.L. Kania of the Supreme Court in the case of *AK Gopalan v. State of Madras* (1950) visualised that, being a part of the Constitution, these Principles "represent not the temporary will of the majority but the deliberate wisdom of the nation expressed through them to be fundamental in the governance of the country." Justice M.C. Mahajan in the *Kameshwar Case* (1952) invoked Art. 39 in support of his contention that the abolition of zamindari had a legitimate public purpose. Justices Hedge and Mukherjee in the *Kesavanand Bharati Case* (1973) observed: "The Fundamental Rights and Directive Principles constitute the 'conscience of our Constitution."

Nehru appreciated the provisions of Part III having fundamental rights as the 'conscience of the Constitution', but Granville Austin places both the fundamental rights and the directives principles in the same category. In his view, "both have been designed as chief instruments in bringing about the great reforms of the social revolution. They have actually done so. The purpose of the Bill of Rights is to create or to preserve individual liberty and a democratic way of life based on equality among the members of society. The fundamental rights have both created a new equality and helped to preserve individual liberty. The number of cases dealing with fundamental rights brought before the Supreme Court and High Courts attest to the value of fundamental rights and their popularity."[14] According to an eminent statesman, "both fundamental rights and directive principle have been the source and inspiration of reform legislation. Under their aegies, the Indian Parliament has been active in the matter of social legislation, whether it be called by the Hindu Code or by any other name."[15]

14. Granville Austin: *The Indian Constitution*, p. 114.

15. K.M. Panikkar: *Hindu Society*, p. 52.

Fundamental Duties

The Forty-second Constitution Amendment Act (1976) has inserted Part IV A with Art. 51A having a set of Fundamental Duties. It says that it shall be the duty of every citizen of India—

(a) to abide by the Constitution and respect its ideals and institutions, the National Flag and the National Anthem;

(b) to cherish and follow the noble ideals which inspired our national struggle for freedom;

(c) to uphold and protect the sovereignty, unity and integrity of India;

(d) to defend the country and render national service when called upon to do so;

(e) to promote harmony and the spirit of common brotherhood amongst all the people of India transcending religious, linguistic and regional or sectional diversities; to renounce practices derogatory to the dignity of women;

(f) to value and preserve the rich heritage of our composite culture;

(g) to protect and improve the natural environment including forests, lakes, rivers and wild life and to have compassion for living creatures;.

(h) to develop scientific temper, humanism and the spirit of inquiry and reform;

(i) to safeguard public property and to abjure violence;

(j) to strive for excellence in all spheres of individual and collective activity so that the nation constantly rises to higher levels of endeavour and achievement; and

(k) As a parent or guardian, to provide opportunities for education to their child or ward from 6 to 14 years of age.

Since these fundamental duties are included in Part IV-A of the Constitution, it is obvious that they have a non-justiciable character. As such, they are hardly of any significance. But their real value cannot be minimised. As Basu says: "The citizen, it is expected, should be his own monitor, while exercising and enforcing his fundamental rights remembering that he owes the duties to the

State and that if he does not care for the duties, he should not deserve the rights .... Of course, the duty as such is not legally enforceable in the Court, but if the State makes a law to prohibit any act or conduct in violation of any of the duties, the Courts would uphold that as a reasonable restriction on the relevant fundamental rights just as they did uphold any law implementing the Directive Principles."[16] The Courts may look at the fundamental duties while interpreting equivocal statutes which admit of two constructions."[17]

The Indian Constitution subscribes to the course of positive liberalism that may be easily identified with democratic socialism. It guarantees essential boons of Justice, Liberty, Equality, Secularism and Socialism which have their conspicuous place in its Part III containing Fundamental Rights as well as in the ideals of social and economic democracy as contained in Part IV having Directive Principles of State Policy. As Ambedkar visualised in his concluding speech in the Con'sembly: "Political democracy cannot last unless there lies at the base of it social democracy. What does social democracy mean? It means a way of life which recognises liberty, equality and fraternity which are not to be treated as separate items in a trinity. They form a union of trinity in the sense that to divorce one from the other is to defeat the very purpose of democracy. Liberty cannot be divorced from equality, equality cannot be divorced from liberty. Nor can liberty and equality be divorced from fraternity."[18]

---

16. D.D. Basu: *Constitutional Law of India,* II ed., 1980, pp. 128–29.
17. P.M. Bakshi: *The Constitution of India,* ed. of 2004, p. 93.
18. *Constituent Assembly Debates,* Vol. XI, p. 979.

9

Indian Union and Federal System

Though a federation, India is neither a 'Confederation' of States like the United States of America and Switzerland, nor is she a 'federation' like South Africa and Germany as declared in their constitutions; she is a 'Union of States' implying two salient points: (*i*) that our federation is not a result of some agreement among the component units, and (*ii*) that no component unit has right to secede from the Union. Thus, Indian Constitution follows the Canadian pattern where the term 'Union' has been preferred to 'Federation'. However, the most outstanding feature of the Indian federation signifying India's being a 'Union of States' has a very significant history of its own that may be placed in two parts: (*i*) integration of the princely States that took place at the time of the making of the Constitution, and (*ii*) further and still further reorganisation of the States that has taken place after the inauguration of our Republic to realise, what Sardar Vallabhbhai Patel once said, "the great ideal of geographical and economic unification of India."[1]

Formation of the Indian Union

At the time of independence, India was not one but two: 'British India' or a great part of the country under British Government, and 'Indian India' or a sizeable part of the country under native princes living under the paramountcy of the British Crown. The two parts of India were also known by the names of the Provinces and the States respectively and their existence on the political map of the country was indicated in red and yellow colours respectively. In the case of the latter, the word 'paramountcy' had its special significance which, though never defined by the British Government

1. V.P. Menon: *The Story of the Integration of the Indian States*, p. 490.

in quite precise terms, meant everything pertaining to the sovereign authority of the English Crown.[2]

A study of the administration of the princely States shows that the Paramount Power had given them almost complete freedom in respect of the internal administration to the extent that British imperial interests did not suffer. For this sake, the British Government had its Political Agents or Resident Commissioners in the States to have a strict watch on the activities of the princely rulers. The Paramount Power was, however, not at all concerned with the issue of good or bad government existing in a State, though it could interfere in matters of maltreatment of the minorities or settlement of the problem of succession. It is well understandable that the Paramount Power "stood out as distant and apparently indifferent spectators so long as the Rulers just carried on, no matter whether their administration of internal affairs was good, bad or indifferent. They intervened only when British imperial interests were at stake, or when the machinery was on the point of collapse, or when gross barbarities were committed."[3]

Thanks to the statesmanship of Sardar Patel and great co-operation given to him by Nehru and Mountbatten that the terribly difficult problem of the integration of the princely States was solved in time. Wisdom prevailed and the princely rulers (excluding those of Junagarh, Hyderabad and Kashmir) bowed their heads to the call of the time.[4] Thus, the period immediately following the transfer of power to India saw "a revolutionary change come over to the Indian States with dramatic speed. Once the States had acceded to India,

---

2. In 1929 Butler Committee endorsed: "Paramountcy must remain paramount; it must fulfil its obligations defining or adapting itself according to the shifting necessities of the time and the progressive development of the States."
3. Dhirendranath Sen: *Revolution by Consent* ?, p.55.
4. That State of Junagarh was integrated with India after the escape of the Muslim ruler Mahabat Ali Khan to Pakistan. A referendum was held that gave its verdict in favour of State's merger with India. The State of Jammu-Kashmir was integrated after its ruler Hari Singh signed the Instrument of Accession on 26 October, 1947. The State of Hyderabad could be integrated in September 1948 when its ruler (Osman Ali Khan) signed the Instrument of Accession.

it was impossible for them to resist such a change, however much they had disliked it."[5]

The integration of the princely States with the Indian Union took place in the following manner:

1. 216 States having a population of over 19 millions were merged with the neighbouring provinces (former British Indian Provinces) that were designated as Part A States.
2. 275 States with a population of about 35 millions were integrated to create new administrative units, namely, Part B States of the Indian Union; some very big States like those of Hyderabad, Mysore and Jammu-Kashmir were also placed in this category; and
3. 61 States having a population of about 7 millions were constituted into Part C States and were like Centrally Administered Areas.

The islands of Andaman and Nicobar were placed in Part D of the Indian Union. The integration of the princely States coupled with its ancillary part of their merger was an *ad hoc* arrangement in view of the fact that unionisation of the units of the 'Indian India' "demanded a fresh approach to the problem of reorganisation."[6] Thus, with a view to make a fresh attempt in the light of new political conditions, the Government of India appointed a commission under the chairmanship of S.K Dar, then a judge of the Allahabad High Court, to examine the case of the reorganisation of the Indian States on the linguistic basis a demand for which had particularly grown up in the south. On 10 Dec., 1948, the Dar Commission submitted its 56-page Report expressing its opinion in favour of the re-organisation of the component units of the Indian federation for the sake of administrative convenience and not at all on the basis of linguistic composition of the area. Unfortunately, politics dominated the wisdom and, in the face of the widespread opposition to the report of the Dar Commission, the Congress (at its Jaipur session in Dec., 1948) took a decision in pursuance of which the JVP Committee (Jawaharlal Nehru, Vallabhbhai Patel and Pattabhi

---

5. M.V. Pylee: *Constitutional Government in India*, p. 162.
6. P.K. Sharma: *Political Aspects of States Reorganisation in India*, p. 44.

Sitaramayya) was set up to re-examine the issue of the linguistic re-organisation of the Indian States.

Categories of Indian States and Centrally Administered Areas in 1953

Categories	*States*
A	1. Assam 2. Bihar 3. Bombay 4. Madhya Pradesh 5. Madras 6. Orissa 7. Punjab 8. U.P. 9. West Bengal 10. Andhra Pradesh*
B	1. Hyderabad 2. Jammu-Kashmir 3. Madhya Bharat 4. Mysore 5. Patiala and East Punjab States Union (PEPSU) 6. Rajasthan 7. Saurashtra 8. Travancore-Cochin 9. Vindhya Pradesh
C	1. Ajmer 2. Bilaspur 3. Bhopal 4. Coorg 5. Delhi 6. Himachal Pradesh 7. Kutch 8. Manipur 9. Tripura 10. Cooch-Behar
D	1. Andaman and Nicobar Islands

* Andhra Pradesh was created in 1953 after cutting a part of the then State of Madras.

The JVP Report appeared on 1 April, 1949. It formally dismissed the idea of the linguistic reorganisation of Indian States, but it conceded that "if public sentiment is insistent and overwhelming, we as democrats, have to submit to it subject to certain limitations in regard to the good of India as a whole." And yet the Report hinted that a shy case might be made for the creation of the Andhra State consisting of the Telugu-speaking people. It left a big handle in the hands of the people of the then Madras State living in the areas now forming part of the Andhra Pradesh. The agitated people took the matters to the streets that culminated in the death of Potti Sriramulu on 15 Dec., 1952 after 56-day hunger strike for the cause. It led to the breaking out of more serious disturbances that forced the Government of India to create the first linguistic State of the Telugu-speaking people after cutting a part of the then Madras State in 1953.

The creation of the State of Andhra Pradesh virtually led to the redrawing of the political map of India as a whole. While speaking in the Parliament on 22 Dec., 1953, Nehru announced the appointment of a commission to examine the whole question of the reorganisation of the Indian States in the light of the dimension of the problem, historical background, existing situation and the bearing of all important and relevant factors thereof. The States Reorganisation Commission under the chairmanship of Fazl Ali and having K.M. Panikkar and Pandit H.N. Kunzru as the two members submitted its report on 30 Sept., 1955. The key recommendation of the SRC. Report was to abolish the A,B,C,D categories of the units of the Indian Union and instead desire their reorganisation in the form of 16 States and 3 Centrally Administered Areas.

The Government of India accepted the recommendations of the SRC Report with certain minor modifications as a result of which the States Reorganisation Act of 1956 was made. It provided for the creation of 14 States, namely, Andhra Pradesh, Assam, Bihar, Bombay, Jammu-Kashmir, Kerala, Madhya Pradesh, Madras, Mysore, Orissa, Punjab, Rajasthan, Uttar Pradesh and West Bengal and 6 Union Territories, namely, Delhi, Himachal Pradesh, Manipur, Tripura, Andaman and Nicobar Islands and Laccadive, Amindive and Minicoy Islands (now Lakshadweep).

Proposed States and Centrally Administered Areas in 1955

Parts	*Units*
States	1. Andhra Pradesh
	2. Assam
	3. Bihar
	4. Bombay
	5. Hyderabad
	6. Jammu-Kashmir
	7. Karnataka
	8. Kerala
	9. Madhya Pradesh
	10. Madras
	11. Orissa
	12. Punjab
	13. Rajasthan
	14. Uttar Pradesh
	15. Vidarbha
	16. West Bengal
Union Territories	1. Delhi
	2. Manipur
	3. Andaman and Nicobar Islands

Even after the reorganisation of the Indian States in 1956, the political map of India continued to change owing to the growing pressure of political conditions and circumstances. A deed of transfer was signed with the Government of France in May, 1956 by virtue of which former French possessions of Chandenagore, Mahe, Yanam and Karekal were merged with the Indian States, while Pondicherry was given the status of a Union Territory. In December, 1961, India acquired the territories of Goa, Daman and Diu by means of police action to overthrow the notorious colonial hold of the Portuguese Government. Thus, Goa, Daman and Diu formed another Union Territory. The bi-lingual Bombay State became the cause of struggle between the Gujarati and Marathi-speaking people as a result of which the State was bifurcated. into Gujarat and Maharashtra States in 1960. Matters flared up in the State of Punjab where the deteriorating situation took a communal turn on account of the demand for a 'Sikh homeland' raised by the Akali Dal under the leadership of Master Tara Singh. Thus, the State was bifurcated in 1966 into the States of Punjab and Haryana leaving the matter of

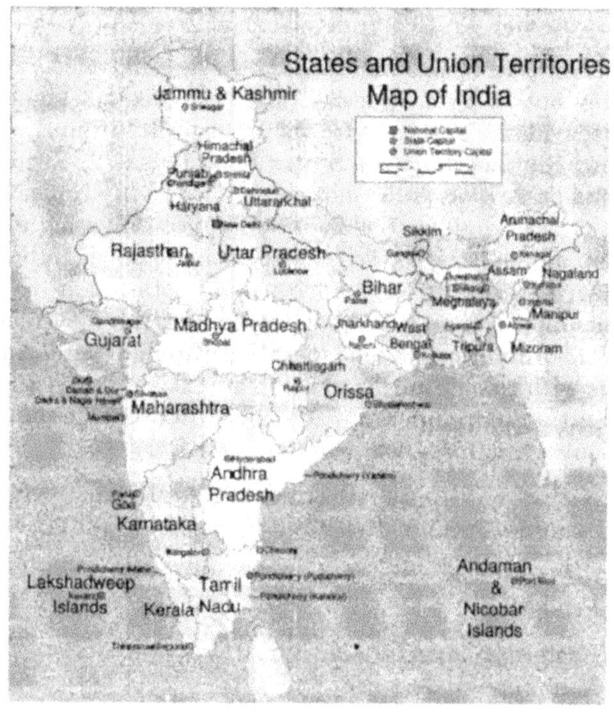

the city of Chandigarh still unsettled and giving some of the hilly areas of Kangra to the then Union Territory of Himachal Pradesh. With a view to satisfy the movement of the hostile Nagas, the State of Nagaland came into being in 1963 after cutting a part of the State of Assam. The State of Assam was further disintegrated to create the Sub-State of Meghalaya in 1969. (In the first instance, it was proposed to create the autonomous State of Meghalaya within the State of Assam.) In 1971, Himachal Pradesh got the status of a State and the north-eastern region of India was reorganised in a way that Meghalaya became a full-fledged State; the Union Territories of Manipur and Tripura got Statehood and the Union Territories of Mizoram and Arunachal Pradesh (former NEF A) came into being. Sikkim got the status of an 'Associate State' in 1974; it became a full-fledged State in 1975. Mizoram got Statehood in 1986; Arunachal Pradesh and Goa got Statehood in 1987. The States of Chhattisgarh, Uttaranchal (now Uttarakhand) and Jharkhand came into being in 2000 as a result of the bifurcation of the States of M.P., U.P., and Bihar respectively.

Zonal Councils

Prime Minister Nehru well realised the fact that a federal system, as pointed out by Prof. Wheare, "after all does not stand for the multiplicity alone. It stands for the multiplicity in unity."[7] Before concluding his speech on the States Reorganisation Report in the Lok Sabha on 21 Dec., 1955, he commended to the House his long-thought plan of dividing the country into four/five big areas and setting up an advisory council in each zone to develop the habit of 'co-operative thinking'. It had its manifestation in the States Reorganisation Act of 1956 that introduced the novel feature of regional co-ordination and co-operation through the formation of the zones with zonal councils to act in an advisory capacity. Sec. 15 of the States Reorganisation Act identified each zone with its constituent units in the following manner:

(*i*) Northern Zone comprising Punjab, Rajasthan, Jammu-Kashmir, Delhi and Himachal Pradesh;

(*ii*) Central Zone comprising Uttar Pradesh and Madhya Pradesh;

(*iii*) Eastern Zone comprising Bihar, Orissa, West Bengal, Assam, Manipur and Tripura;

(*iv*) Western Zone comprising Bombay and Mysore; and

(*v*) Southern Zone comprising Andhra Pradesh, Madras and Kerala.

As the movement for the reorganisation of the States continued in different parts of the country and as some further reorganisation took place under the force of political circumstances, slight changes occurred in the composition of the various Zonal Councils too. For instance, with the bifurcation of Bombay into the States of Maharashtra and Gujarat, the latter became a member of the Western Zone, while Mysore was shifted to the Southern Zone. After the bifurcation of Punjab, Haryana was made a member of the Northern Zone.

However, the most significant development is the creation of the North-Eastern Council on 8 August, 1972, in pursuance of the reorganisation of the North-East region of India in 1971. The

---

7. K.C.Wheare: *Federal Government*, p. 244.

members of the North-Eastern Council are Assam, Manipur, Tripura, Meghalaya, Nagaland, Mizoram and Arunachal Pradesh.[8] Thus, the position, at present, in regard to the scheme of regional co-ordination, as hopefully visualised by Nehru, is as given on the next page.

The functions of the Zonal Councils and North-Eastern Council are almost similar. They are like high-level advisory bodies to provide a forum for the discussion on matters of common interest to the members concerned. The main functions of the Zonal Councils are:

1. To achieve an emotional integration of the people;
2. To help in arresting the growth of acute State consciousness in the form of regionalism, linguism and the like;
3. To help in removing the after-effects of separation;
4. To enable the Centre and the States in economic and social matters and to co-operate and exchange ideas and experience for evolving uniform policies;
5. To co-operate with each other in the speedy and successful execution of development plans; and
6. To secure some kind of political equilibrium between different regions of the country.

Likewise, the functions of the North-Eastern Council are:

1. To formulate a unified and co-ordinated regional plan in addition to State plan covering matters of common importance.
2. In respect of projects or schemes intended to benefit two or more members, to recommend the manner in which they may be executed, managed or maintained, their benefits shared and their expenditures incurred.
3. To supervise the progress of the implementation of the plans and the expenditures thereon; and

---

8. For some time the State of Nagaland remained reluctant to join the North-Eastern Council owing to its 'unfriendly: attitude towards the Centre influenced by the pro-Phizo rebel forces. Sikkim was in the Eastern Zone, but in 2002 it was included in the North-Eastern Council.

Zonal Councils and North-Eastern Council (2014)

Eastern Zone

1. Bihar
2. Odisha
3. West Bengal
4. Jharkhand

Southern Zone

1. Telangana
2. Seemandhra
3. Kerala
4. Karnataka (Mysore)
5. Tamil Nadu (Madras)
6. Puducherry
7. Lakshadweep

Western Zone

1. Gujarat
2. Maharashtra
3. Goa
4. Daman and Diu
5. Dadra and Nagar Haveli

Central Zone

1. Uttar Pradesh
2. Madhya Pradesh
3. Chhattisgarh
4. Uttarkhand

Northern Zone

1. Jammu-Kashmir
2. Haryana
3. Punjab
4. Himachal Pradesh
5. Rajasthan
6. Chandigarh
7. Delhi

North-Eastern Council

1. Assam
2. Manipur
3. Tripura
4. Meghalaya
5. Nagaland
6. Mizoram
7. Arunachal Pradesh
8. Sikkim

4. To review from time to time the measures taken by the Governments for the maintenance and security or public order as and when necessary and to recommend further measures in this behalf.[9]

In general, both the Zonal Councils and North-Eastern Council are high-level advisory bodies with powers to make recommendations with

9. The North-Eastern Council, which came into being in August, 1972 has certain additional functions. It has to formulate a unified and co-operated regional plan (in addition to the State plans) covering matters of common importance. In respect of projects or schemes intended to benefit two or more States, the Council has to recommend the manner in which these may be executed, managed or maintained, their benefits shared and the expenditure thereon

regard to any matter of common interest in the field of social and economic planning, or any matter concerning border disputes, linguistic minorities or inter-State transport, and any matter connected with or arising out of the reorganisation of States for political or security consideration. The personnel of every Council includes:

(*i*) Home Minister or a Minister of the Union Government appointed by the President;

(*ii*) Chief Ministers of the States included in that Zone and two other ministers nominated by the Governor;

(*iii*) In the case of a Union Territory, one member nominated by the President.

(*iv*) Some advisers nominated by the Planning Commission, Chief Secretaries of the States included in the Zone and their Development Commissioners.

The Chairman of each Zonal Council is the Union Home Minister, while the office of the Vice-Chairman is given to the Chief Minister of the States included in the Zone that rotates after every year. The decision of the Council is taken by votes in which the advisers have no role to play. They simply take part in the deliberations. A look at the working of these advisory bodies shows that they have served the useful purpose of settling matters as those relating to boundary demarcation, use of river waters, maintenance of law and order, language issue, and planned regional development. It is hoped that these bodies, as Pandit G.B. Pant observed, would prove an interesting experiment in co-operative federalism.

Indian Union and its Territory

Part I of the Indian Constitution has the following provisions:

1. Art. 1 says: (1) "India, that is Bharat, shall be a Union of States. (2) The States and the territories thereof shall be as specified

---

are supervised by the Council. It also brings about co-ordination among the constituent States and Union Territories. The Council reviews from time to time the measures taken by the States for the maintenance of security and public order and, as and when necessary, recommends further measures in this behalf.

in the First Schedule. (3) The territories of India shall comprise *(a)* the territories of the States, *(b)* Union Territories specified in First Schedule, and *(c)* other territories as may be acquired."

2. Art. 2 says that Parliament may by law admit into the Union or establish new States on such terms and conditions as it thinks fit.

3. Art. 3 says that the Parliament may by law *(a)* form a new State by the separation of territory from any State or by uniting any territory to a part of any State, *(b)* increase the area of any State, *(c)* diminish the area of any State, *(d)* alter the name of any State. Provided that no bill for the purpose shall be introduced in either House of Parliament except on the recommendation of the President and unless, while the proposal contained in the Bill affects the area, boundaries, or name of the States, the Bill has been referred by the President to the Legislature of that State for expressing its view thereon within such period as may be specified in the reference or within such further period as the President may allow and the period so specified or allowed has expired.

4. Art. 4 says that any law made in pursuance of Articles 2 and 3 shall not be deemed as an amendment of the Constitution under Art. 368.

The salient ingredients of the provisions of the Constitution, as given above, may be thus enumerated:

1. It declares that though a federation, India is a Union of States having some Centrally Administered Territories with this line of difference that while the former have their share in the distribution of powers, the latter are under the direct control of the Centre.

2. Indian Union is *highly flexible* in the sense that the Parliament may make changes in the political map of India by means of its unilateral action.

3. The Parliament has the power of a very far-reaching effect in changing the names of the component units; more than that, it has absolute authority in matters of creating a new State by cutting a part of the existing State. What is needed is just a mere reference by the President of India to the concerned

State that is to be affected by the creation of a new State or by the alteration of its boundaries.

4. Though by all means a constitutional amendment, a law made in pursuance of Articles 2 and 3 shall not be taken as an amendment for the purpose of Art. 368 of the Constitution.
5. The requirement that the President must make a reference to the affected State does not cover the case of a Union Territory.
6. The Parliament has full power to decide as to whether a State should be admitted into the Indian Union and, if so, the power of deciding about the time and manner of such admission with or without any condition antecedent or precedent to it lies with it alone.

It is well understandable that the provisions of the Constitution relating to the Indian Union and its Territory, as given in its Part I, not only lay down the framework of a controlled federal system by designating India as 'a Union of States,' they make it very much clear that it "is a union of composite States, of a novel type."[10]

Federal System

Special Characteristics: Though the Constitution of India has adopted federal system, it has its peculiar characteristics which may be thus enumerated:

1. The Indian federal system, as established by the provisions of the Constitution, is *territorial* in the sense that it sets up a dual polity with the Union government at the Centre and the State governments at the periphery, each endowed with sovereign powers to be exercised in the field assigned to them respectively by the Constitution. Thus, the Indian Union, as visualised by the President of the Constituent Assembly (Dr. Rajendra Prasad) is *'indissoluble'* meaning thereby that, barring the cases of emergencies, the Centre and the States remain endowed with the areas of authority allotted to them.
2. Indian federalism is *horizontal* with a strong unitary bias. It implies that though there is the division of powers between

---

10. Basu: *Introduction to the Constitution of India*, XII edition of 1989, p. 62.

the national and constituent governments, the position of the former is unmistakably stronger, perhaps the strongest, if we compare our federal system with such other systems of the world. It has been done to subserve the national interest and not to pay allegiance to some classical standard of federalism at the expense of our requirements. The founding fathers wisely felt that one of the most important lessons of our history was that 'we perish if we make the Centre weak'.

3. Indian federal system is *flexible* in the sense that it can be easily converted into a unitary model particularly in times of emergency. No constitutional amendment is required for this sake. A mere declaration signed by the President is enough to convert the basic structure of the Constitution to meet the imminent danger threatening the independence and territorial integrity of the country. Moreover, the process of constitutional amendment has been so designed that the ratificatory role of the States has been confined to the areas relating to the federal framework alone. Thus, most of the provisions of the Constitution are amendable by the unilateral action of the Parliament.

4. Indian federal system is *co-operative* in the sense that it seeks the collaboration of both the Centre and the States in several matters of common interest. The National Development Council, Inter-State Council, Finance Commission, Zonal Councils etc. may be referred to in this connection. The working of these agencies shows that neither the Centre nor the States can impose their decisions on the other.

5. Last, Indian federal system has become of a *unitarian* type because of the centralised party system. The role of the Congress, the BJP and other parties at the Centre *vis-a-vis* the States has been governed not by the formal constitutional provisions but by the role of the party under the towering leadership of its High Command. It is the supreme leadership of the party that takes a decision about the selection of a Chief Minister, making or unmaking of the new ministries in the States, nomination or recall of the Governors, imposition or revocation of President's rule in a State and the like. Instead of pertaining to the formal federal framework, as obtaining in different countries of the world, it desires a process of bargaining between the Union and the State governments in

which experiment, co-operation and persuasion in place of conflict, competition and coercion are requisitioned both to testify the generally accepted norms and the usual procedural patterns of interaction between national and regional governments. That is, our constitutional system stands on the premises of co-operative federalism what Morris-Jones calls 'bargaining federalism' assuming the interdependence of national and regional governments of a federal union instead of granting them absolute independence in the allotted spheres so as to satisfy the requirements of a classical federal model. With the creation of a very strong Central government, the Founding Fathers have sought to ensure that it "would not necessarily result in weak provincial governments that are large administrative agencies for Central policies."[11]

Features of Formal Federal Framework: A federal system has three essential characteristics and these are very much present in the provisions of the Constitution:

1. A federal system stands for the supremacy of a written and a rigid constitution. A federal state derives its existence from the organic or basic law of the land called the Constitution. It is also required that the Constitution must be written so that the areas of authority of both the national and the regional governments are clearly demarcated. Finally, the Constitution must be rigid so that it cannot be altered now and then having its adverse impact on the sanctity of the distribution of powers between the central and provincial governments. Our Constitution meets this requirement.

2. The very object for which a federal state is formed involves division of powers between the Central and State governments. It is called the 'federal principle' or the method of dividing powers so that the central and provincial governments are each, within the allotted sphere, co-ordinate and independent. There are three lists showing division of powers between the Centre and the States. The administration of the Union List having 97 items of national importance (like defence, war and peace, atomic energy, currency and coinage, railways, post and telegraph, citizenship, foreign trade, ports, airways, communications, broadcasting, external affairs etc.) has been

---

11. Granville Austin: *The Indian Constitution*, p. 186.

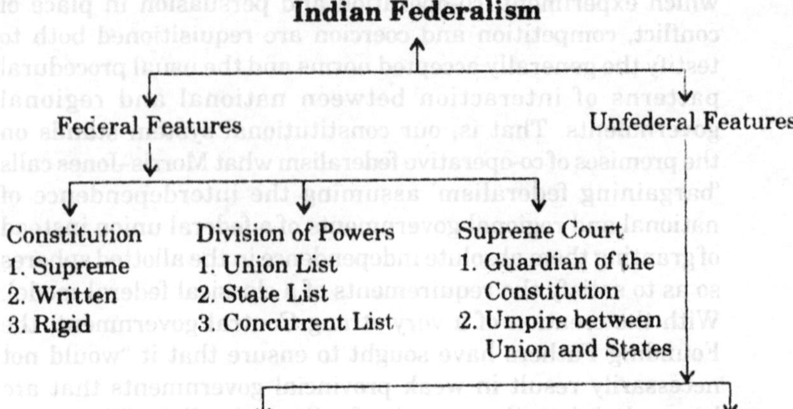

Centralisation

1. Highly unfair division of powers.
2. Dependence of the States on the financial assistance given by the Centre.
3. Alteration in the area and boundaries of the States by the Centre.
4. Centre's heavy hand in making amendments in the Constitution.
5. Unequal representation of States in the Rajya Sabha.
6. Directions of the Centre to be carried out by the States.
7. Executive authority of the States not to impede or prejudice Union administration.
8. Presidential veto-power over State legislation being absolute.
9. Centre's paramount control over States even in normal times.
10. Emergency powers of the President.

Uniformity

1. Single citizenship
2. Single constitutional system
3. Single civil and criminal law and procedure.
4. Singleness in higher public services.
5. Integrated judiciary.

given to the Centre. The administration of the State list having 61 (originally 66) subjects of local importance (like public order, police, jails, agriculture, irrigation, public health, local self-government etc.) has been given to the States. Finally, the administration of the Concurrent list having 47 subjects of common importance (like marriage and divorce, adoption, succession, transfer of property, preventive detention, education, civil and criminal law etc.) has been given to both the Centre and the States with an overriding control of the former. Residuary subjects have been given to the Centre.

3. The last requirement of a federal system is the existence of an independent and impartial judiciary to act as the guardian of the Constitution. Our federal system meets this requirement as well. The Constitution provides a Supreme Court. It has original jurisdiction to settle disputes between the Centre and the States and the States *inter se*. It has been endowed with the power of interpreting the provisions of the Constitution and its judgment is final.

It is, therefore, clear that as the Indian constitutional system meets all the three requirements of a federal system, it cannot be designated as unitary. It also implies that though there are certain serious elements making the position of the Centre very strong at the expense of the area of provincial autonomy, it does not at all render the character of the very constitutional system unitary like that of England or France. Thus, a conscientious student of the Indian constitutional system says that India "is undoubtedly a federation in which the attributes of sovereignty are shared between the Centre and the States."[12]

Elements of Centralisation: A federal system stands for the decentralisation of powers and diversity in administration. Let us now examine the points which support the features of *centralisation* and *uniformity* in the following manner:

1. **Centralisation:** First, we take up the features of the centralisation of powers in the hands of the Union Government so

---

12. C.H. Alexandrowicz : *Constitutional Development in India,* p. 169. Perhaps N.V. Gadgil was right when he echoed the sentiments of the House in these words: "1 doubt whether there is a single individual here or outside, or a party, here or outside, which had stood or even stands for a completely unitary constitution." *Constituent Assembly Debates,* Vol. IX, p. 657.

much so that the autonomy of the States has become of a highly attenuated kind. In this connection, following important points may be enumerated:

(*i*) This distribution of powers is highly unfair from the federal point of view. While the Centre has exclusive control over the Union List consisting of 97 items of national importance and an over-riding control over 47 items of common importance given in the Concurrent List, the States have control over 61 items of local importance contained in the State List. Moreover, even here as, we shall see, the Centre has been endowed with the power to exercise paramount control in an indirect manner. The residuary powers have also been given to the Centre.

(*ii*) The distribution of revenues between the Centre and the States is of such a nature that the States have to depend largely upon the charitable assistance of the Centre.

(*iii*) There is no perpetual guarantee regarding the existence of any State as such. The Centre may redraw the political map of the country.

(*iv*) When we look at the process of constitutional amendment, we find that the States have a very limited say. It is only with regard to certain provisions having their connection with the federal framework of the Constitution where the ratification by half of the States, and that too by simple majority of votes in the Legislative Assembly, is required.

(*v*) In a federal system, as we find in the case of American, Swiss and Australian models, there is the principle of the equality of representation given to the States in the upper chamber of the national legislature irrespective of the size and population of the component units. Contrary to this, in our country the number of the members elected to the Rajya Sabha varies according to the population of the States.

(*vi*) The Union Government has the power to issue directions to the State Governments which they must invariably follow. Its implication is that the failure of the State government in this regard shall be treated as the breakdown of constitutional machinery and that shall enable the President to take over the administration of that State under Art. 356 of the Constitution.

(*vii*) Apart from giving directions to the States, the Centre may delegate some of its functions to them in relation to any matter coextensive with their executive authority. No State law can prevail which is repugnant to the law of the Centre. The States cannot exercise their executive power in a way that goes to impede or prejudice the executive power of the Union government.

(*viii*) It is provided that certain types of bills (like those seeking compulsory acquisition of private property, derogating the power of the High Courts, imposing tax on an item declared essential by the Centre, or likely to be in conflict with a law or policy of the Union government) shall be reserved by the Governor for the consideration of the President. Here President's veto power is absolute.

(*ix*) The Centre may make a law on any item of the State List in case a resolution to this effect is passed by the Rajya Sabha, or there is emergency in the country, or when the Centre desires to implement some international treaty or agreement.

(*x*) The emergency powers of the President are so sweeping in their effect that the very nature of the Indian political system can be transformed from an incidentally federal into a purely unitary system of government.

2. **Uniformity:** The elements of uniformity, which are treated as the hallmarks of a unitary system, are traceable in our federal system and may be thus enumerated:

(*i*) There is single Constitution wherefrom the Centre as well as the State governments derive their powers. That is, the States have no Constitution of their own. The State of Jammu-Kashmir is an exception in this regard, but it cannot have anything repugnant to the Constitution of India.

(*ii*) Despite ours being a federal state, we have single citizenship—the citizenship of India—so as to realise the ideal of 'one people, one country'. That is, there is nothing like the citizenship of States in our country.

(*iii*) This singleness is further visible in the legal institutional framework. There is uniformity in respect of civil and criminal laws and their procedure throughout the country.

(*iv*) The line of singleness in respect of higher public services is also noticeable. The officers of the Indian Administrative and Indian Police Services are recruited by the Union Public Service Commission, they serve State governments and also draw their salaries and allowances therefrom. The Election Commission and the Comptroller and Auditor-General of India are authorities of the Centre, they also serve State governments.

(*v*) Finally, there is integrated judiciary with Supreme Court at the top. The High Courts are under the Supreme Court. The composition of the High Courts and the enlargement of their jurisdiction is in the hands of the Union government.

Such a long list of several weighty points shows that the Indian federal system has notable sub-features of a unitary state. It is the scrutinised study of these significant provisions of the Constitution that enables its critics to designate India as a 'quasi-federal state' or even a unitary state. An English writer says that, "India is a unitary State with subsidiary federal features rather than a federal State with subsidiary features of a unitary state."[13]

Union-State Relations

A study of the Union-State relations covering legislative and administratives spheres as contained in Part XI and financial sphere as given in Part XII of the Constitution should be taken as a supplement to the study of the Indian federal system as given above. The distribution of powers between the Centre and the States bears a clear testimony to the same stand that the Indian federal system subscribes to no classical doctrine; it has a character of its own which, though looking like a unique blending of the unitary and federal systems with a definite bias towards the latter, has been well designed to suit the purposes of a nascent democracy being run by the people of a dynamic and progressive nation. In this part, we shall make a study of Union-State relations in the legislative, administrative and financial spheres so as to have a knowledge of the operation of federal system in our country.

Legislative Relations: As already pointed out, the Centre has the power to make law on any item of the Union List, while the

13. K.C. Wheare: *Federal Government*, p. 28.

States may do the same on any subject of the State List. The Concurrent List has been given to both. It means that both the Centre and the States may make a law on a subject contained in the Concurrent List. In order to prevent conflict between the two, it has been provided that the law of the Centre shall prevail and the State law shall be inoperative to the extent it is inconsistent with the Union law. Residuary subjects are also with the Centre. It has been clearly laid down that the law of the Centre shall prevail and the State law shall be inoperative to the extent of being repugnant to the Union law in the event of any conflict between the two.

What is very important in this direction, however, is that there are certain situations in which the Centre may make a law on a subject of the State List. These are:

1. Art. 249 says that the Rajya Sabha may pass a resolution by the 2/3 majority of its members present and voting and thereby shift any item from the State List to the Union List or to the Concurrent List on the plea that it has assumed national importance. Such a resolution shall remain in effect for a period of one year, but the Rajya Sabha may extend its duration any number of times.

2. Art. 250 says that the Centre shall have the power to make law on a subject of State List during the period of emergency.

3. Art. 252 says that the Parliament may make a law on any subject of the State List in case there is a request to this effect by two or more State governments. Such a law shall prevail in the States being party to the request, though any other State may adopt it after passing a resolution to this effect.

4. Art. 253 says that the Centre may make a law on any item of the State list in order to implement some international treaty or agreement.

In this connection, it should be pointed out that a law made by the Centre on a subject of State List during the period of emergency shall come to an end when the President makes a notification to that effect. It shall cease to have effect after six months of the revocation of emergency at the most. In case a law is made by the Centre on the basis of the special resolution of the Rajya Sabha, it shall come to an end at the most after 6 months of the termination of the period of the resolution. What will happen to a State law already in existence in case a law of the Centre is enforced? The answer is that the law of the Centre shall come into effect immediately and the State law shall remain 'suspended' to the extent it is repugnant to the Central law. It will, however, be revived when the law of the Centre ceases to have its operation.

A critical examination of the distribution of legislative powers between the Union and the States leaves the dominant impression of a very strong Centre endowed with the built-in capacity to impose its will on the component units of the federation by means of its qualified legal sovereignty. The State legislatures have a very truncated area of authority and even that rump area has been further truncated by virtue of serious inroads whereby the Parliament may make more and more encroachments upon the legislative jurisdiction of the States.

Administrative Relations: The provisions of the Union-State administrative relations may be thus enumerated:

1. Art. 256 says that the executive power of every State shall be so exercised as to ensure compliance with the laws made by the Parliament and any existing laws which apply in that State, and executive power of the Union shall extend to the giving of such directions to a State as may appear necessary to the Government of India.
2. Art. 257 says that the executive power of every State shall be so exercised as not to impede or prejudice the exercise of the executive power of the Government of India.
3. Art. 258 says that the President may, with the consent of the government of a State, entrust either conditionally or unconditionally to that Government or its officers functions in relation to any matter to which the executive power of the Union extends.
4. Art. 260 lays down that the Government of India may by an agreement with the government of any territory not being a part of the territory of India undertake any executive, legislative or judicial functions vested in the government of such territory.
5. Art. 261 provides that full faith and credit shall be given throughout the territory of India to public acts, records and judicial proceedings of the Union and of every State.

6. Art. 262 says that the Parliament may by law provide for the adjudication of any dispute or complaint with respect to the use, distribution and control of the waters in any Inter-state river or valley.
7. Art. 263 empowers the President to appoint an Inter-State Council for inquiring into and advising upon disputes which may have arisen between States, investigating and discussing subjects in which some or all of the States, including the Union government, have a common interest, and make recommendations for a better co-ordination between the Centre and the States.

What we have said about the nature of legislative relations, so here it should be repeated that the Centre has a very dominant position so much so that the autonomy of the States is seriously truncated. The States are bound to carry out faithfully all directives issued by the Centre. They cannot take any step that conflicts with the policy of the Centre. The Governor is on the spot to exercise an effective check when he finds that the State government is taking to a course that might create a situation of confrontation with the Centre. Above all, there is the provision of State emergency under Art. 356 whereby a State government may be sacked for any reason that the Centre may interpret as 'breakdown of constitutional machinery there.'

Financial Relations: The salient points of Union-State financial relations may be thus summarised:

1. There are certain taxes which shall be levied and collected by the States and thereby become the sources of State revenues. These are land revenue, taxes on agricultural income, estate duty and tax on buildings, excise on opium and alcoholic goods etc.
2. There are certain taxes which shall he levied and collected by the Union but assigned to the States. These are taxes on railway fares and freights, passengers and goods, and taxes on newspapers and advertisements given therein etc.
3. There are certain taxes levied by the Union and collected and appropriated by the States. These are: stamp duties, excise on medicine and toilet preparation, etc.

4. There are certain taxes which shall be levied and collected by the Union but which may be distributed between the Union and the States. These are taxes on income other than agricultural, duties of excise other than those on medicinal and toilet preparations etc.

5. There are certain taxes which shall be levied and collected and appropriated by the Government of India alone. These are railways, revenues earned from railways, post and telegraph, wireless and broadcasting, foreign exchange, etc.

6. The President may make alteration in the distribution of the revenues earned from income tax between the Centre and the States.

7. The Centre has the power to grant loans and grants-in-aid to the State governments for the welfare of Scheduled Castes and Scheduled Tribes. It may grant special subsidy to the States of Assam, Bihar, Orissa and West Bengal in lieu of income from the export duty on jute.

8. The Centre may impose service tax which may be collected and appropriated by both the Centre and the States.

9. The Union government is empowered to borrow money on the security of the Consolidated Fund of India subject to the limitations laid down by an act of Parliament. No State government can raise loans without the sanction of the Union government.

10. Art. 280 empowers the President to appoint a Finance Commission after every five years, or whenever he deems necessary, to make recommendations regarding the distribution of the net proceeds of taxes between the Centre and the States on the principles which should govern the giving of grants-in-aid to the States out of the Consolidated Fund of India and the like.

Union-State Relations

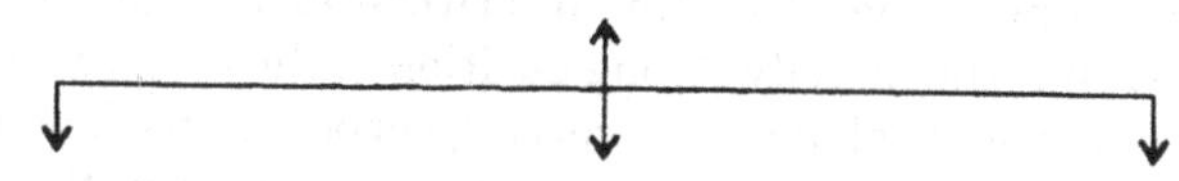

Legislative

1. Union List with the Centre.
2. Concurrent List with both the Centre and the States, with overriding authority of the former.
3. State List with States but under Parliament's power of legislation in these cases:
   (i) After Rajya Sabha passes a special resolution.
   (ii) During emergencies
   (iii) On the request of two or more State legis- latures
   (iv) Implementation of any international treaty or convention
4. Supermacy of Union law over State law in the event of conflict between the two, and
5. Residuary powers with the Centre.

Administrative

1. Executive power of the States to be used in conformity with Union laws.
2. Executive power of the States not to impede or prejudice the Union administration.
3. President's power to delegate or entrust additional powers to State governments with their consent.
4. Union Government's power to take executive, legislative or judicial functions of some foreign country by an agreement.
5. Full faith and credit to be given throughout the country to public acts, records and judicial preceedings of the Union and the States.
6. Parliament's power to make rules for the adjudication of inter-State river water disputes.
7. President's power to create Inter-State Council for maintaining cooperation and coordination between the Centre and the States.

Financial

1. Certain taxes to be levied and collected by the Union whose proceeds may be distributed between the Union and the States.
2. Certain taxes to be collected and levied by the States and thereby forming part of States revenues.
3. Certain taxes to be levied and collected by the Union but assigned to the States.
4. Certain taxes to be levied by the Union but collected and appropriated by the States.
5. Certain taxes to be levied and collected by the Union whose proceeds may be distributed between the Union and the States.
6. President's power to distribute the proceeds of the income tax between the Centre and the States.
7. Giving of grant-in-aid by the Centre to the States with special grants to some States in lieu of export duty on jute.
8. Centre's power to impose service tax to be collected and appropriated by it and by the States.
9. Centre's power to borrow money on the Consolidated Fund of India.
10. Appointment of Finance Commission by the President.

As we have seen in the case of legislative and administrative relations, so here the same line of critical examination should be restressed that the heavily strong position of the Centre has reduced the States to the level of dole-receiving corporations. The resources of the State governments are extremely limited with the result that they are bound to bank upon the charitable assistance of the Centre. Several Central agencies like the University Grants Commission and Central Welfare Board and, above all, the Planning Commission may act in a way so as to influence radically the working of State governments by means of giving them grants-in-laid with virtual strings attached to them. It is also noticeable that, external affairs being a concern of the Centre, all foreign assistance whether from some other country of the world or from some international agency is accruable to the States through the Centre.

Thus, an advocate of federation may say that though component units of the Indian federal system, the State governments have quite often found their hands tied up because of the lack of resources at their disposal entrusted to them by the Union government. Often the State governments have found themselves left with very little discretion in matters of changing the composition of their budgets. The element of politics may have its own role to play. The Centre may replenish some and starve some other States just for the sake of political considerations. Above all, there is the provision of financial emergency under Art. 360 of the Constitution whereby the fiscal autonomy of the States may be finished altogether. Keeping such a contingency in view, Pandit Hridaynath Kunzru had feared that it "would lead to the financial autocracy of the Centre."[14]

A study of Union-State relations in three important directions shows that while the Centre stands like a colossus, the States have a very limited area of authority. Thus, Prof. K.V. Rao calls it a model of *'centralised federalism'*. It is due to this that from time to time several State governments have expressed their deep resentment and demanded more autonomy. The DMK Government of Tamil Nadu appointed a Commission under P.V. Rajamannar in 1970 which submitted a detailed report in regard to the devolution of powers for the sake of more autonomy to the States. The Centre, however, did not honour it. The Union Government has also turned down all proposals for 'suitable amendments in the Constitution

---

14. *Constituent Assembly Debates,* Vol. IX, Part 13, p. 510.

with regard to Union-State relations on the plea that the existing arrangements are adequate. The Sarkaria Commission Report (1987) says that the present arrangement is quite satisfactory and, hence, any more devolution of powers in favour of the States is unwarranted.

A study of the constitutional provisions, as made out in the preceding sections, illustrates that there are two opinions with regard to the nature of our political system hinging on the point of Union-State relations. The one extreme view is that it is highly un-federal or unitary in view of the heavy dependence of the units at the mercy of the Centre. Such an assessment of the Indian constitutional system is hardly convincing. Equally unconvincing is the other view of designating India as *'extremely federal'* as done by Prof. Paul H. Appleby. Instead of going to either of the extremes, one should take a moderate view and then subscribe to the observation of Prof. Ivor Jennings that India is 'a federation with a strong centralising tendency.' Or, as another foreign writer like Selig Harrison says: "The Indian Constitution along with setting up a strong Centre, guarantees built-in-concessions to the federal principle."[15] The nature of the Indian federal principle should be studied in the light of the five peculiar characteristics which we have pointed out above. We should remember that the Supreme Court of India in the *Fundamental Rights (Kesavanand Bharati) Case* of 1973 enunciated the doctrine of the *'basic framework of the Constitution'* and included 'federalism' therein. The fact should be borne in mind that "in spite of federalism, the national interest ought to be paramount."[16]

Reports and Deliberations on Union-State Relations

The issue of relations between the Union and the States has been under discussion ever since the inaugurations of the Contitution in 1950. The opposition parties, particularly the Communists and the ultra-socialists have often said about abolition of the office of the Governor and scrapping of Art. 356 of the Constitution. The leaders of the States have often raised a demand for more autonomy so much so that certain leaders of the National Conference in Kashmir and the extremist sections of the Akali Dal in Punjab have gone to the extent of having a weak Centre as

15. Selig Harrison: *India: The Most Dangerous Decades*, p. 299.

16. Jennings: *Some Characteristics of the Indian Constitution*, p. 55.

envisaged in the Cabinet Mission Plan of 1946. It shall be now worthwhile to have a brief account of the Commissions set up by the Government of India and of some States and the conclaves of the opposition leaders held from time to time. However, their recommendations or observations must be evaluated in the light of this salient fact that autonomy of the States should not be a source of danger or threat to the unity and integrity of the country.

Administrative Reforms Commission Report (1969)

The Administrative Reforms Commission set up by the Government of India submitted its Thirteenth Report to the Prime Minister on 19 June 1969.

1. The Commission put emphasis on the unity of India and the importance of maintaining the same. The Commission was of the view that so far as the constitutional structure was concerned, the Centre must have the power to safeguard the unity of India and make any recalcitrant State conform to the unity of India. As the administrative level, over-concentration of authority should be avoided as it results not only in delay but also causes irritation and friction. A wise and far-sighted administration must be committed to decentralisation of administrative powers.
2. No constitutional amendment was necessary for ensuring proper and harmonious relations between the Centre and the States. The provisions of the Constitution governing the Centre-State relations were adequate for the purpose of meeting any situation or resolving any problem that may arise.
3. It recommended that loans for Planned Schemes should be given only when they are of a productive type. The Planning Commission was to decide whether a scheme was productive or not. The repayment of productive loans should be made over a period of time. It should be insisted that the proper rate of interest is paid within time. Assistance for non-productive capital schemes should be in the form of capital grants.
4. The Finance Commission may be asked to make recommendations on the principles which should govern the distribution of Plan grants to the States. In order to secure

effective coordination of the recommendations of the Finance Commission and the Plan, a member of the Planning Commission should be appointed to the Finance Commission.

5. It further recommended that such as person should be appointed as Governor who has a long experience in public life and administration and can be trusted to rise above party prejudices and predilections. He should not be eligible for further appointment as a Governor. The convention of consulting the Chief Minister before appointing a Governor should be continued. The guidelines on the manner in which discretionary powers should be exercised by the Governors should be formulated by the Inter-State Council.
6. The Inter-State differences should be settled by mutual discussion. These discussions should be held in camera. The Council should consist of the Prime Minister, the Finance Minister, the Home Minister, the leader of the Opposition and others.
7. The use of the naval, military or air force or any other armed forces of the Union in aid of civil power can be made either at the instance of the State Government or *suo moto* by the Centre. The Centre may exercise its discretion to locate such forces in the States and deploy them for maintaining public order for the purposes of the Centre such as protection of Central property. Before issuing any direction to a State under Article 256, the Centre should explore the possibilities of setting points of conflict by all other available means.

Rajamannar Committee Report (1971)

On 22 September 1969, the Tamil Nadu Government set up a Committee consisting of P.V. Rajamannar, former Chief Justice of the Madras High Court, Dr. Lakshmanaswami Mudaliar and P.C. Chandra Reddy to examine the entire question regarding the relationship between the Centre and the States in a federal set-up and to suggest suitable amendments to the Constitution so as to secure utmost autonomy to the States. The Committee submitted its report to the Tamil Nadu Government in May 1971. with these recommendations :

1. The Planning Commission should be made an autonomous body. The Finance Commission should be made a permanent body.

2. The States should be made financially less dependent on the Centre. Some of the subjects should be transferred from the Union List to the State List so that the States become more independent administratively.
3. The appointment of a Governor by the Central Government should be made with the approval of the State Cabinet. If that was difficult, a high powered body may be set up to help the election of an impartial person as a Governor. A person who has once acted as Governor of a State should not be appointed to any other post in the Central Government. The provision that the Ministers hold office during the pleasure of the Governnor, should be deleted.
4. Except in the case of constitutional interpretation, High Courts should have final jurisdiction and no appeal should lie to the Supreme Court.
5. A major part of the Union Government's power of taxation should be transferred to the States.
6. All disputes relating to Inter-State rivers should be taken up by the Supreme Court.
7. All States should be given equal representation in the Council of States and regional representation in the Union Cabinet.
8. Before issuing a Proclamation under Article 356, the President should refer the report of the Governor to the Legislative Assembly of the State. The emergency provisions in the Constitution, especially emergency confined to a State, should be totally repealed.
9. There should be a constitutional provision enabling the President to issue an Instrument of Instructions to the Governors laying down guidelines in respect of matters on which the Governor should consult the Centre or those on which the Centre could issue directions to him.
10. An Inter-State Council should be set up. It should consist of the Prime Minister and the Chief Ministers of all the States. It should discuss and decide all matters concerning more than one State or matters of national importance except defence and foreign affairs. The decisions of this Council should ordinarily be binding on the Centre and the States.

11. State Legislatures should have a voice in the removal of High Court judges.
12. Residuary powers of legislation and taxation should be vested in State Legislatures. State Legislatures should have the power to amend or repeal an Act passed by Parliament under Article 352.

The Government of India ignored the Rajamannar Committee Report. Its contention was that since the Committee was set up by the Government of a State, it had nothing to do with its report. On 13 March 1975, the Government of India accepted the view of the Administrative Reforms Commission that no changes in the Constitution were called for to ensure proper and harmonious Centre-State relations, M.C. Setalvad, former Attorney-General of India, criticized the recommendations of the Rajamannar Committee in these words: "Many of these recommendations for a change in the Constitution ignore the realities of the situation. The question which we have to ask ourselves is whether the situation in India today is one in which we can think of a Central Government less powerful and less involved in the growth and development of the country than at the time of framing the Constitution. The answer of all observers must be an emphatic negative. Fissiparous and divisive tendencies have intensified and taken roots in the factors like linguism, communalism, provincialism, stateism and other narrow loyalties. Far from the Union's power needing curtailment one feels that in many directions they need to be widened. A large section of the community is of the view that these powers require expansion in fields like education, agriculture and the production of articles which are basically needed by the common man. Thus it would clearly not be in the national interest to take steps to amend the Constitution in the manner suggested. Such a step will only result in the opening of the flood-gates of controversy giving an impetus to separatist and fissiparous tendencies and take our energies away from our nation-building tasks."[17] P.B. Gajendragadkar, former Chief Justice of India and Chairman of the Law Commission of India, rejected the suggestion for greater autonomy to the States. "What is necessary is not any radical changes in

17. Setalvad: *Union and State Relations under the Constitution, p. 34*

the Constitution but the development of healthy, federal conventions to regulate the relation between the Union Government and the State Governments. The federal spirit must prevail the conduct of national affairs."[18]

Sarkaria Commission Report (1987)

On 24 March 1983, Prime Minister Indira Gandhi announced the appointment of a Commission under the Chairmanship of Justice Ranjit Singh Sarkaria, a retired judge of the Supreme Court, to examine all aspects of relations between the Centre and the States and make recommendations for change. Its report was made public on 30 January 1988, though it had been submitted on 27 October 1987. Its main recommendations are:

1. The Inter-State Council should be set up under Article 263 of the Constitution. It should consist of a general body which includes the Prime Minister as Chairman and all Chief Ministers and Union Cabinet Ministers as members. It should also have a smaller Standing Committee, consisting of the Prime Minister and six Chief Ministers, one from each zone, elected annually, and six Union Cabinet Ministers, nominated by the Prime Minister. It should provide a forum to senior statesmen for discussing problems of common interest to the Union and the States.
2. While rejecting the demand of some opposition parties for repeal of Article 356, which enables imposition of President's rule in the States, it suggested that it be amended to prevent its arbitrary use. It proposed that the reasons for imposition of President's rule be made public by inclusion in the Presidential proclamation itself, and that the dissolution of the State Assembly be resorted to only after Parliament had approved of the Presidential proclamation.
3. The importance of the All-India Services in discouraging parochial tendencies and maintaining the integrity and cohesion of the administration in the country as a whole was recognised and demands for their disbandment were rejected. The Commission also refused to accept the idea that State Governments be given the choice of opting out of All-India

---

18. *The Hindustan Times*, New Delhi, 26 November 1972

Services. Any weakening of the All-India Services was seen as retrograde and the Commission in fact wanted them to be strengthened and improved through better methods of selection and training.

4. It rejected demands for abolition of the office of Governor. However, it made various proposals for increasing the credibility and dignity of the office. It wanted the Governors to be appointed from among eminent people in different walks of life and not from among politicians belonging to the party ruling at the Centre, especially when the government in the State was in the hands of some other party. It suggested consultation with Chief Ministers before appointment.
5. To solve the vaxed problem of sharing of river waters, it made some important proposals. It suggested that the Inter-State River Disputes Act should be suitably amended to expedite the resolution of conflicts by making it mandatory for the Union Government to appoint a tribunal within one year of the receipt of an application from a State Government and by giving the Union Government the power to appoint a tribunal *suo moto* once it was satisfied that a conflict did in fact exist. The Act should be further amended to make the tribunal's award binding as that of an order or decree of the Supreme Court, to ensure that the award became effective within five years of the date of its constitution, and to make it obligatory for States to furnish necessary data to the tribunal.
6. It suggested that before the Union Government deploys its armed and other forces in a State in aid of the civil administration or declares an area within a State as 'disturbed', it should, wherever feasible, consult the State government and seek its cooperation.
7. It suggested an amendment of Article 217 to ensure that vacancies of High Court judges are filled promptly within a fixed time schedule. It also advised that as a matter of healthy convention the current practice that High Court judges are not transferred without their consent should continue. In addition, a further healthy convention should be established that the Chief Justice of India consults two senior judges of the Supreme Court before forming his opinion on the transfer of a High Court judge.

8. It made detailed suggestions about fixing a time frame for assent and establishing a convention that assent is withheld only on grounds of patent unconstitutionality and not because of policy differences or on the ground that the Union is contemplating a comprehensive law. In any case, the reasons for withholding of assent should be communicated to the States.
9. It advised that the States should be fully involved at all stages of the planning process by the Planning Commission. It also suggested that the National Development Council should be renamed the National Economic Development Council and should emerge as the highest political level inter-governmental body for giving a thrust and direction to planned economic development.
10. It made a number of suggestions for streamlining the allocation of resources, for regularising the overdrafts by States for making foreign exchange available to the States, etc. It suggested the setting up of an expert body to make suitable reforms in the taxation system and the manner in which taxes are shared between the Centre and the States. Financiel Commission's important role was recognised and it was urged that there should be no delay in the implementation of its recommendations.
11. All matters which need to be sorted out between the Union Government and Union Territories with legislatures should be discussed by a Standing Commission for Union Territories.
12. It suggested that the Union Government should have prior consultations with State Governments, individually and collectively, before proposing legislation concerning matters on the Concurrent List. It suggested a more generous use of Article 258 under which the Union government was entitled to confer powers on State governments. Regarding education, it advised that the Union government and professional bodies such as the University Grants Commission should lay down the norms and standards, but leave there implementation to the States.

Apart from this, the Chief Ministers of the States and leaders of the opposition parties had their meetings on different occasions where some decisions were taken. A brief account of such deliberations may be presented.

Recommendations of Southern Chief Ministers (1983): On 20 March 1983, the Chief Ministers of Tamil Nadu, Karnataka, Andhra Pradesh and the Union Territory of Pondicherry met at Bangalore and formed the Council of Southern States Chief Ministers. The Bangalore conference demanded the tranfer of resources to the States on a statutory basis and not in a discretionary way as before. A demand was also made for the appointment of a fiscal commission with adequate representation of State to review the Centre-State relations in fiscal matters. The Constitution should be amended to accommodate and give full meaning to the new definition of Centre-State relationship. A demand was made for modifying the Gadgil formula for the distribution of Planned assistance by the Centre to the States. The needs of Assam, Jammu and Kashmir and Nagaland were to be met through ad hoc assignment out of Central assistance. The balance was to be distributed among the other States as follows: 60 per cent on the basis of population, 10 per cent on the basis of per capita income only to those States whose per capita income was below the national average, 10 per cent on the basis of per capita tax-effort in relation to per capita income, 10 per cent on account of continuing major irrigation and powers schemes and 10 per cent on consideration of special problems of States such as desert areas, tribal areas, drought affected areas. A demand was also made that the limits on ways and means advances to all States should be raised by 50 per cent over the quantum fixed for States in July 1982. Those States which had an over-draft on 30 June 1982, might be given term loans.

Vijayawada Conclave (1983): On 28 May 1983, 14 Opposition leaders met at Vijayawada at the invitation of the Chief Minister of Andhra Pradesh, N.T. Rama Rao. It was asserted at that meeting that the distribution of Centre-State powers must be reviewed, the encroachment of the Centre into the domain of the States must stop and the Centre must consult the States and the Opposition parties before announcing the terms of reference of the Sarkaria Commission.

Srinagar Conclave (1983): The Srinagar Conclave of the Opposition Parties on Centre-State Relations lasted from 5 October to 7 October 1983. The Akalis, CPI, CPM. Bahuguna, Chandra Shekhar, Jagjivan Ram and some other Opposition leaders took part in the Conclave. The Telugu Desam of Andhra Praesh and Akali Dal of Punjab made out a strong case for restricting the

Centre's power to four important subjects leaving the rest to be handled exclusively by the States. The four subjects were defence, foreign affairs, general communications and currency.

Chandrajit Yadav, the Janavadi Party chief, attributed all problems between the Centre and State Governments to the inability of the Union Government to accept the federal spirit. Prakash Singh Badal called for the abolition of the institution of Governor responsible for the abuse of power seventy times so far. Rama Rao criticised the Congress (I) for not eradicating poverty and misery of the people and declared that the people of India had not got their freedom.

The Chief Minister of Andhra Pradesh described the Centre as a conceptual myth. He advocated many amendments to the Constitution to whittle down the powers of the Union and make it a non-entity and ultimately collapse or whither away. Articles 356 and 360 giving emergency powers to the Centre were to be removed from the Constitution. The mass media should be controlled by an independent body not subject to the control of the Centre. State Legislatures were to be made nearly sovereign authorities in practice. The residuary powers were to vest with the States and not with the Centre.

Calcutta Conclave (1984): On 13 January 1984, leaders of 19 Opposition parties and Chief Ministers of some non-Congress (I) States agreed that they must take some concrete action to withstand the onslaught being made against all democratic institutions. The Opposition parties decided to launch a country-wide campaign to mobilise national opinion against the attempt of the Congress (I) to "destroy democracy and expose its incompetence and opportunistic policies which have pushed the nation to the brink of disaster." An Eleven-point Resolution was adopted at the Calcutta Conclave. It included the following main demands: adequate supply of essentials to the consumers at reasonable prices, streamlining and expanding the public distribution system, ensuring adequate purchases for State agencies for providing remunerative prices for agricultural produce, revival of food for work programme, overhauling the existing land reforms legislation, scrapping of the National Security Act and Essential Services Maintenance Act. The conference made a demand to meet emergency situations arising out of natural calamities. A permanent team should be created in the Union Agriculture Ministry to rush to the sites of natural calamities within 48 hours and make a general survey of the damage caused. The conclave appealed for the solution of the Punjab problem.

A critical review of the deliberations and recommendations of these commissions, committees and conclaves shows that these have been inspired by a desire to strengthen the position of the States at the cost of the existence of strong Centre. The recommendation of keeping a weak Centre (as envisaged in the Cabinet Mission Plan of 1946) was rejected by the Constituent Assembly. Most of the politicians operating at the regional levels were like a disgruntled lot and so they made such endeavours. The recommendations of the Sarkaria Commission alone have their significance and some of them have been implemented by the Union Government in course of time. More surprising is the fact that after the decline of the Congress hold, many opposition parties have changed their stand in favour of the existing arrangement. After having the taste of power in coalition governments at the Centre, even vocal sections of the Communist and Socialist parties have put aside their old grievances and assertions for more autonomy for the states.

Inter-State River Water Disputes

Rivers constitute natural resources of the country. Their flow through different regions, provinces, or States is a natural phenomenon and no dispute should arise on the use, distribution and control of their water. The problem may arise when a river passes through different sovereign states, but there should be nothing of this kind if it covers some riparian provinces of a federal polity. In case such a controversy or dispute arises, it should be sorted out in a peaceful and rational manner. For this purpose, Art. 262 of the Constitution empowers the Parliament to make a law for the adjudication of any dispute or complaint with respect to the use, distribution and control of the waters of, or in, any inter-State river or river valley. The Parliament has the power to exclude the jurisdiction of the Courts in this matter.

In pursuance of this provision, the Parliament made Inter-State Water Disputes Act in 1956. Such a dispute shall be settled by a Tribunal set up by the Chief Justice of India. Here the jurisdiction of the Supreme Court has been excluded, but it can direct the Union Government to fulfil its statutory obligations under Sec. 4 of this Act, which is mandatory. An amendment was made in this Act in

2002 which specifies that the Tribunal has to settle the dispute within six years at the most.

The Centre may formulate National Water Policy. It was done in 1987 by the government of Rajiv Gandhi. But the government of Vajpayee revised it in April, 2002. It provides for the setting up of River Basin Organisations by each State of the Indian Union to resolve issues relating to water within that particular State. As river water is a subject of the State List, the Centre may play the role of a 'facilitator'. Now the States shall formulate their own water policy backed by an operational Action Plan (prepared by the Union Ministry of Water Resources) within two years. It lays emphasis on integrated water resources development and management for optimal and sustainable utilisation of the available surface and ground water."[19]

Sutlej-Yamuna Link Canal (SYL) Dispute: The partition of India in 1947 led to the dispute between the two countries on the use of the water of the rivers flowing in Punjab but entering the territory of Pakistan. With the mediation of the World Bank the Indus water treaty came into being in September, 1960. But with the bifurcation of Punjab in 1966, another problem arose that is now known as the Sutlej-Yamuna Link Dispute. Under Sec. 78 of the Punjab Reorganisation Act of 1966, the Government of India issued a notification on 24 March, 1976 whereby water was to be divided between the States of Punjab and Haryana. Under this project, a 214 km. long canal would be constructed that would join the water of Sutlej with the water of Yamuna. The belt of 122 km. would be in Punjab and of 92 km in Haryana, but the entire cost of construction would be met by the Union Government. By the end of 1980, the government of Haryana completed its portion, but the government of Punjab filed a writ petition in the Supreme Court challenging the notification of the Government of India.

A serious roadblock was created by such an action of the Punjab government. And yet the process of conciliation continued intermittently. On 31 December, 1981, the governments of Rajasthan, Haryana and Punjab entered into an agreement with the Union government. It happened at the initiative of Prime

19. Punjab did not give its consent to the draft policy which stipulated that the planning, development and management of water resources need to be governed by national perspective.

Minister Indira Gandhi. Happily, the Chief Ministers of three States signed this agreement with the resolve that the construction work would be completed within two years. Then the Punjab government withdrew its suit. Despite it all, the Punjab government did not honour the terms of this agreement. Then came the Punjab Accord or Settlement signed by Prime Minister Rajiv Gandhi and H.S. Longowal whereby it was agreed upon that the farmers of the three States would continue to have the same amount of water they used to get from the Ravi-Beas system as on 1 July, 1985. It was also decided that the dispute should be referred to a panel headed by a judge of the Supreme Court and the work of construction should be done by 15 August, 1986. In pursuance of this, the Union government issued a notification on 2 April, 1986 whereby the Eradi Tribunal was set up to settle the dispute of water sharing. It submitted its report on 30 January, 1987, but the government of Punjab filed a petition on 9 August, 1987 before the tribunal asking for a review of its award. Thus the matter remained pending.[20]

The stand of the government of Punjab was unwarranted in view of the fact that a big part of the canal had already been constructed and only 10 per cent of work was to be completed within the specified time. Now the government of Punjab came forward with the argument that the construction work was unnecessary, because Haryana was to get additional water from other rivers and, hence, it had no right to get water from river Ravi. The Union government insisted that the remaining work of construction should be completed. Under such conditions, the government of Haryana moved the Supreme Court which ruled that the work of construction of the canal be completed within a year. In its mandatory injunction, the Court also said that the Centre must get it done by its own agency as soon as possible. In stead of honouring the verdict of the Supreme Court, the government of Punjab filed a suit in the Court on 13 January, 2003 (just two days before the line of one year was to expire) questioning the constitutionality of its verdict. It raised the argument of 'changed conditions' and rampant violence in the State. The Court rejected such arguments.

20. The Eradi Tribunal Award distributed water in this manner-Rajasthan-8'60 (MAF), Punjab-5'0 (MAF), Haryana-3'83 (MAF), Jammu-Kashmir-0'65 (MAF) and Delhi-0'20 (MAF).

Having lost its case in the Supreme Court, the obstinate government of Punjab took the last step of scrapping the agreement of 1981. The Legislative Assembly passed the Termination of Agreements Bill on 12 July 2004 and the Governor's assent made it an Act. It was said in the Assembly that the trans-basin diversion of river waters contemplated under the Agreements of 1981 would adversely affect the inhabitants of the basin areas within Punjab and would render nine lakh of farmland dry and barren. It was also pointed out that the total availability of water in Ravi and Beas had been reduced to 14'37 million acre feet (MAF) against 17'17 MAF of 1981. The Chief Minister also argued that Haryana and Rajasthan did not fall in the Ravi-Beas basin.

The Punjab Termination of Agreements Act, 2004 was, indeed, an astounding step taken by the Congress government of Capt. Arminder Singh. But the government issued a press release so as to justify its action. It had these salient points:'[21]

1. Punjab is proud of its position in the Indian Union and has equal concern for its neighbours. As a sovereign authority, Punjab considers it its bounden duty to uphold the Constitution and the laws and to protect the interests of its inhabitants.
2. Indus system which was prevalent before the partition of the country has become irrelevant after partition, since only three east following rivers, namely, Ravi, Beas and Sutlej, out of the six rivers constituting the said system remained within Indian territory for its exclusive use.
3. Presently all the three rivers--Ravi, Beas and Sutlej--flow through the territory of Punjab, None of them flows either through Haryana or Rajasthan and therefore donot constitute their basin areas. Even according to the Irrigation Commission, only 9,939 sq. km. of areas within Haryana fall within the Indus Basin (not within the Ravi and Beas basin), as against 50,304 sq. km. areas within Punjab.
4. Haryana presently utilises about 5'95 MAF of water (about 4'33 MAF from Sutlej and about 1'92 MAF from Ravi and Beas).
5. Punjab's claim of its share in Yamuna water has been turned down even though parts of Punjab fall within Yamuna basin,

---

21. *The Hindustan Times*, (New Dehli), 16 July, 2004

while Haryana and Rajasthan have continued to utilise the waters of rivers Ravi and Beas, though they are neither riparian nor basin States. Punjab as a good neighbour accepted such utilization by Haryana and Rajasthan as usages by sufferance but not as a matter of any recognition of their rights.

6. No reliable and scientific study of hydrological, ecological and sociological impact of large scale trans-basin diversion from Punjab to Haryana and Rajasthan was undertaken when Punjab, Haryana and Rajasthan entered into an agreement on 31-12-1981 allocating 3'5 MAF of water to Haryana and 8'60 MAF of water to Rajasthan out of the surplus flow of the rivers Ravi and Beas, then estimated at 17'17 MAF based on 1921-1960 flow series.

7. Such a huge trans-basin diversion of water is likely to have permanent adverse impact on the irrigation and other requirements within the basin areas of Punjab rendering about 9 lakh acres of the basin areas dry and barren with an adverse impact on livelihood of 1'5 million families. Diversion of water on such a large scale from the donor deficit basin of Ravi and Beas to the surplus basin of the Yamuna river is contrary to national water policy guidelines.

8. There is material and substantial change in ground realities adverse to the interests of Punjab, because the total availability of waters in the rivers Ravi and Beas has reduced from 17'17 MAF (assumed under the Agreement dated 31-12-1981) to 14'37 MAF as per the flow series of 1981-2002. Moreover, under the Yamuna Agreement dated 12-5-1994, Haryana has been allocated 4'65 MAF of water, which will be further augmented by the Sarda Yamuna Link.

9. In the circumstances, the terms of the said Agreement dated 31-12-1981 have become onerous, unfair, unreasonable and contrary to the interests of the inhabitants of the Ravi and Beas basin area, who have lawful rights to utilise the water of the rivers Ravi and Beas.

10. Being conscious of the legal position that the obligations arising from an agreement on a contract do not fetter powers of the Legislature to enact a law in public interest, the Punjab Vidhan Sabha has enacted the Punjab Termination of Agreements Act, 2004.

11. The Punjab Termination of Agreements Act, 2004 fuly protects current utilisation of Ravi, Beas and Sutlej waters by the neighbouring States. Section 5 of the Act clearly stipulates that all existing and actual utilisations through the existing systems shall remain protected and unaffected.

All the arguments furnished by the Punjab government are specious and so unconvincing for these reasons:

1. Agreements once entered into by different parties cannot be revoked unilaterally. It is like a repetition of the callous stand of the government of Karnataka that it would not abide by the verdict of the Cauvery tribunal.
2. The catalogue of arguments contains some objectionable expressions as 'Punjab as a sovereign authority' 'our water' 'diversion of water from a donor-deficit basin to a surplus basin'.
3. No part of the territories of the States of Rajasthan and Haryana fall within the basin areas of Ravi and Beas.
4. India and Pakistan called for the World Bank to mediate in the Indus Water Dispute. An officer of the Government of India (N.D. Gulati) urged Prime Minister Nehru to continue to work on the Sirhind feeder and the Rajasthan Canal before the arrival of the World Bank team that would visit areas of the Indus basin. So a water sharing agreement was drawn up on 29 January, 1955 for the allocation of Ravi-Beas surplus waters between the States of Jammu-Kashmir, Punjab, Rajasthan and Pepsu. It culminated in the signing of the Indus Water Treaty in September, 1960. "A sense of justice and geography prevailed in declaring that Indus basin in India would include Jammu-Kashmir, Himachal Pradesh, Punjab, Chandigarh and parts of Haryana and Rajasthan."[22]
5. There was no Haryana when the Indus Water Treaty was signed by India and Pakistan. Haryana came into being in 1966 and so it has every right to share the water of Punjab rivers. A realisation of this fact had its effect when the agreement of 1981 was hammered out.

---

22. Manvendra Singh: "Flow in the Face of Logic" in *The Hindustan Times*, (New Delhi), 16 July, 2004, p. 10.

It is quite obvious that the stand of the government of Punjab is of "great ilogic, illegality and ill-will towards its neighbouring States. Many arguments flow ironically from the only State which has water as a part of its name."[23]

A critical look at this case shows that the callous leaders of a State government may create an unecessary problem for the federal set up of the country. Moreover it has revealed the ineffectiveness of the party system that is known as the extra-constitutional mechanism of our country. By her influence, Indira Gandhi could bring different parties together to sign the agreements in 1981, but her successors failed to exercise a like influence. The making of an act to terminate the agreements of 1981 "is a powerful assault on the declining authority of the Central Government and the growing incapacity of the two self-proclaimed all India political parties like the Congress and the BJP to tame and control provincial political adventurists who are determined to destroy the delicate balance of federal power in the Indian Constitution."[24]

Cauvery Water Dispute: It is a dispute of the same kind between the States of Karnataka and Tamil Nadu, though the State of Kerala and the Union Territory of Pondicherry are also incidentally involved in it. The dispute is quite old as the low riparian province of Madras had raised its voice in the pre-independence days when the high riparian princely State of Mysore had done something to harm the interest of the Madras Presidency in respect of sharing of water. But then the situation was basically different. The Madras Presidency under a British Governor could have a heavier say in the making of agreements in 1892 and 1924 against the State of Mysore under a feudal chief. Thus, Madras could extract better concessions. It is also a patent fact that Mysore under a native ruler did not require much water for irrigation purposes as the then government of the princely State had not paid sufficient attention towards the development of agriculture.

Things took a turn after the reorganisation of the States in 1956. Now the State government of Mysore (that became Karnataka in 1973) adopted the programme of agricultural and industrial

---

23. *Ibid.*

24. C.P. Bhambhri: *Indian Politics (2001-04): Political Process and Change of Government* (New Delhi: Shipra Pub., 2005), p. 208

development as a result of which it needed more share in the Cauvery water not only for irrigation but also for drinking purposes in many new townships of the State. For this sake, the government constructed large dams and reservoirs. In the 1970s the dispute between the States of Karnataka and Tamil Nadu took a serious shape when the former claimed that it had the right to utilise 465 TMC of water in the basin in order to irrigate 26 lakh acre of land. It started construction work on the Hemavathi, Harangi and Kabini reservoirs. In retaliation the government of Tamil Nadu demanded 489 TMC of water for its cropped area of 28'20 lakh acre.

It led to the dispute on sharing of the Cauvery water. The government of Tamil Nadu requested the Union government to constitute a tribunal for the settlement of this dispute. As the Centre failed to respond, it filed a petition in the Supreme Court. On a direction from the Court, the government of V.P. Singh appointed a tribunal for this purpose in 1990. In June, 1991 the Cauvery Water Tribunal passed an interim order directing Karnataka to release 205 TMC of water to Tamil Nadu in every water year. The government of Karnataka rejected this interim order on the plea that the Cauvery Tribunal had failed to take into account the vagaries of nature and the shortage of river water in the lean years.

In such a situation the government of Tamil Nadu approached the Supreme Court in April, 1997 which asked the Union government to implement the interim award. Thus on 11 August, 1998 came into being the Cauvery River Authority (CRA) having Prime Minister as the Chairman and the Chief Ministers of the concerned States (Karnataka, Tamil Nadu and Kerala) and of the Union Territory of Pondicherry. A Monitoring Committee of the designated officers of the concerned parties was also set up to supervise the release of 205 TMC of the river water. The Union Water Resources Department was also associated with the Monitoring Committee. But the real issue of the implementation of the interim order of the Tribunal remained. The Monitoring Committee has the power to inspect the reservoirs in both the States.

At an emergency meeting of the CRA held in New Delhi under the chairmanship of Prime Minister Vajpayee it was resolved that Karnataka would release at least 0'8 TMC of water per day to provide immediate succour to the delta farmers. The government of Karnataka honoured this settlement, but soon after the farmers started a stir and some of them committed suicide by jumping into the Kabini reservior. Taking note of the deteriorating situation, the government of Karnataka suspended the release of water. It forced the government of Tamil Nadu to once again approach the Union government and the Supreme Court. The issue of water-sharing formula came to be integrated with distress-sharing formula.

On February 5, 2007 the Cauvery Water Dispute Tribunal announced its award which does not seem to have provided the final solution to this century-old dispute. It has been challenged and the grievances have been referred back to the tribunal and the Supreme Court. To start with, the available quantum of water for apportionment (740 tmcft) is based on fifty percent availability, which means that in one out of every two years, there is bound to be a shortfall in this quantity. No clear distress-sharing formula has been given in this award. Its solution calls for a two-pronged approach—(*a*) an additional terminal storage reservoir of at least 50-60 tmcft capacity to store and carry over the flows from a healthy monsoon year to a drought year, and (*b*) inter-basin transfer of water from external catchments into the Cauvery.

A brief study of these two cases informs that such events may occur in other parts of the country as well. The obstinate stands of the governments of Punjab and Karnataka may set a bad precedent. The callous leaders of the States forget that the Constitution is the supreme law of the land and the Supreme Court is its final interpreter and custodian. It may also be visualised that the source of the problem is entry 17 of the State List which makes the State governments the master of the use and control of river water. The Centre may make a law on the subject of regulation and development of inter-State river waters under entry 56 of the Union List, but the State governments may invoke the provision of entry 17 of the State List. It is, therefore, necessary that a constitutional amendment should be made to delete entry 17 of the State List (or to shift it to the Union List or Concurrent List) so that no State government may create a problem for the Centre on this count. While hearing the petition of the government of Tamil Nadu on 2 September, 2002, the judges of the Supreme Court had asked the Solicitor-General (Harish Salve) whether it was possible to bring Inter-State river water under the Union List of the Constitution, as it was going to happen in respect of some other rivers of the country. It was at this time that the Chief Minister of Tamil Nadu (Jayalalitha) had opined that the rivers of the country should be nationalised.

10

Union Executive

Recalling the mind of the Drafting Committee, KM. Munshi said that from the very beginning, it "was decided that the Central Government should be based on the English model."[1] In more forceful words, Sardar Patel observed that it "would suit the condition of this country better to adopt the parliamentary system of Constitution, the British type of Constitution with which we are familiar."[2] The Government at the Centre is called the Union Government. The President is the Head of the State. There is a Vice-President to assist the President and to act as the President during the absence of the latter for any reason. The Council of Ministers with the Prime Minister at the head is to aid and advise the President and is collectively responsible to the Lok Sabha. The indubitable fact that the Indian Constitution has adopted the Westminster model of government places the Head of the State (President) and the Head of the Government (Prime Minister) in the categories of, what Wallter Bagehot said about his English system of government, the 'dignified' and the 'efficient' executives respectively.

President

Election: The President is the head of the Indian republic. He is elected for a term of five years and he may be re-elected any number of times. In order to be elected, he must possess three qualifications. First, he must be a citizen of India. Second, he must have completed the age of 35 years. Last, he must possess all other qualifications prescribed for an elected member of the Lok Sabha

1. *Constituent Assembly Debates*, Vol. VII, p. 984.

2. *Ibid.*, Vol. IV, p. 580.

and that he must not be holding an office of profit.[3] He is elected by an electoral college consisting of the elected members of the Parliament and State legislatures including the Legislative Assemblies of Pondicherry and of the National Capital Territory of Delhi. In this election the value of votes is counted that is drawn according to a formula. In the States, the value of the votes of one MLA is drawn by dividing the population of the State (as given in the last census report) by the total number of elected MLAs and the quotient is further divided by 1,000. In case the remainder is more than 500, then 1 is added to the value of votes. The total value of the votes of all elected MLAs of the country is divided by the total number of elected MPs in order to determine the value of the votes of an MP. Again, in case the remainder is more than half of the denominator, then 1 is added to the value of votes. It is also provided that the election of the President shall be held in accordance with proportional representation with single transferable vote system. The ballot shall be secret.

The makers of the Constitution made a mistake here. The proportional representation system cannot apply where only one seat is to be contested. The question arises as to proportion between whom or what? As a matter of fact, alternative or preferential vote system is used. The voter is given a ballot paper having names and symbols of the contestants with blank columns on the right side where he has to show his preferences by writing the figures of 1,2,

---

3. The term 'office of profit' is very important. It covers all posts where the immediate appointing authority is the Government and where any percentage of his salary or emoluments comes from Government revenue. The Constitution has exempted the offices of the President, Vice-President, Governors, and Ministers of the Union and the States. D.D. Basu makes some more important points to be taken into account in this direction: (1) Actual making of profit by the incumbent is not necessary to make an office of profit; it is enough if the holder of the office may reasonably be expected to make a profit out of it. (2) Profit means any pecuniary gain. (3) It need not be a payment in money. (4) It does not matter whether at the time of holding that office he is making profit or not. (5) A voluntary renunciation of the salary by the holder does not make any difference. (6) The payment, in order to constitute profit, must be made by the person's holding the office. *Commentary on the Constitution of India*, Vol. 2, Ed. V., pp. 569–70.

Presidential Elections

Elections	*Dates*	*Successful Candidates*	*Main Opponent*
First	May, 1957	Dr. Rajendra Prasad	N.N. Das
Second	May, 1962	Dr. Radhakrishnan	Hari Ram
Third	May, 1967	Dr. Zakir Hussain	K. Subba Rao
Fourth	August, 1969	V.V. Giri	N.S. Reddy
Fifth	August, 1974	Fakhruddin A. Ahmed	Tridib Chowdhry
Sixth	August, 1977	N.S. Reddy	(Unopposed)
Seventh	July, 1982	Giani Zail Singh	H.R. Khanna
Eighth	July, 1987	R. Venkataraman	V.R.K. Iyer
Ninth	July, 1992	Dr. S.D. Sharma	G.G. Swell
Tenth	July, 1997	K.R. Narayanan	T.N. Seshan
Eleventh	July, 2002	A.P.J. Abdul Kalam	Mrs. L. Sehgal
Twelfth	July, 2007	Pratibha Patil	B.S. Shekhawat
Thirteenth	July, 2012	Pranab Mukherjee	P.A. Sangma
Fourteenth	July, 2017	Ram Nath Kovind	Meira Kumar
Fifteenth	July, 2022	Draupadi Murmu	Yashwant Sinha

etc. At the time of counting, first preference votes are counted. The winner must secure more than 50 per cent of the votes polled.

In case a candidate manages to secure votes upto the figure of electoral quota, he is declared elected. In case no candidate is able to get votes equal to or more than the figure of electoral quota (as happened in the election of 1969), the candidate having least number of votes is eliminated and his votes are transferred to other candidates according to second preference shown on the ballot papers. Naturally, the votes of other candidates are enhanced. If this step fails to enable a candidate to get votes upto the electoral quota, then a candidate having least number of votes is eliminated and his votes are transferred to other candidates according to second preference shown on his ballot papers, while the votes already transferred according to second preference are now transferred to other candidates according to third preference shown on the ballot papers. If a ballot paper does not indicate subsequent preference, it becomes invalid. This process goes on until a candidate manages to get votes upto the electoral quota, or only one candidate remains after eliminating all other candidates.

The XIII presidential election held on 19 July, 2007 has some striking features. For the first time, this great occasion was boycotted by a number of parties (as Socialist Party, Assom Gana Parishad, Indian National Lok Dal, Trinamul Congress, Telangana Rashtriya Samiti, Telugu Desam Party, Anna-AIADMK, Mizo National Front, Janata Dal (S), and MDMK, though at the counsel of the Election Commission, the A-IADMK changed its stand. The level of canvassing touched a low point when the UPA exploited the issue of 'gender equality' and the leaders of the NDA questioned the 'stature' of Pratibha Patil. As many as 60 members of the electoral college cast their votes by coming out of the jail for this purpose. A very large number of votes were declared invalid. It shows that the elected deputies lacked the knowledge of showing their preference in the ballot paper. For the first time, a woman candidate could have the chance to be the first citizen of the Indian Republic.[4]

The election of Mrs. Pratibha Patil should be taken as the restoration of the system introduced by Indira Gandhi. It was her choice that men like V.V. Giri, F.A. Ahmed and Giani Zail Singh became the head of the Indian Republic. It showed that the President of India was virtually the choice of the real working head of the state. Things had changed to set aside the doctrine of 'PM's President'. But now the same trend has been restored by Sonia Gandhi, the chief of the Indian National Congress and the head of the co-ordination committee of the United Progressive Alliance. The issue of gender equality was not raised in the previous election when Laxmi Sehgal was the candidate, but this time it was forcefully exploited to garner the votes of other parties. The Shiv Sena yielded to the push of regionalism that gave a set back to the votes of the NDA. The leftists could have the chance to rejoice at the success of a woman candidate now whose choice had failed to have its way in the previous election. In the election of 2012 once again the will of the Congress supremo (Sonia Gandhi) prevailed whose nominee Pranab Mukherjee defeated P.A. Sangma supported by the BJP and some regional parties.

---

4. An Indian paper commented: "The biggest loser, of course, may be the nation. India has ended up being burdened by a President who, despite the victory of gender equality, may prove to be a colossal embarrassment especially if a dodgy past is constantly excavated." *The Pioneer* (New Delhi), 22 July, 2007.

Thirteenth Presidential Election (2007)

Legislative Assemblies and Parliament	*Number of Elected MLAs and MPs*	*Total Value of Votes*	*Value of each Vote*	*Pratibha Patil Votes*	*B.S. Shekhawat Votes*	*Invalid Votes*
1. Andhra Pradesh	294	43,512	148	223	2	4
2. Arunachal Pradesh	60	480	8	58	1	–
3. Assam	126	14,616	116	92	20	4
4. Bihar	243	42,039	173	89	145	2
5. Chhattisgarh	90	11,610	129	37	51	1
6. Goa	40	800	20	25	14	1
7. Gujarat	182	26,754	147	57	123	2
8. Haryana	90	10,080	112	74	7	–
9. Himachal Pradesh	68	3,648	51	47	20	–
10. Jammu and Kashmir	87	6,264	72	77	6	2
11. Jharkhand	81	14,256	176	49	28	2
12. Karnataka	224	29,344	131	83	82	–
13. Kerala	140	21,280	152	152	–	5
14. Madhya Pradesh	230	30,130	131	53	162	11
15. Maharashtra	288	50,400	175	223	58	6
16. Manipur	60	1,080	18	55	5	–
17. Meghalaya	60	1,020	17	49	6	4
18. Mizoram	40	320	8	14	–	11
19. Nagaland	60	540	9	42	12	5
20. Orissa	147	21,730	149	46	100	–
21. Punjab	117	13,572	116	45	66	6
22. Rajasthan	200	25,800	129	63	134	3
23. Sikkim	32	224	7	31	1	–
24. Tamilnadu	234	41,184	176	171	59	1
25. Tripura	60	1,560	26	57	–	2
26. Uttarakhand	70	4,480	64	27	41	1
27. Uttar Pradesh	403	83,824	208	251	52	2
28. West Bengal	294	44,394	151	256	–	4

29. NCT of Delhi	70	4,060	58	50	19	–
30. Puducherry	30	480	16	27	3	–
31. Parliament	776	5,49,408	708	442	232	11
Total	**4,896**			**2,931**	**1,449**	**90**

Total Number of Voters		**Total Value of Voters**		**Total Value of Votes Secured by**	
1. Vidhan Sabhas	4.120	MLAs	5,49,474	Pratibha Patil	6,38,116
2. Rajya Sabha	233	MPs	5,49,408	B.S. Shekhawat	3,31,306
3. Lok Sabha	543				
Total	**4,896**		**10,98,882**		

Term: The President holds office for a period of five years from the date he takes the oath in the presence of the Chief Justice of India whereby he swears in the name of God, or solemnly affirms, that he will faithfully execute his office or discharge his functions in a way so as to preserve, protect and defend the Constitution with the best of his ability and devote himself to the service and well-being of the people of India. He may resign his office before the expiry of his term for any reason. The letter of resignation must be addressed to the Vice-President. In the event of vacancy, the Vice-President shall act as the President and in case he is not available, then this opportunity shall be given to the Chief Justice of India and, in the event of his not being available, to any other judge of the Supreme Court according to the principle of seniority. Within next six months the election of the new President must be held.

The President may be removed by the process of impeachment for 'violation of the Constitution'. Any House of Parliament may initiate the proceedings of impeachment. A resolution to this effect must be signed by at least one-fourth members of the whole House and the matter may be taken up for discussion after at least 14 days' notice in writing. After debate such a resolution must be passed by two-thirds majority of the total membership of the House.

If so happens, then the same shall be taken up by other House of Parliament which may investigate the charges, or may cause them investigated by some other authority. It is at this stage that the President shall have the right to appear personally or through his nominee for presenting his defence. In case the motion is passed by the House by two-thirds majority of its total membership, the President shall be removed forthwith from his office.

Functions and Powers: The normal functions and powers of the President may be discussed under five heads-executive, legislative, judicial, financial and others. Art. 52 says that the *executive power* of the Union shall be vested in the President and shall be exercised by him either directly or through officers subordinate to him. The executive functions and powers of the President may be put as under:

1. All administration is conducted in his name; he makes rules for the conduct of government business and allocation of work among the Ministers.

2. He receives information of all important decisions of the Cabinet relating to the affairs of administration and proposals for legislation and he may refer any matter for the consideration or reconsideration of the Council of Ministers.

3. He appoints the Prime Minister; he appoints ministers on the advice of the Prime Minister. Besides, he makes a very large number of appointments as those of the Governors, ambassadors, Chief Justice and Judges of the Supreme Court, Chief Justices and Judges of the High Courts, Chairman and members of the Union Public Service Commission, Chairman and members of a Joint Public Service Commission, Attorney General of India, Chief Election Commissioner and Election Commissioners, Comptroller and Auditor-General of India, Chairman and members of the Statutory Commissions as those of Finance Commission, National Human Rights Commission, National Women's Commission, National Commission for Scheduled Castes, National Commission for Scheduled Tribes, National Commission for Minorities etc. He accepts their resignation also.

4. The administration of the Union Territories and Scheduled and Tribal Areas is done in his name.

5. He maintains foreign relations. For this purpose he appoints ambassadors and envoys for foreign countries and accepts the credentials of the ambassadors and envoys of foreign countries.

6. He is the Supreme Commander of the Defence Forces.

7. He approves rules and regulations for the working of the Supreme Court and other autonomous agencies like the ' Union Public Service Commission.
8. He sends directions and instructions to the State Governments that must be complied with.

Then, in the *legislative sphere,* he performs a number of important functions as under:

1. He summons and prorogues the sessions of Parliament and may dissolve the Lok Sabha.
2. He nominates 12 members of the Rajya Sabha who are distinguished or well experienced in the field of art, literature, science and social service. He may nominate two members of the Anglo-Indian community in case it does not have its adequate representation in the Lok Sabha.
3. The first session of Parliament in a new year or a session held after the general election begins with his inaugural address.
4. A bill passed by the Parliament requires his assent. In case it is a non-money bill, or it is not a constitution amendment bill, he may give his assent, or withhold it, or return the bill for re-consideration of the Parliament.
5. Certain bills (as seeking alteration of the boundary lines of a State) are introduced in any House of Parliament with his recommendation.
6. In case the Parliament in not in session and some law is to be made without any more loss of time, he may promulgate an ordinance having the force of law.
7. In case any House of Parliament is without a presiding officer, he may appoint a *pro tem* Speaker/Chairman.
8. He causes presentation of the reports of various statutory bodies to the Parliament for consideration.
9. He may allow extension, modification or abrogation of any law in case of ports and aerodromes.
10. Certain kinds of bills (as those seeking nationalisation of private property or likely to create a conflict with a law of the Centre) passed by the State legislatures are subject to his absolute veto power.

The President has some *financial powers* which may be put as under:

1. A money bill can be introduced in the Lok Sabha with his recommendation.
2. He keeps control over the Contingency Fund of India. He may make advances out of it to meet unforeseen expenditure pending its authorisation by the Parliament.
3. He causes presentation of the annual financial statement of the government (budget) in the Parliament.
4. From time to time he sets up a Finance Commission for the distribution of the net proceeds of taxes between the Centre and the States and the principles which should govern the grants-in-aid of the revenues of the States out of the Consolidated Fund of India.
5. He may allow determination of the shares of States in the proceeds of income tax and of the amount of grants-in-aid in lieu of jute export duty to the States of Assam, West Bengal, Bihar and Orissa.

The judicial power of the President constitutes his 'prerogative of mercy.' He may grant commutation of sentence, reprieve or pardon to a person held guilty by the highest court of the land in a matter where it comes under the executive authority of the Centre, or where it is a decision of the Court Martial, or where it is a sentence of death.[5]

Besides, the President performs some other functions which may be put as under:

1. He may refer any matter of public importance involving a question of law or fact to the Supreme Court for seeking its opinion.

---

5 The President exercises his prerogative of mercy on the advice of his ministers. But he is expected to assess its effect on the family of the victim and the society at large. The Governor of a State may also exercise such a power, but it cannot be done with the consideration of caste, religion and political loyalty of the person. Hence, the Supreme Court stayed clemency granted by the Governor of Andhra Pradesh for G.V. Reddy known for being a loyal Congress worker. The Court ruled that it could review pardon or clemency. *The Times of India* (New Delhi) 12 December, 2006.

2. He may make rules for the composition and working of the Union Public Service Commission.
3. He may issue directions for the progressive use of Hindi in the light of the recommendations of the Official Language Commission.
4. He may make rules for the administration and control of the Scheduled and Tribal Areas.
5. He may issue notification relating to the control of the Union Government over the administration of Jammu-Kashmir.

Emergency Powers: Now we may have a brief study of the abnormal functions and powers of the President. These are his 'emergency powers' specified in Part XVIII of the Constitution. These powers of the President have, indeed, a very sweeping effect and, for that reason, critical comments about their nature range from one of a protagonist like Sir Alladi Krishnaswami Ayyar who held them as 'the very life-breath of the Constitution' to that of a critic like H.V. Kamath who called it 'a charter of reaction and retrogression'. This part of the Constitution stipulates three kinds of 'emergency' with different effects.

Art. 352 empowers the President to declare *national emergency* whenever he is 'satisfied' that a serious situation has arisen or is likely to arise threatening the security of the country or any of its part by war, external aggression, or armed rebellion. Here the satisfaction of the President implies the satisfaction of his Council of Ministers. The President also has the power to issue another notification so as to vary or revoke his earlier proclamation to this effect. Such a proclamation can be made on the written advice of the Cabinet. It shall remain in operation for one month. But the duration can be extended in case a resolution to this effect is passed by both the Houses of Parliament by special majority (absolute majority of the whole House and two-thirds majority 'of the members, present and voting.) Such an extension may be for six months, but the Parliament may go on extending it again and again. In case the Lok Sabha is dissolved, the Rajya Sabha shall have the power to grant extension, but the time extended by it shall not go beyond 30 days of the commencement of the first session of the new Lok Sabha, unless it is approved by the new House. Moreover, at least one-tenth members of the Lok Sabha may sign a resolution requesting the Speaker (if the House is in session) or to the

President (if the House is not in session) to hold a special session for reconsidering the continuance of such an emergency. The House may revoke emergency by passing a resolution to this effect by simple majority.

In case Art. 352 is invoked, it shall have these effects:

1. The Parliament shall have the power to make a law on any item of the State List. Such a law made by the Parliament shall prevail and a law of the State, if already made, shall remain 'suspended' to the extent of being repugnant to the law of the Centre. The law of the Centre shall prevail at the most for six months after the revocation of this emergency and then the 'suspended' part of the State law would again be operative.
2. The Parliament shall have the power to make law so as to entrust more duties on the offices or public servants of the Union in order to implement such laws made in pursuance of its extended jurisdiction.
3. The Parliament shall also have the power to make a law so as to enhance the term of Lok Sabha beyond five years. It may do the same for extending the tenure of the State legislatures. Thus, elections may be postponed. Such a law shall remain in force for one year at a time, but the Parliament may renew this law again and again. Elections must take place within six months of the revocation of such emergency.
4. The executive power of the Union shall extend to the issuing of any directions or instructions to the State governments as it deems necessary.
5. The President shall also have the power to issue a notification so as to suspend fundamental freedoms enshrined in Art. 19 and their enforcement provided in Articles 32 and 226 of the Constitution. He shall also have the power to suspend the enforcement of Fundamental Rights except those of life and personal liberty provided in Articles 20 and 21 of the Constitution.
6. The President shall have the power to make necessary alteration in the distribution of revenues between the Union and the States.

Such an emergency was proclaimed in Oct., 1962 when China treacherously attacked India. It continued till January 1968 with the result that its invocation could not be done when we had a war with Pakistan in August-September 1965. It was invoked for the second time in December 1971 when Pakistan attack India. In June 1975 this provision was invoked again in the name of grave danger to the internal security of India. Both proclamations ended in March 1977.

Then there is the provision of *emergency in a State* vide Art. 356 in the event of 'breakdown of constitutional machinery' there. Either on the recommendation of the Governor of that State or on the basis of his own 'satisfaction' (that really means the satisfaction of the Union Council of Ministers), the President may take over the administration of that State. He may dismiss the government of that State and may either dissolve the Vidhan Sabha or place it under 'suspended animation'. In case the Vidhan Sabha is dissolved, fresh elections shall take place after the revocation of emergency; in case it is placed under 'suspended animation', the Vidhan Sabha may be revived or dissolved after some time. This arrangement is also known as the 'President's rule'. It does not apply to the State of Jammu-Kashmir.

A proclamation of emergency made under Art. 356 may remain in force for a period of two months. In case the Centre desires to extend this period, it may by done by a resolution of the Parliament passed in each House by simple majority. It is also provided that the period cannot be extended beyond six months in one instance and beyond three years in all. Besides, after giving two extensions, it is also required that further extension can be granted only when emergency is in force, or the Election Commission has given its view that elections cannot be held there due to uncontrollable circumstances. This point may be repeated here that in case the Lok Sabha stands dissolved, the Rajya Sabha shall pass a resolution for the extension of duration of emergency. But the extension so granted by the Rajya Sabha shall not go beyond 30 days of the commencement of the session of new Lok Sabha, unless the new House has passed a resolution to the same effect.

If Art. 356 is put into effect, it shall have these effects:

1. The President shall assume all functions of the State government and conduct its administration through his

Governor or administrator who may be assisted by some advisers.

2. Since the Vidhan Sabha is non-extent, the Parliament of India may make a law on any item of the State List for this State and also pass its budget. As we have already seen, it should be repeated here that a law made by the Centre shall remain in force for six months at the most after the revocation of emergency. Moreover, any part of the State law being repugnant to such a law of the Centre shall remain suspended so long as the law of the Centre is in force.

3. The President may make necessary or incidental or consequential changes in the provisions of the Constitution relating to the administration of the State so as to give desirable effect to the object of his proclamation.

This provision was, for the first time, invoked in 1951 in order to deal with the problem of Punjab and since then it has been invoked on a large number of occasions in the States of the Indian Union.

No doubt, Art, 356 has been grossly abused and misused by the Union executive on a very large number of times. Available figures show that it was invoked 11 times under the regime of Nehru and Shastri, 71 times under the regime of Indira Gandhi and 9 times in a single stroke under regime of Prime Minister Desai. The governments of the Bharatiya Janata Party in the States of Uttar Pradesh, Madhya Pradesh, Rajasthan and Himachal Pradesh were dismissed by the Centre shortly after the demolition of Babri mosque in Ayodhya (UP.) in December 1992. While one could appreciate the dismissal of the government of U.P. in the wake of the fear of communal violence there, the dismissal of other governments was totally unwarranted. The former Chief Minister of Madhya Pradesh (Sunderlal Patwa) challenged the action of the Centre and on 21 April, 1993 the Jabalpur Bench struck down the order of the President on the ground that the Union of India had failed to make out any case or bring forward any material justifying invocation of this extra-ordinary power. Appreciating the stand of the High Court in making Art. 356 justiciable, a leading jurist commended. "In a quasi-federal Constitution like ours, Art. 356 stands out like a sore thumb-it is anti-federal in character and spirit, and it has been one of the most frequently misused provisions of the Constitution. Its manipulation has been the puppet game played by all politicians in power." (Rajeev Dhawan)

This matter was taken to the Supreme Court in an appeal. Since some petitions were already there, the Supreme Court bunched them along with the petition of S.R. Bommai whose government in Karnataka had been dismissed under Art. 356. In March, 1994 its Constitution Bench ruled that Art. 356 was justiciable. It could ask the Centre to produce before it the reasons that so warranted the imposition of emergency in a State. It also ruled that the advice tendered by the Ministers to the President before invoking this provision of the Constitution could be examined in the Court. Appreciating this stand, Rajeev Dhawan commented: "President's rule was and remains the death of federalism. Till this decision the Courts were reluctant to authoritatively say that the Centre's action was wrong. But now it has been laid down that procedural discipline and substantive requirement must be maintained."

Finally, there is the provision *of financial emergency* under Art. 360 of the Constitution. If the President is satisfied that a situation has arisen whereby the financial stability or credit of India or any part thereof has fallen in danger, he can issue a proclamation to this effect that may be varied or revoked by a subsequent proclamation. It is to remain in force for a period of two months. In case the President desires to extend its duration, it may be done by passing a resolution by both the Houses of Parliament by simple majority. Once approval is given by the Parliament, it continues until the government desires to revoke it. The same point should be repeated here that in case the Lok Sabha stands dissolved, the Rajya Sabha may grant extension of time. But the time so granted by the Rajya Sabha shall not go beyond 30 days of the commencement of the session of the new Lok Sabha, unless the new Lok Sabha concurs with the decision of the Rajya Sabha. The proclamation of this kind of emergency shall have these effects:

1. The President shall have the power to lay down canons of financial propriety (to be approved by the Parliament after some time) and to issue necessary directions to the States.
2. The President shall have the power to lay down principles in the light of which salaries and allowances of all public servants including the judges of the Supreme Court and High Courts, may be reduced.
3. The money bills of the State governments shall be under the veto power of the President.

These emergency powers of the President have been criticised in strong terms. It is said that these provisions "enable the federal government to acquire the strength of a unitary system whenever the exigencies of the situation so demand."[6] Recalling the horror of Hitler's Germany, it is feared that these arrangements may create an opening whereby some power-drunk leader may do what was done by the Nazi dictator before the Second World War. Art. 356 is an instrument in the hands of the Centre whereby the existence of any State government can be finished as per the pleasure of the Union government. If the Janata government of Morarji Desai finished 9 Congress (I) governments in 1977 in a single stroke, the Congress (I) government of Mrs. Indira Gandhi did the same just three years after.

It shows that Art. 356 is abused in a very reckless manner for political reasons. The term 'breakdown of the constitutional machinery' has nowhere been precisely defined and it may mean anything to the Union government bent upon sacking a State government by hook or by crook. In other words, the use of such power makes the President like a dictator and lays down the foundation of a 'totalitarian state' in the country. While speaking in the Constituent Assembly, a vocal member (H.V. Kamath) said that "it will be a day of shame and sorrow when the President will make use of these powers having no parallel in any constitution of the democratic countries of the world."[7] But the defenders of these provisions have expressed their own views. For instance, while contradicting the fear of critics like Kamath, Mahavir Tyagi held this part of the Constitution as a 'safety valve.'[8] As eternal vigilance is the price of freedom, he continued, it "becomes the essential responsibility of the people also to see whether the President is really behaving like the highest symbol of democracy."[9]

Actual Position: In the end, we may briefly look into the issue whether the Indian President is a figure-head of the Indian republic having his counterpart in the British monarch, or he is endowed with some independent area of authority where he may, if he so

6. K.V. Rao: *Parliamentary Democracy of India*, p. 259.
7. *Constituent Assembly Debates*, Vol. IX, p. 105.
8. *Ibid*, p. 547.
9. *Ibid*, p. 120.

likes or dares act like a real executive having his counterpart in the President of the United States. Though a member of the Drafting Committee, KM. Munshi brought out a monograph in 1963 in which he categorically affirmed: "In adopting the relevant provision, the Constituent Assembly did not understand that they were creating a powerless President."[10] In 1969, V.V. Giri, the candidate for the Presidential office, gave a public statement that he would not like to be 'a rubber stamp even of God.' P.B. Mukherjee (former judge of the Calcutta High Court) stressed the point that the Indian President "is an independent institution with independent authority and independent functions."[11]

The contention that the President of India may act like a real executive is sustained by some arguments. First, he is endowed with vast authority covering all spheres of administration at the Centre and in the States. Second, he may create conditions where the Prime Minister and the Ministers ditto his line as they can remain in office during his 'pleasure'. Third, as Supreme Commander of the Defence Forces, he may use his military power to establish his autocratic position. Last, he may violate the Constitution and yet create 'conditions that the provision of his impeachment may not be invoked. He may dissolve the Lok Sabha or prorogue the session of the. Parliament in a bid to harass his opponents.

But all these arguments are without much weight. The 42nd Amendment of 1976 has made it binding on him to act according to the advice of the Council of Ministers. The 44th Amendment of 1978 empowers him to return a matter for the reconsideration of the Council of Ministers once and he is bound to act according to the reconsidered advice of his ministers. Second, he cannot make use of his military powers in the fashion of a politically unwise head of the state like President Iskandar Mirza of Pakistan in view of the fact that all such decisions are to be taken by the National Defence Committee having Prime Minister, Defence Minister, the Chiefs of Army, Navy and Air Force, and Secretary of the Defence Ministry. Last, the President is under an oath to preserve, protect and defend the Constitution and, in the event of its violation, he may be removed by the process of impeachment.

---

10. K.M. Munshi: *The President under the Constitution*, p. 9.

11. Mukherji: *The Critical Problems of the Indian Constitution*, pp. 45-46.

The fact stands out that, as B.R. Ambedkar said, the President "is the head of the State, but not of the Executive."[12] The symbolic position of the President was affirmed by the Supreme Court in the case of *Rai Saheb Ram Jawaya Kapur. v. State of Punjab* (1955) in which it observed: "The President has thus been made a formal or constitutional head of the executive and the real executive powers are vested in the ministers of the cabinet." Likewise, in the case of *U.N.. Rao. v. Indira Gandhi* (1971), the Supreme Court reiterated that the Constituent Assembly "did not choose the Presidential system of government." Much, however, depends upon the personality of the holder of this office. Luckily, so far the holders of this office have acted in a very sagacious manner with the result that no acrimony has occurred to vitiate equation of the President with the Prime Minister and his ministers. It is true that Prime Minister Nehru had some differences with President Rajendra Prasad, or Mrs. Indira Gandhi had some differences with President Radhakrishnan, or some differences between Prime Minister Rajiv Gandhi and Zail Singh were publicly aired, but all these instance do not reinforce the contention of powerful presidency in our country.

The real position of the President has undergone a notable change in the present era of coalition politics. The implications of Art. 74 (1) have become fluid and the President has got ample room to exercise his powers in discretion. Happily, the incumbents of this great office have established some healthy precedents that may not at all be taken as aberration in our parliamentary system of government. For instance, in 1996 President Shankar Dayal Sharma refused to sign the two ordinances that were prepared by the government of Narsimha Rao on the plea that with the declaration of the elections the caretaker government could not take up policy matters. (While one ordinance had sought to provide reservations in public services to the Christian Dalits, the second one had sought to reduce the period of election canvassing from three to two weeks.)

---

12. *Constituent Assembly Debates*, Vol. VII, p. 32.
13. In his memoirs written in Hindi *Manzil se Zyada Safar* (Travel Beyond Destination), former Prime Minister V.P. Singh tells us that President Zail Singh had sent him feelers for accepting the office of the Prime Minister after the dismissal of Rajiv Gandhi. He had assured him of the support of 150 MP's. But he (V.P.) declined. *The Times of India* (New Delhi), 26 June, 2006.

He advised Prime Minister Rao to seek the resignation of the Himachal Pradesh Governor (Sheela Kaul) who was found guilty by the Central Bureau of Investigation in a scam relating to the allotment of government flats in the capacity of Minister for Urban Development.

Similarly in 1997, President Narayanan returned the advice relating to the imposition of President's rule in Uttar Pradesh for the reconsideration of the Council of Ministers and he did it again in 1998 in the case of Bihar. On both the occassions he counselled that the Council of Ministers should render such an advice after studying the whole case in the light of the Supreme Court's ruling in the *Bommai Case* of 1994. Not only this, before appointing Vajpayee as Prime Minister in 1998 and again in 1999, he insisted that the parties supporting his government should specify their stand in writing and as such a letter from their chiefs should be submitted so as to offset any foreseeable uncertainty. He expressed his unhappiness at the appointment of National Constitution Review Commission on the plea that the Constitution had not failed us, rather we had failed it. Such well-thought steps taken by the constitutional head of the Indian republic were somehow misconstrued as the case of Presidential activism in our country.

The active role of the President in a coalition system is a natural development. Like Sharma and Narayanan, Abdul Kalam had to take stands that were not appreciated by the head of the real executive. He returned the case of S.L. Bayana to be made a permanent judge of the Delhi High Court on the ground that the strictures were passed against him in the Jessica Lal murder case. He did not favour elevation of Jagdish Bhalla as Chief Justice of the Kerala High Court who was involved in a controversy at the Allahabad High Court. Then, the Collegium of the Supreme Court recommended his appointment as the Chief Justice of the Chhattisgarh High Court. On the basis of the report of the Election Commission, he disqualified Jaya Bachchan from the membership of the Rajya Sabha for holding on office of profit. It created a serious apprehension for a good number of MPs against whom such complaints were pending. Sonia Gandhi resigned and got herself elected so as to save herself from such an onslaught. The government of Manmohan Singh managed to deal with this situation by making an amendment in the law relating to office of profit whereby a number of posts were exempted. When such a bill came before the

President for his assent, he returned it to the Parliament with his remark that its provisions should be comprehensive enough so as to be applicable to the members of Parliament as well as to the members of the legislatures of the States and Union Territories. As a result the bill was repassed by the Parliament with a set of assurances. Then it had the assent of the President. This sagacious action of the President was not appreciated by the leaders of the Congress party and so they disfavoured the proposal of giving second term to him. They desired to choose a President who would invariably move according to their wishes.

As a matter of fact, the Indian President is neither a rubber stamp nor a quiescent volcano. Like the British monarch, he is expected to act as a friend, philosopher and guide of his government. "Instead of hardly remaining insensitive for long to mysterious sense of authority and power emanating from the massive structure of the Rashtrapati Bhavan giving like that of a halo around the head of a god, and thus feeding his vanity and also an incipient hostility towards the real seat of power, he should invariably act in a way that he does not look like a magnificent cypher."[14] The President of the Constituent Assembly, Dr. Rajendra Prasad hopefully visualised that "in our country healthy conventions will grow that will make him a constitutional President in all matters."[15] The Supreme Court in the case of *Shamsher Singh* v. *I.C Agarwal* (1974) well observed: "In short, the President, like the British King, has not merely been constitutionally romanticised but actually vested with a pervasive and persuasive role."

Vice-President

The Constitution provides for a Vice-President. He is elected by an electoral college consisting of the members of both Houses of Parliament in accordance with proportional representation with single transferable vote system. A candidate for this office must possess three qualifications. First, he must be the citizen of India. Second, he must have completed the age of 35 years. Last, he must be eligible for membership of the Rajya Sabha and that he must not be holding an office of profit under the Union or State government

14. H.N. Pandit: *The PM's President*, p. 26.
15. *Constituent Assembly Debates*, Vol. XI. p. 988.

or any other government subject to their control. The term of the Vice-President is of five years. He may tender his resignation to the President. He may be removed from office on some charge if a resolution to this effect is, after 14 days' notice, passed by the Rajya Sabha by its absolute majority and then agreed to by the Lok Sabha by similar majority.

The Vice-President is the *ex-officio* Chairman of the Rajya Sabha. As such, he presides over the session of the House and by virtue of that capacity receives salary and allowances equal to that of the Speaker of the Lok Sabha. In case the office of the President becomes vacant by any reason (like death, resignation, removal, long illness, foreign visit etc.), he acts as the President. He is expected to render full cooperation to the President in matters so referred to him. It is true that the office of the Vice-President is not endowed with politically meaningful authority. But this office cannot be identified with the office of the American Vice-President nicknamed as 'His Superfluous Highness'. Indeed, the Vice-President occupies a position of considerable dignity ranking next to the President in the warrant of precedence.

Prime Minister and Council of Ministers

The Constituent Assembly came to the conclusion that the British system of government would be more suitable for our country in view of our familiarity with it. But one may feel surprise at the fact that while our Constitution has elaborate provisions about many things, the principles of the cabinet system of government have been inexhaustively specified in Articles 74, 75 and 78.[16] It shows that while some essential features have been reduced to writing, many things have been left to the established conventions. Art. 74 says: "(1) There shall be a Council of Ministers with the Prime Minister at the head to aid and advise the President who shall, in the exercise of his functions, act in accordance with such advice. Provided that the President may require the Council of Ministers to reconsider such advice, either generally or otherwise,

16. It may be pointed out here that the Constitution uses the term 'Council of Ministers'. The word 'Cabinet' has been used in the 44th Constitution Amendment Act, 1978. It means a body consisting of the Prime Minister and Ministers of the Cabinet rank· according to Art. 352 (3).

and the President shall act in accordance with the advice tendered after such reconsideration. (2) The question whether any, and if so what, advice was tendered by the Ministers to the President shall not be inquired into any court."

Then, Art. 75 says: "(1) The Prime Minister shall be appointed by the President and the other Ministers shall be appointed by the President on the advice of the Prime Minister. (1 (A)). The size of the Council of Ministers cannot exceed 15 per cent of the strength of the Lok Sabha. (1 (B)). A defector cannot be appointed as a minister until he is re-elected or the House of which he was a member is dissolved, whichever earlier. (2) The Ministers shall hold office during the pleasure of the President. (3) The Council of Ministers shall be collectively responsible to the House of People. (4) Before a Minister enters upon his office, the President shall administer to him the oaths of office and secrecy according to the forms set out for the purpose in the Third Schedule. (5) A Minister who for any period of six consecutive months is not a member of either House of Parliament shall at the expiration of that period cease to be a Minister. (6) The salaries and allowances of Ministers shall be such as Parliament may from time to time by law determine and, until Parliament so determines, shall be as specified in the Second Schedule."

Finally, Art. 78 says: "It shall be the duty of the Prime Minister—(a) to communicate to the President all decisions of the Council of Ministers relating to the administration of the affairs of the Union and proposals for legislation; (b) to furnish such information relating to the administration of the affairs of the Union and proposals for legislation as the President may call for; and (c) if the President so requires, to submit for the consideration of the Council of Ministers any matter on which a decision has been taken by a Minister but which has not been considered by the Council."

Appointment of Prime Minister: We may well take note of the fact that the provisions of our Constitution in regard to the system of parliamentary government are sketchy. All possible situations have not been covered by the written words of the Constitution. Obviously, much has been left to the well-established conventions. The Prime Minister is the head of the Council of Ministers. He is appointed by the President by virtue of being the leader of the party having clear majority in the Lok Sabha. In case no party has absolute majority in the Lok Sabha, the President may invite the leader of the largest party to form the government. Nehru was appointed as the Prime Minister in 1952, 1957 and 1962 for being the leader of the Congress party having clear majority in the Lok Sabha. So was the case with Mrs. Gandhi who was the leader of the Congress party after the general elections of 1967, 1971 and 1979. Since the Congress (I) secured absolute majority in the elections of 1984, its leader (Rajiv Gandhi) was appointed as the Prime Minister.

In case no party is in clear majority in the Lok Sabha, the President may study the situation and then invite the leader of the largest party banking upon the support of other parties so as to be in a position of majority in the Lok Sabha.[17] In 1977 Morarji Desai was appointed as the Prime Minister, for the Janata party had been able to establish its claim as the largest party. In 1989 this post was given to V.P. Singh of the Janata Dal as he could prove majority of the National Front (combination of Janata Dal, Congress (S), Telugu Desam, DMK and Assam Gana Parishad) supported from outside by the BJP and the two Communist parties. The Janata Dal suffered a split in November 1990. A break-away wing under the leadership of Chandra Shekhar (called Janata Dal- Socialist) formed government with the support of Congress (I) led by Rajiv Gandhi. In case the Prime Minister resigns and there is a serious rift in the ranks of the majority party, the President may wait for some time and then on the basis of his own assessment may invite a leader to form the government who may prove his majority in the House and run a 'stable government'. It happened in July 1979 when President Reddy invited Chaudhary Charan Singh to form the government.

The appointment of Prime Minister pertains to the discretionary power of the President, but this discretion must be used with great caution so that his action does not invite the stigma of partisanship. It should not become a matter of public controversy. The President must wait and watch the situation very carefully and then take a decision that wins the confidence of the nation. After the death of Nehru in May 1964 the President (Radhakrishnan) appointed

---

17. So the President appointed P.V. Narsimha Rao as Prime Minister in 1991 as he was the leader of the largest party and he accepted the offer. He was not a member of Parliament at the time of his appointment, but he became a member of the Lok Sabha within next six months.

Gulzarilal Nanda as the acting Prime Minister, but he invited Shastri to form the government after his name was cleared by the Congress Parliamentary Party. Similarly, in January 1966, he appointed Nanda as the acting Prime Minister after the death of Shastri and invited Indira Gandhi to form the government after her name was cleared by the CPP. But in August 1979, President Reddy did not invite Jagjivan Ram to form the government and instead dissolved the Lok Sabha on the advice of the outgoing Prime Minister (Charan Singh) and thereby he faced the criticism of the leaders of the Janata Party.

The President has to move very cautiously and judiciously when no political party has its clear majority in the Lok Sabha. He should call the leader of the largest party to form the government of course. In case a pre-poll alliance manages to secure absolute majority in the House, then its leader should be invited. If neither of the two conditions exists, then he should wait until a common leader of the coalition partners emerges to stake his claim on the basis of specific commitment of the constituent elements to support him. Thus, President Sharma appointed Deve-Gowda as Prime Minister in 1996 after Vajpayee, the leader of the then largest party, failed to have the confidence vote of the House. President Narayanan set up the precedent of having the commitments of the chiefs of the parties going to form such a coalition in writing when he appointed Vajpayee as the Prime Minister in 1998 and in 1999. President Abdul Kalam followed it in 2004 when he appointed Dr. Manmohan Singh as the Prime Minister of a coalition government.

Functions and Position: The first and foremost function of the Prime Minister is to prepare the list of his ministers. He meets the President with this list and then Council of Ministers is formed. Very important ministers are designated as Ministers of the Cabinet rank, others are called Ministers of State, while ministers belonging to third rank are known as Deputy Ministers. It is one of the discretionary powers of the Prime Minister to designate a minister as Deputy Prime Minister as Nehru did for Sardar Patel and Indira Gandhi for Morarji Desai. In a very critical situation the Prime Minister may be forced to have two Deputy Prime Ministers. The Janata Prime Minister (Morarji Desai) had to keep Charan Singh and Jagjivam Ram as his Deputy Prime Ministers. V.P. Singh and Chandra Shekhar did it for Devi Lal and Vajpayee did it for Advani. If we go by the facts, we may say that no Prime Minister desires to

State Structure in India

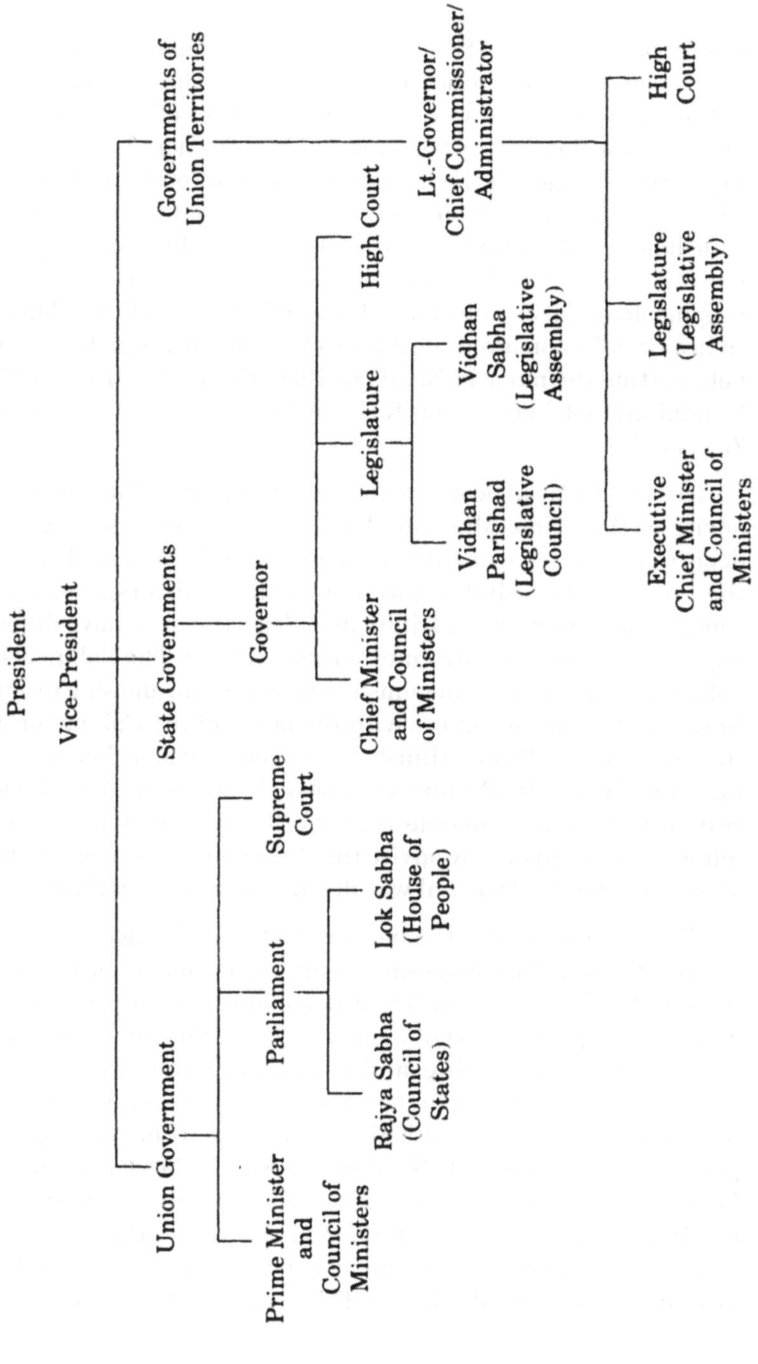

- President
  - Vice-President
    - Union Government
      - Prime Minister and Council of Ministers
      - Parliament
        - Rajya Sabha (Council of States)
        - Lok Sabha (House of People)
      - Supreme Court
    - State Governments
      - Governor
        - Chief Minister and Council of Ministers
        - Legislature
          - Vidhan Parishad (Legislative Council)
          - Vidhan Sabha (Legislative Assembly)
        - High Court
    - Governments of Union Territories
      - Lt.-Governor/ Chief Commissioner/ Administrator
        - Executive Chief Minister and Council of Ministers
        - Legislature (Legislative Assembly)
        - High Court

keep a Deputy Prime Minister until he/she is forced to do so by the compulsions of party politics. It is also one of the discretionary powers of the Prime Minister to keep some ministers of the fourth rank known as Parliamentary Secretaries. The President has hardly any say in the selection of the ministers. It is a different matter that a wise and sagacious President may gently advise the Prime Minister to include or not to exclude a particular name in his list of ministers. For instance, Prime Minister Nehru obliged President Prasad by keeping Jagjivan Ram in 1952, 1957 and 1962 and Prime Minister Indira Gandhi honoured the advice of President Radhakrishnan in not omitting the name of Nanda in 1966. But Prime Minister Rajiv Gandhi did not like to drop K.K. Tiwari so as to oblige President Zail Singh.

The President allocates portfolios among the Ministers on the advice of the Prime Minister. The Prime Minister may keep any department or departments under his control; he may also advise the President to reshuffle portfolios of his ministers from time to time; he may bifurcate or trifurcate a department or have different departments amalgamated into one department. The Cabinet is the policy-making body and all ministers have to swim and sink together. In case a minister disagrees with the policy of the Cabinet or with the views of the Prime Minister, he should resign. For instance, ministers like C.D. Deshmukh, Asoka Mehta and Morarji Desai resigned. It is also possible that the Prime Minister may ask a minister to resign or may advise the President to dismiss a member of his ministry. So Devi Lal was dismissed in August 1990.

The decisions of the Cabinet are virtually the decisions of the Prime Minister. The proposals about appointments of persons to high posts, the determination of home and foreign policies of the government, preparation of budget and introduction of bills in the Parliament, summoning and proroguing the session of the Parliament and a host of other decisions are taken by the Prime Minister in consultation with his close confidants having important positions in the Council of Ministers. In short, in the words of Ramsay Muir, the Cabinet is the steering wheel of the ship of the state and the Prime Minister is its steersman. However, the astonishing feature of cabinet government in our country is that the Prime Minister has 'Presidentialised' his office. Once the Cabinet

Secretariat and now the Prime Minister's Office (PMO) has become the real centre of power with the result that the phrase of Prime Minister's being first among equals has lost its significance.

Theoretically, the Prime Minister is *primus inter pares* (first among equals); in practice, the case is quite different. His pre-eminent position, like his British counterpart, is evident from these points:

1. He is the leader of the party in majority in the popular House of the Parliament.
2. He has the power of selecting other Ministers and also advising the President to dismiss any of them individually, or require any them of to resign. Virtually, the Ministers hold office during the pleasure of the Prime Minister.
3. The allocation of business amongst the Ministers is a function of the Prime Minister. He can transfer a Minister from one Department to another.
4. He is the chairman of the Cabinet, summons its meetings and presides over them.
5. He is in-charge of coordinating the policy of the Government and has accordingly a right of supervision over all the Departments.
6. While the resignation of a Minister merely creates a vacancy, the resignation or death of the Prime Minister means end of the Council of Ministers.
7. The Prime Minister is a link between the President and the Cabinet. Though individual Ministers have the right of access to the President on matters concerning their own Departments, and all important communications, particularly relating to policy, can be made only through the Prime Minister.
8. The Prime Minister is the sole channel of communication between the President and the Ministers and between the Parliament and his Ministers.
9. The Prime Minister is the chairman of many bodies as Inter-State Council, Planning Commission, Nuclear Command Authority etc.

In India, the Prime Minister has all these special powers in as much as the conventions relating to Cabinet Government are in application here.

The credit, or the discredit, for the Presidentialisation of Prime Minister's office goes to Indira Gandhi and her son (Rajiv) who managed the affairs of the country with an arrogant temper and an authoritarian mentality. But the sycophancy and the pusillanimity of the ministers should be held equally responsible for the shrivelling of the Cabinet. As a critic says: "The Cabinet form of government was undoubtedly twisted out of shape during the Premiership of Indira Gandhi, especially after the Congress split in 1969. During the emergency it was reduced to mockery. Rajiv Gandhi has not only restored the Cabinet government, he has further undermined it. His cronies dominate the decision-making process from outside the Cabinet; within the Cabinet ministers are afraid to speak out their mind. Cabinet meetings are not the forums of serious discussion of policies; they are the occasions for the competitive adulation of the leader."[18]

Cabinet Secretariat and Prime Minister's Office

Once a small body formed in October, 1945 under Sir Eric Coates to serve as the co-ordination committee of the War Resources and Reconstruction of the Executive Council headed by Viceroy Lord Wavell, it became Executive Council Secretariat under A.E. Porter in the following year. The then Secretary of State for India (Lord Pethic Lawrence) hoped that this 'good and fair-sized secretariat of its own would function effectively.' When Nehru was appointed as the Vice-President of the Executive Council on 2 Sept., 1946 by Wavell, H.M. Patel replaced Porter. Patel became Private Secretary to Nehru and after some time he was succeeded by Tarlok Singh and Iyengar as Private Secretaries to the Prime Minister. After independence this body became Cabinet Secretariat. Nehru desired to convert it into a high-powered body, but it could not occur owing to the opposition of Sardar Patel. With the advent of independence on 15 August, 1947, Nehru became the Prime Minister and this body assumed a form of its own with the name of Cabinet Secretariat. Its main functions, as described in the Allocation of Business Orders, may be enumerated in brief as under:

18. Madhu Limaye: *Cabinet Government in India,* p. 196.

1. To prepare the agenda of the Cabinet meetings,
2. To provide all information and material considered essential for the deliberations of the Cabinet,
3. To interact with Government agencies and to acquire information about progress made in the implementation of the decision taken by the Cabinet,
4. To provide secretarial assistance to the Committees of the Secretaries constituted. for dealing with the problems and matters relating to inter-ministerial coordination,
5. To finalise and allocate the business of the Government to the Ministries and Departments in accordance with the directions of the Prime Minister,
6. To prepare the minutes of the Cabinet meetings and circulate them among the Ministries and other Departments after their approval by the Prime Minister.

The role of the Prime Minister's Secretariat is to assist the Prime Minster in every possible way. It consists of initiating new policies, review of the working of different ministries, keeping an eye on the Centre-State relations, providing different viewpoints on the proposals received from different ministries from the Cabinet for his own orders. Essentially it has to provide the Prime Minister with inputs for decision-making. It actually consists of two parts–one of the regular secretariat where the senior officials work, and the other at Prime Minister's residence where some secretarial assistance is available. The officials of the Prime Minister's secretariat go to the house of the Prime Minister as needed.[19]

The post of the Cabinet Secretary is very important of course.[20] But his authority is overshadowed by the Private or Personal Secretary to the Prime Minister. It is for this reason that the PM

---

19. B.N. Tandon: *PMO Diary-I: Prelude to the Emergency* (Delhi: Konark, 2003), p. xx.

20. S.S. Khera in his book *The Central Executive* says that the Cabinet Secretary "provides the eyes and the ears for the Prime Minister to keep in touch with the process of official business in the Central Government."

banking upon a bureaucrat occupying this post forms a kind of parallel government. The Cabinet Secretary cannot hope to compete with the Private or Personal Secretary to the Prime Minister. "All important papers pass through the PMO rather than through the Cabinet Secretariat and it is for this reason that the Prime Ministers in India rely more on their Private Secretary in the PMO rather than on the Cabinet Secretary."[21]

Prime Minister Shastri converted the Cabinet Secretariat into Prime Minister's Secretariat. He depended heavily on the advice of L.K. Jha whose best instance was afforded by the Kutch Agreement of 1965 that should be regarded as a contribution of a bureaucrat. Matters reached a point that Michael Brecher designated the Secretariat as 'an interest group in its own right' under L.K Jha and as 'a major power centre in all-India politics.'[22] "The Prime Minister's Secretariat and through it the Prime Minister is the unquestioned supreme power in India today. The Ministers have virtually been reduced to the position of mere camp followers-a far cry from the concept of first among equals." Again, "With the Prime Minister's Secretariat gradually assuming the shape of a miniature government of India, there is a danger of this impersonal aspect being dimmed and a bottleneck being created through most decisions being centralised in the P.M.'s Secretariat. The centralisation is already showing signs of delaying decision-making processes at the Centre, a development which is fraught with dangers to the smooth and efficient working of the administration."[23] Same thing may be said about the role of Brijesh Mishra under Prime Minister Vajpayee. He worked not only as Personal Secretary to the Prime Minister, but also as National Security Adviser. His inefficiency in studying conditions that led to the Kargil War in July, 1999 drew flak and the Subrahmanyam Committee Report (2000) suggested that the office of the National Security Adviser should not be bracketed with the office of Prime Minister's Personal Secretary.

---

21. S.R. Maheshwari: "Cabinet Secretariat and Prime Minister's Office" in *Employment News*, New Delhi, 3–9 August, 1996, pp. 1–3.
22. Brecher: *Succession in India*, pp. 118-19.
23. Dharma Vira: "Note on the Powers of the Prime Minister", *The States* (New Delhi). September 1. 1973, p. 16.

From Cabinet Secretariat to Prime Minister's Office

Prime Ministers		*C.S., PMS., PMO., PMH*
1. Jawaharlal Nehru	...	He operated through Cabinet Secretary and his personal office was headed by a Joint Secretary.
2. Lal Bahadur Shastri	...	He converted the Cabinet Secretariat into Prime Minister's Secretariat by appointing L.K. Jha as its Secretary and then by banking upon his advice in all important matters.
3. Indira Gandhi	...	She converted Prime Minister's Secretariat into Prime Minister's Office and put it under her Personal Secretary P.N. Haksar. Not only that, she created another extra-constitutional centre of power as Prime Minister's House under her younger son (Sanjay Gandhi). The PMH dominated the PMO. Sanjay patronised R.K. Dhawan (Principal Secretary to the PM) and used him as his chief minion. The situation changed after the death of Sanjay in June, 1980.
4. Morarji Desai and Charan Singh	...	The PMO had a low profile as Desai believed in democratic functioning of the government. But his son Kanti Desai operated the PMH. Charan Singh had a very short tenure and he did nothing to elevate or diminish the profile of the PMO.
5. Rajiv Gandhi	...	He packed up the PMO with his friends and trusted aides. Arun Singh was made a minister in the PMO. It outstretched its tentacles so as to deal with all spheres as economy, industry, technology and defence. Sarla Grewal became his Principal Secretary who was replaced by B.G. Deshmukh. But M.L. Fotedar and Capt. Satish Sharma operated the PMH.

6.	V.P. Singh and Chandra Shekhar	...	The PMH was disbanded, but Deshmukh continued to head the PMO. Both Singh and Shekhar desired to keep the PMO as an effective professional body.
7.	P.V. Narsimha Rao	...	Bhuvnesh Chaturvedi, a minister in the PMO, dominated this body, but a bureaucrat like A.N. Verma, Principal Secretary to the PM, called the shots.
8.	Deve-Gowda and I.K. Gujral	...	The PMO lost its vigour under weak Prime Ministers who led the coalitions of shaky partners. Bureaucrats like Satish Chandran and N.N. Vohra dominated the scene.
9.	Atal Bihari Vajpayee	...	Though the head of a coalition government of shaky partners, Vajpayee managed to act like a strong Prime Minister. Vijay Goel worked as a Minister in the PMO, but Brijesh Mishra called the shots. Apart from working as Principal Secretary to the Prime Minister, he also worked as National Security Advisor and did not bother for the recommendation of the Subrahmanyam Committee Report that the two offices should not be combined.
10.	Dr. Manmohan Singh	...	Like his predecessor, Singh headed a shaky coalition; he had chosen B.K. Chaturvedi as his Principal Secretary.
11.	Narendra Modi	...	Heads a Superficial Coalition Government under his dominant leadership, chose N. Mishra as his Principal Secretary

Coalition System

The system of coalition government has now come to stay in view of the fact that now no political party may be in a position to secure absolute majority in the Lok Sabha. If Vajpayee led such a government with the name of National Democratic Alliance, Manmohan Singh's United Progressive Alliance pertains to the same model. The largest party in the House manages to build up a workable alliance with a number of parties, big and small, so as to muster clear majority in the Lok Sabha that enables it to form the government and operate it on the basis of a Common Minimum Programme.

Coalition Government (2009)

Political Parties as Alliance Partners		*Seats*
1. Indian National Congress	(INC)	206
2. Trinamool Congress	(TC)	19
3. Nationalist Congress Party	(NCP)	9
4. National Conference	(NC)	3
5. Jharkhand Mukti Morcha	(JMM)	2
6. Telangana Rashtriya Samiti	(TRS)	5
7. Kerela Congress (M)	(KCM)	1
8. Viduthalai Chiruthaigal Katchi	(VCK)	1
9. Indian Union Muslim League	(IUML)	2
10. All-India Ittehad-ul-Musalmeen	(ALUM)	1
11. Dravida Munnetra Kazhgam	(DMK)	18
12. Rashtriya Lok Dal	(RLD)	3
13. Janata Dal (S)	(JDS)	3
	Total	315

The formation and operation of coalition government shows that political compulsions allow no room for ideological and moral considerations. Once it was anti-Congressism, now it is anti-communalism. All alliance partners condemn the BJP as a party of the Hindu communalists to demonstrate their secular leanings. But the element of hypocrisy cannot be concealed. It may be said that the present government has demonstrated a strong sense of inclusiveness particularly as regards social and religious minorities. The Congress being the largest party has once again shown its remarkable capacity to accommodate and reflect India's diversity or plurality. Like its predecessor, it has registered its unambiguous commitment to the process of economic reforms. Moreover, it would the inclusion of some ministers defeated in the recent elections and the induction of some ministers charge-sheeted in criminal cases cannot be condoned in the name of compulsions of a coalition system.

A line of distinction may, however, be taken note of at this stage if the present system is contrasted with its model as in the past. It is operated by an extra-constitutional centre of power headed by Sonia Gandhi who is the chief of the Congress party and who has picked up Manmohan Singh to lead the government. The Prime Minister in such a situation cannot function independently as he has not only to stick to the terms of the CMP, but also to bow to the whims and caprices of the High Command. The chief of the organisation now acts like the chief of the coordination committee and thereby exercises power without shouldering any responsibility for that. Her most trusted lieutenants have got berths in the Council of Ministers with important portfolios in spite of the fact that some of them were defeated in the recent polls. The leaders of the leftist parties may take benefit of their strong position to dictate their own terms which may be a source of great embarrassment to the Prime Minister. Vajpayee could lead a motley crowd of disparate elements as the BJP had taken to the right-of-the centre approach, Manmohan Singh may not take things as easily in view of the fact that the left-of-the-centre orientation of his party may create a sticky path for him. To deal with the rightist forces is manageable, to deal with the leftist elements is a Herculean task. It is certain that it has led to the creation of one more aberration in our West minster model of government.

Caretaker Government

The system of parliamentary democracy has its celebrated norms in respect of the formation of government, its accountability immediately to the popular chamber of the national legislature and ultimately to the electorate. The operation of a caretaker government begins with the 'appeal to the voters' made by the Head of the State and ends with the installation of a new government having the 'mandate of the masses'. A caretaker government is neither an *adhoc* arrangement, nor a stop-gap mechanism devised to face or deal with a serious situation like war or internal revolt. It is a unique arrangement in the sense that it retains the ministers in office to look after the day-to-day working of the government without taking important policy decisions[24], unless it is so needed by the exigencies of the situation.[25] The term 'caretaker government' became popular after the World War II when Prime Minister Churchill of England (who was till then heading a National Government having some leaders of the Labour Party) sought resignations of the Labour ministers so as to appeal to the electorate of his country for giving their mandate in favour of his Conservative Party. For this sake, he submitted his resignation to the King without consulting his Labour colleagues who were then deliberating at the Blackpool Conference and ostensibly making up their mind to resign before taking part in the general election going to be held in July, 1945. Thus, without waiting for the resignation of the Labour Minister, Churchill resigned. Thereupon, the King commissioned him to form the new Administration that was given the name of 'caretaker government.'[26] Now the Cabinet of Churchill had a few Tory ministers which resolved not to take any policy decision. The notable point is that while Churchill took part in the Potsdam Conference with his Foreign Minister (Anthony Eden) on 17 July 1945 (attended by President Truman of the United States and Prime Minister Stalin of the USSR to deliberate on the fate of Germany), he also took with him the Leader of the Opposition and shadow Prime Minister (Clement Attlee) and his shadow Foreign Secretary

---

24. As former President of India, R. Venkataraman, says: "The Caretaker government cannot take any policy decisions or commit future governments to heavy financial burden". *My Presidential Years,* p. 504.

25. As an official spokesman of the Vajpayee Government, Pramod Mahajan the then Union Minister for Information and Broadcasting) said in New Delhi on 28th April that "what needs to be done in the national interest, will be done." : *The Times of India* (New Delhi), 29 April, 1999 .

26. Prof. Ivor Jennings makes it clear that it "is not the British practice to appoint a caretaker government for the duration of a general election, it was done in 1945 because the War time coalition had broken up. The election had to decide whether they wanted a Conservative Government or a Labour Government and meanwhile the King's services had to be carried on. This was quite exceptional. The Government which advised the dissolution remains in office throughout the election and continues to do so after the election, unless it is defeated." *Cabinet Government,* London, Cambridge Univ. Press, 1965, p. 86, No. 1.

(Ernest Bevin). It highlighted the true character of a caretaker government and the role of Churchill as a true democrat of his country.

Since 1945 the term 'caretaker government' has come into currency in other countries of the world having parliamentary system of government. In India such as arrangement took place without inviting any public controversy during the days of Nehru's towering leadership. It, however, engaged our attention after the decline of the Indian National Congress in the elections of 1967 and then with the growing leadership of Indira Gandhi that was looked at with apprehension by the critical students of Indian politics. The unofficial committee on electoral reforms set up by Jayaprakash Narayan in 1974 under the chairmanship of Justice V.M. Tarkunde took up this issue and in its Report (1975) proposed: "A convention backed by legal sanction should be developed to the effect that the government of the day should function as a caretaker government from the time of the announcement of the dissolution of Parliament or Legislative Assembly, as the case may be, until the polling day. During this period, the caretaker government should not (a) initiate and announce new policies, (b) promise or start new projects, (c) grant allowances or loans, salary increases, and (d) hold official functions attended by ministers."

However, in an official form, it appeared for the first time in the *communique* issued by President Sanjiva Reddy in August 1979 which, while dissolving the Lok Sabha, highlighted two important points:

"1. Elections will be peaceful, free and fair. The revision of the electoral rolls will begin immediately and the election time-table will commence in November, 1979 and be completed by December, 1979.

2. The Government will not take decisions during this period which set new policies or involve new spending of a significant order or constitute measures of administrative or executive decisions. However, work of an urgent nature involving the national interest will not be held up."

Surprisingly, Prime Minister Charan Singh and his Cabinet colleagues like his Foreign Minister (S.N. Mishra) frankly asserted that our Constitution had no such provision and, as such, the government could take any decision. Thus, the government took many crucial decisions as restoration of minority character of the Aligarh Muslim University, job reservations for backward classes on the pattern of the Karpoori Thakur formula of Bihar, and the financing of election expenses of individual candidates by the State. Similar situation arose in 1991 when Prime Minister Chandra Shekhar and his Law Minister (Subramaniam Swamy) reiterated that there was no provision in our Constitution of this nature and so their government could take any decision as it deemed proper or necessary. Thereupon, the government took some such decisions relating to important appointments including those of the judiciary and ordering of some controversial transfers that were objected to by the Election Commission. On the last day of the session in March, 1991 it could have a bill passed by the Parliament in a hurry that sought to grant pension to any member of Parliament, who completed one year, in proportion to the pension available to an M.P. on the completion of four years. In this way, the government created as unseemly controversy and President Venkataraman had to exercise his veto power by not giving assent to the controversial bill passed by the Parliament within a couple of minutes.

No doubt, the caretaker governments of Charan Singh and Chandra Shekhar violated a healthy tradition by adhering to this point that they "were competent to take any decision, including policy decisions"[27]. But the trend continued. The Gujral government did likewise in appointing the Governors of Mizoram and Goa in early 1998 and the Prime Minister (though an elected member of the Rajya Sabha from Bihar) waived central loans worth crores of rupees on Punjab, while he was contesting Lok Sabha election from the constituency of Jalandhar in this State. The appointments of the two Governors were objected to by the new government of Vajpayee and so they had to go after a couple of months.

It is true that the President is the constitutional head of the Indian republic, it is equally true that he has to play a different role

27. M.V. Pylee: "The Caretaker Government: What and Why?" in *Politics India*, New Delhi, April, 1998, p. 19.

during times of crisis. As such, in relation to the operation of a caretaker government he may act on his own, or in consultation with the Ministers may do what he would like to do on his own. Thus, President Sanjiva Reddy explicitly laid down the points in his *communique* of 1979 and President Shankar Dayal Sharma declined to sign the two ordinances in 1996 drafted by the government of Narsimha Rao on the plea that the elections had been declared. (While one ordinance sought to grant reservations in public services to the Dalit Christians, the other one sought to reduce the period of election canvassing from three to two weeks). He may not only specify the terms in his *communique*, he may also issue instructions from time to time, verbal as well as written, so that they are carried out in letter as well as in spirit. As a distinguished leader of our country said: "This is the supreme responsibility which the President undertakes and the Constitution gives him the power to act in times of crisis, particularly to prevent a parliamentary government from becoming parliamentary anarchy or a majority government from indulging in constitutional excesses. The role envisaged by the President in times of caretaker government is a more active one than conventional interpretations of the Constitution would suggest."[28]

It should be borne in mind that the caretaker government is not like a National Government having few ministers of all talents formed to meet the national crisis, it is an interim arrangement to keep the democratic system in operation. It may convert itself into a government proper if it wins the mandate of the people, otherwise its function is to go happily after shaking hands with the new incumbents. We may endorse the view of Prof. Pylee that some provisions should be introduced in our Constitution in this regard so that the concept of a caretaker government "would become more acceptable as an unavoidable adjunct of parliamentary government."[29]

---

28. C. Subramaniam: "Caretaker Government and the President" in *The Hindu.*, New Delhi, 7 January, 1998, p. 10.

29. M.V. Pylee, *op. cit.*, p. 20.

Prime Ministers

	Names	*From*	*To*
1.	Jawaharlal Nehru	15.8.1947	27.5.1964
2.	Gulzarilal Nanda*	27.5.1964	9.6.1964
3.	Lal Bahadur Shastri	9.6.1964	11.1.1966
4.	Gulzarilal Nanda*	11.1.1966	24.1.1966
5.	Indira Gandhi	24.1.1966	24.3.1977
6.	Morarji Desai	24.3.1977	28.7.1979
7.	Charan Singh	28.7.1979	14.1.1980
8.	Indira Gandhi	14.1.1980	31.10.1984
9.	Rajiv Gandhi	31.10.1984	2.12.1989
10.	V.P. Singh	2.12.1989	10.11.1990
11.	Chandra Shekhar	10.11.1990	21.6.1991
12.	P.V. Narsimha Rao	21.6.1991	16.5.1996
13.	Atal Behari Vajpayee	16.5.1996	28.5.1996
14.	H.D. Deve-Gowda	1.6.1996	21.3.1997
15.	I.K. Gujral	21.3.1997	19.3.1998
16.	Atal Behari Vajpayee	19.3.1998	22.5.2004
17.	Dr. Manmohan Singh	22.5.2004	25.5.2014
18.	Narendra Modi	26.5.2014	....

* Nanda worked as Officiating Prime Minister.

Tenures of Lok Sabha

	From	*To*
First Lok Sabha	27.4.1952	4.4.1957
Second Lok Sabha	5.4.1957	21.3.1962
Third Lok Sabha	2.4.1962	3.3.1967
Fourth Lok Sabha	4.3.1967	27.12.1970
Fifth Lok Sabha	15.3.1971	18.1.1977
Sixth Lok Sabha	25.3.1977	22.8.1979
Seventh Lok Sabha	10.1.1980	31.12.1984
Eighth Lok Sabha	31.12.1984	27.11.1989
Ninth Lok Sabha	2.12.1989	13.3.1991
Tenth Lok Sabha	20.6.1991	10.5.1996
Eleventh Lok Sabha	15.5.1996	4.12.1997
Twelfth Lok Sabha	7.3.1998	26.4.1999
Thirteenth Lok Sabha	10.10.1999	6.2.2004
Fourteenth Lok Sabha	17.5.2004	1.6.2009
Fifteenth Lok Sabha	1.6.2009	5.3.2009
Sixteenth Lok Sabha	20.5.2014	....

One important point to be noted here is that with the installation of caretaker government, Art. 74(1) of the Constitution loses its weight. It makes the President free to exercise his individual judgement in crucial matters. He may honour the advice of his ministers in a matter relating to the dismissal of a Governor who would not resign after completing his term of five years so as to make the way clear for the entry of a new incumbent as desired by the Home Minister; he may advise the Ministers not to go ahead with the appointment of new Governors as it amounts to the taking of a policy decision and in stead take to the way of making *ad hoc* appointments of officiating Governors. In a way, it looks like creating a situation of Presidential activism for the time being, for it requires that the government of the day should carry on the administration of the country without making itself accused of acting either actively or passively.

Aberrations in System of Parliamentary Government

The Westminster model of government in its operational form may be said to have three manifestations. First, it is, what Laski calls, parliamentary government in which the Parliament has its upper hand over the ministry. The government is so weak that it, in the real sense of the term, lives on the pleasure of the legislature. Such a government may be easily thrown out as happened with the governments of V.P. Singh, Chandra Skehar, Deve-Gowda, Gujaral and Vajpayee. The second is, what Jennings has termed, the cabinet government. It is a government which has solid majority behind it in the House and so it becomes responsive, though superficially responsible, to the legislature. The Prime Minister is confident of his safe position and so Cabinet works in a manner that is sometimes deprecated as its 'dictatorship'. There is hardly any scope for throwing it out by passing a vote of no-confidence. The governments of Nehru, Shastri and Indira Gandhi may be cited as its examples. Last, it is, what Crossman has designated, a Prime Ministerial government in which its head (Prime Minister) becomes all-powerful so much so that not only Parliament, even the ministers of the Cabinet, become like his palace-guards. What Indira Gandhi did during 1971-76 and then what Rajiv Gandhi did during 1985-89 bears ample testimony to this fact. Such a situation converts parliamentary government into presidentialised form of government.

As a result of the disintegration of the single-dominant party system established by the Indian National Congress, the era of coalition politics has ushered in. Hence, the operation of parliamentary form of government has witnessed some peculiar developments which are described as its aberrations and which may be noted as under:

1. Prime Minister is regarded as the 'keystone of the cabinet arch'; he is taken as 'first among equals', or 'a moon among the lesser stars'; above all in the words of Laski, he is 'central to the life and death of the Cabinet'. Such a situation no longer exists. In a coalition system; it is the coordination committee of the constituent elements which sorts out matters like selection of the ministers, distribution of portfolios, drafting of a common minimum programme and the like. Naturally, the position of the Prime Minister becomes very weak, rather pathetic, and he has to work during the pleasure not of the President but of the constituent elements. Facts show that in every delicate situation Vajpayee had to bank upon the cooperation of a lesser fry like Mahanta of Assam or Naidu of Andhra Pradesh. The chief of the coordination committee becomes a centre of power that controls the working of the government and may even peruse confidential documents without having taken the oath of secrecy.

2. Cabinet government is known for its solidarity. All ministers speak in the same voice. In case anyone differs from the official line, he should quit. But in our country now ministers may be seen speaking in different voices on any crucial issue as the construction of a temple in Ayodhya, the need for a POTA, the enforcement of a uniform civil code, communal riots in Gujarat and the like. The Prime Minister has no real control over his colleagues and he has to soften the tone or reinterpret the statements of his ministers so as to satisfy the critics having their place in the opposition parties.

3. In a democratic system power is wielded as a gift of the mandate of the people. But sharing of power automatically calls for shouldering the responsibility. Those who are in power, they must be accountable to the Parliament. But in our country a new development has occurred in the form of supporting the government from outside. A party having such

Ministries and Departments of the Union Government (2012)

1. Ministry of Agriculture
   (i) Department of Agriculture and Cooperation
   (ii) Department of Agricultural Research and Education
   (iii) Department of Animal Husbandry and Dairying
2. Ministry of Chemicals and Fertilizers
   (i) Department of Chemicals and Petro-Chemicals
   (ii) Department of Fertilizers
   (iii) Department of Pharmaceuticals
3. Ministry of Civil Aviation
4. Ministry of Coal
5. Ministry of Commerce and Industry
   (i) Department of Commerce
   (ii) Department of Industrial Policy and Promotion
6. Ministry of Communications and Information Technology
   (i) Department of Telecommunications
   (ii) Department of Post
   (iii) Department of Information Technology
7. Ministry of Consumer Affairs
   (i) Department of Consumer Affairs
   (ii) Department of Food and Public Distribution
8. Ministry of Corporate Affairs
9. Ministry of Culture
10. Ministry of Defence
   (i) Department of Defence
   (ii) Department of Defence Production
   (iii) Department of Defence Research and Development
   (iv) Department of Ex-servicemen Welfare
11. Ministry of Drinking Water and Sanitation
12. Ministry of Development of North-East Region
13. Ministry of Earth Sciences
14. Ministry of Environment and Forests
15. Ministry of External Affairs
16. Ministry of Finance
   (i) Department of Economic Affairs

(*ii*) Department of Expenditure
(*iii*) Department of Revenue
(*iv*) Department of Disinvestment
(*v*) Department of Financial Services

17. Ministry of Food Processing Industries

18. Ministry of Health and Family Welfare
    (*i*) Department of Health and Family Welfare
    (*ii*) Department of Health Research
    (iii) Department of Ayurveda, Yoga-Naturopathy, Unani, Siddha and Homoeopathy
    (*ii*) Department of AIDS Control

19. Ministry of Heavy Industries and Public Enterprises
    (*i*) Department of Heavy Industries
    (*ii*) Department of Public Enterprises

20. Ministry of Home Affairs
    (*i*) Department of Internal Security
    (*ii*) Department of States
    (*iii*) Department of Official Language
    (*iv*) Department of Home
    (*v*) Department of Jammu and Kashmir Affairs
    (*vi*) Department of Border Management

21. Ministry of Human Resource Development
    (*i*) Department of School Education and Literacy
    (*ii*) Department of Higher Education

22. Ministry of Information and Broadcasting

23. Ministry of Labour and Employment

24. Ministry of Law and Justice
    (*i*) Department of Legal Affairs
    (*ii*) Legislative Department
    (*iii*) Department of Justice

25. Ministry of Micro, Small and Medium Enterprises

26. Ministry of Mines

27. Ministry of Minority Affairs

28. Ministry of New and Renewable Energy

29. Ministry of Overseas Indian Affairs

30. Ministry of Panchayati Raj

31. Ministry of Parliamentary Affairs

32. Ministry of Personnel, Public Grievances and Pensions

(*i*) Department of Personnel and Training
(*ii*) Department of Administrative Reforms and Public Grievances
(*iii*) Department of Pensions and Pensioners' Welfare

33. Ministry of Petroleum and Natural Gas
34. Ministry of Planning
35. Ministry of Power
36. Ministry of Railways
37. Ministry of Road Transport and Highways
38. Ministry of Rural Development
    (*i*) Department of Rural Development
    (*ii*) Department of Land Resources
39. Ministry of Science and Technology
    (*i*) Department of Science and Technology
    (*ii*) Department of Scientific and Industrial Research
40. Ministry of Shipping
41. Ministry of Social Justice and Empowerment
42. Ministry of Statistics and Programme Implementation
43. Ministry of Steel
44. Ministry of Textiles
45. Ministry of Tourism
46. Ministry of Tribal Affairs
47. Ministry of Urban Development
48. Ministry of Urban Employment and Poverty Alleviation
49. Ministry of Water Resources
50. Ministry of Women and Child Development
51. Ministry of Youth Affairs and Sports

Independent Departments of the Central Government

52. Department of Atomic Energy
53. Department of Space
54. Planning Commission
55. Cabinet Secretariat
56. President's Secretariat
57. Prime Minister's Office

a stand does enjoy the fruits of power, but it never desires to shoulder any responsibility for a wrong action of the government.

4. In a coalitional set up minor parties having a local or petty regional base manage to hold ministerial posts. Their outlook is pitiably chauvinistic and so they struggle for the pork barrels. They hardly bother for national interest. Not only this, some elements are so mischievous that they threaten to quit and then the Prime Minister has to somehow satisfy them. Reference may be made to the role of Jayalalitha of the ADMK who withdrew the support of her party as a result of which the government of Vajpayee had its abrupt end in 1998. Such a case presents the peculiar spectacle of the tail wagging the body.

5. Above all, there is the casualty of the principles on which a government works, or it should work. Pragmatism becomes the dominant ideology and all constituent elements throw their commitments to the wind. There is nothing like Rightism, Leftism, or Centrism. It is all a crude hotch-potch of expediencies. The government functions in a directionless situation. The fear of the morrow haunts it and so the power-hungry politicians manage to pull on things as long as it is possible for them to do by any hook or crook.

These are aberrations if one studies them in the light of the operation of parliamentary government since 1952 under the towering leadership of Nehru, Shastri and Indira Gandhi. But those were the days when Congress alone was at the helm of affairs so much so that it was the party, the government, the state, even the country. Things have undergone a basic change now and any idea of restoration of the past would be like a wishful thinking. And yet we should not take it as a sinister development. Our political system is in a melting pot. New things are coming up. Let us hope that in time to come, India would be able to have a model of its own parliamentary government of a country that may be different from the English or the Continental models on account of the peculiar conditions of our country. No model of government can be suitable to another country unless it is carefully chiselled according to the urges and aspirations of its people.

11

Parliament: Evolution, Formation and Role

A study of the rise and growth of parliamentary institutions ever since the establishment of the British rule in India is beset with a strange spectacle of two divergent currents, each pushing things in its own direction, but both ultimately witnessing their confluence into a single channel as a result of which the present bi-cameral model of the Parliament (*Sansad*) came into being. The classical argument of the colonial statesmen based on their conviction that English parliamentary institutions could not be transplanted in a country ridden with social antagonism, economic stagnation and political backwardness assumed a 'modified character' for the better at the hands of enlightened liberal statesmen in the period following the first World War, no matter the dichotomy continued to prevail till the last constitutional dispensation in the form of the Government of India Act of 1935 was offered to placate the agitation of the Indian nationalists.

In this regard, the role of the liberal intellectuals of India has its own place. A concerted movement to transplant parliamentary institutions in this country on the lines of their English counterparts, as emphasised by the liberal statesmen of the country, well synchronised with the approach of the shrewd English statesmen who wanted to strike somehow a balance between their determination to keep the empire intact and, at the same time, to give doses of satisfaction to the Indian leaders agitating for 'Swaraj'. The triumph of the two strands of thought, in this way, found its concrete manifestation in the form of various constitutional experiments made by the foreign power in the pre- as well as post-1857 period. An examination of all this will, therefore, lead us to this conclusion that when the elected representatives of the first Parliament met on May 13, 1952, the day had a great importance of its own in the light of a long historical development of parliamentary institutions in this country; it marked the end of the old and the beginning of a new period.[1]

Constitutional Reforms in the Pre-Mutiny Period

The obdurate view of the classical English statesmen that this country was not suited to the rise and growth of their parliamentary institutions stood defeated in the face of this irresistible fact that the British domination "led to the imposition of British ideas on Indian legislation and legislative machinery."[2] The new industrial class in power in the later half of the eighteenth century could not remain oblivious to the fact that the system of empire-keeping required some more restrictions on the working of the East India Company. Thus, the Regulating Act of 1773 came into being that made drastic changes in the rules relating to the organisation and working of the East India Company. It not only elevated the office of the Governor of Bengal by designating him as the Governor-General but also made him the supreme legislative authority in this country. "By this Act, the legislative power of the Governor-General independently of the Supreme Court, was recognised and confirmed."[3]

---

1. W.H. Morris-Jones: *Parliament in India*, Philadelphia, 1957, p. 43.
2. Parmatma Sharan, *The Imperial Legislative Council of India*, Delhi, 1961, p. 5. The approach of the enlightened statesmen like E.S. Montagu (the then Secretary of State for India) and Viceroy Lord Chelmsford may be seen in their Report of 1918 when they noted; "In fact, the germ of legislative power lies embedded in Elizabeth's Charter (of 31st December, 1600) which authorised the East India Company to make reasonable laws, constitutions, orders, and ordinances, not repugnant to the English law, for the good Government by the Company." *Montford Report*, para 52. On this point C.P. Ilbert comments that the powers of making laws and ordinances granted by the various Charters was similar to those exercised by municipal or commercial corporations and, therefore, the character of laws made under them was akin to that of the bye-law framed by such bodies. *The Government of India*, [Oxford, 1915] p. 9.
3. H. Cowell, *History and Constitution of the Courts and Legislative Authorities in India* (Calcutta, 1936) p. 3.

The new arrangement failed to be satisfactory from every point of view. The most important question that engaged the attention of the Government at that time was related to the organisation and powers of the Legislative Councils. Thus, in the letter of July 14, 1829 addressed to the judges of the Supreme Court, the Government proposed for the reconsideration that the Members of the Supreme Government and the Judges of the Supreme Court of Calcutta should be constituted into a Legislative Council.[4] A successful accomplishment of this move appeared in the Charter Act of 1833 when a Law Member was added to the Governor-General's Council at Calcutta with a specific duty to advise in legislative matters. So far, the Governor-General-in-Council combined in itself executive, legislative and judicial functions. But this Act brought about legislative centralisation by establishing only one Legislative Council for all British territories in India. It effected these important changes in the legislative system of India:

1. The entire legislative power for all the British territories was exclusively vested in the Governor-General-in-Council.
2. The laws passed by the Governor-General-in-Council came to be called 'Acts' and not 'Regulations' as before.
3. The Law Member was added to sit and vote at the meetings of the Council convened for law-making purposes.

The importance of this arrangement lay in the fact that it centralised the law-making function in the Governor-General and his Council and introduced "the first element of institutional specialisation."[5]

The introduction of the Law Member is regarded as the 'first move towards an Indian legislature.'[6] Moreover, the conferment of this distinguished office on Lord T.B. Macaulay made it all the more significant. However, it should be taken note of that this move was dictated neither by any human nor by any political consideration. Nothing but the need for having a technical expert in India to deal with legislative matters was the main consideration that haunted

---

4. *Affairs of the East India Company*, Parliamentary Papers, 1831, Appendix V.
5. Morris-Jones, *op. cit.*, p. 45.
6. *Ibid.*, p. 46.

the minds of the English rulers. The powers of the purse did not belong to the people or their nominees when the seedling of future legislatures took root on the implementation of this Act. An improvement upon this took place when the Charter Act of 1853 came into being. It further distinguished the executive and the legislative aspects of the Governor-General's Council. The size of the Council as a legislative body was further increased by the addition of representative of each Presidency, along with two judges. The Law Member was made a full member of the Council. The Legislative Council became a body of 12 members in all by virtue of having 4 official members representing four provinces appointed by the Governors from amongst persons having been in the service of the Company for at least 10 years and 6 additional members or 'Legislative Councillors'. Another important development was that sittings of the Legislative Council were made public and the proceedings published officially.

As a result of this improved system, the Legislative Council was said to have assumed the airs of a 'petty parliament'[7] The members brought forward motions that had no reference to the measures before them. Sometimes, they even criticised the Executive Council and thereby assumed powers of interpellation. But so far as the question of privileges was concerned this body "behaved like a moderate sovereign legislature. It had framed its own rules of procedure, amended them whenever thought necessary by them, called for information from different governmental organisations, protested against any proposal to restrict its privileges of entertaining petitions and strongly resented the casting of any aspersion on it or attribution of any motive to it in its works."[8]

The role of the Legislative Council as 'a miniature House of Commons' became a source of anxiety to the authorities sitting in England. Sir Charles Wood, the then President of the Board of Control for the East India Company, wrote to Sir Bartle Frere that nobody at the time of the introduction of the Charter Act of 1853

---

7. Allen Gledhill, *The Republic of India*, (London, 1951) p. 20.

8. S.K. Nag, *Evolution of Parliamentary Privileges in India* (New Delhi, 1978), p. 319.

"even dreamt of a debating body with open doors and even of quasi-independence" and in very frank terms, confessed that there was always a sympathy in England for an independent deliberation. His biting indictment may be noticed in his statement: "My intention... was to give to the Council the assistance of local knowledge and legal experience in framing laws. The Council, however, has become a sort of debating society, for petty parliament."[9]

Reforms under the Policy of Association

A definite change in the English colonial policy took place after the enforcement of the Government of India Act, 1858, that terminated the era of the Company rule and instead inaugurated the era of India under the Crown. Aware of the horrors of the 'Mutiny' of 1857, the British statesmen implemented the policy of associating the natives with their system of administration. In pursuance of the 'policy of association', they thought in terms of granting constitutional reforms that would involve participation of the native elements in different branches of administration. Taking note of this fact, Sir Bartle Frere observed: "The addition of the native element (to the Legislative Councils) has become necessary owing to our diminished opportunities of learning through indirect channels what the natives think of our measures and how the native community will be affected by them."[10]

---

9. *Parliamentary Debates* (House of Commons) June 6, 1861, III Series, Vol. 163, Cols 638-42. Compare it with the Report of the Commitee of Parliament on the Affairs of the East India Company in 1833 that defined the new aims of the Supreme Government thus: "On a large view of the state of Indian legislation and of the improvement of which it is susceptible, it is recognised as an indispensable principle, that the interests of the native subjects are to be considered in preference to those of Europeans whenever the two come in competition; and that, therefore, the law ought to be adapted rather to the feelings and habits of the natives than to those of Europeans." See Ramsay Muir, *The Making of British India*, p. 305.

10. See Morris-Jones, *op. cit.*, pp. 46-47. Shrewd English scholars and statesmen as well as their Indian protagonists studied the causes that led to the outbreak of the 'munity' in 1857 and they came to

This was the spirit behind the Indian Councils Act of 1861. By the admirers it was lauded as the 'prime charter of the Indian legislature'. Now the Governor-General's Legislative Council was reinforced by additional members, not less than 6 and not more than 12, nominated by him for two years. Of these, not less than half were to be non-officials *i.e.,* not being in the civil or military services of the Crown. The Governor of a Presidency or the Lt. Governor of a Province also acted as an additional member in case the Council had a sitting within his territorial jurisdiction. Since this was the supreme law-making body of the country, the Governor-General was authorised to appoint a fifth member to his Executive Council who was to be 'a gentleman of legal profession, a jurist rather than a technical lawyer'. It gave to the Governor-General the great power to promulgate an ordinance for the peace and good government of British India or any part thereof that could remain in force for a period of 6 months unless repealed earlier or converted into a law.

The merit of the Act of 1861 lay in inaugurating the system of 'legislative devolution in India'. Though in a halting manner, the start of a representative system may also be discovered herein. It was appreciated for setting 'a new ideal for the educated Indians to make the British Government "responsive to public opinion without in any way affecting its supremacy and authority."[11] However, this act "reached nowhere near the people's aspirations for a more representative legislative body."[12] The English rulers were interested in nothing else than the preservation of their favourites being in the communities of the princes, landlords, dewans and the like, most of whom were ignorant of the English language in which the proceedings were conducted.[13] Thus, most of them played the role of 'magnificent non-entities'.

---

the conclusion that it all happened owing to the exclusion of the distinguished Indians from Indian administation. Thus, Sir Bartle Frere noted that the great evil of the existing system was the entire absence of any element representing the non-official public, native or European, or property or mercantile interests of any kind. Syed Ahmed Khan of Aligarh expressed the same view in his *An Essay on the Causes of the Indian Revolt*, translated from Urdu into English by W.N. Lees, p. 12.

11. S.V. Desika Char, *Centralised Legislation*, p. 332.

12. S.L. Shakdher, *Glimpses of the Working of the Parliament* (New Delhi, 1977) p. 1.

13. C.Y. Chintamani, *Indian Politics Since the Mutiny*, p. 32.

A noticeable change in the evolution of parliamentary system took place after the establishment of the Indian National Congress in 1885. The early liberals like W.C. Bonnerjee, Dadabhai Naoroji, Pherozeshah Mehta, Surendranath Banerjea and Gopal Krishna Gokhle admired the British system of governement and desired its transplantation in this country. At its first session held in the city of Bombay under the presidentship of W.C. Bonnerjee, it registered its faith in the presence of the elected members of the Legislative Councils having right to ask questions and discuss budgetary proposals.. It shows that from its very start the object of the Congress "was to ensure a parliamentary safeguard against bureaucratic actions, such as have lately been witnessed in profusion in the Assembly in respect of the rejection or vetoing of popular demands accepted by a majority and the certification of government demands rejected by people's representatives."[14]

Thus came the Indian Councils Act of 1892 as a marked improvement upon the Act of 1861. It enlarged the size and functions of the Supreme as well as Local Legislative Councils. The members were given the right to ask questions on matters of public interest. For this a notice of 6 days in advance was to be given to the Government. The members were also authorised to discuss budget under certain conditions. The strength of the additional members was also increased. Now it was to be of not less than 10 and not more than 16 members in the Supreme Legislative Council. It was also laid down that two-fifths of the additional members were to be non-officials. A clause, (known as the Kimberley clause) was added whereby the Governor-General was empowered to make regulations concerning the nomination of additional members subject to the approval of the Secretary of State-in-Council.[15]

It may, however, be repeated at this stage that, like other constitutional experiments, the Act of 1892 also failed to meet the expectations of the great Indian liberal leaders. Even under the new set up, the members felt deprived of the status of belonging to a separate and distinct organisation available to a legislative body.

---

14. Dr. Pattabhi Sitaramayya, *The History of the Indian National Congress* (1885-1935), Vol. 1, p. 24.

15. See O.P. Bhatnagar: "The Growth of Parliamentary Institutions and Franchise in India" in A.B. Lal (ed.): *The Indian Parliament*, (Allahabad, 1956) p. 2.

Still the members lacked essential freedom that is the very life-breath of a parliamentary body. On the contrary, the members of the new Legislative Councils ever remained conscious of the fact that they "were nothing more than an appendage to an organ whose main function was not to legislate but to govern."[16] The reason for all this lay in the fact that a government "run by a foreign power cannot afford to arm a subordinate legislature with a complete code of parliamentary privileges as they are possessed by the sovereign parliament unless, of course, the foreign power is prepared to dig its own grave."[17]

Morley-Minto Reforms of 1909

The introduction of the Morley-Minto Reforms in the form of the Indian Councils Act of 1909 has an importance of its own in this regard. While the Reforms certainly contributed to the growth of Indian legislature at the Central and Local levels, they sowed the seeds of communalism by granting separate electorates to the Muslims. In this way, the policy of 'divide and rule' was reinforced by the policy of the 'counterpoise of the natives against the natives'. The official point of view remained embedded in this traditional assumption that English parliamentary institutions could not work in this country. A Government of India dispatch of 1892 had already put it that Indian society was essentially a congeries of widely separated classes, races and communities with divergencies of interests and hereditary sentiments.'[18] Representing the same standpoint, Lord Morley said in the House of Lords: "If it could be said that this chapter of reforms led directly or necessarily to the establishment of a parliamentary system in India, I for one would have nothing at all to do with it."[19]

---

16. S.K. Nag, *op. cit.*, p. 321.
17. *Ibid.*, p. 322.
18. Cited in Reginald Coupland: *The Indian Problem.* p. 24,
19. Cited in *Indian Statutory Commission Report.* 1930, Vol.1, para 119. Compare it with the affirmations of Lord Dufferin who in 1896 said: "It is not necessary that there should be no mistake about our aims, the Act of 1892 was not to be regarded as an approach to English Parliamentary Government. India is an integral part of the mighty British Empire and the Government of India is responsible not to any local legislature but to the Sovereign and to the British Parliament." See Morris-Jones, *op. cit.*, p. 47.

The Act of 1909 enlarged the size of the Supreme Legislative Council. Now it could have 37 official members (28 nominated by the Governor-General and 9 *ex-officio* members-Governor-General himself, 1 extra-ordinary member and 7 ordinary members) and 32 non-official members (5 members to be nominated by the Governor-General and the rest to be elected for a term of 3 years by Provincial Legislative Councils, landholders, Muslims, Chambers of Commerce of Bombay and Calcutta etc.) For the first time, the system of separate electoral representation was accorded whereby seats were allotted to different communities, castes, classes and interests. The Governor-General-in-Council, with the approval of the Secretary of State for India, was empowered to make regulations as to the conditions under which and the manner in which persons resident in India might be nominated or elected as members of the Supreme Legislative Council (or to any of the Provincial Legislative Councils) along with the qualifications of the elected and nominated members.

The Act of 1909 also enhanced the rights of the members to ask questions and their supplementaries and discuss budget. They could move a resolution desiring alteration of taxation, raising of any additional grant to local government proposed or mentioned in the financial statement or explanatory memorandum. But they were not permitted to discuss expenditure on interest on debt, ecclesiastical affairs, railways etc. The member-in-charge of a department could refuse to answer a supplementary question off-hand or demand some time for this purpose. The members got the right to raise a definite issue in the House by putting a resolution which the President could disallow, in full or part, without assigning any reason. No discussion was permitted on any subject falling outside the competence of the Council, or on any matter affecting relations of the Government of India with any foreign power or Princely State, or any other matter under judicial examination or settlement.

The system of Morley-Minto Reforms was appreciated by the English writers as well as by the leaders of the Muslim League and leading leaders of the 'Moderate School'. For instance, the authors of the Montford Report visualised that now the members of the Councils, Supreme as well as Provincial, were given "a real opportunity of exercising some influence on questions of administration and finance."[20] The Muslim communalists expressed their profound satisfaction with the system of weightage given to their co-religionists. This, Mian Muhammed Shafi, in a letter to Dunlop Smith dated April 30, 1909, said that the provisions of the Act "gave full expression to their grateful feelings and we thought that separate representation at all stages had become a settled fact."[21] Among leading liberals of that time, Surendranath Banerjea hailed these Reforms as "crowning triumph of constitutional agitation" and urged upon the Congressmen to express their deep gratitude to the Government of India for granting "most valued concessions." Likewise, Gokhale admired them for affording the people of India "an occasion to have a responsible association with the Indian administration."[22]

But this system was vehemently attacked by the fiery nationalists of the country. Pandit Madan Mohan Malaviya in his Presidential address at the Lahore Congress of 1909 denounced these Reforms for creating communal dissensions and laying down unnecessarily narrower and arbitrary restrictions on the choice of the electors."[23] On this occasion M.A. Jinnah moved a resolution (that was seconded by Harul Haque and Hasan Imam) that desired immediate scrapping of the notorious system of communal representations to the Muslims.[24] There was no dearth of the critics who could discover herein a peculiar reconciliation of the principles of autocracy and constitutionalism. They could take it for granted that, though elected, the European elements were as good as the official; the landlords and the Muslims "were admittedly there for their 'service to the Empire'; and were bent upon improving the future of their own classes by proving their loyalty still further."[25]

---

20. *Montford Report,* para. 6. An English writer Morris-Jones also says that the "experience communicated and gained through these early Legislative Councils was limited but far from negligible." *Op. cit.*, p. 49.
21. See M.N. Das, *India under Morley and Minto.* p. 224.
22. J.S. Hoyland, *Gokhale: His Life and Speeches,* p. 130.
23. See A.C. Banerjee. *Indian Constitutional Documents,* Vol. II, pp. 169-70.
24. See Lal Bahadur, *Muslim League,* p. 82.
25. S.R. Sharma, *A Constitutional History of India,* p. 148.

Neither Lord Morley (the then Secretary of State for India), nor Lord Minto (the then Viceroy and Governor-General of India) should be credited with having an enlightened point of view in taking things in right direction. Prof. Coupland has endorsed the fact that Morley's ideas on Indian Government "had nothing to do with democracy."[26] But Minto was a man of different inclinations. In his despatch to Lord Morley dated November 27, 1909, he said: "I am afraid when the position is clearer, we may fairly owe so much in India... I should say that if the Government of India was biased in any direction, it was towards Muhammedan interests."[27]

However, the most outstanding contribution found place in the historic declaration of Montagu who could extract such a monumental signal from the reluctant war Cabinet.[28] On August 20, 1917 he said: "The policy of His Majesty's Government, with which the Government of India are in full accord, is that of increasing association of the Indians in every branch of administration and the gradual development of self-governing institutions with a view to the progressive realisation of responsible government in India as an integral part of the British Empire." This important declaration marked "the end of one epoch and the beginning of a new one."[29] The authors of the Montford Report themselves acknowledged the fact that the Morley-Minto Reforms of 1909 had made the Government of India "a benevolent despotism tempered by a remote and only occasionally vigilant democracy which might, as it saw fit, for purposes of enlightenment, consult the wishes of the subjects."[30]

---

26. Coupland, *The Indian Constitutional Problem*, p. 34.

27. S.D. Waley, *Edwin Montagu*. p. 136.

28. See Das, *op. cit.* p. 248.

29. *Montford Report,* para 7.

30. *Ibid.*, para 81. Taking a critical view of the working of Legislative Councils made under the Act of 1909, two English writers Ilbert and Meston commented that "a handful officials and two or three complaisant Indian gentlemen sat around a table and read manuscript speeches in turn." *The New Constitution of India* (1923), p. 91.

Montford Reforms of 1919

Thus, inauguration of a 'new policy' took place. It appeared in the form of Montagu-Chelmsford Reforms embodied in the Government of India Act of 1919 Now it appeared, as eulogised by some English commentators, that "it was not a question primarily of how to make the autocracy work more smoothly, it was a question rather of finding a way towards the transfer of power."[31] For the first time, the principle of bi-cameralism was adopted whereby Indian legislature was given a Central Legislative Assembly as the lower and Council of State as the upper chambers. The Council consisted of not more that 60 members of whom nct more than 20 were officials. Its electorate was so designed as to give it a character distinct from the Assembly. Its constitution was so framed as to make it a representative house of big landlords, capitalist class, and mercantile aristocracy. High property qualifications were fixed and separate representation was given to the Sikhs and the Muslims, while special constituencies were created for the European and non-communal interests. Franchise was also given to the past and present presidents and vice-presidents of local bodies, members of the university senates etc. Its term was of 5 years, though the Governor-General could extend its life or dissolve it earlier. He appointed its presiding officer from amongst its members.

The Central Legislative Assembly consisted of 140 members of whom 100 were elected, 26 official and 14 nominated members. Instead of doing away with the notorious system of communal representation, now it was further extended to cover the Sikhs, Europeans, Christians, and the Anglo-Indians. Landholders and the

---

31. As per rules and regulations framed by the Viceroy-in-Council, the number was fixed at 41 nominated and 144 elected members. In the Assembly there were 30 seats elected by the Muslim voters. 2 from the Punjab elected by the Sikhs and 9 by the Europeans; 7 members were the representatives of landholders and 4 of the Indian commerce. The Governor-General nominated 5 members to represent Indian Christians, Anglo-Indians, Depressed Classes, labour and Associated Chamber of Commerce. In the Council of State, 16 seats were reserved for the Muslims and 1 for Sikh from Punjab. Maurice Gwyer and A. Appadorai: *Speeches and Documents on the Indian Constitution*. Vol. I, pp. 35-36.

institutions of chambers of commerce also retained their privileges. The 26 official members included most of the members of the Governor-General's Executive Council. The other official members were either important members of the Secretariat of the Government of India such as Military Secretary and Foreign Secretary, or were nominated as the representatives of different Provincial Governments.[32] The number of seats allotted to every province varied according to its size and importance and so was the case with the voting qualifications. Franchise was given to those who paid income tax or municipal tax or land revenue of a higher standard. The normal term of the Assembly was of three years, but the Governor-General had the power to extend it or dissolve it earlier. It was also laid down that after its dissolution, fresh elections would take place within next six months, or within 9 months with the approval of the Secretary of State for India.

One important development at this stage should be seen in the evolution of the office of the President of the Assembly. The Act provided that after four years of the commencement of this Act, the Assembly would elect its presiding officer. The Governor-General nominated Sir Fredrick Whyte in 1920 for this post, but it was held by Vithalbhai J. Patel after him who laid the foundation of the great office now belonging to the Speaker of the Lok Sabha.[33] Patel interpreted the rules and orders of the Assembly literally in order to safeguard the rights of non-official members of the House thereby upholding the dignity of the legislature. To the great dismay of the Governor-General, he exercised his casting vote against the Public Safety Bill on September 24,1928.

Shortly after, in March 1929 when a motion to take into consideration the Report of the Select Committee on the Second Public Safety Bill was moved in the House, President Patel took the view that the subject of the Bill was identical with what was called the Meerut Conspiracy Case and, as such, it was not possible to discuss the provisions of the Bill without referring to the

32. Morris-Jones, *op. cit.*, p 51.

33. For a detailed study on this subject see Maya Dube, *The Speaker in India* and J.N. Singh Vadav: *The Indian Speaker: Crisis of Identity*.

proceedings in the said case that was then *subjudice*. He, therefore, ruled the motion out of order and decided not to place it before the House. Thus irked, the Viceroy himself addressed the Assembly the next day and pointed out that the action of the President was contrary to the spirit of the rules of the Assembly. Then, Patel took strong exception to the action of the Governor-General of India.[34]

The Act of 1919 enhanced the powers of the Indian legislature to a considerable extent. Now they could make laws for all persons, courts, places and other things within British India and for all subjects of His Majesty beyond as well as within British India. They could ask questions and their supplementaries on matters of public importance; they could table adjournment motions and place resolutions, discuss votable parts of the budget and debate matters in the Standing Committee. The Assembly could pass a vote of censure against the Government. Two committees of the House-Finance Committee and Committee on Public Accounts—exercised some influence over the Executive Councillors. However, the powers of the Assembly were circumscribed by a number of limitations.

The Governor-General could give his assent to a bill passed by the Central legislature, or return it for reconsideration, or veto it, or reserve it for the consideration of His Majesty. His prior sanction was required to introduce a bill that affected public debt or public revenues, or impose any charge on the Indian revenues, religion or religious rites of any class or community, discipline or maintenance of defence forces, external relations of the Government of India or its relations with the princely States, repeal or amendment of a law made by a provincial legislature and the like. It was within his power to authenticate a bill, whether money bill or not, passed by the Legislature as passed even if it had been rejected, though such a matter was subject to the final assent of His Majesty.

---

34. See Shakdher, *op. cit.*, p. 4. To cite another case, it may be given here that when it was suggested to Patel that he should invite the members of the Simon Commission (1928) to the Assembly he insisted that they should call on him first. Sir John Simon appreciated Patel's stand and went to see him. It "clearly demonstrates that under the new Act, the legislature had grown in stature and dignity". See Nag, *op. cit.*, p. 324.

Council of State (1929)

Constituencies	*Nominated*		*Elected*					
	Officials	*Non-Officials*	*Non-Muslims*	*Sikhs*	*Muslims*	*Non-Communal*	*Europeans. Commerce*	*Total*
Govt. of India	11	–	–	–	–	–	–	11
Madras	1	1	4	–	1	–	–	7
Bombay	1	1	3	2	–	–	1	8
Bengal	1	1	3	2	–	–	1	8
U.P.	1	1	3	2	–	–	–	7
Punjab	1	3	1	2	1	–	–	8
Bihar and Orissa	1	–	2	1	–	–	–	4
C.P. and Berar	–	2	–	–	–	1	1	4
Assam	–	–	–	1	–	–	–	1
Burma	–	–	–	–	–	1	1	2
N.W.F.P.	–	1	–	–	–	–	1	2
Total	17	10	16	10	2	2	4	62

In spite of all this, it may be admitted that the Indian legislators found the first remarkable opportunity to make use of legislative bodies for their purpose. To cite an instance, we may say that in February 1921, Kamath moved a resolution "recommending to the Governor-General of India that rules may be framed to ensure that no action, administrative or legislative, be taken on the reports of the Commissions and the Committees appointed by the Secretary of State for India, until an opportunity shall have been given by the Government to the Indian legislature to express its opinion thereon."[35] As feared, it was opposed by the Government of India, but ultimately a compromise was struck and the House adopted the resolution in a modified form. Then it said: "This Assembly recommends to the Governor-General-in-Council that, as far as practicable, steps may be taken to ensure that no action, administrative or legislative, be taken on reports of the commissions and committees appointed by the Secretary of State for India or the

35. File No 77/27, Home Government (Spl.). *Ibid.*

Government of India until an opportunity shall have been given by the Government to the Indian legislature to express its opinion thereon."[36]

Central Legislative Assembly (1929)

	Nominated		*Elected*							
Constituencies	*Officials*	*Non-Officials*	*Non-Muslims*	*Muslims*	*Sikhs*	*Europeans*	*Land holders*	*Indian Commerce*	*Total*
Govt. of India	14	5	–	–	–	–	–	–	19
Madras	2	--	10	3	–	1	1	1	18
Bombay	2	1	7	4	–	2	1	2	19
Bengal	2	2	6	6	–	3	1	1	21
U.P.	1	2	3	6	–	1	1	--	14
Punjab	1	2	3	6	2	–	1	–	15
Bihar and Orissa	1	1	8	3	–	–	1	15	15
C.P. and Berar	1	1	3	1	–	–	1	–	14
Assam	1	–	2	1	–	1	–	–	5
Burma	1	–	3	–	–	1	–	–	5
Delhi	–	–	1	–	–	–	–	–	1
Ajmer-Merwara	–	–	1	–	–	–	–	–	1
N.W.F.P.	–	1	–	–	–	–	–		1
Total	26	15	52	30	2	9	–	4	145

The Central legislature could now take the form of a controlled parliament of India inspite of the fact that its working was disturbed to some extent by the Swarajists led by Motilal Nehru. A substantial body of useful legislation could take place in the form of Workmen's Compensation Act of 1923, Criminal Law Amendment Act of 1923, Cantonment Act of 1924, Indian Trade Union Act of 1926, Child Marriage Act of 1926, Indian Bar Councils Act of 1926, and the Factories Act of 1926. Enthused with their victory in the elections

36. *Ibid.*

of 1923, the Swarajists with a contingent of 45 members and by having an alliance with the Nationalists and the Independents could have a resolution passed by the House on February 18, 1924 wherein it was recommended that a Round Table Conference be held for making a new constitution with a view to establish full responsible government in the country. The Swarajists could reject the budget of the Government of India for 1924-1925 and thereby compel the Government of India to invoke its power ofcertification.' Then, a resolution moved by C.D. lyengar was adopted by 58 votes to 45 that urged the suppression of the Bengal Ordinance by an Act of the Legislature. In February, 1925 the House passed bills moved by Vitahalbhai Patel for the repeal of the State Prisoners' Act and the Prevention of Seditious Meetings Act. Keeping all these facts in view, it was commented: "Violent speeches were made from time to time on the Left; but the spokesmen of the Government were usually heard with patience and often with assent. Between 1921 and 1937, the Viceroy used his over-riding power of 'certification' only ten times."[37]

Government of India Act of 1935

And yet the dichotomy between the British point of view maintained by the system of empire-keepers, on the one hand, and the seekers of Swaraj, on the other, could not be alleviated. The British authorities noted with anxiety the fact that a clearly marked tendency had been developing in the Indian legislature to attempt to interfere with the details of administration. On the contrary, the nationalist opinion was expressing its dissatisfaction with the system of a truncated legislature. The authors of the Simon Report studied it all and when they attended the sessions of the Indian legislature in 1928-29, they "were more impressed by its differences than by its resemblance to the Parliament to which they themselves belonged." The nationalist leaders of India were equally annoyed at the role of the Governor-General of India who "had been literally making use of these over-riding powers in the face of a hostile Assembly."[38]

At this stage, the report of the Simon Commission came as a note of despair. It represented the classical English view that the

---

37. R. Coupland; *The Indian Problem, 1833-1935*. p. 77.

38. M.V. Pylee, *The Constitutional History of India*, p. 64.

people of India were not at all capable of having parliamentary institutions the type of which they had developed in their own soil. The Commission noted that it "was a difficult and delicate operation to transplant in India forms of government which are native to British soil. The British parliamentary system has developed in accordance with the day-to-day needs of the people, and has been fined like a well-worn garment to the figure of the wearer, but it does not follow that it will suit everybody. British parliamentarism in India is a transition, and in even the best translations the essential meaning is apt to be lost.'[39]

The matter relating to the preparation of a new constitution acceptable to all sections of the countrymen was discussed at the first, second and third Round Table Conferences held at London respectively in 1930, 1931 and 1932. However, nothing fruitful could emerge on account of the obdurate colonial policy of the English rulers who had forced the leaders of the Indian National Congress to demand nothing short of complete independence after the Lahore Congress of 1929. As a matter of fact, British statesmen at this stage desired a workable compromise between refining the organisation and working of the legislative bodies in India so as to placate the demands of the nationalists, on the one hand, and to preserve the system of executive dominance as the *sine qua non* for the safety of their empire on the other.

Thus, the Joint Parliamentary Committee of the British Parliament on Indian Constitutional Reforms (1934) admitted that, in spite of disadvantages of dyarchy (introduced in the provinces under the Act of 1919) on which Simon Commission laid much stress, "Indians have shown since 1921 a marked capacity for the orderly conduct of parliamentary business—a capacity which has grown with the growth of their experience."[40] And yet feeling bound by the limitations of their interest, the JPC noted: "We have no wish to underrate the legislative function in our judgment of over-riding importance. In the absence of disciplined political parties, the sense

39. *Indian Statutory Commission Report* (1930), Vol. II, pp. 6-7. As late as in 1946 Henry Sharp published a book *Goodbye India* and harped on the same theme that Western democracy "is ill-suited to the traditions and institutions of India."

40. *Report of the Joint Parliamentary Committee on Indian Constitutional Reforms*. 1934. Vol. I, para 20.

of responsibility may well be of slower growth in the legislature and threat of dissolution can scarcely be the same potent in a country where, by the operation of a system of communal representation, a newly elected legislature will often have the same complexion as the old."[41]

It is for this reason that the Government of India Act of 1935 failed to go beyond extending the number of seats in the two Houses of the Cer.tral Legislature and that too owing to population increase than extension of franchise. A minor change was that the name of the Central Legislative Assembly now became House of Assembly. Since the strength of both the Houses was increased, it was laid down that the Council of State would have at the most 260 members—156 for the British Indian Provinces and 104 for the princely States. Moreover, out of 156 seats, 6 were reserved for nominations to be made by the Governor-General in his discretion. It was to be a permanent body not subject to dissolution, though 1/3 members were to retire every third year. The method of election of its members was mostly direct, while the representatives of the princely States were to be nominated by the rulers thereof. It was provided that the representatives of the Provinces would be elected by the voters with high property qualifications. But the system of communal and separate representation was retained with the result that seats were reserved for Sikhs, Muslims, and Scheduled Castes.

The House of Assembly was to consist of 375 members out of whom 250 were allotted to the Provinces and 125 to the Indian

41. *Ibid.*, para 23. It went on to say: "As our enquiries have proceeded, we have been increasingly impressed not by the strength of the Central Government as at present constituted, but by its weakness... It is confronted by a legislature which can be nothing but(in Bagehot's words) 'a debating society adhering to an executive'...the members of the legislature have shown themselves prone to regard support to Government policy as a betrayal of the national cause. It is no wonder that the criticism offered by the members of such a legislature should have been mainly destructive, yet it is abundantly clear from the political history of the last twelve years that criticism by the Assembly has constantly influenced the policy of Government, and disharmony between Government and legislature has tended to keep the efficiency of both. Indeed, the main problem which, in this sphere, Parliament has now to consider is how to strengthen an already weakening Executive." *Ibid.*, para 4.

States. It was to sit normally for a term of five years unless extended or dissolved earlier by the Governor-General. The members were to be elected indirectly on provincial-cum-communal basis. The members of the provincial Legislative Assemblies were to elect the members of this House by a system of proportional representation with a single transferable vote.

No important change took place in the functions and powers of the Central Legislature under the Act of 1935. However, as it proposed a federal system for the country with compulsion for the Provinces and option for the princely States to join it, it was laid down that the Central Legislature could make a law on any item of the Central and Concurrent Lists and for the Chief Commissioners' Provinces on all matters and for the federating States on all subjects handed over to the Federation under the Instrument of Accession. It was required that a bill be passed by both the Houses before it could be sent to the Governor-General for his assent. In the event of a deadlock between the two Houses, the Governor-General could call a joint session. The members of both the Houses had the power to ask questions and their supplementaries from the ministers, including Executive Councillors, move resolutions, table adjournment motions, but the Assembly alone could censure the government. A money bill could originate in the Assembly only; otherwise the powers of both the Houses were equal in financial matters.

But the powers of the Central legislature remained circumscribed. No bill could be moved in either House if it sought to repeal or amend any law made by the English Parliament or an order promulgated by the Governor-General in his discretion, or affected an area of the discretionary powers of the Governor-General, touched a law relating to police administration or the procedure of criminal proceedings in which Europeans were involved, or provided for discriminatory taxation, or covered income taxed or taxable in the United Kingdom. Likewise, it had no power to make a law affecting the Royal Family or succession to the English Crown, or the sovereignty of the Crown over India or her part, or the Army Act, or the law of prize or prize court, or any order-in-council made by the Secretary of State for India. The Governor-General had the power to distinguish between votable and non-votable parts of the budget and thereby prevent discussion on any part of the annual financial statement of the

Council of State (1935)

S.N.	*Provinces and Communities*	*Total*	*General*	*Sch. Castes*	*Sikhs*	*Muslims*	*Women*
1.	Madras	20	14	1	–	4	1
2.	Bombay	16	10	1	–	4	1
3.	Bengal	20	8	1	–	10	1
4.	U.P.	20	11	1	–	7	1
5.	Punjab	16	3	1	4	8	1
6.	Bihar	16	10	–	–	4	1
7.	C.P. and Berar	8	6	1	–	1	–
8.	Assam	5	3	1	–	2	–
9.	N.W.F.P.	5	1	–	–	4	–
10.	Orissa	5	4	–	–	1	–
11.	Sind	5	2	–	–	3	–
12.	British Baluchistan	1	–	–	–	1	–
13.	Delhi	1	1	–	–	–	–
14.	Ajmer-Merwara	1	1	–	–	–	–
15.	Coorg	1	1	–	–	–	–
16.	Anglo-Indians	1	–	–	–	–	–
17.	Europeans	7	–	–	–	–	–
18.	Indian Christians	2	–	–	–	–	–
19.	Nominated by the Governor-General	6	–	–	–	–	–
	Total	156	75	7	4	49	6

Government. He could also stop discussion on a bill or veto it after it was passed by both the Houses on the plea that it was necessary for the discharge of his special responsibilities. Not only this, he could 'authenticate' a bill and give to it the shape of a law by his discretionary authority even if that bill was rejected by the Legislature. It was also given that in case the Legislature refused or reduced a grant, the Governor-General could declare it to be necessary for the discharge of his special responsibilities and authorise the expenditure in spite of the adverse vote of the Legislature.

Central Legislative Assembly (1935)

S.N.	*Provinces and Communities*	*Total Seats*	*General Seats*	*Sch. Castes*	*Sikhs*	*Muslims*	*Anglo Indians*	*Europeans*	*Indian Christians*	*Commerce & Industries*	*Land-holders*	*Labour*	*Women*
1.	Madras	37	19	4	–	8	1	1	3	2	1	1	2
2.	Bombay	30	13	2	–	6	1	1	1	3	1	1	2
3.	Bengal	37	10	3	–	17	1	1	1	3	1	2	1
4.	U.P.	37	19	3	–	12	1	1	1	–	1	1	1
5.	Punjab	30	6	1	–	14	–	1	1	–	1	–	1
6.	Bihar	30	16	2	6	9	–	1	1	–	1	1	1
7.	C.P. and Berar	15	9	2	–	3	–	–	–	–	1	1	1
8.	Assam	10	4	1	–	3	–	–	–	–	–	1	–
9.	N.W.F.P.	5	1	–	–	4	–	–	–	–	–	–	–
10.	Orissa	5	4	–	1	–	–	–	–	–	–	–	–
11.	Sind	5	1	–	–	3	1	–	–	–	–	–	–
12.	British Baluchistan	1	–	–	–	1	–	–	–	–	–	–	–
13.	Delhi	2	2	–	–	1	–	–	–	–	–	–	–
14.	Ajmer-Merwara	1	1	–	–	–	–	–	–	–	–	–	–
15.	Coorg	1	1	–	–	–	–	–	–	–	–	–	–
16.	Non-Provincial State	4	4	–	–	–	–	–	–	3	–	1	–
	Total	250	105	19	6	82	5	7	9	11	7	10	9

It all shows that the Act of 1935 provided the model of a quite unrepresentative and powerless parliament. The so-called representative system, as provided for the composition of the two Houses, was nullified at the outset by the insertion of a solid non-elected and non-representative reactionary bloc in each House, replacing the old official bloc-but more reactionary and constituting a much larger proportion than under the old Montford Reforms. The provision that the Governor-General could decide about the votable and non-votable parts of the budget showed that he could deprive the legislature of having any discussion on about 80% of the budget.[42] The first elementary condition for any representative organ

42. G.N. Joshi: *Indian Administration*, p. 69.

of finance was completely absent when we take note of the fact that the Governor-General could 'authenticate' any expenditure even if its grant was refused by the Legislature and that his Finance Member of the Executive Council and his Financial Advisers were not accountable to it.[43] In a word, the Central Legislature, as contemplated under the Act of 1935, "was more a legislature by courtesy than by its powers."[44]

The federal part of the Act of 1935 could not be implemented owing to its inherent abnormalities coupled with the uncooperative attitude of the rulers of the princely States. In this respect, as V.P. Menon says, it remained like a 'lost ideal'. Since the whole scheme of a 'bastard federation' remained a 'tragic casualty',[45] the provisions of the Act of 1919 remained in force with necessary modifications till the advent of independence. A real change occurred after the composition of the Constituent Assembly in December, 1946. The Grand Con'sembly was given the place of a 'Provisional Parliament' of India and it assumed a sovereign status after the declaration of independence on 15 August, 1947. Now the representatives of the Indian people got the long-desired opportunity of framing their Constitution. Since a very large number of the leading members of the Con'sembly like Nehru, Patel, Munshi, Ambedkar, Ayyangar, Krishanamachari, Azad etc. favoured the system of English government, the model of Parliament was shaped accordingly.

One may say that the bi-cameral model of the Indian Parliament is like a refined version of what was given to us under the Acts of 1919 and 1935. However, the correct version would be that the founding fathers were so much impressed by the Westminster system under the British rule that they deliberately chose it in spite of the vehement opposition of those who invoked the remarks of Gandhi that the English Parliament was like a 'sterile woman' or a 'prostitute today under Asquith tomorrow under Balfour.' Rebutting all fears and charges of this type, K.M. Munshi said: "We must not forget a very important fact, that during the last one hundred years Indian public life has largely drawn on the traditions of English constitutional law. For the last thirty or forty years, some kind of

43. R.P. Dutt, *India Today*, p. 507.

44. Pylee, *op. cit.*, p. 86.

45. V.P. Menon: *Transfer of Power in India*, p. 57.

responsibility has been introduced in the governance of this country. Our constitutional traditions have become parliamentary."[46]

Parties/Groups in the Central Legislative Assembly

Period	*Parties / Groups*	*Number of Members*	*Name of Leaders*
First Assembly (1921-23)	Democratic Party	48	Dr. H.S. Gour
Second Assembly (1924)	1. Swarajists	28	Motilal Nehru
	2. Independents	40	M.A. Jinnah
	3. European Group	9	Sir Darcey Lindsay
Third Assembly (1927-30)	1. Swarajists	38	Motilal Nehru
	2. Nationalists	18	M.M. Malaviya
	3. Central Muslim Party and some non-partymen	22	Sir Zafrullah Khan
	4. Independents	13	M.A. Jinnah
	5. European Group	9	Sir Darcey Lindsay
Fourth Assembly (1931-34)	1. Nationalists	40	Dr. H.S. Gour
	2. Independents	30	Sir Abdur Rahim
	3. European Group	9	Sir Leslie Hudson
	4. Landholders Group	8	Raja Sri Vasudev
Fifth Assembly (1935-45)	1. Congress Party	44	Bhulabhai Desai
	2. Independents	22*	M.A. Jinnah
	3. Congress Nationalists	11	M.S. Aney
	4. Landholders Group	9	Sir Leslie Hudson
Sixth Assembly (1945-47)	1. Congress Party	59	Sarat Chandra Bose
	2. Muslim League	30	M.A. Jinnah
	3. European Party	8	Sir P.J. Griffith
	4. Independents	3	
	5. Akali		

*Of the 22 members 18 were Muslims. In 1939 Jinnah formed the Muslim League with 26 Muslim members who were earlier Independents.

Source : S.C. Kashyap: *History of the Parliament of India*, Vol. I p. 134.

46. *Constituent Assembly Debates*, Vol, VII, p. 984.

In this way, a brief survey of the evolution of Indian Parliament shows a peculiar reconciliation of the enlightened view of the English liberal statesmen who played a very important role in the grant of doses of constitutional reforms from time to time, on the one hand, with that of their Indian counterparts who not only appreciated all colonial gifts with a critical point of view but also pushed things in a direction that ultimately the pattern of the masters was adopted so as to make it in tune with the requirements of, as Nehru said, 'a vital and dynamic nation.'

Formation under the Present Constitution

The structure and composition of the legislative institutions as provided by the Government of India Acts of 1919 and 1935 failed to furnish any satisfactory basis on which independent India's national legislature could be devised. Without taking any vital inspiration from the past. Sir B.N. Rau, the Constitutional Advisor to the Constituent Assembly, circulated a questionnaire on 17 March, 1947 inviting views of the members on various matters as utility of bi-cameralism, representation of different communities and interests in the chambers, making of constituencies and method of election, allocation of seats and terms of the two houses, relative powers of the two houses and the formula of resolving the deadlock and the like. After this, he prepared a memorandum for the use of the Union Constitution Committee. Herein he suggested a legislature with two chambers-Senate having 280 members of whom 168 were to be from the Provinces and 112 from the States elected for a term of 9 years, 1/3 retiring after three years, and House of Representatives having elected delegates of the Provinces and the States in the proportion of not less than one representative for every million of the population and not more than one for every 7,50,000, the ratio to be adopted to be uniform throughout the country. To a considerable extent it coincided with the memorandum on the principles of the Union Constitution prepared by Sir Alladi Krishnaswami Ayyar and N. Gopalaswami Ayyangar. According to this joint scheme, the Senate was to be a permanent body, one third of its members retiring every year, but the House of Representatives was to have a term of five years.

The Union Constitution Committee considered these proposals at its meeting held on 9 June, 1947. The main points which were emphasised in the course of this meeting were:[47]

---

47. B. Shiva Rao: (ed.): *Framing of India's Constitution*. Vol. V, p. 422.

1. That the two chambers should be named as the Council of States and the House of the People.

2. The Council of States would have 250 members. It would not be liable for dissolution, but its 1/3 members to retire after every two years. The Vice-President of India would be its *ex-officio* Chairman.

3. The House of the People would consist of 400 to 500 members directly elected by direct suffrage from territorial constituencies for a term of 4 years.

4. The two chambers would have equal powers except in respect of money bills and deadlock between the two would be resolved by joint meetings.

5. Money bills would be introduced in the House of the People, but the Council of States would have the power to suggest amendments which the House may accept or not.

The case of bi-cameralism for India was seriously debated. A large number of members expressed their misgivings about the feasibility of the second chamber as it 'might prove a clog in the wheel of progress.'[48] It was also said that its existence would involve expenditure without anything to add to the efficiency of work. But all such misgivings were removed by the reply of N. Gopalaswami Ayyangar. Said he: "Therefore, what we really achieve by the existence of this second chamber is only an instrument by which we delay action which might be hastily conceived, and we also give an opportunity, perhaps, to seasoned people who may not be in the thickest of the political fray, but who might be willing to participate in the debate with an amount of learning and importance which we do not ordinarily associate with a House of the People."[49]

In this way, the Constituent Assembly opted for a bi-cameral legislature with the Council of States and Central Legislative Assembly. It did not appreciate the idea of calling the lower house 'National Assembly' as presented by some members. It was also agreed upon that the strength of the second chamber should be equal to half of the strength of the House of the People and that its

---

48. *Ibid.*, p. 423.

49. *Constituent Assembly Debates*, Vol. IV, pp. 924–28.

members should come from the Provinces in proportion to 1 to a million and from the States in a way that 60% of them belong to the former and 40% to the latter. The representatives of the Provinces would be elected by the members of the Provincial Legislative Assemblies. But what became the point of debate was the proposal of Sir B.N. Rau and endorsed by the Union Constitution Committee that 25 members of the Council of States should be returned by functional constituencies or panels on the lines of the Irish constitution of 1937. For the representation of the functional interests, it was provided in the draft that five panels should be drawn up before each biennial election. These panels would contain the names of persons with knowledge of political experience in (a) national language and culture, literature, art, education and such professional interest as might be defined by an act of the Legislature, (b) agriculture and allied interests, (c) labour, (industry and commerce including banking, finance, accountancy, engineering architecture, and (e) public administration and social service. But Sir B.N. Rau changed his mind when the Irish President de Valera, during a course of a meeting, advised him not to proceed ahead in this direction that had created a lot of trouble in his country.[50]

While the idea of functional representation was eventually discarded, the Union Constitution Committee desired nomination of 15 members to this chamber by the President so as to represent special interests. It was appreciated, but the number was restricted to 12 members having special knowledge of/or experience in the field of science, literature, art and social service. It was also agreed upon that the members of the Council should be elected by proportional representation with single transferable vote system, but the rider of Prof. K..T. Shah was not appreciated that cumulative vote system should be provided in stead of single transferable vote system. The proposal of Begum Aizaz Rasul was not accepted that the Parliament should be called the 'Indian National Congress' as the Congress was a movement rather than a party. Ananthasayanam Ayyangar feared that it would sound the death-knell of the Indian National Congress as a party, which would now carry on its crusade against reactionary and anti-national forces in the country.[51]

50. B. Shiva Rao, *op. cit.*, p. 429.

51. *Ibid.*, p. 431.

The term of the House of the People was preferred to be of five years unless sooner dissolved, but the Assembly thought it expedient to empower the President to extend the life of the House by a year at a time during emergency. On the suggestion of Ambedkar, this power was vested in the Parliament. The issue of laying down qualifications for the membership of Parliament was also taken up. Sir Rau suggested that the qualifications should be so precisely formulated that an election tribunal would be able to say in a particular case whether or not the candidate satisfied them. However, the general view was that only some broad qualifications should be laid down in the Constitution as citizenship of India and a minimum age of 25 years for the House and of 30 years for the Council, and all other points should be left to be determined by a law of the Parliament. This suggestion of Prof. K.T. Shah was not appreciated that the Constitution should have a provision for the Parliament being in continuous session. But the suggestion of H.V. Kamath that there should be at least three sessions of the Parliament in a year was modified for two sessions in a year. The issue of the codification of the privileges of the members of Parliament was also left to be taken up by the legislatures established under the new Constitution. The Assembly did not appreciate the proposal of Prof. K.T. Shah that the election expenses of all candidates standing for election should be paid from the public exchequer according to a prescribed scale.[52]

The decisions of the Con'sembly taken after thoughtful deliberations, therefore, fulfilled what was contained in Para 4 of the Objectives Resolution moved by Nehru on 13 December, 1946 that "all power and authority of the Sovereign Independent India, its constituent parts and organs of government is derived from the people." Dr. Rajendra Prasad, the President of the Assembly, visualised in his valedictory address on 25th November, 1949: "Thus, it is the will of the people as expressed by their representatives in the popular chamber that will finally determine all matters, The second chamber and the President can only direct reconsideration and can only cause some delay, but if the popular chamber is determined, it will have its way under the Constitution. The Government... will rest on the will of the people which will be

52. *Ibid.*, p. 437.

expressed from day to day through their representatives in the legislatures and occasionally directly by them at the time of general elections."[53]

The Constitution came into effect on 26th January, 1950 and elections to the Parliament were held in 1952. At that time, the Council of States had representatives from A, B, and C States. As per Art. 80(4), the representatives of Part A and Part B States were elected by the members of the Legislative Assemblies of these States in accordance with the system of proportional representation by means of single transferable vote, but the representatives of Part C States were to be chosen in a manner as prescribed by a law of Parliament. As per Art.81, the House of the People was to consist of 500 members at the most directly elected by the voters of the States. The States were to be grouped or formed into territorial constituencies and the number of members to be allotted to each such constituency was to be so determined as to ensure that there would be not less than one member for every 75,000 of the population and not more than one member for every 5,00,000 of the population. The ratio between the number of members allotted to each territorial constituency and the population of that constituency would, as far as possible, be the same throughout the country. But the representation of any territory not included in any State would be determined by a law of Parliament.[54]

---

53. *Constituent Assembly Debates,* Vol. XI, p. 990. Dr. Rajendra Prasad in his concluding address on 25th November, 1949 called it a 'regret'. Said he "It is anomalous that we should insist upon high qualifications for those who administer or help in administering the law but none for those who make it except that they are elected. A law giver requires intellectual equipment but even more than that capacity to take a balanced view of things, to act independently and above all to be true to those fundamental things of life-in-one word-to have character. It is not possible to devise any yardstick for measuring the moral qualities of man and so long as that is not possible, our Constitution will remain defective." *Ibid,* p. 993.

54. On 14 May, 1954 the Speaker (G.V. Mavlankar) announced in the House that henceforth House of People would be known as the Lok Sabha. Similar announcement was made in the Council of States on 23 August, 1954 and so it became Rajya Sabha. Kaul and Shakdher: *Practice and Procedure of Parliament,* IV ed., 1991: p. 12 n 1.

Allocation of Seats in the Council of States (1950)

Category	States	Seats	Category	States	Seats	Category	States	Seats
A	1. Assam	6	B	1. Hyderabad	11	C	1. Ajmer	1
	2. Bihar	21		2. Jammu-Kashmir	4		2. Coorg	
	3. Bombay	17		3. Madhya Bharat	6		3. Bhopal	1
	4. Madhya Pradesh	12		4. Mysore	6		4. Bilaspur	1
	5. Madras	24		5. Patiala and East Punjab States Union (PEPSU)	3		5. Himachal Pradesh	
	6. Orissa	9		6. Rajasthan	9		6. Cooch-Behar	1
	7. Punjab	8		7. Saurashtra	4		7. Delhi	1
	8. United Provinces	31		8. Travancore-Cochin	6		8. Kutch	1
	9. West Bengal	14		9. Vindhya Pradesh	4		9. Manipur	1
							10. Tripura	
Total		**145**			**53**			**7**

Total of all seats—205

To supplement the provisions of the Constitution, the provisional Parliament made Representation of the People Act, 1950 which provides that all seats allotted to the House of the People shall be filled by persons chosen by direct election from parliamentary constituencies in the States. Every such constituency shall be a single-member constituency. Any State to which only one seat is allotted shall form one parliamentary constituency. The composition of the House of the People should be read with Art. 330 of the Constitution that provides for reservation of Seats in favour of Scheduled Castes and Scheduled Tribes and then Art. 331 which provides the same for the members of the Anglo-Indian community. Initially, it was a temporary arrangement made for first ten years from the commencement of the Constitution, its period may be extended by a constitutional amendment. It is due to this that its duration has been extended after every 10 years and so now it is till 2010. The work of the delimitation of constituencies has been entrusted to a commission appointed for this purpose, but the Election Commission may correct any patent mistake, if so necessary.

The composition of the Parliament has changed from time to time. The system of A, B, C, States was terminated with the enforcement of the States Reorganisation Act or Seventh Constitution Amendment Act in 1956 as a result of which 14 States and 5 Union Territories came into being. With the passage of time, the number of States increased and now it has reached the figure of 28, while the number of the Union Territories is 7. The number of seats allotted to each State in the Rajya Sabha is contained in Fourth Schedule. Each State has to be given one seat at least, but the number may increase as the allocation of seats is done on the basis of demographic figures. It is due to this that while Uttar Pradesh has 31 seats, Goa, Manipur, Tripura, Meghalaya, Nagaland, Sikkim, Mizoram and Arunachal Pradesh have one seat each. The Parliament may by its law allot a seat or some seats to a Union Territory. Thus, Pondicherry has one seat, while Delhi has 3 seats in this House. It should also be noted here that while the representatives of the States are elected by the members of the State Legislative Assemblies by means of proportional representation with single transferable vote system, the representatives of the Union Territories are elected in a manner as laid down in a law of Parliament. The representatives of Delhi are elected by the members of the Legislative Assembly by the plurality of votes system.

The number of seats of the Lok Sabha has also changed from time to time. It was 500 at the most in the beginning; it became 520 for the States and 25 for the Union Territories; and then it became 525 for the States' Now it has at the most 530 for the States and 20 for the Union Territories. As changed first by the Seventh Amendment Act of 1956 and then by the Thirty-fifth Amendment Act of 1974, Art. 82(2) provides: (a) There shall be allotted to each State a number of seats in the House of the People in such manner that the ratio between the number and the population of the State is, so far as practicable, the same for all States, and (b) each State shall be divided into territorial constituencies in such manner that the ratio between the population of each constituency and number of seats allotted to it is, so far as practicable, the same throughout the State. It is also provided that these provisions shall not be applicable to a State if its population exceeds six millions. It was provided in the 42nd Amendment Act of 1976 that till 2000 reference to the population of a State would mean the census of 1971 till the publication of the figures of first census taken after 2000. Now the 84th Amendment Act of 2002 provides that for the figures 2000,2026 shall be substituted. It simply means that the strength of the Lok Sabha shall remain unchanged till 2026.

Multifunctional Role

The significance of the Parliament consists in its multifunctional role about which an eminent writer says that it "is a pivot on which the political system of the country revolves."[55] In a traditional sense, the Parliament is just a law-making organ of the state. But in a modern empirical study, it is a multifunctional institution. Obviously, we have to examine the role of the Parliament in the operation of the political system in these important directions:

Legislation: The Parliament can make a law on any item of the Union List and Concurrent List; it can also make a law on any residuary item; under certain conditions it can make a law on any item of the State List as well. A bill to this effect must be passed by both the Houses of Parliament and then assented to by the President. Since, it can make a law, it can also change or repeal it. It may also empower the executive departments to issue necessary circulars and notifications while putting a law into effect. All such circulars

55. S.C. Kash[illegible] *P[illegible]ment*, p. [illegible].

and notifications must be approved by it afterwards. It signifies control of the Parliament over delegated legislation. It is true that in a cabinet government, this inherent function of the Parliament is usurped by the executive in view of the fact that bills introduced by the ministers are passed and it is very rare that a bill moved by a private member is adopted. It, however, does not mean that the executive becomes the law-making department of the state.

It is required that a bill prepared by the experts of the Law Department and well considered by the Cabinet is introduced by some minister and then is passed by both the Houses. During the course of discussion, some important changes may be proposed which eventually go into the text of the bill. It is not necessary that a bill moved by a minister is passed by both the Houses in a wav he pleases. Some amendments may be made, in it during the course of its passage, or the Government may decide to withdraw a bill even at the introduction stage in view of the opposition by a sizable number of the members. It is also possible that a bill passed by one House may be returned by the other House and as a result of the difference between the two, a joint session be held as happened in 1961 over the Dowry Prohibition Bill, in 1978 over the Banking Service Commission (Repeal) Bill, and in 2003 to pass a bill that became POTA. An ordinance promulgated by the President has the force of law, but it cannot go beyond 6 weeks from the commencement of the Parliamentary session. The Parliament may either pass it in the form of a bill or reject it.

The law-making power of the Parliament includes its constituent power as well in view of the fact that a bill of constitutional amendment must be passed by both the Houses by special majority in most of the cases. It is also possible that a government bill may not be passed due to the lack of special majority. For instance, in 1989 the Rajya Sabha rejected two government bills-one seeking to change the structure and enhance the powers of the village panchayats and the other one seeking reconstitution and enlargement of the powers of the units of urban local administration. It is also possible that the government may well calculate the mood of the members in opposition and then make necessary amendments in the bill so as to have its smooth passage by both the Houses. For instance, the Janata government agreed to delete five important portions of the 45th Constitution Amendment Bill and then it could be passed by the Rajya Sabha. (On receiving President's assent it was renumbered as 44th Constitution Amendment Act.). Reference should also be made to this important point that all pending bills lapse in case the Lok Sabha is dissolved except one that is introduced in the Rajya Sabha and is pending there.

Control over Administration and Finance: All acts of commission and omission of the government are discussed in the Parliament. The ministers have to answer questions and their supplementaries asked by the members During the question hour a piercing searchlight is thrown on every nook and corner of the vast length and breadth of administration. Thus, scandals are exposed as a result of which a minister (like T.T. Krishnamachari or V.K.K.Menon) may have to go. It is true that an adjournment motion may be moved only in the Lok Sabha. but the members of both the Houses may table resolutions, or move calling attention motions, or may demand half-an-hour discussion on any matter of urgent public importance. When the budget is discussed, the members of the Lok Sabha may refuse to vote supplies or make a cut amounting to the defeat of the government. The members of the Parliament may expose the role of a minister (K.D. Malaviya) in the Serajuddin Affair, or of another minister (L.N. Mishra) in the rags scandal. During 1986 the proceedings of the Parliament were often disturbed on the issue of alleged scandal in the purchase of guns from the Bofors. The leaders of the opposition parties felt emboldened after irregularities in the deal were pointed out in the report of the Comptroller and Auditor-General of India. The Parliament has been able to throw out governments (as Janata Dal government in 1990, the U.F. government in 1997, and the NDA government in 1998 and 1999) by showing its want of confidence in it and it has very much showed its power of surveillance of administration that is also known as administrative accountability to the Parliament.

Adjudication: The Parliament exercises some judicial powers as well. It may expel a member on the ground of some serious charge. If a person commits breach of privileges or contempt of the House, he may be brought before the House and then he may be either admonished, or reprimanded, or imprisoned till the continuance of the session. In case a member of the House is found guilty on this count, he or she may be expelled. For instance, Mrs. Indira Gandhi was expelled from the Lok Sabha in 1978. (It is a different matter that the House rescinded this resolution in 1981.)

It is also possible that a member may be disqualified on the ground of holding an office of profit as happened in the cases of H.G. Mudgal (member of the Provisional Parliament) in 1951 and of Mohanrangam and Jaya Bachchan (members of Rajya Sabha) in 1982 and 2006.

Control over Foreign Policy: Another important direction should be traced in Parliament's control over Government's foreign policy and diplomacy. The Prime Minister takes regular care to keep the Parliament in confidence in respect of his policy towards other countries of the world, particularly the great powers. Some members of the Parliament are associated with the Consultative Committee of the Ministry of External Affairs. It holds its meetings from time to time in which the Minister for External Affairs briefs the members about international commitments and the attitude of the Government towards them. It is a fact that despite his immense personal prestige, Nehru always took care to give the formulation of foreign policy a broad base not only within the Cabinet but also in the Parliament. It is for this reason that the Parliament supported the Government, when India's diplomacy was successful in the signing of the Treaty of Peace, Friendship and Cooperation with the USSR and our victory in the Bangladesh war in 1971. The Parliament may also go to the extent of expressing its profound shock and resentment at the failure of India's diplomacy as happened in our defeat at the hands of China in 1962. In view of the sentiments expressed in the Lok Sabha, the Government took 'police action' to secure the liberation of Goa, Daman and Diu from Portuguese colonialism in 1961. In 1962 the Lok Sabha passed a resolution condemning Chinese aggression on Indian territory and endorsed the determination of the Government to make every possible effort to secure territories forcibly occupied by the Chinese. Statistics show that in 1966 out of 16,972 questions asked by the members of the Lok Sabha, 823 were related to external affairs. Moreover, the Public accounts Committee and the Estimates Committee indirectly influence the working of the External Affairs ministry by making comments on policies which are haphazard and uneconomical.[56]

Conflict-Resolution and National Integration: Every society is ridden with conflicts and tensions. As such, there should be some

56. See N.M. Khilnani: "The Role of Parliament in Foreign Affairs" in *Journal of Constitutional and Parliamentary Studies*, New Delhi, Vol. VI, No. 4, 1972, pp. 52

machinery to resolve such contradictions in a civilised way. The accurrence of conflicts is not bad; their resolution through constitutional means is called for. The Parliament provides a forum where elected members may bring their issues of conflict and then resolve them in a democratic manner. It helps the process of national integration. The Parliament has a brilliant record of its own in this important direction. For instance, it resolved tangled issues (as those of Telangana and Nagaland) by holding discussion and adopting necessary measures. The problems of Assam, Mizoram and Manipur could be sorted out by Government in this way. It is well observed: "Parliamentary democracy is considered to be a better and pure civilised system of government in as much as under it debate and discussion on the legislative floor take the place of physical strife on the stress or on the battlefields. Debates and discussions bring out into the open underlying tensions and resentment in society. Parliament becomes legitimate areua for power struggle, for crystallisation of political activity or for acting out the conflicting roles and interest with the parliament and procedures, facilitating eventual reconciliation. Instead of fighting to annihilate each other, the parties tend to agree to disagree and to accommodate and tolerate each other. It is on the legislative floor that some delicate problems get resolved. The contending forces struggle to have their way and finally get reconciled. In performing this conflict-resolutat in role, the parliamentary institution acts as a great national integrator and mediator in change. This conflict-resolution and integrational role Parliament is specially significant in the context of our highly pluralistic society."[57]

Representational and Educational: Finally, Parliament is the grand inquest of the nation. "It is not only a microcost of the people, but also a barometer of their mood and puse."[58] A look at the sociological composition of the Parliament shows that its membership is being shared by the hitherto neglected sections of the society. It is true that some seats are reserved for Scheduled Castes and Scheduled Tribes, but the democratisation of the process of election has made it possible for the people living in remote rural areas and without any impact of the Western culture to occupy the seats of this national democratic organisation. It is thus imparting

---

57. Kashyap, *op. cit.*, p. 46.

58. *Ibid.*, p. 44.

a kind of political education to the people of the country. So it is observed: "Parliament is becoming more representative of the people of India, of the level of their political awareness, of their lack of sophistication, and of their problems, hopes and aspirations. Elitist politics is gradually giving way to a healthy ruralised politics. The polished urban lawyer who knew the law and the niceties of parliamentary procedure is being replaced by the village farmer or the political/social worker with his innate commonsense and acute awareness of what the people need. The foreign educated, public or convent school trained upper middle class urban elite are being elbowed out by the rural educated, indigenous counter-elite."[59]

After seeing this, we may easily form the impression that the Parliament has its own significant place in the constitutional structure of our country. It is well observed: "Nevertheless, Parliament occupies a pivotal position in the present-day Indian polity and constitutional limitations on its sovereign authority are themselves to be understood with important qualifications. Such powers as Parliament possesses under the Constitution are immense and it fulfils the role which a sovereign legislature does in any other independent country."[60]

59. *Ibid.*, pp. 44-45.

60. Kaul and Shakdher: *Practice and Procedure of Parliament,* ed. IV, 1991, pp. 1-2.

12

Parliament: Composition, Working and Decline

Art. 79 of Chapter II headlined 'Parliament' contained in Part V titled 'The Union' provides for the Constitution of the Union legislature called Parliament (*Samsad*) consisting of the President, the Rajya Sabha (Council of States) and the Lok Sabha (House of People) respectively as the upper and lower chambers. The President is an integral part of the Parliament, though he is not a member of any House, for the reason that he summons and prorogues the session, may dissolve Lok Sabha, delivers inaugural address and may send messages and, finally, places his signatures to authenticate the bills passed by the Parliament. However, the peculiar thing about our Parliament is that while its general pattern is like that of the English Parliament, it is a non-sovereign law-making body like the American Congress.

Rajya Sabha

The Parliament is a bicameral body. Its upper chamber is the Rajya Sabha. It consists of 250 members at the most. Out of this 12 members are nominated by the President from amongst persons distinguished in the field of literature, art, science and social service. The remaining members are the representatives of the States and Union Territories. The number of representatives, as specified in IV Schedule of the Constitution, varies from State to State as the number of seats allocated to them is based on the factor of population. It is due to this that while a small State like Nagaland has only one seat, a very big State like that UP has 31 seats. The members are elected by the members of the State Legislative Assemblies in accordance with proportional representation with single transferable vote system. The Parliament may make some other arrangement for the representation of Union Territories.[1] It is due to this that the party-wise composition of the Rajya Sabha reflects the party-wise composition of Vidhan Sabhas in the country.

A member of the Rajya Sabha must possess three qualifications. First, he must be a citizen of India. Second, he must have completed the age of 30 years. Last, he must possess all other qualifications laid down in an act of Parliament. The condition that a person contesting election must ordinarily be a resident of that State has been done away with.[2] Open ballot system has also been provided now. The disqualifications for the membership of this House are: holding an office of profit under the Government of India or of any State except that of a minister or any other exempted by a law of Parliament, being of unsound mind or an undischarged insolvent as declared by a competent court, being an alien or a non-citizen, and being disqualified under any law of the Parliament.

The Rajya Sabha is a continuing chamber. Its one-third members retire after every second year and elections are held for the vacant seats. Thus, a member of the Rajya Sabha has six years to serve, but he may be re-elected any number of times. (It applies to the nominated members as well). A member of the Rajya Sabha may tender his resignation or cease to be its member in case he incurs some disqualification as provided in Art. 101 of the Constitution.

---

1. For instance, the three members of the National Capital Territory of Delhi are elected by its Legislative Assembly according to first-past-post system.
2. The removal of the qualification of 'ordinary residence' in a State by an amendment in the Representation of the People Act in 2003 was challenged by Kuldip Nayyar on the ground that a member of the Rajya Sabha must be a resident of the State which he represents. He contended that the amendment affected the basic structure of the Constitution. The Supreme Court dismissed the petition on the ground that residence or domicile "is not the essential ingredient of the structure and the composition of the upper house. Residence is neither a constant factor nor a constitutional requirement, but a matter of qualification prescribed by Parliament in exercise of its power under Art. 84. The Rajya Sabha does not act as a champion of local interests and voting in the house cannot be compared with general election." *The Times of India* (New Delhi), 22 August, 2006.

That is, a member of this House shall forfeit his membership in case he becomes a member of the Lok Sabha or of any State legislature, or has voluntarily acquired the citizenship of a foreign State, or is under any acknowledgement of allegiance or adherence to a foreign State, or remains absent from all meetings of the House and its committees for a period of 60 days without any reason conveyed to the House, or he is expelled from the membership of the House, or is held a political defector by the Chairman of the House.

Though a House of the Elders, the Rajya Sabha is regarded as a weak chamber in comparison to the Lok Sabha for these reasons:

1. A money bill cannot be introduced in the Rajya Sabha and when such a bill is referred to it after it is passed by the Lok Sabha it has to pass it within a period of 14 days. The Rajya Sabha may return a money bill with some recommendations, but the Lok Sabha may accept them or not while reconsidering the same bill.
2. A non-money bill may be introduced in any House of Parliament and here the Rajya Sabha is again a weak, though not very weak (as in the case of passing a money bill) chamber. In case there is disagreement between the two chambers, the President may convene a joint session of Parliament. Such a session (as occurred in 1961 in the case of Dowry Prohibition Bill, in 1978 in the case of Banking Service Commission (Repeal) Bill, and in 2003 in the case of POTA Bill) shall be held under the chairmanship of the presiding officer of Lok Sabha (Speaker) and the matter shall be decided by the majority of votes. The Speaker alone has the right to decide whether a bill is money bill or not. It is provided that the Rajya Sabha must pass a bill already passed by the Lok Sabha or return it to Lok Sabha for consideration within six months.
3. The Rajya Sabha cannot pass a motion of no-confidence against the government. Its members cannot put adjournment motion which, indeed, amounts to a censure motion. At the most, they may criticise and thereby embarrass the government.

But in some other directions, the Rajya Sabha has powers equal to those of the Lok Sabha and, in that respect, it cannot be termed as a weak chamber. These are:

1. A bill of constitutional amendment requiring special majority (absolute majority of the whole House coupled with two-thirds majority of the members, present and voting) for its adoption must be passed by both the Houses. If there is disagreement between the two chambers in passing such a bill, joint session of the Parliament cannot be held. Thus the Rajya Sabha could show its 'teeth' by rejecting the 24th Constitution Amendment Bill (seeking abolition of the privy purses and privileges of the former rulers of princely States) in 1970 and the 64th Constitution Amendment Bill (seeking reorganisation of Panchayati Raj) and the 65th Constitution Amendment Bill (seeking restructuring of urban municipal boards) in 1989.
2. The Rajya Sabha has equal powers with Lok Sabha in matters like electing the President and Vice-President, impeaching the President, judges of the Supreme Court and High Courts and other high officers, approving proclamation of emergency and extending its duration, considering the reports of various commissions and autonomous bodies, setting up martial law courts during national emergency for dealing with the offences committed by the civilians and indemnifying officers for their acts done in good faith, taking away an item from the purview of the Union Public Service Commission, and exercising control over delegated legislation.

But there are some areas in which the Rajya Sabha has special powers and thereby appears more important than the Lok Sabha.

1. Vide Art. 249, it may pass a resolution by its two-thirds majority so as to shift an item of the State List to the Union List or to the Concurrent List on the plea of its 'expediency' in the national interest. Such a resolution shall remain in force for one year, but it may renew it again and again.
2. Vide Art. 312, it may pass a resolution by its two-thirds majority so as to propose the creation of an all-India public service to be regularised by a law of Parliament in time to come.
3. It may initiate a move for the removal of the Vice-President. Such a resolution is to be passed by the Rajya Sabha by its absolute majority and then agreed to by the Lok Sabha.
4. In case the Lok Sabha stands dissolved, the Rajya Sabha may permit extension of the time of 'emergency' declared by the President.

Allocation of Seats in Parliament

States and Union Territories		*Rajya Sabha*	*Lok Sabha*
States			
1.	Andhra Pradesh	18	42
2.	Arunachal Pradesh	1	2
3.	Assam	7	14
4.	Bihar	16	40
5.	Chhattisgarh	5	11
6.	Goa	1	2
7.	Gujarat	11	26
8.	Haryana	5	10
9.	Himachal Pradesh	3	4
10.	Jammu and Kashmir	4	6
11.	Jharkhand	6	14
12.	Karnataka	12	28
13.	Kerala	9	20
14.	Madhya Pradesh	11	29
15.	Maharashtra	19	48
16.	Manipur	1	2
17.	Meghalaya	1	2
18.	Mizoram	1	1
19.	Nagaland	1	1
20.	Orissa	10	21
21.	Punjab	7	13
22.	Rajasthan	10	25
23.	Sikkim	1	1
24.	Tamil Nadu	18	39
25.	Tripura	1	2
26.	Uttar Pradesh	31	80
27.	Uttarakhand	3	5
28.	West Bengal	16	42
Union Territories			
1.	Andaman and Nicobar Islands	–	1
2.	Chandigarh	–	1
3.	Dadra and Nagar Haveli	–	1
4.	Daman and Diu	–	1
5.	Delhi	3	7
6.	Lakshadweep	–	1
7.	Puducherry	1	1
	Nominated	12	2
	Total	245	**545**

It shows that the Rajya Sabha is neither a weak chamber like the British House of Lords, nor is it powerful chamber like the American Senate. It is expected to be a house of the seasoned and elderly leaders. It is true that the Rajya Sabha has failed in living like a 'house of angels', it has certainly not been a gathering of reactionary and raw elements. Though its members are inducted by indirect election in which State Assemblies have their part, it "does not seem to have made the floor of the Council a battleground between Centre and States; a defence of States' rights an expression of the regional demands, that is just likely to be heard in the other House."[3]

Lok Sabha

The Lok Sabha is the popular chamber having at the most 550 elected members (530 from the States and 20 from the Union Territories). The President may nominate at the most two members of the Anglo-Indian community in case he finds it not adequately represented therein. The members of this chamber are elected directly by the voters. The whole country is divided into territorial constituencies in a manner that the ratio between the number of the representatives and the size of the population is, as far as practicable, the same throughout the State. Moreover, under the Delimitation Commission Act of 1962, the Election Commission is authorised to determine forthwith the number of seats in the Lok Sabha on the basis of the latest census figures having regard to the constitutional provisions on the subject. Some seats are reserved for Scheduled Castes and Scheduled Tribes.[4]

A member of the Lok Sabha must be a citizen of India and that he must be above 25 years age. He should not be holding an office of profit, nor should he meet any disqualifications as already pointed

---

3. W.H. Morris-Jones: *The Parliament in India*, p. 256.

4. The 42nd Amendment of 1976 provided that until the relevant figures for the first census taken after the year 2000 had been published, it would not be necessary to readjust the allocation of seats in the House to the States and the division of each State into territorial constituencies under this provision. The 84th Amendment of 2002 makes it 2026.

out in the case of a member of the Rajya Sabha.[5] The normal term of the House is of five years to be computed from the date of its first sitting. The President may dissolve this House at any time. In case proclamation of emergency is in force, the Parliament may make a law to extend the life of the Lok Sabha (as happened in 1976). Such a law shall remain in force for one year, but it may be readopted.[6]

The Constitution provides that the sessions of the Parliament should be held in a way that intervening period is of not more than six months. It means that the Parliament must meet at least twice a year. Both the Houses hold their session normally thrice a year known as the budget session, monsoon session, and winter session.

---

5. The office of the Minister is excluded from the office of profit. On 30th September, 1982 the President disqualified a member of the Rajya Sabha (M.R. Mohanrangam) as he was holding the post of special representative of the government of Tamil Nadu in Delhi. It was taken as an office of profit. So happened with Jaya Bachchan in 2006 and with K.M. Moghi in 2007. The Representation of the People Act, 1951 lays down certain conditions for disqualification which are applicable to the members of Parliament and State legislatures. These are:

   (a) He must not have been found guilty by a Court or an election tribunal of certain election offences or corrupt practices in the elections.

   (b) He must not have been convicted by a Court of any offence and sentenced to imprisonment for a period of at least two years.

   (c) He must have not failed to lodge an account of his election expenses within the time and in a manner prescribed by law.

   (d) He must not have been dismissed for corruption or for disloyalty from Government service.

   (e) He must not be a director or a managing agent, nor hold an office of profit under any Corporation in which the Government has any financial interest.

   (f) He must not have any interest in Government contracts, execution of Government work or services.

6. The Government of Vajpayee committed an act of constitutional impropriety by extending the winter session of the Parliament from 23 December, 2003 to 5 February, 2004. A new session of a new year must be inaugurated by the President, but in this case it was not

In each House the quorum is one-tenth of its total membership. Any member may raise the issue of quorum. If there is no quorum, the Chairman/Speaker may ring the quorum bell to ensure minimum attendance of the members or adjourn the sitting for some time.

The functions and powers of the Lok Sabha must be understood in the light of what we have already said about the functions and powers of the Rajya Sabha. The Lok Sabha is known as the powerful chamber of the Indian Parliament for these reasons:

1. It has control over the government. The Council of Ministers is collectively responsible to the Lok Sabha. As such, the ministry may be thrown out in case this House passes a motion of censure or no-confidence, or makes a cut in the budget, or disapproves of the policy of the government. The members may put the ministers to gruelling tests by asking questions, tabling motions (calling attention and adjournment), demanding half-hour discussion etc.
2. The Lok Sabha has a better position in the joint session by virtue of its numerical strength.
3. The Lok Sabha has control over the purse of the nation. A money bill (and so a budget) can be introduced in the Lok Sabha with the recommendation of the President and, when passed by it, it has to be passed by the Rajya Sabha within 14 days.

However, a comparative study of the functions and powers of the two Houses leads to this unmistakable impression that the Lok Sabha is a powerful chamber as compared to the Rajya Sabha. There should be no doubt about Rajya Sabha being the upper chamber and

---

done. It was interpreted as the continuation of the winter session. The Lok Sabha was prematurely dissolved the next day. The extension of the session was, indeed, an act of impropriety. The President did not honour the view of the Leader of the Oppositon (Sonia Gandhi) who had raised this issue. But he acted on the advice of the Prime Minister in dissolving the Lok Sabha. This matter was challenged in the Supreme Court through a PIL petition filed by Vipul Sharma. The bench of Chief Justice Khare (with Justices Kapadia and Brijesh Kumar) dismissed it on the ground that the matter fell within the discretionary powers of the President. *The Times of India* (New Delhi), 14 February, 2004.

Lok Sabha being the lower chamber of the Parliament. However, the two chambers should not be designated as such with a mind to exalt one and denigrate the other that goes to intensify the bitter tradition of rivalry. What should prevail is the convention of harmony and cooperation between the two. Prime Minister Nehru well counselled on 6 May 1953 that we must not blindly follow the English practice in every way. As he said: "Our guide must, therefore, be our own Constitution which has clearly specified the functions of the Council of States (Rajya Sabha) and the House of the People (Lok Sabha). To call either of these Houses an upper house or a lower is not correct. Each House has full authority to regulate its own procedure within the limits of the Constitution...That the Constitution treats the two Houses equally except in certain financial mattrs which are to be within the sole purview of the House of People."

No doubt, the Parliament is the pivot around which the whole structure of democratic government revolves. It may be lauded as nation in miniature. As a learned writer comments: "Parliament of India, representing as it does all constitutionally organised shades of public opinion at the national level, occupies a pre-eminent and central position in Indian polity. Members of Parliament, as elected representatives of the people, ventilate the people's grievances and opinions on various issues, scrutinise the functioning of the government on the floor of the Houses of Parliament and enact laws. Parliament functions as the grand inquest and watchdog of the nation."[7]

Speaker

The office of the presiding officer of the Lok Sabha (called the Speaker) is of great honour, dignity and authority. In the order of precedence, he is ranked seventh and is bracketed with the Chief Justice of India.[8] His office is modelled on the office of the English Speaker with regard to which Prime Minister Nehru, while unveling

7. S.C. Kashyap: *Our Parliament*, pp. 33-34.

8. The order of precedence is—(1) President, (2) Vice-President, (3) Prime Minister, (4) Governors, (5) Ex-President, and Ex-Governors, (5a) Deputy Prime Minister, (6) Lt.-Governor, (7) Chief Justice of India and Speaker of Lok Sabha.

the portrait of Vitthalbhai J. Patel on March 18, 1948, said these impressive words: "I hope that those traditions will continue, because the position of the Speaker is not an individual's position or an honour done to an individual. The Speaker represents the House. He represents the dignity of the House and, because the House represents the nation, in a particular way, the Speaker becomes the symbol of the nation's liberty and freedom. Therefore, it is right that it should be an honoured position, a free position and should be occupied always by men of outstanding ability and impartiality."

The Speaker is elected by the House from amongst its members. He holds his office until he ceases to be a member, or he himself resigns his office, or he is removed from his office by a resolution of the house passed by a majority of all the then members of the House. He continues in office notwithstanding the fact that the House has been dissolved as he vacates it immediately before the first meeting of the new House after general election. It is required that at least 14 days' notice should be given to the Speaker in case a motion of no-confidence is brought to remove him from office. It is also provided that the Speaker shall not preside over the house in case such a motion is under consideration, although he will have the right to present himself in the House for saying anything in his defence. Thus, the normal term of a Speaker is that of five years. There is, however, no restriction on his seeking another term or terms. The letter of his resignation must be addressed to the Deputy Speaker.

The Speaker occupies an office that carries both great dignity and high authority. The powers of the Speaker may be roughly classified into four parts for the sake of a convenient study with sub-heads like regulatory, supervisory and censuring, administrative, and special or miscellaneous.

1. The regulatory powers of the Speakers includes his authority of as well as responsibility for conducting the business of the House in an orderly manner. Thus, he maintains order and decorum in the House. He allots time for the debates and discussions and allows the members to express their views within the time allotted by him. He interprets the rules of the Constitution and of the Procedure for the guidance of the members. He puts matters for division and announces the result. In case of tie, he exercises his casting vote. It is within

his powers to admit motions, resolutions and points of order and then make arrangements for discussion on them.

2. Allied with the regulatory powers of the Speaker are his supervisory and censuring powers. The Speaker is the head of the Parliamentary Committees. Some important committees like Rules Committee and Business Advisory Committee work under his chairmanship. He appoints the chairmen of various committees of the House and may issue instructions and decisions for their guidance. He may ask the Government to supply such information to the House or to its committees that is so essential in the public interest. He sees to it that no member speaks unparliamentary language, or he becomes unnecessarily argumentative or verbose in his expressions. He may force a member to withdraw his indecent expressions or make amends, or he may order expunction of some words and phrases from the records of the debates. He may issue warrants of arrest for bringing an alleged offender of the privileges of the House and it is his function to implement the decision of the House with regard to the punishment given to a person for the breach of the privileges or contempt of the House.

3. The Speaker has some administrative powers as well. He keeps control over the Secretariat of the Lok Sabha. He makes provisions for the accommodation and other amenities of life granted to the members of the House. He regulates the lobbies and galleries meant for the press and the public. It is his duty to make arrangements for the sittings of the House and its committees. He is the custodian of the honour of the House.

4. Finally, we come to the miscellaneous or special powers of the Speaker. He gives his certificate to a bill that is passed by the House. He alone can decide whether a bill is a money bill or not. He presides over the joint sessions of the Parliament. He can correct patent error in a bill after it has been passed by the House, or make such other changes in the bill consequential on the amendments accepted by the House.

Such a long catalogue of the powers of the Speaker should be treated as widely illustrative but by no means exhaustive. A study of the powers of the Speaker, in practice, shows that he has not been able to gain that high level of dignity which is enjoyed by the English Speaker for the obvious reason that we have remained far from being able to develop the sound tradition of Speaker's being a non-party man. That is why, there have been occasions (as in December 1954) when a move for removing the Speaker from office was made, or that some angry members went to the final length of undermining the high office of the Speaker until they were forcibly taken out of the House by the watch and ward staff headed by the Marshal.

The office of the Speaker is of great authority and dignity. But it requires that he should be known for his impartiality. "Confidence in the impartiality of the Speaker is an indispensable condition of the successful working of the procedure and many conventions exist which have as their object not only to ensure the impartiality of the Speaker but also to ensure that his impartiality is generally recognised."[9] Unfortunatelly, this noble tradition is dishonoured when the members of the House use unparliamentary expressions and make an exchange of fists and blows on any issue like the disqualification of a member on the ground of his holding an office of profit or location of a Maritime University in Chennai or Kolkata. So Speaker Chatterji regretted. "It is a very sad day. This is not the way the MP's should behave. We should be role models for the entire country."[10]

Legislative Process

The story of legislation begins with the introduction of a non-money bill in any House of Parliament and of a money bill in the Lok Sabha with the prior recommendation of the President. It is a fact that the functioning of cabinet form of government has so much changed that the executive has usurped the inherent function of the legislature. For this reason, we may unhesitatingly add that the government bills are invariably passed by the Parliament. According to the policy of the ministers, the work of drafting is done by the experts of the Ministry of Law. The ministries concerned

---

9. Sir Erskine May: *Treatise on the Law, Privileges, Procedure and Usages of Parliament*, XVII ed., p. 247.

10. *The Times of India* (New Delhi), 14 March, 2007.

and the Attorney-General of India may be consulted, if necessary. The final draft of a bill is discussed and approved in the Cabinet meeting and then the way is cleared for its introduction in the Parliament. The minister concerned is required to give 7 days' notice to introduce the bill. (It may be two days' notice with the permission of the presiding officer of the House.) It is included in the List of Business on a date fixed by the presiding officer of the House.

On the appointed date just after the question hour or at a time specified in the business of the day, the minister concerned is called upon by the Chairman/Speaker to ask for leave of the House for moving his bill. It is possible that the minister may, apart from reading out the title and objects of the bill, also deliver a brief speech so as to highlight its salient features within a span of 10 minutes. In case the bill before its introduction in the House is published in the Gazette of India with the permission of the Chairman/Speaker, then the formality is avoided. There is no discussion at this stage. This is known as 'first reading' of a bill. It is very rare that a bill is rejected at the first reading stage.

The crucial stage in the life of a bill is its 'second reading'. Now the bill is taken up for detailed discussion. All principles of the bill are thoroughly debated. Amendments may also be moved. The House may take one of the three options. The bill should be passed in view of its great importance; it should be referred to a Select Committee of the House or, if it is very important, to a Joint Committee of both the Houses; it may be circulated to elicit public opinion. Generally, the bills are referred to the Committees where detailed discussion takes place and the fate of the bill is finally decided. The Committee may pass the bill as it is, or may make some amendments in it, or may keep it in abeyance for a long time so much so that the Lok Sabha is dissolved and the matter lapses. In case the committee returns the bill to the house, then second reading has its second instalment. Now the bill is discussed clause by clause and closures may be applied so as to finish the work within time.[11]

---

11. Closure motions are resorted to in order to cut the debate and finish the business before the House within time. Any member of the House may put a closure motion requesting that the matter be put to vote. Such a motion may be put at any time subject to the condition that if some member is holding the floor, he should be allowed to conclude his statement. In case the presiding officer

Then, on a date fixed by the Business Advisory Committee, the bill is taken up for the 'third reading'. This is the last stage and this is again a formality like the first reading. No discussion takes place and within a couple of minutes this formality is done. Thereafter, the bill goes to the second House where it passes through similar stages. In case the bill has been cleared by the Joint Select Committee of the Parliament, then there is no need to refer it to a select committee. The other House may pass that bill or return it with its recommendations. In that case the first House may pass it again accepting the recommendations of the other House and in case it sticks to its earlier recommendations, there is a situation of disagreement or deadlock. The President may call a joint session of both the Houses to resolve this crisis. The Speaker shall preside over the joint sitting and the decision shall be taken by the majority of votes. But a joint session can be held only in the case of a non-money bill to be passed by simple majority.

The last stage in the life of a bill is the assent of the President. When a bill is passed by the Parliament, it is referred to the President

---

feels that ample discussion has taken place on the matter, he may permit this motion. In case he feels that the matter has not been fully discussed, or the House is not in favour of appreciating the closure motion, he may reject it. It should, however, be noted that a closure motion cannot be put so as to infringe the right of a reasonable debate. Closure motions are of four kinds. A 'simple' closure is one when a member moves "That the matter having been sufficiently discussed be now put to vote'. It is also possible that before the commencement of discussion on a bill or a very long resolution, its clauses are grouped into parts. The debate covers the part as a whole and the entire part is put to vote. This is called 'closure by compartments'. It is also possible that only important clauses are taken up for discussion and voting and the intervening clauses are skipped over and taken as passed. It is called 'kangaroo' closure. Finally, there is 'guillotine' closure. When the time allotted for the debate is over, the presiding officer puts all clauses to vote and declares the result. It means that whatever remained undiscussed, let it remain so. It is generally applied when the budget is passed by the House. A study of the working of our Parliament shows that with the coming into being of the Business Advisory Committee in 1953, the practice of resorting to the device of closure motion "has practically gone out of use and is now resorted to rarely." Kaul and Shakdher: *Practice and Procedure of Parliament*, p. 750.

who may give his assent, or refuse to give his assent, or return it for reconsideration. It shows that the veto power of the President is absolute as well as qualified. For instance, in 1986 Zail Singh returned the Postal Amendment Bill for reconsideration. In such a situation it depends upon the view of the Council of Ministers to proceed ahead or not. In case the same bill is passed again by the Parliament with or without accepting the recommendations of the President, he must give his assent. After receiving the assent of the President, the bill becomes an act and is placed on the statute book.

Procedure in Respect of Money Bill

India has a special procedure in respect of financial business. A money bill is introduced in the Lok Sabha. Since it can be introduced with the prior recommendation of the President, it is always a Government bill. Art. 110 defines a money bill as one dealing with the imposition, abolition, remission or alteration of any tax, or regulation of borrowing of money by the government, or the payment of moneys into or their withdrawals from the Consolidated or Contingency Fund of India, or declaring an item to be a charge on the Consolidated Fund of India and the like. It is also given that in the event of any controversy as to whether a bill introduced in the Parliament is a money bill or not, the Speaker shall decide and his ruling shall be final. In case such a bill is introduced in the Rajya Sabha and during the course of discussion it is disputed that it is a money bill, the Chairman shall stop the discussion and refer the matter for the decision of the Speaker. In case the Speaker rules that it is a money bill, the bill shall stand as withdrawn from the House.

A money bill, like any bill, must be passed by both the Houses of Parliament. The Rajya Sabha must pass it within 14 days. In case it returns the bill with some recommendations, the Lok Sabha may accept them or not. The bill shall not be referred to the Rajya Sabha again. The President has no power to veto such a bill. The budget or annual financial statement of the Government is presented in two parts. On some date in the last week of February, the Railway Minister presents his budget. But on the last day of this month at 5'00 p.m. the Finance Minister presents the general budget. He also delivers a long speech highlighting the salient points of his budget. After a gap of few days the Business Advisory Committee specifies a time of about 4 days for a general discussion of the budget. The members have the occasion to speak in favour or against the provisions of the budget. It is followed by voting on the demands for grants.

The members of the opposition parties now take the opportunity of moving cut motions. The functioning of various ministeries is now hotly debated. It is possible that in view of the mounting criticism the Government may agree to have a cut in the demands of some ministry in the name of 'economy'. In case the cut motion is passed against the wishes of the ministers, it amounts to a vote of no-confidence in the government. Since the time is short and the discussion may go on for any length of time, simple closures may be applied and the demands be put to vote. Even then the work of elaborately discussing the demands of all ministries remains unfinished. Hence, at a time as specified in the List of Business, discussion is closed and all demands are put to vote. It is known as the application of 'guillotine' closure.

The budget has two sides–revenues and appropriations. Thus, the budget is converted into two bills. The Finance Bill incorporates all financial proposals of the government for the ensuing year. Discussion on this bill covers matters relating to general administration. It must be passed by the Parliament and assented to by the President within a period of 75 days. The expenditure side of the budget is covered by the Appropriations Bill. It incorporates all the demands for grants voted by the Lok Sabha alongwith expenditure charged on the Consolidated Fund. Discussion on this bill affords another chance to the members of the parties in opposition to criticise the administration in general. The Government sees to it that both the Bills are passed by the Lok Sabha. The Rajya Sabha is given a chance to discuss the budget and pass the bills within 14 days. It may return the two bills with some recommendations which may or may not be appreciated by the Lok Sabha. Since both the bills are money bills, these receive the assent of the President.

A pertinent question at this stage arises as to what would happen in case the budget is not passed by the Parliament before the commencement of the next financial year, or what would happen in case the Government feels the need for more money to be raised and appropriated on certain unforeseen conditions as those of war or national calamity. Art. 116 has a special provision for 'vote on account'. It empowers the Lok Sabha to sanction any grant in advance for a part of any financial year pending the completion of the budgetary process. Normally it is taken for two months and it should be roughly equal to 1/6 of estimated expenditure for the entire year under various demands for grants. This period may be enhanced to 3 or 4 months in the case of special urgency. What is to be noted here is that the vote on account is done after a general discussion of the budget and, by way of a practice, it is not discussed in the Lok Sabha.

It is also possible that some critical situation may arise (as caused by war or national calamity) calling for the passage of a supplementary budget. (Art. 115) While discussing supplementary demands for grants, the members of the Lok Sabha cannot reopen the debate already held in the House, they may only criticise the new demands or the purpose behind them as claimed by the Government. At this stage general grievances cannot be ventilated. It is a different matter that some members may refer to previous assurances of the Government so as to reinforce their arguments. Art. 116 says about votes on account, votes of credit and exceptional grants for a particular purpose that does not form part of the ordinary expenditure of the financial year. For this the House may grant separate funds. The Lok Sabha also passes the budgets of the Union Territories and of a State under President's rule.

Committee System

Legislatures all over the world work with the help of their committees both for the economy of time and for detailed discussion on a matter which is not possible in the House on account of heavy load of work. Moreover, the members of the committees are generally the experts of their chosen areas and they may discuss a matter in a committee room where they have more time to speak and also, in most of the cases, they are not bound by the party whips. We have already seen that a bill after being discussed in and passed by the House in the first instalment of the second reading is generally referred to a Select Committee for detailed discussion. Apart from this, the House has a large number of other Committees. Both the Houses of Parliament have their committees, but a Joint Committee of the two Houses may also be formed for passing a bill of great significance within a short time.

The number of the members of the committees varies. The members of the committees are elected by the House. They may also be nominated by the presiding officer. Casual vacancies in the committees are filled up by the presiding officer or by the House on a motion made to this effect. In case a bill is referred to a Select Committee, it invariably includes the minister concerned if it is a government bill; in case it is a Private Member's bill, the minister concerned may be included in it. In the case of a Joint Committee of Parliament the members are appointed on a motion adopted by one House and agreed to by the other House. The committees are formed in proportion to the strength of the parties' in the House. The quorum is one-third of the members in the House. The ruling party has a safe position in the committees on account of being in majority in the House. itself. In most of the committees the ministers are not included, unless so necessary. The whips are issued very sparingly. The backbenchers have a chance to play a noticeable role in the committees.

Known as the Financial Committees of Parliament, three committees are very important. The Estimates Committee has 30 members annually elected by the members of the Lok Sabha from amongst themselves according to proportional representation with single-transferable vote system. It examines the estimates referred to it by the House or by the Speaker and the estimates which it may deem fit with a view to effect economy in expenditures. The Public Accounts Committee has 15 members from the Lok Sabha and 7 from the Rajya Sabha elected annually by the members of the House from amongst themselves according to proportional representation with single transferable vote system. As per practice, its Chairman is a member of the party in opposition and that its members are given a term of two years by re-election to ensure continuity. It examines the report of the Comptroller and Auditor-General of India and sees whether the money was spent according to the provisions of the budget passed by the Parliament. It also examines the statement of accounts showing income and expenditure of autonomous and semi-autonomous bodies. The Committee on Public Undertakings has 15 members elected from the Lok Sabha and 7 from the Rajya Sabha by the members from amongst themselves. It examines the accounts and reports of Public Undertakings allotted to it.

Delegated Legislation

Delegated, or subordinate, or executive, or administrative legislation may be defined as rules, regulations and orders framed by the executive departments under the authority drawn from the statutes made by the Parliament for the purpose of supplementing the provisions of 'blanket' legislation. It is said that a law made by the Parliament is like a 'blanket'. That is, it contains outlines only. It needs details to be filled in when it is put to implementation. Thus, circulars, notifications, regulations etc. are issued by the executive departments from time to time so that the law made by the Parliament, or 'parent act' as it is called, does not fall short of its proper implementation. As a result, we have two forms of legislation—the laws made by the Parliament and the regulations issued by the concerned departments to supplement the provisions of the 'parent law'. The latter makes subordinate legislation. It is also called 'delegated legislation', because the departments have authority in this regard delegated to them by the Parliament itself.

However, this delegation of authority is subject to these limitations:[12]

1. Within the allotted field of legislature, the delegation may be limited or unlimited.
2. The legislature cannot transfer its powers without performing its essential functions.
3. In delegating its authority to some executive department, the Parliament does not abdicate its authority and, for this reason, it may either withdraw its delegation, or entrust the same to another agency.
4. The regulations issued by the departments mut be in accordance with the wishes of the Parliament as contained in the 'parent act'.
5. Delegated legislation is subject to the approval of the Parliament. Moreover, as the Courts may look into the constitutional validity of a law made by the Parliament, they may do the same in the case of delegated legislation.

---

12. See V.N. Shukla; *Commentary on the Constitution of India*, VI Ed. of 1975 edited by D.K. Singh, p. 420.

As pointed out above, delegated legislation is subject to the control of the Parliament. All directions and regulations issued by the departments are submitted to the Parliament for approval. Any member of the House may raise a question and then a regulation of the department may be repealed in case the House finds it contrary to the letter or spirit of the parent law. For this purpose, the Parliament has a committee (called committee on subordinate legislation) which examines the rules and regulations issued by the departments and then submits its report to the House. In this way, the Parliament continues to keep its control over the delegated legislation.

The critics point out that delegated legislation has assumed a very serious form now. It has made the executive departments powerful enough to issue directions, that may go even to the extent of undermining the authority of the Parliament. To say that this legislation is subject to the control of the Parliament does not hold good in modern times, because it has very limited time and the approval of the Parliament for departmental regulations is just a matter of formality. Chief Justice Lord Hewart of England has, for this reason, called delegated legislation as an instrument of 'new despotism'. Though the criticism is quite weighty, it cannot be forgotten that delegated legislation has now become an inescapable necessity. What is, therefore, needed is that there should be a strong public opinion in the country. The press should be free and the people be vigilant to fight for their rights and liberties. As Prof. D.C. Sharma says: "The people, the press and the Parliament must all keep a vigilant eye on the executive and the rules framed by it if delegated legislation is to be immune from the infection of official despotism."[13]

The Opposition

If the people are to retain control over their government, those set in authority must, from time to time, be made to account for their stewardship. In order to secure this end, different devices have been made. Referendum may be one such device whereby a bill passed by the legislature is subjected to the final verdict of the

---

13. D.C. Sharma; "Delegated Legislation" in A.B. Lal (ed.): *The Indian Parliament*, p. 178.

people. In a parliamentary form of government, the opposition is given a sanctified place so that it may attempt to curb the excessive use of authority by a system of checks and balances.

The story of the opposition in India begins from 1952 when the Congress party gained overwhelming majority in the first general election and thus placed all opposition parties in a very weak position. Opposition to the ruling party ran into three directions. While the newly formed Bharatiya Jana Sangh took to the course of the right, the Communists adopted the line of the left, and the Praja-Socialists adopted the curious line of supporting and opposing the ruling party on issues and merits.

An improvement in this direction took place after the second general election of 1957. The victory of the Communists in the State of Kerala strengthened their position in the Parliament also. Moreover, with the birth of the Swatantra Party in 1959, Congress came to have a formidable opposition. The Jana Sangh and the Swatantra thus drew close and their opposition to the Congress rule found expression in their attack on some progressive and socialistic policies like nationalisation of private industry, co-operativisation of agriculture, and imposition of more and more restrictions on economic freedom.

But the reverses of the Congress in the third general election of 1962 coupled with our defeat at the hands of China thereafter made this party's rule highly unpopular. What added fuel to fire were the schemes of compulsory deposits and gold control initiated by the then Finance Minister (Morarji Desai) that irritated the people and that had their impact on the bye-elections held in the summer of the following year. The victory of Rammanohar Lohia, Acharya Kripalani and Minoo Masani from the constituencies of Kanauj, Amroha and Rajkot respectively signified the triumph of three great opposition leaders whose entry in the Lok Sabha meant the existence of a formidable opposition to the government of Nehru. In the monsoon session of 1963, it was for the first time, that these towering leaders of the opposition moved a censure motion. Though the motion was defeated, it did give a bold indication of the growing strength of an effective opposition in the country.

The reverses suffered by the Congress in the fourth general election of 1967 signified an astounding improvement in the position of the opposition. The Congress government was vehemently criticised for its injudicious policy of taking part in the Islamic summit held at Rabat in 1969. The leaders of the opposition sought to have enquiries into several shoddy affairs like those of the Jayanti Shipping Company and Prime Minister's shares in the National Herald. A peculiar development took place in Nov., 1969 when the Congress had a split and the Congress (O) joined the opposition ranks leaving the ruling Congress (N) in a position of minority. For the first time, Ram Subhag Singh was designated as the Leader of the Opposition.

While the New Congress could emerge triumphant in the elections of 1971, it also sharpened the vigour of the leaders of the opposition. The defeat of the Grand Alliance did not mean total liquidation of the opposition, rather it made the opposition leaders more vocal as well as violent in censuring the conduct of the Congress government with regard to affairs of the Maruti and Nagarwala. Thus, the opposition forced the government to allow it to have a look into the papers relating to the rags scandal in which the hand of the then Commerce Minister (L.N. Mishra) was too obvious.

It was towards the end of 1974 that the attitude of some of the opposition parties became quite militant and that made it impossible for the then Congress Government to go ahead, in its usual manner, with the doctrine of viscosity—the ease with which business is carried through the Parliament. The role of the opposition reached formidable heights by the middle of the following year that exhausted the patience of the then ruling party. Thus happened the unfortunate event when after the proclamation of national emergency on 25 June, 1975, the opposition was virtually outlawed. Most of the opposition leaders were placed behind the bars and the Parliament held its sessions without question hour and unofficial business.

A notable change took place in 1977, when the hitherto ruling party formed the opposition. Surprisingly, most of the hitherto opposition parties captured power after merging themselves in a new entity called the Janata Party. The august office of the Leader of the Opposition again came into being under Y.B. Chavan of the Congress (N). Indeed, this was a very remarkable development that could test the capabilities of the hitherto opposition parties that had now assumed power and also afforded a long-awaited opportunity to study the political behaviour of the Congress as a party in the opposition.

However, the role of the opposition became effective, in the real sense of the term, in 1989 when no party could secure clear majority in the Lok Sabha and the highly fluid situation signified the existence of a 'hung' Parliament for the first time in the parliamentary history of our country. In spite of being the largest party in terms of numerical strength, the Congress (I) declined to form the government. Then, V.P. Singh, the leader of the Janata Dal, next to the largest party, in collaboration with some other parties (which constituted the National Front) formed the government, while Rajiv Gandhi of the Congress (I) became the Leader of the Opposition. The Singh ministry dwindled when the BJP withdrew its support and the House removed the government by not passing the motion of confidence tabled by the Prime Minister in November, 1990. Then, Chandra Shekhar of the Janata Dal (S) formed the government banking on the support of some other parties from 'outside'. This government fell after a few months when the Congress (I) withdrew its support. The Opposition could throw out two governments within six months. The BJP emerged as the second largest party in the election of 1991 and so while P.V. Narsimha Rao of the Congress (I) formed the government, L.K. Advani of the BJP became the Leader of the Opposition. After some time, he relinquished this post on being the President of the BJP and then this office was given to A.B. Vajpayee.

The events of the following years demonstrated that the opposition had been able to assert itself in a situation when a government depended upon the cooperation of other parties from inside or outside, or it had a very slender margin which a Prime Minister of a majority government like P.V. Narsimha Rao could cover up by purchasing the loyalty of some influential leaders of other political parties.

The opposition became very vocal when Deve-Gowda formed coalition government in 1996. It was followed by a coalition government headed by Gujral about a year after. The Congress withdrew its support on the plea that the DMK had no right to be in a government whose hands were tainted with the blood of Rajiv Gandhi. It was contended on the basis of an inference drawn by the Congress party from interim report of the Jain Commission. After the fall of the Gujral government, Vajpayee formed another coalition government. When the A-DMK withdrew its support, the government had to seek confidence vote of the Lok Sabha. It could not occur and hence the government of Vajpayee was thrown out. Vajpayee formed another coalition government in 1999. In May, 2004 another coalition government came into being headed by Manmohan Singh of the Congress banking upon the support of a number of leftist parties and outfits as a result of which the BJP got the chance to head the opposition under the leadership of Advani.

The effective role of the opposition in the age of coalition governments is a natural development. The government is operated by a conglomerate alliance of more than half a dozen parties and petty outfits and a crisis is arisen when any major constituent gets out of the alliance. Such a rainbow coalition puts the government in a very imbecile position so much so that the model of cabinet government loses its shine and the role of a reckless opposition becomes the order of the day. The agitated members stall the proceedings of the House for days together for any reason like inquiring into some shoddy deal or removing the 'tainted' ministers. Hence, Prime Minister Manmohan Singh in his first address to the nation said: "It should be a matter of deep concern for all of us when established mechanisms for a constructive dialogue and critique, which are vital for a parliamentary democracy, are disrupted and not allowed to operate."[14]

Parliamentary Privileges

The members of Parliament have certain privileges without which they cannot discharge their duties properly. The members have a set of special rights and immunities which "exceed those possessed by other bodies or individuals."[15] Thus, Art. 105 lays down:

1. Subject to the provisions of this Constitution and to the rules and standing orders regulating the procedure of Parliament, there shall be freedom of speech in Parliament.
2. No member of Parliament shall be liable to any proceedings in any court in respect of anything said or any vote given by him in Parliament or any committee thereof, and no person shall be so liable in respect of the publication by or under the authority of either House of Parliament of any report, paper, votes or proceedings.

---

14. *The Times of India*, New Delhi, 25th June, 2004.

15. Erskine May: *op. cit.*, p. 42.

3. In other respects, the powers, privileges and immunities of each House of Parliament, and the members of the committees of each House, shall be, as may from time to time, be defined by Parliament by law, and, until so defined, shall be those of that House and of its members and committees immediately before the coming into force of Section 15 of the Forty-fourth Amendment Act of 1978.
4. The above provisions shall apply in relation to persons who by virtue of this Constitution have the right to speak in, and otherwise to take part in the proceedings of a House of Parliament or any Committee thereof as they apply in relation to Members of Parliament.

It is obvious that the powers, privileges and immunities of the members of Parliament have been inexhaustively specified in Art. 105. (Art. 194 has the same provision for the members of State Legislatures). The Forty-fourth Constitution Amendment Act has deleted the phrase that 'until defined by an Act of Parliament, the privileges of the members of Parliament would be the same as those of the British House of Commons'. What is still a matter of difficulty in this connection is that the privileges of the members of Parliament have not yet been exhaustively enumerated in a code. They have their source in some of the provisions of the Constitution, in some legal measures of the country, as well as in the various reports of the Parliamentary Committees and the interpretations of the Courts. The important privileges of the members of Parliament as well as of its Committees may be enumerated as under:

1. Freedom to speak in the House and its Committees.
2. Immunity from any proceedings in any court in respect of anything said or vote given by them in the House or its Committees.
3. Immunity from proceedings in any court in respect of the publication by or under the authority of the House of any report, paper, notes or proceedings.
4. Prohibition on the courts to inquire into the proceedings of Parliament and its Committees.
5. Freedom from arrest in civil cases during the continuance of the session of the House and 40 days before its commencement and 40 days after its conclusion.

6. Exemption from liability to serve as jurors.
7. Right of the House to receive immediate information of the arrest, detention, conviction, imprisonment and release of a member.
8. Prohibition of arrest and service of legal process on the members within the precincts of the House without the permission of the presiding officer.
9. Prohibition of disclosure of the proceedings or decisions of a secret sitting of the House by the members.
10. Right to refuse to give evidence or produce documents in the courts of law relating to the proceedings of the House without the permission of the presiding officer.
11. Right not to attend as witnesses before the other House or of a House of the State Legislature or its Committee without the permission of the House, nor can a member be compelled to do so without his consent.
12. Power of the House and its Committees to send for persons, papers, records, and other relevant material, including witnesses.
13. Administration of oath of affirmation by a Committee of the House before examining a witness.
14. Prohibition of publishing any evidence or statement relating to the reports and proceedings of a Committee before its tabling in the House.
15. Right of the House to regulate its proceedings, its own procedure and conduct of business, and
16. Right of the House to exclude strangers from the House and to a person, whether a member of the House or not, for a breach of privilege or contempt of the House.

It is true that the privileges of the members of Parliament and of State Legislatures are not yet codified. But the dominant view, all along, has been that any codification "is more likely to harm the sovereignty and prestige of Parliament/State Legislatures without any benefit being conferred on the Press and that in the present circumstances, codification of Parliamentary privileges is neither necessary nor desirable."[16]

Parliamentary Improprieties

The Parliament is lauded as a nation in miniature. In the glorious words of Rousseau, it represents the 'general will' of the community. The National Constitution Review Commission Report (2002) desired that like Caesar's wife the members of Parliament should be above suspicion. They should voluntarily place themselves to public scrutiny through Parliamentary ombudsman. It also suggested that Art. 105 (2) of the Constitution should be amended to clarify that the immunity enjoyed by the MP's under Parliamentary privileges does not cover 'corrupt acts' committed by them in connection with their duties in the House or otherwise. However, what happened in the recent past is certainly an unfortunate development if we look at three cases in this regard.

1. **Cash for Query Scam:** The members of Parliament have the right to ask questions and supplementary questions so as to seek information from the ministers. They represent the electorate and get salaries and allowances in addition to many other perks or benefits. It is expected that they perform their duties in an upright manner so as to maintain the dignity of their great democratic assignments. They should not take any money from their clients for asking a question or raising a matter of urgent public importance in the House. But in 2005 a number of MP's were caught taking huge amounts of money from some persons for this work. Their actions were video-filmed. The Ethics Committee of the Rajya Sabha (headed by Dr. Karan Singh) and a similar committee of the Lok Sabha (headed by P.K. Bansal) found the evidence sufficient and so recommended expulsion of such members from the House. As a result, 10 members of the Rajya Sabha and 1 member of the Lok Sabha were expelled. One of them filed a petition in the Supreme Court to challenge the verdict of the House, but it was rejected. No doubt, it was a climactic moment in India's Parliamentary history.

2. **Local Area Development Scheme:** In 1993 the government of Narsimha Rao started this scheme whereby an MP is given a sum of Rs. two crores (originally one crore) to spend that amount

---

16. Kashyap, *op. cit.*, p. 195.

on the welfare activities of his constituency. Under the rules framed by the government, not more than one-tenth of the amount can be spent on a particular project and that this money cannot be spent for private or religious or communal purposes. In course of time, it appeared that either the money remained unspent, or the recipients of this money misused it in their own ways. The National Constitution Review Commission Report (2002) suggested that this scheme should be scrapped. The Administrative Reforms Commission headed by Veerappa Moily in its report (2007) has reiterated it, while a committee of the Parliament has desired its enhancement to the tune of Rs. 5 crores a year for each MP.

The inherent defects of this scheme have come into lime light. It breeds corruption and misuse of public funds. There is no arrangement for the audit of such expenses. The amount is given out of the funds allocated by the Centre to the States. As such, the interest of the States suffers and a principle of federalism is violated in a certain respect. As the MP's spend it on some local projects, a parallel power structure is established at the grass-roots level. Above all, the function of the MP's is to pass grants and not to implement them. This scheme transforms MP's into benevolent feudal lords who can dole out public funds at their discretion. The money sanctioned by the Parliament should be spent by the executive authorities who can be held accountable for the embezzlement or misappropriation of funds. But in this case a separate rule is envisaged for the legislators which is inconsistent with their role as representatives of the people.

A pertinent question arises as to what should be done to prevent such unfortunate developments. Punitive action against the erring MPs may not help the Parliament to rid it of its deep rooted malaise. As S.C. Kashyap says, it "needs path-breaking Parliamentary reforms to put the House in order. The presiding officers only have to will it."[17] The words of the Speaker (Somnath Chatterjee) are worth quoting: "The people's right to recall a representative who fails to live upto their expectations is an important democratic tool. I plead for its inclusion in the electoral system. Survival of democracy depends upon people's faith in the system, and it can be ensured only if leaders, particularly the people's representatives, conduct themselves as role models."

---

17. *The Times of India* (New Delhi) 4 December, 2005.

Office of Profit : The job of the legislators is to make laws, not to execute them. An executive function makes it office of profit which has three ingredients. The immediate appointing and dismissing authority is the government. The incumbent receives some amount in the form of salary or allowance or perks from the public treasury regardless of the fact that he actually receives it or not. Last, he performs some duties of an executive nature. The Constitution has various provisions disabling a person from becoming the President (Art. 58 (2)), Vice-President (Art. 66 (4)), the members of Parliament (Art. 102 (1) (a)), and of State legislatures (Art. 191 (1)). The purpose behind such an arrangement is to ensure separation of powers so that the legislators can perform their duties without any fear or favour independent of the Central and State governments. But the Parliament and the State legislatures have the power to make laws and amend them from time to time so as to exempt any office or offices from the purview of the said provisions.[18]

On 24 August, 1954 the Bhargava Committee was appointed to consider a comprehensive bill on disqualifiactory exceptions. In its report submitted to the Parliament in September, 1958, it broadly justified exclusion from disqualification of the Ministers, while underlining that governmental largesse should not pick and choose the members of Parliament to whittle down their independence. Facts indicate that both the Parliament and State legislatures have framed laws and also amended them from time to time so as to exempt some office or offices from the grip of the constitutional provisions. For instance, the post of the Deputy Chairman of the Planning Commission was exempted when its incumbent (R.K. Hegde) was disqualified in 1989. Not only this, the disqualification of a person can be held with retrospective effect as happened in the Kanta Kathuria Case in 1969 and the Jaya Bachchan Case in 2006.

The issue of the office of profit took a serious form in 2006 when a number of leading members of Parliament were found involved in it after the disqualification of Jaya Bachchan. Taking a cautious view of the state of affairs, Sonia Gandhi resigned and got herself

18. It is for this reason that the offices of the President, Vice-President, Ministers of the Union and the States, and the Governors of States have been exempted by the provisions of the Constitution.

re-elected and thereby she set a good precedent. Jaya Bachchan was re-elected as her case had become a matter of prestige for the Samajwadi Party in U.P. However, two important points engage our attention at this stage. First, the Union and State legislatures should not have unfettered power in this regard. The way the Parliament and also some of the State legislatures amended their laws so as to save a number of eminent figures from disqualification on the recommendation of the Election Commission by the President of India cannot be appreciated by a serious student of constitutional law. Second, in view of the expanding role of the welfare state, the definition of the office of profit should be suitably revised without killing the spirit of constitutional law.[19] It is for this reason that President Abdul Kalam returned the bill passed by the Parliament for reconsideration with this suggestion that its provisions should be very comprehensive. He gave his assent to it after it was re-passed by the Parliament with an assurance that such a case would be looked into by a committee of the Parliament.[20]

Decline of Parliament

A critical examination of the functions and powers of the Parliament, in practice, confirms this astonishing impression of modern writers that the old distrust of the executive has been replaced by the new confidence in its leadership. The strong position of the cabinet working under the unflappable leadership of the Prime Minister in a parliamentary form of government, recently rechristened as the Prime Ministerial form of Government, confirms the doctrine of Ramsay Muir that it "has to a remarkable extent diminished the power and prestige of Parliament, robbed its proceedings of significance, made it appear that Parliament exists mainly for the purpose of maintaining or of somewhat ineffectually

---

19. Way back in *Madhukar's Case* (1977) Justice V.R. Krishna Iyer warned: "We have to bear in mind that our Constitution mandates the state to undertake multi-form public activities on a massive scale. In such an expanding situation, can we keep out of elective posts an army of non-officials who are wanted in various fields not as full-time government servants but as part-time participants in people's projects sponsored by the government."

20. Rajeev Dhawan: "Money Matters: Rules for MP Ineligibility to be Clarified" in *The Times of India* (New Delhi), 21 March, 2006.

criticising an all good but omnipotent Cabinet and transferred the main discussion of political issues from Parliament to platform and the members."[21]

The fact of the decline of Parliament finding, its manifestation in our constitutional system looking like a dull, meaningless and routine affair, draws its support from these points:

1. The Supreme Court (and also High Courts) are empowered to look into the constitutional validity of laws made by the Parliament. The judiciary has been empowered to apply the doctrine of legislative competence in order to pronounce its verdict whether a law made by the Parliament, partly or wholly, is *intra vires or ultra vires* of the Constitution that is the supreme law of the land. By virtue of Art. 13 (2) the judiciary can strike down any law made by the Parliament in case it, in its esteemed judgment, is inconsistent with Part III of the Constitution dealing with Fundamental Rights. The climax of this prerogative of the supreme judiciary reached in the *Golak Nath Case* of 1967 when the Court ruled: "Parliament will have no power from the date of this decision to amend any of the provisions of Part III of the Constitution so as to take away or abridge the Fundamental Rights enshrined therein."
2. The area of authority originally belonging to the Parliament has been usurped by the Cabinet.[22] It is true that the instrument of judicial review places a very heavy hand of the judiciary on the supremacy of the Parliament, it is equally true that the over-riding control of judiciary can be over-ridden by the Parliament itself acting at the behest of the Cabinet. The result is that the Parliament has come to live under the redeemable control of the judiciary on the one hand and of the generally irredeemable control of the Cabinet on the other. The rashness with which the Government of Mrs. Gandhi managed to have the 24th and 25th Constitution Amendment Acts in 1971 and

---

21. See Ramsay Muir: *How Britain is Governed*, Ch. III.

22. As K.C. Wheare says: "The exercise by the executive of law-making powers probably by the growth of delegated legislation has meant that the legislature no longer makes all the laws or even all the important laws." *Legislatures* (London: Oxford University Press, 1968), p. 149.

the 38th and 39th Amendment Acts in 1975 constitutes a concrete evidence of the political axion that the Cabinet can make use of the Parliament for repudiating the challenge of the judiciary. It is the Cabinet that initiates a bill and it is the Cabinet alone that has to see that its bill is passed by the Parliament. Not only that, it is the Cabinet that decides about the time when the bill has to be moved and debated and finally adopted by the Parliament. It is thus enough to say that the Cabinet, under the leadership of strong Prime Ministers like Nehru, Indira and Rajiv Gandhi could well become the first and also the last chamber of our law-making mechanism.

3. Let us look into the pitiable position that the members of the Parliament really enjoy. Though one may not concur with the rash impression of a Communist member that "to the present rulers the Opposition is an ulcer which they want to remove."[23] He will agree with the observation that the leaders of a deplorably fragmented Opposition, as it obtains in our country, have hardly been able to learn the counsel, what Sir Alec Douglas-Home once said, that they must not exploit the Parliamentary situation in a way that good government is made difficult.[24] The result is that the ruling party by means of its strong and effective organisational machinery has been able to keep its members tied up in a form of discipline as desired by the unflappable Prime Minister. The use of whips in a rigorous manner and the off and on admonitions by the Prime Minister and his senior lieutenants to accord verbal punishment to the members of Parliament seeking to assert their independence to any degree whatsoever are enough to confirm the impression of a critic that the members of the Parliament have been reduced to the level of the 'robots'.

4. The dignity of an office depends upon its deeds. Everyone knows that the function of the Parliament is to deliberate, discuss and decide matters relating to the interest of the nation as a whole. In recent times one may feel taken aback at the poor quality of debates, niggardly attendance of the members,

---

23. A.K. Gopalan: "The Opposition" in A.B. Lal. (ed.) *The Indian Parliament*, p. 71.

24. Kenneth Young: *Sir Douglas-Home*, p. 121.

unruly behaviour of some extra-vocal leaders quarrelling for their partisan interest in the name of 'public good' and the like. In March, 1991 the Parliament created a bad history by passing as many as 18 bills without discussion within a couple of minutes. Important financial business as voting on demands for billions of rupees for the Union, vote on account for 1991–92, coupled with supplementary grants for 1990–91 and the budgets of four States and one Union Territory under President's rule were passed without any scrutiny or discussion. Most astounding of all, both the Houses passed a bill within seconds that sought to provide them proportionate pension for life on completing only one year as a member which fortunately was vetoed by the sagacious President. The ninth Lok Sabha was thus out setting a dismal record of sorts, but the eleventh one went steps farther. Then it saw its end after 15 months, Madhu Limaye lamented at its 'inglorious exit'.

5. One more cause should be traced in the marvellous development of information technology. Parliament was lauded as the committee of grievances where high officers of the State were impeached. Now that role of the Parliament has been taken over by the critical press and agencies of mass media. Not the Houses of Parliament or their Committees but the newspapers, radio and television are within the reach of a common man. The proceedings of the House may be secret or confidential, inaccessible to an ordinary man, but information technology may expose any scandal from Watergate in America to Tehelka in India. Due importance should be given to the role of many non-governmental organisations like Common Cause, People's Union for Civil Liberties, People's Union for Democratic Rights and the like which take the matter to the Courts and thereby tarnish the image of the Parliament whose crafty members try their best to conceal their misdoings. It shows that the functions of the Parliament have now been shared with other bodies."[25]

6. The patent reality cannot be overlooked that the number of such members of Parliament is steadily increasing who have

---

25. K.C. Wheare: *op. cit.*, p. 156.

hardly any knowledge of the laws, rules and regulations and the norms of parliamentary behaviour. They often remain absent from the session and take pleasure in leavng the chamber after making a disorderly scene; sometimes, they thump their desk when it is an occasion for shedding tears. The members of the opposition parties are equally to be blamed. At the time of passing the budget in 2004, they committed an act of constitutional impropriety by pressurising the Prime Minister in his office to incorporate into the budget appropriations as they liked without any debate or discussion in the House. It is well observed: "The larger issue is that all MPs should be accountable for thier actions in Parliament and face recall in the event of their failure. They should be enjoined to spend a minimum amount of time in the House, just as office-goers in the public sectors report to work. They should mandatorily participate in the debates of the House and its committees and their views be placed in record for public consumption."[26]

7. Recent developments show that the pace of decline has become more rapid owing to the entry of social and economic wrong-doers into the legislative chambers of the country. The Election Commission regretted in 1997 that the Lok Sabha had as many as 40 members against whom criminal proceedings were going on in different courts of the country. Keeping it in view, a perceptive analyst comments: "But now we seem to have arrived in a blind alley. We have to think of the future of parliamentary institutions and of the ideals of freedom and democracy, stability and accountability. In a parliamentary democracy there can be nothing sadder or more dangerous than the representative credentials of the representatives becoming suspect and an ever-increasing alienation taking place between the people and their representatives. Today we are in a situation where sanctity of means has lost all value, meaning and relevance. If dacoits, smugglers, gangsters and foreign agents can help put or sustain in power, we are prepared to compromise with them. We are prepared to buy stability of our chairs by bribing fellow legislators. The people feel that in the face of personal ambitions the new breeds of politicians in

26. *The Times of India*. New Delhi, 26 August, 2004.

all parties are selfish, power hungry, greedy, dishonest, hypocrites and power merchants for whom the nation comes last and the welfare of the people is at the bottom of priorities. Theirs only concern is to amass wealth and somehow get to and stay in power. They are so busy in the struggle for survival that they have no time or energy left for serving the people."[27]

What James Bryce had bemoaned in his *Modern Democracies* (1921) has now become a patent reality. In his pathological study of some legislatures of the world, he highlighted the fact of the 'decline' of legislatures which saw its coincidence with the observation of an eloquent Congressman of America (Elijah Pogram) who sarcastically remarked that 'their bright home is in the setting sun.'[28] John Stuart Mill in his *Considerations on Representative Government* had made a normative assertion in the later part of the nineteenth century that the 'function of a legislature is to be a congress of opinions', and Walter Bagehot in his work *The English Constitution* admired the 'expressive and teaching functions of the House of Commons'. However, the fact of 'decline' should not be identified with 'demise'. Lowenberg insists that the institution of legislature 'still seems to be one of the most enduring and widely applicable inventions of political man.'[29] And he makes the case quite plain by endorsing: "Decline is in the eye of the beholder and depends on his analytical perspectives."[30]

---

27. S.C. Kashyap: "Parliament: Changing Face and Functions" in V. Narayanan and Jycti Sabherwal (ed.): *India at 50: Bliss of Hope and Burden of Reality* (New Delhi: Sterling Publishers, 1997), p. 48.

28. K.C. Wheare, *op. cit.*, p. 149.

29. H. Gerhard Lowenberg: *Modern Parliaments: Change or Decline* (Chicago: Aldine Althestor Inc., 1971), p. 19.

30. *Ibid.*, p. 15.

13

State and Local Governments

The framework of the State governments is almost the same as we have seen in the case of the government at the Centre. Some minor points of difference may, however, be noted. For instance the Governor is the constitutional head of the State government, but he is not elected, he is appointed by the President and may be recalled, or reappointed, or transferred by him from one State to another. The Governor performs the same functions what the President does at the Centre with this difference that he has no 'emergency' powers. Each State has a Vidhan Sabha, but in some States, the legislature is bicameral having Vidhan Parishad and Vidhan Sabha respectively as upper and lower chambers. All Vidhan Sabhas have a normal term of five years, but the Vidhan Sabha of Jammu-Kashmir has a term of six years. Since we have a unified judiciary, the High Courts are not the third organ of the State governments in the correct sense of the term, they constitute the sub-part of the Union judiciary. Above all, since we have a federal system with a strong Centre, the State governments do not have such autonomy that is ejoyed by the States of the USA or the cantons of Switzerland due to the overriding and over-arching control of the Centre in many areas of the administration of the States.

Governor

Each State has a Governor. There may be a common Governor for two or more States for some time. He is appointed by the President on the advice of the Union Council of Ministers for five years. A person to be appointed for this post must be a citizen of India; he must be above 35 years of age; and he must not be holding any office of profit. Two usages have developed in this direction. First, the person to be chosen for this post must not be a domicile of the State. For instance, a Maharashtrian should not be appointed as the Governor of Maharashtra. Second, before making this appointment, the Union government must consult the Chief Minister of the concerned State just for the sake of courtesy. It does not mean that the Chief Minister may dictate his will in this matter; it is simply a gesture of goodwill that the Centre should show to the real head of the State government. Unfortunately, the second usage has not been observed scrupulously on several occasions.[1] Not only that, the Centre has failed to evolve a clear-cut-policy about the selection of persons for this post. Facts illustrate that this post has been given to persons ranging from eminent public figures and seasoned bureaucrats to burnt-out politicians and fallen horses. A noted jurist like M.C. Setalvad regretted that since the advent of independence, many of those selected for the post "have fallen short of the required standard, largely due to the lowly place given to the office which has come to be treated as a sinecure for mediocrities or as a consolation prize for burnt-out politicians."

The Sarkaria Commission Report (1987), in very clear terms, says that the Governors should be persons who have not taken too great a part in politics generally and particularly in the recent past. Then, the National Constitution Review Commission Report (2002) reiterates: "By and large, the picture has not been an inspiring one. This is because very often active politicians defeated at the polls and men lacking in integrity and fairness and individuals not possessing an understanding of the constitutional system–persons who are more interested in their personal career than public good–are chosen for this office."

The functions and powers of the Governor cover executive, legislative, judicial, financial and other spheres. In the *executive sphere*, his functions are as under:

1. He is the executive head of the State government. The executive power of the State is vested in him that he has to

---

1. The appointment, transfer or recall or the Governors is concern of the Centre. For courtesy's sake the Union Home Minister may have a talk with the Chief Minister of the concerned State. On 29th October, 2004 the Supreme Court dismissed a petition filed by the Government of Tamil Nadu that the Centre should be restrained from transferring its Governor (P.S. Rammohan Rao) without consulting the Chief Minister. A little earlier, Union Home Minister (Shivraj Patil) had informed Chief Minister Jayalalitha on telephone: "This is the way we usually do things."

exercise directly or through officers subordinate to him. All executive actions of the State government are taken in his name. He makes rules for the transaction of business of the government and for the allocation of work among his ministers.

2. He appoints the Chief Minister and on his advice appoints other ministers. He administers to them the oaths of office and secrecy. He accepts their resignations. He may dismiss the Chief Minister or any minister on the advice of the Chief Minister. He makes appointment of high officers of the State like Advocate-General, Chairman and members of the State Public Service Commission, Election Commissioner of State, Chairman and members of State Finance Commission etc. and is consulted by the President in the appointment of the judges and Chief Justice of the High Court of his State.
3. He may call for information from the Chief Minister relating to the affairs of administration and proposals for legislation. He may refer any important matter for the consideration of the Ministers so as to seek their advice.
4. He acts as the Chancellor of State universities.
5. In case he is satisfied that constitutional machinery in his State has broken down, he may write to the President recommending invocation of Art. 356 of the Constitution. If it happens, he acts as the 'agent' of the President in running the administration of the State.

Then, he performs important functions in the *legislative sphere* as under:

1. He is an integral part of the State legislature without being its member. He summons the session of the legislature and prorogues it. He may dissolve the Vidhan Sabha at any time on the advice of the Chief Minister.
2. He may nominate one member of the Anglo-Indian community to the Vidhan Sabha in case he finds it not adequately represented in it. If the State legislature is bicameral, he nominates about one-sixth of its members from amongst persons distinguished in the fields of art, literature, science, social service and cooperative movement.
3. On the advice of the Election Commission, he can decide a matter relating to the disqualification of a legislator of his State.

4. The first session of the legislature of a new year and a session after general election begins with his inaugural address.
5. He may send messages to the legislature for consideration.
6. In case the legislature is not in session and some law is necessarily to be put into force, he may promulgate an ordinance having the force of law. It may be withdrawn at any time by him, but it can remain in force at the most for six weeks after the reassembling of the State legislature.
7. The annual reports of various bodies like State Public Service Commission and Auditor-General are submitted to him that he causes to be laid before the legislature for consideration.
8. He has veto power. As such, he may give assent to a non-money bill, or withhold his assent, or return it for the reconsideration of the legislature.
9. In case he finds that a bill passed by the State legislature seeks abolition of private property, or derogates the jurisdiction of the High Court, or imposes tax on an item declared 'essential' by a law of the Parliament, or is likely to be in conflict with any law or policy of the Union government, he may 'reserve' it for the consideration of the President of India.

Like the President, in the *judicial sphere*, he has 'prerogative of mercy'. He may grant pardon to a person convicted by the Court or may remit or commute the sentence, provided all judicial remedies have been exhausted and the matter falls within the executive authority of the State government. He can decide matters relating to the appointments, postings and promotions of district judges and other judicial officers. He enjoys personal immunity from all civil and criminal proceedings during his term of office.

In the *financial sphere*, he has some powers. A money bill can be introduced in the Vidhan Sabha with his recommendation. He causes the annual financial statement or budget of the State government laid before the Vidhan Sabha. The Contingency Fund of the State is at his disposal and he can make advances out of it to meet an unforeseen expenditure pending its authorisation by the State legislature.

Besides, the Governor has some discretionary powers. He may study the situation prevailing in his State and on the basis of his 'satisfaction' may advise the President to invoke Art. 356 of the Constitution. The Governors of Assam, Arunachal Pradesh and Nagaland have special powers to deal with anti-national elements. In case he is given the charge of an adjoining Union Territory, there he may act independently in the capacity of its Lt.-Governor or Administrator. He may permit initiation of legal proceedings against the serving or ex-Chief Minister involved in some alleged scandal or criminal wrong. In case he is satisfied that the Chief Minister has lost majority in the Vidhan Sabha, he may either dismiss him, or ask him to prove majority in the House at an early date.

The Governor acts in a dual capacity. On the one hand, he acts as the constitutional head of the State government. As such, he is expected to act on the advice of the Chief Minister. Here his position may be identified with the British monarch. But a critic may go to the extent of calling this post as a sinecure job or a gubernatorial assignment. Since the Governor has to act invariably on the advice of the Chief Minister, his position may be compared, in the words of a former Governor of UP (Mrs. Sarojini Naidu), with 'a bird in the golden cage'. On the other hand, the Governor acts like the agent or 'the eyes and the ears of the Centre.' Since he can live in office during the 'pleasure' of the President, he must look towards the Centre in each and every delicate or sensitive situation. Whenever a critical situation arises, the Governors rush to New Delhi and try to settle it in a way appreciable to the Central leaders.

The Governors spoil the image of their office by not according permission to prosecute an ex-Chief Minister or a Minister for political reasons. The provision of Sec. 197 of the Criminal Procedure Code remains unimplemented owing to the obstinate and clearly partisan view of the Council of Ministers on whose advice he acts. Thus, while sending a clear indication to the politicians in power, the Supreme Court ruled that the Governr could accord permission for the prosecution for an alleged illegal act even if his Ministry did not like it. Presiding over a Constitution Bench of five judges, Justice Variava observed: "Democracy itself will be at stake if the Governor refuses to accord sanction for prosecution against a Minister in matters where *prima facie* a clear case for prosecution is made out. It may then lead to a situation where people in power may break law with impunity."[2]

---

2. *The Times of India* (New Delhi) 6 September, 2004.

In 2005 the Governor of Bihar (Buta Singh) committed an act of great impropriety by advising the Centre to dissolve the Legislative Assembly as no party was in a position to form the government. He should have followed the established tradition of inviting the leader of the largest party to form the government and instructing him to seek confidence vote of the Assembly within a specified time. The view of the Governor was palatable to the Centre and so the Assembly was dissolved. It is the first instance when the elected representatives could not enter the House at all. The decision of the Governor was challenged in the Supreme Court. The Court held the Governor guilty of acting in 'undue haste'. His drastic and extreme action misled the Cabinet. The Constitution bench headed by Chief Justice Sabherwal passed serious strictures against the Governor and chided the Union Cabinet for acting on such a bad opinion of the Governor as a 'gospel truth'. Then, the Governor had to resign. It was editorially commented: "It is expected of such handpicked Governors that they protect the interests of their party rather than the Constitution."[3]

It is for this reason that the office of the Governor becomes the subject of criticism particularly when the State government is run by a party which is not in power at Centre. It is a fact that a person may serve as a Governor only when he manages to keep both the Prime Minister and the Chief Minister in good humour. A Governor has to go in case he forfeits the pleasure of the President implying the pleasure of the Prime Minister as happened with the Governors of Goa, Haryana, Gujarat and U.P. in July, 2004. It is also possible that sensing the mood of his Council of Ministers, the President may tacitly or indirectly advise the Governors to resign instead of facing premature exist. It is also a fact that a person in the good books of the Prime Minister may continue as a Governor either in a particular State or be shifted to another State with every prospect of reappointment. Keeping it all in view, this fact "must be accepted that the Governor today is the hare in a puppet show—his role depends upon what the man behind is doing with the strings."[4]

3. *The Times of India* (New Delhi), 26 January, 2006.

4. K.V. Rao: "The Role of State Governors in India" in *Indian Political Science Review*, Delhi, April-Sept., 1968, p. 175. Throwing light on the present state of affairs, Soli J. Sorabjee in a press statement said: "No institution has seen greater debasement than the office of the Governor. It has declined into a cheap political post. There have been many instances when ministers dismissed from the government for strictures passed on them, have got promotion to the office of the Governor." *The Times of India*, New Delhi, 19 January, 1995.

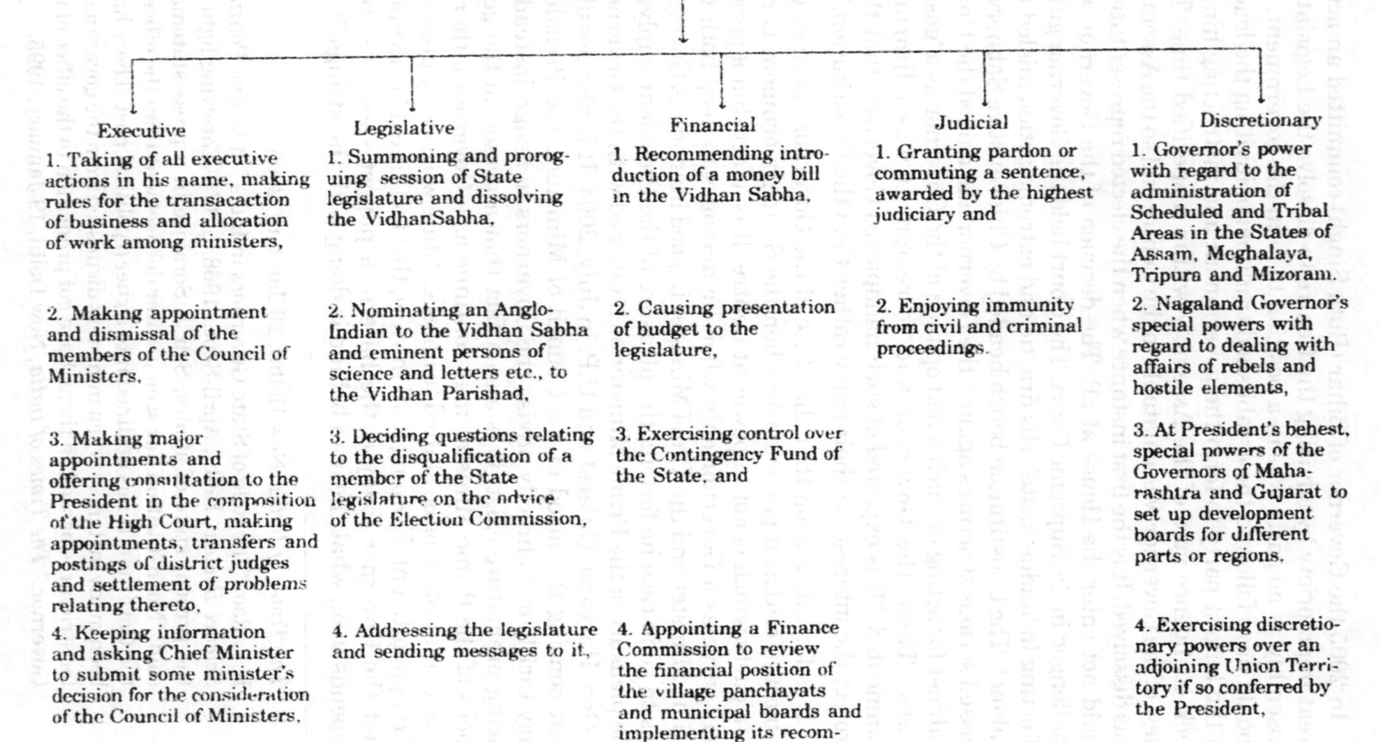
GOVERNOR'S FUNCTIONS AND POWERS
Executive
1. Taking of all executive actions in his name, making rules for the transacaction of business and allocation of work among ministers,
2. Making appointment and dismissal of the members of the Council of Ministers,
3. Making major appointments and offering consultation to the President in the composition of the High Court, making appointments, transfers and postings of district judges and settlement of problems relating thereto,
4. Keeping information and asking Chief Minister to submit some minister's decision for the consideration of the Council of Ministers,
Legislative
1. Summoning and proroguing session of State legislature and dissolving the VidhanSabha,
2. Nominating an Anglo-Indian to the Vidhan Sabha and eminent persons of science and letters etc., to the Vidhan Parishad,
3. Deciding questions relating to the disqualification of a member of the State legislature on the advice of the Election Commission,
4. Addressing the legislature and sending messages to it,
Financial
1. Recommending introduction of a money bill in the Vidhan Sabha,
2. Causing presentation of budget to the legislature,
3. Exercising control over the Contingency Fund of the State, and
4. Appointing a Finance Commission to review the financial position of the village panchayats and municipal boards and implementing its recommendations.
Judicial
1. Granting pardon or commuting a sentence, awarded by the highest judiciary and
2. Enjoying immunity from civil and criminal proceedings.
Discretionary
1. Governor's power with regard to the administration of Scheduled and Tribal Areas in the States of Assam, Meghalaya, Tripura and Mizoram.
2. Nagaland Governor's special powers with regard to dealing with affairs of rebels and hostile elements,
3. At President's behest, special powers of the Governors of Maharashtra and Gujarat to set up development boards for different parts or regions.
4. Exercising discretionary powers over an adjoining Union Territory if so conferred by the President,

5. Reporting to the President with regard to the breakdown of constitutional machinery in the State on the advice of the Chief Minister, and	5. Exercising veto power—absolute as well as suspensive and reserving a non-money bill for the consideration of the President,		**5. Reserving any bill for the consideration of the President in the name of its being in conflict with a law or policy of the Union Government,**
6. Acting as the Chancellor of State Universities.	6. Promulgation and revocation of ordinances, and		**6. Reporting to the President with regard to the breakdown of constitutional machinery in the State even without or against the advice of the Chief Minister,**
	7. Causing presentation of the reports of various bodies to the legislature for consideration.		**7. Taking decision in the event of a conflict between the Union and State Government over the issue of their respective executive authority.**
			8. Seeking instructions from the President before promulgating an ordinance dealing with certain important matters,
			9. Dissolving the Vidhan Sabha, and
			10. Allowing initiation of legal proceedings against the serving or former Chief Minister.

As constitutional head of a state government, the office of the Governor has its unique significance. Its holder must realise the moral aspect of his role. As President Abdul Kalam in his message to them observed: "The Governor's role is to distil the best aspirations of the people from the vicissitudes of politics. It is like preserving the light of Dharma; his office is like a beacon light in the affairs of the state... You have to decide whether you rise to be a first citizen or remain caged in the confines of your political or any other ancestry. If you continue to nurture certain affiliations, many will hesitate in approaching you with suggestions and problems. You will be isolated from a large number of people."[5]

Recommendations of the Governors Committee (1971)

On 30 November, 1970 the President (V.V. Giri) appointed a committee of five Governors to study and report on the appointment of the Council of Ministers by the Governor, for summoning, proroguing and dissolving the Vidhan Sabha, and failure of constitutional machinery in a State.[6]

It submitted its report on 26 November, 1971 having these important recommendations:

1. The functions and powers of the Governor are clearly laid down in the Constitution and, for this reason, he cannot be taken as the 'agent' of the Centre, even when State is under President's rule. He is expected to act on the aid and advice of the Council of Ministers, but in exceptional situations he may take action according to his discretionary powers. Mutual trust between the Governor and his Council of Ministers should be maintained.

2. If no party commands clear majority in the Vidhan Sabha, the Governor may invite the leader of the largest party to form the government. But it is not necessary in each case. On the basis of his independent judgement, he may choose a person for the post who may secure confidence vote of the House and run a stable government.

---

5. *The Times of India* (New Delhi), 15 June. 2005.

6. It consisted of the Governors of Jammu and Kashmir (Bhagwan Sahai), of Uttar Pradesh (B. Gopala Reddy), of Kerala (V. Vishwanathan), of Maharashtra (Ali Yavar Jung) and of West Bengal (S.S. Dhawan). The Governor of Jammu-Kashmir was its chairman.

3. A nominated member of the State legislature should not be appointed as the Chief Minister. In case a person appointed as the Chief Minister is not a legislator, he should get himself elected within the prescribed period of 6 months.
4. The advice of the Chief Minister for the dissolution of the Vidhan Sabha should not be accepted in case there is the possibility of forming an alternative government, or the budget is to be passed.
5. Only as a last resort, the Governor should recommend to the President for the invocation of emergency in his State under Art. 356.

Chief Minister and Council of Ministers

Since parliamentary form of government has been established in the States as at the Centre, so the provisions of the Constitution in this regard resemble, though we may come across certain variations as well. Art. 163 (1) says that there shall be a Council of Ministers with the Chief Ministers at the head to aid and advise the Governor in the exercise of his functions except in so far as he is by or under the Constitution required to exercise his functions or any of them in his discretion. It is given in Cl. (2) that if any question arises whether a matter falls within his discretionary power, his decision shall be final. Last, Cl(3) makes it clear that the advice tendered by the Ministers shall not be inquired into any court. Then, Art. 164, as affected by the 91st Amendment of 2003, lays down:

1. The Governor shall appoint the Chief Minister and appoint other ministers on the advice of the Chief Minister and they shall hold office during the pleasure of the Governor. But in the States of Madhya Pradesh, Bihar and Orissa there shall be a Minister in-charge of tribal welfare who shall also look after the welfare of the Scheduled Castes and other backward classes or any other work.

(1A) The total number of the Ministers, including the Chief Minister, shall not exceed fifteen per cent of the total number of the members of the Vidhan Sabha of that State, provided that the total number of the Ministers, including the Chief Minister, shall not be less than twelve.

(1B) A defector cannot be appointed as a Minister unless he seeks re-election or the House of which he was a member is dissolved, whichever earlier.

2. The Council of Ministers shall be collectively responsible to the Vidhan Sabha.

3. The Governor shall administer the oaths of office and secrecy to all the Ministers and after that they shall enter upon their office.

4. If a Minister is not a member of the legislature of his State at the time of his appointment, he must have its membership within a period of six consecutive months.

5. The salaries and allowances of the Ministers shall be determined by a law of the State legislature and until so determined, shall be as specified in the second schedule of the Constitution.

The Chief Minister is the real head of the State government. He is appointed by the Governor. In accordance with the principle of parliamentary government, the Chief Minister must be the leader of the party having majority in the Vidhan Sabha. In case a political party manages to secure clear majority in the Vidhan Sabha, its leader is invited by the Governor to form the government. In case no party gets absolute majority in the Vidhan Sabha, then a coalition government is formed. Two or more parties may form a coalition and then their chosen leader is invited by the Governor to form the government. If no party gets clear majority and there is no chance of the formation of a coalition government either, the Governor may advise the President to invoke Art. 356. The Governor appoints ministers on the advice of the Chief Minister. Since the ministry lives in office during the 'pleasure' of the Governor, he may dismiss the Chief Minister in case he forfeits the claim of being the leader of the party having majority in the Vidhan Sabha, or when there is a serious split in the ranks of the party having clear majority there.

Like the Prime Minister at the Centre, the Chief Minister is the real head of the State government. He advises the Governor to appoint ministers and deputy ministers and to distribute portfolios among them. He may advise the Governor to dismiss a minister in case he differs from the policy and working of the Council of Ministers. He acts as the channel of communication between the

Governor and the Council of Ministers and also between the Council of Ministers and the State legislature. He advises the Governor to make high appointments, to summon the session of the State legislature, and to dissolve the Vidhan Sabha.

However, his actual position depends upon three situational variables. In case he is a powerful leader of the party having comfortable majority in the Vidhan Sabha and is also in the good books of the Prime Minister, he behaves like a 'showman' of his government. All ministers work under his leadership and the Vidhan Sabha cannot present to him a formidable challenge. In case he is a strong leader of the party having comfortable majority in the Vidhan Sabha but in opposition at the Centre, his position becomes weak owing to the hostile attitude of the Central government. In such a situation he manages to act like a 'spokesman' of his party. With tact as well as with worldly wisdom, he may prove his strong hold over the government of the State. But in case he is the leader of a coalition government with different constituents pulling in different directions coupled with the hostile attitude of the Centre, his position is quite vulnerable on every front and thus he plays, in the words of Jyoti Basu, the role of a 'postman'. The experiences of the days of Congress hegemony show that most of the Chief Ministers happily devalued themselves as 'chief messengers' of the supreme leader of their party and the Prime Minister of the country.

The Council of Ministers is the team headed by the Chief Minister to aid and advise the Governor in the exercise of his functions, except where he has the power to act in his discretion, and it is collectively responsible to the Vidhan Sabha. It is necessary that all ministers must be the members of the State legislature. In case the Chief Minister or any minister is not a member of the legislature, he must secure its membership within a period of 6 consecutive months. It is also given that in the States of Bihar, Orissa and Madhya Pradesh, there shall be a minister in charge of tribal welfare who may in addition be in charge of the welfare of the Scheduled Castes and backward classes or any other work.

The Council of Ministers is the policy-making body. The Chief Minister presides over the meetings of the cabinet and every member is bound to honour the decisions taken therein. In the event of differences of views, the minister should resign. The Governor may refer any important matter for the consideration of the Council of Ministers. If a question arises whether there is any matter in respect of which the Governor is required to act in his discretion, the decision of the Governor shall be final and thevalidity of anything done by the Governor shall not be called in question. The question whether any, and if so what, advice was tendered by the ministers to the Governor shall not be inquired into any court. In case the Governor asks for any information relating to the affairs of administration or proposals for legislation, the Chief Minister is duty bound to supply it to him. However, the 'pleasure' of the Governor does not involve the element of arbitrariness or anything like subjective assessment, because it is for the Legislative Assembly to enforce the principle of collective responsibility.

Legislature

Each State of the Indian Union has a Vidhan Sabha, but six States (Bihar, UP, Karnataka, Maharashtra, Jammu-Kashmir and Andhra Pradesh) have an upper chamber (Vidhan Parishad) as well. As per Art. 169, the Centre has the power to create or abolish Vidhan Parishad in case a resolution to this effect is passed by the Vidhan Sabha of that State by special majority (absolute majority of the whole House as well as 2/3 majority of the members, present and voting). Hence, the Parliament made laws to abolish the Vidhan Parishads of West Bengal, Punjab, Andhra Pradesh and Tamil Nadu. It is also possible that the Centre may adopt a dilatory attitude and in the meantime the newly constituted Vidhan Sabha may rescind the earlier resolution and thereby save the Vidhan Parishad as happened in the cases of UP and Bihar. It is also possible that a Vidhan Parishad may not be created in a State in spite of its provision in the Constitution as we may note in the case of Madhya Pradesh.

It was recreated by an act of Parliament in Tamilnadu in 2010, but it has not yet been established there.

Vidhan Parishad: The strength of Vidhan Parishad varies from State to State. It is provided that the strength of the Vidhan Parishad may be at least 40 and at most not more than one-third of the strength of the Vidhan Sabha of the State. The composition of this chamber is determined by a formula involving the method of indirect election in some and direct election in some other categories, leaving the case of some members to be nominated by the Governor. It is as under:

1. About one-third members are elected by the Vidhan Sabha from amongst persons who are not its members.
2. About one-third members are elected by the local bodies of the State like municipal boards, zila parishads or any other authority as specified in a law of Parliament.

3. About one-twelfth members are elected by persons of at least 3 years' standing as teachers in educational institutions not lower in standard than that of a secondary school.
4. About one-twelfth members are elected by the university graduates of at least 3 years standing in the State.
5. About one-sixth members are nominated by the Governor from amongst persons possessing special knowledge of or experience in the fields of art, literature, science, social service and cooperative movement.

A member of the Vidhan Parishad must have three qualifications. First, he must be a citizen of India. Second, he must be above 30 years of age. Last, he must possess all other qualifications as laid down in a law of Parliament. A person cannot be a member of both the Houses of Parliament, or of both the Houses of State legislature, or of a House of a State legislature and a House of Parliament at one and the same time. The Vidhan Parishad is a permanent chamber. Its one-third members retire after every second year. As such a member enjoys a tenure of six years. He may be re-elected any number of times. The Parishad elects its Chairman and Deputy Chairman.

Composition of Vidhan Parishads

States	*Total Seats*	*Nom. by Governor*	*Elections*			
			by Assembly	*by Local Bodies*	*by Teachers*	*by Graduates*
1. Bihar	75	12	27	24	6	6
2. Uttar Pradesh	100	10	36	38	8	8
3. Karnataka	75	11	25	25	7	7
4. Maharashtra	78	12	31	21	7	7
5. Jammu-Kashmir	36	6	21	7	2	--
6. Andhra Pradesh	90	12	31	31	8	8
7. Madhya Pradesh	90	12	31	31	8	8
8. Tamilnadu	78	12	26	26	7	7

The Vidhan Parishad has no effective powers. It has to pass a money bill passed by the Vidhan Sabha within 14 days and a non-money bill passed by the Vidhan Sabha within 3 months. In case the Vidhan Parishad rejects or returns a non-money bill, the Vidhan Sabha may readopt it and the Vidhan Parishad has to pass it within a period of one month. There is no provision for joint sitting in such a matter. A money bill cannot be introduced in the Vidhan Parishad. In case it returns it, the Vidhan Sabha may pass it again after accepting or rejecting such recommendations. The Council of Ministers is collectively responsible to the Vidhan Sabha. As such, it may put the government to some inconvenience at the most by throwing critical light on its acts of commission and omission. The members of this House do not take part in the election of the President and of the members of the Rajya Sabha. In short, the Vidhan Parishad cannot override the will of the Vidhan Sabha. Keeping in view its insignificant position and condemning it as a rendezvous of retired and burnt-out politicians, it is said that the Vidhan Parishads are not even like an ornamental chamber. "Should they prove inoffensive, they might be retained. If not, they can be abolished without much trouble".[7]

Vidhan Sabha: But the Vidhan Sabha is the popular and powerful chamber of the State legislature. It may have at the most 500 members and at the least 60 members depending upon the demographic composition of the State. (The strength of the Vidhan Sabhas is specified in a law of the Parliament that may fix a strength of even less than 60). The members are elected directly by the voters of the State, but the Governor may nominate one Anglo-Indian as a member in order to give representation to this community. Some seats are reserved for Scheduled Castes and Scheduled Tribes except in the State of Assam where special provisions have been made for the sake of Scheduled Tribes. After each census the total number of seats in each State and the division of seats into territorial constituencies is readjusted by the Election Commission in accordance with the law of Parliament. It is essential that the ratio between the population of each constituency and the number of seats allotted to it must be, as far as practicable, same throughout the State.

A member of the Vidhan Sabha must be a citizen of India; he must be above 25 years of age; and that he must fulfil all other qualifications as laid down in an act of Parliament. No person can be a member of the two Houses, including the Parliament, or some other State legislature at the same time. The normal term of the Vidhan Sabha is of five years. It begins from the date of its first meeting. In case proclamation of emergency is in force, the Parliament may extend the life of Vidhan Sabha by one year by making a law in this regard. Such a law may be renewed again and

7. M.P. Sharma: *The Government of the Indian Republic,* V ed., p. 256.

again. But within 6 months of the termination of emergency, elections must take place. The Governor has the power to dissolve the Vidhan Sabha at any time. In case Art. 356 of the Constitution is invoked, it depends upon the text of the proclamation of emergency to place the Vidhan Sabha under 'suspended animation' or to effect its dissolution. The House elects its Speaker and Deputy Speaker who are accountable to it. That, is, the Vidhan Sabha may remove its presiding officers by passing a vote of no-confidence against them by its absolute majority.

As already pointed out, the Vidhan Sabha is a powerful chamber. A money bill and a budget are introduced in it. Its members take part in the election of the President of India and of the members of the Rajya Sabha and the Vidhan Parishad (if it is there) in accordance with proportional representation with single transferable vote system. Since the ministry is accountable to the Vidhan Sabha, it may throw out the government by passing a vote of no-confidence against it. It may express its lack of confidence in the government by rejecting an official bill, or by making a cut in the budget, or by disapproving the policy of the cabinet, or by passing the motion of censure. It considers reports submitted by the State Public Service Commission, Auditor-General, State Human Rights Commission, State Women Commission etc. In case the Centre desires to make alteration in the name, area or boundary lines of a State, the President shall refer that proposal to know the view of its Vidhan Sabha before recommending its introduction in the Parliament. He may also fix a time limit within which the Vidhan Sabha has to give its view. The Vidhan Sabha gives its view on such a proposal, but the Centre is not bound to honour it. In the case of a constitutional amendment bill referred to it for ratification under Art. 368, it passes a resolution by simple majority to endorse it or not.

On the whole, the position of the State legislatures is very weak. They can make a law on a subject of the State List. They can make a law on a subject of the Concurrent List also. In case a law on a subject of the Concurrent List has already been made by the Centre, then the bill passed by the State legislature shall be 'reserved' by the Governor for the consideration of the President of India. Moreover, in the event of any conflict between the Central law and the State law on a matter of Concurrent List, the former shall prevail and the latter shall remain inoperative to the extent of being repugnant to the former. We have also seen conditions in which the Centre can make a law on a subject of the State List and here in the event of any conflict between the Central law and State law, the latter shall remain 'suspended' to the extent of being repugnant to the former and be effective again after the revocation of the former. It may also be kept in view that the Governor is duty bound to keep any bill passed by the State legislature 'reserved' for the consideration of the President in case he finds it likely to be in conflict with any law or policy of the Centre. Thus, the operation of the legislative process at the Central as well as at the State levels "reinforces the Union predominance in the legislative field".[8]

Allocation of Seats in State Legislative Assemblies

States	*Seats*	*States*	*Seats*
1. Andhra Pradesh	294	2. Assam	126
3. Bihar	243	4. Chhattisgarh	90
5. Gujarat	182	6. Haryana	90
7. Himachal Pradesh	68	8. Jammu-Kashmir	89
9. Jharkhand	81	10. Karnataka	224
11. Kerala	140	12. Madhya Pradesh	230
13. Maharashtra	288	14. Manipur	60
15. Meghalaya	60	16. Nagaland	60
17. Orissa	147	18. Punjab	117
19. Rajasthan	200	20. Sikkim	32
21. Tamil Nadu	234	22. Tripura	60
23. Uttar Pradesh	403	24. Uttarakhand	70
25. West Bengal	294	26. Mizoram	40
27. Arunachal Pradesh	60	28. Goa	40

Though the component units of a federal system, the State governments do not have the type of autonomy that is enjoyed by the states of America or the cantons of Switzerland. There are many inroads through which the Centre may exercise its dominance over the States in normal as well as abnormal times. Not only this, the States must carry out the directives sent to them by the Centre, otherwise it would be taken as the 'breakdown of constitutional machinery' there and then the Centre shall have the power to

8. Alice Jacob: "Centre-State Relations in the Indian Federal System" in Jain, Kashyap and Srinivasan (ed.) *The Union and the States*, p. 31.

dismiss a State government under Art. 356. The President is the head of the Indian republic and the Governor, while being the constitutional head of the State government, acts as the 'eyes and the ears' of the Centre. Despite this all, our State governments cannot be identified with the provinces of Canada which, in the words of Dawson, 'are like glorified municipalities'. It is true that such a statement has now become outdated as the Canadian provinces have gained more powers, still they have no autonomy as is available to the states of America, Australia and Germany. In fine, the position of the States of the Indian Union falls somewhere between the states of America on the one side and of the provinces of Canada on the other.

Union Territories

Originally known as the 'Scheduled Districts' under the Scheduled Districts Act of 1874 and then as Chief Commissioners' Provinces, and finally, as 'Part C' and 'Part D' States in the post-independence period, certain areas under the direct control of the Centre have assumed the nomenclature of 'Union Territories' after the enforcement of the Seventh Constitution Amendment Act in 1956. The peculiarity of the establishment of these central enclaves may be discovered in a variety of reasons like special treatment and care of the very backward and tribal people, or a pattern of cultural distinctiveness as applicable to the former Portuguese and French possessions like Daman and Diu and Pondicherry respectively, or some strategic consideration applicable to the case of Andaman and Nicobar Islands and Lakshadweep and, finally, purely political and administrative considerations which may be seen in the inclusion of Chandigarh and Delhi in this category. That is, a variety of reasons may be traced for the placement of certain parts of the country under the direct control of the Government of India.

Save as otherwise provided by a law of Parliament, every Union Territory shall be administered by the President, acting to such an extent as he thinks fit, through an Administrator to be appointed by him with such designation as he may specify. The President may appoint the Governor of a State as the Administrator of the adjoining Union Territory and where a Governor is so appointed, he shall exercise his functions as its Administrator independently of his Council of Ministers. The status of the Administrator is not similar to that of the Governor or the Government of a State.

The President may make regulations for the peace, progress and good government of the Union Territories of the Andaman and Nicobar Islands, Lakshadweep, Dadra and Nagar Haveli, Daman and Diu and Pondicherry. Provided that when any body is created under Art. 239 A to function as a Legislature for the Union Territory of Pondicherry, the President shall not make any regulation for the peace, progress and good government of that Union Territory with effect from the date appointed for the first meeting of the Legislature. Provided further that whenever the body functioning as a Legislature for the Union Territory of Pondicherry is dissolved, or the functioning of that body as such Legislature remains suspended on account of any action taken under any such law as referred to in clause (1) of article 239 A, the President may, during the period of such dissolution or suspension, make regulations for the peace, progress and good government of that Union Territory. Any regulation so made may repeal or amend any Act made by Parliament or any other law which is for the time being applicable to the Union Territory and, when promulgated by the President, shall have the same force and effect as an Act of Parliament which applies to that territory. The regulation-making power of the President is plenary and a regulation can be made for a Union Territory on all subjects on which Parliament can make laws. Thus, a regulation can be issued on any item of the Union List, Concurrent List, or State List. The Supreme Court has held that when a law prevalent in a State is extended to a Union Territory under this provision, and if the said law is declared unconstitutional as being beyond the legislative competence of the enacting State, the Act in the Union Territory will not be affected, for there the question is to be judged not with reference to the power of the State legislature but with reference to that of Parliament.

Finally, the Parliament may by law constitute a High Court for a Union Territory or declare any court in any territory to be a High Court for all or any of the purposes of this Constitution. Delhi has its High Court, while all other Union Territories have been put under the jurisdiction of the High Court of an adjacent State.

Art. 239 A provides for the creation of a Legislative Assembly and a Council of Ministers or both for the Union Territory of Pondicherry. Thus, Parliament may by law provide for it a body, whether elected or partly nominated and partly elected, to function as its Legislature, or a Council of Ministers or both with such constitution, powers and functions as may be specified in the law.

The Sixty-ninth Constitution Amendment Act of 1991 provides for a special set-up for Delhi renamed as National Capital Territory of Delhi. The Administrator of Delhi shall be designated as the Lt.-Governor. It shall have a Legislative Assembly consisting of the members directly elected by the people of the Territory from territorial constituencies. The total number of seats in the Assembly, the division of the territory into territorial constituencies and the reservation of seats for Scheduled Castes and all other matters relating to the functioning of the Assembly shall be regulated by a law of Parliament. In matters of election the provisions of Part XV (relating to the jurisdiction and powers of the Election Commission) shall apply, but any reference to 'appropriate Legislature' shall be deemed to be a reference to the Parliament of India. Subject to the provisions of the Constitution, the Assembly of Delhi shall have the power to make laws for the whole territory of Delhi or any of its parts with respect to any matter contained in the Concurrent List and State List in so far as any such matter is applicable to Union Territories except matters with respect to entries 1 (public order), 2 (police), and 18 (land revenue and land acquisition) of the State List and entries 64 (offences against laws), 65 (courts), and 66 (fees other than court fees) of the same List in so far as they relate to the said entries 1, 2 and 18. But nothing shall derogate from the powers of Parliament to make laws with respect to any matter for a Union Territory or any part thereof.

It provides a Council of Ministers consisting of not more than ten per cent of the total number of members in the Legislative Assembly, with the Chief Minister at the head to aid and advise the Lt.-Governor in the exercise of his functions in relation to matters with respect to which the Legislative Assembly has the power to make laws, except in so far as he is by or under the law, required to act in his discretion. Provided that in the case of difference of opinion between the Lt.-Governor and his Ministers on any matter, the Lt.-Governor shall refer it to the President for decision and act according to the decision given thereon by the President and, pending such decision, it shall be competent for the Lt.-Governor in any case where the matter in his opinion is so urgent that it is necessary for him to take such action, or give such direction in the matter as he deems necessary. The Chief Minister shall be appointed by the President and the other Ministers shall be appointed by the President on the advice of the Chief Minister and the Ministers shall hold office during the pleasure of the President. The Council of Ministers shall be collectively responsible to the Legislative Assembly.

Finally, we come to Art. 239AB that provides for President's rule in the case of failure of constitutional machinery. If the President on the receipt of a report from the Lt.-Governor or otherwise is satisfied that a situation has arisen in which the administration of the National Capital Territory of Delhi cannot be carried on in accordance with the provisions of article 239AA or any law made in pursuance of that article; or that for the proper administration of the National Capital Territory, it is necessary or expedient to do so, the President may by order suspend the operation of any provision of article 239 AA or of all or any of the provisions of any law made in pursuance of that article for such period and subject to such conditions as may be specified in such law and make such incidental and consequential provisions as may appear to him to be necessary or expedient for administering the National Capital Territory.

It is obvious that a difficult feature of the administrative system of 7 Union Territories finds place in the sphere of great diversity. That is, there is no uniformity in matters of administration as we find in the case of the States of the Indian Union. We may put the administrative set-up of the Union Territories into three categories. First, the administrative set-up of Delhi is of a very developed type. It has its Legislative Assembly, Council of Ministers and High Court. Second, comes the case of Puducherry that has its Legislative Assembly and the Council of Ministers, but is attached to the High Court of Madras. The common point is that both Delhi and Puducherry are under the headship of a Lt.-Governor and a bill passed by the Assembly shall be reserved by him for the consideration of the President. Last, the remaining five Union Territories are bereft of any popular set up. Here the highest functionary is the Chief Commissioner or the Administrator who is assisted by advisory committees. The purpose of these committees is to discuss matters relating to the interest of that territory and then refer it to the Union Home Ministry for necessary action.

Administrative Set-Up of Union Territories

	Union Territories	*Executive*	*Public Services*	*Legislature*	*Judiciary*
1.	Andman and Nicobar Islands	Chief Commissioner	Recruitment through UPSC	X	Under Calcutta High Court
2.	Chandigarh	Chief Commissioner	"	X	Under Punjab and Haryana High Court
3.	Dadra and Nagar Haveli	Administrator	"	X	Under Bombay High Court
4.	Delhi	1. Lt.-Governor 2. Chief Minister 3. Council of Ministers	"	Legislative Assembly	High Court
5.	Daman and Diu	Administrator	"	X	Under Gujarat High Court
6.	Lakshadweep	Administrator	"	X	Under Kerala High Court
7.	Puducherry	1. Lt.-Governor 2. Chief Minister 3. Council of Ministers	"	Legislative Assembly	Under Madras High Court

The administration of all the Union Territories is under the control of the Union Government. That, is, these units have no autonomy as is available to the States of the Indian Union.[9] The Lt.-Governor does not act as the nominal head like the Governor of a State, rather he acts like the agent of the President. The Parliament is competent to make law on any item of the three Lists for the Union Territories. Here the system is of unitary type and the existence of Legislative Assembly or Council of Ministers does not diminish the constitutional position of the Union Government. Thus, the "truly distinguishing attribute of a Union Territory is its direct administration by the Central Government and, in this way, existence of these Territories constitutes a conspicuous departure from federalism in India; the government of India is plainly unitary in so far as the relationship between New Delhi and these Central Enclaves is concerned."[10]

Undeniable is the fact that the administrative system of these seven Union Territories is full of several structural deficiencies which demand progress in the direction of remodelling their administration. It may, however, be borne in mind that the policy of the Union Government has been to develop the administration of these special areas in a way so that eventually they get Statehood as has happened in the cases of Himachal Pradesh, Manipur, Tripura, Arunachal Pradesh, Mizoram and Goa. The notable point in this regard is that the people of Union Territories either desire a progress towards Statehood or retention of the existing arrangement but not at all their amalgamation with an adjoining State of the Indian Union.

Democratic Decentralisation

A democratic polity involves decentralisation or deconcentration of powers in a way that the local affairs of the people are managed

---

9. In 1994 Municipal Corporation has been provided to the Union Territory of Chandigarh. The Union Territories of Andaman and Nicobar Islands, Daman and Diu Dadra and Nagar Haveli and Lakshadweep have an Advisory Council each headed by the Administrator. These bodies have the right to discuss and make recommendations about matters in so far as they relate to their respective territories.

10. S.R. Maheshwari: *State Governments in India*, p. 118.

by means of their positive participation. Known by the popular name of democratic decentralisation, it implies extension of democracy at the grass-roots level in view of the fact that people's participation signifies the constitution of a democratic government not merely at the top but also at the foundation-level of the political system. It signifies marked devolution of power from the higher to the lower levels in a way that the units of local government exercise their power with the participation of the people of that area with occasional control and supervision of the provincial and central governments. Thus, Panchayati Raj was introduced in our country in the light of the recommendations of the Balwantray Mehta Committee Report (1957) which failed to achieve the desired result. Hence, the government of Rajiv Gandhi introduced the 64th and the 65th Constitution Amendment Bills in the Lok Sabha in 1989 which, though passed by it, could not be adopted in the Rajya Sabha. The effort failed. The government of P.V. Narsimha Rao took up the issue with the same motive and the two bills moved in the Parliament could be adopted which became the 73rd and the 74th Constitution Amendment Acts of 1992 now placed in Part IX and Part IX A of the Constitution.[11]

Village Panchayats: The 73rd Constitution Amendment Act inserts provisions into Part IX of the Constitution. It empowers the State Legislatures to make laws for the organisation of Panchayats at the village level as well as at the higher levels of a district. Such laws shall define the mode of composition, strength of the members including reservation of seats for Scheduled Castes, Scheduled Tribes and other weaker sections of the community. The members shall be elected directly by the voters of the territorial constituencies, but the law of the State shall lay down the method of the inclusion of the MPs and MLAs of that area in such bodies and the representation of the chairpersons of such bodies at the intermediate or higher levels of Panchayati Raj in a district. The chairperson of a village Panchayat shall be elected directly by the voters of a constituency, but the law of the State government shall determine the method of the election of the chairpersons of higher units of Panchayati Raj in a district. The law of the State Government shall

11. The original Constitution of India had Part IX relating to the administration of the territories belonging to Part D of the First Schedule and other territories not specified there. It was deleted by the Seventh Constitution Amendment Act, 1956.

also provide for reservation of seats for Scheduled Castes (excluding Arunachal Pradesh) and Scheduled Tribes in proportion to their population in the State, but 1/3 seats shall be reserved for women under such a category. The reservation system shall come to an end if the provision for such reservations, as given in Art. 334 of the Constitution, comes to an end.

The normal duration of a Panchayat has been fixed at 5 years from the date of its first meeting. But the State government shall have the power to dissolve it earlier. If so happens, next elections shall take place within 6 months, provided that where the remainder of the period for which the dissolved Panchayat would have continued is less than 6 months, it shall not be necessary to hold any election under this clause for constituting it. But a new Panchayat constituted upon the dissolution before the expiration of its duration shall continue only for the remainder of the period for which the dissolved Panchayat would have continued, had it not been dissolved. A person shall be disqualified for being a member of the Panchayat if he holds any office of profit under the Central or State government, or is declared by a competent court to be of unsound mind, or is an undischarged insolvent, or is not a citizen of India, or is disqualified under any law in force. Any dispute of this kind shall be referred to the Governor and his decision shall be final.

The State Legislatures may make laws for the conferment of such powers and authority on these bodies as may be necessary to enable them to function as units of self-government and such a law may contain provision for the devolution of powers and responsibilities upon Panchayats at the appropriate level, subject to such conditions as may be specified thereunder, with respect to:

(*i*) the preparation of the plans for economic development and social justice and (*ii*) the implementation of schemes for economic development and social justice as may be entrusted to them including those in relating to the matters listed in Schedule XI. The State legislatures may also make a law to:

(a) authorise a Panchayat to levy, collect and appropriate such taxes, duties, tolls and fees in accordance with such procedure and subject to such limits;

(b) assign to a Panchayat such taxes, duties, tolls and fees levied and collected by the State Government for such purposes and subject to such conditions and limits;

(c) provide for making such grants-in-aid to the Panchayats from the Consolidated Fund of the State; and

(d) provide for constitution of such Funds for crediting all moneys received respectively by or on behalf of the Panchayats, and also for the withdrawal of such money therefrom, as may be specified in the law.

However, the most important feature of this arrangement is related to financial autonomy granted to such bodies. Within one year of the commencement of this Amendment Act and thereafter at the expiration of every fifth year, the Governor shall have the power to set up a Finance Commission to review the financial position of the Panchayats and to make recommendations to the Governor as (a) to the principles which shall govern (i) the distribution between the State and the Panchayats of the net proceeds of the taxes, duties, tolls and fees leviable by the State, which may be divided between them under this part and the allocation between the Panchayats of all levels of their respective shares of such proceeds, (ii) the determination of the taxes, duties, tolls and fees which may be assigned to or appropriated by the Panchayats, (iii) the grants-in-aid to the Panchayats from the Consolidated Fund of the State; (b) any other matter referred to the Finance Commission by the Governor in the interest of sound finance of the Panchayats. The composition, jurisdiction and the procedure of working of the Finance Commission shall be determined by the law of the State. It shall submit its report to the Governor who shall cause it to be laid before the State legislature together with an explanatory memorandum as to the action taken thereon. The State Legislature shall also make law for the maintenance of accounts of these bodies under the superintendence, direction and control of the Chief Electoral Officer of the State.

The provisions of this Constitution Amendment Act may apply to the Union Territories as well with any number of exceptions and modification made by the President of India in it. But these provisions shall not be applicable to the States of Nagaland, Meghalaya, Mizoram, Tripura, Arunachal Pradesh, the Hill Areas in the State of Manipur and the Hill Areas of the District of Darjeeling in West Bengal. The Legislatures of these States may empower the District Councils with such facilities for the sake of decentralisation of power after passing a resolution by absolute majority of the whole House and 2/3 majority of the members, present and voting. The State Legislature shall also provide by law for the settlement of electoral disputes, but the delimitation of constituencies and the allotment of seats in these bodies shall not be questioned in any court of law.

This Act introduces XI Schedule into the Constitution conferring 29 functions on Panchayats as agriculture and agricultural extension, land improvement and soil conservation, minor irrigation and water management, animal husbandry, fisheries, social and farm forestry, minor forest produce, small-scale industries, khadi and cottage industries, rural housing, drinking water, fuel and fodder, roads and other means of communication (like bridges, ferries, waterways etc.) rural electrifcation, non-conventional energy sources, poverty alleviation programmes, primary and secondary education, technical training and vocational education, adult and non-formal education, libraries, cultural activities, markets and fairs, health and sanitation including primary dispensaries and health centres, family welfare, women and child development, social welfare, welfare of the weaker sections, public distribution system, and maintenance of community assets.

Municipalities: The 74th Constitution Amendment Act inserts Part IX A as to specify the organisation and working of local self-government in the urban areas known by the name of Nagar Panchayats or municipalities/municipal boards/councils/corporations. The State Legislature shall by law determine the strength of these bodies, the number of seats reserved for Scheduled Castes, Scheduled Tribes and other weaker sections of the community in proportion to their population in the State, including women. These members shall be elected directly by the voters of the territorial constituencies including the chairpersons of such bodies. The State Legislatures may by law also provide for the making of committees at the ward level or other levels within the territorial area of the Municipality including their powers and the elections of their chairpersons.

The accounts of the Municipal Corporations or boards shall be subject to auditing according to the rules framed by the Governor after consulting the Comptroller and Auditor-General of India. The Comptroller and Auditor-General of India shall cause the accounts of the said Municipal Corporation or board to be audited in such a manner as he may deem fit and the report of the Comptroller and Auditor-General shall be submitted to the Governor of the State who shall cause it to be laid before the Legislature of his State and the Municipal Corporation concerned.

The normal tenure of these bodies shall be of five years from the date of their first meeting. In case a body is dissolved earlier, election shall be held within next six months from the date of dissolution. Provided where the remainder of the period for which the dissolved body would have continued is less than six months, it shall not be necessary to hold any election under the clause for constituting it. But such a body constituted upon its dissolution before the expiration of its duration shall continue only for the remainder of the period for which the dissolved body would have continued. A person shall be disqualified from the membership of this body if he holds any office of profit under the Central or State government, is declared of unsound mind by a competent court, is an undischarged insolvent, is not a citizen of India, or is disqualified under any law in force. Any dispute of this kind shall be referred to the Governor whose decision shall be final.

Subject to the provisions of the Constitution, the State Legislatures may by law endow (a) the Municipalities with such powers and authority as may be necessary to enable them to function as institutions of local self-government and such law may contain provisions for the devolution of powers and responsibilities upon Municipalities subject to such conditions as may be specified therein with respect to (i) the preparation of plans for economic development and social justice, (ii) the performance of functions and the implementation of schemes as may be entrusted to them including those in relation to the matters listed in Schedule XII, (b) the Committees with such powers and authority as may be necessary to enable them to carry out the responsibilities conferred upon them including those in relation to matters listed in Schedule XII. Besides, the State Legislature may by its law (a) authorise a Municipality to levy, collect and appropriate such taxes, duties, tolls and fees in accordance with such procedure and subject to such limits, (b) assign to a Municipality such taxes, duties, tolls and fees levied and collected by the State Government for such purposes and subject to such conditions and limits, (c) provide for making such grants-in-aid to the Municipalities from the Consolidated Fund of the State and (d) provide for constitution of such funds for crediting all moneys received respectively by or on behalf of the Municipalities and also for the withdrawal of such money therefrom as may be specified in the law.

Within one year of the commencement of this Act and thereafter at the expiration of every fifth year, the Governor shall set up a

Finance Commission to review the financial position of these bodies and to make recommendations as to (a) the principles which should govern (i) the distribution between the State and the Municipalities of the net proceeds of the taxes, duties, tolls and fees leviable by the States, which may be divided between them under this part and the allocation between the Municipalities at all levels of their respective shares of such proceeds, (ii) the determination of the taxes, duties, tolls and fees which may be assigned or appropriated by the Municipalities, (iii) the grants-in-aid to the Municipalities from the Consolidated Fund of the State, (b) any other matter referred to the Finance Commission by the Governor in the interest of sound finance of these bodies. Moreover, the State Legislature shall by law define the composition, strength and procedure of working of the Finance Commission. It shall submit its report to the Governor who shall cause it to be laid before the State Legislature with an explanatory memorandum as to the action taken thereon.

The State Legislatures shall have the power to make laws relating to elections to these bodies under the superintendence, direction and control of the chief electoral officer of the State. The provisions of this Act shall apply to all Union Territories and the President of India shall have the power to make necessary alterations or modifications in their application. But the validity of any law relating to the delimitation of constituencies or the allotment of seats shall not be questioned in any court. The State Legislatures shall make law for the settlement of election disputes. The provision of this Act shall not apply to the existing municipalities, but the State Legislatures shall have the power to dissolve them before the expiration of their term and to implement the provisions of this Constitution Amendment Act. The provisions of this Act (the 74th Constitution Amendment Act of 1992) shall not apply to Scheduled and Tribal Areas, though the Parliament shall have the power to apply them to such areas with some exceptions and modifications.

It inserts Schedule XII into the Constitution which assigns 18 functions to Municipalities as urban or town planning, regulation of land use and building construction, planning for economic and social development, roads and bridges, water supply for domestic and commercial purposes, public health and sanitation including conservancy and solid waste management, fire service, urban forestry and promotion of ecological aspects, safeguarding the interests of weaker sections of society including physically handicapped and mentally retarded, slum improvement and upgrading, urban poverty alleviation, urban recreational facilities, promotion of cultural and educational activities, burial and cremation grounds, cattle pounds and prevention of cruelty to animals, and vital statistics including registration of births and deaths.

Critical Appreciation: The structure of the Panchayati Raj, according to the provisions of the Seventy-third Constitution Amendment Act is required to be a three-tiered one with elected bodies at the village, block and district levels. While one-third of all the seats are reserved for women, reservations for Scheduled Castes and Scheduled Tribes have been provided in proportion to their population at each level. This Act came into effect on 24 April, 1993 and it was stipulated that all the States (excluding Jammu-Kashmir, Meghalaya, Mizoram, Nagaland and certain Scheduled Areas of some other States) should either make new laws or suitably amend their existing laws so as to bring them in conformity with the provisions of this Amendment Act. To facilitate quick action by the States, the Union Ministry of Rural Development had circulated a model bill prepared by the National Institute of Rural Development, Hyderabad. Happily this could be done within a year and 24th April, 1994 became 'a day to remember'. Consequently, elections to the institutions of Panchayati Raj took place within next six months and the State Governments set up their Election Commission and Finance Commission for the specified purposes. Thus, the task of granting constitutional status to Panchayati Raj is now accomplished.

No doubt, the provisions of Part IX and Part IXA have their own significance in the sphere of democratic decentralisation in our country. For the first time, the units of local self-government in the rural and urban areas have been accorded a constitutional status. Now their existence is not dependent on the whims and caprices of the rulers of the States. Obviously, it would strengthen democracy at the grass-roots level. And yet a critic may throw light on certain weak points. It may be feared that the innocent people living in the rural and urban areas would suffer from the hazards of struggle for power in which violence would have its own part in vitiating the peaceful atmosphere of the rural and underdeveloped areas of the country. It may also be feared that these institutions of local self-government would be grabbed by crafty and mischievous politicians who would abuse their powers recklessly by committing acts of impropriety like misappropriation of public funds. The judiciary would not appreciate the provision that any law made by a State Legislature for the delimitation of territorial constituencies or the allotment of seats in the rural and urban bodies shall remain immune from its scrutiny.

The whole arrangement looks like a distortion of the dream of *gram swaraj* as seen by Mahatma Gandhi and his followers of the Sarvodaya movement like Acharya Vinoba Bhave and others. Real *swaraj* would prevail if it moves from the bottom to the top. But in this case it has been imposed by the top on the bottom. The politicians occupying high offices would like to induct men of their choice at the base who would throw leaders of their choice at the regional or provincial levels so as to secure their position at the top. Nothing but politicisation at each level would be the net result of this arrangement. As former President of India R. Venkataraman, in the course of his suggestions for the restructuring of Indian polity, has observed: "The Indian ethos has been in favour of panchayat administration and not party administration. We must, therefore, devise a system in which there would be adequate participation of all sections rather than rule by the majority party."[12]

Administration of Scheduled and Tribal Areas

India is a vast country and some of her areas are not as developed as others are. Moreover, the people of different areas have their distinctive social and cultural traits. Keeping this in view, the makers of the Constitution evolved a system that is democratic as well as federal so that the people of different areas have their say in the administration of their affairs and they may also maintain their social and cultural identity. Part X of the Constitution has some provisions for the administration of Scheduled and Tribal Areas which have their elaborate expression in fifth and sixth Schedules. These are "are treated differently from other areas in the country, because they are inhabited by aboriginals who are socially and economically rather backward and special efforts are required to improve their conditions of life. Therefore, the whole of the administrative machinery operation in a State is not extended to the Scheduled Areas, and the Central Government has somewhat greater responsibility for these Areas."[13]

12. *Indian Express* (New Delhi), 23 April, 1995, p. 9.

13. M.P. Jain: *Indian Constitutional Law*, III ed., 1978, p. 214.

The provisions of V Schedule shall apply to the administration and control of the Scheduled Areas and Scheduled Tribes in any State other than the States of Assam, Meghalaya, Tripura and Mizoram. But the provisions of VI Schedule shall apply to the administration of the tribal areas in the States of Assam, Meghalaya, Tripura and Mizoram. A novel experiment was made in 1969 to create a sub-state within the State of Assam with the name of Meghalaya, but in 1971 it became a full-fledged unit of the Indian federal set up.

What has been given above has its supplementary part in Fifth Schedule that covers all States excluding the States of Assam, Meghalaya, Tripura and Mizoram. The executive power of the State shall extend to these areas subject to the provisions of this Schedule. The Governor of each State having Scheduled Areas therein shall annually, or whenever so required by the President, make a report to the President regarding the administration of the Scheduled Area in that State and the executive power of the Union shall extend to the giving of directions to the State as to the administration of the said area. Part C of this Schedule has the definition of Scheduled Areas. It says that in this connection the expression 'Scheduled Areas' means such areas as the President may by order declare.

Part B of this Schedule makes elaborate arrangements for the creation of Tribes Advisory Councils. It lays down:

"1. There shall be established in each State having Scheduled Areas therein and if the President so directs, also in any State having Scheduled Tribes but not Scheduled Areas therein, a Tribes Advisory Council consisting of not more than 20 members of whom, as nearly as may be, three-fourths shall be the representatives of the Scheduled Tribes in the Legislative Assembly of the State provided that if the number of the representatives of the Scheduled Tribes in the Legislative Assembly of the State is less than the number of the seats in the Tribes Advisory Council to be filled by such representatives, the remaining seats shall be filled by the other members of those tribes.

2. It shall be the duty of the Tribes Advisory Council to advise on such matters pertaining to the welfare and advancement of the Scheduled Tribes in the States as may be referred to them by the Governor.

3. The Governor may make rules prescribing or regulating as the case may be, (a) the number of the members of the Council, and the mode of their appointment, and the appointment of the Chairman of the Council and of the officers and servants thereof, (b) the conduct of its meetings and its procedure in general, and all to other incidental matters."

In order to maintain the autonomy of such areas, paragraph 5 of this Schedule empowers the Governor of the State to declare by a public notification that such a law made by the Parliament or the State Legislature shall not apply or apply with certain modifications and exceptions to a Scheduled Area or a part thereof and any direction given by him to this effect may come into effect with a back date. The Governor may make regulations for the peace and good government of any area in a State declared as Scheduled Area. Such a regulation may (a) prohibit or restrict the transfer of land by or among the members of the Scheduled Tribes in such area, (b) regulate the allotment of land to members of the Scheduled Tribes in such area, (c) regulate the carrying on of business as money-lender by persons who lend money to members of the Scheduled Tribes in such area. In making any such regulation the Governor may repeal or amend any Act of Parliament or of the State Legislature or any existing law which is for the time being applicable to the area in question. All such regulations made by the Governor shall be submitted to the President forthwith and unless assented to by him, shall not be put into effect. Moreover, the Governor is required to consult the Tribes Advisory Council where it exists before making any regulation in this regard.

What has been given above finds its supplementary part in Sixth Schedule. It covers the case of the administration of the Tribal Areas in the States of Assam, Meghalaya, Tripura and Mizoram. Paragraph 20 has a table specifying the district of North Cachar Hills and the Karbi Anglong in Part I, the District of Khasi Hill, Jaintia Hills and Garo Hills in Part II, and Tripura Tribal Areas District in Part IIA, and the District of Chakma, Mara and Lal in Part III. Each district shall be an 'autonomous district'. If there are different Scheduled Tribes in an autonomous district, the Governor may by public notification, divide the area or areas inhabited by them into autonomous regions. The Governor may by a public notification include any area or any of its parts in the said table or exclude any area or its part therefrom, create a new autonomous district, increase or diminish the area of any autonomous district, unite two or more autonomous districts or parts thereof so as to form one autonomous district, alter the name of any autonomous district or re-define its boundary line. But the Governor shall be able to do so after obtaining the report of a Commission appointed by him. He shall also have the power to make necessary modifications in the provisions of the para 14 of this Schedule as may deem necessary to him.[14]

Paragraph 2 of this Schedule provides for the creation of District Councils and Regional Councils. It says that there shall be a District Council for each autonomous district consisting of not more than 30 members of whom not more than 4 persons shall be nominated by the Governor and the rest shall be elected on the basis of adult suffrage. There shall be separate Regional Councils for each area constituted as autonomous region. The Governor shall make rules for the constitution of District Councils and Regional Councils in consultation with the existing Tribal Councils or other representative tribal organisations within the autonomous districts or regions concerned and such rules shall provide for

(*a*) the composition of the District Councils and Regional Councils and the allocation of seats therein;

---

14. It says that the Governor may at any time appoint a Commission to examine and report on any matter specified by him relating to the administration of the autonomous districts and autonomous regions in the State, including matters specified above, or may appoint a Commission to inquire into and report from time to time on the administration of autonomous districts and autonomous first regions in the State generally and in particular on (a) the provision of educational and medical facilities and communications in such districts and regions, (b) the need for any new or special legislation in respect of such districts and regions, and (c) the administration of the law, rules and regulations made by the District and Regional Councils, and define the procedure to be followed by such Commission. The report of every such Commission with the recommendation of the Governor with respect thereto shall be laid before the Legislature of the State by the Minister concerned together with an explanatory memorandum regarding the action proposed to be taken thereon by the Governor of the State. In allocating the business of the Government, the Governor may place one of his Ministers specially in charge of the welfare of the autonomous districts and autonomous regions in the State.

(*b*) the delimitation of territorial constituencies for the purpose of elections to those Councils;

(*c*) the qualifications for voting at such elections and the preparation of electoral rolls thereon;

(*d*) the qualifications for being elected at such election as members of such Councils;

(*e*) the term of the office of members of Regional Councils;

(*f*) any other matter relating to or connected with elections or nominations to such Councils;

(*g*) the procedure and the conduct of business including the power to act notwithstanding any vacancy in the District and Regional Councils;

(*h*) the appointment of officers and staff of the District and Regional Councils.

The elected members of the District Councils shall hold office for a term of five years from the date appointed for the first meeting of the Council after the general elections to the Council unless sooner dissolved under paragraph 16 and a nominated member shall hold office during the pleasure of the Governor.

What the President can do under. Art. 356 to suspend or sack the government of a State, the Governor may do the same for these District Councils and Regional Councils under the provisions of VI Schedule. In a way, these powers of the Governor may be termed as his emergency powers in relation to the administration of Scheduled and Tribal Areas. Paragraph 15 says that if at any time the Governor is satisfied that an act or a resolution of a District or a Regional Council is likely to endanger the safety of India, or is likely to be prejudicial to public order, he may annul or suspend such act or resolution and take such steps as he may consider necessary including the suspension of the Council and the assumption to himself of all or of any of the powers vested in or exercisable by the Council to prevent the commission or continuance of such act, or the giving of effect to such resolution. Any order so made by the Governor together with the reasons therefore shall be laid before the Legislature of the State as soon as possible and the order shall, unless revoked by the Legislature of the State, continue to be in force for a period of twelve months from the date on which it was made. Provided that if and so often as a resolution approving the continuance in force of such order is passed by the legislature of the State, the order shall unless cancelled by the Government continue in force for a further period of twelve months from the date on which it would otherwise have ceased to operate.

Paragraph 16 empowers the Governor to dissolve a District Council on the recommendation of a Commission appointed under paragraph 14 and by a public notification direct that a fresh general election shall be held immediately for the reconstitution of the Council, or subject to the prior approval of the State Legislature assume the administration of the area under the authority of such Council himself, or place the administration of such area under the Commission appointed vide paragraph 14 or any other body considered suitable by him for the period not exceeding twelve months. Provided that when an order is so made, the Governor may take action with regard to the administration of the area in question pending the reconstitution of the Council after general election. It is also necessary for the Governor to take such a drastic action after giving an opportunity to the District Council or Regional Council so as to enable it to place its views before the State Legislature.

If at any time the Governor is satisfied that a situation has arisen in which the administration of an autonomous district or region cannot be carried on in accordance with the provisions of the Schedule, he may by a public notification assume to himself all or any of the functions or powers vested in or exercisable by the District Council, or as the case may be, the Regional Council declare that such functions and powers shall be exercisable by such person or authority as he may specify in this behalf, for a period not exceeding six months. Provided that the Governor by a further order or orders may extend the operation of the initial order by a period not exceeding six months on each occasion. Every such order of the Governor with reasons therefore shall be laid before the State Legislature and shall cease to operate at the expiration of 30 days from the date on which the State Legislature first sits after the issue of the order, unless before the expiry of that period it has been approved by the State Legislature.

No doubt, these provisions of the Constitution boldly demonstrate the fact that the tribal people of our country have been given a kind of special treatment so that they may maintain their distinctive social and cultural patterns and enjoy autonomy in the administration of their local affairs. When the Constituent Assembly adopted these provisions, Rev. J.J.M. Nicholas-Roy (representing Assam) on 8 November, 1948 said: "I must especially thank the Drafting Committee for accepting the draft for the creation of the District Councils with autonomy in the hill districts of Assam which in the VI Schedule are called 'Autonomous Districts.' These hill districts inhabited by the tribal hill people will, under this Constitution, be able to develop themselves according to their own genius and culture".[15] The Governor has been given the power to make regulations for the peace and good government of a Scheduled Area after consulting the Tribes Advisory Council. In case his regulation is assented to by the President, it may repeal or amend any law of the Centre. Paragraph 7 of Schedule V and paragraph 21 of Schedule VI make it very clear that any law made by the Parliament to change or repeal any provision of these Schedules shall not be taken as amendment of the Constitution for the purpose of Art. 368. It is quite clear that the Scheduled and Tribal Areas of these States shall be governed by special provisions not applicable to the States and Union Territories. Schedule VI has been appreciated for having a self-contained code for the governance of the tribal areas.

15. *Constituent Assembly Debates*, Vol. VII, pp. 327–28.

14

Judicial System

As already pointed out, we have a unified judiciary with Supreme Court at the apex, the High Courts just below it, and district courts at the base. The rulings and directions of the Supreme Court must be honoured by all the courts of the country. The decisions of the district courts can be challenged in the High Courts. The decisions of the High Courts can be taken to the Supreme Court in appeal and its decision is final. The jurisdiction of the Supreme Court is India-wide. While the composition of the district courts is a subject of the State List and, as such, it comes under the purview of the State governments, the composition and jurisdiction of the High Courts is a matter of the Union List and, as such, it comes under the domain of the Union government. The High Courts do not have autonomous position as they should have in a federal system. The power of 'judicial review' has been given to the Supreme Court as well as to the High Courts.

Supreme Court

Composition : The Supreme Court stands at the apex of the Indian judicial system. It consists of a Chief Justice and 25 other judges. The President appoints the Chief Justice of India after 'consulting' the judges of the Supreme Court. He appoints the judges with the 'consultation' of the Chief Justice of India. The President may appoint *ad hoc* judge or judges at the request of the Chief Justice of India. Only a working judge of some High Court or a retired judge of the Supreme Court can be appointed on *ad hoc* basis. It should be noted that matters relating to the appointment of the judges of the Supreme Court relate to the discretionary powers of the President and the provision that he should consult judges of the Supreme Court or of the High Courts, as he may deem necessary, in the event of selection for the post of the Chief Justice of India is of a recommendatory and not of a mandatory character.

Here the provision of Art. 124(2) clashes with the provision of Art. 74(1). While the latter desires the President to act on the advice of his Council of Ministers that is binding, the former requires that the President must always consult the Chief Justice of India whose advice cannot be binding in the like manner. In the *S.P. Gupta Case* (1982) the Supreme Court ruled that the advice of the Chief Justice was not binding on the President. But in the *Supreme Court Advocates-on-Record Association Case* (1993), it ruled that the advice of the Chief Justice was effective and hence binding. It created a complicated situation. Thus, President Narayanan referred this matter for the advisory opinion of the Supreme Court in 1998. Also known as the *Third Judges Case*, the Court laid stress on these two points.

1. The consultation process to be adopted by the Chief Justice of India requires consultation of the plurality of the Judges. The role of the CJ alone does not constitute the consultation process.
2. In matters relating to the appointment of the judges of the Supreme Court, the Chief Justice of India should consult four senior-most judges, and if two of them give an adverse view, then the CJI should not send that recommendation to the President.

It has further complicated the situation and the solution to this problems lies only in making a suitable amendment in the relevant provisions of the Constitution.

A person to be appointed as a judge of the Supreme Court must possess two qualifications. First, he must be a citizen of India. Second, he must have served as a judge in a High Court for at least five years, or practised in a High Court as an advocate for at least ten years, or must be a distinguished jurist in the view of the President. As a matter of practice, one of the judges must be a Muslim so as to ensure secular character of the supreme judiciary.

The judges of the Supreme Court retire on completing the age of 65 years. A judge may resign by addressing a letter to the President of India. It is also provided that a judge of the Supreme Court may be removed by the process of impeachment. For this purpose, the Parliament may pass a special address by its absolute majority coupled with two-thirds majority of the members, present and voting, on charging a judge with 'proved misbehaviour' or 'incapacity'. As per the Judges Inquiry Act, 1968 it is necessary that before the matter is taken up for discussion in any House of Parliament, it must be looked into by an inquiry committee consisting of the Chief Justice or a senior judge of the Supreme Court, Chief Justice or a senior Judge of a High Court, and a distinguished jurist of the country.

Jurisdiction : The jurisdiction of the Supreme Court is of three kinds—original, appellate, and advisory.

1. Its original jurisdiction covers cases of constitutional law or fact between the Centre and the States, or between the States. Here it acts as an umpire between the Union and the States. The matters relating to election disputes of the President and Vice-President may be tried in the Supreme Court alone.
2. The appellate jurisdiction of the Supreme Court covers cases decided by the High Courts. The judgement of a High Court can be taken to the Supreme Court in appeal in case the High Court itself certifies that the 'case is fit for appeal', or the Supreme Court gives its leave for this purpose. In civil and constitutional cases, an appeal shall lie to the Supreme Court against the judgement of a High Court if it is satisfied that the case involves a substantial point of law as to the interpretation of the Constitution. In criminal cases, it has to be seen whether the High Court has in appeal reversed the order of acquittal of an accused person delivered by a district court and sentenced him to death, or has withdrawn for trial before itself any case from any court subordinate to its authority and has in such a trial convicted the accused person and sentenced him to death. It shows that a person cannot move the Supreme Court in appeal as a matter of right. The Court may issue prerogative writs for the protection and enforcement of fundamental rights. Under Art. 136 the Supreme Court can allow special leave to appeal against the judgement of any court or tribunal in the territory of India.
3. Under Art. 143 the President may refer any matter of law or a fact of considerable public importance for taking the opinion of the Court that is not binding, though it has great persuasive value. This is known as advisory jurisdiction of the Supreme Court. The court may decline to give its advisory opition as it did in the Babri Masjid Reference Case (1995).

Chief Justice of India: The office of the Chief Justice of the Supreme Court is of great dignity and real authority. He is regarded as the highest custodian of the dignity of the temple of justice. As such, his position is not that of a *primus inter pares* (first among equals) *vis-a-vis* other judges of the Court. He remains like a judge of the Court after holding the office of the Chief Justice, and all provisions from Clause (2) to Clause (7) of Art. 124 apply to him as they apply to all other judges of the Court. And yet his position is different from them in respects more than one. As already pointed out, he is always 'consulted' by the President of India in matters relating to the appointment of other judges of the Supreme Court and the Chief Justices and the judges of the High Courts. Apart from this, he has some special functions and powers emanating from the provisions of the Constitution as well as from certain statutory and non-statutory arrangements which may be put as under:

1. Vide Art. 60, he administers the oath of office to the President or any person acting as the President or discharging the functions of the President of the Republic. In the event of vacancy and non-availability of the Vice-President, the office of the President shall be conferred on him.
2. Art. 146 lays down that the appointment of the officers and servants of the Supreme Court shall be made by the Chief Justice of India or such other judge or officer of the Court as he may direct subject to the rules and regulations laid down by the President in consultation with the Union Public Service Commission. It is further provided that the Chief Justice shall lay down the service conditions of the officers and servants of the Court subject to the provisions of law made by the Parliament. He may authorise any judge or an officer of the Court to do so.
3. Vide Art. 258, the President may with the consent of any State government, entrust, either conditionally or unconditionally, to that Government or to its officers functions in relation to any matter to which the executive power of the Union extends. For this purpose, the Centre shall pay an amount to the State government as agreed upon. But in the case of any dispute relating to the determination of the amount or its payment, the matter shall be decided by an arbitrator appointed by the Chief Justice of India.

4. Vide Art. 290(b), the Chief Justice of India shall appoint an arbitrator to determine the amount to be charged on and paid out of the Consolidated Fund of India or of any State or of States, as the case may be, if there is a default in regard to contribution in respect of the expenses or pensions as may be agreed upon.

5. Vide Art. 317, the President may refer a case to the Supreme Court for inquiring into the charge of 'misbehaviour' levelled against the Chairman or a member of the Union Public Service Commission or of any State Public Service Commission or of a Joint Public Service Commission. In such a case, the Chief Justice shall nominate a judge or some judges of the Court and then submit report to the President.

6. Under the Veerraswami ruling (1991), the consent of the Chief Justice is required before initiation of criminal proceedings against a judge of the Supreme Court or High Court.

7. Under the Judges Inquiry Act of 1968, the presiding officer of any House of Parliament constitutes a committee of three judges to investigate the alleged charges with the consultation of the Chief Justice of India. It means that the Chief Justice has a role in constituting the impeachment committee in case such a process is initiated in the Parliament.

8. Under the rules of the Supreme Court, the Chief Justice allocates work among the judges of the Supreme Court.

9. As the holder of the highest judicial office, the Chief Justice may do something on his own for maintaining the dignity of the judiciary. For instance, Chief Justice Mukherji set up an informal committee of judges in 1990 to conduct a sort of pre-investigation so as to determine whether any work be allotted to a judge against whom impeachment proceedings had started in the Parliament. He did not proceed in this direction as this committee reported on 21 December, 1990 that it could not come to any definite conclusion and the then Chief Justice (Ranganath Mishra) accepted it.

10. The Chief Justice of India has to perform some other functions conferred on him by statutory arrangements. For instance, he is a member of the Committee that recommends the name of a person to be appointed as the Chairman of the National

Human Rights Commission. A law of Parliament may assign some functions to the Chief Justice of India. When a tribunal is set up for adjudicating inter-State river water dispute according to the provisions of such a law of 1956, its member (s) is (are) nominated by the Chief Justice. Sec. 3A of the Legal Services Authorities Act of 1987 says that the members of the Supreme Court Legal Services Committee shall be nominated by the Chief Justice. He may constitute a committee to look into allegations against a judge of some High Court.

The powers of the CJI are quite limited. V.N. Khare said: Give some powers to the Chief Justice. What powers does the C.J.I. have? Despite repeated requests, nothing has been done. How do I control the situation and how much can be done to control such a situation by passing orders on the judicial side. You (government) do not know with how much difficulty I secured the resignations of two High Court Judges earlier."[1]

Expanding Jurisdiction : As a matter of its *Dharma* (pious obligations), the judiciary cannot deny justice to a person or a party that knocks at its door. Art. 142 of the Constitution specifically empowers the Supreme Court to render 'complete justice' to the aggrieved person. The problem arises when some act of injustice occurs inside the legislative chambers and the aggrieved party moves the Court. In many cases the Courts have taken the view of not entering into the validity of proceedings of the House. In the *A.G. Kher Case* (1954), the Allahabad High Court observed that it had no jurisdiction to issue a writ, or a directive, or an order relating to a matter which affected the internal affairs of the House. In the *MSM Sharma Case* (1960) the Supreme Court observed. "No court can go into the question which are within the special jurisdiction of the legislature itself which has the power to conduct its own business." But when it comes to the protection of fundametal rights, the Court takes a different view. Thus, in the *Keshav Singh Reference Case* (1964) the Supreme Court gave the opinion that the High Court had the power to stay service of the warrants of arrest issued by the Speaker of the U.P. Vidhan Sabha against Keshav Singh who had committed 'contempt' of the House and his two lawyers who had defended him in the Lucknow bench of the Allahabad High Court.

---

1. *The Times of India*, New Delhi, 24 February, 2004.

The deplorable fact is that very large number of the legislators disturb the proceedings of the House and flout the rules of procedure as well as celebrated norms of parliamentary democracy. The Governor takes a patently partisan stand in appointing a person as the Chief Minister or the Speaker disqualifies some members of the House on flimsy grounds so as to save the government in a division. When such a matter is brought before the Court, it has to apply the principle of natural justice without offending the authority of the House. For instance, in 1998 the Governor of Uttar Pradesh dismissed Kalyan Singh and appointed Jagdambika Pal as the Chief Minister. In this case the Supreme Court directed that a special session of the Assembly be held to test the majority behind the Chief Minister and an observer be appointed by the Governor to submit his report as to how the proceedings were conducted. It was like a strange counsel of the Court which was honoured by the Speaker and then the House could express its verdict against the newly appointed Chief Minister. Similarly, in 2005 the Court ordered the Governor of Jharkhand to hold a session of the House so as to test majority behind the Chief Minister (Shibu Soren). The Court also ordered that a video film of the proceedings be prepared. Apprehending the consequences, Soren resigned and then the Governor had to appoint the leader of the BJP as the Chief Minister. It shows that the Supreme Court cannot tolerate anything that amounts to a fraud on the Constitution or constitutes a case of institutional self-aggrandisement.

The members of the legislative chambers try to justify their wrong actions in the name of anything like 'mandate of the people' or 'sovereign authority' of the legislature. In Rajasthan in 2006 some members of the Vidhan Sabha had the audacity to criticise the functioning of the High Court in violation of Art. 211 of the Constitution as a result of which the Court had to write a letter to the Speaker to explain it. The deplorable fact is that such members have no knowledge of law, rules and regulations and, more than that, they have no sense of propriety. The members of the higher judiciary are well versed in law and they are obligated to maintain the 'rule of law'. In the *Gopalan Case* (1950), the Supreme Court had ruled that all organs of government must act within their sphere and that the judges must observe the norm of self-restraint. Keeping it in his view, Somnath Chatterjee (the Speaker of the Lok Sabha and also an eminent jurist by profession) said these words: "I appeal to all arms of democracy to work within the constitutional provision helping each other. If this is not followed and everyone tries to do the work of others leaving its own, the country will face a difficult situation and it will lead to a serious crisis. I have immense respect for the judiciary. I have nothing to say against the judiciary. What I am stressing upon is that any wrong, if committed, weakens the spirit of the Constitution. The Constitution clearly states that all its major pillars should work independently showing respect to each other. It means that the legislature, the executive and the judiciary should be working harmoniously. But if any of the pillars tries to cross its *Lakshman Rekha* (boundary line) and interferes in the working of others, it is bound to create problems for all."[2]

Critical Estimate : A critical evaluation of the working of the Supreme Court shows that it has done well as the cutodian of the supreme law of the land. It has protected the fundamental rights and liberties of the people and put an effective check on the arbitrary actions of the Union and State governments. A citizen can resort directly for relief to the Supreme Court under Art. 32 of the Constitution. It has ruled in several cases that the executive and the legislative organs should remain within the allotted spheres. There should be no transgression of power and, if it heppens, it can strike down the law or order of the state as it did in the *Privy Purse Case* of 1971. In several cases, it upheld the laws for the abolition of private property, but ruled that the compensation paid to the affected persons should be just or adequate. The Court cannot allow a fraud on the Constitution.

However, three points of criticism may be furnished at this stage:

1. The Court has changed its stand from time to time which has unsettled the process of judicial thought in our country. For instance, in the *Sankari Prasad Case* (1951) and in the *Sajjan Singh Case* (1964) it ruled that the word 'law' occurring in Art. 13 (2) and Art. 368 had different implications, but in the *Golak Nath Case* (1967) it ruled that both had the same implications. On that basis it ruled that no amendment in the Constitution could be made to curtail the scope of fundamental rights and the Court could examine its constitutional validity. It created a situation of confrontation between the Union Government and the Supreme Court.

---

2. *The Times of India* (New Delhi), 22 March, 2005.

2. The Court may ask the executive and the legislative wings to work within their respective areas, but who can keep it within the sphere allotted to it. Sometimes, the Court has ruled what is not permissible under the Constitution. For instance, Art. 74 (2) says that the advice of the Ministers given to the President cannot be called in question in any court. But in the *Bommai Case* (1995) it ruled that the Court could look into the advice of the Ministers whereby Art. 356 was invoked in the State. It implies that the Court may look into the proclamation of emergency made by the President and may strike it down if the step is *mala fide*. In the *Judges Reference Case* (1999) it gave an opinion that before recommending the name of a judge for appointment in the Supreme Court, the matter shall be considered by a panel of five judges headed by the Chief Justice and its recommendation shall be 'effective' if supported by all or four members of the panel. It is patently against the provision of Art. 124 (2) which says that the President of India shall always take the advice of the Chief Justice (not of any panel) before appointing a judge of the Supreme Court.
3. In recent years the Supreme Court has widened its jurisdiction by entertaining petitions under the PIL and even issuing *suo moto* orders or directions to various functionaries of the Union and State governments. In Plato's ideal state, the philosophers (Guardians) shall guard the state. The question arises as to who shall guard the Guardians? Vide Art. 142, the Supreme Court may take any necessary step for the sake of ensuring 'complete justice', but who is there to look into the constitutional validity of such a step?

Such fears may be dispelled if we appreciate the view of Chief Justice Patanjali Sastri given in *Gopalan Case* (1950) that in the absence of any constitutional restraints, the judges should themselves work with self-restraint. It is the same thing that, as said by Gandhiji, self-control precedes swaraj. No doubt, the Supreme Court has acted with admirable restraint in certain delicate situations. It has enunciated the doctrine of 'basic structure of the Constitution' and kept with it the power of defining its implications and contours. No doubt, the invention of this peculiar doctrine has put an effectice check on the ambitions of the power-drunk politicians who have no hitch in fiddling with the provisions of the fundamental law of the land. This is the reason that while the people in general have lost their faith in the ministers (including bureaucrats) and the legislators of the country, they have unflinching faith in the verdicts of the highest judiciary. The judges have often drawn the attention of the law-breakers to these judicious words of Chief Justice Sir Edward Coke: "Be you ever so high, but the law is above you."[3]

High Courts

The Constitution provides for a High Court for each State; there may be a common High Court for two or more States as well as for a Union Territory. A High Court consists of a Chief Justice and some other judges as the President may determine from time to time. The judges retire at the age of 62 years. It is also provided that the President may appoint additional judges to clear the arrears of work for a term of two years subject to the age limit of 62 years. The President may also appoint temporary judges to fill casual vacancies in the cadre of permanent judges caused by the reason of absence or any other factor. While appointing a judge, the President consults the Chief Justice of India, the judges of the Supreme Court, the Chief Justice of the High Court and the Governor of the concerned State. Art. 217 says that before appointing a judge of the High Court, the President must consult the Chief Justice of India, but it does not specify whether the advice of the CJI is binding. In the *Judges Reference Case* (1998), the Supreme Court has stressed these points:

1. In matters relating to the appointment of High Court judges, the CJI must consult two senior-most judges of the Supreme Court and their opinion must be unanimous.

---

3. In 2000 the Supreme Court celebrated its 50 years in commemmoration of which a book was released. In the 'Preface', former Chief Justice Dr. A. S. Anand observed: "In retrospect, it is satisfying to see that its achievements have been significant in all areas of national life. As an independent judiciary under the scheme of the Constitution, the Court has played its role effectively in acting as a watchdog through judicial review over the acts of the legislature and the executive. The major contribution of the Supreme Court has been to uphold the Constitution by delineating the role of the three organs of the State. When two organs of the State fail to perform their duties, the judiciary cannot remain a mute spectator." S.K. Verma and Kusum (eds): *Fifty Years of the Supreme Court (Its Grasp and Reach)*, (Delhi: Oxford University Press, 2000), pp. v–vi.

2. In matters relating to the transfer of a judge from one High Court to another, the CJI must, in addition to the collegium of four senior-most judges of his Court, also consult the Chief Justice of the two High Courts—one from which the judge is to be transferred and the other receiving him.
3. A matter relating to the transfer of a judge from one High Court to another would be reviewable on the ground that the process of consultation was not followed. But the Supreme Court alone can look into this matter.

A judge of a High Court must possess two qualifications. First, he must be a citizen of India. Second, he must have held a judicial office in the country, or practised as an advocate in some High Courts for at least 10 years. A judge may resign his post by writing a letter to the President of India: he may be transferred from one High Court to another; he may be appointed as a judge of the Supreme Court; he may be removed by the process of impeachment as applicable to a judge of the Supreme Court discussed above.

The jurisdictional competence of the High Courts still remains as it was before the commencement of the Constitution. As a result, while the High Courts of Calcutta, Bombay and Madras have both original and appellate jurisdiction (in civil cases of the value of more than Rs. 2000 and in criminal cases referred to them by the Presidency magistrates and other cases of revenue), all have limited original jurisdiction in cases relating to admiralty, will, divorce, marriage, company law and contempt of court. All High Courts have appellate jurisdiction in civil and criminal cases. Like the Supreme Court, the High Courts have the power to issue prerogative writs for the protection and enforcement of fundamental rights in the nature of *habeas corpus*, *mandamus*, prohibition, *certiorari*, and *quo warranto*. Unlike the Supreme Court, they may also issue such writs 'for any other purpose'. The original jurisdiction of the High Courts also covers election disputes of the members of Parliament and State Legislatures. Like Supreme Court, each High Court is a court of record.

The decisions of the district courts can be challenged in the High Court. The High Court can call from the subordinate courts returns, issue general rules and forms to regulate their proceedings, prescribe for them account forms and books, and settle the table of fees allowed to the clerks and officers of such courts and to the pleaders practising therein. It has the power of superintendence and control over the

High Courts in India

Names	*Year of Establishment*	*Territorial Jurisdiction*	*Seats*	*Bench or Benches at*
1. Allahabad	1866	Uttar Pradesh	Allahabad	Lucknow
2. Andhra Pradesh	1954	Andhra Pradesh	Hyderabad	—
3. Bombay	1861	Maharashtra, Goa, Dadra and Nagar Haveli, and Daman and Diu	Mumbai	Nagpur, Aurangabad and Panaji
4. Calcutta	1861	West Bengal, Andaman and Nicobar Islands	Kolkata	Port Blair
5. Delhi	1966	Delhi	New Delhi	—
6. Guwahati	1948	Assam, Manipur, Nagaland, Meghalaya, Tripura, Mizoram and Arunachal Pradesh	Guwahati	Kohima, Aizwal, Itanagar, Imphal, Agartala, and Shillong
7. Gujarat	1960	Gujarat	Ahmedabad	—
8. Himachal Pradesh	1971	Himachal Pradesh	Shimla	—
9. Jammu-Kashmir	1928	Jammu-Kashmir	Srinagar	—
10. Kerala	1956	Kerala and Lakshadweep	Ernakulam	—
11. Madhya Pradesh	1956	Madhya Pradesh	Jabalpur	Gwalior and Indore
12. Madras	1891	Tamil Nadu and Puducherry	Chennai	—
13. Mysore	1884	Karnataka	Bangalore	—
14. Orissa	1948	Orissa	Cuttack	—
15. Patna	1916	Bihar	Patna	—
16. Punjab and Haryana	1947	Chandigarh	Punjab, Haryana and Chandigarh	—
17. Rajasthan	1949	Rajasthan	Jodhpur	Jaipur
18. Sikkim	1975	Sikkim	Gangtok	—
19. Jharkhand	2000	Jharkhand	Ranchi	—
20. Uttarakhand	2000	Uttarakhand	Nainital	—
21. Chhattisgarh	2000	Chhattisgarh	Bilaspur	—

lower courts within their areas except military courts. If a High Court is satisfied that a case pending before any subordinate court involves a substantial question of constitutional law, it can take up the case and decide it itself, or may send it back to the subordinate court, in question, after deciding the question of law involved therein.

Judicial Review

It may be defined as the power of the court to look into the constitutional validity of an impugned law or executive action and hold it unconstitutional and, for that reason, unenforceable to the extent it is inconsistent with the fundamental law of the land. It is an invention of Chief Justice Marshall of the American Supreme Court and now it has been adopted in the constitutional systems of many countries like Canada, Australia, Germany, Japan and India. The reason behind it is that in a country having a written constitution the ordinary law must be subordinate to the higher (constitutional) law of the land. No organ of government can transgress its areas of authority and in case it occurs in the form of a law made by the legislature or some other organ having authority delegated to it, or if some administrative action is taken in violation of the doctrine of 'competence', it may be challenged in the Court and then the Court may declare it null and void to the extend of its being repugnant to the Constitution or due process of law. Such a unique function of the judiciary "stems from a feeling that a system based on a written constitution can hardly be effective in practice without an authoritative, independent and impartial arbiter of constitutional issues and also that it is necessary to restrain governmental organs from exercising powers which may not be sanctioned by the Constitution."[4]

The source of the power of the judicial review is contained in Art. 13 (2) of the Constitution. It says that "all laws in force in the territory of India immediately before the commencement of this Constitution, in so far as they are inconsistent with the provisions of Part III shall, to the extent of such inconsistency, be void. The State shall, not make any law which takes away or abridges the rights conferred by this Part and any law made in contravention of the clause, shall to the extent of the contravention, be void. Unless the context otherwise requires, the word 'law' includes any ordinance, order, bye-law, rule, regulation, notification, custom or usage having in the territory of India the force of law. It also includes 'laws in force' or laws made by a Legislature or a competent authority in the territory of India before the commencement of this Constitution and not previously repealed, notwithstanding that any

4. M.P. Jain: *Indian Constitutional Law*, III ed., 1978, p. 669.

such law or any part thereof may not be then in operation either at all or in particular areas."[5]

Whether the word 'law' used in this Article means ordinary law or constitutional law, it is not clear. The Supreme Court in the leading case of *Sankari Prasad* v. *The Union of India* (1951) and again in the case of *Sajjan Singh* v . *The State of Rajasthan* (1965) held the view that the word 'law' occurring in Art. 13 meant ordinary law. But in the case of *Golak Nath* v. *The State of Punjab* (1967) it ruled that the word 'law' occurring in Art. 13 and in Art. 368 meant the same. As such, even a law of constitutional amendment could not be valid if it was inconsistent with Part III of the Constitution having fundamental rights. In this case the Supreme Court subscribed to the doctrine of prospective overruling as established in the American jurisprudence. It means that a law could remain in operation in spite of being unconstitutional as much work had already been done and that could not be reversed, but in future no such law could be made. In order to demolish this barrier, the Twenty-fourth Constitution Amendment Act came into being in 1971. It provides that the Parliament may amend any part of the Constitution if it deems proper or necessary.

The power of judicial review is vested in the High Courts and the Supreme Court. As such, an aggrieved party may challenge a law or any executive order on the ground of its being inconsistent with the provisions of the basic structure of the Constitution. It is true that our Courts cannot invoke the plea of 'due process of law' as it is invoked by the American Supreme Court for the reason that they are specifically bound to follow 'procedure established by law'. It appears that the judiciary is virtually under the sway of the legislature. However, this point should not be understood in a way to minimize the position of the judiciary. The Courts may also look into the fact that the procedure established by law is not a fraud on the Constitution. In the case of *Kesavanand Bharati* v. *State of Kerala* or *Fundamental Rights Case* (1973) the Supreme Court laid down

---

5. In a case the Supreme Court observed: "An order which the Court can make under Art. 142 of the Constitution in order to do complete justice between the parties must not only be consistent with the fundamental rights guaranteed by the Constitution but also with the substantive provision of the relevant statutory law." *K.M Nanavati v. State of Bombay*, AIR 1961 SC 112.

the doctrine of the 'basic structure of the Constitution'. It is true that the Court did not clearly define the term 'basic framework or structure', but it is very clear that it could establish its powerful position *vis-a-vis* the power of the legislature. The judgement of the Court in this case may be regarded as our Republic's greatest contribution to jurisprudence, and its underlying philosophy as of momentous significance for the survival of democracy in our country.

While exercising the power of judicial review, the Courts are guided by certain maxims. For instance, the point of 'competence' is taken into consideration. The Court examines whether the law-making or order-issuing authority has acted within its jurisdiction or not. It is also known as the doctrine of pith and substance. The Court also distinguishes between the good and bad parts of an impugned law and, as such, it may declare only its bad part void. The Court may declare a law void in case it transgresses the authority of the legislature or of the executive. For instance, the Supreme Court invalidated a decree of the President (1970) that derecognised all former rulers of the princely States and thereby made them ineligible for privy purses and privileges. The Court may also see whether a law or decree is bad in part and may then strike it down as it invalidated some parts of the law whereby 14 banks were nationalised in 1969. In case the Parliament makes an amendment in the Constitution, or it makes a change in a law in rectification of a mistake for which the Court had invalidated a particular law, then the Court will not strike down an impugned law or administrative action. Moreover, the Court may change its view from time to time in the light of new conditions or circumstances.

The position of the Courts with regard to the exercise of the power of judicial review, as it obtains in our country, is well evident from the observation of Justice S.K. Das in the case of *A.K. Gopalan* v. *State of Madras* (1950); "In India the function of the judiciary is somewhat between the Courts in England and the United States. While, in the main, leaving our Parliament and State Legislatures supreme in their respective legislative fields, our Constitution has, by some of its Articles, put upon the Legislature certain specified limitations. The point to be noted, however, is that in so far as there is any limitation on the legislative power, the Court must on a complaint being made to it, scrutinise and ascertain whether such limitation has been transgressed and if there has been any transgression, the Court will courageously declare the law unconstitutional, for the Court is bound by its oath to uphold the Constitution. But outside the limitation imposed on the legislative powers, our Parliament and State Legislatures are supreme in their respective legislative fields and the Court has no authority to question the wisdom or policy of the law duly made by appropriate legislature. Our Constitution, unlike the English Constitution, recognises the Court's supremacy over legislative authority, but such supremacy is a limited one, for it is confined to the field where the legislative power is circumscribed by limitations upon it by the Constitution itself."

The power of judicial review, as exercised by the Supreme Court and the High Courts, has been criticised as well as defended by the writers on constitutional law and politics. It is said that judicial review opens the flood-gates for more and more judicial debate signifying a "lawyers' paradise". It leads to judicial despotism that virtually results in a confrontation between the executive and the judicial departments of the State. It is also commented that judicial review becomes an effective instrument in the hands of the vested interests owing to the highly conservative attitude of the Courts. Further, the Courts, instead of giving stability to judicial thought, tamper it with their shifty stands as a result of which uncertainty prevails in the realm of law and justice. Above all, it elevates the position of the Courts to act like the 'powerful third chamber' or the 'super-master of the legislature'. As a learned writer remarks: What is distinctive to the Indian experiment....is the fact that the Indian Supreme Court has functioned largely in an inapposite Westminster model of parliamentary democracy."[6]

However, viewed in a correct perspective, judicial review looks like an essential instrument in the hands of the judges to work as the protectors of our democratic system as enshrined in the provisions of the Constitution. It is by virtue of this power that the judiciary can save the ordinary people from the onslaught of executive or legislative despotism. What is really needed is that the custodians of the Constitution must not exercise their power in a way that would lead to the intrusion of their personal philosophy into the social philosophy of the nation and thereby cause a sort of confrontation between the two organs of the political system.

---

6. Upendra Baxi: *The Indian Supreme Court and Politics*, p. 31.

Independence of Judiciary

We may now enumerate some provisions of the Constitution which ensure independence of the judges of the Supreme Court and the High Courts as under:

1. Though made by the President on the advice of the Ministers, the appointments of the judges are regarded as 'constitutional'; they are governed by specific high qualifications pertaining to the realm of law and justice which a person must possess.
2. The judges are paid salary and allowances as determined by a law of the Parliament and, until it is done, as specified in Second Schedule of the Constitution. It also includes their right to leave and pension. These cannot be varied to their disadvantage after their appointment. The provision of Art. 360 is an exception when during financial emergency the President may reduce the salaries and allowances of all public servants, including the judges. It is also given that the salaries, allowances and pensions of the judges and all administrative expenses of the Supreme Court shall be charged on the Consolidated Fund of India and of the judges of the High Courts on the Consolidated Fund of the concerned State.
3. It is also given that a judge may be removed on the charge of 'proved misbehaviour' or 'incapacity' or both if the resolution of impeachment is passed by both the Houses of Parliament by special majority. The Judges Inquiry Act makes it binding that the matter must first by investigated by a high-powered inquiry committee. The process of impeachment of the judges is quite tedious.
4. Art. 220 puts restriction on private legal practice by a judge who retires from service in the Supreme Court. But a retired Chief Justice or a judge of a High Court may do it in the Supreme Court or in any High Court excluding the High Court or High Courts where he had served in a permanent capacity.
5. The constitution and jurisdiction of the Supreme Court and the High Courts is a Union subject. As explained by Sir Alladi Krishnaswami Ayyar, the placement of the High Courts under the control of the Union in certain important matters had been done in order to keep them outside the range of 'provincial politics'.

6. The conduct of the judges cannot be discussed in any State Legislature; it can be discussed in the Parliament only when a substantive motion for the removal of a Judge is under consideration.

Critical Appreciation

It is true that the provisions of the Constitution have made effective arrangements for keeping the judges independent so that they may perform their duties fairly and impartially. But some deficiencies may also be pointed out. Since the judges are appointed, transferred and promoted by the President and since he invariably acts on the advice of his Ministers, one may easily diagnose the fact that politics is injected into the process of the appointment, transfer and promotion of the judges of the High Courts. The Law Commission of India in its XIV Report (1958) regretted that "communalism, regionalism and political patronage have in a considerable measure influenced appointments to the High Court judiciary." It expressed its distress over the fact that the judgeship of a High Court "has become a post to be worked and canvassed for." Unfortunately, the policy of reservations in favour of certain castes, tribes and classes in the name of 'social justice' has its own deleterious effect on the functioning of judiciary where nothing but the considerations of merit and ability should prevail.

One important point that applies to the judges of the Supreme Court but not to the judges of the High Court should also be taken into account. It is related to doing practice of law after retirement. The judges of the High Courts should have been placed in the same category as we find in the case of the judges of the Supreme Court. That is, they may take an unfair advantage of their high connections made in the past. It is also a fact that the standards of the integrity of the judges are not as high at the lower level as they may be seen at the higher level of the judicial structure. Quite often we come across the allegations of rampant corruption in the judiciary at the lower levels. The bar associations often make agitations and demonstrations for the removal of a judge on some charge of nepotism or corruption. The practising advocates go on strike continuing for many days as a result of which the work of the courts remains paralysed. Unfortunately, what is at the top of judicial hierarchy is not available at its lower strata in the country.

However, on certain occasions, the role of an over-active judiciary has been a matter of concern. The growing trend of judicial assertiveness has not been appreciated by those who desire to see that all organs of a political organisation should remain in a state of, what the Americans call, 'checks and balances'. The Supreme Court has been very sensitive in respect of protecting its area of authority. As such, it invalidated the provision of the Forty-second Amendment of 1976 laying down that a law of constitutional amendment could not be challenged in the Courts. Sec. 7 of the anti-defection law empowers the presiding officer of a House of Parliament or State Legislature to disqualify a person from the membership of the House on the ground of being a defector. But it invalidated a part of this law specifying that such a decision could not be challenged in a Court. It forced the Speaker of Manipur Legislative Assembly (Dr. Borababu Singh) to appear before it in a contempt of court case as he had not followed its directives. In the *Bommai Case* (1994) it went to the length of holding that Art. 356 was justiciable and that the advice tendered by the ministers to the President before the invocation of this provision of the Constitution could be requisitioned in the Court. It ruled that the Presidential proclamation issued under Art. 356 could be put into effect after its approval by the Parliament It certainly amounted to the circumvention of the provisions of the Constitution.[7]

The range of subjects on which the Supreme Court has pronounced verdicts over the last few years "is mind-boggling; it has decided whether Speakers have acted properly in applying the anti-defection provisions; whether the Central Government acted rightly in taking over State Legislature; whether contracts have been properly awarded; how and when foreigners should be permitted to adopt Indian infants; when prisoners should be hand-cuffed; which quarries should be permitted in the Doon valley; whether decisions

---

7. So Madhu Limaye commented: "The judgment should be generally approved, but I differ on one point—the Assemblies not to be dissolved till Parliamentary approval is given to the proclamation of President's rule. This point is not in the Constitution and even the highest court in the land is not authorised to remake the Constitution." *The Sunday Times of India*, New Delhi, 20 March, 1994. So comments S.C. Kashyap: "How has the Bench circumvented provision that the advice tendered to the President by the Council of Ministers will not be brought before a court of law?" *Ibid.*

of the Election Commission are valid."[8] Why has it come to occur? The same writer well answers: "Disillusionment with politicians, disgust with government apathy and the ability of the courts to respond, have all led to the acceptance of an enormous *de facto* enlargement of the powers of the courts and almost constituted courts into a super-legislature and a super-executive. A working democracy, no doubt, requires an independent judiciary; it also requires an effective executive and a responsive legislature. The legislature and the executive represent the people who periodically elect them; judges are appointed and are thus not representatives."[9]

Such a confrontation between the executive and the judiciary is a natural development in a democratic and social welfare state. What is required is that both should take things in right earnest and not let them drift into channels of discord and disharmony. On 8 April, at the Conference of the Chief Ministers and Chief Justices of the High Courts in New Delhi, Prime Minister Manmohan Singh said; "The dividing line between judicial activism and judicial over-reach is a thin one. A take-over of the functions of another organ may at time become the case of over-reach." Chief Justice K.G. Balkrishnan observed; "The application of judicial review to determine constitutional validity of legislation and to review the executive decision sometimes creates tension between the judges and the legislative and executive branches. Such tension is natural and to some extent desirable in a democracy."[10]

Subordinate Courts

Chapter VI of Part VI of the Constitution has provisions for the subordinate courts of a State. Art. 233 says that appointments of persons to be, and the posting and promotion of districts judges in any State shall be made by the Governor of a State in consultation with the High Court exercising jurisdiction in relation to such State. A person not already in the service of the Union or of the State

---

8. Atul Setalvad: "An Active Judiciary" in *The Times of India*, (New Delhi), 17 May, 1994.

9. *Ibid.*

10. *The Times of India*, (New Delhi), 9 April, 2007.

shall only be eligible to be appointed a district judge if he has been for not less than seven years an advocate or a pleader and is recommended by the High Court for appointment. Art. 233 A provides for the validation of appointments and judgements etc. delivered by district judges in certain cases.

Art. 234 provides for recruitment of persons other than district judges to the judicial service of the State. It says that the appointment of persons other than district judges to the judicial service of a State shall be made by the Governor of the State in accordance with rules made by him in that behalf after consultation with the State Public Service Commission and with the High Court exercising jurisdiction in relation to such State. Finally, Art. 235 says about the control over subordinate courts. The control over district courts and other courts subordinate thereto, including the posting and promotion of persons belonging to the judicial service of a State and holding any post inferior to the post of a district judge, shall be vested in the High Court, but nothing in this article shall be construed as taking away from any such person any right of appeal which he may have under the law regulating the conditions of his service or as authorising the High Court to deal with him otherwise than in accordance with the condition of his service prescribed under such laws.

The object of these provisions is to secure the independence of subordinate judiciary from the executive and to that extent to effect separation of powers. Since the Governor has to exercise his powers in consultation with the High Court, it has been held by the Supreme Court that it must be "effective" as it is mandatory. In this context, the High Court means full court of all the Judges. Consultation with a sub-committee of the High Court or of some other body would be invalid in case of any appointment made by the Governor. But the judgement delivered by a district judge whose appointment is subsequently held invalid would not be taken as invalid. Moreover, the Governor cannot make any rule in this regard that is violative of the provisions of the Constitution.

Administrative Tribunals

Part XIV A of the Constitution inserted by the Forty-second Amendment of 1976 "opens a new chapter in Indian constitutional and administrative law by substantially excluding judicial review of administrative decisions".[11] In pursuance of Art. 323A (which provides for adjudication or trial by the Administrative Tribunals of disputes and complaints relating to recruitment and conditions of service of persons appointed to public services and posts in connection with affairs of the Union and State government), the Administrative Tribunal Act, 1985 came into effect. (It was amended in the following year.) It sets up Central Administrative Tribunal to provide speedy and inexpensive justice to the employees of the Central Government in respect of their service matters. The principal bench of the CAT is at New Delhi. It has other regular benches at the principal seats of the High Courts. These benches also hold circuit sittings at other seats of High Courts where workload for the tribunal is less.

Sec. 4(2) of this Act provides for the setting up of Administrative Tribunals in the States by the Union Government in respect of specific requests made by any State government. Accordingly , such tribunals have been set up in Himachal Pradesh, Orissa, Maharashtra, Karnataka, Madhya Pradesh, Tamil Nadu and Andhra Pradesh. Like CAT, the State administrative tribunals have the power of all courts except that of Supreme Court in regard to service matters of the employees of the State government. However, the important point to be noted is that these tribunals have got the jurisdiction to settle disputes relating to service matters of the government employees. What the civil courts and the High Courts could do, has new been entrusted to the tribunals. They may grant relief to the aggrieved party as well. The decisions of the CAT can be taken to the appropriate High Court in appeal.

Lok Adalats

Justice should neither be costly nor delayed. It should be within the reach of a common man and that it should be available to the aggrieved person or party within a reasonable time. For this sake, many suggestions have been made. One of the points of Gandhi's non-cooperation programme of 1920 was to advise the litigants to withdraw their suits from the courts of law and to get them settled with the help of arbitrators. The old panchayat system of India was based on the principle of mutual settlement with the role of chosen arbitrators. But it was replaced by the judicial system enforced by the British rulers. As a result of this, justice became a very costly

---

11. D.D. Basu: *Indian Constitutional Law*, ed. VI of 1991, p. 379.

affair. The distance between the aggrieved person and the deliverers of justice became too wide and, more than that, due to the intricacies of law it became unduly delayed. The work-load of the law courts went on increasing . As a solution to this problem, the idea of People's Courts (Lok Adalats) gained prominence and its implementation in our country in the 1980s created a new experiment in the sphere of para-judicial mechanism.

The source of the origin and growth of people's courts may be traced in the efforts of the Government, Central and State, as well as in the role of some unofficial organisations engaged in the movement for reforming judicial administration of the country.[12] In 1958, Justice D.A. Desai, the Chairman of the Law Commission of India, on the subject of 'Reform of Judicial Administration' observed: "In view of the ever-rising graph of arrears tinkering and the fringes, far from yielding the desired results, have further aggravated the situation. The consumers of justice have been patiently waiting for justice to become people-oriented." However, the movement gained momentum in the 1970s when the Government of Gujarat set up a committee of the legal experts to ponder over this question and a similar committee was set up by the Government of India with Justice P.N. Bhagwati and Justice V.R. Krishna Iyer as its members. In its report the Committee said: "The legal and judicial system, therefore, needs to be reformed and changed so that it becomes more suited to our socio-economic culture and can become an effective instrument for delivering justice to the poor and the disadvantaged. It must be resolved that a twentieth century service cannot be produced from an unaltered nineteenth century mould."[13]

---

12. Reference should be made here to a clause of the Forty-second Constitution Amendment Act of 1976 that inserted Art. 39A in the list of Directive Principles of State Policy. It reads: "The State shall secure that the operation of the legal system promotes justice, on a basis of equal opportunity, and shall, in particular, provide free legal aid, by suitable legislation or scheme or in an any other way, to ensure that opportunities for securing justice are not denied to any citizen by reason of economic or other disabilities."

13. The people's courts started functioning in the State of Gujarat in March 1982 under the leadership of Justice M.P. Thakkar. The first camp of this kind was held at Una in Junagarh district. Then, it was followed in other States and Union Territories of our country.

An important recommendation of another Committee set up under the headship of Chief Justice Bhagwati in 1980 was that the village panchayats should be entrusted with judicial functions. The Law Commission of India in its 114th Report (1986) on the subject of village court (*gramnyayalaya*) did not appreciate the idea of abolishing *nyaya panchayats*, rather it laid stress on people's participation in the administration of justice.

Notable event in this regard is the making of Legal Service Authorities Act in 1987. Its objective is "to provide free and competent legal services to the weaker sections of the society, to ensure the opportunity for securing justice are not denied to any citizen by reason of economic or other disabilities and to organise Lok Adalats to secure that the operation of the legal system promotes justice on a basis of equal opportunity." Sec. 19(1) of this Act provides: "(1) The State or district authorities may organise Lok Adalats at such intervals and place and for exercising such jurisdiction and for such areas as they think fit. (2) Every Lok Adalat organised for an area shall consist of such judicial officers of the area as may be specified by the State or district authorities organising the Lok Adalats and such other members possessing such qualifications and experience as may be prescribed by the State Government. (3) A Lok Adalat shall have jurisdiction to determine and arrive at a compromise or settlement between the parties to a dispute in respect of any matter falling within the jurisdiction of any civil or criminal or revenue court or any tribunal constituted under the law for the time being in force in the area for which the Lok Adalat is organised."

Then, Sec. 21 of this Act says: "Every award of the Lok Adalat shall be deemed to be a decree of a civil court or order of any other court or tribunal and where a compromise or a settlement has been arrived at by a Lok Adalat in a suit or proceeding transferred to it under sub-section (I) of Section 20, the court fee paid in such a suit or proceeding shall be refunded in the manner provided under the Court Fees Act of 1870. Every award made by a Lok Adalat shall be final and binding on all the parties to the dispute, and no appeal shall lie to any court against the award. Sec. 22 specifies the powers of the Lok Adalats. For the purpose of holding any determination under the Act, these courts shall have the same powers as are vested in a civil court under the Code of Civil Procedure (1908) while trying a suit in respect of any of the following matters:

(a) the summoning and enforcing of attendance of any witness and examining him on oath,

(b) the discovery and production of any document,

(c) the reception of evidence or any public record or document or copy of such record or document from any court or office, and

(d) such other matters as may be prescribed.

The Lok Adalat may adopt its own procedure for the settlement of any dispute before it.

The Lok Adalat is constituted by the district judge who may engage the services of any subordinate judge or a magistrate for this purpose. The concerned judge or magistrate fixes a particular date and place to hold his Lok Adalat so as to get the matter pending in his court settled with the consent of the parties. The seat of such a court may be anywhere in the district according to the convenience of the judges and magistrates as far as possible. The notable point is that such a court works as a friend and guide of the litigants so that they may arrive at a point of compromise or settlement. The lawyers may also appear in such a court not for the purpose of entering into arguments or wordy duels but to persuade the parties to somehow arrive at a point of reciprocal agreement. The litigants may withdraw their suits from a court of law and get them settled here by their consent. As such, the award of the people's court is binding on the concerned parties and they have no right to challenge it in a court of law by filing an appeal.

From the above, it is clear that a Lok Adalat functions on the basis of some positive norms as:

1. It asks the consenting parties to appear before it on a particular date and at a particular place for the settlement of their dispute.
2. It asks the consenting parties for the elucidation of the points of dispute in a way leading to their settlement.
3. The judge and the other members of the Lok Adalat try to offer concrete guidelines for the parties so as to get at the truth of the matter.
4. The Lok Adalat may offer a solution so as to resolve the dispute in case the parties face difficulty in arriving at a point of agreement.

5. As a result of such endeavours of the Lok Adalat, a deed of agreement is finally drawn that is acceptable to both the parties. It is duly signed by them and a copy of the same is sent to the regular court of law.

6. If the Lok Adalat issues a decree, it is enforced by a regular court according to the rules of the Civil Procedure Code.

7. After the resolution of the dispute, the court fee paid by the litigants to a regular court is refunded as per rules.

The operation of the system of Lok Adalat obviously demonstrates the phenomenon of a para-judicial process that is like as well as unlike the operation of a judicial system in these respects:

1. A Lok Adalat is not a court of law as understood by the common people, though it may have the attribute of the same. It hardly has anything in common with the regular court except that both are tools in the legal system to deliver justice. The point of difference is that while a law court sits at its premises where the litigants come with their lawyers and witnesses to seek justice, the Lok Adalat itself goes to the people to deliver justice at their doorsteps.

2. In order to ensure that the settlement is fair and according to law, the forum may consist of legally trained people who are respected in the community where the Lok Adalats are constituted. The functions of a Lok Adalat is not to act as a law court but to enable the respective parties who voluntarily seek its intervention with a view to understand their respective rights and obligations relating to the disputes brought before it and to help it to keep the dialogue going on in a fair manner.

3. It makes another alternative to justice by a regular court of law for the sake of delivering informal, cheap and expeditious justice to the common man by way of settling the dispute which is pending in the court and also those which have not yet reached the courts by negotiations, conciliation and by adopting persuasive common sense and human approach to the problem of the disputants with the assistance of specially trained and experienced members of a team of conciliators.

4. The true basis of the settlement of disputes by the Lok Adalat is the principle of mutual consent and voluntary acceptance of the solution with the help of the conciliators. It revolves around

the principle of creating an awareness among the disputants to the effect that their interest lies in arriving at a peaceful settlement of their dispute without losing more time unnecessarily.

5. The system of Lok Adalat has its origin not in any statute or law, it is devised and developed by the people themselves as a participatory instrument of democratic judicial decision-making.

The Lok Adalats are like para-judicial institutions devised and developed by the social activists and the people themselves. The system is still in a stage of infancy, though it is trying to find an appropriate structure and procedure in the fight of the common people for the cause of social justice. By all means, a Lok Adalat is a unique institution which not only settles the disputes of the parties and their points of contention, it also contributes to their well-being in several other ways. It meets the aspirations of the people by delivering them economic and social justice. Their main aim is to settle the dispute in such a manner that the mutual relations of the disputants remain primarily the same as existed before the commencement of such a dispute.[14]

Since the system of Lok Adalat forms a variety of the Alternative Dispute Resolution, a distinguished writer enumerates its advantages as under:

1. It can be used at any time, even when a case is pending before a court of law.
2. It can provide a better solution to disputes more expeditiously and at less cost than litigation.
3. ADR programmes are flexible and not afflicted with rigours of rules of procedure.
4. The freedom of the parties to litigation is not affected by ADR proceedings.
5. ADR can be used with or without a lawyer.
6. ADR procedures help in the reduction of the work-load of the courts and there-by help them to focus attention on the cases which ought to be decided by the courts.

---

14. N. Madhava Menon: "Justice Sans Lawyers: Some Indian Experiments" in *Indian Bar Review*, Vol. 2, 1985, p. 446.

7. ADR procedures permit parties to choose neutrals who are not specialists in the subject-matter of the dispute. Lawyers will have to adapt their role to ADR requirements.[15]

It may be hopefully visualised that the experiment of Lok Adalats would contribute to the making of justice available to a common man at a low cost and within due time. It would carefully strengthen the faith of the ordinary people in the system of justice in the country. "Lok Adalat has the potential for social construction and legal mobilisation for social change. It can influence the style of administration of justice and the role of lawyers and judges in it. It can take law closer to the life of the people and reduce disparity between law in the books and law in action."[16]

Public Interest Litigation

Popularly known as the PIL, it may be defined as litigation undertaken for the purpose of redressing public injury, enforcing public duty, protecting social, collective and diffused rights and interests or vindicating public interest.[17] In the beginning it was confined to a few cases as those of combating inhuman conditions inside the jails or horrible exploitation of the bonded labour. But now its scope has become wider so as to include any situation calling for speedy trial, right to legal aid, right to livelihood, right to protection of life from pollution of air and water or environmental hazards, right to lead a life of dignity or fulfilment of basic needs and the like. No doubt, a surprising degree of willingness has been shown by the Indian judiciary in altering the rules of procedure whenever necessary so much so that now actions may be commenced not only by way of a formal petition, but also by way of letters addressed to the court or to a judge who may choose to treat it as a writ petition.[18]

---

15. Dr. P.C. Rao: "Alternatives to Litigation" in *The Hindustan Times*, New Delhi, 1 October, 1995, p. 13.

16. N.R. Madhava Menon: "Lok Adalat: People's Programme for Speedy Justice" in *Indian Bar Review*, Vol. 13, No. 2, 1986, p. 140.

17. Sonia Hurrah: *Public Interest Litigation* (Ahmedabad: Mishra and Co., 1993), p. 4.

18. Notable is the fact that several actions have been taken on a post card written to a judge, and by one judge converting a letter to the editor of a newspaper into a public interest litigation writ petition. Prof. Upendra Baxi has termed it 'epistolary jurisdiction' of the Court.

Obviously, the case of public interest litigation militates against the traditional doctrine of *locus standi* which signifies that only an aggrieved person or a directly affected party may move the court. That is, unless a person or a party is directly affected by the action of the other party, it has no right to come to the court for seeking relief or for redressal of the wrong done to him. Appreciating the new trend, V.R. Krishna Iyer says: "Restrictive rules about standing are, in general, inimical to a healthy system of administrative law. If a plaintiff with a good cause is turned away, merely because he is not sufficiently affected personally, that means some government agency, is left free to violate law and that is contrary to public interest." Litigants are unlikely to expend their time and money unless they have some real interest at stake. In the rare case where they wish to sue merely out of public spirit, why they should be discouraged."[19]

The development of public interest litigation has occurred in many developed countries of the world in recent times. While its emergence is widely appreciated as a necessary rejection of the *laisez faire* doctrine, its goal is hailed as the creation of a system which would provide legal relief without back-breaking formality and costly procedures of law.

However, the points of limitations may be enumerated as under:

1. The Court must see that the member of the public who approaches it in a case is acting bonafide and not for a personal gain or private profit, or political motivation, or any other oblique consideration. This right to move the Court cannot be used for any extraneous purpose as preventing the government of Rajasthan from shifting its Public Health Engineering Department from Ajmer to Bhilwara.

2. The Court must not allow its process to be abused by crafty persons just for political considerations or by some others to delay any legislative or administrative action for the sake of achieving some political end. Nor should the Court overstep the limits of judicial functions and trespass into areas reserved for the executive or the legislative organs of the government.

---

19. V.R. Krishna Iyer: *The Integral Yoga of Public Law and Development in the Context of India*, p. 5.

3. Any conscientious person may move the Court for securing the writ of *quo warranto* in order to quash a wrong appointment that would cause harm to the interest of the public. But the petitioner should not do so with a selfish motive of his own. The argument of a petitioner that while he had not applied for the post of a lecturer in the University as he knew in advance that a person with lesser qualifications would be appointed, he moved the Court in the name of public interest for issuing a writ of *quo warranto*. He lost the case. The Court took it as attempt on the part of the petitioner to have his own axe to grind.
4. The Court may take an action *suo moto* as well after seeing something shocking in the newspapers with a view to do justice to the aggrieved party.
5. A tax-payer may file a writ petition against an authority as the municipal board for asking it to do what it is required to do. In such a case the Court would see whether the life of the people of the locality, as alleged, is in danger and, if in danger, then it would issue the writ of *mandamus* asking that authority to do something. The Court may also entertain the petition of a prisoner drawing its attention to the torture of his fellow prisoners in the jail.

The case of public interest litigation has its weak and strong sides. Arguments against it may be enumerated as under:

1. It misuses and over-burdens the courts by asking them to resolve questions which belong more appropriately to the executive and legislative departments of the State. It is argued that the liberalisation of the rule of standing will provide more opportunity for interference with the working of other organs of the State which is against the theory of separation of powers. As Justice R.S. Pathak observed: "In the process of correcting executive error or removing legislative omissions, the Court can so easily find itself involved in policy-making of a quality and to a degree characteristic of political authority and indeed run the risk of being mistaken for one."[20]

---

20. Cited in M.N. Chaturvedi: "Liberalising the Requirement of Standing in the Public Interest Litigation" in *Journal of Law Institute*, New Delhi, Vol. 26 (January-June, 1984), p. 53.

2. It is also possible that in this process such lawyers may intervene in the judicial process who do not really represent public interest. It is feared that the adoption of a liberalised rule of standing, as Prof. M.N. Chaturvedi says, "will encourage vexatious litigants to file non-meritorious challenges in a large number thus allowing them to abuse the process of the court, and also cause further delay in the administration of justice."[21]

3. It has been suggested that a liberal rule of standing may lead to immobility and inefficiency in the sphere of administration. Excessive judicial interference in administrative matters is likely to affect creative responsibility of those who have been authorised by law to run the administration of the country. The result of this "may be that the government may not be able to implement social welfare schemes, because it will be very easy for any person to allege wasteful expenditure of public money and thus the official machinery will be afraid of implementing any progressive policies."[22]

4. It is desired that all the three departments of State act in harmony and coordination. Hence, it is argued that involving the jurisdiction of the Courts to sit in judgement over the actions of the political branches is likely to lead to confrontation between the judiciary, on the one hand, and the executive and the legislature on the other. The effect of such confrontation may undermine the prestige of judiciary and impair its ability to discharge its traditional function. Therefore, as a matter of caution and prudence, the Courts should not judge the legality of the actions of public authorities until they are called upon by persons actually affected by the actions."[23]

5. Law is not the best way to undertake matters of social change or socio-economic modernisation of the country. The root cause of social and economic injustice cannot be attended through judicial process. A word of caution should be added here. It is well commented: "These trends are doubtless

---

21. *Ibid*, p. 50.

22. *Ibid*, p. 51.

23. *Ibid*.

welcome, but while welcoming them, one has to be realistic and factually assess the potential of judicial process in order to see the limits within which such liberalisation will have to function. This will prevent undue complacency. Public interest litigation and liberalisation of *locus standi* are methods of increasing accountability of the government. But they are not the panacea for social injustice. There are limits to what can be achieved through judicial process."[24]

The weight of the above arguments cannot be dismissed easily. At the same time, the merits of the public interest litigation should not be lost sight of. There seems to be a general agreement that the requirement of *locus standi* should be relaxed or liberalised so far as case of the protection and enforcement of the fundamental rights of the poor and backward sections of the community is concerned. Similarly, depending upon the facts of the case, in matters involving public wrong or injury, the courts should relax the requirements of standing where the issue requires judicial determination. Such areas of public interest litigation "need encouragement and support. But it should not be used for policing the corridors of power. Judicial activism is desirable for protecting the citizen, not for policing the government."[25]

Judicial Activism

The trend of 'judicial activism', as it has developed over the recent years in our country, should be taken as the assertion of the "supremacy of the wise men' over the 'system of laws'. It is informed by this judicious maxim that, in the words of Sir Fredick Pollock, it "is the duty to keep the rulers of law in harmony with the enlightened common sense of the nation". Law is said to be blind, but the judges have the eyes to see it in its applied form so that the 'will of the state' is not perverted by those who have no scruples in converting it into a 'highway robbery', or, in the words of St. Augustine, transforming this earth into a 'city of the ungodly'. Law creates distinction between a condition of 'license' as understood by Hobbes and a state of liberty as conceived by Hobhouse. It accepts the pattern

---

24. *Ibid*, p. 52.

25. S.P. Sathe: "Public Participation in Judicial Process: New Trends in Law of Locus Standi with Special Reference to Administrative Law." *Ibid.*, p. 12.

of its justice the morality of the community whose conduct it assumes to regulate."

The roots of judicial activism may be traced in the role of the Supreme Court and the High Courts in exercising the power of 'judicial review' as well as in making wider interpretations of the Constitutional provisions while entertaining public interest petitions and trying them in an expeditious manner. By making a liberal interpretation of the rule of standing (*locus standi*) and, more than that by making an expanding concept of the fundamental rights of the citizens in their view, the Courts have gone to the extent to looking into many areas as vires of telecom policy, allotment of official accommodation to the public servants, cause of the spread of an epidemic hazardous to human life, distribution of petrol dealerships and gas agencies, protection of the environment, involvement of politicians in any *hawala* transaction,[26] any scam relating to animal fodder or Ayurvedic medicines etc. It all shows that the Courts have expanded their jurisdiction to any conceivable extent in the name of doing complete justice to the aggrieved party that moves them or to any public-spirited organisation that does the same for or on behalf of such a person or party. Such a role of the high judiciary has been regarded as 'active', even adventurous, which though widely appreciated by the common people, is not absolutely immune from its inherent weaknesses.

Certain eventualities may, however, be conceived when the judiciary may have to over-step its normal jurisdiction and intervene in areas otherwise falling within the domain of the legislature:

(i) When the legislature fails to discharge its responsibilities.

(ii) In case of 'hung' legislature when the government it throws up is weak, insecure and busy only in the struggle for survival

---

26. *Hawala* trade is a system of bypassing the official foreign exchange channel. Operators in the field take payment in rupees and supply dollars against it abroad. Thus, trade runs through the networks of agents under an operator's control. Payments made in dollars abroad cannot be transferred to India and the beneficiary is paid in rupees. Thus, it is a method of laundering money. Dollars can be purchased at a lower rate through *hawala* than the official one. Foreign exchange drawing limits can also be bypassed. *Hawala* rates often differ from place to place and within a country. Some exporters and importers resort to *hawala* in other ways as well.

and therefore unable to take any decision which displeases any caste, community, or other group.

(iii) Those in power may be afraid of taking honest and hard decisions for fear of losing power and, for that reason, may have public issues referred to Courts as issues of law in order to make time and delay decisions or to pass on the odium of strong decision-making to the Courts.

(iv) Where the legislature and the executive fail to protect the basic rights of the citizens like the right to lead a decent life, a healthy surrounding or to provide an honest, efficient and just system of laws and administration.

(v) Where the Court of law is misused by a strong authoritarian parliamentary party government for ulterior motives as was sought to be done during the emergency aberration.

(vi) Sometimes, the Courts themselves knowing or unknowingly become victims of human, all too human, weaknesses of craze for populism, publicity, playing to the media and hogging the headlines.[27]

Taking into considerations what the Courts have done so far, we may trace the cause and decipher some established maxims sustaining judicial activism in our country as under:

1. There arise situations when the people cry for justice. But when they find that the legislative and the executive authorities do nothing for them, and, more than that, do for the worse, they perforce move the Courts. In such a sensitive situation, the Courts have to do justice in stead of asking the aggrieved persons or parties or someone acting on their behalf to go elsewhere or to keep quiet.[28]

---

27. S.C. Kashyap: "Judiciary–Legislature Interface", *Politics India*, New Delhi, April, 1997, p. 22.

28. Bindeshwari Pathak: "Judicial Activism: It's Right, My Lord" in the *The Hindustan Times*, New Delhi, 28 April, 1996, p. 13. Passing critical remarks against top bureaucrats, this writer goes to the extent of saying: "IAS officers who have been given constitutional protection, have only become an extension of political parties, spineless and subservient, they no more provide the steel-frame of the administration."

2. When a matter comes before the Court, it carefully sees whether it falls within its jurisdiction or not. Hence, the learned judges dismiss a petition filed for the sake of luxurious or frivolous litigation, or if it is politically motivated. The Court has made it clear that it cannot go into policy matters relating to fiscal resources. But, short of that, it may go ahead in doing justice so as to give relief to the petitioner.
3. The judiciary scrupulously observes the rule of self-imposed limitations. While recognising that it may exercise its jurisdiction in the matter, it is guided by the norm of implementation. That is, while exercising its jurisdiction, it also keeps it in its view that it has to ensure the implementation of its decisions as there is no sense in laying down a proposition that is incapable of operation at the ground level. The notable point is that the judges do not act like politicians under the cover of political considerations.
4. It is true that in the name of hearing a public interest petition, the Courts would do their best as to render justice to the aggrieved party even by relaxing the rigours of procedure, their purpose is not to meddle with the jurisdiction of the legislative and executive authorities deliberately and indiscriminately.
5. Strong judicial orders in the exercise of contempt jurisdiction must not be taken as the instances of judicial activism. For instance, the Supreme Court summoned the Speaker of the Manipur Legislative Assembly (Dr. Borababu Singh) for not implementing its orders for the payment of salaries and allowances to some members of the House who had 'wrongly' been disqualified by him on the charge of committing the act of political defection.

The case of judicial activism has its positive and negative aspects. On the positive side, it may be affirmed that it has widely captured the public imagination as the only ray of hope piercing through the clouds of an otherwise overcast sky. The fairly swift and dramatic decisions of the Courts have highlighted not just the largest activist role that the judiciary appears to have assigned to itself but also the unresponsiveness of the legislature, the executive, the bureaucracy and the police to the crying needs and grievances of the common people. By imposing a fine of Rs. 50 lakh on the former

Union Petroleum Minister (Capt. Satish Sharma) for abusing his discretionary power in the allotment of gas agencies and petrol dealerships and a fine of Rs. 60 lakh on the former Minister for Urban Housing and Development and the then Governor of Himachal Pradesh (Mrs. Sheila Kaul), the Supreme Court has established the 'supremacy of law' over the 'supremacy of man' . The Courts have instructed the public servants to do their duty faithfully and by taking immediate and effective action against the wrong-doers, they have earned the trust of the common people in the system of justice in the country.

On the negative side, it is said that judicial activism amounts to judicial excessivism or judicial adverturism inherent with the pernicious tendency of judicial despotism. A noted jurist of the country (N. A. Palkhivala) deprecated it in the name of the violation of the celebrated principle of separation of powers in that justice given by a dictator should not be similarised with the justice of a democratic organisation. The people, in his view, should know that even judiciary cannot transgress its limitations in a democratic set up.

However, the trend of judicial activism should be evaluated in the light of this irrefutable fact that the law-makers "are invariably handicapped by the limitations of human foresight."[29] The legislators and the administrators of the country are politicians by profession. They may do anything for a populist cause, but the judges constitute the sober element of the state and so they, in the words of Justice Frankfurter of the American Supreme Court, "decide matters in accordance with the standards and values of the reasonable men."[30]

Fast Track Courts

It is a new venture in the sphere of judicial reforms. We know that the courts of the country are over-loaded with work as a result of which judicial process has become time-consuming. Under a scheme launched by the Union Law Ministry vide directive dated 8

29. Mendelson: "Judicial Activism" in David I. Sills(ed.): *International Encyclopaedia of the Social Sciences* (New York: Macmillan and Free Press, 1968), Vol. 8, p. 320.

30. Prof. Andre Betaille: "Future of Institutional Autonomy," *The Times of India,* New Delhi, 11 December, 1995, p. 10.

January, 2001, the Chief Justice of a High Court may assess the position of cases pending in the courts and then prepare a plan for the establishment of such courts in various places of the State. Since the Union Law Ministry pays for the expenses of such courts, the Chief Justice appoints judges for such courts on a contract basis for two years. The courts may hear and decide civil and criminal cases. It is required that such a court must dispose of at least 14 civil and at least 14 criminal cases in a month. The cases are referred to them by the High Court.

The success of this venture may be seen in the fact that in 2002 166 such courts were functioning in the country and 175 cases had been decided by them. In Gujarat such courts disposed of 8,771 out of 29,302 cases transferred to them by the High Court. Such a court at Vadodra created history by disposing of *Best Bakery Case* within a couple of hours after hearing 21 accused persons and one investigating officer and acquitted all of them. West Bengal has 152 sanctioned courts, though only 59 could be identified and only 52 were functional. Rajasthan has 83 sanctioned courts. All are functional and have decided 7,386 out of 11,986 cases transferred to them by the High Court. Surprisingly, such a court at Alwar heard and decided a rape case within three weeks. The accused person was given the sentence of life imprisonment.

Justice delayed is justice denied. It is equally true that justice done in haste is justice undone. So the matter of establishment of fast track courts was challenged in the Supreme Court. A bench of three judges (consisting of B.N. Kripal, K.G. Balakrishnan and Arijit Pasayat) described the whopping acquittal rate of 90 to 95 per cent as a 'serious problem' and undertook the task of framing guidelines for the High Courts on the appointment and monitoring of these courts.[31]

Code of Ethics for Judges

(Statement of the Values of Judicial Life adopted at the annual conference of the Chief Justices held in New Delhi in the first week of December, 1999, chaired by Dr. A.S. Anand, Chief Justice of Supreme Court of India).

---

31. *Bar Council of India* v. *Union of India and others*, Newsletter of the Indian Law Institute, Vol. II, October-December, 2001.

1. A judge should not contest elections to any office of a club, society or any other association.
2. He should not hold any elective office except of a society or an association connected with law.
3. Close association of a judge with individual members of the bar, particularly those who practise in the same court, must be eschewed.
4. A judge should not permit any member of his family such as spouse, son, daughter, son-in-law, daughter-in-law or any other close relative of he or she is member of the bar, to appear before him or even be associated in any manner with a case to be dealt with by him.
5. A member of a judge's family, if he or she is a member of the bar, should not be permitted to use the residence in which the judge actually resides.
6. A judge should practise a degree of aloofness consistent with the dignity of his office.
7. A judge should not hear or decide a matter with which a member of his family, a close relative, or a friend is concerned.
8. A judge must not enter into public debate or express his views in public on political matters or on matters that are pending, or are likely to arise for judicial determination.
9. A judge is expected to let his judgments speak for themselves, he should not give interviews to the media.
10. A judge will not accept gifts or hospitality except from his family, close relatives and friends.
11. A judge will not hear and decide a matter of a company in which he holds shares or is concerned with it, unless he has disclosed his interest and no objection to his hearing the matter is raised.
12. A judge must not speculate in shares, stocks or the like.
13. A judge should not engage directly or indirectly in trade or business either by himself or in association with any other person. (Publication of a legal treatise or any activity in the nature of a hobby will not be construedas trade or business.)

14. A judge should not ask for, accept contributions, or otherwise actively associate himself with the raising of any fund.
15. Every judge must at all times be conscious that he is under the public gaze and there should be no act or omission by him which is unbecoming of his office.

Accountability of Judges

The Santhanam Committee Report (1964) endorsed all-pervasiveness of corruption in our country. Former Chief Justice S.P. Bharucha publicly regretted that about 20 per cent of judiciary was in its grip. Some unsavoury reports about the 'misdemeanours' of the Judges of High Courts of Punjab, Karnataka and Rajasthan also came into limelight. Hence, the issue of the accountability of the Judges has come up and the general view is in favour of the appointment of a National Judicial Commission. A bill to this effect was moved in the Lok Sabha in 1990 by the then Law Minister (Dinesh Goswami), but it lapsed owing to the dissolution of the House in the following year. The issue of the appointment and transfer of High Court Judges has come to be bracketed with it and so it is suggested that an independent body should recommend the names of the persons for appointment as the Judges of Supreme Court and High Courts as well as transfer of the Judges from one High Court to another and make, when required, a thorough inquiry into the alleged act of 'misdemeanour' against a Judge. Such a step should not be taken as an innovation in view of the fact that in Canada a Judicial Commission set up in 1971 has the power to recommend the names of guilty judges for removal after making a thorough inquiry. The same job is done by a Constitutional Commission in Australia.

Happily, judiciary in our country has remained immune from corruption that is so pervasive in the domains of the executive and the legislature. If there have been some cases to tarnish the names of the higher judiciary, the reason for this should be traced both in the process of appointment as well as in the personal weaknesses of the incumbents. The power of appointment of the Judges is vested in the President who acts on the advice of his ministers. It is for this reason that the President appointed V. Ramaswamy as a judge of the Supreme Court in flagrant disregard to the views of the then Chief Justice E.S. Venkataramaiah who was later found guilty by the Sawant Inquiry Committee.

Surprisingly, in 1993 the motion of impeachment could not be passed in the Lok Sabha due to want of requisite majority as the then Prime Minister (Narsimha Rao) issued a verbal whip to the Congress MPs to walk out of the House at the time of division. We have seen that the Supreme Court in the *S.P. Gupta Case* (1982) ruled that the matter relating to the transfer of Judges fell within the discretionary power of the President. In the *Supreme Court Advocates-on-Record Association Case* (1993), it held that the President should honour the advice of the Chief Justice as it was 'effective' under Art. 124 (2). The Court complicated the situation yet more by holding in the *Special Reference Case* of 1998 that the Chief Justice of India should constitute a panel of Judges under him (consisting of 4 senior-most Judges) and then recommend anybody's name for appointment as a Judge of Supreme Court provided it is accepted by all or by 4 of the 5 members. In a case relating to the appointment of a Judge for a High Court, the Chief Justice must consult two senior-most judges of the Court and a name should be recommended to the President if it is cleared unanimously. Then, in a matter relating to the transfer of a High Court judge, the Chief Justice must consult 4 senior-most Judges of the Court and the two Chief Justices of the High Courts—one from which the judge is to be transferred and the other receiving him.[32] By doing so, the Supreme Court crossed the bounds of its domain and so it was not appreciated by leading jurists of the country like H.M. Seervai and N.A. Palkhivala.[33]

---

32. With a view to make the apointment process of the judges of the Supreme Court and High Courts quite apparent, the Supreme Court in this *reference case* observed that the process "must be initiated well in time to ensure its completion at least one month prior to the date of an anticipated vacancy, and the appointment should be announced soon thereafter to avoid any speculation or uncertainty. This schedule should be followed strictly and invariably in the appointment of the Chief Justices of the High Courts and the Chief Justice of India to avoid the institution being rendered headless for any significant period. In the case of the appointment of the Chief Justice of a High Court to the Supreme Court, the appointment of the successor Chief Justice in that High Court should be made ordinarily within one month of vacancy."

33. It is not judicious to vest the power of appointment of Judges in the head of the state in the name of his 'discretionary' jurisdiction that becomes virtually vested in the Ministers in a parliamentary form of government. In England, judges are appointed by the Lord Chancellor who is a Cabinet Minister. A voice has been raised against it. The Bar Council appointed an Inquiry Commission

As corruption is a matter of choice, it reflects human weakness. Self-restraint forms part of the moral code of conduct and, as a matter of fact, it is the most effective remedy. Justice Frankfurter of the American Supreme Court aptly visualises: "All power is of an encroaching nature. Judicial power is not immune to this human weakness. It must also be a guard against encroaching beyond its proper bounds and not the less so, since the only restraint upon it is self-restraint" But statutory checks are also required so as to discourage an incumbent from falling prey to material temptations. For this purpose, Art. 124 (4) provides for the impeachment of a judge. But this process is cumbersome. A judge with a vitiated mind knows that his conduct cannot be discussed in the Parliament unless there is a substantive motion before the House (Art. 121) and that the procedure of impeachment cannot be easily made use of as the Ramaswamy affair has shown.[34] Hence, the appointment of a National Judicial Commission is the need of the hour. The National Constitution Review Commission Report (2002) has endorsed it.[35] We may appreciate the view of a former judge: "There is an insistent public demand now that matters connected with appointments and misdemeanours of the Higher Judiciary need to be dealt with by an independent body using transparent means instead of the present unsatisfactory mechanism shrouded in secrecy.[36]

---

under Iain Glidewell, a former Justice of Appeal, which commented: "It was politically unacceptable for a member of the Government to continue to appoint high ranking Judges. The present practice is not wholly satisfactory to the 21st century".

34. Inflated ego informed by vitiated mind plays its own part in this regard. As Dr. A.S. Anand, former Chief Justice of India, observed: "Our function is divine, but the problem begins when we start thinking that we become divine."

35. Former Union Law Minister Shanti Bhushan well points out: "The time has come for civil society and the media to realise their strength and use it to compel Parliament to amend the Constitution and put in place a National Judicial Commission as a permanent body for the appointment and removal of Judges." Refer to his paper "Clean Up the Judiciary" in *The Times of India* (New Delhi), 12 October, 2007

36. Rajinder Sachar: "National Judicial Commission" in *The Hindu*, New Delhi, 28 March 2003, p. 10.

15

Public Services

One of the salient features of the Indian Constitution is that it incorporates chapters on some such subjects which ought to have been covered by the process of ordinary legislation or administrative action or both. Part XIV titled 'Services under the Union and the States' is a case in point. What had an impact of its own on the minds of the Makers was to have independent, impartial and efficient public services in the country going to adopt a constitution irrevocably wedded to the ideals of a democratic, secular and social welfare state after overthrowing the vestiges of a long colonial rule that had converted the top administrative class into a 'new caste' of autocrats ruling over the destiny of the teeming millions of India.

Kinds of Public Services

Our Constitution establishes three kinds of public services—All-India Public Services, Central Services and States Public Services. Art. 310 specifies the tenure of persons serving the Union or State Governments. It lays down:

1. Except as expressly provided by this Constitution, every person who is a member of a defence service or of a civil service of the Union or an all-India services or holds any post connected with defence or any civil post under the Union holds office during the pleasure of the President and every person who is a member of a civil service of a State or holds any civil post under a State holds office during the pleasure of the Governor of the State.

2. Any contract under which a person, not being a member of the defence services or of an all-India service or of a civil service of the Union or a State, is appointed under this Constitution to hold such a post, may, if the President or the Governor, as the case may be, deems it necessary in order to

secure the services of a person having special qualifications, provide for the payment to him of compensation, if before the expiration of an agreed period the post is abolished, or he is by reason not connected with any misconduct on his part, required to vacate the post."

However, what really ensures security of service to all civil servants is Art. 311 which lay down:

"1. No person who is a member of a civil service of the Union, or of an All-India service or the services of a State, or holds a civil post under the Union or a State shall be dismissed or removed by an authority subordinate to that by which he was appointed.

2. No such person aforesaid shall be dismissed or removed or reduced in rank except after an inquiry in which he has been informed of the charges against him and given a reasonable opportunity of being heard in respect of those charges.

3. If in respect of any such person as aforesaid, a question arises whether it is reasonably practicable to hold such inquiry as is referred to in clause (2), the decision thereon of the authority empowered to dismiss or remove such person or to reduce him in rank shall be final."

Then, Art, 312 empowers the Rajya Sabha to pass a resolution by 2/3 majority of the members, present and voting, for the creation of an All-India Public Service in the national interest.

This point should be taken into account here that since members of the All-India services are common to the Union and the States, the posting of a member of such Services, working in a State, to a post under the Union should be considered as on deputation, unless the order of posting says so specifically.

Public Service Commissions

Art. 315 contains provisions for the constitution of Public Service Commission for the Union as well as for the States, including a Joint Public Service Commission for two or more States. The Chairman and the members of the Union Public Service Commission and of a Joint Public Service Commission shall be appointed by the President and of a State Public Service Commission by the Governor of the State. The Constitution does not specify the strength of Public

Service Commissions, but it lays down that, as nearly as possible, half of the members of a Commission shall be persons who at the date of their respective appointment have held office for at least ten years either under the Government of India or under the Government of a State, and in computing the said period of ten years any period before the commencement of this Constitution during which a person has held office under the Crown in India or under the Government of an Indian State shall be included.

It is also provided that if the office of the Chairman of the Commission becomes vacant, or if the chairman is by reason of absence or for any other reason unable to perform the duties of his office, those duties shall, until some person appointed under clause (1) to the vacant office has entered on the duties thereof or, as the case may be, until the Chairman has resumed his duties, be performed by such one of the other members of the Commission as the President in the case of the Union Public Service Commission or a Joint Public Service Commission and the Governor of a State in the case of a State Commission may appoint for the purpose. The Chairman and the members of a Public Service Commission shall hold office for a term of six years from the date on which they enter upon office or until they attain the age of 65 years in the case of Union Public Service Commission, and 62 years in the case of a State Public Service Commission or a Joint Public Service Commission, whichever earlier. Provided that a member of a Public Service Commission may in writing under his hand addressed to the President in the case of Union Public Service Commission or a Joint Commission, and in the case of a State Public Service Commission to the Governor of the State, resign his office or may be removed in the manner provided in clause (1) or clause (2) of Art. 317. A person who holds office as a member of Public Service Commission shall, on the expiration of his term of office, be ineligible for reappointment to that office.

The Chairman or a member of a Public Service Commission may be suspended or removed from his office by an order of the President on the ground of 'misbehaviour' after the Supreme Court, on reference being made to it by the President in that behalf under Art. 145 reported that the Chairman or such member, as the case may be, ought to be removed on any such ground. The President in the case of the Union Public Service Commission or Joint Public Service Commission and the Governor in the case of State Public

Service Commission may suspend from office the Chairman or any other member of the Commission in respect of whom a reference has been made to the Supreme Court under clause (1) until the President has passed orders on receipt of the report of the Supreme Court on such reference. Notwithstanding anything in clause (1), the President may by order remove from office the Chairman or any other member of a Public Service Commission if the Chairman or such other member, as the case may be, (a) is adjudged an insolvent, or (b) engages himself during his term of office in any paid employment outside the duties of his office, or (c) is, in the opinion of the President, unfit to continue in office by reason of infirmity of mind or body. If the Chairman or any other member of the Public Service Commission is or becomes in any way concerned with or interested in any contract or agreement may by or on behalf of the Government of India, or participates in any way in the profit thereof or in any benefit or emolument arising therefrom otherwise than as member and in common with the other members of an incorporated company, he shall for the purpose of clause (1) be deemed to be guilty of misbehaviour.

Art. 318 empowers the President in the case of Union Public Service Commission and a Joint Public Service Commission and to the Governor in the case of a State Public Service Commission, as the case may be, to determine the number of members of the Commission and their conditions of service and to make provisions with respect to the number of members of the staff of the Commission and their conditions of service. Provided that the conditions of service of a member shall not be varied to his disadvantage after his appointment.

In order to ensure impartiality and integrity of the members of the Public Service Commission, a bar has been put on post-retirement appointment under the Union or State Governments. Art. 319 lays down that the Chairman of the Union Public Service Commission shall be ineligible for further employment either under the Government of India, or under the Government of a State. The Chairman of a State Public Service Commission shall be eligible for appointment as the Chairman or a member of the Union Public Service Commission, or as the Chairman of any other State Public Service Commission, but not for any other employment either under the Government of India or under the Government of a State. A member, other than the Chairman of the Union Public Service

Commission shall be eligible for appointment as the Chairman of the Union Public Service Commission or as the Chairman of a State Public Service Commission, but not for any other employment under the Government of a State. A member, other than the Chairman of a State Public Service Commission, shall be eligible for appointment as the Chairman or a member of the Union Public Service Commission, or as the Chairman of that or any other State Public Service Commission, but not for any other employment either under the Government of India or under the Government of a State. Obviously, the object of this provision is to ensure impartiality of the members of the Public Service Commissions by keeping them immune from any allurement of employment under the Government after termination of their office in the Commission.

The functions of the Public Service Commissions have been spelt out in Art. 320 of the Constitution as under:

1. It shall be the duty of the Union and State Public Service Commissions to conduct examinations for appointment to the services of the Union and the services of the States respectively.
2. It shall also be the duty of the Union Public Service Commission, if requested by any two or more States so to do, to assist those States in framing and operating schemes of joint recruitment for any services for which candidates possessing special qualifications are required.
3. The Union Public Service Commission or the State Public Service Commission, as the case may be, shall be consulted–
   (a) on all matters relating to methods of recruitment to civil services and for civil posts;
   (b) on the principles to be followed in making appointments to civil services and post and in making promotions and transfers from one services to another and on the suitability of candidates for such appointments, promotions and transfers;
   (c) on all disciplinary matters affecting a person serving under the Government of India or the Government of a State in a civil capacity, including memorials or petitions relating to such matters;

(d) on any claim by or in respect of a person who is serving or has served under the Government of India, or the Government of a State, or under the Crown in India, or under the Government of an Indian State, in a civil capacity, that in any costs incurred by him in defending legal proceedings instituted against him in respect of acts done or purporting to be done in the execution of his duty, should be paid out of the Consolidated Fund of India, or, as the case may be, out of the Consolidated Fund of the State;

(e) on any claim for the award of a pension in respect of injuries sustained by a person while serving under the Government of India or the Government of a State, or under the Crown in India, or under the Government of an Indian State, in a civil capacity, and any question as to the amount of any such award.

Art. 323 says that it shall be the duty of the Union Public Service Commission to present annually to the President a report as to the work done by it and on receipt of such report the President shall cause a copy thereof together with a memorandum explaining, as respects the case, if any, where the advice of the Commission was not accepted, the reasons for such non-acceptance to be laid before each House of Parliament. So the State Public Service Commission shall submit its annual report to the Governor (and a Joint Public Service Commission shall submit its annual report to the Governors of the concerned States) who shall cause it to be laid before the State Legislature together with a memorandum explaining the reason for not accepting the advice of the Commission in any case or cases.

The Public Service Commissions have the power to adopt any method for selection and recruitment of public servants, provided it is not arbitrary or unfair, or *ultra vires* of the laws and rules of the country. In the matter of selection by promotion, it would not be arbitrary because it is based solely on service records. It is required that the Public Service Commission be consulted in the matter of suitability of candidates for appointment, promotion, transfer etc. But there is no requirement that the Commission must interview the candidates, or permit a selection committee to do this job. It shall suffice if the Commission reserves to itself the right to approve or disapprove the report of the selection committee and thus take responsibility for the discharge of its functions.

Acting under Article 320, the President of India made in 1958 the Union Public Service Commission (Exemption from Consultation) Regulations. Those Regulations provide that it shall not be necessary to consult the Union Public Service Commission in regard to any of the matters mentioned in Article 320 in the case of the following services and posts:

1. Posts in respect of which the authority to appoint is specifically conferred on the President by the Constitution.
2. Posts of Chairman or members of any Board, Tribunal, Commission, Committee or other similar authority created by or under the provision of a statute.
3. Posts of Chairman or members of any Board, Tribunal, Commission, Committee or other similar body appointed by or under the authority of a resolution of either House of Parliament or by a resolution of the Government for the purpose of conducting any investigation or enquiry into or for advising Government on specified matters.
4. Posts of Heads of Diplomatic, Consular and other similar Indian Missions in countries abroad, e.g., Ambassadors, High Commissioners, Ministers, Commissioners, Consul-General; Representatives, Agents.
5. Posts on the personal staff attached to the holders of the posts mentioned in items 1 to 4 above.
6. Posts in the Secretariat of the Lok Sabha and Rajya Sabha.
7. All technical and administrative posts in or under the Atomic Energy Commission.
8. Judicial Commissioners and Additional Judicial Commissioners, District Judges and Additional District Judges in the Union Territories.
9. Subordinate Judges and Munsifs in the Union Territories of Manipur, Tripura.
10. All Class III and Class IV Services and posts.
11. Any service or post concerned with the Administration of the North-East Frontier Agency.
12. Any service or post or class of posts in respect of which the Commission has agreed that it shall not be necessary for it to be consulted.

It shall not be necessary to consult the Union Public Service Commission in regard to the selection for a temporary or officiating appointment to a post which is not to last for more than one year.

The UPSC may appoint committees and to implement their recommendations so as to streamline the system of competitive examinations. It set up the Kothari Committee in 1974 and then introduced in 1979 the system of holding preliminary tests so as to flush out the undeserving candidates. In 1988 it set up the Satish Chandra Committee and as per its recommendation, introduced the compulsory paper of essay in the main civil services examination so as to weed out the candidates who have no capability to write notings on the files. Then, it set up the Alagh Committee in 2000 to review the present scheme of selection to higher civil services like IAS, IPS and other Central Services through the Civil Services examination.

The Alagh Committee submitted its report on 22 October, 2001 showing an attempt to review and redesign the scheme in all its aspects including eligibility parameters. It has desired characteristics in terms of knowledge, skills, attitudes, values and the testing instruments and modalities necessary for identifying the most suitable candidates for higher civil services. It has also recommended as far more elaborate and objective methodology for personality assignment as against the present interview based personality test. The tread of reforms is sought to be completed through recommendations on post-induction training and issues relating to the management of services, since it has felt that recruitment, training and management are components of the same system and reforms in one cannot succeed without reforms in the other. In brief, the Alagh Committee has desired a scheme aimed at identifying younger candidates with the desired qualities of heart and mind for taking the civil services away from the perceived negative influences and shaping them into instruments of reforms while ensuring continuity, stability and security of society and country at large.[1]

The Constitution has some important provisions so as to ensure independent functioning of the Public Service Commissions. These are:

---

1. *Employment News* (New Delhi), 9-15 February, 2002.

1. The Chairman and other members of the Commission are appointed by the President in the case of the Union Public Service Commission and of a Joint Public Service Commission and by the Governor in the case of the State Public Service Commission. The conditions of service of the Chairman or of any other member cannot be varied to his disadvantage during his term of service. He may be removed on the charge of 'misbehaviour' after it is investigated and proved by a Judge of the Supreme Court and the President alone can remove a member of any Public Service Commission on the basis of the inquiry report. The Governor may suspend the Chairman or a member of the State Public Service Commission, but the dismissal can be done by the President.
2. Certain disabilities are imposed on the Chairman and members of the Public Service Commissions. For instance, the Chairman of the Union Public Service Commission cannot take any Government employment after retirement and a member of the UPSC may be appointed as the Chairman of this body or of a State PSC. So the Chairman or a member of the State PSC may be appointed as a member of the UPSC, or a member of the PSC may be appointed as the Chairman of the same or of some other PSC of a State. This has been done to keep the members of the Public Service Commissions immune from all allurements.
3. All expenses of the Union Public Service Commission including any salaries, allowances and pensions are a charge on the Consolidated Fund of India and so of a State Public Service Commission on the Consolidated Fund of the State.

Bureaucracy

By bureaucracy is meant a government run by tenured public servants selected or picked up on the basis of merit and promoted on the basis of efficiency as well as length of service, but who are not accountable to the people or their elected deputies. The bureaucrats are 'officers' in spite of the fact that they are regarded as 'public servants' in terms of the law; they run administration of the country according to 'rules'; their service conditions and emoluments are well-defined; and they can be punished in the event of a wrong done by them after a proper enquiry is made and the relevant procedure is followed. They are supposed to serve leaders elected by the people without involving themselves into the tugs and pulls of politics and thereby maintain their 'integrity' that is defined as their 'neutrality' in the traditional sense of the term. However, an empirical study of bureaucracy has shown that the concept of neutrality has either been mistaken, or it requires to be understood in a different perspective.

A study of bureaucracy in India should be made covering three important spheres–sustenance of the elite political culture, problem of neutrality versus commitment, and its role like a pressure group in its own right. On account of being a legacy of the British imperial system as well as owing to the increasing State activity in the name of rendering social welfare services, bureaucracy has been able to control the levers of power at all levels of administration. The officers belonging to the Indian Administrative Service, Indian Police Service and a host of other civil services occupy key positions of power. Though they work under the control and direction of the political chiefs, they manage to retain their strong and unassailable position by virtue of the security of their service and efficiency of work. In most of the cases the ministers may be compared with the 'caps' and the bureaucrats working under them with the 'brains' of the governments.

All important papers are prepared by high officers or the bureaucrats who play a very important part in the decision-making activities. As Ramsay Muir says, the ministers mostly sign on the dotted lines. There are few instances when a capable minister like Kidwai, Pant and Shastri could exercise his hold over the bureaucrats or a Prime Minister could dispense with the services of a bureaucrat as Jawaharlal Nehru did for Mathai or Indira Gandhi for N.B Banerjee.[2] In many other cases, seasoned bureaucrats (like V. Shankar, B.K. Nehru, K. Vishwanathan, L.K. Jha, Rajeshwar Prasad, D.P.Dhar, P.N. Haksar, T.N. Kaul, L.P. Singh, R.K. Dhawan, G.K. Arora, Brijesh Mishra etc.) could demonstrate their strong position in the governance of the country. As such, bureaucracy is said to be an 'elite group', "It is an absolute misconception that bureaucracy in India is a weak social group. More than 400 IAS officials who stand at the apex of the bureaucratic pyramid are truly an elite group."[3]

---

2. See. N.B. Banerjee: *Under Two Masters*, pp. 227–39.

3. C.P. Bhambhri: *Politics in India, 1947-87*, p. 106.

Then, we may have a look into the problem of commitment of public servants. The traditional view is that the bureaucrats should maintain their political neutrality. But this view should be understood in a different perspective as well. What the word 'commitment' implies in relation to a communist or a fascist state should not be taken here. Commitment in a different sense implies dedication and devotion of the public servants to the fulfilment of tasks enjoined upon them. As such, the bureaucrats in our country must show their commitment to the ideals of the Constitution as well as to the successful implementation of the projects of public welfare. "A certain commitment to the goals and objectives of the State policy is inescapable; neutrality cannot be allowed to degenerate into disinterestedness; nor political sterilisation allowed to slip into political desensitisation."[4] Perhaps with this conviction in 1969 Prime Minister Mrs. Gandhi issued the call for the commitment of public servants that could not be understood by her critics in a correct perspective.

The issue of neutrality versus commitment of bureaucracy in our country should be studied in a different or particular manner. India is a social welfare state. Here all developmental programmes require considerable direct involvement and participation of bureaucracy at all stages of formulation and implementation. "In the context of these new responsibilities the bureaucracies in the developing countries, particularly in India, are confronted with a series of problems. In its new setting the bureaucracy could not maintain its earlier colonial image of power, nor could it continue to exist as a high prestige class, enjoying exceptional privileges. It needed a closer identification with the masses and in shedding of its former paternalistic and authoritarian tone of administration. Although bureaucracy did concede the desirability of such a change in the theoretical and emotional plane, yet at the same time it developed a system of rationalisation to justify the maintenance of the status quo. A great hiatus still persists within the Indian bureaucracy between its emotional awareness of the desirable and the willingness to accept it in practice."[5]

---

4. R.B. Jain: *Contemporary Issues in Indian Administration*. p. 154.
5. R.B. Jain and O.P. Dwivedi: "Bureaucracy in India: The Developmental Context" in R.B. Jain (ed.) *Bureaucratic Politics in the Third World* (Delhi: Gitanjali, 1989), p. 285.

However, the most interesting part of this study must be seen in evaluating the role of bureaucracy as an interest group in its own right. The bureaucrats have a sharp sense of 'fraternity'. They have their groups which may be used as instruments of exercising pressure on the political chief. It is possible that the bureaucrats secretly pass on information to the leader of the Opposition or may do anything to put a particular minister in trouble. The bureaucrats of the Defence Ministry supplied secret information to the leaders of the Opposition in 1959 who could criticise the doing of the defence department under V.K.K. Menon in disregard to the wishes of the Army Chief Thimayya and some of them visited the public gallery of the Lok Sabha to watch proceedings with motives. L.P. Singh (Home Secretary) created a situation as a result of which Home Minister Gulzarilal Nanda had to quit in November, 1966. The Prime Minister's Secretariat run by L.K. Jha, Rajeshwar Prasad and C.P. Srivastava prepared all important papers and thereby strengthened the position of Prime Minister Shastri. It became Prime Minister's Office afterwards. The bureaucrats of the PMO in due course became so powerful that they overshadowed the authority of cabinet ministers. A paper prepared by a bureaucrat (M.S. Ahluwalia) of the PMO hit at the approach paper prepared by the Planning Commission in 1990.

Unfortunately, in recent years, bureaucracy has become a partner in political corruption owing to the growing power of money and muscle. Facts may be gathered to highlight that senior administrators not merely establish proper linkages with politicians, they are also successful in establishing proper liaison with private industry for employment after their retirement. It is enough to substantiate that "private business has to deal with government for licenses, import of raw materials and financial resources from public credit institutions and in it the help of politicians and administrators is needed. Obliging civil servants are rewarded appropriately by their clients who are captains of industry and trade."[6] But at the lower level of administration the bureaucrats have to maintain links with the politicians and the criminals. One swallow cannot make a summer, so a single Dharam Singh Rawat could not force the government of Uttar Pradesh to rectify land deal wrongs made

6. R.L. Hardgrave, Jr.: *India: Government and Politics in a Developing Nation*, p. 108.

in violation of the urban land ceiling laws. So the voice of G.R. Khairnar could hardly move the government of Maharashtra to check rampant corruption in the Bombay Municipal Corporation. The bureaucrats know that "responsibility is diluted in delays and in action, in implementing an administrative policy the administrators adjust and adapt themselves to the informal political goals of leadership."[7]

Such a strong position of bureaucracy may be said to be a definite result of India's commitment to follow the 'ideology of development.' The evil of 'red-tapism' contributes to the encrichment of the bureaucrats as a result of which 'bureaucratic bourgeoisie' comes into existence. The evil of 'self-aggrandisement' contributes to the trend of bossism of the officers that causes marginalisation of the masses. More and more schemes are formulated by the politicians in the name of 'public interest' which virtually contribute to the interest of the clever leaders and astute bureaucrats. In a state of under-development maladministration grows and that swells corruption in the sphere of public administration. Whereas the politicians articulate broad and diffuse interest of unorganised individuals, bureaucrats mediate narrow, focussed interests of organised clientele. As a consequence occurs the bureaucratisation of politics and the politics of bureaucratisation. The nexus between the politician and the bureaucrats is established; and since the politicians have their nexus with criminals, the nexus between the bureaucrats and the politicians is also established in an indirect manner. In case a 'garrison state' (military dictatorship) comes into being, military bureaucracy joins the same stream.

However, what is now worrying is that in our country bureaucracy is growing more and more immune from the bond of accountability for these reasons. First, the general calibre of the political chiefs (ministers) is declining steadily. The new breed of politicians lacks the ability and integrity of men like Nehru, Shastri, Pant and Kidwai. They also lack in respect of commitments and convictions; most of them are self-seekers who would like to remain in power by following dubious means. Surprisingly, many of them "have ceased to feel embarrassed when their names are associated

7. C.P. Bhambhri: *Politics in India*, p. 69.

with reports of such other misuse of powers."[8] Second, most of the bureaucrats prefer to keep the political chiefs in good humour for the sake of reaping tangible benefits like staying in Delhi or heading a public sector undertaking. In such bodies as the State Electricity Board, Development Authority, Transport Corporation and the like the bureaucrats live like monarchs "where they flourish in the total absence of accountability." Last, the bureaucrats, who were once supposed to be a class apart immune from any degeneration caused by material temptations, have now become worldly wise in respect of sailing according to the winds of time. Most of the high-ranking public servants willy-nilly go to the extent of rigging elections just to oblige a powerful politician. As one IAS officer told M.K. Tikku: "How can a politician, however high and mighty he may be, do it (rigging) on his own? On the ground, it is we who let it happen."[9]

Critical Appreciation

No doubt, the Constitution has made elaborate and effective arrangements to ensure impartiality and efficiency of the public servants, but some weak points must be mentioned at this stage:

1. The authority of the Public Service Commissions has been eroded to a great extent by making a provision that the government is not required to consult them in matters relating to reservation of posts in favour of Scheduled Castes, Scheduled Tribes and other backward classes. By doing so the scope of reservations has been widened more and more just for political considerations by the leaders in power that has put a big premium on the element of merit and efficiency of the public servants.

2. It is a queer arrangement that while the Governor appoints the Chairman and other members of his State Public Service Commission, he cannot remove them. He may at the most pass interim order of suspension on the ground of 'misbehaviour' and then it is for the President to set up an inquiry commission and take the final decision on the basis of its report.

---

8. M.K. Tikku: "Bureaucracy: What is Going Wrong?" *in The Hindustan Times*, Sunday Magazine Section, New Delhi, 4 April, 1993, p. 5.

9. *ibid.*

3. The actual role of most of the public servants shows that they strive to render assistance to the leaders of the party in power with the hope of getting certain benefits of their patronage. Unfortunately, in 1969 Prime Minister Indira Gandhi raised the bogey of 'committed bureaucracy' in the country. The Bombay session of the Indian National Congress (New) held under the presidentship of Jagjivan Ram endorsed it. Since such a move was widely decried, the leaders in power came ahead with this interpretation that they never intended to have the type of public servants as in a Fascist or a Communist country, they just wanted that all public servants ought to be committed to the values and ideals of the Constitution, only then the programmes of social and economic reconstruction of the country could be implemented properly. It is because of the political patronage of the leaders in power that corruption in public services has become 'institutionalised.' The Gorwala Report (1951) stressed the point that 'corruption in all guises stalks the land unashamed.'[10]

In spite of some glaring points of weakness in the bureaucratic compositiion and functioning in our country, it may be pointed out that our public services cannot be regarded as 'committed', if the word 'commitment' means the same thing what is taken in a country having a non-democratic form of government. In general, public services are independent and neutral and the evils of red-tapism, procrastination, frustration, corruption, and above all, politicisation are a legacy of the foreign rule coupled with the undersirable role of the politicians, particularly at the level of the States. Though the critics have dubbed some State Public Service Commissions as 'packed houses,' it cannot be said about the Union Public Service Commission that has been lauded as 'the bulwark of democracy,'[11] and 'one of the four pillars of democracy, others being the Supreme Court, Election Commission and the Comptroller and Auditor-General of India.'[12]

---

10. Cited in C.N. Bhalerao: *Public Service Commission in India*, p. 193.
11. M.A. Mutallib: *The Union Public Service Commission*, p. 179.
12. Batuk Singh: *The Union Public Service Commission*, p. 1. In the words of Surinder Nath, former Chairman of the UPSC, "every citizen can participate in the administration of the country for which the UPSC provides a gateway." *Employment News* (New Delhi), 9-15 February, 2002

The aim of the UPSC is to recruit persons who may prove ideal civil servants with qualities of head and heart. In an interview the Chairman of this body (Surinder Nath) enumerated the merits or qualities of such a person. "An officer must be a gentleman. He should possess good character and have the courage of conviction, intellectual and moral capabilities, leadership qualities and capabilities of taking right decision at the right time. He should have in-depth professional knowledge, self-confidence, good communication skills; he should be analytical in his thinking, flexible and not rigid, must be able to inspire and motivate his colleagues and subordinates. There should be balance between judgement and decision-making."[13]

13. *Employment News* (New Delhi), 9-15 February, 2002, p. 16.

16

Political Parties and Pressure Groups

Modern democratic system cannot operate without the role of political parties. A pluralistic social order has a number of organised interest groups that play a part of their own in the political process of the country in alliance, open or secret, with political parties. A two-way traffic can be noted in that while the political parties need followers and resources which groups provide, the groups require leadership and direction which is provided by the parties. The groups articulate their interests and the parties aggregate them. Thus, interaction takes place that has its visible form in the role of political parties and its invisible form in the role of organised (catalyst) groups. Since India has a pluralistic society and a democratic welfare state, the role of political parties and pressure groups deserves a particular study.

Characteristic Features of Party System

In order to make an empirical study of the Indian party system, we may enumerate its characteristics as under:

1. India has neither a single party system as prevailling in a communist country like China, nor does it have a bi-party system as prevailing in Britain and the United States. Here operates a multi-party system as prevailing in many countries of the world. If a complete catalogue of Indian political parties, whether big or small, recognised or registered with the Election Commission or not, is prepared, the number may exceed the astonishing figure of 500. At the national level, we may mention the names of Indian National Congress, Janata Dal (S), Janata Dal (U), Nationalist Congres Party, Bharatiya Janata Party, Communist Party of India and Communist Party of India-Marxist. At the regional level we may refer to National Conference in Jammu-Kashmir, Shiromani Akali Dal in

Punjab, Telugu Desam (N) in Andhra Pradesh, Dravida Munnetra Kazhagam and Anna-DMK in Tamilnadu, Biju Janata Dal in Orissa, Rashtriya Janta Dal in Bihar, Forward Bloc and Forward Bloc-Marxist in West Bengal, Mizo National Front in Mizoram, Sikkim Democrative Front, Assom Gana Parishad in Assam, Samajvadi Party and Bahujan Samaj Party in U.P. etc. Besides, there are many parties like *ad hoc* and fringe organisations.

2. A multi-party system is one in which different parties have the chance to be in power. Power alternates from one party to another. We may take note of the multi-party system at the national and regional levels. Since 1996 coalition politics has come to stay and so the Prime Ministers like Deve Gowda, Gujral, Vajpayee and Manmohan Singh led a government constituted by about 20 parties.

3. A new development has taken place that may be visualised in the formation of some loose organisation within or outside a political party which may, and also may not, be identified with a political party. In 1988 some members of the Parliament (V.P. Singh, Arun Nehru, Arif Muhammad Khan etc.) left the Congress Party and formed Jan Morcha (People's Front) for this purpose. It is also possible that a shrewd dissident leader may float a Manch (Forum) inside the party to work as a ginger group. A Vikas Manch (Development Forum) floated by Dr. Jagannath Mishra in Bihar and another by Bansilal in Haryana are its instances.

4. Ideology plays an important part in the organisation and working of political parties. But the element of ideology cannot be traced in many political parties of India. Leaving aside the BJP on the right and two Communist parties on the left, all parties are like ideologically neutral organisations. Their commitments to the principles of social, economic and political significance are so flexible that they may be termed non-ideological organisations. Moreover, with the making of an amendment in the Representation of the People Act in 1988, every political party is required to have its faith in and allegiance to the Constitution of India and endorse its commitment to democracy, secularism and socialism. As such,

rightism, leftism and centrism have lost their sanctity; expediency and pragmatism have taken the place of commitment to certain principles.

5. The factor of 'personality' has a place of its own in the operation of Indian party system. Congress is a party of Sonia Gandhi, BJP of Vajpayee, RJD of Laloo Prasad, SP of Mulayam Singh, BSP of Mayawati, Shiva Sena of Bal Thackeray etc.

6. We may also find some political outfits where the boundary line between a political party and a pressure group is quite blurred. Hence, one may take them as either this or that. Its instances are as Majlis-i-Ittehad-ul-Musalmeen and Telangana Rashtriya Samiti in Andhra Pradesh, Lok Jana Shakti in Bihar, Muthu Dravida Munnetra Kazhgam in Tamilnadu etc. Surprisingly, in this era of fractured mandate, they manage to secure some seats in the legislature and thereby play the role of institutional pressure groups.

7. Above all, we may take note of the perplexing fact of frequent disintegration and polarisation of political parties. There are two Congresses, two Communist parties, two Janata Dals, two DMKs, three Akali Dals, three Muslim Leagues, about half a dozen socialist parties etc. Most of these parties are sustained by the factor of anti-Congressism or anti-BJPism. Politics means struggle for power and struggle for power requires combination of strange partners. Thus, *ad hoc* alliances are formed.

Leading Political Parties

India has multi-party system. The number of major parties operating at the national and regional levels is quite limited, but at the regional and sub-regional levels it is frightening. If a catalogue of all political parties, big and small, is prepared, the total number may exceed the astonishing figure of 100. Since the element of ideology has almost disappeared, it is very difficult to distinguish one party from the other. Sheer pragmatism is the dominant factor that has led to the germination of bad trends and tendencies in the operation of our country's party system. Secularism and pseudo-secularism have become synonymous. All organisations invoke the name of socialism without bothering for the real implications of this social, economic and political tendency. Above all, democracy is a pet invocation, while each party is ridden with the tendencies of authoritarianism. A brief account of some of the major national and regional political organisations deserves its place.

Indian National Congress: It is the oldest party of India. It was founded in 1885 to organise constructive and sane nationalism in the country. It became the vehicle of national movement under the leadership of Mahatma Gandhi who converted it into a mass organisation of all 'hues' of people. The Congress became like a huge umbrella under whose cover people of diverse backgrounds and different 'ideologies' could come to play their part in the freedom struggle of the country. Its leadership fell into the hands of Nehru after independence. He sought to make it a socialist organisation without giving to it the name of a socialist party. Due to this, the Congress stole the thunder of the socialist parties. As a matter of fact, the Congress cannot be designated as a socialist organisation for the obvious reason that its socialistic professions are too vague and, more than that, different factions operating within its fold try to pull things in different directions. These factions have different approaches to the matters of social and economic significance and they "interact in a continuous process of pressure, adjustment and accommodation to provide an in-built opposition.[1]

We may thus describe the Congress as a party of the parties having various competitive factions within its fold; we may also describe it as a party of the Prime Minister controlling the federal constitutional system of the country through the mechanism of his party at the Union and State levels. The Prime Minister and his loyal lieutenants have all the powers and resources; they may attract any number of careerists by the charm of their 'patronage', who are not swayed by ideological considerations and who are in the Congress, because it brings them additional power and prestige. The underlying current of the entire politics of the Congress leaders hinges on the point of reaping the fruits of influence by living in power through the mechanism of party.

What is the ideology of the Congress party? We may say that it is an ideologically neutral organisation. It subscribes to certain policies and programmes of social, economic and political significance

1. Rajni Kothari: "Party System" in the *Economic Weekly* (Bombay, 3 June, 1961), p. 849.

that display a curious blending of three different currents–Gandhism with its emphasis on rural reconstruction on the lines of decentralisation of power and economic self-sufficiency; Liberalism recognising the right of free enterprise in a mixed economy; and Socialism with its emphasis on State ownership and control of the means of production and distribution. It is the radicalism of the Congress that has had its manifestation in the nationalisation of some major private establishments and that attributed to this party the label of a left-of-centre organisation..

The leaders of the Congress make use of the term 'ideology' in a particular sense so that the amorphous character of the organisation is maintained. Its ideology stands on the pillars of parliamentary democracy, democratic socialism and enlightened secularism.

The main points of the ideology of the Congress are thus highlighted in its manifesto issued on the eve of Lok Sabha elections in 1998:

1. **Stability:** It implies continuity of the ideas, policies and programmes. It is not an end in itself but a means to an end–growth, human development and social justice.
2. **Secularism:** Democracy and social harmony can never flourish in a society that is not secular. It rejects communalism of all kinds. It regards all citizens as equal and yet it recognises minorities because of the special disadvantages with which they sufer and the special help they need.
3. **Economic Agenda:** It desires to restore confidence among the farmers, workers, domestic entrepreneurs, industrialists and foreign investors.
4. **Political Agenda:** It desires to restore governance and impart a sense of coherence and national purpose to government's functioning. It includes strengthening of local bodies and to set up the office of the Lok Pal for checking corruption.
5. **Social Agenda:** It wants to be in the forefront of a new social reforms movement against *sati,* dowry deaths, female infanticide and child marriage. It is committed to implement the programmes for the welfare of Scheduled Castes, Scheduled Tribes and Other Socially and Educationally Backward Classes, including women and children.

6. **Unity in Diversity:** It is committed to the maintenance of parliamentary democracy and federal system. The oneness of the people has to be preserved and strengthened.
7. **Foreign Policy:** It advocates the policy of non-alignment that should be redefined in the present age of liberalisation and globalisation.

At its Panchmarhi meet held under the chairmanship of Sonia Gandhi in September, 1998, it expressed its commitment to the following points:

1. Strengthening parliamentary democracy, encouragement to secularism, establishment of socialist system on the basis of equality and social justice.
2. Opposition to any cut in reservation quotas for Scheduled Castes, Scheduled Tribes and other Socially and Educationally Backward Classes or weaker sections of the community.
3. Priority to women in the organisation and distribution of tickets.
4. Increase in the representation of the youth in the organisation.
5. No party ticket to any person having more than two children.
6. Setting up a committee for electoral reforms so as to prevent money power in elections, and
7. Meeting demand for national water supply and settling inter-state river water disputes.

At the Shimla Meet (July, 2003), the leaders of this party formally recognised the existing political reality and thus accepted the course of coalition system that has now come to stay. But at its Hyderabad session held in January, 2006 under the presidentship of Sonia Gandhi, it made it clear that all parties in such an adjustment must follow a basic discipline and not cross the line of constructive criticism. The dynamism of this party may be seen in the fact that while it runs a coalition government at the Centre with the help of some parties, it has no hesitation in being against any of the constituents at the State level. Such a change in its ideology and strategy is due to its recognition of the political reality of the day.

Janata Dal (S): We may have a brief study of the other national and secular political parties as well. On 11 October, 1988 (birthday of Jayaprakash Narayan) a new party came into being with the merger of three parties (Janata Party, Jan Morcha and Lok Dal) under the leadership of V.P. Singh. The policies and programmes of this party cover social, economic and political spheres and they look like based on the foundations of democracy, secularism and socialism. In the political sphere, it desires restoration of civil liberties and extension of the rights of the people, eradication of corruption, revitalisation of parliamentary institutions, reversal of over-centralisation process, more autonomy to the States and decentralisation of powers, solution of national problems through the process of national consensus and reconciliation, social justice to the weaker sections of the community, incorporation of right to work in the list of Fundamental Rights, curbs on the use of Art. 356 sanctioning President's rule in the States, reorganisation of Panchayati Raj, establishment of a responsive administrative structure etc.

In the economic sphere, it desires prevention of concentration of wealth in the hands of few people, encouragement to small-scale and cottage industries, more production of basic consumer goods, land reforms, crop insurance system, maximisation of employment opportunities, alleviation of poverty and indebtendness, rationalisation of tax system etc. In the social sphere it desires preferential opportunities and concessions to Scheduled Castes and Scheduled Tribes, improvement of the status of women, social security for the physically handicapped people, vocation-oriented education etc. In the words of the then leader of this party (Chandra Shekhar): "Mending of broken hearts and propping up human dignity and self-respect is the essence of the policy of the new party."

The Manifesto issued by this party on the eve of Lok Sabha elections in 1998 opens with the exhortation that it "derives a vision from its commitment to Democratic Socialism based on Freedom, Democracy, Equality, Social Justice and Solidarity." It declared its programme as under:

1. **Economic Agenda:** It desires primacy to agriculture and rural development, modernisation of industry, maximisation of employment opportunities, and adoption of a balanced approach towards liberalisation and globalisation in view of India's autonomous development.

2. **Social Agenda:** It desire welfare of the Scheduled Castes, Scheduled Tribes and other weaker sections of the community, improvement of public health and standard of living, expansion of employment opportunities, gender equality and justice and protection of environment.

3. **Political Agenda:** It desires cooperative federalism so that the States may have an effective say in the decision-making process, devolution of financial powers in favour of the States, making panchayati raj more effective, guarantee of right to information, creation of the office of the Lok Pal for prevention of corruption, and formation of smaller States of the Indian Union.

4. **Foreign Policy:** It desires to follow a policy of peace, friendship and cooperation with all countries of the world. It lays stress on the need for disarmament and arms control and to bring about a new and just international order. Very cordial relations should be established with some of our immediate neighbours like Nepal, Bhutan and Bangladesh. The United Nations system should be restructured or reformed.

Bharatiya Janata Party: The Bharatiya Jana Sangh founded by Shyama Prasad Mukherji in 1951 lost its identity when it was merged with the Janata Party in 1977. But after the failure of the Janata experiment, it had its revival in 1979 under the leadership of Atal Behari Vajpayee with the name of Bharatiya Janata Party.[2] It expresses its commitment to five ideals—nationalism and national integration, democracy, positive secularism, Gandhian socialism,

---

2. The Bharatiya Janata Party alone frankly shows its commitment to Hindutva which should not be identified with Hindu communalism as advocated by Veer Savarkar. As explained by its stalwarts like L.K. Advani, K.R. Malkani and Murli Manohar Joshi, it is the substitute of India's cultural nationalism. In the *Manohar Joshi Case,* the Supreme Court has appreciated it as the synonym of 'Indianness'. Even among its votaries there is no unanimity in view of the fact that their interpretations vary from the pole of Hindu communalism on the one extreme to that of enlightened cultural nationalism akin to secularism on the other. Thus, Hindutva "poses a formidable, intelectual and political challenge in contemporary India today." Jyotirmaya Sharma: *Hindutva: Exploring the Idea of Hindu Nationalism* (New Delhi: Penguin Viking India, 2003), p. 1.

and value-based politics. It reposes its faith in democratic norms with the hope that it would attempt to create a consensus on all major issues and compete with others if situations of conflict arise. However, as national consensus cannot be built on mere struggle for power, it must be based on certain principles and national objectives. The people of different faiths and ideologies should be able to coexist in peace and harmony, but those who have extra-territorial loyalties or engage in anti-national activities cannot be expected to contribute to national consensus and, for this reason, would have to be kept out.

As a believer in democracy, the BJP fights against all trends of fascism and authoritarianism. Its commitment to positive secularism implies a rejection of what the Congress has been advocating so far. It rejects the case of appeasement towards any community and instead supports the idea of full protection to the life and property of the minorities. It desires distillation of common moral values whether derived from different religions or from other historical and civilisational experiences and approaches, which have always remained integral to Indian nationalism. While accepting the doctrine of Gandhian socialism, it seeks to replace both capitalism and statism by the principle of a cooperative system and a form of trusteeship in all fields of economic activity. Finally, it desires value-based politics. It means that social and political life should be guided by a set of norms and values the abridgement of which should bring forth social sanction and punishment.

A leading figure and a former President of this party (Murli Manohar Joshi) has laid stress on these points while analysing the ideology of his party:

1. It desires a stable country, a stable government, and a stable economy.
2. Our brand of *swadeshi* means empowering the people. We welcome foreign investments in those areas where we lack experience.
3. Liberalisation means freeing the country from present bureaucratic stranglehold. Our motto is—"liberalise, modernise, globalise."
4. We believe in the credo of 'justice for all, appeasement of none'.

5. India has never been a Hindu state. India can never be a theocracy, because the Hindu mind is secular. Uniform Civil Code should be enforced throughout the country.
6. Women empowerment should be a reality so that they may participate in the decision-making process.
7. All leaders subscribe to the tradition of the RSS, but they are not controlled by it.

The party defines Hinduism or *Hindutva* in terms of Indianness or cultural nationalism which has four essential elements, namely, *suraksha* (security), *Schuchita* (welfare), *swadeshi* (use of home-made goods and economic self-reliance) and *samrasta* (social harmony). Its motto is–'one people, one nation, one country, one culture'.

Communist Parties: Both Communist Parties claim Marxism-Leninism as the foundation of their ideology. According to its constitution, the Communist Party of India "is the political party of the Indian working class, it vanguard, its highest form of class organisation. It is a voluntary organisation of workers, peasants and toiling people in general, devoted to the cause of socialism and communism." The policies and programmes of the CPI cover political, economic and social spheres. In the political sphere, it desires restructuring of the federal system in a way so as to ensure autonomy of the States, abrogation of Art. 356 sanctioning President's rule, abolition of the office of Governor, introduction of proportional representation with list system, enlargement of democratic rights of the people, making justice inexpensive and easily available, ensuring freedom of the press and repeal of all 'black' laws, pursuance of the policy of peace and friendship with socialist countries.

In the economic sphere, the CPI desires curbs on monopolies and transnational giants, nationalisation of major industries (sugar, textile, steel, jute and vanaspati) and foreign trade, State take-over of trade in foodgrains, strengthening the network of public distribution system, need-based minimum wages for low paid factory workers, encouragement to cottage and small-scale industries, protection of the trade union rights of the workers, participation of workers in the management of industry, employment programme for rural workers and educated youth including unemployment allowance etc. Finally, in the social sphere, it desires free education of all children upto secondary stage, economic assistance in matters of education for low income groups, security of the person and honour of the people belonging to weaker sections, social insurance in the event of accident or disability, ban on communal and obscurantist organisations, secularisation of the polity etc.

The Communist Party of India–Marxist (CPM) claims itself as the genuine leftist party based on the ideology of Marxism-Leninism. It frankly accuses the CPI of being a gathering of the opportunists and class collaborationists working in alliance with feudal-bourgeois elements having their place in the Indian National Congress. Its social, economic and political commitments are more or less the same as espoused by the CPI. However, what is striking about the CPM's ideology is that it seeks to keep itself in equidistance from the 'rightism' of the BJP, 'centrism of the Congress' and so-called 'leftism' of the CPI.

The dividing line between the two Communist Parties was their disposition towards the two great Communist powers–the Soviet Union and China. While the CPI was pro-Soviet Union, the CPM was pro-China. This was the crucial issue that had inspired a section of the CPI to have its way in 1963. But this dividing line became irrelevant after the disintegration of the USSR in 1991. The coalition government formed by Deve-Gowda in 1996 had some ministers of the CPI and it banked on the support of the CPM from outside. It continued its support to the government of Gujral. Both the communist parties took the stand that they wanted to keep the Congress and the BJP out of power. As a similar line was adopted by other leftist organisation like Revolutionary Socialist Party and All-India Forward Bloc, all the four parties issued a joint manifesto on the eve of Lok Sabha elections in 1998. It had these important points:

1. **Secularism:** They have full faith in secularism that expresses the reality of the daily life and experience of the millions of the countrymen who live and work harmoniously together irrespective of caste, creed and religion. The forces of communaliam should be defeated and the dispute of Ram Mandir at Ayodhya be settled by the Supreme Court.
2. **Federalism:** They deprecate a highly centralised and undemocratic system of the concentration of powers at the Centre. The States should have more powers and, for this

sake our Constitution should be amended. The National Development Council and Inter-State Council should be made more effective. The abuse of Art. 356 should be checked. The States should have an effective say in the operation of Union-State relations.

3. **National Unity:** The feelings of neglect and separatism are rampant in some parts of the country like Jammu-Kashmir and the North-East. More autonomy should be given to the States and infrastructural facilities should be provided for their development. The problems of the North-East should be solved by means of negotiations.
4. **Economic Policy:** Efforts should be made for speedy implementation of land reforms, self-sufficiency in the production of food grains, guarantee of minimum wages to agricultural workers, ban on foreign investments, and strengthening public distribution system.
5. **Social Policy:** They desire free and universal education, protection of public health, availability of drinking water, housing facility for all, gurantee of right to work as a fundamental right, abolition of child labour, population control, women empowerment, safeguarding the rights of the minorities, welfare of the Scheduled Castes and Scheduled Tribes and other weaker sections of the community, protection of environment and development of sports.
6. **Political Agenda:** They desire establishment of the office of the Lok Pal for preventing corruption, ban on the entry of criminals into politics, introduction of proportional representation with partial list system, state assistance to people fighting elections in the form of necessary material, constitution of a National Judicial Commission for the selection of the judges of the Supreme Court and High Courts and suitable amendments in the anti-defection law.
7. **Foreign Policy:** They desire that India should follow an independent policy in international sphere, should not sign the NPT and the CTBT, should not enter into military cooperations with the United States, improve relations with immediate neighbours like China and Pakistan, make SAARC more effective and work for the dismantling the American military base at Diego Garcia.

It is surprising to see that the 'red ink' of the two Communist parties has run out. The Communist party gave support from outside to the minority government of Indira Gandhi and also appreciated imposition of emergency by it in 1975, while the CPM remained strongly critical of it. The CPI joined the governments of Deve-Gowda and Gujral and the CPM gave its support from outside. Now both the Communist parties are giving support to the Manmohan Singh government from outside. The CPM-dominated government has solicited investment of foreign capital in the State of West Bengal and both parties now favour direct investment of foreign capital in selected areas. The Government of West Bengal has given big plots of land in Singur and Nandigram to the Tatas. But both the Communist parties are very critical of the civilian nuclear deal between India and the USA. It shows that now sheer pragmatism is the ideology of both the parties.

Regional Political Parties: We may also have a brief study of the regional political parties in India. Since most of these parties operate in a particular State, Morris-Jones has preferred to call them "One-State parties." In this connection reference may be made to National Conference in Jammu Kashmir, Shiromani Akali Dal in Punjab, DMK and Anna-DMK in Tamil Nadu, Telugu Desam and Telangana Rashtriya Samiti in Andhra Pradesh, Assom Gana Parishad in Assam, Sikkim Democrate Front, Shiv Sena in Maharashtra, Biju Janata Dal in Orissa, Rashtriya Janata Dal in Bihar, Samajvadi and Bahujan Samajvadi Party in U.P., Indian National Lok Dal in Haryana, People's Party in Manipur etc. In some parts of the States sub-regional political parties may be referred to as Gorkha League in West Bengal and Gondwana Party in M.P. A study of these regional and sub-regional organisations shows that they have now become a force to reckon with in the political system of our country. It is well pointed out: "No academic endeavour to analyse or evaluate the dynamics of Indian politics today can be valid if it ignores what may be described as the regional perspective and fails to take adequate account of the increasingly critical role played by the regional political parties."[3]

---

3. K.R. Bombwall: "Regional Parties in Indian Politics: A Preview" in S. Bhatnagar and Pradeep Kumar (ed.s.): *Regional Political Parties in India*, p. 1.

The emergence and the increasingly important role of these political parties may be said to be a consequence of these reasons. First, India is virtually a land of many regions. The fact of diversity may be noted in respects of languages, customs, cultures and, above all, levels of social and economic development. A powerful national party like the Indian National Congress could give a setback to the destructive forces of regionalism by preaching as well as sincerely sticking to the way of 'unity in diversity.' But as a result of the decline of this party, regional organisations naturally raised their head and managed to defeat the Congress in various States of the Indian Union. Second, these regional organisations successfully exploit the fact of local, regional and parochial grievances. The leaders of these organisations well thrive on the propaganda of 'regional imbalance' in respect of economic development caused by the negligent attitude of the Centre. Last, the rise and growth of such parties is also sustained by the existence of primordial loyalties exploited by communal and ethnic forces. It is for this reason that the regional leaders fail to broaden their area of operation to other parts of the country.

It is a patent fact that the identity of a regional political party is marked by its area of operation. But in the case of some parties we may also take note of their eagerness to improve their image by establishing links with an all-India party either for the sake of bettering their electoral prospects or for having a mark of national recognition.

The regional political parties may be called 'grievance groups,' for their aim is to thrive on the exploitation of local and parochial discontent of the people. Very often they demand amendments in various provisions of the Constitution particularly those which create a strong Centre in our federal system. Since politics means struggle for power, even national and secular parties try to establish links with these regional organisation by espousing their cause in an indirect or covert manner. The leaders of the Janata Dal, BJP, CPI and CPM often make sophisticated expressions to usher in a true or genuine federal system in the country ensuring 'autonomy' of the States.

However, the role of regional parties should not be studied with a sense of undue apprehension in each and every case. There is nothing wrong if a particular party fights for the interest of its own people without endangering the unity and integrity of the nation.

In case a regional political party can give a better and stable administration to the people of a particular State by working within the framework of the Constitution of India, it should be appreciated as a development in the direction of a healthy and viable federal system. On the other hand, in case a regional political party distorts the provisions of the Constitution and fails in suppressing anti-national elements, its role should be denounced. Only in the latter direction, the role of regional political parties should be seen with a sense of apprehension. One thing is, however, certain that regional political parties have come to stay like a prominent and durable feature of India's political landscape.

Critical Appreciation

A critical study of the Indian party system shows that it suffers from certain weaknesses.

1. The fact of ideological orientation is missing in most of the parties operating at the national and regional levels. Leaving aside the BJP on the rightist and the two Communist parties on the leftist spectrums, all other parties are ideologically neutral organisations more concerned with their attitude towards 'personalities' than with a clear-cut commitment to some particular type of social and economic philosophy. The requirement of the amended Representation of the People Act (that every political party seeking its registration with the Election Commission must have a constitution of its own expressing its commitment to Democracy, Secularism and Socialism) has made the line of distinction between parties further blurred.
2. Frequent events of fragmentation of parties and then move for polarisation of like-minded parties disturbs the stasiological map of the country from time to time. One faces difficulty in preparing a list of all kinds of 'socialist' parties in the country.
3. Above all, each party is ridden with rampant factionalism. Consequently, the opportunists and careerists have been able to establish their hold over the organisation. In recent years a more pernicious trend may be noted in the growing nexus between the politicians and the criminals. The sanctity of elections has been vitiated by the criminalisation of politics to a great extent. These developments stand as powerful barriers in the growth of a healthy party system in the country.

Pressure Groups

A number of organised groups play their own part in the political process of the country. Since these groups are organised on the basis of some 'interest,' they are known as 'interest groups,' and since they adopt pressure tactics to protect and promote their specific interest, they are generally taken as 'pressure groups'. Here we have to see the role of numerous associations of the businessmen, industrialists, workers, peasants etc. We may enumerate these characteristic of pressure group politics in our political system as under:

1. As we have a loose, disorganised and fragmented multi-party system, so we have numerous groups, big and small, with long as well as ephemeral durations, living in conflict with one another, appearing and disappearing in response to the prevailing conditions and, above all, riven with shifting political allegiances. It presents a very confusing as well as a perplexing spectacle. Though we may make a list of such groups for the sake of a convenient study, it is a tedious job to prepare their taxonomic illustration as most of them may be found cutting across the boundaries of their real political character. In addition to that, the shifting affiliations of the groups with political parties and the penetration of the influence of the political leaders into the functioning of these groups further adds to our difficulty.
2. The organised groups, like political parties, lack definite political commitments. Their political loyalties are shifting and that contributes to their unstable political culture. Their attitudes towards political parties as well as their faith in the strategies and techniques lack definite commitments in respect of which rigid norms cannot be laid down. For instance, if we take up the case of the business groups, we may take note of the fact that they "are divided politically and have conflicting views about strategy towards particular parties and also about the potential consequences of the support that they give to any of the major parties."[4]
3. Owing to the absence of clear-cut ideological commitments, most of the groups feel interested in creating conditions of

---

4. S.A. Kochanek: *Business and Politics in India*, p. 4.

anarchy and lawlessness. They have less, rather very little, faith in the use of constitutional methods as adopted in democratic countries. It appears that they have no hesitation in indulging in activities of an extra-constitutional and unconstitutional nature. Strike is a favourite weapon in their hands that sometimes assumes the form of *bandh* (complete closure); demonstrations and long marches are undertaken. The groups may unhesitatingly take to the ways of arson and violence causing great damage to people's life and property. More than this, recourse to rank militancy may display overtones of anomie and anti-nationalism. It may, therefore, be admitted that violence has come to occupy a special place in the political process of our country.[5]

4. The point of 'bi-culturalism' may also be discovered in the political behaviour of the groups. That is, while they try to operate on modern lines, they cannot give up their traditional mores or primordial loyalties. They may have their registered offices; they may openly or clandestinely finance political parties and try to induct men of their choice into the legislative and executive organs of the government, or they may adopt the ways of keeping the bureaucrats in good humour by paying them in cash or kind. And yet they may not make themselves totally free from religious, communal, regional, sub-regional or parochial attachments. Thus, the elements of traditions as well as of modernity may be traced in the political behaviour of most of the groups playing their part in the political process of the country.

5. Above all, the role of the groups can be termed non-autonomous. They prefer to work under the leadership of some political party and be guided by its directions. The fear psychosis has its indelible effect so much so that while playing their definite role in the politics of the country, they not only pretend to be neutral in political matters, they try to change the label of their political affiliations in response to the requirements of a rank opportunistic policy. It enables the ruling party to set the parameters within which the groups in loyalty towards the parties in opposition have to operate.

---

5. Myron Weiner says that "an anomic outburst is unplanned and is analogous to the temper tantrum of a child whose violence is directed at all objects within reach." *The Politics of Scarcity*, p. 204

As already pointed out, organised groups may be horizontally classified as business groups, labour groups, peasant groups, professional groups and the like. Almond has classified them as associational, non-associational, institutional and anomic groups. Some groups may also be termed as religious, communal, tribal, ethnic, linguistic, cultural and the like. For the sake of a convenient study, we may put them under these broad heads:

First of all, we may refer to a number of business groups or the organisations of the industrialists and capitalists. We have three great organisations–Federation of the Indian Chambers of Commerce and Industry with its major constituents like Indian Merchants Chamber of Bombay, Indian Merchants Chamber of Calcutta and Southern Indian Chamber of Commerce of Madras; Associated Chamber of Commerce having its major constituents in Bengal Chamber of Commerce of Calcutta and its lobby (Central Commercial Organisation in Delhi), and All-India Manufacturers Organisation with its headquarters in Delhi and its branches in Kolkota and Mumbai.

It is a paradox that while all business groups detest 'socialism,' they have to support this or that political party frankly subscribing to it as a matter of compulsion. Socialism is an instrument of mass appeal and, for this reason, every political party feels bound to invoke its name in order to collect the votes of the hungry millions. And yet every party knows that elections cannot be fought without financial resources that may come from big business houses. On the other hand, the business houses understand that Indian socialism permits the system of 'mixed economy' in which their interests remain safe.

The business groups contribute to the funds of the political parties with the hope of getting their support when they are in power. Pragmatism may be termed as the ideology of the Indian business groups. Most of the business groups support the party in power as their policy is to salute the rising sun. They also try to have good relations with important ministers and bureaucrats with obvious motives. Weiner says: "Since they have no effective influence on law-makers, Indian businessmen establish high particularistic relationships with individual administrators, who are appealed to on the basis of blood relationship (when it exists), personal friendship, or most often financial rewards."[6]

---

6. Weiner, *op. cit.*, p. 130.

The trade unions play the part of pressure groups of the working class. Here two points are noticeable. First, such organisations act like the labour wings of different political parties and, for this reason, the relationship between a trade union and a political party is invariably static. For instance, the Indian National Trade Union Congress is the labour wing of the Indian National Congress; the All-India Trade Union Congress is the labour wing of the CPI; the United Trade Union Congress is the labour wing of the CPM; the Bharatiya Mazdoor Parishad is the labour wing of the BJP; and the Socialists have their Hind Mazdoor Sabha. Second, the labour groups adopt the methods of strike, *gherao* (encirclement of the officer concerned for compelling him to meet their demands,) *bandh* (complete strike), demonstrations, marches etc. and may go to the extreme of damaging public property by violent means. They fight for the security of employment, better emoluments, more bonus, housing and medical facilities, adequate compensation in the event of death or physical disability of a worker etc.

The trade union movement in our country is marked by rivalry and factionalism as a result of which labour groups often fail to have what they struggle for. Weiner rightly points out: "The Indian trade union movement is one of the most maligned in the world. Unions are poorly organised, membership turn-over is great, dues-paying is limited to strike, demonstrations and election work. Only rarely does a union provide services for its members. Rival unionism is rampant, unions are led by outsiders, and control of the unions is often in the hands of political parties seeking to use them for their own ends. Employers, political parties, trade union leaders (with the exception of communists), and government officials all lament the politicisation of trade unions; but the trend has been towards a more fragmented trade union movement paralleling the fragmented party system of India."[7]

Then, we may look at the role of peasant groups or farmers' organisations. The Indian National Congress established its peasant wing (All-India Kisan Congress) that after some time became All-India Kisan Sabha, The Socialists set up their Hind Kisan Panchayat and the Communists formed their United Kisan Sabha. All-India Kisan Sammelan was organised under the leadership of Chaudhry

7. *Ibid.*, p. 109.

Charan Singh in 1978. Recently some more organisations have come up as Shetkari Sanghthan under Sharad Joshi and Bharatiya Kisan Union under Mahendra Singh Tikait. These peasant groups fight for their own interests like availability of seeds and fertiliser at a cheap rate, remunerative prices for agricultural products, development of irrigation and agriculture, rural credit scheme, insurance of crops, supply of electricity at cheaper rates, representation of the farmers in all decision-making bodies of the government, waiver of loans given to small farmers, implementation of the scheme of land reforms etc. However, like the groups of the workers, the groups of the farmers have not been able to assert effectively due to mass ignorance, casteist rivalries, inadequate financial resources, rampant factionalism etc.

Finally, we may refer to a very large number of professional and anomic groups. The lawyers have their bar associations. The medical practitioners have their Indian Medical Association and also a large number of subsidiary organisations. The teachers have their own groups. So is the case with other professionals like engineers, technicians, artists etc. The students unions may also be included in this category. The Hindus have their religious organisations like Bajrang Dal and Vishwa Hindu Parishad, the Muslims have their Jamaat-i-Islami; the Christians have their Roman Catholic Association; the Parsis have their Anjuman; the Shiromani Gurdwara Prabandhak Committee protects the interest of the Sikhs; the Republican Party of India fights for the interest of the depressed classes.

In fine, Indian political system provides considerable freedom to different sectors of society to make demands upon its operators. The groups articulate their 'specific' interests and the political parties manage to aggregate them so that the process of accommodation of diverse interest remains undisturbed. But the unfortunate thing is that the decision-makers do not understand the gravity of the situation until organised groups take matters to the streets and public peace is disturbed.

Political Pluralism and Parliamentary System

Modern democracy is 'representative government' as nomenclatured by John Stuart Mill. It is run by political parties, which capture power of the state by constitutional means and then implement their declared programmes in the name of the 'mandate of the masses', or what, in the romantic expression of Rousseau, also known as the 'poet of politics', may be designated as the 'general will' of the community. Since party system has its operational nexus with the political system, it becomes all the more necesssary that it should be regulated by the provisions of law in case the network of healthy conventions is not there. The British people may boast of their healthy conventions, but it is not so with other countries, as Germany and Austria, where statutory arrangements have been made in this regard. A study of party system vis-a-vis parliamentary system in our country has, therefore, its own relevance and, at the moment, in the context of rampant corruption and criminalisation, calls for its reform and regulation.

Statutory Arrangements: One of the salient features of the Indian Constitution is its bulky character. Its detailed provisions, supplemented with numerous sections and sub-sections and qualifying clauses and sub-clauses, make it the lengthiest constitution in the world. It covers many subjects, such as citizenship, public services, official language, elections, etc., which could have been covered by means of ordinary legislation or administrative action. But it does not cover party system which has emerged like an extraconstitutional development without its rules and regulations and which has assumed formidable proportions in the absence of healthy traditions. The Constitution of India, in its original form, did not incorporate the term 'political party'. It is said to have been covered under Article 19 (1) (c) which guarantees freedom to form associations and unions.[8] The 32nd Amendment Bill (1973) made the first attempt ot incorporate the term 'political party' and to define it in loose terms. But this attempt failed.[9] Then,

---

8. But this freedom, like other freedoms, is subject to reasonable restrictions imposed by the state in the interest of public order, decency or morality, sovereignty and integrity of India, security of the state, friendly relations with foreign states etc. Thus, this freedom "will not entitle any group of individuals to enter into a criminal conspiracy to form any association dangerous to the public peace or to make illegal strikes or to commit a public disorder, or to undermine the sovereignty or integrity of India." See D.D. Basu, *Introduction to the Constitution of India*, 1989, p. 97.

the 52nd Amendment of 1985 (Schedule X of the Constitution), also known as anti-defection law, has incorporated the term 'political party' without giving its precise definition. Section 1 (b) of this Act defines political party as "a group consisting of all members of that House for the time being belonging to that political party." However, a proper definition of the term 'political party' has been avoided and the Election Commission has been given the power to recognize or derecognize a political party according to the rules in force.[10]

---

9. With a view to implement the recommendations of the Chavan Committee though with certain modifications, the government of Mrs. Gandhi introduced in the Lok Sabha on 16 May 1973 an anti-defection bill in the form of 32nd Constitution Amendment Bill. The term 'political party', as defined in this bill, meant (i) a political party classified as a recognized political party under any law or any rule, regulation, order or notification having force of law with respect to matters relating to or in connection with elections to either House of Parliament, (ii) any other political party which is recognized by the Chairman or, as the case may be, by the Speaker of such House as a political party and which on the basis of such recognition consists of not less than one-fifteenth of the total number of members of such House.

10. The Election Commission of India has the power to recognize and derecognise a political party vide Election Symbols (Reservation and Allotment) Order, 1968. Its old rules were revised in March 2001. Now, under Rule 6A, a party may be recognized as a 'national party', if it satisfies one of the two conditions. First, candidates set up by it in any four or more States in the last general election to the Lok Sabha or Vidhan Sabha, have secured at least 6 percent of the total valid votes polled in their respective States, and it has returned at least four members to the Lok Sabha in the last general election from any State or States. Second, it has secured at least 2 percent of the total seats of the Lok Sabha, any fraction exceeding one-half being counted as one; and the said candidates have been elected to the Lok Sabha from at least three States. Then, under Rule 6B, a party may be recognised as a 'state party', if it satisfies one of the two conditions. First, candidates set up by it in the last general election to the Lok Sabha or Vidhan Sabha have secured at least 6 percent of the total valid votes polled in that State, and it has returned at least two members to the Vidhan Sabha. Second, it secures at least 3 percent of the total number of seats in the Vidhan Sabha, any fraction exceeding one-half being counted as one, or it has secured at least three seats in the House, whichever is more, in the last general election.

We may refer to an important change made in the Representation of the People Act, 1951 as amended in 1988, It requires that a political party seeking its registration with the Election Commission must submit a copy of its constitution expressing its faith in and commitment to democracy, secularism and socialism. One may wonder whether such an attempt has yielded any positive result so far. The political parties have revised their constitutions so as to meet this formality, but all has happened in name only. The Election Commission has formulated its own rules to recognise/derecognise a political party on the basis of its performance in the elections to Union and State legislatures which has nothing to do with its behaviour being consistent with the norms of democracy, secularism and socialism or not. The Election Commission has very cautiously avoided to open the Pandora's box on this count and, for this reason, some political parties (as Muslim League, Shiva Sena, Hindu Mahasabha, and some outfits of the extremists) have not been derecognised by it in spite of the dubious nature of their democratic and secular credentials. Since political parties work in alliance with numerous organised groups, the association of some recognised political parties with certain communal and terrorist organisations is a matter of patent reality and yet the Election Commission due to its limitations has not sought to question the identity of such political parties and organisations in the light of the above requirement

The 52nd Amendment has, however, yielded some positive results in curbing the evil of political defections. It is the only part of the Constitution where the term 'political party' has been used. Surprisingly, section 1 of this Act, containing 'interpretations' of all important terms used in this Act, does not provide a precise definition of political party and, for this reason, it offers no solution to certain problems that have arisen in course of time. For instance, it does not make it clear whether any political outfit having the name of a 'Manch' (Forum) or 'Morcha' (Front) can be taken as a political party or not. We may refer to the Haryana Vikas Manch of Bansi Lal and Bihar Vikas Manch of Dr. J.N. Mishra in this regard. Herein lies a clear opening and a shrewd politician may take advantage of saving himself from the penalty clause of the anti-defection law while being as well as not being in such an organization, by all means a political party, in the absence of an authentic definition of the term, other than one what this law calls the 'original party' or a party on whose ticket a person is elected to any house of the Parliament or State legislature. The legislator may also take advantage of a situation in which he is expelled from the party and then becomes an 'unattached' member of the house. In such an event also, the penalty clause of this law shall not apply. Such an opening is not provided by the law nor by the rules framed under it, and yet it has occurred in the past confirming the fact of no limit to man's political ingenuity. The anti-defection law had provided that an action would not attract the penalty clause in an event of 'split'. But, another opening had been discovered. The bosses of a political party could forestall such an eventuality by expelling some leading figures of a group of the apprehended defectors so as to frighten their followers and also to frustrate the possibility of a split. "This almost suggests that the party constitution provides a legitimate methodology for doing so."[11]

The crucial problem of the Indian party system lies in its dysfunctional role owing to low level of the political culture of the country. Not that the voters in general are influenced by the charisma of a particular leader, or they are swayed by the orations of the demagogues, the painful fact stands out that their communal, casteist, racial, clannish, tribal and communitarian attachments can easily be exploited by the crafty politicians. The 'vote bank' consists mostly of the socially and educationally backward people of the country whose 'will can be purchased at a very low price, or who can be easily coaxed and cajoled by the charm of petty material temptation, or coerced by the fear of intimidation and violence. Frequently, we hear about the events of large-scale rigging, booth capturing and violence which may be taken as serious symptoms of a disease afflicting the democratic system of our country. All possible attempts are made to win election by hook or crook and surprisingly political parties have no reservation in fielding certain notorious figures as their worthy candidates. As a result of this, politics no longer remains the way of rendering social service as said by Gandhiji; it becomes perverted and criminalized by the role of such party leaders.

Degeneration of the System: A parliamentary government is a responsible government. Since it is operated by the political parties, it automatically implies that the parties should use power delegated to them by the people in a serious and responsible manner. As late

11. Subhash C. Kashyap, "Anti-Defection Law Does Not Apply", *The Times of India*. New Delhi, 7 November 1990, p. 6. The 91st Amendment of 2003 has omitted the provision of 'split'.

as on the occasion of the golden jubilee celebrations of Indian independence, the Lok Sabha at the end of its special session on 1 September 1997, adopted a momentous resolution called 'Agenda for India' which, *inter alia,* says: "That continuous and proactive efforts be launched for ensuring greater transparency, probity and accountability in public life so that the freedom, authority and dignity of Parliament and other legislative bodies are ensured and enhanced, that more especially, all political parties shall undertake all such steps as will atain the objectives of ridding our polity of criminalization or its influence."

The expectations of the founding fathers seem to have been badly frustrated now. All political parties prefer candidates who have prospects of victory at the polls regardless of the fact that most of them are history-sheeters, murderers, rapists, extortionists, abductors, and the like. The National Police Commission, in its second report of 1979, with special reference to Bihar noted: "The manner in which different political parties have functioned, particularly on the eve of periodic elections, involves free use of musclemen and *dadas* (hoodlums) to influence the attitude and conduct of the sizeable sections of the electorate." Former Chief Election Commissioner M.S. Gill publicly said that seats of about 40 MPs and 200 MLAs were occupied by such criminal elements. The Vohra Committee Report (1993) is an eye-opener. It is stated: "In certain States like Bihar, Haryana and Uttar Pradesh, these gangs enjoy the patronage of the local-level politicians, cutting across party lines and the protection of governmental functionaries. Some political leaders became the leaders of these gangs/armed senas and over the years got them elected to local bodies, State Assemblies and the national Parliament."[12]

The present state of affairs is highly pathetic. A large number of persons against whom criminal cases are pending in the courts have turned law-makers and ministers after winning elections. It "has not only seriously jeopardized the legal process, but has posed far-reaching ethical dilemmas and concerns."[13] The old saying stands discredited that crime never pays. Instead, the present reality is that the shining record of crimes alone is the best qualification for

---

12. See S.C. Kashyap (ed.), *Eradication of Corruption and Restoration of Values*, (New Delhi: Sterling, 2001), Annexure 4.

13. R.B. Jain, *"The Art of Political Corruption"*. *Ibid.*, p. 109.

securing party tickets and grabbing ministerial berths after winning elections by all possible means. "The countryside is brimming with gun-carrying criminals, trotting as politicians. Crime is their source of livelihood, but politics provides them the necessary amphibious; he combines two occupations at the same time."[14]

In view of the rampant corruption and electoral malpractices leading to the victory of the majority of the candidates on the minority of votes, "even their representative character has come to be seriously doubted."[15] Luckily, the Supreme Court has come to our rescue. In a leading case, it ruled that the MPs and the MLAs were 'public servants' under section 2(c) of the Prevention of Corruption Act of 1988.[16] In another case[17] it relied on the seven principles of the Nolan Committee Report of 1994.[18] However, it created history in the Poll Reforms case by issuing a directive to the Election Commission on 2 May 2002 to call for full information, on an affidavit signed before a first-class magistrate, from every candidate filing nomination paper for election to Parliament or State legislature.[19] The information should cover many things like the record of convictions and acquittals in any criminal offence including the cases pending in the courts, assets in the form of movable and immovable property and bank balance belonging to him as well as to his spouse and dependents, liability to public institutions and government dues, and educational qualifications.

It came as a bolt from the blue for the politicians regardless of their party affiliations. Eminent politicians cutting across party lines

---

14. S.R. Maheshwari, "Political Reforms for True Governance" in T.N. Chaturvedi (ed.), *Towards Good Governance*, (New Delhi: Indian Institute of Public Administration, 1999), p. 57.

15. S.C. Kashyap, "Towards Good Governance: Need for Political Reforms". *Ibid.*, p. 68.

16. *Narsimha Rao* v. *Union of India*, 1998, 4 SSC 626.

17. *Vineet Narain* v. *Union of India*, 1998 I SCC 226.

18. It was a committee of the British Parliament set up under the chairmanship of Lord Nolan which recommended in 1994 seven principles to be applied to all aspects of public life-selflessness, integrity, objectivity, accountability, openness, honesty and leadership.

19. *Union of India* v. *Association for Democratic Reforms*, 2002.

had a meeting with the Union Home Minister and they showed rare unanimity in demanding that the directive of the Supreme Court should be circumvented by a law of the Parliament. Thus, an ordinance was issued (that was subsequently converted into a law) which introduced an amendment in section 33 of the Representation of People Act of 1951. It provided that a person after being a member of any house of Parliament or State legislature would supply such information to the presiding officer of the house (not on an affidavit). As expected, the Supreme Court struck it down in March 2003 and thereby it proved its credentials of being sentinel on the *qui vive*.

Remedial Measures: Then, what is the way out? We may advance a number of suggestions in the light of which the constitutional/legal system of our country should be reformed:

1. While the right to vote should remain available to every adult citizen, right to fight elections should not be the privilege of all. Since administrative system requires recruitment of the experts and since this rule is invariably followed in the sphere of administrative and judicial departments, legislature should be no exception to it. That is, those who desire to be the members of the rule-making department of the state should know about the operation of the legislative system of their country. Hence, right to fight elections should be given to those who have at least an elementary knowledge of reading and writing. More than this, those who win election must undergo a training for a period of about six months so that they acquire first-hand knowledge of the Constitutions as well as of parliamentary procedure and conduct of business. For this purpose, a high-powered body like a Legislative Service Commission should be set up to hold preliminary tests from time to time and those who qualify be permitted to file their nomination papers at the time of elections. That is, nobody should be allowed to seek election unless he or she obtains a certificate of eligibility from the Commission. As its adjunct, an Institute of Parliamentary Work should also be created for imparting training to the new recruits and also for arranging refresher courses for the new and old legislators from time to time.
2. Every political party has a staff of its own whose members are recruited on the basis of 'spoils system'. The 'favourites' of the great leaders are inducted to carry on party work and

who, in most of the cases, have hardly any merit equal to the task assigned to them. Their terms of service are not specified; their salaries and allowances are also not mentioned in clear terms. In spite of all this, people accept a job in the party office with certain ulterior motives. By getting close to the levers of power, they enhance their social status and then by resorting to unethical and undesirable practices they manage to make hay even when there is no sunshine. Hence, this point should be repeated that all registered political parties recruit staff from amongst persons selected by a statutory body like the Legislative Service Commission and so their service conditions be governed by the statutes of the country. Besides reforming and regulating the working of political parties in an appreciable measure, it shall also solve the problem of unemployment to some extent.

3. The accounts of political parties should be subject to public audit. Black money generated by the people is partially donated to party funds, or the parties manage to collect hush money from big business houses and other unknown sources. This money is spent, rather squandered, according to the whims and caprices of the few leaders. Facts reveal this unfortunate fact that no party desires to spend any amount of money on the maintenance of a good library or a reading room or a centre of advanced study and research, while it may easily and promptly spend a big chunk of its funds on taking out a procession, organizing a *mela* (fair), holding a convention, according reception to its supremos and the like. To a certain extent, the expenses of the parties should be subsidized by the state on the basis of their election results as we find in the case of Germany.

4. Power is the source of attraction. A seat in the legislature has its own charm; the office of a minister has a greater attraction. Te party leaders and their zealous followers have their eyes set on the legislative and ministerial berths without paying any regard to this maxim: "first deserve, then desire". There should be specific rules that a person cannot avail more than two or three terms as a legislator or a minister or both; that defector shall not be entitled for a post unless he completes a probation period of at least two or three years; that the total strength of the ministry should not be more than one-tenth of

the total strength of the house(s) of legislature; that a person should not be given such a dignified post unless he emerges innocent in civil and criminal proceedings, if going on against him in the courts of the country; that the sons and daughters of the legislators/ministers should not be allowed to have a seat along with their parents; and that the legislators/ministers should be required to declare their assets and liabilities annually in their income tax returns.

5. A democratic system is also known by the name of, what Dicey called, the 'rule of law' which is the antithesis of the rule of lawlessness. As such, any party indulging in acts of violence and terrorism of any kind should be placed under an effective ban. There should be a high-powered statutory body to examine the democratic and secular credentials of a political party and necessary action should be taken by the Government in the light of the findings and observations of this autonomous authority. It should also be entrusted with the task of looking into all sorts of irregularities and those found guilty on a serious count should not be allowed to fight elections for a period of ten years.
6. The rules relating to recognition and derecognition of political parties should also be revised in a way that right to fight elections should be available only to political parties recognized by the Election Commission. No party should be allowed to seek its registration with the Election Commission unless it has a standing of at least three years. One person should be allowed to fight election from one constituency at a time. The code of conduct issued by the Election Commission should be binding on all parties.
7. The evil of political defections should be curbed in all possible respects. The present anti-defection law has some loopholes which should be plugged. For instance, no office should be given to a defector unless he has a standing in some other party for at least two years; an independent member of the house, whether elected or nominated, should not be allowed to join any other party; and the phrase 'violation of the whip' (as used in this context and on the basis of which the presiding officer may disqualify a person from the membership of the house) should be defined in clear terms.

8. The membership of a political party should be given on the basis of some well-defined rules and regulations. It should not be like a privilege to be conferred in a quick and reckless manner. The applicant should be placed on a term of probation for some time so that he may acquaint himself with the ideology and working of the party. Election to various posts should also be held as provided in its constitution so as to do away with the practice of sheer ad hocism. There should be inner-party democracy. The working of the parties should be reviewed from time to time by the Election Commission or some other statutory body meant for this purpose. It should also study the annual report of the activities of all recognized and unrecognized parties and then it should submit its report and observations to the head of the state for any necessary follow-up action.
9. The requirement that political party seeking registration with the Election Commission should express its faith in socialism be removed in view of the fact that 'socialism' lacks a precise connotation and that it has unfortunately become an instrument of political blackmail at the hands of party politicians. It should be substituted by a better term 'social justice'.
10. In order to keep the government and the party as two distinct entities, it would be better if persons holding ministerial positions are not allowed to hold offices in the party organization.

The above suggestions are only illustrative, by no means exhaustive, and many more constructive points may be added. Some of the objectives may be realized by the growth of healthy conventions. In the absence of such a situation, however, statutory arrangements are called for. The provisions of the Constitution should be revised or reformed and a statutory mechanism be evolved to supplement them if the experiment of parliamentary democracy is to be made successful in our country. A critic may burst out that some of the suggestions, listed above, are either utopian or fantastic having no place in the advanced democratic countries of the world. But a suitable reply to such a criticism would be that even in the advanced democratic countries, party system is regulated by some kind of statutory mechanism that is supplemented with a large number of conventions sustained by the high level of political culture of the people. Democracy is an ideal to be pursued and realized in degrees and, for this sake, every country should strive in its own way keeping in view its social setting and political milieu. So is the case with our country. A party system reformed and regulated in accordance with the proposals given above would certainly yield the desired results. Hopefully, it would signify a movement from 'de-institutionalisation'[20] to 're-institutionalization' of party system in our country worthy of being what is now ardently desired as a segment of the vision for the next two decades of the present century.

20. L.I. Rudolph and S.H. Rudolph used this term in the context of 'de-institutionalisation' of the Indian National Congress under the leadership of Indira Gandhi and Rajiv Gandhi'. See *In Pursuit of Lakshmi: The Political Economy of Indian State*, p. 144.

17

Elections

Part XV of the Constitution titled 'Elections' constitutes a glaring instance of departure from the usual practice in view of the fact that it does not treat the subject of elections as a matter of comparative unimportance that should have been left to the jurisdiction of the executive and legislative departments of the state. The fact that detailed provisions in this regard have been made in the Constitution shows how anxious the Constitution-makers had been to safeguard this political right as an integral part of the Constitution itself. It is for this important reason that the subject of elections has been accorded constitutional recognition in our country.

Underlying Principles of Election

In the pre-independence days, franchise was a restricted affair. Even under the Government of India Act of 1935, it was about 14.1% of the total population of the country. Moreover, it was highly vitiated by the arrangement of separate and communal electorate system. When the Constitution-makers were discussing the issue of universal adult franchise, some members registered their scepticism in this regard and some others, supporting the case of a Gandhian constitution, desired the adoption of indirect election system in a pyramid-like polity with village panchayats at the base and a national panchayat at the top. However, such considerations were rejected and ultimately the Constituent Assembly decided to adopt the principle of universal adult franchise in deference to what Nehru and other great leaders had been emphasising for the last many years.

Considering that a vast majority of the people of this country are illiterate, tradition-bound and without experience of democratic processes, such a resolve amounted to a momentous decision. The President of the Assembly (Dr. Rajendra Prasad) visualised : "I am not dismayed by it..........I know the village people who constitute the bulk of this vast electorate. In my opinion, people possess intelligence and commonsense. They also have a culture which the sophisticated may not appreciate but which is solid..........They are able to take the measure of their own interest and also of the interests of the country at large if things are explained to them."[1]

As a result of this, Art. 326 of the Constitution came into being. It says: "The elections to the Lok Sabha and to the Vidhan Sabha of every State shall be on the basis of adult suffrage; that is to say, every person who is a citizen of India and who is not less than 18 years of age on such date as may be fixed in that behalf by or under any law made by the appropriate legislature and is not otherwise disqualified under the Constitution or any law made by the appropriate legislature on the ground of non-residence, unsoundness of mind, crime, or corrupt, or illegal practice, shall be entitled to be registered as a voter at any such election."

By all means, the provision of universal adult suffrage is one of the most important features of the Constitution that is lauded as an organisation of individual liberty and an instrument of political power. Thus, the idea of Nehru has been materialised that "only a legislature elected by the voters of the country as a whole would be far more interested in the economic and social problems of the masses, than in the petty communal issues which affect small groups." But the critics have expressed their misgivings in this regard. Their argument is that the principle of universal adult suffrage has dragged all sorts of Toms, Dicks and Harries into the vortex of electoral politics most of whom have no knowledge at all

1. *Constituent Assembly Debates*, Vol. XI, p. 989. On 18 November, 2004, in a message delivered by President Abdul Kalam it was counselled: "By casting your vote for a candidate who in your opinion can represent you in the Lok Sabha, you are sowing seeds for the creation of a prosperous India, a happy India, a safe India, a secure India and, above all, India with nobility. The right to vote is a sacred right and an onerous responsibility that you owe to the motherland. Hence, exercising your franchise must become a priority and you should cast your vote positively." *The Times of India* (New Delhi), 19 April, 2004.

of what they are expected to do. The result is that several local, communal and regional organisations have come up to vitiate the democratic system of the country. It has led to the emergence of the forces of factionalism, communalism, casteism and regionalism.

At this stage, it shall be worthwhile to mention a few fundamental principles underlying elections to the Lok Sabha and State legislatures:

1. There is one general electoral roll for every territorial constituency. No person is ineligible for inclusion in an electoral roll on the grounds of religion, race, caste, sex etc.

2. Voting right has been given to every citizen of India above 18 years of age. A citizen may, however, be deprived of this right on some grounds like unsoundness of mind, conviction by a court for at least two years, or a declaration of his being an undischarged insolvent, held guilty by a court for some illegal or corrupt act or any other like ground defined in the law of the land.

3. The Election Commission has the power to waive disqualification of a person for reasons to be recorded by it in writing.

4. No person can be registered as a voter in more than one constituency. He/she may contest election to the Lok Sabha or to the Vidhan Sabha if he/she is above 25 years of age.

5. The State may make reservation of seats for Scheduled Castes and Scheduled Tribes in the Lok Sabha and Vidhan Sabha of every State.

6. No candidate should commit a 'corrupt' practice which involves payment of bribery including gift, promise or some gratification for affecting the electoral process, exercise of undue influence or any such thing going to interfere with the free exercise of a person's franchise, spreading feeling of enmity or hatred between different classes of citizens on the grounds of religion, caste, community, language and the like, indulging in bride-burning or *sati,* publication of any false statement going to affect the personal character or conduct of a candidate, hiring or procuring vehicles by a candidate for the purposes of fetching voters to the place of polling, expending an amount more than

authorised for election purpose, and obtaining any assistance, other than that of voting, for the furtherance of electoral prospects of a candidate.

It is obvious that these arrangements have been made in the Representation of the People Acts of 1950 and 1951, as amended from time to time, for the sake of ensuring free and fair polls in the country.

Election Commission

To ensure free and fair elections, the Constitution provides an important body called the Election Commission. It is an autonomous body having all-India jurisdiction over elections to the Parliament, State legislatures and offices of the President and Vice-President. Thus, it is a central body entrusted with the work of conducting elections for State legislatures as well. Though it looks like violation of the federal system to some extent, the reason for having an all-India body to supervise and conduct elections, rather than having separate bodies to organise elections in each State, is, as Prof. M.P. Jain observes, that "some States have a mixed population, as there are the native people as well as others who are racially, linguistically or culturally different from the native people. In order to prevent injustice being done to any section of the people, it was thought best to have one central body which would be free from local influences and have control over the entire election machinery in the country."[2]

Art. 324 of the Constitution says that the superintendence, direction and control of the preparation of the electoral rolls and the conduct of all elections to the Parliament and to the Legislature of every State, including the offices of the President and Vice-President, shall be vested in the Election Commission which shall consist of the Chief Election Commissioner and other Election Commissioners, if necessary, as the President may fix from time to time. The appointments of the Chief Election Commissioner and other Election Commissioners, including some Regional Election Commissioners working under him, shall be governed by the law of the Parliament. In the absence of any such law, the mode of the

2. Jain: *Indian Constitutional Law*, 1978, p. 394.

appointment and terms and service conditions etc. of the Chief Election Commissioner and Election Commissioners shall be governed by an order of the President.[3]

The head of the Election Commission is the Chief Election Commissioner. He is appointed by the President and holds his office for a term as determined by a law of Parliament. He may tender his resignation at any time he so likes, or he may be removed by the President after a special address (or impeachment motion) is passed by both the Houses of Parliament by special majority (that is, absolute majority of the whole House and 2/3 majority of the members, present and voting). It is also laid down that, during his tenure, his service conditions or his emoluments cannot be varied to his disadvantage. In case, the President desires to take disciplinary action against any Election Commissioner, he shall do so after obtaining the recommendation of the Chief Election Commissioner. It is also laid down that the President and the Governor, as the case may be, shall, when so requested by the Election Commission, make available to the Chief Election Commissioner or to an Election Commissioner such staff as may be necessary for the discharge of functions conferred on the Election Commission.

The functions and powers of the Election Commission are given below:

1. It is its duty to get the electoral rolls for elections to the Parliament and all State legislatures, prepared and revised subject to the provisions of the Constitution and the laws made by the Union and State Legislatures.

2. Subject to the provisions of the Constitution and other laws made by the Parliament and State Legislatures, it exercises superintendence, direction and control over all matters pertaining to the elections of the President, Vice-President, Parliament and State Legislatures.

---

3. In 1993 Parliament made a law for the appointment of two Election Commissioners. Regional Election Commissioners may also be appointed by the President in consultation with the Chief Election Commissioner to assist the Election Commission on the eve of the general election.

3. It advises the President and the Governors regarding the incurring of disqualifications by a member of the Union or State Legislatures, as the case may be, subsequent to his election.
4. It is its duty to appoint election officers for inquiring into doubts and disputes arising out of or connected with the election arrangements.
5. It may advise the President to appoint Regional Election Commissioners in a sufficient number to help it in the performance of its duties on the eve of elections to the Lok Sabha or to the Vidhan Sabhas of the States.
6. It may requisition from the President and the Governors, as the case may be, such staff as it may deem necessary for conducting elections.
7. It may settle a dispute regarding reservation and allotment of symbols to the parties in the event of a split.
8. It may postpone the dates of elections for some reasons or cancel an election in case it is satisfied with the complaints of rigging, booth-capturing, use of violence and the like. It may issue orders for repolling.
9. It reserves the right to prepare a roster for Central broadcasts and telecasts allocating particular days and time to particular parties.
10. It may order for the rectification of a clerical mistake made by the Delimitation Commission with the prior approval of this authority.
11. It may visit the disturbed areas and make appeals through the mass communication media to pacify the people crying for the rectification of electoral records or procedures.
12. It may exempt a person from the disqualification imposed by a judicial decision.
13. It may waive the conditions of holding an election until the electoral rolls are revised. In exceptional situations, it may order repoll.
14. If the Government wants to extend the duration of emergency in a State (under Art. 356 of the Constitution) beyond one

year, it can be done with the approval of the Parliament. But such a proposal of the Government must be supported by the advice of the Election Commission that prevailing conditions donot warrant possibility of holding elections in that State for certain pertinent reasons, or if emergency is in force.

15. After the election results are declared, it issues a notification that the House is duly constituted.

It may be added that important arrangements have been made to ensure independence and impartiality of the Election Commission. For instance, the CEC is appointed by the President and can be removed from office by following special procedure of impeachment. The other Election Commissioners are appointed by the President and may be removed by him on the advice of the CEC. Their salaries and allowances are a charge on the consolidated fund of India. Some members of the Constituent Assembly like Pandit Hridaynath Kunzru and Shibbanlal Saksena had expressed a fear that the appointment of this high officer by the President on the advice of the Prime Minister "may make room for the exercise of political influence."[4] It is also apprehended that while advising the Government for extension of the duration of emergency in a State on certain grounds, or while ordering repoll in a constituency, this officer might be dragged into the vortex of politics. It is, however, a matter of satisfaction that the President, acting on the advice of the Prime Minister, has so far appointed men of unquestionable integrity and highest judicial probity to this office and thus "various apprehensions regarding political influences creeping in the appointment of the Chief Election Commissioner have also been belied in practice."[5]

Election Procedure

The election procedure is determined by several important statutory arrangements. We may refer to the Representation of the People Acts of 1950 and 1951, as amended from time to time, in this connection. The Parliament has been given the power to make laws for electoral arrangements in the country relating to the composition of Union and State Legislatures. However, it may

4. *Constituent Assembly Debates,* Vol. VIII, pp, 907–8 and 921–922.

5. R.P. Bhalla: *Elections in India*, p. 9.

authorise State Legislatures to make certain incidental laws for the same purpose subject to the provisions of the Constitution and the laws made by it already in force. A study of the election procedure should be made in the light of these important points:

1. Delimitation of constituencies is the first essential step in this regard. The Parliament has the power to make laws for the composition and functioning of the Delimitation Commission after every decennial census. Thus, the demarcation of constituencies is done by a statutory body after every decennial census.
2. The President issues a notification of the general election whereby the polling schedule is announced by the Election Commission. Accordingly, the Election Commission appoints returning officers in all parts of the country. The political parties start the work of distributing tickets. Nomination papers are filed by the candidates after they are duly proposed and seconded by the voters whose names are given there in the electoral rolls.
3. The Election Commission has the power to issue guidelines on the eve of the elections which must be observed by all. In case a candidate is found to have made use of any 'corrupt' practice, his election may be declared invalid by the High Court and the Supreme Court.
4. Election canvassing must come to a stop 48 hours before the close of the elections.
5. Nomination papers filed by the candidates are properly checked. A person may withdraw his nomination paper within the specified time. It is after the date of scrutiny and final withdrawal that the nomination of candidates is declared and then proper election canvassing begins. Candidates nominated by the recognised parties have their reserved symbols, while candidates of unrecognised parties and non-partymen, known as 'independents', choose their symbols out of the list made by the Election Commission. All disputes relating to the allotment and reservation of symbols are settled by the Election Commission.
6. The Government of India may declare certain constituencies 'reserved' for Scheduled Castes and Scheduled Tribes.

7. Elaborate polling arrangements are made by the District Election Officers. Polling booths are made where polling officers are stationed. On the polling date, enrolled voters are given right to vote. Their particulars are checked by the men on duty and then ballot papers are given to them. The voter must affix the seal of 'X' against the name of the candidate of his/ her choice and then cast it into the ballot box. The authorised agents of the candidates have the right to challenge the bonafides of a voter. A person may be arrested and then prosecuted on the charge of impersonation.
8. After the polling is over, the ballot boxes are sealed and brought to the district headquarters. Then counting begins. A candidate securing highest number of votes is declared elected. The defeated candidate or candidates may challenge the election in the High Court of the State. The decision of the High Court can be reversed by the Supreme Court in appeal.
9. After election, every candidate has to submit an account of his election expenses within a specified period. In case he/ she makes an expenditure of more than the specified limit, his election may be set aside. However, the expenses made by the party in the election of a candidate shall not be counted in the expenses made by him. Moreover, the work of election shall be taken to have begun from the date of the actual nomination of the candidate.
10. The publication and preservation of the ballot papers, including electoral rolls and other necessary papers, is the job of the Election Commission. The Election Commission may issue necessary instructions from time to time. Recently, the Election Commission has made an experiment with electronic voting machines in selected constituencies of the country.

The Election Law has recently undergone some important changes which are given below:

1. Any conviction under Section 2 (offence of insulting the National Flag or the Constitution of India) or Section 3 (offence of preventing singing of National Anthem) of the Prevention of Insults to National Honour Act of 1971, shall hereafter entail disqualification for contesting elections to Parliament and State legislatures for a period of six years from the date of such conviction.

2. The amount of security deposit which a candidate at an election to the Lok Sabha or a State Legislative Assembly has to make has been enhanced as a measure to check the multiplicity of non-serious candidates. Now the amount of deposit for Lok Sabha election is Rs. 10,000 (Rs. 5,000 for a person belonging to SC or ST) and the amount for a Vidhan Sabha seat is Rs. 5,000 (Rs. 2,500 for a person belonging to SC or ST). In case a candidate fails to secure at least 1/6 of the valid votes polled, his security deposit shall be forfeited. It is also provided that the nomination paper of a candidate should have the signatures of at least 10 proposers if he has not been set up by a recognised National or State party. In the case of a candidate of a recognised party, only one proposer is enough.
3. Minimum interval between the last date for withdrawal and the holding of polls has been reduced from 20 to 14 days. Now a person cannot contest election from more than two constituencies whether it is a general election, or a bye-election to the Lok Sabha or Vidhan Sabha, or it is biennial election or a bye-election to the Rajya Sabha or the Vidhan Parishad of a State.
4. Now the names of the candidates shall be printed on the ballot paper in a particular order—first the name of candidates belonging to 'recognised political parties', then of 'recognised registered parties' and then of other (independent) candidates.
5. No election will be countermanded on the death of a candidate. In case the deceased candidate was set up by a recognised National or State Party, the party concerned will be given an option to nominate another candidate within 7 days of the notice issued to this effect by the Election Commission.
6. Bye-elections to the Parliament or State legislatures will now be held within six months of the occurrence of vacancy. This stipulation will not apply where the remainder of the term of the member is of less than one year, or the Election Commission informs the Government of India about the impossibility of holding bye-election within the said period.
7. An amendment has been made in the Presidential and Vice-Presidential Election Act whereby a person seeking election must deposit a security amount of Rs. 15,000 and his nomination paper must be signed by at least 50 electors as

proposers and 50 other electors as seconders in the case of Presidential election and by 20 electors as proposers and 20 as seconders in the case of Vice-Presidential election.

8. Section 29 A of the Representation of the People Act provides for the registration of political parties by the Election Commission. The Commission may recognise or derecognise a political party under the Election Symbols (Reservation and Allotment) Order of 1968. Under the existing rules (as revised in March 2001, a party must secure at least 6 per cent of the valid votes polled in any four or more States or Union Territories in Lok Sabha or Vidhan Sabha elections. Also, it must win at least 4 seats in the Lok Sabha from any State or States. Or, it must secure at least 2 per cent of the seats in the Lok Sabha provided its 4 members are elected from at least three different States. If so, it shall be recognised as a national party. To be recognised as a State-level party, it must secure at least 6 per cent of the valid votes polled in the State in Lok Sabha or Vidhan Sabha elections of that State. Besides, it must also win at least two seats in the Assembly. Or, it must win at least three per cent of the seats in the Vidhan Sabha or at least 3 seats, whichever is more. Now a party losing its recognition as a national or State-level party would not lose its reserved symbol immediately. It would be given a period of 6 years to retrieve its position, though it would not be entitled to the facilities available to a recognised party at the time of elections.

Electoral Reforms

A look at some defects of the system coupled with the allegations of misuse of official machinery and role of black money in the elections has informed a good number of people to think in terms of electoral reforms. The JP Movement, started in 1974, popularised this theme very much. All-India conferences, seminars, debates, discussions etc. were organised by many official, semi-official and non-official agencies and institutions. While all reposed their faith in the democratic system and appreciated the general framework of statutory provisions, they offered numerous suggestions of reform like introduction of proportional representation with single transferable vote and list systems, state subsidy for election expenses, facilities for broadcasting and telecasting programmes to all political parties, complete ban on the use of official machinery for electoral purposes, reduction of the minimum age of the voters from 21 to 18 years, reorganisation of the Election Commission so as to have a multi-member Election Commission, legal prohibition of defections, statutory ban on political donations and flow of foreign money, audit of funds of political parties, establishment of special courts for the speedy disposal of election petitions, enhancement of ceiling on the permissible expenditure made by a candidate in his election, etc.[6]

Instead of making a big catalogue of all such proposals of reforms advanced by numerous people, it shall now be worthwhile to refer to some important suggestions made by the former Chief Election Commissioner (R.K. Trivedi):

1. Election law should be changed so as to define the term 'political party' and its area of operation.
2. Election Commission should have the constitutional authority to make regulations for *(i)* compulsory registration of political parties. *(ii)* compulsory maintenance of accounts including all receipts and donations and minute books, *(iii)* open acceptance of donations from companies and individuals under the receipts subject to suitable regulatory conditions including tax relief with a ceiling in the case of individual donors, *(iv)* compulsory audit and accounts by an agency to be named by the Commission, *(v)* submission of periodic reports to the Commission, and *(vi)* residuary powers relating to the role of political parties.
3. Misuse of official machinery by a candidate should be defined as a 'corrupt' practice attracting legal provisions of the Representation of the People Act, 1951.
4. Art. 324 (6) of the Constitution should be so amended that the Election Commission may utilise the services of the polling staff of one State for election work in another State with the consent of the Governor of the concerned State.
5. Referring to the special case of Assam, the CEC desired a change in the election law to the effect that a minimum number

6. Most of such recommendations were contained in the Tarkunde Committee Report of 1975.

of seats be laid down on whose filling up the Election Commission may issue notification of the due constitution of the House.[7]

It is a matter of satisfaction that recently important changes have been made in the Representation of the People Act, 1951, so as to implement some important measures of electoral reforms. There are:

1. Sec. 8 of the Act includes a larger number of offences which can disqualify a candidate from contesting elections. These are related to indulging in terrorist activities, burning and torturing brides, glorifying *sati* cases, booth-capturing, rigging elections by a candidate or his agents, importing and exporting prohibited goods, and violating Narcotic Drugs and Psychotropic Substances Act and Foreign Exchange Regulation Act.
2. Sec. 29 A has been inserted to provide for registration of political parties. Now a political party seeking registration with the Election Commission is required to include in its rules and regulations a specific provision that it shall bear true faith in and allegiance to the Constitution of India and to the principles of secularism, socialism and democracy.
3. Among other measures, we may refer to the use of electronic voting machines in 'sensitive' constituencies to ensure free and fair elections. The penalty for disturbing election meetings has been raised from Rs. 250 to Rs. 1,000. The designated officers and staff of the State governments have been taken under the direction, control and superintendence of the Election Commission while discharging their duties in elections.

In 1990, the Dinesh Goswami Committee was set up which made these important recommendations:

1. The Election Commission should be a multi-member body having a Chief Election Commissioner and two Election Commissioners.

---

7. *The Times of India* (New Delhi), 28 March, 1983.

2. There should be a fresh delimitation of constituencies on the basis of last decennial census and the seats reserved for the Scheduled Castes and Scheduled Tribes should be rotated from time to time. The political parties should distribute more tickets in favour of women.
3. A person should not be allowed to contest election from more than two constituencies of the same category.
4. The model code of conduct issued by the Election Commission on the eve of elections should be given a statutory backing.
5. A bye-election should be held within six months of the occurrence of a vacancy and election petitions pending in the High Courts should be disposed of expeditiously. For this sake special courts or tribunals may be set up.
6. The law should ban donations to political parties by the companies, but the State may grant subsidies to recognised political parties in the form of material as free supply of vehicles, petrol, diesel, stationery etc.
7. The minimum age of the candidates should be reduced as from 30 to 25 for election to the Rajya Sabha and Vidhan Parishads and from 25 to 21 for elections to Lok Sabha and Vidhan Sabhas.
8. Stringent punishment should be given to those who commit acts of booth-capturing, rigging the polls, terrorising the voters etc.
9. The security deposit of the candidates should be enhanced so as to discourage non-serious candidates.
10. The law should be suitably amended for imposing a ban on the transfer of civil and police officers connected with the work of elections for a specified period.

It is good that some of the recommendations of this report have been implemented in due course, though its recommendation relating to the State funding of elections on the pattern of Germany and Austria in a poor country like ours may be disputed. It was already contained in the Tarkunde Report of 1975 and, as we shall see later, it was accommodated in the Inderjit Gupta Committee Report of 1999.

We may also refer to the recommendations of the Inderjit Gupta Committee Report (1999) the most important of which are following:

1. Since political parties perform a vital public function of sustaining democracy, they should be financed from public fund. The Centre should create a separate election fund with a corpus of Rs. 600 crore annually with another Rs. 600 crore chipped in annually by the States. But it should be available to the candidates of parties recognised by the Election Commission. Moreover, this assistance should be in the form of material, not cash, as rent-free accommodation in State capitals, petrol, diesel, jeeps, stationery etc.
2. Elections should be made free from the influence of criminals and use of money and muscle power should be checked.
3. Restrictions should be imposed on wall writing and displays of banners and a reasonable number should be fixed for taking out processions and holding of public meetings.
4. All donations from Rs. 10,000 upward should be accepted by cheques or drafts and the name of donors be disclosed.
5. Political parties must file a return of their income and expenditure after every general election to the Election Commission.

Activism of the Election Commission

The functions and powers of an institution or its functionary may be elaborately written in a statute, but the real nature of the office is determined by the personal equation of its holder. The Government of India Act of 1858 had entrusted the power of superintendence, direction and control of the administration of India to a British Cabinet Minister (Secretary of State for India) who could stretch his jurisdiction to any extent in the name of these three important terms. The same expression is contained in Art. 324 of the Constitution whereby the Election Commission has the power to superintend, direct and control elections to the Union and State legislatures apart from Presidential and Vice-Presidential elections. Credit goes to Chief Election Commissioner T.N. Seshan and his worthy successors who very cautiously but steadily expanded their area of authority and that came to be called by many a critic as its 'activism'. It may be noted in several significant directions:

1. By enforcing the Reservation and Allotment of Election Symbols Order in 1968, it has taken upon itself the power of

recognising and derecognising political parties and to settle any dispute in this regard. It may amend such rules as it did in 2001.

2. It may make a change in the date of declared elections, may stop polling or recounting of votes if the conditions so warrant. It may requisition staff from the State governments and instruct the Chief Secretaries of the States to punish persons on duty for any act of insubordination or wilful negligence. In this way, it has established its disciplinary jurisdiction. As clarified by the Supreme Court, (in *Election Commission v. Union of India*) the disciplinary jurisdiction of the Election Commission over officers, staff and police deputed to perform election duties during the period of election shall extend to

   (a) suspending any officer/for insubordination or dereliction of duty,

   (b) substituting any officer/official/police personnel by another such person and returning the substitute individual to the cadres which he belongs,

   (c) Making recommendations to the competent authority for taking disciplinary action for any act of insubordination or dereliction of duty. Such recommendations shall be promptly acted upon by the disciplinary authority and action taken will be communicated to the Election Commission within a period of six months.

   (d) The Union Government will advise the State governments that they too should follow the above principles and decisions, since a large number of election officials are under their administrative control.

3. By its prompt decision and follow-up actions, the Election Commission has maintained its autonomy. The Chief Election Commissioner J.M. Lyngdoh regretted inability to hold elections in strife-torn Gujarat in 2003. He put aside the argument of the then Union Home Minister (Advani) that the elections should be held as early as possible so that the intervening period between the two sessions of the Assembly does not exceed the limit of six months as required under Art. 174 of the Constitution. The argument of the Minister was patently wrong in view of the fact that such a requirement did

not apply to a dissolved Vidhan Sabha. The CEC expressed the view that such a constitutional problem could be solved by extending the duration of President's rule under Art. 356. In stead of honouring the sane view of the Chief Election Commissioner, the irate Minister reacted that it was no business of the CEC to advise the government. With a view to attract the votes of the poor and innocent people to the side of his party, Lalji Tandon of the BJP distributed *sarees* on the occasion of his birth day in April 2004 in Lucknow. In the stampede about 21 women were killed. The Commission took it as an attempt to bribe the voters and a violation of the Code of Conduct. It asked the Government of Uttar Pradesh to register a case under Sec. 171-B of the Indian Penal Code against Tandon and to transfer the Collector and Police Superintendent from Lucknow.

4. The Election Commission has taken up a number of measures to check misuse of public money by the politicians particularly during election campaigns. After taking the office of the Chief ElectionCommissioner, T.S. Krishnamurthy on 8 February, 2004 said: 'My personal view is that, as far as possible, tax payer's money should not be used for electoral advantages." The Commission rejected the proposal that the Deputy Prime Minister could use air force planes for electoral purposes. On 27 February 2004, the Commission put a clamp on election advertisements on television channels. It held that Rule 7 (3) of the Cable Television Network Rules (1994), prescribed under Sec. 6 (advertisement code) of the Cable Television Network Regulations Act of 1995 which prohibits advertisements on cable television networks of a political nature or towards any political end should continue to be on the statute book. The action of the Commission was appreciated by the Supreme Court when it, on 2 April, 2004, put a ban on the telecast of all political advertisements on cable networks and television channels which offend morality, decency and religious susceptibilities of the viewers. Such a stand was taken by the Court to provide a level playing field for all political parties.

5. The assertive role of the Election Commission is a source of trouble for the politicians of the country who want to push matters in their own way. Hence, Yashwant Sinha, former Union Minister in the NDA government of Vajpayee expressed

his reaction thus: 'The EC must stop taking on powers of the executive. In our country, a fractious and weakened executive has, over a period of time, surrendered its authority in various matters to the other organs of governance. The first constitutional question which arises, therefore, is whether one constitutional authority can compel another, especially Parliament to do its bidding. By not holding elections within six months from the date on which President's rule was first imposed in Bihar, the EC did precisely that. In other words, it arrogated to itself the power of Parliament to extend President's rule. This amounts to a mockery of our nation's constitutional jurisprudence."[8]

Critical Appreciation

A study of the system of elections and electoral process in our country has its own strong and weak aspects. While it is true that ours is a democratic set up and fortunately it has been steadily moving towards the goal, some points of weakness may be enumerated as under:

1. In the electoral politics much belaboured and carefully prepared election manifestoes play an insignificant role. They are neither widely publicised to reach the common voter, nor do the candidates care to enlighten the masses.

2. Timely events and popular slogans influence and attract the voters more than the permanent values. These slogans invoke socialism, democracy, secularism, proletarianism and exploitation and eradication of communalism.

3. The election results also reveal that the number of seats won by a political party do not correspond to the percentage of votes polled by it. A reason for this is division and consequent loss of opposition votes.

4. Failure of the opposition parties may be assigned to their inability in making a broad-base covering the rural and urban areas, and also their apathy towards conveying their ideology and programmes to the people. The success of the various regional and local parties is primarily due to their capacity of manoeuvring the inflated protest votes.

---

8. *The Hindustan Times* (New Delhi), 8 September, 2005.

5. Ideological flexibility among the rank and file of the party cadre helps members to defect and change party loyalty freely and frequently.

6. The Election Commission has been successful in checking the role of muscle power in the elections. Owing to its active and effective role, leaders like Laloo Prasad Yadav in Bihar and Mulayam Singh Yadav in Uttar Pradesh had to be out of power. But the same thing can not be said about its check on the role of money power. The law of ceiling on poll expenses is very much there, but its sincere implementation is yet to take place. In *G.Y. Kanakkarao Case* (1991) the Supreme Court observed: "The prescription on the ceiling of expenditure is a mere eyewash. This lacuna in the law is, however, for the Parliament to fill lest the impression is reinforced that its retention is deliberate for the convenience of everyone. If this is not feasible, it may be advisable to omit the provision to prevent the resort to indirect methods for its circumvention and submission of law. This provision has ceased to be even a fig leaf to hide the reality."

18

Good Governance and its Problems

Good governance has now become the topic of the day. Democracy is the best form of government of course, but good governance has now come to be its integral feature. Social and political thinkers have, in their own ways, sketched the models of good governance, without bothering for any particular form of government in which it alone would be possible. In recent times, the concept of development has engaged the attention of social scientists who have linked it with the element of sustainability. Likewise, the administrative thinkers have come forward with their models of good governance despite the fact that to tread such a path is to embark on an endless journey. As Prof. T.N. Chaturvedi says: "The search for good governance seemingly is an endless one. Ensuring goodness in governance and raising its levels—intensity-wise and coverage-wise—has been aspiration of the people and a persistent demand of the articulate section of any society."[1]

Meaning of Good Governance and Case of India

Mere governance is not enough, it should be good as well. The old saying has a sense that it is nice to be important, but it is more important to be nice. So this concept implies that the governance of a country should be neither malfunctional, nor dysfunctional, nor even functional for its own sake, it should be well-functional. Good governance is not simply something that governments achieve or do by themselves. It very much depends upon the cooperation and involvement of a large number of citizens and their organisations. These requirements are considered not only essential for good governance but are also important for sustainable human development. The essential elements of good

1. T.N. Chaturvedi: *Towards Good Governance*, p. vii.

governance are contained in the reports of the World Bank released in 1991, 1992 and 1994 and they touch many significants points ranging from accountability of the rulers and the bureaucrats to that of citizen-government interface.

According to the Reports of the World Bank, these indices of good governance have been identified for both the developed and the developing countries:

1. Political accountability including acceptability of the political system by the people and regular elections to legitimise the exercise of political power.
2. Freedom of association and participation by various religious, social, economic, cultural and professional groups in the process of governance.
3. An established legal framework based on the rule of law, independence of judiciary to protect human rights, secure social justice and guard against exploitation and abuse of power.
4. Bureaucratic accountability ensuring a system to monitor and control the performance of government offices and officials in relation to quality of services, inefficiency and abuse of discretionary power. The related determinants include openness and transparency in administration.
5. Freedom of information and expression needed to the formulation of public policies, decision-making, monitoring and evaluation of government performance. It also includes independent analysis of information by the professional bodies, including the Universities and others needed for a civil society.
6. A sound administrative system leading to efficiency and effectiveness. This, in turn, means the value of money and cost effectiveness. The effectiveness includes the degree of global achievement as per the stated objectives and also the administrative system which is able to take secular and rational decisions and the system which is self-propelling to take corrective measures.
7. Cooperation between the government and civil society organisations.

In short, the concept of good governance implies a system of administration which is good in every possible respect. It "derives its relevance in the context of misgovernance which involves non-feasance, over-feasance, and malfeasance."[2]

The ideal of having good governance in our country may be traced in the text of the Preamble as well as in Art. 38 of the Constitution which enjoins upon the state to create a social order in which justice-social, economic and political-shall inform all institutions of national life. However, its comprehensive expression may be seen in the text of a long resolution adopted by the Lok Sabha on 1 September, 1997 on the occasion of Golden Jubilee of Independence captioned 'Agenda for India'. It *inter alia* states that "continuous and proactive efforts be launched for ensuring greater transparency, probity and accountability in public life so that the freedom, authority and dignity of Parliament and other legislative bodies are ensured and enhanced; that, more especially, all political parties shall undertake such steps as will attain the objective of ridding our polity of criminalisation or its influence... That, finally, the essence of participatory democracy be seen in the inculcation of our national spirit of self-reliance in which our citizens are equal partners in all spheres of our national endeavour, and not simply the beneficiaries of governmental initiatives."

Good governance is an ideal which can be realised only in a truly representative democracy in view of the fact that it ensures establishment of responsible government and prevalence of the rule of law. Our Constitution establishes such a system. Not only that, laws made by the state from time to time have supplemented what is given in the bare provisions of the Constitution. Reference may be made to the Representation of the People Act of 1950, Representation of the People Act of 1951, Protection of Civil Rights Act of 1955, Prevention of Corruption Act of 1947 and 1988, Harijan Act of 1990, Right to Information Act of 2005 etc. Besides, a number of statutory commissions have been set up for the purpose of protecting the rights of the minorities, women, Scheduled Castes, Scheduled Tribes, human rights etc. The aim of all such measures is to ensure a clean and transparent administration with a human face in the country.

But much remains to be done in this important regard. We may throw focus on some of the problems which stand in the way. Apart

2. Ashok Mukhopadhyaya: "Re-inventing Government for Good Governance", *ibid*., p. 30..

from the traditional evils of casteism, communalism and regionalism, which are rooted in a tradition-bound society, we find the growing trend of corruption and maladministration at all levels of government in the country. The nexus between the politicians, bureaucrats and criminals of the country has become the biggest problem in this regard, Statutory measures have fallen short in dealing with such menaces and the steps taken by Supreme Court, High Courts and the Election Commission have not been able to hit the malady at its root. The democratic system has, therefore, come to face the crisis of governability. The salient feature of citizen-government interface is woefully lacking that smacks of the absence of an agile society in the country. Taking it into his view, Prime Minister Manmohan Singh desired in his first address to the nation on 24th June that "our democracy needs more professionals to become more engaged and active in politics."[3]

Political Corruption

Corruption and criminalisation are the ways of life and so they are as old as human civilisation. It is a different matter that their nexus has now become a topic of the day. Law is made to check corruption and to punish the criminals. So both the corrupt public functionaries and the criminals find their in the breach of law, or in its distortion in a way that their innocence and involvement become inter-connected, the former overshadowing the latter. Crime becomes a profitable business and its arch-businessmen enter into the domain of politics so as to immunise themselvs from the clutches of law. The law-breakers become the law-makers; they occupy the posts of the ministers and the Chief Ministers and thereby manage to demolish the sanctity of this celebrated maxim given by Sir Edward Coke of England: "Be you ever so high, but the law is above you." The paradox of a democratic system is that while in name it is operated by the will of the people that is identifiable with the will of God, in practice it is a plaything of the corrupt and crafty politicians of the country who convert the State into their 'fief' and surprisingly manage to deify their devildom publicly. The vast field of politics thus becomes a fertile ground for corruption as well as criminalisation and the two depict the commercialisation of a market society. As

3. *The Times of India* (New Delhi), 25th June, 2004.

a learned figure observes: "From politics of corruption, the path to criminalisation of politics is only a stone's throw away. What we refer to as criminalisation of politics or politicisation of crime is really the commercialisation of both crime and politics."[4]

Meaning and Dimensions : As pointed out above, corruption is as old as man's social life. Kautilya in his *Arthasastra* regards it as an irremediable problem of public administration. History is full of accounts to prove that the honest rulers awarded exemplary punishments to their corrupt servants. Civilised societies developed norms to humiliate or segregate corrupt officials. In modern times, statutory mechanism has been designed to deal with this problem. But human ingenuity makes all such mechanisms inadequate as a result of which arrangements after arrangements have been devised to deal with this chronic evil. However, as this evil has its place in the mind of man, or in the words of Plato in the human soul, its only remedy is internal purification which is very rare or whose possibility is limited to a saint or a philosopher.

The ramifications of corruption are so wide that they cover different facets and so only a person can immunise himself from it in case he neither speaks ill, nor sees ill, nor hears ill like the three monkeys of Mahatma Gandhi. Like diabetes it eats into the vitals of the state and may become the cause of the destruction of a big empire. Keeping it in his view, Dr. S. Radhakrishnan in his address on the midnight of 14–15 August, 1947 said. "Unless we destroy corruption in high places, root out every trace of nepotism, love of power, profiteering and blackmarketing which have spoiled the good name of our country in recent times, we will not be able to raise the standards of efficiency in administration as well as in production and distribution of necessary goods of life."[5]

Corruption is a household word, but it cannot be defined in precise terms. It is concerned not merely with the taking of a graft or doing favour in a matter of employment. It also covers every instance of man's material and moral degeneration. The undressing of Draupadi

4. T.N. Chaturvedi: "Corruption in India: An Overview" in S.C. Kashyap (ed.): *Eradication of Corruption and Restoration of Values* (New Delhi: Sterling Publishers, 2001), p. 44.

5. Cited in Kashyap, *op. cit.*, p. 3.

in the court of the Kauravas was an act of corruption. The way Warren Hastings recognised the widowed Begum of Bengal as the inheritor of her husband's property was a clear case of corruption, though it was sought to be white-washed with the execution of an innocent man named Nand Kumar. The Keeler affair was another example of corruption that saw the fall of British Prime Minister Macmillan in 1963. The act of bugging done by the supporters of Nixon in the American Presidential election of 1972 was an act of corruption that became known by the name of Watergate scandal. Such examples may be multiplied, but the crux of the matter remains that corruption is an omnibus term that covers physical, mental, moral and spiritual aspects of a man's personality. However, in general terms, corruption may be defined as "a deliberate and intentional exploitation of one's position, status, or resources, directly or indirectly, for personal aggrandisement whether it be in terms of material gain or enhancement of power, prestige or influence beyond what is legitimate or sanctioned by commonly accepted norms to the detriment of the interest of other persons of community as a whole."[6]

To attempt to define corruption in precise terms is to open a Pandora's box. Subjectivity stands in the way as a result of which the author knowingly or unknowingly takes some and ignores some other implications or dimensions of corruption. A practical viewpoint was taken at the 19th Conference of European Ministers of Justice held in Malta in 1994, where it was agreed upon: "Bribery and other behaviour in relation to persons entrusted with responsibilities in public or private sector which violates their duties that follow from their status as a public official, private employee, independent agent or other relationship of that kind and is aimed at obtaining undue advantages of any kind for themselves or others." T.N. Chaturvedi tries to offer a comprehensive definition of this term in these words: "Apart from outright graft or bribery (willing, induced, or extorted), the use,

6. A. Avasthi and S.R. Maheshwari: *Public Administration*, 1971 ed., p. 342. "It is a fundamental assumption of the modern state that public offices (and associated powers) should not be used for private gain by the incumbents of such offices what would normally be called corruption." A. Leftwich: "Theorising the State" in Peter Burnell and Vicky Randall (eds): *Politics in the Developing World* (Oxford: Oxford Univ. Press, 2003), p. 142.

abuse and non-use of power, legal or political, for personal or private gain to one-self or others not rightfully entitled to it, does cover the various hues and nuances of corruption. Corruption, or the obverse of it, probity, even if not apparent to the naked eye, makes its presence felt like power in the electric bulb. That is why, it is said that even discretion, vested legally in a decision-making authority, is to be exercised with discretion. Discretion cannot be exercised indiscreetly or dicriminatingly. In a way, the abuse of power of authority, accountability and the implicit action in the case of lapse implied therein, constitute basic elements of any discussion, debate or discourse on corruption."[7]

The Prevention of Corruption Act, 1947 defines corruption as 'an act of criminal misconduct'. The Santhanam Committee Report (1964) says that "any action or failure to take action in the performance of duty by a Government servant for some advantage is corruption." Sec. 161 of the Indian Penal Code says: "Whoever, being or expected to be a public servant, accepts or obtains, or agrees to accept, or attempts to obtain from any person for himself or any other person, any gratification whatever, other than legal remuneration, as a motion or reward for doing or forbearing to do any official act, or for showing or forbearing to show, in the exercise of his official functions, favour or disfavour to any person, or for rendering or attempting to render any service or disservice to any person, with the Central or any State government or Parliament or the Legislature of any State, or with any local authority, Corporation or Government Company referred to in Sec. 21 or with any public servant, as such, shall be punished with imprisonment of either description for a term which may extend to three years, or with fine, or with both."[8]

---

7. Chaturvedi, *op. cit.*, p. 41.

8. In this definition, the term 'public servant' is very important which according to Sec. 21 covers any commissioned officer in the defence services, a judge or a juryman or an assessor or an arbitrator empowered to perform judicial functions of any kind, any authority who may keep a person under confinement, any employee empowered to assess, collect and spend the amount of taxes, any authority entrusted with the duty of preparing electoral rolls and conducting elections, and any person serving in the government or some

(contd.)

Efforts for Prevention: During the World War II, people minted money by many dubious means. The Government of India took a serious view of it and in 1946 it set up an anti-corruption police organisation known as the Delhi Special Police Establishment (DSPE) which was made a part of the Central Bureau of Investigation (CBI) set up in 1963. In 1947 came the Prevention of Corruption Act. Then, in 1952 came the Feroze Gandhi Act or Commission of Inquiry Act. Departmental Committees were set up and rules were framed as All-India Services Conduct Rules, 1954, Central Civil Services Conduct Rules, 1954, Railway Services Conduct Rules, 1956 etc. The Gorwala Report (1951) admitted, "Yet even after considering all these circumstances, a sub-structure of truth still remains out of the many allegations of lack of integrity throughout the country."[9]

The issue of political corruption became a matter of wide discussion. In July, 1959 C.D. Deshmukh, Finance Minister in the Nehru Cabinet, offered to submit evidence regarding certain lapses of the high ups if a standing judicial tribunal was set up for inquiring them. Nehru did not appreciate it. But the matter was taken up in the meeting of the Congress Working Committee on 14 June, 1960. The Congress President N. Sanjeeva Reddy announced that the CWC had authorised him "to set up a permanent machinery to examine the merits of complaints of corruption against ministers and other responsible Congressmen." By another resolution, the CWC authorised the Congress President "to require the Congress Ministers of Central and State governments and Congress MPs and MLAs and MLCs to submit to him annual statements of their assets, income and expenditures." On 28 June, 1960 he announced the formation of a panel of five eminent jurists.

---

corporation on the payment of fees or commission". It is for this reason that the members of Parliament and State legislatures are not taken as 'public servants' under the IPC. But the Supreme Court has ruled that they are public servants and their case is covered by the Prevention of Corruption Act. 1947. *K.Karunanidhi* v. *Union of India*, 1979, 3 SCR 254. The Supreme Court has reiterated this view in another case by ruling that the MPs and the MLAs fall within the category of public servants vide Sec. 2 (c) of the Prevention of Corruption Act, 1988, *Narsimha Rao* v. *Union of India*, 1993, 4 Sec 626.

9. A.D. Gorwala: *Report on Public Administration*, 1951, p. 64.

A Committee on Prevention of Corruption was set up by the Government of India in 1962 under the chairmanship of K. Santhanam. It submitted its report on 31 March, 1964 wherein it held that while it was true that the securing of some kind of pecuniary or other material advantage directly or indirectly for oneself or family, or relatives or friends, constituted the most common form of corruption, other forms of the evil were coming into existence in the ever-increasing complexities of modern society. It endorsed: "There is a widespread impression that failure of integrity is not uncommon among ministers and that some ministers who have held office during the last 16 years have enriched themselves illegitimately, obtained good jobs for their sons and relations through nepotism, and have reaped other advantages inconsistent with any notion of purity in public life."

The Committee gave some significant suggestions 'in the interest of the future of public life.' These are:

1. A code of conduct for ministers, including public servants, relating to acquisition of property, acceptance of gifts, and disclosure of assets and liabilities should be drawn up.
2. Specific allegations of corruption on the part of a minister at the Centre or in a State should be promptly investigated by an agency whose findings must command respect.
3. The integrity of the members of Parliament and State legislatures will be a great factor in creating a favourable social climate against corruption.
4. It has to be frankly recognised that political parties cannot be run and elections cannot be fought without large funds. But these funds should come openly and it should be regulated by some rules.
5. Art. 311 of the Constitution should be amended so as to simplify the procedure for handling corruption cases relating to public servants.
6. Sec. 21 of the IPC should be amended in a way that a public servant is one who is in the service or pay of any Government — Central, State or Local — or of any Government Company.
7. An independent body (Central Vigilance Commission) should be set up to investigate the cases of corruption involving public servants of the Government of India.

The recommendations of the Santhanam Committee could not be appreciated by the politicians running the Government for reasons known to all. The CVC was set up in 1965 of course, but it could not meet the expectations of the authors of the Report in view of its limitations some of which have been removed now due to the intervention of the Supreme Court. So, in 1998 the CVC was been made a multi-member body and given a statutory status.

Efforts for the prevention of corruption went on. The Administrative Reforms Commission set up by the Government of India under the chairmanship of Morarji Desai in its report (1966) suggested the creation of the office of the Ombudsman (Lok Pal) at the Centre and of the Lok Ayuktas in the States to deal with the evil of corruption. It is a pity that the Lok Pal Bill was moved in the Parliament again and again, but it could not be passed. It lapsed with the dissolution of the Lok Sabha. Happily, some State governments have set up their Lok Ayuktas, but they have hardly been able to achieve the desired purpose on account of the unhelpful, rather dilatory and obstructive, role of the ministries concerned.

It is also a deplorable fact that senior bureaucrats develop nexus with the politicians who occupy ministerial posts and thereby subvert the administrative process. "A senior official of the Government of India is reported to have remarked that 'we are well trained but some of us like to become pets.' It is the 'pet' relationship that is suspect."[10]

The fact stands out that there is no political will to check the demon of corruption. Prime Minister Nehru took recourse to procedural requirements and thereby saved Krishna Menon whose involvement in the 'jeep scandal' was so obvious. Indira Gandhi saved her minister L.N. Mishra whose role in the 'rags scandal' was a patent reality. Rajiv Gandhi played a role that the CBI made him the central figure of the 'Bofors scandal'. Narsimha Rao crossed all records by inviting the verdict of conviction by a subordinate court. The 'Tehelka episode' exposed the misdoings of the President of the BJP (Bangaru Laxman) and of Vice-President of the Samata Party (Jaya Jaitley) in 2000 and yet nothing occurred except for the exit of Defence Minister (George Fernandes) for a couple of months.

10. B.P.R. Vithal: "Envolving Trends in the Bureaucracy" in Partha Chatterjee (ed.): *State and Politics in India*, (New Delhi: Oxford University Press, 1988), p. 219.

Vice-President Bhairon Singh Shekhawat minced no words when he said in a public interview: "On the issue of corruption, for instance, we have got to ask ourselves why is it that people in high places, whether in politics, or bureaucracy or police, routinely get away despite having cases registered against them? In the last 55 years hardly any influential people have been sentenced for corruption. I would like Parliament to apply its mind to it so that the guilty are not allowed to get away lightly."[11]

Law-Makers and Corruption : To call the administrators as a corrupt lot is not to make any revelation. A public functionary is like a fish which lives in water and drinks it whenever it likes. But the legislators should not be painted with the same brush. It is taken for grant that they represent the will of their electors. The chosen deputies occupy the great offices of the head of the state, head of the government and head of the departments. Their position is so sacrosanct that they enjoy 'privileges' and they may punish anybody if he commits their breach or contempt of the house. If a member of the house commits an act amounting to the breach of privilege or contempt of the House, then the House alone may award him suitable punishment. This celebrated position stands as a powerful shield in the hands of the people's deputies who occupy the seats of the law-makers and the ministers and rule with this impression in their mind that they are above the law of the land. This is really a very unfortunate situation which calls for a proper rectification, sooner the better.

The British Parliament is regarded as the 'mother of Parliaments'. Hence, our Constitution-makers initiated and imitated it. They put into Art. 105 (3) that the privileges of the members would be defined by a law of Parliament and, until so defined, they would enjoy the same privileges as those available to the members of the House of Commons of the United Kingdom. This reference to the British practice created many problems and so it was deleted by the forty-fourth amendment of 1978. The new assumption all over the world is that the legislators should not be treated as persons above law. Hence, Foreign Corrupt Practices Act came into effect in 1977 in USA. Now the American companies which break the law are liable to fine upto 2 million dollars per violation and individuals

11. *The Times of India*, New Delhi, 7 April, 2003, p. 12.

holding any portion upto 1 million dollars and also imprisonment upto five years. This gift of the Jimmy Carter Administration has done something to check foreign bribery and reform the behaviour of the men-in-authority roles.

Such problems arose in Britain as well. Keeping the precedents of other countries in his view, Justice Buckley in *Exparte Greemay Case* (1992) held that an MP against whom there is a *prima facie* case of corruption should be immune from prosecution in a court of law is, to my mind, an unacceptable proposition at the present time."[12] The British Attorney-General in a submission to the privileges committee of the House of Commons expressed the view that an MP "could be prosecuted under the present law only if the complete offence could be established without reference to any debates or proceedings in Parliament and the House of Commons in a particular case would expressly waive privilege."

Earlier, both the Solomon Commission and the Nolan Committee had taken the view that the Parliament should consider whether its members should be brought within the criminal law of corruption. The Nolan inquiry was a result of the 'cash for questions' scandal which mentioned that some MPs were in the pay of the businessmen who could collect vital information from the Parliament through these paid legislators.[13] The Nolan Report focussed on internal and administrative enforcement of standards and then a law was made to implement its recommendations.[14]

An enumeration of scandals in our country since independence presents a very sad spectacle. The names of some Prime Ministers and their Ministers at the Centre and so of some Chief Ministers and their Ministers in the States along with the names of MPs, MLAs and MLCs figure therein. The woefully surprising aspect is that while the administrative and legal machinery remains at work and some of the big sharks are caught and convicted, nothing occurs

---

12. See Erskine May's *Treatise on the Law, Privileges, Proceedings and Usages of Parliament*, 22nd ed., pp. 114–15.

13. The Nolan Committee has recommended seven principles which apply to all aspects of public life. These are Selflessness, Integrity, Objectivity, Accountability, Openness, Honesty, and Leadership.

14. P.P. Rao: "Corruption in High Places" in S.C. Kashyap, *op. cit.*, p. 78.

to debar them from the political arena. On the basis of his personal experiences, Ved Marwah, a retired Police Commissioner, said: "Many of the tainted politicians have been re-elected. By and large, the voter has ignored the criminal charges against them. Facing serious charges of corruption, the more notorious among them have done rather well at the hustings. They are now strutting about on the national scene as king-makers.... There is something radically wrong with a system that allows law-breakers to become law-makers in such large numbers.... Corruption will continue to be one of the most important issues standing in the way of development."[15]

Major Cases and Inquiry Commissions

Commissions	Year	Purpose
1. Chagla Commission	1958	Investment of Rs. 3 crores in the Mundhra shares and involvement of Union Finance Minister T.T. Krishnamachari in a deal with the Chairman of Life Insurance Corporation of India.
2. Das Commission	1963	Allegations of corruption against Chief Minister Sardar Pratap Singh Kairon of Punjab.
3. Ayyangar Commission	1965	Allegations of abuse of office and acquisition of wealth against Chief Minister Bakshi Ghulam Muhammed of Jammu-Kashmir .
4. Aiyer Commission	1967	Allegations of corruption against Chief Minister of Bihar K.B. Sahay and five of his ministers.
5. Mudholkar Commission	1968	Allegations of corruption against Chief Minister Mahamaya Prasad Sinha and his 13 ministers of Bihar .
6. Mudholkar Commission	1968	Allegations of corruption against Chief Minister Dr. H.K. Mahtab of Orissa .

15. *Ibid., p.79.*

7. Kapoor Commission	1968	Allegations of corruption against Chief Minister Dayanand Bandodkar of Goa .
8. Sarkaria Commission	1976	Allegations of misuse of official position and taking of bribe against M. Karunanidhi, former Chief Minister of Tamilnadu.
9. Grover Commission	1977	Allegations of corruption against Dev Raj Urs Chief Minister of Karnataka and some of his ministers.
10. Vimada Lal Commission	1977	Allegations of corruption against Vengala Rao Chief Minister of Andhra Pradesh and some of his ministers.
11. Reddy Commission	1977	Allegations against Kanti Desai (son of Prime Minister Morarji Desai) for wielding extra-constitutional authority and interference in the affairs of the Union Government.
12. Vaidyalingam Commission	1979	Allegations relating to a contract entered or signed by the Government of India during Bansi Lal's tenure as Defence Minister.

Major Scams

Name	Year	Description
1. Jeep Scandal	1949	A scam of Rs. 216 crore in the purchase of jeeps for Indian military from a British firm in which India's High Commissioner to the UK (V.K.K. Menon) was involved.
2. Mudgal Affair	1951	M.C. Mudgal, a member of the Provisional Parliament was charged with agreeing to canvas support and make propaganda on behalf of the

		Bombay Bullion Association on a payment of Rs. 20,000. The Krishnamachari Committee Report described his role as a liasion officer of a Bombay firm as derogatory to the dignity of Parliament and so he resigned.
3. Serajuddin Affair	1956	K.D. Malaviya, Minister of Mines and Fuels in the Nehru Cabinet took a huge amount from a firm of Calcutta (Serajuddin and Co.) as donation for elections which was not duly accounted in the funds of the Congress party.
4. Nagarwala Episode	1971	R.S. Nagarwala fraudulently withdrew Rs. 60 lakh from the State Bank of India, Parliament Street Bronch, New Delhi by making a confidential telephonic call to its Manager to give this money to him out of the account of 'Mataji'. He was caught and after some time died in the Tibar jail of Delhi.
5. Tulmohan Ram Case	1971	Tulmohan Ram forged the signatures of 21 MPs and obtained import licenses from the Government of India.
6. Antulay Case	1982	A.R. Antulay, the Chief Minister of Maharashtra, charged fees for granting licensed cement and industrial alcohol and extorted crores of rupees in the name of Indira Pratisthan and resigned after an adverse court verdict.
7. Churhat Lotteries Case	1982–83	Allegations against Arjun Singh, Chief Minister of Madhya Pradesh, for collecting Rs. 5.4 crore through the Churhat Children's Welfare Society.

8. The Bofors Deal	1987	Payment of Rs. 65 crore as bribe for securing Rs. 1600 crore contract by the Swedish Company (Bofors) in which the Government of Rajiv Gandhi was alleged to have been involved.
9. Westland Helicopters Deal and Fodder Scandal	1991	The purchase of outdated Westland helicopter and fodder scandal alleged to be promoting the interest of a foreign company by waiving import duty in return for fodder making machines in which Speaker Balram Jakhar was alleged to be involved.
10. Securities Scandal	1992	A Joint Parliamentary probe into the multicrore scandal indicted Union Minister of State for Finance (Rameshwar Thakur) and an amount of Rs. 132 crore was diverted from the Oil India Development Board to Syndicate Bank for investment in the Stock Market in which Harshad Mehta a broker of Bombay played the big role.
11. Classic Computer Deal	1992	Chief Minister B.B. Bangarappa of Karnataka resigned after being accused of involvement in this deal.
12. Sugar Muddle	1994	A Rs. 650 crore scandal in which Union Minister Kalpnath Rai had to go after the Gian Prakash Committee Report described lack of timely imports as the main reason for the escalation of sugar price.
13. Telecom Scandal	1994–96	Union Communications Minister Sukh Ram was accused of having favoured Himachal Futuristic Communications Ltd. and thereby amassing huge wealth.

14. Fodder Scandal	1995–96	Fraudulent withdrawal of funds from Bihar Government treasuries belonging to the Animal Husbandry Department by former Chief Minister Jagan Nath Mishra and his successor Laloo Prasad Yadav.
15. The JMM Bribery Case	1996	Four MPs of the Jharkhand Mukti Morcha took huge bribe to vote against the no-confidence motion and thus save the Rao Government. According to CBI, it involves a scandal of Rs. 3.5 crore.
16. The Urea Scandal	1996	Advance payment of Rs. 133 crore to a little known Turkish firm for import of urea which was never delivered. It had the involvement of Prabhakar Rao (son of Narsimha Rao) and some high officials.
17. The Mumbai Port Trust Scandal	1996	The Chairman and Deputy Chairman of the Trust allegedly allotted prime commercial space to its counsel Kiran Chaudhuri (daughter-in-law of Bansi Lal) at a throw away price of Rs. 57 per sq. metre compared to the market rate of Rs. 1,000 per sq. metre.
18. Hawala Scandal	1995–96	A 65-crore scandal by the Hawala agents (S.K. Jain and J.K. Jain) showing involvement of politicians and bureaucrats in making illegal transactions and receipts of money through hawala.
19. The Jayalalitha Case	1996	Case under Prevention of Corruption Act, 1988 for depositing a demand draft for 300,000 dollars in her name and cases relating to Tansi land deal.

20. Housing Scandal	1996	Union Minister Sheila Kaul made allotment of government flats and bungalows in violation of the rules and regulations and for which the Supreme Court imposed a fine of Rs. 50 lakh on her.

Causes and Cure : Why does acts of corruption occur? Manifold are its reasons which range from poverty or poor economic condition of the people to lust for acquiring wealth by any hook or crook. Cumbersome administrative procedures and delays breed corruption. Causing unnecessary delay in the performance of a duty puts the persons concerned in a condition of inconvenience and so they prefer to get the things done on the payment of a hush money. Administrative power and growth of distortion vested in the officials provide opportunities and scope for harassment, malpractices and corruption. At the top people preach integrity more often than not they lack the virtue of example. The unwillingness to deal drastically with corrupt and inefficient public servants is also a factor. The continuous decline of moral standards in public life has its own place in this regard.

Corruption is world-wide and so is the case of fight against it. Transparency International is a Berlin-based non-profit private organisation which regularly publishes its 'Corruption Perception Index' which is called a 'pole of polls'. Its chairman (Dr. Peter Eigen) has given the exhortation: "Wake up, call for political leaders and the public at large to confront the abundant corruption that prevails in so many countries." As per its index Denmark tops the list of honest countries, but Nigeria has its first position in the category of the corrupt countries. India has the 8th rank on the most corrupt list of 50 countries. A global conference on the theme of corruption was held at Lima in Peru from 7 to 11 November, 1997 in which 93 countries participated. A declaration was adopted at the end which "recognised that corruption apart from augmenting the bank accounts of corrupt officials, erodes the moral fabric of every society and violates the social, and economic rights of the poor and the vulnerable. Fighting corruption is everyone's business, it is imperative that top leadership set the tone."[16]

16. O.P. Tandon: "Corruption in Administration and National Security" in Kashyap, *op. cit.*, p. 164.

A 2-day National Convention on Eradication of Corruption and Restoration of Values was held in New Delhi on 25–26 November, 1998 in whice leading luminaries of the country like Dr. Karan Singh, Dr. Subhash C. Kashyap, Justice J.S. Verma, T.N. Chaturvedi, Prof. R.B. Jain and a host of eminent figures participated. As a result of deliberations, the Convention had a general consensus on these points:[17]

1. The Government and the administration should become more citizen-friendly and responsive to the needs of the common man.
2. As the illiterates and the uneducated are more prone to be victims of corruption, highest priority should be given to education.
3. The provisions of the Constitution should be suitably amended so as not to give any incentive or scope to corruption.
4. A candidate seeking any election from Parliament to a Panchayat must disclose his assets and liabilities at the time of filing his nomination paper and it should be made public as per the terms of a law.
5. If the court takes cognisence of a crime, the accused person should not be allowed to fight any election.
6. There is need for regulating political funding and audit of party and campaign funds.
7. Corruption can be controlled when it ceases to pay and then social sanctions against it become strong and prompt.
8. Prompt investigation and deterrent punishment in cases of corruption would go a long way towards controlling the situation.
9. The Official Secrets Act of 1993 should be repealed or drastically transformed to ensure maximum transparency in public dealings by the administration and a free flow of information to the people.
10. The Lok Pal Bill pending in the Parliament should be expeditiously passed.

---

17. *Ibid.*, pp. 235–36.

11. Vigilance Commission and Lok Ayukta institution should be established at all State levels.
12. At all offices with public dealings, the services available and the duties and responsibilities of the officers and the legal and legitimate rights of the citizens must be prominently displayed.
13. The Government should be drastically reduced and it should withdraw itself from non-essential areas.
14. Monopoly of power at any level is dangerous. It should be eradicated.

The list is praiseworthy but not exhaustive. Any conscientious person may add some more points to it. But the basic question is whether the purpose as a whole can be achieved by recourse to rule of law. Locke is right in saying that where law ends, tyranny begins. Aristotle's dictum is more meaningful that law is reason, not passion. It implies that a brute law is no law and so, in the words of Mahatma Gandhi, 'disaffection is a virtue under a satanic rule'. Law and ethics are twins in regulating the behaviour of man. Where one ends, the other begins. So it is well observed, "But the mutuality of the two is to be appreciated and the move towards the generation and promotion of values and ethics in different ways has to be crystallised and institutionalised to ensure a value-based and corruption-free society, economy and polity."[18]

Political Criminalisation

Corruption is a curse, it may become a cause of catastrophe when mixed with criminalisation. That is, the former is like pthysis, the latter is like cancer. Both are mortal enemies of the body politik. Administration is established to book the criminals and the courts enforce the laws made by the legislature. But the entire apparatus of state is vitiated when the law-breakers enter the legislative chambers, occupy ministerial berths, and then subvert the judicial process. The cases pending in the courts are withdrawn, the prosecution is made weak, the witnesses are terrified or purchased, the evidence is destroyed, the judges are influenced, and every possible effort is made to immunise the social and economic offenders from the clutches of law and justice. If a lower court gives an adverse verdict, it is taken to the higher courts in appeal and so the matter remains in abeyance.

18. T.N. Chaturvedi, *op. cit.*, p. 48.

At the time of elections, events of violence occur like intimidiation of the voters, capturing of booths, casting of fake ballots etc. so as to ensure the victory of the mafia dons. The services of anti-social and anti-national elements are requisitioned who are paid in good coins after such persons occupy high places in the government. The criminalisation of politics "has played havoc with the administration of criminal justice and the situation today is that it has become most difficult, if not well-nigh impossible, to secure conviction of major culprits guilty of offences like murder, grievous hurt, intimidation and rape because of the political interference with the police investigation of the crime. In many States, the former history-sheeters against whom criminal cases are still pending in the courts have turned law-makers and ministers after winning elections, which has not only seriously jeopardised the legal process, but have also posed far-reaching ethical dilemmas and concerns."[19]

The tragedy of blasts in Bombay in January, 1993 engaged the attention of the Government of India and so a committee was set up under N.N. Vohra, the then Union Home Secretary. Known as the Vohra Committee, it submitted its report having startling revelations. Since Secretary, Ministry of Revenue of the Government of India, Director of the Information Bureau, and Director of the CBI were associated with it, it could have a tough investigation and came to these conclusions:

1. In certain States like Bihar, Haryana and U.P. these gangs enjoy the patronage of the local level politicians, cutting across party lines and the protection of Government functionaries. Some political leaders become the leaders of these gangs/armed senas and over the years get themselves elected to local bodies,

---

19. R.B. Jain: "The Art of Political Corruption" in S.C. Kashyap, (ed.): *Eradication of Corruption and Restoration of Values,* pp. 108–09. There is no effective legislative provision to prevent the criminals from contesting elections. So Chief Election Commissioner T.S. Krishnamurthy suggested: "Candidates against whom charge sheets have been framed by competent courts for certain serious offences should be disqualified from contesting elections. Such recommendations have been made more than once to the Government of India. It is very unfortunate that there is no political consensus to bring about a quick legislation in this regard. So long as law is not amended, the problem will continue to exist." *The Times of India* (New Delhi) 9 March, 2005.

State Assemblies and the national Parliament. Resultantly, such elements have acquired considerable political clout, seriously jeopardising the smooth functioning of the administration and the safety of life and property of the common man, causing a sense of despair and alienation among the people.

2. The big smuggling syndicates, having international linkages, have spread into and infected the various economic and financial activities, including *havala* transactions, circulation of black money and operation of a vicious parallel economy causing serious damage to the economic fibre of the country. These syndicates have acquired substantial financial and muscle power and social respectability and have successfully corrupted the Government machinery at all levels and yield enough influence to make the task of investigating and prosecuting agencies extremely difficult: even the members of the judicial system have not escaped the embrace of the mafia.

3. Certain elements of the mafia have shifted to narcotics, drugs and weapon smuggling and established narco-terrorism networks, especially in the State of Jammu-Kashmir, Punjab, Gujarat and Maharashtra. The cost of contesting elections has thrown the politicians into the lap of these elements and led to a grave compromise by officials of the preventive/detective systems. The virus has spread to almost all the centres in the country: the coastal and the border States have been particularly affected.

4. The Bombay blast case and the communal riots in Surat and Ahmedabad have demonstrated how the Indian underworld has been exploited by the Pak ISI and the latter's network in UAE to cause sabotage, subversion and communal tension in various parts of the country. The investigations into the Bombay blast cases have revealed extensive linkages of the underworld in the various governmental agencies, political circles, business sector and the film world.

The Vohra Committee Report (1993) is an eye-opener document and its seriousness has been realised by a very large number of conscientious citizens as well as by the learned judges of the High Courts and the Supreme Court. Thus, higher judiciary has come to our rescue. In the *Narsimha Rao Case* (1998), the Supreme Court ruled that the MPs and the MLAs were 'public servants' under Sec. 2(c) of the Prevention of Corruption Act. 1988, though not under Sec. 21 of the Indian Penal Code. In its judgment, the Court has filled up a caveat by ruling that although there is no written provision specifying as to whose prior permission is required for prosecuting an M.P., it may be done with the permission of the presiding officer of the House. Then, in the *Vineet Narain Case* (1998), the Court relied on the seven principles of public life set out in the Lord Nolan Committee Report of 1994.

The Supreme Court created history by delivering its verdict in the *Association for Democratic Reforms Case* on 2 May, 2002 in which it directed the Election Commission of India to call for following information on an affidavit from every person filing nomination paper for election to the Parliament or State legislatures:

1. Whether the candidate is convicted/acquitted/discharged of any criminal offence in the past–if any, whether he is punished with imprisonment or fine.
2. Prior to six months of filing of nomination, whether the candidate is accused in any pending case, of any offence punishable with imprisonment for two years or more, and in which charge is framed or cognizance is taken by the court of law. If so, the details thereof.
3. The assets (immovable, movable, bank balance etc.) of the candidates and his/her spouse and that of the dependants.
4. Liabilities, if any, particularly whether there are any overdues of any public financial institution or government dues.
5. The educational qualifications of the candidate.

The Election Commission was already aware of the ground reality and the verdict of the Supreme Court strengthened its hands. Chief Election Commissioner M.S. Gill had publicly said in 2000 that there were about 40 MPs and 200 MLAs in the States having criminal record. The Commission took a broad view of the language of Art. 324 of the Constitution and construed that the 'superintendence, direction and control' of the elections meant holding free and fair elections in the country. Now the Supreme Court gave to the Election Commission what was direly needed and so it issued a detailed proforma that was to be filled up by a candidate on an affidavit seeking election. Naturally, it came as abolt from the blue for the politicians. The leaders of all political parties had a meeting with the Union Law Minister and came to this unanimous decision that the will of Parliament could not be overshadowed by a directive of the Supreme Court given to the Election Commission.

So the NDA Government issued an ordinance which was converted into a statutory provision after some time. It dispensed with the requirement of filling up the proforma on an affidavit. It introduced an amendment in Sec.33 of the Representation of the People Act, 1951 which provided that a person after being a member of the Parliament or State legislature would supply information to the presiding officer of the House (not on an affidavit) about his antecedents and assets as well as liabilities. By all means, it was a shameless move of the politicians of the country and, as expected, this amendment was struck down by the Supreme Court in March, 2003. Hence, the Election Commission has revived the proforma. It demostrates the victory of good sense over the evil designs of the politicians who desire neither purity nor transparency in the democratic system but invariably strive to fish in dirty water.[20]

As per the new guideliness issued by the Election Commission, each candidate seeking election to the Parliament or State legislatures would have to furnish full information in his nomination paper on an affidavit signed before a first class magistrate, or a public notary, or a commissioner of oath appointed by the High Court of the State. In this document he would supply complete information about the criminal cases in which he is involved including cases in which cognisance has been taken by the Court, the punishment that has been awarded to him by any Court, his assets and liabilities and educational qualifications. The copies of such an affidavit would be made available to any rival candidate as well as to the representatives of the print and electronic media. If any rival candidate furnishes information to the contrary by means of a duly sworn affidavit, then this document would also be made available to others. The returning officer would have the power to reject a nomination paper in case a candidate suppresses facts or does not supply full information as required. It is hoped that the norms laid down by the Election Commission in pursuance of the directive of the Supreme Court shall serve the desired purpose to a considerable extent.

---

20. *The Times of India*, New Delhi, 1 April, 2003.

The crucial issue before us is as to how the malady of political criminalisation be effectively checked. Some suggestions may be given, though some of them may be criticised for being impracticable in the present conditions or undemocratic by the persons involved in this nasty exercise.

1. The political parties should allow admission to persons with a clean record of public service. Election tickets should be given to the persons known for their ability and integrity of character. Disciplinary action should be taken against those found delinquent on this count. What is needed is that political parties should have a lofty vision. In his message given on the eve of the Republic Day in 2004, President Abdul Kalam counselled: "Every political party must clearly state its vision, action plan and approaches for developing India—Vision 2020—and how fast they can realise these missions in quality and quantity."[21]
2. The floors of the legislative chambers should be closed for social and economic offenders. Strict statutory arrangements should be made. A person should not be permitted to contest elections, and a legislator should not be permited to enter the chamber after charges have been framed against him by a sessions court in a criminal case. The judicial process should be streamlined so that such cases are disposed of within a couple of months. A person found guilty in such a case should not be allowed to contest elections or secure a political appointment for 25 years.
3. The funds and assets of all political parties should be subject to audit and public scrutiny. Money plays the most important part in fighting and winning elections. Hence, the resources of political parties should be thoroughly scrutinised and a party found guilty on this count should be derecognised by the Election Commission.
4. The antecedents of the persons contesting elections should be given to the press and also telecast so that the people may be aware of the black deeds of their political carrer. If a legislator indulges in horse-trading or in a scam like cash for query or human trafficking, he should be disqualified from the

21. *The Times of India* (New Delhi), 26 January, 2004.

membership of the House and salary and allowances received by him since the date of disqualification should be recovered from him. While presenting awards to the outstanding parliamentarians for the years 1999, 2000, 2001 and 2002 on 21 March 2005, President Abdul Kalam said: "The arithmetical computations of incremental numbers and the alleged tradeability of certain legislative seats won through means allegedly dubious and undemocratic, have many a time created doubts in our democratic system in the public eye. When politics degrades itself to political adventurism, the nation would be on the calamitous road to inevitable disaster and ruination. Let us not risk it."[22]

5. All legal loopholes should be carefully plugged so that the crafty politicians may not be able to twist the arms of law by hook or by crook. The laws relating to election and prevention of corruption should be revised so as to meet every possible deficiency. In a case the Supreme Court has observed: "As the law stands today, anybody, including a smuggler, criminal or any other anti-social element may spend any amount over the election of any candidate in whom such a person is interested, for which no account is to be maintained, or to be furnished and any such expenditure shall not be deemed to have been expenditure in connection with the election under Sec. 77(1) so as to amount to corruption within the meaning of Sec. 123 (6). If the call for purity of election is not be reduced to a lip service or a slogan, then the person investing funds in furtherance of the prospects of the election of the candidate, must be identified and located. But this has to be taken care of by the Parliament."[23]

Needless to say that the growing trend of political criminalisation is posing a very serious threat to the operation of our democratic system and it must be effectively checked, sooner the better.

Crisis of Governability

The case of good governance in India is very much vitiated by the crisis of governability. Gunnar Myrdal puts India in the category

---

22. *The Hindu* (New Delhi) 22 March, 2005.

23. *G. Narayanswamy* v. *Jaffer Sharief*, AIR, 1994 SCC 170 Supp.

of a 'soft state', while J.K. Galbraith labels India as a 'functional anarchy'. What the imperatives of a liberal democracy demand and what actually occurs in our country makes it amply clear that any talk about good governance here is like rambling in a dreamland or parading in the field of hypocrisy. Rajni Kothari calls it 'politics of postures', while Atul Kohli designates it as the 'crisis of governability'. Populism has overshadowed the domain of performance. The fact of radicalisation of democracy at the base but authoritarianism at the top cannot be overlooked by a critical student of Indian politics. It may also be termed as politics of 'deceit' or 'manipulation' reinforced by the single factor of the politics of survival. Kothari throws focus on three kinds of crises:[24]

1. *Crisis of Institutions*: It signifies too much emphasis on leadership, too little on institutions along with their integrity and autonomy.
2. *Crisis of People's Participation*: It smacks of increasingly personalised and plebiscitary politics on the one hand with a tendency to overlook and in effect undermine institutions and traditions and parochialised politics on the other with a tendency to negotiate political and economic issues with local potentates rather an all-India elite.
3. *Crisis of Values:* It signifies that the state is shorn of the normal imperatives and nuances and also the controls that go with it, becomes totalitarian in the midst of all constitutional and legal instruments of a liberal democratic order.

The dreams of the founding fathers stand unrealised. The nexus between the politicians, the bureaucrats, the businessmen and the criminals has frustrated the expectations of those who had desired proper governability in the country. The makers of the Constitution "sacrificed stability for the sake of accountability. They did not, however, seem to have foreseen a situation where the concept of collective ministerial responsibility to the legislature would tend to absolve the Ministers of all responsibility to the people at large and where the government would become so very desperately dependent on shifting party loyalties and temporary majorities in august House, that the Ministers would have to remain preoccupied with

---

24. Rajni Kothari: "The Decline of the Modern State" in Zoya Hasan (ed.): *Politics and the State in India*, pp. 199–200.

efforts to continue in power and would have little time or patience left for the business of governance or development. Also they could hardly visualise how with all the electoral corruption and malpractices and with the majority of members getting elected on minority of votes, even their representative character would come to be seriously doubted."[25]

The whole case of good governance in our country is like a dreamflower or, in the words of Prof. O.P. Minocha, is like 'new public management perestroike' about which regrets occur at every turn of discussion. The statutory arrangements are circumvented and the judicial process is subverted by Machiavellian methods as a result of which the offenders remain 'innocent' and they manage to grab high offices of the state. The old saying that 'crime never pays' is replaced by a new aphorism that it alone pays. Rational planning and irrational politics become inseparable parts of the very logic of the Indian state that conducts a kind of, what Gramsci calls, 'passive revolution'. The vast difference between theory and practice of politics tarnishes every feature of good governance in our country. As Chatterji says: "What is science in one domain becomes rhetoric in the other: what is the rational will of the whole in the one becomes the contingent agglomerative of the particular will in the other. The two together—this contradictory, perenially quarrelsome couple—comprise the identity of the developmental state in India today."[26]

25. S.C. Kashyap: "Towards Good Governance: Need for Political Reforms" in Chaturvedi (ed.): *Towards Good Governance*, pp. 67-68.

26. Partha Chatterji: "Development Planning and the Indian State" in his (ed.) *State and Politics in India*, p. 297.

19

Crises of Integration

Modern state is a nation-state. It is first a national and then a political entity. The realisation of the goal of integration is essential for its survival and development. For this reason, nation-building activities have their start in every newly created state. The rulers and the leaders take a very serious view of the fissiparous and disruptive forces so as to bring about conditions of unity and harmony in the country. The people are counselled to discard their narrow or parochial loyalties or to subordinate them to the higher goal of national integration in all aspects. The forces of casteism, communalism, racialism, regionalism, sub-regionalism, linguism and the like may be referred to at this stage which, if not put under effective control in time, may convert the process of political development into that of political decay. The role of such forces creates the crises of integration in the politics of a country and leads to the destabilisation or disruption of a modern secular and democratic polity. In this chapter an attempt has been made to discuss the forces of casteism, communalism and regionalism in the politics of our country creating obstacles in the way of national integration.

Casteism

An account of the role of caste in contemporary Indian politics forms part of a very important as well as an interesting study. Examined from the standpoint of political sociology, it is found that abundant material is available for collation, hypothetisation and empirical analysis in this area of study.[1] Leaving aside the case of politics at the national level, the role of caste seems to be very conspicuous above the small circle of the village where caste groups interested in politics seem to have resembled the occupational, other

1. Rajni Kothari: *Politics in India*, p. 225.

pressure and electoral groups found elsewhere in developing democratic societies.[2]

Meaning of Caste and its Transformation: Caste society signifies a population with a common general culture, divided by social barriers into endogamous units each of which possesses some peculiar cultural specialities. History tells us that kinship and social control organisations split the people into segments separated by differences in rituals, morals and canons of exclusiveness. These units (sub-caste organisations) are usually hierarchised according to their rank of purity. Some specially out-caste groups are also characterised by their social status. Viewed thus, caste in India may be defined as a homogenous, endogamous social control organisation with distinctive rituals, especially those pertaining to a religious purity. Each caste and sub-caste is given an official status, rating high or low, according to the date of its origin, its supposed one time occupation and the strictness of its morals and religious codes.[3]

The term 'caste' has been derived from the Portuguese word 'casta' meaning breed, race, kind. Now it is employed to define a concept of Hinduism, in particular, for which several indigenous words are in currency. Certain it is that caste is an endemic feature of Hindu life and, as it is known in this country, it is exclusively an Indian phenomenon. However, it has now effectively pervaded all strata of our society so much so that it is found among other religious orders like Muslims and the Sikhs. An indigenous word for caste is *jati* in Sanskrit or *zat* in Persian meaning race, a fact which has led some scholars to posit a racial or tribal origin for castes according to which the Aryan priests, warriors and traders formed the Brahmin, Kshattriya and Vaishya segments respectively, while the people belonging to the slave component of the Aryan camp were called the *Sudras* and the aboriginal and uncivilised tribes constituted the *puncham* or outcaste class.

Caste being an ubiquitous institution and a steel-frame of Hindu society is rightly considered as a system where society is immutably graded and divided. A working definition of the term caste may, therefore, be furnished: "A caste is an endogamous

---

2. Granville Austin: *The Indian Constitution: Cornerstone of a Nation*, p.47.

3. See H.P. Fairchild (ed.): *Dictionary of Sociology*, p.33.

group, or a collection of endogamous groups, bearing a common name, membership of which is hereditary, imposing on its members certain restrictions in matters of social intercourse; either following a common traditional occupation or claiming a common origin, and generally regarded as forming a single homogeneous community."[4]

What is, however, important at this stage is to take note of the fact that the traditional concept of caste as a segmented division of society in which an individual can live his life fully has undergone a serious transformation. A large number of differentiations have emerged within the caste groups as a result of which deviation from caste norms is possible with impunity with regard to occupation, commensuality, everyday social intercourse and even with regard to intermarriage, though to a lesser extent. Now one may easily take note of the fact that the elders cannot exercise their authority over their youngers with the same degree of command and confidence as they did in the past and a man's educational accomplishments, his service status and financial position assign him a very respectable position irrespective of his caste attachments. This may be described as the phenomenon of caste transformation.

It may, nevertheless, be added that the case of caste transformation should not be appreciated to the extent of being taken as a mark of the termination of caste system. The lower castes have ever tried to emulate the ways of the higher ones. Prof. M.N. Srinivas has called it 'Sanskritisation'. What has really suffered is the pollution aspect of caste identity. As Prof. Srinivas observes: "There is a widespread impression among educated Indians that the caste is on its last legs and that educated, urbanised and westernised members of the upper classes have already escaped its bond. Both these impressions are wrong. These people may observe very few dietetic restrictions, marry outside caste and even religion but this does not mean that they have escaped the bonds of caste entirely. They show caste attitudes in surprising contexts."[5]

---

4. Refer to E. Blunt (ed.) : *Social Service in India*, Ch. XI

5. M.N. Srinivas: "The Indian Road to Inequality" in *Economic and Political Weekly* (Bombay), Vol. XII (Special Number of June, 1960), pp.867–72.

Interaction of Caste and Politics : If it is a truism that much of the caste system that one finds operating in the Indian political system today is far from being traditional, it is equally upright to hold that with the inauguration of the Constitution of the Indian Republic envisaging reservations and safeguards in favour of certain castes and tribes it seems to have found wider scope to operate as well. Curiously, it has operated more effectively than before and seems to have been gaining a tighter grip on the body politic. It has penetrated so deep into Indian society as to intermingle with several other trends such as communalism, regionalism and linguism. The reason for this lies in the fact of interaction of caste and politics in our country. It confirms the impression that where a democratic polity consciously resolves to build a modern nation, the result is a progressive fusion of various elements. It is for this reason that while caste "has been politicised, in the process it has provided Indian politics with processes and symbols of political articulation."[6]

Caste in contemporary Indian politics plays a very important role behind the facade of parliamentary democracy. The political behaviour of people is influenced by caste considerations as is quite evident at the time of distribution of election tickets and composition of ministries. It is found that the persons of a caste vote *en bloc* for a candidate of their own caste, if so available, or for some other candidate in pursuance of the decision of their caste panchayat or some other body. As far as possible and practicable, the people prefer a candidate of their own caste irrespective of his merits and demerits. Hence, while selecting a candidate for a particular constituency, it is foreseen whether he would be able to get the support of his caste or not. Similar regard is paid when the list of party's office-bearers is prepared. More so, when a single party is not in a position to have its own candidates, alliances are formed on the basis of caste to recommend the name of a person after arrangements of give and take are made to the satisfaction of the constituents. It is only in a strife-ridden situation that people have the unusual course of shaking off their caste orientation and, what is euphemistically said, vote according to their conscience.

---

6. Rajni Kothari and Rushikesh Maru: "Caste and Secularism in India" in *Journal of Asian Studies*, Nov., 1965, p.33.

But the fact remains that caste politicisation is not at all a one-sided affair. If caste orientation involves politics, politics in turn leaves its effect upon caste solidarity and hierarchy. A caste conscious of the fact of social stratification strives to better its position for the sake of modernising the life of its members and thereby saving itself from the onslaught of social injustice. Believing that it is quite eligible for participation in a representative democracy like other advanced castes, it asks even for representation in government through the membership of a political party irrespective of its position in the traditional social stratification. A successful assertion of privileges made by a caste is in many ways comparable to the extension of corporate liberties characteristic of the growth of English liberalism. For instance, the Shanans (traditionally low caste South Indian tappers of toddy) had a series of riots until the feudal potentate of Travancore conceded that their womenfolk could cover their bosoms in any way but different from the women of the upper castes.[7]

In a word, new conditions of independent India have given a fresh vigour to the politicisation of caste as a result of which it (caste) has begun to manifest itself as a regional, rather than a local, force increasingly independent of competitiveness in relation to other castes rather than a natural social group. "The central discovery is that politics is more important to caste and castes are more important to politics than before."[8] It is also commented that top political leaders may proclaim the goal of a casteless society, but the newly enfranchised rural masses know only the language of traditional politics which so largely turns about caste....Behind the formal list of party candidates nominated for the contests, there is probably an inside story of careful calculation in terms of caste appeal."[9]

A comprehensive study of caste in Indian politics reveals certain underlying characteristics. These are:

1. Caste politicisation has occurred like a two-way traffic. One has affected the other and thereby opened a new direction for the study of politics in our country. The operation of competitive politics has drawn caste out of its apolitical context and given to it a new status and identity hitherto unknown that has begun to disintegrate.

---

7. See Edgar Thurston : *Castes and Tribes*, Vol. VI, p. 365.

8. W.H. Morris-Jones: *The Government and Politics of India*, Ed. I, p. 65.

9. *Ibid*., p. 66.

2. Evidence shows that caste associations pass resolutions, submit memorandums and undertake other courses for protecting and promoting their specific interests like arrangements of separate electorates, reservation of seats in educational institutions and public services, removal of disqualifying clauses, and the like.

3. Caste politicisation has a very marked appearance at the time of elections when cries of 'a Jat for a Jat', 'an Ahir for an Ahir', 'a Brahmin for a Brahmin' and the like are made. Several caste associations may be found forcing their members persuasively to exercise their franchise in a particular direction.

4. Traditional caste rivalries have an impact of their own on the politics of our country. For instance, the Kammas and the Reddies are the two major castes of Andhra Pradesh. It is because of the fact of traditional rivalry between the two that while the Congress thrived on the support of the Reddies, the Communists on that of the Kammas. Likewise, the case of Lingayats and Vokaliggas in Karnataka may be referred to.

5. The relationship between caste and politics has been of a dynamic type. It has, by and large, been determined by the factor of expediency and pragmatism. In other words, it changes with the rise and fall of new entrepreneurs and innovators of politics. Thus, we find that while the Scheduled Castes or Harijans, as they are called, generally voted for the Congress party, they did not do so in the elections of 1977 and that they once again switched back their loyalty to the Congress led by Mrs. Gandhi (a Brahmin) in the elections of 1979 despite the fact that the hitherto ruling party (Janata) was led by a great Harijan leader (Jagjivan Ram).

To sum up, caste occupies a very important place in the politics of our country at local and regional levels. It is traceable in various important events like selection of candidates for elective offices, formation of groups and factions, canvassing campaigns, exercise of franchise, making of ministries, securing government favours and the like.

Constitutional Sanction and Party Politics : Caste system received a shattering blow when the British administration put an effective check on its horizontal tendency by introducing new means of transport and communications, law and justice and bureaucratic organisation. The civil and criminal law abolished caste panchayats and established the principle of equality before law irrespective of all caste considerations. The introduction of Western education affected increased economic mobility and weakened orthodox notions of social life. The system of decennial census indicated respective progress of different castes and thereby opened a new era of class conflict. In a word, it was the establishment of *Pax Britannica* which set the classes free from the territorial limitations inherent in the pre-British political system. Curiously, the British rule freed the jin from the bottle."[10]

Whereas the British administration put a strong check on the horizontal tendency and traditional bonds of caste system became weak with the introduction of many reforms, the result of Mutiny drove home to the British rulers the impression that the safety of their regime was integrally connected with the keeping of Indian people divided on the lines of religions and castes. Some upper castes like Brahmins and Kayasthas not only made use of the Western education but assumed the leadership of nationalist movement and thereby incurred the displeasure of the British rulers. The way-out was a firm adherence to a policy of divide and rule. As such, once again caste gained prominence for the British masters who knew it well that in our society it divided the people into small groups and thereby obstructed the emergence of nationalist sentiment.[11]

The Montford Reforms of 1919 imparted an unprecedented political push in this regard by conceding mixed electorates to non-Brahmins. It had its profound impact in South India where Brahmanical supremacy faced a final blow at the hands of all other castes which, under the changed circumstances, clamoured for special representation in legislative bodies and public services. As a result, the anti-Brahmanical movement gathered big momentum hitherto unseen and, with the shift of authority, the Brahmins had to suffer many losses in public services regardless of their efficiency and merit. The deteriorating situation could be checked only by the role of the Indian National Congress which gave a crushing defeat to this anti-Brahmin caste politics in the elections of 1937 as a result of which more moderate non-Brahmins in Bombay joined the Congress and they soon assumed a dominant position, while the

10. M.N. Srinivas: *Caste in Modern India*, Ch. 1.

11. G.S. Ghurye: *Caste and Classes in India*, pp. 175–76.

extremist elements "joined the Dravida Kazhagam under the leadership of E.V. Ramaswamy Naicker of Madras—a militant, atheistic, anti-Aryan, anti-north Indian and anti-Brahmin movement."[12]

The Constitution of India based on the ideals of Justice, Liberty Equality and Fraternity has given an irreparable damage to caste politics prevalent under the British administration by abolishing untouchability and prohibiting discrimination on various grounds (including caste), introducing universal adult franchise, terminating system of separate electorates and guaranteeing liberty of thought, expression, faith, belief and worship. India is a secular, democratic and socialist state allowing no room for the politics of caste and communalism. However, in practice things are not so and it may be pointed out with confidence that caste politics has risen from the ashes in a new form. It may be seen in the implementation of the doctrine of 'protective discrimination' whereby reservations have been conceded to the persons of Scheduled Castes, Scheduled Tribes and other socially and educationally backward classes (OBCs) in matters of admission to educational institutions and recruitment to public services. Thus, "within the new context of political democracy, caste remains a central element of India's society even while adapting itself to the values and methods of democratic politics."[13]

Two important points may, however, be taken note of while throwing light on the policy of reservations for Scheduled Castes, Scheduled Tribes and OBCs and their plausible justification. First, it is all meant for those who have been socially discriminated against and denied opportunities for educational advancement. Second, these measures are not meant for economic advancement of the persons so appointed but to ensure representation in public services of those who, due to historical reasons, have been deprived of the opportunities to serve the country like upper caste people. Keeping such points in view, Jagjivan Ram argues that caste, not economic prosperity, determines the status of an individual in the society. Says he: "It is obvious that in all matters in society, caste predominates, but when it comes to reservation in services for those

12. Srivinas, *op, cit.*

13. See L.I. Rudolph and Susane Rudolph : "The Political Role of India's Caste Associations" in *Pacific Affairs*, Vol. XXXIII, No. 1 (March, 1960).

sections of society which have been wronged all along, some other criteria is sought to be introduced. It is, therefore, not irrational or unreasonable to interpret the move as a sinister one to deprive the Scheduled Castes and Scheduled Tribes of an opportunity to secure some place in society which will afford them status and responsibility. Those who have for many years usurped the share of these communities are reluctant in their selfishness to part even with that which is not legitimately theirs."[14]

The basis of electoral politics is manipulation. Naturally, those castes have now become more important which constitute a 'vote bank'. Power is no longer based on blood prestige, familiarity with the nature of administrative machinery, or ability and courage to contact the high bureaucrats as was the case in pre-independence era. Now it is based on the numerical strength regardless of the fact that the leaders are westernised or not. Special concessions accorded to the backward and depressed classes have, in fact, acted as a special catalyst of political mobilisation in as much as many social groups (previously unaware of their strength and barely touched by the political changes which have now taken place) have now realised that they are in a position to wield power. It is owing to this fact that the political position of the Dalits (Harijans) and of the tribal people is very much ahead of either social status or their economic condition as compared to their special bargaining power in politics, the co-operation of their leaders into competing coalition networks and the need felt by higher caste politicians to solicit their support.

It is by all means amazing to see that the Indian National Congress succumbed to the temptations of caste at the expense of its modernising influence. A reference to the elections of 1937 shows that the Bihar Pradesh Congress Committee had to take caste labels into consideration in certain constituencies as the success of its candidates depended upon such considerations.[15] Similarly, in spite of a clear directive issued at the Avadi annual session of 1955, the Congress leadership, particularly in the State of Andhra Pradesh, on the eve of second general election, held off the decision of selecting its candidates until the Communist Party of India had filled its list and "then candidate for candidate matched the CPI state with the

14. Jagjivan Ram: *Caste Challenge in India*, pp. 94-95

15. Rajendra Prasad: *Autobiography*, p. 429.

slate of Congress supporters belonging to the identical caste."[16] So in the State of Rajasthan it was quite clear that Hiralal Shastri played the dominant role in finalising the list of Rajput ex-rulers in the State by accommodating their interests in the process of selection.[17]

Political articulation of caste finds its highest water-mark when a certain party is set up to protect and promote the interests of its members. Caste associations, in this way, establish an institutional means of their own to capture power and thereby force other political parties to recognise their existence. The Justice Party of Madras and the Independent Labour Party of Bombay are such examples of the pre-independence era. Frustrated with the achievements of their caste associations, the Vanniyars of Madras convened in 1951 a major gathering of the Vanniyakulu Kshattriya Sangam on a State-wide basis and then resolved that they should contest elections in co-operation with the toiling masses and thereupon they formed a political party (Tamilnadu Toilers Party) whose support was required by the Congress-led coalition government of Rajagopalachari followed by Kamaraj Nadar. The name of the Bahujan Samaj Party of U.P. may be cited in this regard. However, the strength of such a party varies with the numbers it may attempt to mobilise with the degree of self-consciousness and effectiveness of the leadership, with the degree of internal cohesiveness and with the power of countervailing other political processes. The Naga National Organisation as a body of the Nagas in Nagaland and the Gorkha League of the Gorkhas of West Bengal, in particular, may also be referred to in this connection.

Caste Politics at Regional and Local Levels : A study of caste politicisation in India has a salient characteristic of its own in this regard that while it has a major role at the local and regional levels, it is marginal at the all-India level. It is also found that while sub-castes tend to decrease, caste groups increase in importance at the higher levels in the political system.[18] One more striking feature, in this direction, is that while no State of the Indian Union may be said to be free from the shackles of caste politics, it is noteworthy that

---

16. Hugh Tinker: *India and Pakistan*, p. 149.

17. *Link* (New Delhi), Nov. 26, 1961.

18. P.R. Brass: *Fractional Politics in India*, p.16.

caste politics has been of maximum intensity in south of the Vindhya mountains where the first post-independence phase saw a struggle to dispossess the Brahmins of power and position "that phase is now almost ended, and a struggle between the newly dominant 'middle' classes and the submerged mass of lower castes and untouchables has only just begun."[19]

Let us, therefore, have a bird's eye view of the role of caste in the politics of leading States of the Indian Union in the following manner:

From this standpoint, Bihar represents the scene of a clash among major castes as Ahirs, Brahmins, Rajputs, Kayasthas and backward tribals. The Adivasis or the backward tribal people of Bihar-Orissa border organised themselves into a political party (Jharkhand) which in the elections of 1957, had been able to capture most of the seats reserved for the tribals and backward sections of the society and with its increased strength intensified the demand (under the leadership of a Hindu-turned-Christian named Jai Pal Singh) for a separate Tribal State of Jharkhand comprising all tribal areas of Bihar, Orissa and Madhya Pradesh. It afforded a potential challenge to the Congress party. In order to face the situation, the Congress leaders of the High Command deputed a Christian lady. (Rajkumari Amrit Kaur) to visit the tribal areas in order to wean away many tribesmen (particularly those converted in Christianity) from the growing influence of this new organisation. Thus, the Congress succeeded in depleting the ranks of this tribal party which in a truncated form became divided into many factions.

Three important castes (Marathas, Brahmins, Mahars) have played a leading part in the politics of Maharashtra. The most important part has been played by the Brahmins on account of their being much advanced in the sphere of educational accomplishments. However, their influence has, by and large, been confined to the urban areas. The Marathas have played the same important role in the rural areas particularly of Satara and Kolhapur. The Mahars (untouchables) have the third place in this regard. By joining army services in a considerable number and also by serving as labourers in many industrial units and commercial organisations, they have assumed a privileged position for the purpose of a 'vote bank'. While

19. Tinker, *op. cit.*, p. 147.

the Congress party had tried to maintain a balance between the position of various caste elements within its fold, sometimes splits occurred when a certain section has felt dissatisfied with the character of this party. For instance, in April 1948 a large bloc of the Marathas left the Congress and formed a new organisation (Peasants' and Workers' Party) under the leadership of K. Jedhe and S.S. More, while the untouchables joined the Scheduled Castes Federation in which Dr. B.R. Ambedkar played a very significant part and converted it into Republican Party.

The Dravidians have their own record in the State of Tamilnadu. In the pre-independence era, they formed Justice Party and then had their Commonweal and Toilers' Party. However, most of them joined the Dravida Kazhagam of Naicker—'an anti-Hindu, anti-Hindi and anti-Hindustan organisation.' A split occurred in its ranks when a large section of the party left it and joined the Dravida Munnetra Kazhgam led by C. Annadurai. Then, one more faction parted company with the DMK and became Anna-DMK under the leadership of M.G. Ramachandran.

The role of caste in the politics of Kerala received a major setback owing to the confrontation of the Hindus with the Christians in the West Coast and with the Muslims in the northern part of the State. With the amalgamation of the Travancore-Cochin princely states, Kerala became the biggest Malayalam-speaking State with an overwhelming population of the Hindus divided into many castes like Brahmins (chiefly Namboodiripads), Nairs and Izhavas or Tiyyans (a backward class with traditional occupation of toddy tapping). It may, however, be pointed out that the sociological make-up of the Hindus of Kerala shows that here politics is dominated more by consideration of religion than that of the caste. Herein may be discovered the source of the success of Muslim League. The Christians supported the Congress in the beginning. However, they shifted their political loyalty when the Congress leaders desired to adopt a new policy of controlling the administration of educational institutions run by the Christian missionaries.

In the State of Karnataka one may take note of the traditional rivalry going on between two castes—the Lingayats or Veersaivas and Vokkaligas. The Vokkaligas (dominant in the area of Mysore and worshippers of Lord Vishnu) still harbour old fear that they would always remain dominated by the Lingayats in the large Kannada-speaking State and for this reason they supported the idea of a separate State for them called Dakshina Pradesh. On the other hand, the Lingayats (worshippers of Lord Shiva) have been in a very powerful position in the areas of Bangalore. They have opposed the idea of Dakshina Pradesh and yet desired the formation of a large State of the Kannada-speaking people. An instance of the traditional rivalry between the two dominant castes of Karnataka may be seen in the fall of K. Hanumanthayya. His crime was that as the Chief Minister of this State he incurred the displeasure of the Vokkaligas by giving support to the demand for a greater Kannada-speaking State.

Caste politics in the State of Andhra Pradesh looks like a game of cock-fighting between the Kammas (dominant in the Krishna-Godavri delta also known by the nickname of the Kamma Rashtra) and the Reddies dominant in other areas (called Rayalseema). It is on account of the fact of traditional rivalry between the two dominant castes that while the Communists have banked on the support of the Kammas, the Congress has done the same by depending on the support of the Reddies. Curiously, a very small section of the Brahmins has reaped political gains out of the prevailing tug-of-war between the two dominant castes. Realising this political fact, the Congress High Command deputed S.K. Patil to visit the areas and somehow weaken the hold of the Communists. He could succeed by requisitioning the support of a Kamma leader (N.G. Ranga) on the eve of the second general election in 1957. The position of the Reddies improved much with the inclusion of Telangana region in Andhra Pradesh and this went to the positive advantage of the Congress party. Moreover, it was because of the growth of the position of the Reddies that a man of average significance like N. Sanjiva Reddy became the President of the Indian National Congress.

In this connection, it may also be added that in certain situations the element of caste rams into the sphere of religion and thus gives a new dimension to the case of caste politicisation. For instance, Sikh is a religion, a caste, a community. The Sikhs are a separate entity, as most of them claim, as well as they are a part of the Hindu community. We may, therefore, take note of the prevailing rivalry between the Sikhs and non-Sikhs, Akalis and non-Akalis. It is due to this that while a very small section of the extremists sometimes aired demand for a separate and sovereign State (Sikhistan), the moderate elements in majority felt satisfied with the creation of a 'Punjabi Suba' as an autonomous State within Indian Union. It may also be visualised that while the Sikhs struggled for the cause of Punjabi language, others desired the same for Hindi. Hence, Gurdwara politics versus Arya Samaj politics dominated the scene.

Interlinking of Castes and Classes : In a literal sense, castes and classes have different implications. But in the politics of our country they have come to be identified with each other. Even Courts have accepted the view that in certain situations the class as a whole may be taken as a caste and thus a caste may be entitled for the benefits of reservation that are available to a 'backward class'. In pursuance of Art. 338, the Government of India appointed a Backward Classes Commission in 1953 under the chairmanship of Kaka Saheb Kalelkar which submitted its report in 1955. With a view to identify socially and educationally backward classes, it adopted a 4-point criteria: (*i*) low social position in the traditional caste hierarchy of Hindu society, (*ii*) lack of general educational advancement among the major sections of a caste or community, (*iii*) inadequate or no representation in Government service, and (*iv*) inadequate representation in the field of trade, commerce and industry. In its report the Commission related social backwardness of a class to its low position in the traditional caste hierarchy of Hindu society; treated all women as a 'backward class'; desired reservation of 70 percent seats in all technical and professional institutions for qualified students of backward classes and minimum reservation of vacancies in all government services and local bodies for other backward classes in this manner: Class I—25 percent; Class II—33.1/3 percent; and Class III and Class IV—40 percent. The report failed to be unanimous and the Government of India rejected its basis of identification of castes. As such, the report of the Kalelkar Commission failed to serve any purpose.

The Janata Government set up the second Backward Classes Commission under the chairmanship of B.P. Mandal in 1978 which submitted its report in 1980. It adopted a set of 11 'indicators' in the social, educational and economic spheres for the determination of backwardness. In the social sphere, it accepted 4 points: (*i*) Castes/Classes considered as socially backward by others; (*ii*) Castes/Classes which mainly depend on manual labour for their livelihood; (*iii*) Castes/Classes where at least 25 percent females and 10 percent males above the state average get married at an age below 17 years in rural areas and at least 10 percent females and 5 percent males do so in urban areas. (*iv*) Castes/Classes where participation of females in work is at least 25 percent above the State average. In the educational sphere, it adopted 3 points: (*v*) Castes/Classes where the number of children in the age group of 5–15 years is at least 25 percent above the State average; (*vi*) Castes/Classes where the rate of student dropout in the age group of 5–15 years who never attend schools is at least 25 percent above the State average;(*vii*) Castes/Classes amongst whom the proportion of matriculates is at least 25 percent below the State average. Finally, in the economic sphere, it adopted 4 points: (*viii*) Castes/Classes where the average value of family assets is at least 25 percent below the State average; (*ix*) Castes/Classes where the number of families living in kuchcha houses is at least 25 percent above the State average; (*x*) Castes/Classes where the source of drinking water is beyond half a kilometre for more than 50 percent of the households; (*xi*) Castes/Classes where the number of households having taken consumption loan is at least 25 percent above the State average.

The chairman of the Commission submitted his report with the note of dissent given by a member (L.R. Naik). It recommended 27 percent of the seats to be reserved for other socially and educationally backward classes. It put special emphasis on the fact that while these 'backward classes' constituted 52 percent of the population, they could not be entitled for that much of percentage in matters of reservations in view of the fact that 22 1/2 percent of the seats were already reserved for the Scheduled Castes and Scheduled Tribes and that the Supreme Court had given a ruling in the *Balaji Case* (1963) the total reservations could not exceed the limit of 50 percent of seats.

The report was submitted in Dec. 1980, but it remained in abeyance until the Government of V.P. Singh issued an order on 13 Aug., 1990 for the reservation of 27 percent of the vacancies in civil posts and services under the Government of India and in all public sector undertakings and financial institutions. Soon riots broke out in different parts of the country. The matter was challenged in the Supreme Court that granted stay of its implementation. But in its judgment delivered two years after, the Court held the impugned order as constitutionally 'valid'. It also said that the benefit of reservations could not be given to the 'creamy layers' or economically well off segments of the other backward castes. It asked the State Government to appoint commissions for the identification of the OBCs and their 'creamy layer' that could be looked into by the Courts.

Distribution of Indian Population of Religious and Caste Groups

	Groups	Status (Sections)	%
1.	(*i*) Scheduled Castes	Scheduled Castes	15.05
	(*ii*) Scheduled Tribes	Scheduled Tribes	7.51
		Total	22.56
2.	(*i*) Muslims (other than STs)	Non-Hindu Communities (0.02) Religious Groups etc.	11.19
	(*ii*) Christians (other than STs)	,, (0.44)	2.16
	(*iii*) Sikhs (other than STs)	,, (0.22)	1.67
	(*iv*) Buddhists (other than STs)	,, (0.03)	0.67
		Total	16.16
3.	(*i*) Brahmins (including Bhumihars)	Forward Hindu Castes and Communities	5.52
	(*ii*) Rajputs	,,	3.90
	(*iii*) Marathas	,,	2.21
	(*iv*) Jats	,,	1.00
	(*v*) Vaishyas-Banias etc.	,,	1.88
	(*vi*) Kayasthas	,,	1.07
	(*vii*) Others	,,	2.00
		Total	17.58
4.	Remaining OBCs	Backward Hindu Castes and Communities	43.70
5.	52% of Religious Groups under Section 2 may also be treated as OBCs	Very Backward Non-Hindu Communities	8.40
6.	Others	The approximate derived population of OBCs including non-Hindu Communities	52%

*Figures given in brackets show the population of SCs and STs among these non-Hindu communities.

Source: *Mandal Commission Report*, Chapter XII.

It created a new situation described as the 'Mandalisation of politics'. Prime Minister V.P. Singh justified this action in the name of bringing about 'social justice' in the country. Rajni Kothari termed the riotous situation in the country as 'the great secular upsurge' in the form of 'a message that rejects pan-Indian *Hindutva* and makes caste a bulwark against religious fundamentalism and its fascist overtones.'[20] But others said that "few will relish the civilisational havoc that is likely to result from making a virtue of the cultural attributes of backwardness."[21] A surprising, rather shocking, development may now be seen in the growing trend of de-Sanskritisation. That is, some advanced castes have come out with a demand for their inclusion in the category of the OBCs. Thanks to the factor of caste politicisation, the Jats and some other hitherto advanced castes have been able to win their game in some States as Rajasthan and U.P. Certain sections of the Rajputs and the Brahmins have raised a similar demand in the name of their 'economic backwardness' in spite of the fact that the Supreme Court has ruled it out in the *Mandal Case*.

No doubt, the judgment of the Supreme Court in the *Mandal Case* shattered the hopes of the sensible people. The Court did not take into account the fact that the reservation of seats for the OBCs would have a deleterious effect on the efficiency of public services and do a lot of injustice to the deserving people of the country.[22] It did not appreciate the argument that the enlistment of 3,743 socially and educationally backward castes in the Mandal Report was based on the data of the Census Report of 1931 and, for that reason, had now become obsolete to a very large extent. Most of the so-called 'backward castes', as listed in

20. Rajni Kothari: "Caste and Politics" in *The Times of India*, New Delhi, 28 September, 1990.

21. Swapan Dasgupta: "Curse of Mandal" in *The Times of India*, New Delhi, 13 Aug., 1990.

22. In one of his letters written to the Chief Ministers of the States dated 27 June, 1961, Prime Minister Nehru said: I react strongly against anything which leads to inefficiency and second-rate standards. I want my country to be a first-class country in everything. The moment we encourage the second rate, we are lost. The only real way to help a backward group is to give opportunities of good education, this includes technical education which is becoming more and more important. Everything else is provision of some kind of crutches which do not add to the strength or health of the body." *Letters to the Chief Ministers*, 1947–1964, Vol. 5 (Oxford University Press, 1989), pp. 456–57.

the Report, had become advanced since the advent of independence and they had no right to be treated as such. So an Indian sociologist rightly pointed out: "There is considerable social and economic heterogeneity in each of these castes (as kurmis, lodhas, ahirs etc). Hence the dubbing of an entire caste as 'backward' by the Mandal Commission is highly irrational. The benefits are likely to go to the better-off and more influential in these castes at the expenses of the poor and backward ones. At the same time, very poor individuals from castes not dubbed backward are excluded."[23] Taking into account the highly subversive effects of such a move, another cirtic said: "If caste has acquired a new lease of life in independent India, this is almost entirely because of the increasing use made of it in politics..... The most serious implication of extending caste quotas is that all public institutions will by that process come to be cast in the mould of political councils and committees. Universities, hospitals, scientific research laboratories, defence establishments and courts of justice will all come to look more and more like representative political bodies. If they are constituted so as to maintain a balanced representation of castes, it will not be long before they begin to function like them. Every public institution will then be riddled not only with caste but also with politics, for caste has no function today except in politics."[24]

Critical Appreciation : The spectre of caste has increasingly come to haunt both Indian politics and Indian political analysis. A proper study of this momentous subject of Indian political sociology, however, shows that while the role of caste in the political process of the country has been decried as a fissiparous threat to national unity, it has also been lauded as a channel of communication that acts as a link between the most elaborate and the new democratic processes and makes them comprehensible in traditional terms to a population still largely politically illiterate. The paramount fact remains that caste is so tacitly and so completely accepted by all, including most vocal in condemning it, that it is everywhere the unit of social action. Let us, therefore, look into the good and bad aspects of caste politicisation.

23. M.N. Srinivas: "The Mandal Formula" in *The Times of India*, New Delhi, 17 Nov., 1990.

24. Andre Betaille: "Caste Politics" in *The Times of India*, New Delhi, 11 Sept., 1990.

Indisputable is the fact that caste has demonstrated itself as an undesirable, even harmful, asset of Indian politics. It has cultivated and invigorated the evil of caste patriotism by putting group loyalty above merit and competence and narrow selfishness over public well being all set for jeopardising the effectiveness of government's vital functions. Any tendency undermining or destroying liberal-democratic values should be discouraged and, as such, any positive contribution of caste to the politics of our country becomes incomprehensible. None can deny that the politics of group selfishness is morally degrading, intellectually unsatisfactory, socially criminal, politically undesirable and aesthetically displeasing. Hence, the statesmen, economic planners, civil servants and other enlightened persons are fully justified in repudiating the demands put by various caste organisations for the benefit of their particular class of people alone. By all means, it signifies a system of 'instituted' or 'legal' inequality.

The case of caste politicisation should also be studied in a different perspective. Caste in the traditional sense should go; caste in the modernised sense should survive to exert a liberating influence. If caste politics means group selfishness, it ought to be deplored in the name of social duty and discipline. But if it may imply an institutional arrangement of bringing about political democracy inculcating egalitarian aspirations among the members of a particular group, it becomes a mechanism exerting a liberating influence. Keeping the spirit of political pluralism in view, it may be said that all social groups and institutions have a personality of their own and they are entitled for the allegiance of the people in as much as they satisfy the needs of their members. Thus studied, it may be hoped that caste associations "may play a vital role in the exercise of political freedom through group; self-government, which contributes to the process of finding approximation of the public good, provides a means for furthering group purposes independent of, as well as supplementary to, the state and helps to protect the liberties of both the associations and the individuals.[25]

It follows that the momentous subject of the interaction of caste and politics in our developing country should be re-examined in the

25. Rudolphs, *op. cit.*

light of the new approach of J.D.B. Miller who holds that the business of politics is to deal with conflicts. The pattern of our representative democracy with its basic principle of 'one man, one vote' disallowing every artificial ground of discrimination, has drawn the social institution of caste into the web of electoral politics. Hence, many caste groups have made use of the opportunity of asserting their real weight that remained forbidden to them during the pre-independence period. Truly speaking, they are the new entrepreneurs of politics, the real actors of political drama and the new contestants of power. Herein they find an extremely vocal and flexible basis of their political generation. As Prof. Kothari visualises : "By drawing the caste system into web of organisation, politics finds material for its articulation and to mould it into its own design."[26]

What is, therefore, needed is that castes should be deprived of all exclusive privileges given to them because of some political considerations in as much as such an arrangement kills the spirit of an egalitarian society. It is also warranted by the fact that castes deriving immense benefits from certain special arrangements show reluctance to give up the privilege of their backwardness. Whatever be the theoretical justification for the retention of certain reservations and safeguards, it should never be lost sight of that intelligence and commonsense "are not harnessed in combating inequality."[27] It is quite necessary for the proper utilisation of the secular potentialities of our society based on the astonishing foundation of 'unity in diversity'.

---

26. Kothari: *Politics in India*, p. 225

27. M.N. Srinivas, *op. cit.* It is well suggested: "Thus a suitable system of reservation is one which (*a*) takes care of the downtrodden and the poor through creation of opportunities at the educational and the first job stage ; (*b*) identifies the poor by the level of poverty and not by caste; (*c*) graduates the economically weak as they become stronger; (*d*) provides through coaching, hostel facilities and scholarships and stipends at the scholastic stage; (*e*) arranges training programmes to the weak preparatory to admissions to jobs in the public and the private sectors and generally promotes self-reliance rather than doles and crutches." A.M. Khusro; "Pro-Side, Con-side and Inside" in *Indian Express*, New Delhi, 13 Sept., 1990.

Communalism

Communalism may rightly be described as another puzzling idiom of Indian politics. Like casteism, it poses a formidable challenge to our political system established on the lines of democrary and secularism, though a student of political sociology may discover herein also a channel of increasing politicisation of the people and, on that basis, may not treat communalism as an absolute evil by all means. As a matter of fact, it looks like sworn to negate what the enlightened builders of our nation have so ardently desired in the form of realising the ideal of 'Fraternity assuring the dignity of the individual and unity and integrity of the nation' as so gloriously enshrined in the Preamble to the Constitution. Hence, an attempt has been made to study the role of religious and sectarian fanaticism, called communalism, that "presents a real threat to Indian secularism."[28]

Nature and Essential Implications: In quite simple terms, communalism may be defined as a person's attachment with the good of his 'community'. However, in the realm of politics it has very sinister implications in view of the fact that it "is generally associated with a narrow, selfish, divisive and aggressive attitude on the part of a religious group."[29] It is, for this reason, obvious that in the field of politics, communalism does not convey a simple sense of designating the existence of heterogeneous social groups or organisations based on the lines of communal make-up. It is true that communalism, in general, stands for the protection and promotion of the specific interests of a particular community; however its manifestation in the realm of politics has a negative, and rather a disastrous, dimension in as much as it seeks to foster the interests of a section of the population presumably to the detriment of society as a whole. It also acts in the name of some religion or tradition that opposes social change along constructive and progressive lines. For this reason, as Richard D. Lambert says, it "is an epithet implying anti-social greed and reactionary social outlook."[30]

---

28. D.E. Smith: *India as a Secular State*, p. 454.
29. *Ibid.*
30. See Lambert: "Hindu Communal Groups in Indian Politics" in Park and Tinker (ed.): *Leadership and Political Institutions in India*, p. 211.

Implicit in the meaning of communalism is, therefore, a sense of blind loyalty towards the community that may go to the extent of subordinating one's higher loyalty to his nation or society as a whole. Instead of having an attitude towards a particular religion enlightened enough so as to circumvent any possible feeling of orthodoxy, it leads to the inculcation of wrong orientations that have their manifestation in the form of fanaticism or religious orthodoxy. The feelings of social unity and harmony are subverted and in their place sentiments of hatred or enmity towards other religious and cultural orders hold a strong place in the minds of the people. As such, communalism refers to the attitude of the people and their groups when they "place their loyalty to the community above the loyalty to the body politic (Nation) to which they belong, or else when they develop active hostility towards other communities living within the same body politic."[31]

Fanaticism and orthodoxy, in this way, provide the ground on which the tendency of communalism stands and finds its sustenance. Various organisations dedicated wholly to the cause of their communal uplift may, however, be ignored in a study of politics unless they show their involvement in the political process and activity of the country in some measure. Moreover, since the basis of communalism is the consideration of the interest of the community above everything else, including the overall interest of the nation as a whole, and since the term 'community' refers to a religious order as well as a sub-division of its own in the form of caste or creed, the term 'communal' in our country also covers the case of caste and similar other organisations.

In the typical Indian context the meaning of 'communalism' is thus given by an Indian writer: "Adherence to religion and religious system is not communalism. Exploitation of religion is communalism. Attachment to a religious community or religiousity is not communalism. Using a religious community against other communities and against a federal nation is communalism. Communalism is conversion of religiousity into political bellicosity. Communalism is the enemy of progress, democracy, secular culture and federal nation-state building on rational scientific line. Communalism envisages a religious community alone as a base

31. Hans Kruze: "Some Problems of Independent India" in *South Asian Studies*, IV, New Delhi, 1968, p. 51.

and universe of its political ambition and action. For a communalist, religious community is the only relevant and valid category in politics and in state affairs. Communalism is a political orientation that recognises religious community and not the nation or the nation-state as the terminal community—the final point of political allegiance. Therefore, communalism is a political strategy opposed to nationalism as a process of unifying multi-ethnic, multi-religious and multilingual communities. Communalism is opposed to secularism as a pattern of socio-cultural coexistence and political integration. Communalism is opposed to a rational civic basis of party formations and political system."[32]

If the term 'communalism' is applied to a study of the Indian stasiological system, it becomes akin to the element of 'ideology' in a narrower sense. Here the area of concern is with the claims of a distinct religious community. Viewed in a broader sense, it covers what is generally known by the name of the 'right' or 'rightist ideology'. A study with this standpoint shows that while some major organisations like the Muslim League may be included in the former category, others like Akali Dal and Dravida Munnetra Kazhagam may be included in the latter. All rightist organisations may be termed 'communal' for the reason of drawing sustenance from the consideration of a particular religious or caste system. [33]

Hindu Communalism : The study of communalism in the politics of our country engages our attention in the direction of examining it on two main fronts—Hindu and Muslim. A call for joining the national mainstream relates to the role of the two communities in such a way that without interfering with each other's religious beliefs, the two communities should give an abundant proof of the sense of a common heritage. However, it all does not happen to the desired extent in which the guilt of fanaticism on both sides may be found. A brief look at the development of communalism in the pre-independence phase shows that, despite vigorous implementation of the British policy of divide and rule, most of the Hindus and Muslims jointly and whole-heartedly fought for the national liberation,

---

32. Resheeduddin Khan: "Political Integration in Federal India" in *The Times of India*, New Delhi, 19 November, 1992.

33. W.H. Morris-Jones: *The Government and Politics in India*, Ed. I of 1964, p. 159.

while a militant section of both communities adhered to the course of separatism that served the nefarious purpose of the colonial power. Hence, it cannot be lost sight of that the two communities "took parallel lines and communalism is, therefore, also a phase of nationalism."[34]

Great leaders of the Hindu Maha Saba like Savarkar sharpened the trend of Hindu communalism. Savarkar defined a Hindu as "one who treats India as his *Matrubhu* (motherland) as well as his *Punyabhu* (holy land)."[35] Such an interpretation was distinctly anti-Islamic, because the Muslims could never agree to regard Bharatvarsh as their holy land, though they could have no reservation in regarding it as their motherland. Savarkar frankly repudiated the possibility of any conversion in the Muslim mind on account of their concepts of *Dar-ul-Islam* (land of Islam) and *Dar-ul-Harb* (land of struggle), the latter applicable to every place where Islam was not in power. So he said: "Consequently, territorial patriotism is a word unknown to the Muslim—nay is tabooed unless in connection with a Muslim territory Afghans can be patriots, for Afghanistan is a Muslim territory today."[36]

Savarkar offered a new concept of Hindu nation by holding that the idea of Hindu Rashtra referred to a people united by a common country, blood, history, religion, culture and language. It signified that the Hindus "are a vastly more than a religious community, they are a nation." Further elaboration in the same regard implies that while the "Hindus are a nation, the Muslims only a community." In his presidential address at the session of Hindu Maha Sabha at Karnavati (Ahmedabad) in October, 1937, he went to the length of saying: "India cannot be assumed today to be unitarian and a homogeneous nation but on the contrary there are two nations in the main; the Hindus and the Muslims." [37] Naturally, the Hindu Maha Sabha expressed its profound shock and resentment at any talk about the partition of the country and came out with the call of 'Akhand Hindustan' (Undivided

34. Bakar Ali Mirza: *Hindu-Muslim Problem*, p. 54.

35. Savarkar: *Hindutva*, edited by V.G. Ketkar, 1942, p. 4.

36. Savarkar: *Rashtravad* edited by Satya Prakash p. 72.

37. Savarkar: *Hindu Rashtra Dashan* (Hindi), edited by L.G. Khare, p. 26.

India). In the post-independence era, it made no inhibitions in saying that it "stands for establishing Hindu Raj in Bharat, with a form of government in accordance with Hindu conceptions of polity and economy." [38]

The case of the Rashtriya Swayam Sevak Sangh (RSS) may also be studied in this very connection. It was founded in 1925 at Nagpur by Dr. K.B. Hadgewar with the objective of reorganising and militarising the Hindu community. It has concentrated its efforts on the development of a tightly disciplined corps of well-indoctrinated, physically fit, devoted volunteers to the Hindu youth who represent *Sangathan* ideal of the Hindu society in miniature. "Convinced that the political power cannot effect the necessary revitalisation of the Hindus, the RSS has sought to create a model society which will eventually expand to include the entire Hindu nation." [39]

In defining the concept of Hindu Rashtra, the RSS leaders like M.S. Golwalkar, Deoras, Rajendra Singh, Advani, Malkani and Sudershan adopt the same line. Nation is a cultural entity and not merely a political unit and on this basis they describe Hindu community as a 'nation' in existence even before the advent of Islam in India. With such an interpretation they alienate the non-Hindus from the Hindu nation and lay emphasis on the assimilation of the minorities as happened in the United Kingdom, France and the United States. Golwalkar says: "The non-Hindu people in Hindustan must either adopt the Hindu culture and language, must learn to respect and hold in reverence Hindu religion, must entertain no ideas but those of the glorification of the Hindu race and culture; that is, they must not only give up their attitude of intolerance and ungratefulness towards the land and its age-old traditions but must also cultivate the positive attitude of love and devotion instead—in a word, they must cease to be the foreigners, or must stay in the country wholly subordinated to the Hindu nation, claiming nothing, deserving no privileges, far less any preferential treatment—not even citizen's rights." [40]

---

38. Smith, *op. cit.*, p. 461.
39. Smith, *op. cit.*, p. 465, For a pioneering study, see J.A. Curran: *Militant Hinduism in Indian Politics: A Study of the R S S*, 1951. Also see Govind Sahai: *RSS*: Ideology, *Technique and Propaganda*.
40. Golwalkar: *We or Our Nationhood Defined*, pp. 55–56.

Hindu communalism has now come to be known as *Hindutva*. In simple terms, it implies Hinduism, Bharatiyata, Indianisation and the like. It stands for cultural nationalism of India sustained by the force of classical Hinduism (Sanatam Dharma) as a religion as well as by the centuries-old traditions of the country. In a strict sense, it suggests the character of being Hindu. But in the context of India's partition and its vehement criticism by the devotees of Akhand Hindustan, it assumes ostensibly anti-Muslim overtones. *Hindutva* is not anti-Muslim or anti-Christian and the like; it is certainly pro-Hindu and here it stands for, what Sri Aurobindo called, 'larger Hinduism. The main implications of *Hindutva* may be thus enumerted:

1. It stands for a typical meaning of 'secularism'. In the West secularism stands for complete separation of state and religion, Church and State, and hence becomes an irreligious ideology. In India secularism stands for equal respect for all religions. It does not advocate the case of irreligiousity, though it frankly rejects the case of a theocratic state. Thus, religion or *Dharma* as a way life and the country with its polity, economy and social order cannot be separated from each other.

2. It calls for a tolerant way of life. Hence, there is no question of its being opposed to the basic tenets of any other religion. It is mistakenly seen as anti-Muslim. The enemies of *Hindutva* deliberately distort its real meaning. In fact, it enjoins upon every citizen of the country to be an Indian, first and last. The Sikhs, the Buddhists, and the Jains are the segments of the Hindu order.

3. Not only this, *Hindutva* regards even non-Hindus, particularly Muslims, as the sons of the same soil and appreciates the expressions of intelligent and enlightened Muslim leaders in this regard. For instance, it admires the frankness of a great leader of Muslim renaissance, Sir Syed Ahmed Khan of Aligarh, who on one occasion stunned the audience of Gurdaspur in Punjab by asking 'Am I not a Hindu?' in reaction to his reference as a great Muslim leader. So a devotee of *Hindutva* would admire the couplet of Iqbal that 'India is proud of Rama, men of understanding address him as the hero of India."[41] For truth to tell , all Indians are Hindus—by culture and nationality.

---

41. As the couplet reads: "Hai Ram ke wajud pe Hindostan ko nazz; ahle nazar samajhte hain usko Imam-i-Hind.'

4. It stands for national integration in a way that the Indian way of life becomes manifest in all walks of people's life. And since Hindu civilisation and culture constitute the foundation of nationalism, the pattern of people's life should be based on it accordingly. Moreover, as non-Hindu ways of life also prevail in the country. they should try to reconcile themselves with the basic norms of this country's civilisation and culture. That is, the other ways of life should not be mercilessly suppressed or discarded or even undermined, what is needed is the harmonisation of all in a way that the foundational features are not destroyed. For instance, the Muslims should practise and profess their faith, but they should not behave in an anti-Hindu manner.

5. It has been the sustaining force of our nationalism in the past and, as such, is should continue to be the force of our social, economic and political regeneration. As Malkani says: "Basically, *Hindutva* is India's agenda for coming into its own after centuries of vicissitudes. If a person seeks votes in the name of Ram or Rahim, he is obviously violating both, religion and politics. But if a person talks of Ram Rajya, or Kingdom of God on Earth, or Nizam-e-Mustafa, he is only setting up idealistic goals, and he cannot be faulted."[42]

6. Finally, it stands for the consolidation of unity in the ranks of the Hindu society. It militates against the tendency of dividing Hindu society in the name of castes and communities. A well organised Hindu society will attract, even force, non-Hindu people to feel in a different way. As prof. Rajendra Singh (Rajju Bhaiya) argues: "If the solidarity of the Hindu society is maintained, all others in the country, including the Muslims, will feel that they are also a part of it."

As such, now *Hindutva* has become an ideology which the RSS is propagating as a matter of its unflinching faith in it and the BJP is sticking to it without any inhibition. If it was Gandhism yesterday, *Hindutva* is today, as hopefully and zealously asserted by its protagonists.

In short, the advocates of Hindu communalism desire to establish a new form of social and political order in the country that is distinctly

---

42. *The Hindustan Times*, New Delhi, Sunday Magazine, 29 August, 1993, p. 5.

based on the fundamental principles of Hinduism. In this regard they go to the extent of lauding the Hindu kingdom of Nepal as the only mark of a Hindu State in the world. India, that is Bharat or Aryavarat, is one and indivisible and, for this reason, any talk of its fragmentation is a crime, a sin, and an act of infidelity.[43]

Muslim Communalism : Muslim communalism should be treated as a sharp rejoinder to its Hindu counterpart with this point of distinction that here the source of inspiration is the religion that is exploited for political purposes. We have already seen that shrewd English mind could thrive on the support that it got from the 'loyal' Muslims in the pre-independence era. It is also evident from the fact that the suspicious communal mind did not pay heed to the sane advice of Maulana Abul Kalam Azad that, in the post-independence phase, the Muslims should join the national mainstream as the best way to protect and safeguard their legitimate interests. The result is that in "the post-partition India, the Muslims are certainly in a dilemma."[44]

The Muslim League founded in 1906 played, as we have already seen, a very unfortuante part in the partition of the country. In the post-independence period its remnant in the South survived that gained some weight in the years to follow. However, it is the Jamaat-i-Islami founded by Maulana Maudoodi in 1941 and led by Abul Lais Islahi after the Maulana migrated to Pakistan in 1948 that deserves a special mention here. It should be taken as an "ideological party" of the Muslim communalists that has no reservations in saying that the Muslim can secure political power by establishing a State of their own in accordance with the *Quran* and *Shariat* and thereby demonstrating the futility of secular democratic government. Co-operation with any un-Islamic government is '*haram*' or prohibited by religion.[45]

The orthodox school of the Muslim communalists makes out a powerful case against nationalism, secularism and democracy as all repugnant to Islam. The only alternative is to accept the Divine Guidance as promised in the holy books. It offers an alternative to

43. See K.M. Munshi: *Akhand Hindustan*, p. 96.

44. Moin Shakir: *Muslims in Free India*, p. 46.

45. *Ibid.*, p. 50.

all—Liberalism, Communism, Socialism and Democracy. The Jamaat represents its total opposition to any idea of having even a coalition (muahedah) with the Hindus or un-Islamic elements. Different from this is the stand of the Jamaat-ul-Ulema-i-Hind led by Maulana Asad Madni that believes in the principle of 'muahedah' or coalition with the non-Muslims. Moreover, it has faith in the establishment of a secular state in India. The Indian Union Muslim League is purely a political organisation that frankly appreciates the course of coalition with like-minded political organisations.

Mention, at this stage, may be made of several religious-cultural organisations of the Muslims that, though having a non-political character, do provide cadre support to the political organisations of the Muslims. The Tablighi Jamaat initiated by Maulana Ilyas advocates that Islam is a complete practical code of life and the Muslims should take the responsibility of enforcing the Islamic practices for the good of mankind. The Tamir-e-Millat and Majlis-i-Ittehad-ul-Mussalmeen are the two such organisations founded and led by the prominent Muslims of Hyderabad which lay emphasis on the need for change within the Islamic framework and reconstruction of the Muslim society along modern lines without injuring the basic tenets of Islam. It shows that there is a sharp difference of opinion among various Muslim religio-cultural organisations so far as the issue of modernisation of the community is concerned. However, for our purpose, it is noteworthy that all such organisations take inspiration from the fundamentalism of Islam and lay emphasis on the need for reorganising the Muslim community for the ultimate purpose of being in a position of dominance.

After making a brief study of different Muslim organisations, whether political, para-political or pseudo-political, or even purely religious and cultural, which may be used for the purposes of cadre support by the political organisations, and their divergent points of view in regard to the social, economic and political issues of the country, certain common points may be earmarked so as to lay focus on the main tenets of Muslim communalism. These are: [46]

1. The Muslim communalists believe that they have a mission to perform. It implies that the Muslims must ever understand the message of Islam.

46. *Ibid.*, pp. 83–86.

2. Muslim communalism is sustained by the sense of separatism and exclusiveness. The communalists do not believe in integration or assimilation and instead want to maintain their separate and distinct identity. The burden of their argument is that the Hindus and the Muslims are two parallel societies and, as such, there can be no synthesis between the two.

3. The Muslim communalists demand separate electorates for them as they had during the pre-independence days. Their argument is that only Muslims can represent their interests in the law-making bodies of the state. They have come out with a demand for adequate representation of the Muslims in government services and other areas of public employment, including police and defence.

4. The Muslim communalists take a very conservative view in maintaining their age-old practices. They detest any change in their personal law relating to marriage, divorce, inheritance, succession etc. For this very reason, they oppose any idea of modernisation of the community even if it is preached by the enlightened Muslim leaders and intellectuals like M.C. Chagla, A.A.A. Fyzee, A.G. Noorani, M. Imam, Dr. Rafiq Zakaria, Prof. Tahir Mahmood, Maulana Waheeduddin Khan, Asghar Ali Engineer, Ali Sardar Jafri and others.

5. The Muslim communalists look towards all Muslim countries with a nostalgic sense. Their interest in the Muslim world is evident. For this very reason, they want India's intimate friendship with all Muslim countries, with Pakistan in particular.

The keynote of Muslim communalism may, therefore, be discovered in its determined bid to create a force as a counterblast to the force of the Hindus. Any idea of secularism, nationalism, democracy and modernisation is not appreciated by the Muslim communalists. At the base is the fear psychosis that creates in their minds a sense of insecurity and loss of faith in the leadership of genuine secularists. Such reiterations may be seen in the deliberations of Muslim Conventions held at Aligarh in 1953 and in New Delhi in 1961. Any issue like giving due place to Urdu language takes a communal turn. Even sane counsels of eminent Muslims like Maulana Azad, Dr. Zakir Hussain and Maulana Waheduddin Khan fail to have their impact. It all shows that the Muslim communalists, like their Hindu counterparts, miserably fail in understanding the voice of reason or realising the hard facts of life.

The various communal organisations play a nefarious part in fomenting tension or reacting to such things engineered by the opposite camp. It well illustrates that "their main burden can be discerned to be that of activating the Muslim community to the position of a pressure group so as the secure political and other special rights calculated to nurture and develop group identity as a separate entity for the Muslims in India."[47]

Sikh Communalism : The case of Sikh communalism has a peculiarity of its own. The Sikhs are a religion, a community, even a caste within the broad fold of Hinduism. That is, they have a separate identity of their own, even not. They have anti-Muslim postures in some and anti-Hindu posture in some other respects. However, they have full faith in the tenets of nationalism, though a microscopic section may be seen in having different designs—an element that may also be discovered in the ranks of the communalists belonging to other varieties discussed above. The reason of this lies in the peculiar conditions under which Sikhism came into being. According to a learned authority on this subject, the Sikhs "are the most outstanding example of Hindu renaissance produced by Islam—an edifice built as it were with Hindu bricks and Muslim mortar."[48]

The fact that the Sikhs claim themselves as a separate entity and believe in the sense of separatism becomes evident from their opposition to the idea of their assimilation into or integration with the Hindu community on the plea that it would amount to the loss of their identity. Khushwant Singh has given vent to such a fear over the relapsing back of the Sikhs into the fold of Hinduism and, with a word of caution, commented that if this process "continues at the present pace, within a short period of history (fifty years at the most) we may witness the remarkable phenomenon of a religious community, which achieved the semblance of nationhood, disappear in the quick-sands of Hinduism."[49]

Such an apprehension lurks in the minds of the diehard Akali elements. For instance, in 1955 Master Tara Singh said that the

47. G.S. Ghurye: *Social Tensions in India*, p. 429.

48. Khushwant Singh: *The Sikhs*, p. 29.

49. *Ibid.*, p. 180.

Punjab Congress and the Legislative Assembly of the State were dominated by the Hindus who wished to finish the Sikhs. He found its solution in the creation of a state of the Sikhs so that the Sikhs could have effective power and be assured of the means necessary to protect the gurdwaras. He declared: "The greater the interference in our religion by the government with its political power, the greater the need of the political power to protect our religion from this satanic interference."[50]

It is for this reason that the Sikh communalists have criticised laws relating to Gurdwara administration. In very harsh terms, Masterji criticised the Sikh Gurdwara (Amendment) Act of 1959 that liberalised provisions enabling the entry of even the non-Sikhs in the sphere of the administration of the Sikh temples and also increased the strength of the official nominees therein. In the wake of 1960, the Masterji and his group boldly charged that the then Congress government led by Pratap Singh Kairon aimed at setting up a Hindu Raj in the country and he demanded immediate formation of the Punjabi Suba.[51] So great was the effect of the reiterations of the Masterji that he and his faction secured overwhelming success in the elections to the Shiromani Gurdwara Prabandhak Committee.

The frankly anti-Hindu postures of the Sikh communalists led to the creation of their rift with the leaders of the Arya Samaj. The issue of Punjabi versus Hindi controversy dominated the scene. Thus, while the Sikh leaders insisted on the imposition of the Gurmukhi language at all levels in the State of Punjab, the Arya Samajists fought for the status of Hindi language. The management of the D.A.V. educational institutions took the matter to the judiciary and won as a result of the interpretations made by the Supreme Court. The Court invented the concept of 'regional minority' and on the plea held that Gurmukhi language could not be imposed on the Arya Samaj institutions which were a linguistic minority in the

---

50. *The Hindu* (Madras), August 14, 1955.

51. For instance, an Akali like Balbir Singh Mann then regretted: "India claims to be a secular state. At present Hindus are in majority in every state of the Union. The unilingual principle has been applied to all States except the Punjab. The Punjab is the only State where application of the unilingual principle may reduce Hindus to a minority community." *The Punjabi Suba Morcha*, p. 15.

State of Punjab.[52] The matter of dispute could be settled when the bifurcation of Punjab took place in 1966 as a result of which the Punjabi-speaking State of the Indian Union, and not at all a Sikh State, came into being.[53]

Obviously, the creation of Punjab as a unilingual State could satisfy the Akalis to some extent. It did not entail full satisfaction in view of the fact that the Akalis had to reinterpret their demand for Punjabi Suba so as to make it bereft of communal overtones. That is, they had to realise the hard facts of life and thereby modify their struggle so as to make it in line with the concept of nationalism and secularism as embodied in the provisions of the Constitution of India. Obviously; as said by a spokesman of the Sikh Youth Federation, such a switch over involving a change in the basic objectives, however is hard to believe, for the proposed State would have a Sikh majority.[54]

More than this, Sikh communalists have raised the demand for a constitutional recognition of the separate and distinct identity of their community. For this purpose, the extremist elements come forward with demand for amending Art. 25 in a way that a reference to the 'Hindus' is not to be construed as a reference to the Sikhs and for this purpose the term' Hindu religious institutions' does not cover the case of the religious institutions of the Sikhs. The moderate sections of the Sikh community do not agree with such a contention. However, keeping in view the tense situation of Punjab, the Centre expressed its willingness to concede this demand of the Akali Dal if the leaders of the party accepted the course of negotiations in an atmosphere of peace and goodwill for the solution of the tangle in which the State was caught up. Such political developments of Punjab have done damage to this impression that the Sikh community as a whole appreciates the values of secularism, nationalism, democracy and modernisation.

---

52. *D.A.V. College of Jalandhar v. The State of Punjab* (1971) 2 SCC 269.

53. Smith, *op. cit.*, p. 466. He further says that many Silks "See the creation of their own State as the only possible means of checking the forces which threaten to dissolve the distinctive unity of the *Panth.*" *Ibid.*, p. 450.

54. *Ibid.*, p. 450.

Christian Communalism : Basically different from Hindu, Muslim and Sikh communalism is the case of the Christian communalism. The Christians are a peace-loving people and believe in the propagation of their religion by peaceful means. However, they have faith in the principles of democracy and nationalism. It is evident from the fact that in the deliberations of the Round Table Conferences held at London (1930–32), eminent figures like Dr. S.K. Dutta and K.T. Paul opposed the system of separate electorates. Likewise, Dr. H.C. Mookerjee opposed the principle of communal representation in the Constituent Assembly.[55] The Christians appreciated the system of secularism as embodied in the Constitution that did not interfere with their right to propagate their religion and appreciated that in this regard, our fundamental law is based on the principle that "so long as religion is religion, conversion by free exercise of the conscience is to be recognised."[56]

It may, however, be pointed out that although the Constitution has guaranteed right to religion and also recognised right to propagate it by peaceful means, it does not mean that no restriction can be imposed on the activities of the religious missionaries. The Government of India placed restrictions on the role of Church missionaries when it was brought to its notice that they were involved in the work of proselytisation either forcibly or through fraud and temptation of monetary and other gains. The Government took the view that by converting illiterate aboriginals and other backward people, these agencies were offending the feelings of the non-Christians. It is for this reason that the Niyogi Committee appointed by the Government of Madhya Pradesh in April, 1954 attracted wide attention and the then Union Home Minister (Dr. K.N. Katju), while appreciating the philanthropic services of the Christian institutions, said that "if they come here for evangelistic work, then the sooner they stop, the better."[57] Likewise, Prime Minister Shastri took exception to the activities of the church

55. *Constituent Assembly Debates*, Vol. VIII, pp. 310–11.

56. D.N. Bannerjee: *Our Fundamental Rights*, p. 275.

57. See D.E. Smith, *op. cit.*, p. 201.

missionaries in the State of Nagaland as a result of which Bishop Scott had to leave the country in 1965.[58]

The Christians of India are a small minority and, for this reason, they are not interested in having a political party of their own. The National Christian Council of Bangalore is a body of the Protestant Christians that has frankly expressed its disapproval of such an idea. For instance, in a policy statement in 1956 it said: "In a country where communalism is the bane of politics, the Christian community should not organise itself as a Christian political party or association to fight for Christian interests in the State."[59] Similarly, the Roman Catholic Church has taken the view of having no political party of the Christians as such. However, the difference between the view of two Christian organisations may be discovered in the fact that the latter has not disharboured the idea of taking an indirect part in the politics of the country. The Roman Catholic Church has exercised influence over the voting behaviour of its members which is mostly visible in the State of Kerala. The Christians have, for this reason, opposed moves for the officialisation of their educational institutions in the name of interference with their management. The St. Xavier's Education Society of Ahmedabad won a case agianst the State of Gujarat in 1974. The Supreme Court has ruled that the State can not interfere in the management and administration of institutions run by the minorities.[60]

---

58. We may refer here to an incident that occurred in Raipur on the Independence Day in 1957. The organisers of a programme staged a scene depicting worship of a Hindu goddess at the stage. Since the place of holding the function was the Gass Memorial Centre, it was objected to by the Superintendent of the institution The result was sudden resentment that caused severe damage to the property of the Christian institution. The local newspaper *Mahakoshal* published inflammatory articles. But the Bhatt Commission set up by the Madhya Pradesh Government virtually 'exonerated' all. It could go to the extent of admitting the hand of 'some persons acting secretly that had incited the students'. However, the members of the Christian community found the report extremely disappointing as it had failed in fixing the responsibility and thereby clearing the way for punishment of the wrong doers. *Ibid*, p. 43.
59. See Smith. *op. cit.*, p. 436.
60. *Ahmedabad St. Xavier's College Society v. The State of Gujarat* (1974) 1 SCC. 717.

However, the Christians of India have expressed their resentment whenever the Government has tried to curtail their freedom of propagating their religion. Great uneasiness was roused among the Christian community by the Freedom of Religion Bill of 1978 moved by a member of the then ruling party (Janata) named O.P. Tyagi. The bill sought to make it a criminal offence punishable with imprisonment if religious conversion was done by means of force, fraud or inducement. All sections of the Indian Christians strongly opposed the Bill on the ground that it would interfere with their right to religion which also included right to propagate it. They argued that the philanthropic activities of Church institutions, which provided 20% of the hospital beds and running of many educational institutions in the country, would also be regarded as 'inducement' and thereby make them liable for punishment and that legislation to prevent forced conversion already existed in the Indian Penal Code. A mass protest demonstration was organised in Delhi on May 14, 1979 and then a delegation met the then Prime Minister (Desai) who assured that the controversial bill would be withdrawn, though the Government might bring another bill on more or less similar lines. This bill lapsed with the dissolution of Lok Sabha in 1979. The atrocities on the Christians and desecration of their churches in the States of Orissa and Gujarat have forced them to fight for the security of their religious places by peaceful means. But their opposition to prevention of religious conversion laws of a State and demand for reservations in public services are certainly sustained by communal considerations.

Critical Appreciation

From what we have said above, three broad varieties of communalism may be identified. First, there is the communalism of the majority community manifesting itself in the form of movement for Indianisation, *Bharatiyata, Hindutva*. It desires a common life-style or culture for all people of the country belonging to any community, caste, tribe, denomination and the like. In the view of its protagonists, Hinduism is not a religion, it is a civilisation, a culture of this country called Bharatvarsh or Aryavarta and, hence all people of this country must adopt the same way of life. Those who do not, they must do so. It may be labelled as 'assimilative communalism'. Second, there is the tendency on the part of some minority religious communities to define themselves as 'nations', not as 'communities' and even to go to the length of demanding a separate and sovereign 'homeland'. This should be designated as 'secessionist communalism'. However, in this variety, a sub-variety may also be noticed. The moderate elements demand not a separate and sovereign state but a fully autonomous province in the form of a separate administrative arrangement within the federal set up of the country. That is, they demand a semi-sovereign status of their desired political unit. Last, invoking religion as the source of social discrimination and economic disparity, special treatment is demanded from the state to uplift their socio-economic conditions by some religious collectivities which may be called 'welfarist communalism.' If and when the state or political parties respond favourably to these demands of deprived religious minorities, it is labelled as pseudo-secularism by the advocates of the assimilative communalism.[61]

It is, indeed, a matter of pity that the ghost of communalism is still haunting us despite the fact that the framers and pursuers of the pernicious policy of divide and rule have gone and a new generation has grown up which had not been exposed to the divisive influence of an alien government and which spent its younger days in the comparatively harmonious period between 1950 and 1960. But the matter of profound shock is that it is precisely this generation which is found in the forefront of communal disturbances. Prof. Rasheeduddin Khan has studied the case from a different standpoint. His view is that the process of nation-building in a widely fragmented and plural society passes through the phases of 'fission' and 'fusion' as a result of the conflict between democratic political institutions and modernised political system on the one hand and a pre-democratic social organisation and the traditional psychological environment on the other. Though in the short span, these phases of fission and fusion "appear as a negation of each other, yet in the

---

61. T.K. Oomen: "Types of Communalism:Value of Empowering Minorities" in *The Times of India*, New Delhi, 2 March, 1994, p.12. While we may appreciate the three-fold categorisation of communalism in India, we may not appreciate the view that communalism of the majority community is the most dangerous of all. Communalism of any hue is a curse which Ooman should take note of when he aggues: "That majority communalism is more dangerous is a correct empirical assertion,because it has tremendous striking power, the potentiality to become hegemonic and oppressive and ultimately authoritarian and fascist." *Ibid.*

complementarity and their alternating occurrence is intrinsic in the development of a plural polity towards its political integration."[62]

However, it should be borne in mind that the virus of political strife and intolerance stands as a far more serious challenge than the problem of Hindu-Muslim confrontation. The demolition of Babri Masjid on 6 December, 1992 by the Hindu fundamentalists and its consequences stand as its clear testimony. Communalism is just an offshoot of a bigger malady that is eating into the vitals of our national integration and political development. Politics looks like becoming more narrow-minded than the narrow-mindedness of communalism. It may be discerned in the fact that bitterness of the political rivalry is causing violence to such an extent that the ascerbity of communal, caste and language disputes pales into insignificance. Nothing but the bringing about of social and economic equality is called for so as to inaugurate, what Gandhiji said, "a non-violent democracy."[63]

Regionalism

Regionalism is a fairly widespread phenomenon of Indian politics. In spite of the political reorganisation of the country on the basis of linguistic consideration, we take note of this surprising fact that as more and more development programmes are carried out by the Central and State governments, regional disparities become more and more marked and they engender a sense of cumulative deprivations in the minds of the people of certain areas called 'regions'. In this way, regionalism becomes a quite significant subject of the politics of our country. Movements going on for the creation of a separate unit after cutting a part of the existing State or States drawing sustenance from the factor of language or socio-economic grievances, of a struggle for substituting existing arrangements like Regional Commitees by some more appropriate agencies in the form of Autonomous Development Councils for the betterment of the lot of the people living in a particular area, called 'region', therefore engage our attention in an empirical study of contemporary Indian

---

62. Khan: "Understanding India's Communal Politics" in *Mainstream* (New Delhi), March 1, 1969.

63. See Vira Michels Dean: *New Pattern of Democracy in India*, p. 205

64. S.R. Maheshwari: *State Governments in India*, p. 219.

politics. Thus, a region, "acquires an altogether new dimension in the state's spectrum of politics and government."[64]

Nature and Essential Implications : The term 'region' lends itself to a multiplicity of meanings, the only common thread which runs through them is a basic cultural assumption that it is relatively smaller in size than the area in the context of which it is used. It may mean a part of the district, a part of a state but more than a district, a State or even a zone. It also means a large tract of land, a more or less defined portion of the earth's surface specifically distinguished by certain natural features, climatic conditions, a spatial fauna or flora or the like; an administrative division of a city or district. The essential point is that a region is characterised, more than anything else, by a widely shared sentiment of 'togetherness' in the people, internalised from a wide variety of sources which might even include common prosperity, comraderie developed in a common struggle etc., and what is more a 'separateness' from others.

In other words, a region is marked by 'maximum homogeneity within' drawing sustenance from language, dialects, social composition, ethnicity, demographic complexion, geographical contiguity, cultural pattern, economic life, historical antecedents, political background and psychological make-up or recongnised consciousness of group identity.[65] By all means, such an interpretation of the meaning of the term 'region' covers within itself a broad spectrum which may be applied to any part of the world. However, while keeping our attention confined to the case of our own country, we may say that a region signifies a part of the existing State or States marked by distinct homogeneity in respect of language, culture and social and economic backwardness of the people. It is a different matter that the Planning Commission has taken different zones of the Indian Union (Eastern, Western, Southern and Central) as regions for the sake of its convenience.[66]

The concept of regionalism, therefore, draws sustenance from the factors of geography, topography, religion, language, culture, economic life, customs and mores, political traditions and shared historical experiences. Not one but several variables play their part in this direction. The factor of diversity makes the people of a

65. Rasheeduddin Khan: "The Regional Dimensions" in *Seminar*, New Delhi, No. 1164, April, 1973, p. 39.

66. *The Fourth Five Year Plan*, 1969, p. 398.

particular area or region distinct from other regions and the factor of 'disparity' inculcates in their minds a sense of social and economic injustice. The twin effect is that the people feeling bound by certain ties come out to fight for the sake of their 'regional cause' and their behaviour in this regard illustrates positive as well as negative dimensions of the case of regionalism. Thus, "diversity and disparity feed and sustain regionalism."[67]

The term 'regionalism' has its wider and narrower connotations. In the former sense, it covers the case of a movement directed against 'centralism'; in the latter sense, it refers to the attachment of the people with the interests of a local or topical singificance and in that respect it becomes analogous to localism or sectionalism. In a bid to define the term in a quite comprehensive sense, Hedwig Hintze says: "In a general way, regionalism may be defined as a counter-movement to any exaggerated or aggressive form of centralisation. It must not, however, be considered, solely from the viewpoint of political control or governmental administration. Regionalist problems arise only when there is a combination of two or more such factors as geographical isolation, independent historical traditionalism, racial, ethnic or religious peculiarities and local or economic class interests."[68]

If so, regionalism may be distinguished from certain related themes as nationalism, localism,sub-regionalism and the like in the following manner:

1. Regionalism is different from nationalism in the sense that while the latter desires subordination of sectional and regional loyalties to the wider loyalty to the nation, the former seeks to lay more emphasis on local loyalties even at the expense of national loyalties in certain cases. In this way, sectional interests may transcend national interests in the case of regionalism.

2. Regionalism also differs from sectionalism or localism. While the latter is based on some very narrow interest of a class or community, the former is based exclusively on certain ethnic or cultural factors like linguistic or traditional peculiarities which provide a basis for, what is often termed, a 'sub-nationality'.

---

67. Maheshwari, *op. cit.*, p. 186.

68. Hintze: "Regionalism" in E.A.R. Seligman (ed.): *Encyclopaedia of the Social Sciences*, Macmillan, New York, 1967, Vol. 7, p. 209.

3. Regionalism may also be distinguished from 'sub-regionalism', though one may well point out that the differentiation between the two may hardly be done in a precise manner and that too in the context of contemporary Indian politics. However, with a view to differentiate the two, at least on a theoretical plane,we may say that a sub-region refers to a small area within a region which for certain factors of its own is aware of possessing a distinct identity. Thus, the Telangana movement, being a part of the Telugu-speaking region of Andhra Pradesh, constitutes the case of sub-regionalism.

However, a study of regionalism in the context of Indian politics should be made with certain important points in mind. First, regionalism in our country is, to a very large extent, linguistically bound.[69] As such, in most of the cases, regional boundaries are those of major languages. The result is that a struggle for the redressal of economic grievances in a part of a State, as happened in the area of Telangana, leads to the issue of 'sub-regionalism' and thereby makes the whole case of regionalism a complicated affair. The movement of sub-regionalism sometimes gives birth to some political parties or pressure groups like Telegana Praja (Rashtriya) Samiti which show parochialism in their affiliations than the State-wide parties. Second, regionalism in Indian politics should not be treated as an evil. It has its constructive aspects as well, so far as it has its reconciliation with the task of nation-building. It was well endorsed by the States Reorganisation Commission in 1955 that national loyalties do not demand that other loyalties should be eliminated.[70] Above all, India being a country with great diversity, in several respects, has witnessed the rise of regionalism in some of her parts in a way that it has assumed the shape of infra-nationalism that sometimes touches the verge of secessionism. The case of the north-eastern region of the country may be refered to in this connection.[71]

Salient Characteristics and Supporting Factors : Regionalism is a world-wide phenomenon. We sometimes hear about

69. W.H. Morris-Jones : "Language and Region Within the Indian Union" in Philip Mason (ed.): *India and Ceylon: Unity in Diversity*, pp. 51-66.

70. *Third Five Year Plan*, 1964. p. 151.

71. See J.C. Johari: "Creation of Nagaland: Triumph of Ebullient Infra-Nationalism" in *Indian Journal of Political Science*, Vol. XXXVI, No. 1, 1975, pp. 13-38.

the agitation of the Scots in the United Kingdom, the Kurds in Iraq, the Karens in Myanmar, the French in the Quebec province of Canada, the Tamils in Sri Lanka, the Baluchis and Pashtus in Pakistan and the like. The reason of this should be traced in the dissatisfaction of the people in minority with the behaviour of those in majority. That is, regionalism becomes the voice of the people in minority who desire to redress their grievances, mainly social and econimic. Sometimes, their movement assumes a formidable form and forces the rulers to suppress it by force in the name of being an anti-national activity.

We may, however, point out the salient charctierstics of the politics of regionalism in our country and also examine the factors that play a very important role in their generation. These may be reckoned as under:

1. Regionalism in India is an essential product of her diversity. Ours is a big country having diversity on a massive scale. The people of our country speak different languages, have different ways of life, observe different social customs and, above all, are in varying stages of social and economic development. Not only this, even after the political re-organisation of the country on linguistic ground we find that the people of one part of the State have a sense of separateness from those living in another part of the same State. Thus, agitations or movements for the cause of a regional interest take place. A Vidarbha or a Marathwada in Maharashtra, a Saurashtra in Gujarat, a Bundelkhand in Uttar Pradesh, a Darjeeling in West Bengal, a Ladakh in Jammu-Kasmir etc. may be referred to in this connection.

2. Linguistic attachment may be treated as another important factor in this regard. Though the ruling party (Indian National Congress) appreciated the key recommendation of the Dar Commission in 1948 against creating units of the Indian Union on the basis of linguistic consideration, Nehru, Patel and Pattabhi did endorse a shy case of a Telugu-speaking State in this regard. The result was fierce agitation in the then State of Madras and due to that occurred the creation of Andhra Pradesh in 1953. It vitually opened the way for the political reorganisation of the country as a whole on linguistic ground.

3. Another reason should be discovered in the fact of economic injustice. When the people of one part of a State thrive and

others suffer, a sense of dissatisfaction naturally develops. Thus, the people of Telangana resented the misuse of their surplus funds. It was for the sake of protecting the economic interests of the Maharashtrians that Shiv Sena created a stir against the non-Maharashtrians in the State of Maharashtra and the agitators of All-Assam Students Union and All-Assam Gana Sangram Parishad did the same in Assam. The implementation of the doctrine of protecting the interests of the 'sons of the soil' thus becomes an integral part of the politics of regionalism.

4. The factor of social injustice is naturally allied with the above point. The fact of social backwardness, coupled with that of economic degradation, inculcates in the minds of the suffering people a sense of struggle for the cause of their own area or region. Thus, the tribals of the southern parts of Bihar cried for Jharkhand State and got it. The people of Meghalaya fought for such a cause and ultimately got a separate State of their own.

5. Above all, there is the political factor. We may take note of the fact that some local or regional leaders fight for a sectional interest with a long-range view of their own interests. Sometimes, it appears to them that they might be having a better and superior position in the political hierarchy if they have a State of their own choice. A minority in a particular State may become a majority in a State of its own choice. Hence, an agitation for a Bodoland in the State of Assam.

What has really contributed to the politics of regionalism in our country is the existence of a democratic and federal system which inspires interested people to fight for their local, sectional or regional interests. The party system of the country is also affected by the currents of regionalism. All major national and secular organisations of the country have to do hobnobbing with regional and sub-regional, even communal and parochial forces. The result is a multi-way traffic that either leads to the further alteration of the political map of the country or the suppression of an agitation by force in the overall interest of the nation. In short, cultural diversity, economic and social disparity and, above all, federal democratic polity feed and sustain the politics of regionalism in our country.

Regionalism and Constitutional Recognition : It is true that the Constitution of India nowhere uses the term 'region' or 'regionalism' like the Charter of the United Nations; it also does not eliminate the case of regionalism as well. A careful study of Art. 3 in this direction has an importance of its own. By virtue of this provision, the Centre may create a new State, or change the name or boundary lines of an existing State. It shows that the power of political reorganisation of the country for the sake of some regional consideration lies with the Centre. Though it has been given that the President will seek the opinion of the going-to-be affected State before giving his recommendation to introduce a bill in this regard in the Parliament, it is also given that the Government of India is not bound by the opinion thus elicited. Thus, the power relating to the reorganisation of the units of the Indian Union lies with the Centre.

However, the fact of constitutional recognition of the case of regionalism came into limelight not in 1953 when the State of Andhra was created as in 1956 when the seventh constitutional amendment in the form of States Reorganisation Act came into force. It devised a novel scheme of zonal councils with the result that the newly created units of the Indian Union were regrouped into five zones—Eastern, Western, Northern, Southern and Central. As already pointed out, the Planning Commission took these zones as 'regions' just for the sake of its convenience.

What is really significant in this direction is the establishment of Regional Committees in the States of Punjab and Andhra Pradesh in 1957 and 1958 respectively vide Presidential orders issued under Art. 371 of the Constitution. These attempts were designed to protect the special interests of the regions in the two States by enabling their represntatives in the State legislatures (organised in the form of regional committees) to advise the legislative and executive departments of their State for taking administrative and statutory actions in regard to a number of 'scheduled subjects'. The whole purpose of this arragement was to concede a certain measure of autonomy to the regions in the economic, social and cultural spheres without crating a sub-federation in these two States of the Indian Union.

The Regional Committees for the Hindi and Punjabi-speaking areas in the State of Punjab were intended to transfer autonomy in socio-economic spheres and thereby act as a safeguard against separatism. The two committees consisted of Hindi-speaking and Punjabi-speaking areas. The Chief Minister, the Speaker and members of the Legislative Council were excluded from these bodies. The ministers could take part in the proceedings, but they could vote only in the committee of which they were members. Each regional committee had its own chairman and deputy chairman. The main functions of these committees were: (*i*) to consider bills other than money bills which contained provisions dealing with 'Scheduled matters', (*ii*) to consider and pass resolutions recommending to the State government any legislative or executive action affecting the regions concerned in respect of any the 'scheduled matters'[72]

Likewise, the Regional Committee of Andhra Pradesh (called Telangana Regional Committee) consisted of all legislators belonging to the region of Telangana. It, however, did not include the Speaker, the Chief Minister and the members of sthe Legislative Council. Its functions were the same as we have seen in the case of Regional Committes of Punjab.

The staus of these committees was purely of an advisory type. That is, they were more or less like Scottish Grand Committee of the House of Commons. They could have their meetings in camera and keep their deliberations and resolutions secret until the legislative and executive departments of the state could take any action in that regard. It was expected that their recommendations would normally be accepted by the State, the matter would go to the Governor whose decision would be final. It is by virtue of this arrangement that the Governor could discharge his 'special responsibilities'.

The experiment of regional committees, however, could not make success to the desired extent. The regional committees could not meet the purpose for which they were intended. Suspicions about their effectiveness in protecting and promoting the cause of the 'region' persisted. A sort of tug-of-war between the regional committees on the one hand and the Legislative Assembly and the Council of Ministers on the other continued. The leaders of the regional committees also tried to complicate the matters so that the people, in general, could be provoked to fight for the cause of a

72. The 'scheduled mattters' were : local self-government, public health and sanitation, hospitals and dispensaries, primary and secondary education, agriculture, protection and improvement of livestock, prevention of cattle trespass, veterinary training and protection of wild life, fisheries, cottage and small-scale industries, markets and fair, inns and inn-keepers, co-operative societies, religious institutions and charitable endowments and development and economic planning.

full-fledged State of their own. Thus, happened the bifurcation of Punjab in 1966 and with it the regional committees came to an end. The Telangana Regional Committee had the same fate in 1974. In this way, the experiment of sub-federalism failed to have a fair trial.

Linguistic Regionalism : As already pointed out. regionalism in Indial has four main dimensions—linguistic, socio-economic, cultural-communal and tribal-communitarian. In the first place, let us examine the role of language in the politics of regionalism. We have seen that the Indian National Congress had accepted the principle of linguistic reorganisation of the country in the 1920's. Naturally, a demand in this regard gained momentum when India came on the threshold of independence. The Constituent Assembly desired to obtain an expert opinion on this important matter. Thus, the Dar Commission was appointed in 1948. Justice Dar in his report rejected the idea of political reorganisation of the country along linguistic lines on the plea that it would do immense harm to national unity. And yet politics dominated. The JVP Committee (consisting of Jawharlal Nehru, Sardar Patel, and Pattabhi Sitaramayya) endorsed in 1949 the case of a Telugu-speaking State.

While the JVP Report was accepted by many important leaders of various organisations, the Telugu-speaking people living in the then State of Madras failed to resist their resentment. The inference of the JVP Report provided than an irresistible invitation to bend their energies to closing the mind of the leaders in the right direction.[73] Prime Minister Nehru suggested the course of patient discussion so that any decision taken in regard to the bifurcation of any unit of the Indian Union should be done by the wishes of the people concerned.

Unfortunately, the sane advice of Nehru could not be properly appreciated by the impatient people demanding nothing short of a separate Telugu-speaking State at the earliest possible moment. What, however, worsened the case was the exploitation of the situation by the Communists and the demand of the Telugu-speaking people for the merger of the 'B' class state of Hyderabad with their desired Andhra State. A veteran Congress leader like Swami Sitaram started a series of organised popular campaigns to pressurise the Government of India

73. W.H. Morris-Jones: *The Government and Politics of India,* Ed. III, p. 96.

on the basis of Nehru's assurances regarding the creation of Andhra State as early as possible. He started his fast from August 16, 1952 and broke it after 35 days at the intervention of Acharya Vinoba Bhave. When nothing could happen to the satisfaction of the Telugu-speaking people, Poti Sriramulu started his fast unto death. Unfortunately, he died after 56 days of fasting on December 15, 1952. Then, the Parliament passed the bill whereby Andhra State was created on October 1, 1953 with its capital at Kurnool.

In order to solve this gigantic problem, the Government of India appointed States Reorganisation Commission under the chairmanship of Justice Fazl Ali (with K.M. Panikkar and H.N. Kunzru as members) to re-examine the question of linguistic reorganisation of the Indian States while bearing in mind "consideration of national security, need to preserve and enhance national unity, viability of the units and welfare of the people, including linguistic minorities." The Government of India accepted the recommendations of this Commission with certain modifications as a result of which 14 States and 5 Union Territories came into being in 1956.

Though the political reorganisation of the country took place on linguistic ground, the problem remained unsolved. It had its first formidable manifestation in the bilingual State of Bombay. The Gujarat Maha Sabha started agitation for a Gujarati-speaking State, while the Sampooran Maharashtra Samiti desired the retention of Bombay as a bilingual State. Tension reached a point that Centre had to agree to the bifurcation of this State in 1960. Thus, the Gujarati-speaking people got a State of their own. Similar trend developed in the State of Punjab. The extremist sections of the Akali Dal intensified the situation to an extent that the State was bifurcated in 1966. Thus, Haryana State of the Hindi-speaking people came into being.

The linguistic reorganisation of the States, despite being the best arrangement under the obtaining conditions, is said to have been fraught with great danger. A study of regionalism in this regard poses an important question whether it has succeeded in forging a sense of integration among the reorganised units or it has given a fillip to the phenomenon of sub-nationalism.[74] It is said that it has unnecessarily entailed a radical recasting of the units of our federal

74. See Iqbal Narain : *State Politics in India*, Edition II of 1976, p. xxii

system and produced a situation as "if bones are broken for the simple fun of resetting them again."[75] When the situation in this regard deteriorated in various parts of the country, Prime Minister Nehru had to say in a speech at Gokak: "Remember we are parts of one body. If a single finger is hurt, the pain affects the whole body. India is the body and the States are its limbs."[76] Recent developments have revealed the fact that the effect of the territorial reorganisation of the country on linguistic lines has given a more intensely regional character to politics and made the States a much more important lever of power.[77]

Protective Regionalism : What really gives a sharpening edge to the politics of regionalism is the prevalence of social and economic injustice. A study of the politics of regionalism in our country, therefore , informs us to look into the agitations for the sake of redressal of social and economic injustice even by militant and violent means. The role of Shiva Sena (SS) in Maharashtra, of Telangana Praja Samiti (now Telangana Rashtriya Samiti) in Andhra Pradesh and All-Assam Students Union (AASU) and of All-Assam Gana Sangram Parishad (AAGSP) in Assam may be referred to in this connection. Here we may find abundant material showing the rise and growth of populist movements in the country, or 'parochialism run mad' and the exploitation of genuine social and economic grievances of the people by a "combination of local chauvinism, demogoguery, good organisation and strong-arm tactics."[78]

The Shiva Sena created a massive stir in Maharashtra in 1967 and 1968 by organising demonstrations, *bandhs*, strikes, picketing, riots and the like. Its main target was the community of non-Maharashtrians particularly the South Indians whom the followers of Thackeray contemptuously called 'loongiwallahs'. In a rounded reference, 'Kapilacharya' said: "We are opposed to those who come here specifically to amass wealth by fair or foul means and transfer the benefit of the riches to their own provinces." In March 1968, it

---

75. Krishna Kodesia, *The Problem of Linguistic States in India*, p. 32.

76. *Ibid*, p. 38.

77. Hugh Tinker : *India and Pakistan*, p. 137.

78. *Daily Telegraph* (London), June, 6, 1968.

captured 53 out of 135 seats in the Greater Bombay Municipal Corporation. The Shiva Sena that was once like a militant pressure group thriving on the support of 'rightist organisations like the Swatantra party became a political party in due course. It could, however , not make much headway as the victory of the Congress party in the Lok Sabha elections of March,1971 gave a shattering blow to its hold and which gave a more serious blow to it in the State Assembly elections in the following year. Thus, the pernicious trend set by this fascist organisation to destroy the cosmopolitan character of Bombay and giving a bold indication of the misdirected angle of regionalism could be effectively checked.

Another example of protective regionalism in India should be seen in the Telangana Movement that broke out in 1968 and captured the attention of the people for a period of about next four years. While the formation of the State of Andhra in 1953 marked the victory of the Telugu-speaking people who could now fell riddance from the fear of any possible exploitation at the hands of advanced Tamilians of the erstwhile. Madras State, in due course certain misgivings developed in the minds of the relatively backward Telanganaites about the possibility of their fresh exploitation at the hands of advanced Andhraites. Recognition given to the residential qualifications or Mulki Rules by the Government of India in 1957 and the establishment of a Regional Committee (as we have seen above) failed to allay the fears because of the considerations that various vested interests developed in the struggle for a separate State of their own.[79]

The struggle for the cause of Telangana State witnessed a clash between the separationists on the one hand hailing mainly from the Telangana region and the integrationists on the other. In order to strengthen their claim, the separationists accused the Regional Committee of doing nothing to protect their legitimate interests. The issue of the misuse of 'Telangana Surpluses' was exploited. It

79. The Mulki Rules owed their origin to a *firman* issued by the Nizam of Hyderabad in 1919 that laid down the rule of a mulki on four grounds—birth, domicile, descent and marriage. Only the domiciliatory qualification survived, for other grounds were taken as *ultra vires* of the Constitution. Thus, a *mulki* was one who had taken up his residence in the Telangana area for 15 years and given an affidavit that he had abandoned the idea of returning to his native place.

was also contended that the Andhraites had not properly honoured the condition of gentlemen's agreement whereby it was stipulated that revenues of the State government would be divided between Andhra and Telangana in a ratio of 2 to 1. The Wanchoo Commission set up in April, 1969 to settle the tangled issue somehow could suggest only this much that all appointments to the local government offices should be made by the head of each office in every district.

What sparked the problem was the invalidation of the mulki rules by the Supreme Court in 1969 on the ground of being discriminatory. Thus, the movement took a serious turn. In April, 1969 all ministers belonging to the Telangana region banking on the support of K.V. Ranga Reddy tendered their resignations and demanded the exit of Chief Minister Brahmanand Reddy—a non-Telanganaite. The problem could be sorted out with the intervention of Prime Minister Mrs. Indira Gandhi when a Telanganaite (Narsimha Rao) was appointed as the Deputy Chief Minister. It entailed peace for the time being , though skirmishes continued.

Under these circumstances, Prime Minister Mrs. Gandhi offered her six-point formula envisaging that the mulki rules would go in a phased manner by 1980, Telangana Regional Committee would be disbanded, local candidates would be given preference for direct recruitment to non-gazetted posts, a high-power Tribunal would be set up to deal with grievances of the Telanganaites relating to public services, a State-level Planning Board would be set up to deal with the problem of backward areas, a new Central University would be established at Hyderabad to augment existing educational facilities and preference would be given to local candidates for admission to educational institutions, and, finally the Constitution would be amended for this purpose. Thus, the 33rd Constitution Amendment Act came into being in 1973 that solved the problem and entailed end of the agitation for Telangana. But the Telangana Rashtriya Samiti has revived it.

The problem of protective regionalism in the State of Andhra Pradesh could be solved by the timely action of the Government of India. Different is the case of Assam where such a movement erupted towards the end of 1979. The coalition government headed by Chaudhry Charan Singh failed to take a timely action with the result that the political situation in Assam deteriorated more and more. The indications of this movement hinging on the detection and deportation of all 'foreigners' from the State of Assam were available when Chief Minister J.Hazarika said that his government "will never compromise on the issue of the deportation of foreign nationals."[80] Then, in a memorandum submitted to the Central Election Committee, Manihar (General Secretary of the State's People's Party) sought deletion of the names of all immigrant voters from the electoral rolls.[81]

Whereas the Shiva Sena fought for the interests of Maharashtrians and directed its movement mainly against the 'South Indians' and the people of Telangana struggled for the interests of the people of their own area and for this sake directed their fight against the Andhraites, the agitators of Assam did the same for protecting their legitimate interests and found their foes in the community of the 'foreigners', mainly Bengalis, whether Hindus or Muslims, who came from West Bengal or from East Pakistan now Bangladesh. It was just for the sake of giving a soft form to their demands that they often clamoured from their house-tops that their movement was not directed against Indian nationals coming from other parts of the country and that their sole purpose was to guard 'Assamese culture.'

The violent activities of arson, loot, riots, forceful picketing, sabotage, traffic blockade and the like did a lot of harm to the community of the 'foreigners', particularly the Bengali-speaking people. It was owing to this that retaliation from the side of the Bengalis living in Assam as well as in the adjoining State of West Bengal added to the stock of complications. It was, however, a wrong impression that this movement was being backed by the upper-caste Hindus, though one could rightly hit at the hidden hand of certain hostile foreign elements. Thus, a counter-movement from the side of the minorities started gathering weight which made the matters more complicated. Fortunately, the good sense prevailed and the problem could be solved in a peaceful manner by the strenuous efforts of the regional and national leaders as earlier happened in the case of Telangana movement.

Communal Regionalism : The case of communal regionalism in Punjab finds place in the role of the Shromani Akali Dal—a political-religious organisation of the Sikhs having its headquaters at Amritsar'-

80. *The Hindustan Times* (New Delhi), October, 20, 1979.

81. *The Statesman* (New Delhi), October, 2, 1979.

the Mecca of the Sikhs'—for the cause of achieving a 'sikh homeland' called 'Punjabi Suba.'[82] For our purpose, the peculiar thing in this connection is not a struggle for a State based on a distinct language as we saw in the movement for a Gujarati-speaking State in the bilingual State of Bombay or prior to that in the struggle for carving a Telugu-speaking State out of the then State of Madras, but an attempt to have a state of the people of a particular community who no doubt speak the same language. Thus, communal factor dominated the factor of language. It is by all means a fact that the Akali Dal's main objective is the protection of the *Panth* that lies in protecting the rights of the Sikhs and ensuring their continued existence as an independent entity.[83] Hence, in a study of regionalism at this stage, this paramount fact should be borne in mind that though the Sikhs were quick to fasten their resentment on the language issue, the Akali Dal espoused the cause of the Sikh community and the demand for Punjabi Suba was, in fact, one of Sikh State ; language was only a sugar-coating.[84]

Ever since Master Tara Singh lost his case in his dialogue with the Cabinet Mission in 1946 (when he had raised the demand for independent Sikhistan in retaliation to the demand of the Muslim League for Pakistan), the Akali Dal desired a State of the Sikhs without making it above board whether it should be a sovereign entity or a unit of the Indian Union, though on most of the occasions the demand for 'Punjabi Suba' was given the latter interpretation. Since the Congress party was in a very weak position in running the government owing to intra-group rivalries,it had to bank upon the support of the Akali Dal. Thus, the Akalis managed to secure several concessions in the form of 'service formula'(providing for proportion in public services), 'Parity formula'(providing for proportionate representation in the ministry) and, above all, 'Sachar formula' providing for the eventual division of Punjab into Punjabi and Hindi-speaking regions.

The Akali Dal fought the first general election in 1952 on the clear issue of having a Punjabi-speaking State within the Indian Union. However, the Congress secured victory and with the installation of Pratap Singh Kairon as the Chief Minister in 1954,

82. See B.R. Nayyar : "Punjab" in Myron Weiner (ed.) : *State Politics in India,* p. 488.

83. Khushwant Singh : *A History of the Sikhs,* Vol. 2, p. 294

84. *Ibid,* p. 295

the movement of the Akalis could be suppressed. The Akali Dal presented its case to the States Reorganisation Commission in the form of the demand for a Greater Punjab which was not accepted. Thus, Masterji characterised the SRC Report in relation to Punjab as a bilingual State as 'a decree of annihilation' and sought to launch the movement with greater vigour.[85] The strong hands of Kairon frustrated their all efforts. Meanwhile, Sant Fateh Singh emerged on the scene who gave a soft complexion to the struggle for Punjabi Suba by defining it in very clear terms as a State within the Indian Union of the Punjabi-speaking people. His group captured the Shri Gurdwara Parbandhak Samiti in the elections of January, 1965.

The Akalis managed to have an upper hand after the death of Nehru in 1964 which also entailed the fall of Kairon in Punjab after the Das Commission had passed strictures against him. Sant Fateh Singh threatened to immolate himself in the Golden Temple of Amritsar in case the Government of India did not concede his demand for a Punjabi Suba after 15 days of fasting beginning from September 10, 1965. However, he postponed the idea in view of the Indo-Pak war. When the war was over, Prime Minister Shastri took a realistic view and he appointed a committee of three ministers (Indira Gandhi, Y.B. Chavan and Mahavir Tyagi) to consider the issue in all of its perspectives. Moreover, a Parliamentary Committee of 22 members was also set up under the chairmanship of the then Speaker (Sardar Hukam Singh) to tender assistance to the committee of three ministers.

The Congress High Command also studied this problem. It set up a committee of three leaders (K. Kamaraj, U.N. Dhebar and Gulzarilal Nanda) to deal with the opposition of those Congressmen who wanted to keep Punjab united. On March 9, 1966, the Congress Committee recommended the formation of a Punjabi-speaking State. The Parliamentary Committee also recommended the creation of a unilingual State, the hill areas to be merged with the then Union Territory of Himachal Pradesh in view of the factor of linguistic and cultural affinity and the remaining Hindi-speaking areas of Punjab to be formed as a separate State of Haryana. The Government of India accepted in principle these recommendations. Thereupon, a commission under Justice J.C Shah was set up (with Subimal Dutt and M.M. Philip as the members) to demarcate the

85. See Ajit Singh Sarhadi: *Punjabi Suba*, p. 255.

boundary lines. The Commission did its job in time. As a result of this, the Parliament passed the Punjab Reorganisation Bill in August, 1966. It received Presidential assent and thus the Punjabi-speaking State or 'Punjabi Suba' came into being on November 1, 1966. In this way, the Akali Dal got a predominantly Punjabi-speaking State of its own for the satisfaction of the members of its community.

In 1981 Akali extremism resurfaced itself with a call for the acceptance of its demands contained in the Anandpur Saheb resolution of 1973. As subsequently modified, this important and comprehensive resolution incorporated demands, some of which were astounding as drastic devolution of power in favour of the States amounting to their full autonomy, inclusion of all Punjabi-speaking areas in the State of Punjab, giving away of Chandigarh to Punjab, representation to the Sikhs in all public and defence services according to their numerical strength so as to undo long injustice to them, imposition of ban on smoking in all public places in Punjab, enactment of an All-India Gurdwara Act, abrogation of Mrs. Gandhi's award on the water of Ravi and Beas, *kirpan* to become an integral part of the Sikh soldiers, a foreign policy of good relations with all States where Sikhs are settled or their shrines are situated, abolition of capitalism by eradicating concentration of wealth in few hands, ceiling of 30 standard acres of land for each family, free movement of food stuffs throughout the country, removal of regional economic imbalance, and recognition of distinct and independent identity of the Sikh community.

Though the resolution was passed in October, 1973, it came into lime-light in 1983 when the extremist elements of the Akali Dal resorted to the use of terroristic methods. Assassinations of the leaders critical of these demands became a routine matter. Appreciation of these activities by some elements living abroad gave an indication of support to this movement from some 'foreign' powers through Jagjit Singh Chauhan settled in the United States and Ganga Singh Dhillon in England.

In early June, 1984 military action had to be taken as a result of which, according to the White Paper of the Government of India, 493 persons were killed and 86 injured inside the Golden Temple. Gradually the situation improved. In 1985 Prime Minister Rajiv Gandhi signed an accord with Sant Longowal. But the policy of the Government of India succeeded in suppressing and flushing out the terrorists in the 'Operation Black Thunder' in 1998. Situation returned to normalcy and a popular government could be installed in Punjab in 1992.

But the case of Kashmir is different. Here the movement of the Kashmiris may be seen channelled in three directions. First, the sane and moderate elements appreciate the fact of Kashmir's accession to India and want to operate within the framework of the Constitution of their own state and of the Constitution of India, though they desire some effective dose of autonomy. Second, the soft-core extremists have reservations on the issue of accession, but they like to strike a compromise on the issue of 'autonomy' implying semi-independent status of this State. It may be a stop-gap arrangement for them so as to unleash second instalment of agitation in the direction of complete independence after some time. But the hard-core elements openly refute the fact of accession and declare their aim of creating a sovereign state of their own by means of violence.

In the case of Kashmir, politics of regionalism has taken most dangerous form by touching the verge of secessionism. The demand for 'autonomy' of the State may be understandable, but the agitating elements should also make it clear as to what they really mean by it. If it means granting of some more powers, as available to the States of the United States or to the Cantons of Switzerland, matters may be sorted out across the table. But if it means delegation of powers to the extent of making them fully independent, it cannot be accepted. What has made the whole matter so delicate and dangerous is the way of *ad hocism* adopted by the Government of India.

The destructive politics of regionalism could have its end in Punjab for the reason that it was not appreciated by the majority of the people, including sane and moderate elements of the Sikhs, coupled with Government's clear-cut policy of suppression of such elements. In Kashmir the case is much different. Here the Hindu-majority areas of Jammu and the Buddhist-majority areas of Ladakh are peaceful. The Muslim-majority areas of Kashmir are the trouble spots due to the activities of the fundamentalists and the terrorists, banking on the support of Pakistan. The saner elements of the Muslim populace have been over-awed by the militants, though they may be waiting for the opportune time to reveal their real inclinations.

Tribal and Communitarian Regionalism : The politics of regionalism in the case of Punjab and Kashmir blended itself with communalism and went to the last extent of coverging itself with secessionism. Communalism is an evil in itself in as much as it creates divisive tendencies and inspires its protagonists to adopt anti-national postures. Thus, the militant Akalis of Pubjab and a number of such outfits in Kashmir, inspired by the tenets of religious fundamentalism, no longer kept themselves away from indulging in anti-national activities.[86] The term 'communitarian regionalism' has different implications. The sentiment of communitarianism does not create sharp divisions in the society as the sentiment of communalism does, nor does it inspire its protagonists to indulge in brazenly anti-national activities. The agitators may adopt some tactics of the terrorists in a mood of frenzy, but the interest of the country as a whole, sooner or later, haunts their minds. So, such elements may be designated as 'insurgents' who stop their movement when their demands are satisfied or when the voice of reason prevails. They never think in terms of having a separate and sovereign state of their own, though their agitation for 'autonomy' may signify their demand for having a State of their own like other States of the Indian Union. The movements for Jharkhand and Uttarakhand may be referred to in this direction.

During the period of our freedom struggle the two major tribal movements—the Birsa Movement (1895-1900) and Tana Bhagat Movement (1914 onwards)-occurred. Both the Birsa Movement of the Mundas in the Ranchi district and the Tana Bhagat Movement of the Oraons in the western part of Chhotanagpur were directed

---

86. We may differentiate the cases of Punjab and Kashmir on this important ground as well that while in the former the militants were organised as a single force, in the latter there are several outfits having no unity among themselves. The names of Jammu-Kashmir Liberation Front, Hizbul Mujahideen, Al-Umar, Ilkhwanul Musalmeen, Al-burg, Mulsim Mujahideen, Tehrik-ul Mujahideen, Al-Jihad and Al-Faran may be referred to. Often the incidents of group clashes occur and mutual accusations and denunciations may also be taken note of. The militants of one group may go to the extent of killing or abducting men of other groups. The All-Party Hurriyat Conference has failed to create a united front of all such militant outfits.

against the oppressions of the British government and the local landlords. No doubt, the Birsa Movement had an anti-British edge, but the Munda Movement was not so in its real character. The Mundas did not fight for any nation-hood. In fact, at their stage of historical development, they were not aware of such a concept. But the anti-British content of the movement found an echo in the Tana Bhagat Movement led by Jatra Bhat. They were called 'Tana' meaning to pull together and Jatra tried to pull all tribals (Oraons) together. The subsequent Indian freedom movement and the Jharkhand movement were inspired by the Birsa Movement, the former stressing its anti-British content and the latter its exclusiveness. Right from its inception, the Jharkhand movement was primarily concerned with a separate administrative unit of the tribals that assumed the form of demand for a separate autonomous province under the leadership of Jaipal Singh Munda, respectfully addressed as the 'Father' of the movement, and M. Horo popularly regarded as the 'grand old man' of the movement.

Like other sub-regional and sub-nationalist movements going on in other parts of the country, the Jharkhand movement stood for the creation of a separate state of the tribals living in the areas of Bihar, Orissa, Madhya Pradesh and West Bengal. The curious development was that the tribals had been able to win the support of the non-tribals of this region for the sake of realising their cherished dream of a separate autonomous State within the Indian Union.

The history of the Jharkhand movement is quite old. The Christian missionaries did a lot of work to organise the tribals and inculcate in them a kind of political consciousness as a result of which their organisations came into being as the Tribal Christian Students Union in 1911, the Chhotanagpur Unnat Samaj in 1928 and Chhotanagpur Catholic Sabha in 1930. These were amalgamated as a result of which the Chhotanagpur Adivasi Mahasabha came into being in 1938. Ignes Beck played a very important role in the making of this greater body. After 1940 when the Muslim League raised the demand for a separate and sovereign state of the Muslims, the leaders of all such Christian-dominated organisations also raised their claim for a separate and sovereign state of the Christians. However, after independence, the leaders of these tribal organisations changed their stand and they thought in terms of having a province of their own with the name of Jharkhand.[87] The Adivasi Mahasabha became the Jharkhand Party in 1950 with anti-Congress orientation.

But the disgruntled elements of the Jharkhand Party launched a new body called All-India Jharkhand Party under N.E. Horo in the Chhotanagpur division, and a dissident wing floated its own outfit called Hul Jharkhand under Bagun Smbrui with a promise to adopt some 'radical methods to fulfil its demand" of a separate State for the tribals as well as non-tribals who thought it expedient to join hands with the former on account of the compulsion of living in this area. As a result of this, the tribals also gave up their opposition to be ruled by those non-tribals whom they resentfully called the 'Dikus'(aliens). But both the wings of the Jharkhand failed to make any noticeable success in the elections. In 1973 the leftist and militant elements formed Jharkhand Mukti Morcha under the leadership of Sibu Soren who exhorted his followers to forcibly harvest the crops on land which the tribals had lost to landlords and money-lenders. In no time he became the hero of tribals with the revered appellation of Sing Bonga or 'Guruji' by virtue of advocating strong-arm tactics and extra-legal methods. In the elections of 1990 the Jharkhand Mukti Morcha could capture 19 seats in the Bihar Legislative Assembly.

In view of the fast deteriorating situation in this part of the country, the Central government decided to form an Autonomous Council for the region on the pattern of the Gorkhaland Hill Development Council of Darjeeling. It was passed by the Bihar Legislature and then sent to the Centre for its approval. Under the terms of this arrangement the Council could prepare its own annual budget and the State government could provide funds for development. The Council could prepare long-term and short-term plans to be incorporated into the State plans. It could plan and monitor development schemes for agriculture, animal husbandry, forest (excluding the right of settlement), minor irrigation, public health, tourism and trade, urban and rural roads, water supply,

---

87. The word '*Jhar*' literally means thick and thorny bush and the word '*khand* means the tract of land. Since the tribals live in such a tract, they called it '*Jharakhand*' implying a place quilted with very thick cluster of bushes and woods. The Church leaders in the initial phase had thought in terms of having a Christian State of their own on the model of Pakistan of the Muslims.

small and cottage industries, education upto secondary level, social welfare, maintenance of irrigation projects etc. It could meet at the district headquarters of Chhotanagpur and Santhal Parganas after every three months by rotation. This move was not appreciated by the JMM that wanted nothing short of a State of their own.

While the bill passed by the State legislature in 1991 was pending consideration of the President of India, the Centre was putting pressure on the government of Bihar to expedite adoption of the Jharkhand Autonomous Council Bill which envisaged the formation of a Development Council for the tribal areas of the State. On this crucial issue even the Congress leaders of Bihar were sharply divided. But the State government, in stead of passing a new bill to this effect, desired that the Centre should return the bill lying with the President with certain amendments as desired by it. The bill became an act and then in August, 1995, the Bihar government set up the Jharkhand Area Autonomous Council. Things reached a happy end with the creation of the State of Jharkhand in 2000 without including the areas of Orissa, Madhya Pradesh and West Bengal as claimed by the leaders of this movement.

The agitation for Uttarakhand, also called Uttaranchal by the BJP leaders, became the latest addition to the politics of communitarian regionalism in our country. The generally peace-loving people of the 8 hill districts of Western Uttar Pradesh, hitherto so taken for granted with impunity by the ruling classes, had struck back with the kind of assertiveness that nobody in the State or at the Centre could have suspected them of possessing it. The decision of the U.P. Government for reservation of 27 per cent of seats in favour of other socially and educationally backward castes or classes in educational institutions ignited the slumbering resentment of the people of these districts who rightly feared that its implementation would pave the way for the influx of such people from other districts of the State of U.P. in view of the fact that in this region such persons constituted only 3 per cent of the population.

The anti-reservation agitation started on 2 August, 1994 with a fast-unto-death by seven leaders of Uttarakhand Kranti Dal (U.K.D) in Puari district. The agitation quickly spread to others parts of this region like Dehradun and Nainital. The situation became very serious when the police fired on the peaceful marchers and misbehaved with the womenfolk in Muzaffarnagar and Dehradun on 1 and 2 October, 1994 who were moving towards Delhi to engage the attention of the

Government of India. Throwing light on the quick development, an independent MLA from Lansdowne (Surendra Singh Negi) said: "The sheer extent of the popular involvement in the agitation is unprecedented in the history of the hill areas of Uttar Pradesh."[88]

The demand for the State of Uttarakhand comprising some hill districts of Uttar Pradesh was sustained by several factors constituting its separate identity from administrative point of view. It is true that in view of the above factors, this area could be said to have its own identity, but some other factors relating to socio-economic injustice were also to be taken into account as :[89]

1. The increasing denudation of forests due largely to commercial felling, the migration of able-bodied males to other parts of the country in search of jobs, and the emergence of a 'money order economy' played their own part in this regard. The two disciples of Mahatma Gandhi (Merabehn and Savitabehn) had drawn the attention of the people of Garhwal much earlier as a result of which first Dev Suman and then Pandit Sunderlal Bahuguna launched 'chipko' movement with the object of preventing the outsiders from cutting trees indiscriminately and thereby disturbing the ecological balance of this area.

2. The young elements were facing the problem of unemployment. There was great potential for developing the industries of electronics and tourism which were pollution-free and which would generate employment here, but very little work had been done in this regard. It was readily acknowledge that there was no regional planning with the name for these hill areas. As the feeling of neglect persisted, the inescapable conclusion was that all this wisdom had largely remained on paper and had not been backed by effective administrative arrangements for putting these ideas into practice.

---

88. *The Sunday Times of India,* New Delhi, 11 September, 1994, p. 17

89. C.H. Hanumantha Rao: "Uttarakhand Agitation: Viability of Small State" in *The Times of India,* New Delhi, 19 April, 1995. The demand for this State rested on ecological ground. India should honour the provisions of the Mountain Agenda of the United Nations (1995) adopted at the Earth Summit held at Rio de Jenerio which enjoins that the people of the mountain areas should not be marginalised, they should have their control over the management of their natural resources. Annpurna Nautiyal: "Uttarakhand: So Near Yet So Far Away," in *Politics India,* New Delhi, September, 1997. p. 37.

3. The basic explanation for the failure to formulate and implement effectively the regionally relevant plan was simply this that the power to formulate and implement such a plan was not vested in the region itself. The potential district-level plan outlays accounted for only about 25 to 30 per cent of State plan outlays. This means that as much as 70 to 75 per cent of the outlays was still planned and allocated at the State-level for various infra-structural items including, particularly, power and major and medium irrigation which had a bearing on the development of the individual districts. Besides, the levels and patterns of private investments, which were important determinants of development, could only be influenced by policies at the State level.

What was really problematical in this context, as in the context of similar movements in other parts of the country, was that the Centre sought to undertake steps in the light of political or partisan considerations alone. Prime Minister Rao strongly rejected the move of his party unit in U.P. to dismiss the Mulayam Singh ministry under Art. 356 of the Constitution in view of the atrocities of the police on peaceful marchers, including women. Above all, he paid no heed to the fact that a resolution for the creation of Uttarakhand State had been adopted by the Lagislative Assembly of U.P. twice in the recent past. As in the case of Jharkhand so here, matters reached a happy end with the creation of the State of Uttaranchal in 2000.

Movements for regional autonomy have been in existence in many parts of the country, but the common feature of all may be traced in the component of 'anti-migrantism.' Everywhere some ethnic or 'sons of the oil' component becomes the sustaining force. It was not so in the case of this movement. Hence, what distinguished the Uttarakhand movement from similar movements going on in the States of Andhra Pradesh, Assam, Madhya Pradesh and Bihar, was perhaps its totally non-violent, spontaneous and non-political character. The entire thrust was on the economic and administrative neglect of the region largely due to its topographically distinct location in the then State of Uttar Pradesh.[90]

Critical Appreciation : A study of regionalism in the politics of our country, as contained in the preceding sections, leaves these broad impressions :

90. Pradeep Kumar: "Uttarakhand: Frittering Away of a Democratic Movement" in *Politics India*, New Delhi, February, 1998, pp. 34-35.

1. Regionalism in India is not a very precise and clear-cut affair in view of the fact that it cuts into sub-regionalism, sub-nationalism, communalism, even infra-regionalism, and secessionism in certain situations. Though it is found to be sustained by the factors of culture, geography, historical antecedents, political peculiarities and social and economic conditions of the people which may be said to have played an important part in this regard, it becomes very difficult to include all case studies in a single chapter. However, it certainly appears that regionalism is a dynamic and pragmatic concept which seldom sustains itself on a single factor. It rather sustains itself on a coalition of factors and circumstances including politicisation of the region and a sense of economic retardation is invariably at the back of regional reassertions.
2. Regionalism in the politics of India is an essential product of great diversity in social and cultural spheres. That is, it draws sustenance from the facts of our life. All great leaders, writers Statesmen have taken due note of this fact and also lauded it. At the same time, they have ardently desired 'unity in the midst of diversity'. Thus, regionalism is not an evil as such, it is an essential part of our life as well. What is required is that there should be harmony between regionalism and nationalism so that progress of the country as a whole takes place. An over-all development of the country usually involves the development of the regions within its fold.
3. The fact of regional imbalance prevailing in the country cannot be lost sight of. Hence, if the people of a particular region or a sub-region struggle for the protection or promotion of their genuine interests, their case should be properly studied and supported. It is also necessary that in a democratic set up mattters should be settled in a peaceful and constitutional way. The movement for the State of Chhattisgarh was not so volatile and yet the Centre realised its case and created it in 2000. Thus, it is not politics of regionalism as such as the politicisation of regional issues by self-seeking politicians that has brought a bad name to the case of regionalism.
4. The policy of creating regional development councils or boards for the part of a State as Vidarbha in Maharashtra or Gorkhaland in West Bengal would not pay dividends in the long run. It is like a stop-gap arrangement. Once such an

institution is created, half of the aim of the agitators is achieved and, after some time, they think in terms of restarting their agitation for a full-fledged State. It is happening in West Bengal where Ghishing as chairman of the Gorkhaland Development Council and his zealous supporters often express their grievances and desire their prompt redressal by the State government. It is quite likely that the leaders of such a regional body may create problems for the State government and may pick up cudgels with the State Governor.[91]

5. Above all, the politics of regionalism has its constructive and destructive aspects. In its former aspect it should be appreciated, in the latter aspect it should be deprecated. Thus, while the Government is expected to sort out the matters in an amicable way if the agitators adhere to its constructive aspect, it has every right to suppress by all possible means those whose activities blend regionalism with anti-nationalism or secessionism. No sovereign state can tolerate its disintegration. Thus, even the most repressive measures of a state adopted for protecting its territorial integrity cannot be denounced in the name of the violation of 'human rights'.

A detailed study of regional movements in the politics of our country indicates that the problems of the States have been subordinated to excessive political pressures that have led to a mass-scale agitation and consequent disintegration and destruction. The statistics of massive destruction are also an eloquent testimony to heavy drain on the public exchequer. In fact, the outlook of the separationists and disruptionists has resulted in a severe damage to the efforts of a State for its development.

National Integration

A study of the momentous subject of national integration should be regarded as a complementary part of what we have seen in the previous sections in view of the fact that in a developing country like India, 'nation-building' and 'national integration' look like two sides of the same phenomenon. Like 'nation-building', the term 'national integration' requires its understanding in a comprehensive

---

91. N.A. Palkhivala: "Development Boards : Risky Remedy for Regional Ills" in *The Time of India*, New Delhi, 8 Aug., 1990.

sense so as to cover its ramifications even in directions other than political. If so, our study in this significant direction automatically involves something more than what we have seen above. An attempt should be made to discuss the subject of national integration in a broad theoretical framework followed by an elaborate discussion of the matter in various important spheres as desired by our great leaders to realise the ideal of 'Fraternity assuring the dignity of the individual and unity and integrity of the nation.'

Nature and Essential Implications : Though the term 'national integration' has been defined in different ways by different writers, it is not a difficult job to devise a synthetic view of the same. The reason behind it is that almost all writers on this momentous subject take the term 'nationalism' so as to signify the existence of state as the impersonal and ultimate arbiter of human affairs.[92] In this way, it may involve the process of nation-building which suggests bringing together, culturally and socially, discrete groups into a single territorial unit and thereby securing the establishment of a national identity. Naturally, the tenet of political unity or the existence of a 'nation-state' figures in. As such, the term 'national integration' "refers specifically to the problem of creating a sense of territorial nationality which overshadows—or eliminates—subordinate parochial loyalties."[93]

One point may be repeated here that as the idea of nationalism has its two different connotations—'western' and 'eastern'—that have their relevance in the process of 'nation-building', so the idea of 'national integration' has its two broad varieties. In other words, there are two public policy forms and strategies for the achievement of the goal of national integration. The first is the elimination of the distinctive cultural traits of the minorities into some kind of, what the leaders in power call, 'national' culture which is invariably that of the group in majority. It may be defined as national assimilation, though in the context of a particular country it may have the appellation of anything like 'Americanisation', 'Russianisation', 'Germanisation', 'Vietnamisation' and the like. The second is the course of having 'unity in the midst of diversity'. Here

92. K.H. Silvert (ed) ; *Expectant Peoples: Nationalism and Development*, p. 19.

93. Myron Weiner : "Political and Social Integration: Forms and Strategies" in E.A. Nordlinger (ed): *Politics and Society*, p. 197.

we find synchronisation or ordering of national loyalties without eliminating subordinate cultures.[94]

The case of national integration in India falls in the latter category where instead of assimilation or absorption of the minorities, the ideal of 'unity in diversity' has been adopted. All great leaders have minced no words in reiterating that there exists a running thread of unity even among the most vulnerable forces of disunity. They have also emphasised that regional or linguistic plurality and racial or casteist multiplicity do not pose a noticeable danger to the forces of national integration. Social conflicts and even group tangles resulting from such diversity are the natural outcome of social stratification and political injustice. As a great national leader, Nehru realised this fact fully and went on laying stress everywhere on the unity of the country and on the need to fight all disruptive forces like communalism, casteism, provincialism, separatism and the like.

Viewed thus, the concept of national integration, as given by the secularist and democratic leaders of the country, is quite different from one given by the communalists and the sectionalists. It does not imply 'Hinduisation' of the people as desired by the leaders of the Hindu Maha Sabha, nor can it have any reconciliation with the 'Islamisation' of the country as suggested by the leaders of the Jamat-e-Islami. However, one may not easily object to the case of the 'Indianisation' of the people if this term is understood in the proper perspective like asking and expecting every citizen of the country to be "Indian first, Indian second, and Indian last."[95]

It follows that the idea of national integration in our country has certain important implications. These are :

1. The idea of 'integration' does not imply 'absorption'. The purpose is not to have uniformity at the cost of unity. What is really required is that there should be unity in the midst of diversity. Let the people with their own religion, caste language, culture and the like exist and yet they should

---

94. *Ibid.*, p. 200.

95. P.B. Gajenderagadkar : *The Philosophy of National Integration—Its Broad Imperatives,* Third Jawaharalal Nehru Memorial Lecture delivered under the auspices of the Institute of Constitutional and Parliamentary Studies, New Delhi, Nov. 27, 1972, Mimeographed, p. 24.

harmonise their varying loyalties in such a way that the nation-state is strengthened.

2. Whereas the idea of national integration implies harmonisation of the loyalties of the people in a particular way, it also calls for the suppression and eradication of anti-national forces at work that play a very heinous role in disrupting the unity and integrity of the nation. That is, the idea of national integration is not merely a normative affair; it has its empirical dimension as well. Mere laying emphasis on unity in diversity is not enough. What is equally necessary is that concerted efforts should be made to deal with the disruptionist forces.
3. The concept of national integration is quite comprehensive. It covers all dimensions—political, economic, social, cultural, legal, educational and psychological. That is, it does not merely desire the existence of a strong and viable nation-state; it also aspires for social, economic and cultural integration. Above all, it desires emotional integration of the people. Thus, it comes to involve a value system as well.

The idea of national integration desires neither mal-integration, nor para-integration, nor over-integration. It simply desires proper integration of the people in diverse spheres of life so that all may happily join the national mainstream and thereby contribute their due share to the security and prosperity of the nation. It implies a sense of belonging, a feeling of togetherness, and unity. It means creating a sort of climate in the country in which all citizens, irrespective of their social status or economic position, may lead a life of peace and honour and feel like devoted entirely to the common purpose of building a strong and united India. It was nothing but the sheer absence of such an ideal situation about which Nehru once regretted "I know there is India, but I want to know where are the Indians."[96]

Major Dimensions : As already pointed out, the idea of national integration is quite comprehensive. It not merely covers the area of politics, it has its economic, social, cultural, ethical and psychological dimensions as well. Obviously, in the realisation of such a goal, several serious hurdles come up which demand their solution at an earliest

96. *Ibid*., p. 4.

possible time. We may also take note of the fact that if gigantic hurdles in this regard are not surmounted in time, national disintegration takes place. Hence, we shall now examine the case of national integration in our country in its broad dimensions and also throw some focus on the problem coupled with the solutions devised for this purpose.

1. **Political Dimension :** First of all, let us examine the case in the sphere of territorial integration of the country or what is also known by the name of 'state-building'. We have seen that state-building is a pre-requisite to the ideal of nation-building in view of the fact that the goal of national integration cannot be achieved until the people have a strong territorial unit of their own called the state. The fluctuating boundaries of historic empires and the fuzziness at the peripheries, where kinship ties and tributary arrangements mark the end of a state, are no longer acceptable arrangements in the modern world. Sovereignty is characterised by an exclusive control over territory. Facts illustrate that the establishment of a territory precedes the establishment of subjective loyalties. For instance, a Congo nation cannot be established without there being a Congo state. Fortunately, political integration of our country has taken place. The most serious problem in this regard relating to the integration of former princely States could be tackled well in time. Subsequently, the reorganisation of States along linguistic lines took place in 1956. In order to satisfy the legitimate demand of Gujarati-speaking people of the bilingual State of Bombay, bifurcation of the State took place in 1960. Similarly, Punjab was bifurcated in 1966 so as to satisfy the claim of people speaking Punjabi language, while the Hindi-speaking people got the State of Haryana. Apart from linguistic consideration, the Government of India has also taken the factor of administrative efficiency and economy in its view and thereby done political reorganisation of the country. It was for this sake that the State of Meghalaya first as a 'sub-State' within the State of Assam was made in 1968 and then it was given the status of a full-fledged State of the Indian Union.

2. **Economic Dimension:** A study of national integration also reveals the fact that the poor, hungry, naked, shelterless and economically downtrodden people cannot understand the value of national unity and integrity. As Marx said, the workers know no fatherland. To such people, fighting demon of starvation is more important than dying for the cause of the country. A portrait of Mao

became more important to the people of Vietnam, because herein they found a message of hope. It is for this reason that the nation-builders strive hard to bring about an economic revolution in the country. If so, economic backwardness acts as a serious impediment to the growth of national integration and it may be seen having a weight of its own in the Indian context. Sometimes we also learn about the fact of the regional economic imbalance, want of employment opportunities, fight for the cause of jobs to the local people or 'sons of the soil,'poverty of the people and want of economic justice.For this sake, the Planning Commission has framed plans. Community Development Projects and National Extension Services have also been launched. Growth of the public sector is also a noticeable fact here.

3. **Social Dimension:** No less important is the sphere of social justice. National integration requires social integration of the people as well. That is, the people of a country should not be divided on the lines of religion or caste. All should have liberty as well as equality. In this way, the forces of racial or communal segregation or social alienation cause a lot of damage to the existence of national unity. Viewed in this context, one may easily look at the pernicious role of communalism and casteism as a result of which some sections of the people have been in a position of advantage and thereby exploited and oppressed the downtrodden people of the country. Regional and social imbalance may also be taken note of in this connection when we find that the position of the people living in the plains is far better than that of the tribals. This should go. Fortunately, we have been able to solve the problem of social disintegration to a very large extent. The Constitution has adopted the ideal of secularism and granted boons of Liberty and Equality to all. However, in order to give a special lift to the position of the poor and weaker sections of the society, reservations and safeguards have also been made. The purpose behind it is not to violate the sanctity of the principle of equality but to make special provisions for the betterment of the lot of the people belonging to Scheduled Castes, Scheduled Tribes and other socially and educationally backward classes.

4. **Cultural Dimension:** The culture of a people embracing language, script, customs, ideas and the whole way of life plays a very significant role in achieving the goal of national integration. So deep is the attachment of the people with their distinct language, script, customs and the entire way of life that they strive to maintain their separate existence as we may see in the behaviour of the

French people living in the Quebec province of Canada, or of the Germans living in the state of Bavaria in Germany. Luckily, we have been able to solve the problem of national integration in this sphere to a great extent. The ideal of secularism as embodied in the Constitution has done a great deal in this regard. All people have the right to maintain and preserve their distinct language, script and culture and the State has been deprived of the right to interfere with the management of educational institutions run by the people in minority for this purpose.

5. **Ethical Dimension :** Now we enter into the domain of value system. Values have a very important place in the life of human beings; moreover, these change with the passage of time. For instance, what was appreciated by the people of the nineteenth century is decried now. The people of the feudal era and its replacement by the age of socialism has given place to several values of libertarianism and egalitarianism. What was once done at the behest of an all-powerful despot is now done by means of consensus. That is, singularity has yielded place to plurality in the sphere of decision-making. With the growth of representative system transposition in the ranks of the elites has also become a routine affair. Thus, elite-mass integration has also become another imperative of national integration in a modern democratic system. National integration in our country in this important sphere has, however, not been to the desired extent the reason for which should be traced in the remnants of the feudal order and the colonial system under which we remained for a period of about two hundred years. Particularly in the rural areas, feudal values like taking of forced labour or *begaar*, exploitation of the landless peasantry and suppression of the weaker communities still persist. It often leads to social conflicts having repercussions in the field of politics the examples of which we could see in the Naxalite revolts in various parts of West Bengal, Bihar, Andhra Pradesh and Kerala. The value system obtaining in a developed part of the country is different. The rich and advanced people living in urban areas have given up much of the traditional habits and ways of life. They may be said to have developed a different set of values hovering between the systems of liberalism and socialism.

6. **Psychological Dimension:** Finally, we take up the role of sentiments and emotions of the people in achieving the goal of

national integration. As a matter of fact, national integration is an idea which can be realised only when the people understand it and make necessary sacrifices for its cause. It is for this reason that national goals, symbols, anthems, emblems, flags, figures, slogan etc. are devised. The role of the psychological dimension in bringing about unity and integrity of the people cannot be undermined by any stretch of imagination. Unless the people have emotions springing from their unshakable love for the motherland, they cannot know the difference between the portraits of Gandhi and Mao, between the crescent and the *chakra*, between Curzon and Kasturba. We may safely affirm that all activities going to disrupt the unity and integrity of the nation issuing in the form of communalism, casteism, linguistic chauvinism, separatism, secessionism and the like have their source in the non-existence of the feelings and sentiments of nationalism. Thus, after the settlement of the vexed problem of political reorganisation of the country on linguistic lines in 1956, Nehru strongly desired; "Political integration has already taken place to some extent, but what I am after is some thing much deeper than that—an emotional integration of the Indian people so that we might be welded into one, and made into one strong national unit, maintaining at the same time all our wonderful diversity."[97]

In brief, the ideal of national integration in our country has been realised to a considerable extent. Several gigantic problems have been solved. It is mainly in the economic field where much still remains to be done and if the desired success has not been achieved, the reason for this may be discovered partly in the legacy of the colonial system and partly in the lack of consensus over the adoption of a particular economic system. In this connection, it should also be brone in mind that our goal of national integration is not merely confined to having a united nation but more than that to make it useful for the service of humanity as a whole. As Nehru once exhorted: "We have to build up the great country into a mighty nation, mighty not in the ordinary sense of the word, that is, having great armies and all that, but mighty in thought, mighty in action, mighty in culture and mighty in its peaceful service of humanity."[98]

Critical Appreciation : Our study of national integration in India, as contained in the preceding sections, leads to the conclusion

---

97 Nehru : *Speeches*, Vol. III, p. 35

98 *Ibid.*

that the ideal has, by and large, been realised and most of the problems coming in its way have been solved. Moreover, the running trend shows that problems in the sphere of socio-economic integration of the people, though quite formidable, may be solved by the rulers with the co-opertion of the people.Let us hope that an enlightened conscience will develop so as to make the people aware of the course of secularisation of our polity, implying growing capacity of the people to make use of reason in determining their national goals and then making concerted efforts for their realisation.

Educational institution have to play their own part in bringing about internal purification and thereby emotional integration of the people. This is a big cause in which ministers, legislators, bureaucrats, judges, teachers, workers, businessmen,farmers, in a word, people belonging to any walk of life have to play their constructive part in order to create a new order composed of all citizens of the country, residing in different regions, professing allegiance to different religions and speaking different languages into one brotherhood of Indian citizens who believe in the paramount importance of national unity and political, social and economic justice.

It should also be remembered that national integration is not merely an ideal that should be pursued and, after having realised it, the matter comes to an end. As a matter of fact, it is future-oriented as well. The essential task is to have a united and strong nation; allied with it is the task of facing new and still newer challenges through democratic means so as to tread the path of modernisation. Thus, secularisation and modernisation of the polity go together. As Gajendragadkar says: "Those who believe in national integration must be committed to the task of creating new India of tomorrow."[99]

Above all, our concept of national integration has a moral aspect too which should not be lost sight of. When we fought for independence, we were guided by the glorious value of *Swaraj* which meant by all means more than national liberaton. Gandhiji defined it as a capacity of each individual to remain free and also to resist the abuse of power. Viewed thus, our concept of national integration has a high moral over-tone. It is well contained in this noble reiteration of Gandhiji: "The union we want is not a patched up

---

99 Gajendragadkar, *op.cit.*, p. 57

thing, but a union of hearts based upon a define recognition of the indubitable proposition that *Swaraj* for India is not an impossible dream without an indissoluble union. It must be partnership between equals, each respecting the other and the other's way of life. What we need is not to be one but to be able to tolerate one another and live in amity and peace."

Thus, we may appreciate the view of an eminent Indian writer that India "is not a simple nation in the conventional sense of the word. India is a federal nation. And because it is the world's largest and most complex federal nation, the problems, aspects and dimensions of political integration are many and challenging. A federal nation is a mosaic of many segments—ethnic, religious, caste, tribal, linguistic, regional and cultural. Autonomy and respect for segments have to go hand in hand with political unity, federal integration, and pan-Indian solidarity and fraternity. .... In the semantics of functional politics, the term 'national integration' in India means, and ought to mean, cohesion but not fusion, unity but not uniformity, reconciliation but not merger, agglomeration but not assimilation, solidarity but not regimentation of the many segments of the people constituting our continental diverse polity. Federal India must resort to federal solutions, and not resort to unitarian and simplistic solution imposed authoritatively without democratic sensitivity."[100]

100. Resheeduddin Khan: "Political Integration in Federal India" in *The Times of India*, New Delhi, 19 Nov., 1992.

20

Electronic Governance and Information Technology

Politics is the study of power and power is the 'ability to use and develop human capacities.'[1] Since pursuit of power has no rest and no end, man remains engaged in the discovery as well as invention of new sources of power and their better application so as to enhance the sphere of his influence. Invention and innovation go together. New instruments are created and the mode of their operations is also streamlined. With the growth of democracy, politics has become a concern of every active citizen who desires to know what the rulers do and, in turn, in order to provide legitimacy to their rule, the rulers seek to honour the reactions of the ruled as far as possible. The result is that technology and informatics have now come to require their proper study in the domain of politics. It is not confined to the advanced countries of the West, it is equally important for a non-Western country like India where "the technological revolution brings closer the realisation of their concept of the human essence."[2]

Technological Revolution and Democracy

Contemporary politics is very much different from the politics of ancient, medieval, and even early modern and recent times. Its reason should be traced in the marvellous success of the technological revolution. F.D. Roosevelt won the presidential election in the United States in 1932 by making use of radio and Jimmy Carter could have an easy victory against Gerald Ford in the presidential election of 1976 on the basis of his impressive performance on the television. The press, the radio and the television disseminate information relating to the political events of the country as well as of the whole world to a common man. As a result, the popularity of

1. C.B. Macpherson: *Democratic Theory: Essays in Retrieval* (London: Oxford Clarendon Press, 1973,) p. 39.

2. *Ibid*, p. 38.

democracy has overshadowed all other forms of government. What was once a matter of academic exercise as done by Mill and Bryce has now become a theme of empirical investigation for Downs and Dahl. As C.B. Macpherson says: "But this change has become more urgent now, because of the conjecture of two changes in our society, namely, the increasingly democratic temper of the world as a whole, and the technological revolution of our time. The two changes are not unrelated."[3]

If technological revolution has brought about such a momentous change in the politics of the Western countries, India can be no exception. Invention of new sources of power with their application creates a technological revolution. It metamorphoses the world of communications. Thus, informatics becomes a new and significant theme of study. The use of mechanical methods lightens the burden of work and economises time as a result of which a man may channelise his energy into some other useful vocations and thereby raise his standard of living. Data can be computerised and its information may be delivered to the person seeking it at a little expense of time and money. Votes can be cast by means of electronic machines and results may be declared as expeditiously as possible. In the legislative chambers electronic voting may be adopted. What is contained in the huge pile of files may be sorted out by means of computers and its information may be made available on the internet or the website. It is due to this that the results of the examinations conducted by some university or public service commission can be made available to persons living thousands of miles away in not much time.

Hence, electronic voting devices have been adopted in the Parliament and State legislatures. The Election Commission makes use of electronic voting devices in sensitive constituencies and now a demand has gathered weight that it should cover all constituencies of the country. The Central Government has made two important laws for this purpose, namely, Information Technology Act, 2000 and Right to Information Act, 2005. The Supreme Court has ruled that right to information is a fundamental right and is covered under Act. 19(1) (*a*) of the Constitution.[4] It is on this ground that it issued

---

3. *Ibid*. p. 36.

4. *S.P. Gupta* v. *Union of India*, AIR 1982 SC 149.

a directive to the Election Commission in a leading case on 2 May 2002 to ask a candidate seeking election to the Parliament or State legislatures to furnish full information about his criminal antecedents, moveable and immovable assets and liabilities and educational qualifications. A voter's or a little man's right to know it all "is much more fundamental and basic for the survival of democracy."[5]

In fine, the information technology revolution, that has swept across the world, "has changed the way the governments work and interact with their stake holders. This explains why digital government or electronic government (e-government) has become one of the most important topic in the public sector reform agenda. Such an e-transformation in government has its roots in the 1950s when some few professionals and academics started to speak about the computerisation of public organisations. For several decades discussion was concerning mainly in the use of computers in international organisation accounting and record keeping. Wider perspectives started to gain ground as late as 1980s in the wake of the introduction of personal computers and the merger fo computers and telecommunications. Yet the most fundamental recent turn in the information technology revolution was the Great Internet Explosion of 1993-94 and the increased popularity of the World Wide Web (WWW) in particular. Since then the transformative power of e-government has been generally recognised."[6]

E-Governance

Simply stated, electronic is the ability of government to provide access to services and information to the people round the clock. As democracy is the rule of the people, they should have all kinds of information so that they may enable themselves to be active participants in public affairs. E-government may turn democracy into E-democracy representing the use of information and communication technologies and strategies by those who play the role of the actors in the operation of this system like political parties, organised groups, agencies of mass media, elected members of the

5. *Union of India* v. *Association for Democratic Reforms* (2002) SC 294.

6. Ari-Veikko Anttiroiko and Matti Malkia (eds) ; *Encyclopaedia of Digital Government* (London : Idea Group Reference, 2006), Vol. I, Preface by the Editors, p. xxxvii.

legislature and the authorities of the government. In the words of Steven Clift, it "suggests greater and more active citizen participation enabled by the internet, mobile communications and other technologies in today's representative democracy as well as through more participatory or direct forms of citizen involvement in addressing public challenges."

With the use of new techniques of information technology and internet, private and public sectors can be brought closer to each other. It is the transformation of the internal and external relationships of the public sector through net-enabled operations, information technology and communications, to optimise Government service delivery, constituency participation and governance. According to Christopher Baum, "True e-government requires transformation of all the system involved in processing a transaction, not just those facing citizens and business." If so, some features of e-governance may be pointed out. First, it is the use or application of the emerging information and communication technologies to facilitate the governmental process and public administration. Second. it is about providing citizens with the ability to choose the manner in which they wish to interact with their government. Last, it is about the choices the government makes about how information and communication technologies may be deployed to meet the choices of the people. In short, e-governance establishes close relationship between the rulers and the ruled through the network of information technology.

Electronic governance has assumed a significance of its own in the present age of advanced information technology. Popularly known as e-governance, it implies a system that makes the functioning of the government known to the people by means of using electronic means. Information must be disseminated so that the people in general may know about the doings and misdoings of their government and then may behave like enlightened citizens in making their administration accountable to them in the real sense of the term. It provides creative opportunities to both the rulers and the ruled to have a first-hand knowledge of the actions and reactions of one another. If the people acquire information about the policy or programme going to be adopted by the government or about the actions taken by it in order to implement the recommedations of some commission or committee and the like, the government, in turn, may have full information about the demands and reactions of the people who desire a transparent and responsive governance in their country. Obviously, e-governance is another technological name of open government that is responsible as well as responsive to those with whose will it is instituted. It is well observed: "The new thinking that is new evolving within the Government about having an open Government, one that is responsive and effective, calls for people's access to information"[7]

The sole aim behind the whole mechanism of e-governance is to bring about a situation of government-citizen interface. It is a matter of duty, rather obligation, on the part of the government to provide information to the citizens through National Information Centres and, in turn, the citizens may also have access to such information when they so require. If the hackneyed rules and regulations of the departments stand in the way, they should be streamlined. 'Smart Cards' should be introduced which "will help the citizen to interact for utilities and services, make bill payments, vote electronically, obtain ration cards, passports and driving licenses. All these would ensure that the citizen's rights are well protected and documented in an electronic environment."[8]

It may be inferred that e-governance adds a new, though ancillary, wing to the administration of the country. The ministers may formulate a policy, the legislators may make a law, the planners may chalk out a plan, the courts may deliver a verdict in a typical case of corruption of cyber crime, it is required that there must be a body of competent staff to maintain all records and feed it properly which may be loaded and unloaded in a website or a computer. The purpose can be achieved if the records generated through e-governance are carefully managed through systems providing constant intellectual and physical control. "It is not something that can be supplemented and managed by a group of information technology professionals alone, record managers also have a key role to play along with the planners and developers of e-governance programme. Awareness needs to be created at two levels for

7. N. Vittal and S. Mahalingam: *Information Technology* : *India's Tomorrow* (New Delhi: Manas Publications, 2001, p. 42.

8. Kinkini Dasgupta and Misra: "Electronic Governance", *Employment News*, New Delhi, 11-17 May, 2002., p. 1.

e-governance to succeed in practical context. While the first would be at the governmental or operational level, the other has to be at the level of the public, the users and the beneficiaries."[9]

In short, e-governance is the application of information and communication technologies to transform the efficiency, effectiveness, transparency and accountability of informational and transactional exchange within government, between government and non-government agencies at national, regional and local levels, between citizens and businesses, and to empower the people through access to and use of information. But it should also be taken into consideration as to what e-governance is not. Terms such as 'data resale', 'digital democracy' and 'e-politics' are also frequently mentioned within the same breath as 'e-governance'. Neither of these terms, however, observes the principle of leveraging the internet to simplify the process of government. Digital democracy is, in fact, 'e-politics' rather then 'e-government; that is leveraging the Internet to simplify the electronic process (rather than government). It is important that these terms donot muddle the objectives of e-governance.

Case of India

"Information technology is nothing but a happy marriage of computes and telecommunications."[10] In the last fifty years, it is the one technology which has grown dramatically and affected practically every aspect of life in information technology. It is, therefore, natural that information technology affects public governance. Many governments are increasingly resorting to the use of information technology. India has also witnessed in the last fifty years the increasing impact of information technology in different aspects of governance. It is interesting to note that the functions of the government and the strengths of information technology seem to be made for each other. Governments as a part of their functioning have to deal with mass of data, for they deal with a very large number of people. Apart from the large amount of data to be processed in order to ensure that the administration acts in a fair manner, they need to keep records. and it is the keeping of the records that leads to the occupational hazard of the governance which is cynically called 'red tape'.[11]

9. *Ibid.*

10. N Vittal : "Information Technology and Administration in Government" in *Yojana* (New Delhi), November, 2007, p. 23

11. *Ibid.*

The significant leverage provided by the Information Technology for economic growth is the result of an evolution significantly guided by a conscious governmental planning process towards an eventual self-guided market. Nucleated in the mid-fifties by Homi Jehangir Bhabha and P.C. Mahalanobis, nutured in the sixties by Vikram Sarabhai and M.G.K. Menon, focused for growth of applications in the seventies by the Electronics Commission, the eighties and the early nineties saw government-steered liberalisation, preparing the ground for the boom of the nineties, whose momentum has sustained unabated to the present day. Credit goes to the Homi Bhabha Committee that realised the need for focus on electronics and computers. On 26 June, 1970 came into being the Department of Electronics under Prime Minister Indira Gandhi with Prof. G.K. Menon as the Secretary as well as Chairman of the Electronics Commission. The New Computer Policy adopted by the Government of Rajiv Gandhi on 19 November 1984 followed by the Software Export and Training Policy adopted two years after, "kick-started the Indian IT story."[12]

India became the twelfth nation in the world to have an Information Technology Act in 2000 so as to address the growing e-commerce and e-business and the attendant cyber security e-governance initiatives like e-Seva in Andhra Pradesh (in 2002) and Bhoomi (land records) in Karnataka (in 2003) followed by the establishment of National Institute of Smart Governance at Hyderabad in 2006. The government of Vajpayee realised the importance of information technology and so the National Information Technology Task Force was created in 1998 and the new National Telecom Policy produced the liberalisation and globalisation ambience that nurture the initiative of thousands of IT enterprises whose combined effort has put India as the vanguard of the global IT and ITES outsourcing.

Apart from making laws, as referred to above, notable steps have been taken by the Central and State governments in this regard. On 15 July, 2002 the Union Ministry of Information Technology organised the first National Conference in New Delhi of IT Ministers of various States for arriving at a Common Action Plan. On this occasion, some important decisions were taken as : (*i*) full deregulation of National Long Distance Operations, (*ii*) complete de-monopolisation of undersea optical fibre connectivity for ISPs, and (*iii*) setting up of a Task Force

12. S. Sadagopan : 'Fifty Years of Indian IT' in *Yojana* (New Delhi) November, 2006, p. 18.

on human resource development in IT. Accordingly, a Common Action Plan was adopted. Then, the IT Ministry set up a Working Group on IT for the Masses. In its report it has set up a target of 100 million Internet connections by the end of 2008 and one million Internet enbled IT Kiosks/Cyber cafes to be set up in the country. Its main recommendations are :

1. To establish IT infrastructure in 60,000 schools over a period of five years,
2. Web enabled citizen-oriented Government services,
3. No licenses and controls for setting up IT infrastructure and services,
4. To promote development of Indian Language content over Internet.
5. To launch mass awareness campaign through IT *Yatras* and other programmes,
6. To set up an IT Mission for five years to carry out the porgramme recommended by this report and follow up its other recommendations,
7. Compulsory IT literacy for Government recruitment,
8. Earmarking upto 5 per cent budget for IT induction in Government,
9. State Government Portals to help rural artisans and entrepreneurs,
10. Internet Portal for one point Government Information and services.
11. All Government Information to be on Internet,
12. All Government payments on Internet, and
13. Results of Public Services examinations to be made available on Internet.

National Informatic Centre (NIC) at present provides computer support to Departments of the Government of India, of State Governments and of District Adminstration in 540 districts. New districts are being created for this purpose. It has set up a satellite based computer communication network for providing E-mail, Internet, File Transfer, access to National and International database (including bio-medical, land records etc.), Electronic Data Interchange, Video-conferencing facility etc. It has been training Government employees on a regular basis to enable them to use computerised MIS and database. It has computerised Supreme Court, 18 High Courts and 430 lower courts in the country to streamline functioning and providing transparency to the litigants and legal database.

The Department of Information Technology has set up Community Information Centres (CISs) at 487 block headquarters in the seven north-eastern States and Sikkim which can help in combating escalating crisis in health, energy, water, education and literacy as well as alleviation of poverty. These bodes would also provide internet connectivity, e-mail facilities, interface between citizen and government, distance-learning programmes, information on national programmes, disaster management system and public health awareness, as a new initiative in the context of bringing the digital divide, the Government of India has collaborated with Media Lab. of Massachusetts Institute of Technology of USA with a view of form Media Lab Asia which is proposed to be a network of national as well as overseas prople, projects land laboratories dedicated to bringing the benefits of the most advanced information technologies to the people. It has been designated as an Asian Regional Hub of the UN ICT Task Force for coordinating activities of academia and the private sector in the area of IT for the masses. The Indian Computer Energy Response Team (CERT) is being set up to ensure that India's information assets in every sphere are provided the necessary protection. To integrate technology into the learning environment, the Department of Information Technology has formulated two specific programmes, namely 'Vidya Vahini' and 'Gyan Vahini' to provide connectivity to schools across the country and IT infra-structure at all the institutions of higher learning in the country respectively.[12]

No doubt, the entire programme of e-governance has brought about an astonishing change in the process of administration at the Centre as well as in the States. For instance, in Hydrabad through e-Seva, the people can view and pay bills for water, electricity and telephones, besides municipal taxes. In Gujarat there are websites where the people can log on and get access to the concerned departments of the government on issues such as land, water and other taxes. Through Mahiti Shakti, people may make a request for government documents

12. Rajiv Rastogi: "India's Advancement in the IT Sector" in *Employment News*, New Delhi, 29 March-4 April, 2003, p. 1.

on line. In Karnataka Bhhomi enables the people to see centuries-old land records. Similarly, Jan Mitra in Rajasthan, Gyan Doot in Madhya Pradesh, Lok Mitra in Himachal Pradesh, Nai Disha in Haryana, Automatic Vehicle Tracking System in Delhi, e-Shrankhala in Kerala, Rasi Maiyams-Kanchipuram in Tamilnadu, Community Information Centre in Arunachal Pradesh, Infotech Information Society in Chhattisgarh, Dharani Project in Goa and SETU in Maharashtra may be referred to. It all shows that e-government is gradually changing its role from an implementer to that of a facilitator and regulator. It is all the more important that public-private participation (PPP) is constantly growing.

The IT software and services industry in India accounted for about 2 per cent of the country's GDP during 2001-02. Indian IT software and services exports accounted for over 18 per cent of India's total exports during 2001-02. It is expected that by the year 2008, Indian IT software and services industry will account for 17 per cent of India's GDP and 35 per cent of its total export. The Nascom McKinsey Report (2002) has reiterated that despite the recent slowdown, the Indian IT services (ITS) and IT-enabled services (ITES) industry is poised to meet its long-term exports potential 57 US billion dollars, though the service line mix is likely to be different.[13]

Numerous are the benefits of information technology that has changed the entire process of goveranance. It has brought about a set of new responsibilities for the administrators of the country which must be realised and properly discharged by them. But it requires a new mindset and a new work culture allowing no room for intertia. It also requires skilled navigation to ensure a smooth transition from old processes and mutual operations to new automated services without hampering the existing servies. Each step should be in the direction of learning about the impediments and to improve the style of functioning in terms of directions and magnitude. Needless to say that the objectives of achieving e-governance and transforming India go far beyond mere computerisation, they require the new role of adminstrators as well as private entrepreneurs.

Statutory Arrangements—Right to Information Act (2005)

The advancement in the sphere of information technology has a profound impact on the economy of the country and the quality of

---

13 *Ibid.*

work and life of the people. The convergence of computer, communication and content creates tremendous opportunities as well as challenges. The IT revolution has opened up new possibilities of economic and social transformations from which both developed and developing countries can potentially benefit. For this sake, it is required that there should be some statutory arrangements. First of all, we may refer to the Information Technology Act, 2000. In order to facilitate growth of e-commerce, electronic communication through network and acceleration induction or IT in critical sectors of the economy, this law has come into effect. It provides legal framework to facilitate e-commerce and e-transaction and aims at recognising electronic contracts, prevention of computer crimes, e-filing/documentation, digital signature etc. Rules for its implementation have been made and the Controller of Certifying Authority has been appointed. Then, the semiconductor Integrated Circuits Lay-out Design Act, 2000 came into being. It provides for protection of semi-conductor integrated layout-design and for some incidental matters connected therewith. Rules for its implementation have been framed.

An important step in this regard was the Freedom of Information Act, 2002, which covered the entire country except the State of Jammu-Kashmir. It provided that all citizens would have freedom of information. Its main features were :

1. Every public authority (*i*) would maintain all records and publish them at times the particulars of its organisation, functions and duties; (*ii*) the powers and duties of its officers and employees and the procedure followed by them in the decision-making process; (*iii*) the norms set for the discharge of its functions; (*iv*) rules, regulations, instructions, manuals and other categories of records under its control used by its employees for discharging its functions; (*v*) the details of facilities available to citizens for obtaining information, (*vi*) the name, designation and other particulars of public information officer.

2. Every public authority for this purpose could appoint one or more Public Information Officers who could provide the required information to the person who asked for it and also provide reasonable assistance to him. In this task he could seek the assistance of any other officer as he considered necessary. A person desiring such information would make a

request in writing or through electronic means to the concerned PIO. The information could be supplied to him expeditiously but within 30 days of the receipt of the request, on the payment of required fee, or he could refuse to do so on some valid ground. Where the information sought for concerned the life and liberty of a person, it should be provided within 48 hours of the receipt of the request.

3. The PIO could refuse to give information the disclosure of which would prejudice the sovereignty and integrity of India, security of the state, strategic, scientific or economic interests of India or conduct of international relations. Any such information could not be given that prejudicially affected public safety and order, Centre-State relations, detection or investigation of an offence or the trial of a case in the court. Moreover, such information could not be supplied that was related to Cabinet papers, trade or commercial secrets or breach of parliamentary privileges.
4. Besides, the PIO could also reject the request in case it was already published in a newspaper or in some document issued for public circulation, or it was of too general a nature, or it could cause unnecessary diversion of resources of the public authority or interfere with the discharge of his authority, it could make an unwarranted attack on the privacy of a person.
5. In case the request was rejected, the person concerned, within next 30 days, could make a representation to a higher authority as prescribed. In case the representation was rejected, he could file an appeal within next 30 days to the Central Government, or to the State government, or to any other competent authority.

The Freedom of Information Act of 2002 created by the Vajpayee government remained unimplemented. It was never notified and so the Right to Information Act, 2005 repealed it. Applicable to India as a whole except Jammu and Kashmir, it covers all Central and State Government bodies and, in addition to the executive, it also applies to the legislature and the judiciary. Moreover, it covers all bodies owned, controlled and substantially financed, either directly or indirectly by the government and non-governmental institutions, and other private bodies substantially funded directly or indirectly by the Central or State governments. It would seem to include private schools, hospitals and other commercial institutions that have got subsidies in the form of land at concessional rates or tax concessions among others. Apart from these, it interestingly covers the private sector as it provides the citizens access to all information that the government can itself have through any other law currently in force.[14] Its main features may be noted as under:

1. It has a comprehensive definition of the term 'information'. It includes all opinions and advices, suggestions or counsels subject to disclosure. It also covers right to inspect work and documents and allows the extraction of certified samples for verification. Notings on the files may be seen except when specifically exempted. In a broad sense, it includes right to *(i)* inspect works, documents and records, *(ii)* take notes, extracts or certified copies of documents or records, *(iii)* take certified samples of material, and *(iv)* obtain information in the form of print outs, diskettes, floppies, tapes, video cassettes or in any other electronic mode or through print outs.

2. The Union Government as well as State Governments, including the governments of the Union Territories, shall appoint their Public Information Officers who will accept requisitions and provide information to a person seeking it within 30 days, though on some relevant grounds extension may be allowed. However, the information relating to the life and liberty of a person must be supplied within 48 hours.

3. Certain categories of information have been exempted from disclosure. No information can be given that would prejudicially affect the sovereignty and integrity of India, the security or strategic or scientific or economic interests of the state, adversely affect good relations with a foreign state or lead to incitement of an offence, or which is

---

14 Though the Act came into force on 12 October, 2005 (120 days after its enactment on 15 June, 2005,) some of its provisions came into effect immediately, namely, obligations of public authorities, designations of Public Information Officers and Assistant Public Information Officers, Constitution of Central Information Commission, non-applicability of the Act to the Intelligence and Security Organisations, and power to make rules to carry out the provisions of the Act.

forbidden by a court and whose disclosure may amount to contempt of court, or which may amount to the breach of privilege of Parliament or State legislatures, or confidential correspondence with foreign governments, or any information that would obstruct the process of investigation of a case, or endanger the identity or safety of a person involved in the process of prosecution, and minutes of the meetings of the Council of Ministers.[15]

4. Discretionary powers have been given to the Public Information Officers who may study a case on its own merits and then deny or supply some information in the 'public interest'. Information relating to commercial confidence, trade secrets or intellectual property are included in this category. Any information that can be supplied to a member of Parliament or State legislature can be supplied to any other person. So not the minutes of the meetings of the Cabinet but information relating to the decision taken on that basis can be supplied. It may be done even in violation of the provisions of the Official Secrets Act of 1923 in the name of 'public interest'. However, most of the 'exempted' information can be made available after the lapse of 20 years.

5. Under this Act, the Centre shall set up its independent Information Commission having a Chief Information Commissioner and some Commissioners. So the States shall set up their Information Commissions having a Chief Information Commissioner and some Information Commissioners not exceeding ten.

---

15. Apart from it, certain intelligence and security agencies of the Government of India, specified in the Second Schedule of the Act (as Information Bureau, Research and Analysis Wing, Directorate of Revenue Intelligence, Central Economic Intelligence Bureau, Directorate of Enforcement, Narcotics Control Bureau, Aviation Research Centre, Special Frontier Force, Border Security Force, Central Reserve Police Force, Indo-Tibetan Border Police, Central Industrial Security Force, National Security Guards and Assam Rifles) have also been kept out of the purview of this Act. Agencies specified by the State governments through a Notification. Infomation relating to the allegation of the Central and State Information Commissions, as the case may be, shall also be excluded.

6. A person can lodge his complaint with the concerned Public Information Officer who must supply the requisitioned information. If he does not oblige, then appeal may be filed before a senior officer. If he takes no action, then the matter may be filed before the State Information Commission. It is provided that the appeal be disposed off within 30-45 days. The Information Commission may impose a penalty of Rs. 250 per day on a delinquent Public Information Officer that may be Rs. 25,000 at the most. This amount shall be deducted from his salary. But the PIO may be condoned for delay if his action is done in good faith.
7. Reasonable fee may be charged for supplying requisitioned information that must be waived for persons below the poverty line. The public authorities are obligated to publish a great deal of information suo moto and should take care of creating awareness among the people in this regard.
8. According to sec. 26 of this Act, the Central and State governments should take necessary steps to (*i*) develop educational programmes for the public especially disadvantaged communities about it, (*ii*) encourage public authorities to participate in the development and organisation of such programmes, (*iii*) promote timely dissemination of accurate information to the public, (*iv*) train officers and develop training matters, (*v*) compile and disseminate a User Guide for the public in the respective official language, and (*vi*) publish names, designations, postal addresses and contract details of the Public Information Officers and other information such as notices regarding fees to be paid, remedies available in law if request is rejected etc.

No doubt, this law shall prove its worth in making the administration transparent and thereby put an effective check on the corruption and maladministration in the country. But its inherent weaknesses should also be taken into account. First, it creates a very difficult situation for the public servants who are bound to follow the provisions of the Official Secrets Act. The line of demarcation between the Official Secrets Act of 1923 and the Right to Information Act of 2005 is very thin, even blurred. A move taken by a public servant according to his best judgement may be a cause of trouble for him. Second, the list of exemptions is so big that in many cases the requisitioned information may not be supplied to the applicant. Much depends upon the interpretation of the case by the Public Information Officer and the Information Commission. Third, the schedule of charging fee is not clear. The authority concerned may enhance it in an arbitrary manner. An application fee of 10 rupees has to be paid to avail information from a department of the Government of India. Besides, a payment of two rupees per page is also to be made by the applicant. But it varies from State to State. Above all, the Government is not prepared to show the 'file notings' and more than that, it may enlarge the list of exemptions to any possible extent.

The Right to Information Act has a significance of its own in present times known as the 'era of information technology.' It is expected that this law shall prove to be a powerful instrument of democracy. It shall provide power to the people in general to obtain official information and inspect official papers and records that would make the administration transparent. By all means, it is a big improvement on the Freedom of Information Act of 2002 which could not be implemented due to lack of political will on the part of the then NDA government. Available figures show that in Maharashtra and Delhi there were about 15,000 requisitions within a span about 15 months. "If effectively implemented, it may change the nature of governance in India. It could start a process of transparent and inclusive governance that could gradually shift the Indian democracy from being almost totally a representative one to a vigorously participatory one."[16]

Not the bare provisions of a law but the manner of its implementation by the government as well as the role of the social activists have their place in changing situation in the desired direction. The names of Aruna Roy of Rajasthan and Anna Hazare and Shailesh Gandhi of Maharashtra may be referred to who came out to raise their voice against any act of diluting the provisions of this Act. For instance, the view of the Prime Minister to exclude 'file notings' from the purview of this law was strongly criticised. It is true that in pursuance of this law, the Centre and

---

16. Shekhar Singh and Nisha Singh: "Changing Governance for Ever" in *Yojana*, New Delhi, January, 2006, p. 35.

the State governments appointed their Public Information Officers and also set up their Information Commissions, it could shock a number of conscientious people to see that they were staffed by the seasoned bureaucrats like Wajahat Habibullah at the Centre and Suresh Joshi in Maharashtra. All such bodies have been headed by the members of the Indian Administrative Service and so it "has raised fears that the RTI regime may become just another means for the bureaucracy to tighten its monopoly over government information."[17]

---

17. I.J. Mistry: "Breaking the Bureaucratic Mould", *ibid.*, p. 11.

21

India and the World

An account of the foreign policy and diplomacy of a country forms an integral part of the study of its domestic policy for the obvious reason that the former is an extension of the latter in the sphere of international relations and politics. The rulers or policy-makers are not only concerned with running the administration of their country, they also think in terms of the furtherance of, what is generally called, national interest in their dealings with other states of the world. As the making of the foreign policy of a state is the job of its rulers and as policy, whether internal or external, is formulated and pursued in the midst of numerous intra- and extra-societal constraints and limitations, an integral connection between the spheres of domestic and foreign policies of a country can be easily understood.

Foreign Policy and Diplomacy

In simple terms, foreign policy may be defined as a systematic statement of a deliberately chosen course by a nation for the protection and promotion of its interest by means of playing an intelligent role in the sphere of world politics. Obviously, foreign policy and diplomacy are the two sides of the same coin: while the former consists in the taking of rational or deliberate decisions to protect and promote national interest, the latter is the art of realising the purpose that informs the statesmen to select relevant options or alternatives. As such, the making of foreign policy by the statesmen of a country and its implementation through its diplomats suggest similarity as well as distinction between national and international politics.

In a technical sense, the term 'foreign policy' may be roughly defined as a set of planned guidelines for exercising as much control as possible over existing anticipated or unforeseen circumstances in the international environment.[1] It is also defined as "a system of activities evolved by communities for changing the behaviour of other states and for adjusting their own activities to the international environment."[2] The aims of the foreign policy of a state are many like maintaining defence and integrity of the country, dispelling threats to its national security, developing its power so as to enhance its national prestige, strengthening political system and also desiring its 'export' to other countries, and striving for the emergence and consolidation of a new international order. The sum-total of these objectives constitutes a country's national interest; all decisions taken to protect and promote it constitute its foreign policy, while the technique and the strategy to implement them make its diplomacy. In short, foreign policy "is the use of political influence in order to induce other states to exercise their law-making power in a manner desired by the state concerned."[3] Moreover, as it changes form time to time in response to new pressures of domestic and external constraints, it "constitutes an endless dialogue between the powers of continuity and the powers of change."[4]

Non-Alignment

Faced with the emerging conditions of the Cold War after the termination of the second World War, India preferred the course of keeping herself away from the awfully destructive politics of bipolar diplomacy. Representing the stand of the country, Prime Minister Nehru made it clear that India would not join the military blocs of either of the two super-powers and, at the same time, pursue the path of international peace and cooperation. Soon after India's independence, both the super-powers (the USA and the USSR) strongly desired and unsuccessfully sought to entrap her in their military blocs and so, in a mood of frustration, both condemned the course of an independent foreign policy as 'immoral' comparable with 'sitting on the fence', or 'being in secret alliance with the opposite camp.' Undeterred by such allegations, Nehru repeatedly

---

1. James Rosenau : *The Scientific Study of Foreign Policy*, p. 217.
2. George Modelski : *The Theory of Foreign Policy*, p. 3.
3. F.S. Northedge. "The Nature of Foreign Policy" in his (ed.) *The Foreign Policy of the Powers*, p. 9.
4. *Ibid.*, p. 11.

affirmed his determination to pursue an independent foreign policy. Its two essential features were: (*i*) non-alignment with the military blocs of either of the two super-powers, and (*ii*) examining each international issue on its merit and expressing opinion on it frankly without fear or favour.[5]

As a matter of fact, India was presented with a challenge right from the very beginning of her independence to choose a foreign policy in accordance with her national interest in the context of a world divided between communism and anti-communism. India had to take a stand on this issue, because the attitudes of the principal powers of the world were bound to be determined by that stand."[6] That the critics of this policy showed their unwillingness to understand the implications of this stand and, instead, identify it with some other terms as neutrality, neutralisation, unilateralism, isolationism, splendid isolationism, non-involvement, non-commitment, passivism and the like. But Nehru refused to identify his concept of non-alignment with any of the so-called related terms. While speaking at the Columbia University in September, 1949, he said: "The main objectives of this policy are: the pursuit of peace not through alignment with any major group of powers but through an independent approach to each controversial or disputed issues; the liberation of subject peoples; the maintenance of freedom, both national and individual; eradication or racial discrimination; and the elimination of want, disease and ignorance which afflict the greater part of world's population."[7]

It is for this reason that India denounced the system of military groups like NATO formed in 1949, SEATO formed in 1954 and the Baghdad Pact of 1955 (which became Central Treaty Organisation in 1958) by the United States and similar commitments made by the USSR with China in 1949, with North Korea in 1950, and the making of Warsaw Pact in 1955. Instead India sought to maintain good relations with all countries of the world as far as possible on the basis of equality and mutual benefit. India did not like to interfere in the internal affairs of China when the Chinese forces intervened in Tibet. In April 1954 India signed a trade agreement with China in whose preamble five principles were incorporated:

5. B.S.N. Murti : *Nehru's Foreign Policy*, p. 68.
6. J.C. Kundra : *Indian Foreign Policy*, p. 3.
7. *Nehru's Speeches, 1947-53*, p-401

1. Mutual respect for each other's territorial integrity and sovereignty,
2. Non-aggression,
3. Non-interference in another's domestic matters,
4. Equality and mutual benefit, and
5. Peaceful coexistence.

Henceforth, non-alignment signified a set of these five principles that came to be known as 'Panchsheel' to which some other principles were attached as condemnation of colonialism and racial discrimination in any part of the world, resort to pacific settlement of international disputes, call for universal disarmament and concerted efforts for strengthening the United Nations.

Non-Alignment Policy During the Cold War Era

The Korean war of 1950 provided the first occasion when India's policy of non-alignment was put to test. India took no sides in this war and criticised the action of both the super-powers in aggravating the situation. When the United Nations adopted collective security measures, India supported them and contributed her part to the U.N. forces. In 1956 India condemned the joint attack of Britain, France and Israel on Egypt. She supported the action of Col. Nasser in nationalising the Suez Canal. Once again, she supported the preventive diplomacy of U.N. Secretary-General (Dag Hammraskjold) to restore peace in the area. But when the armed forces of the USSR suppressed the movement of the people of Hungary in the fall of the same year, India refused to condemn this action of intervention in the domestic affairs of another state by a super-power. It provided a powerful handle to the critics who dubbed it as a distinct tilt towards the Soviet Union. Thus, even a seasoned diplomat of India had to confess: "Nothing has caused so much misunderstanding regarding India's foreign policy than her attitude towards the Hungarian revolution."[8]

When civil war broke out in Congo in 1960 that resulted in the assassination of Prime Minister Patrice Lumumba, India denounced the revolt of the leader of the Katanga province (Tshombe). She contributed her share to the U.N. forces to restore peace there so as

8. K.P.S. Menon: *India and the Cold War*, p. 48.

to bring about the territorial integrity of this African state. Though India ever stood for the pacific settlement of international disputes, Prime Minister Nehru showed change in the way of his thinking in response to several compelling reasons like growing weight of the public opinion in the country as to throw off Portuguese colonialism by all possible means, suppression of the freedom struggle in Goa by the government of Portugal by repressive means, demand of the African nationalists to defeat Portuguese colonialism in India so as to strengthen their case in Angola and Mozambique, reports about secret hobnobbing between Portuguese and Pakistani authorities in Goa likely to pose threats to India's security in time to come, Portugal's membership of the NATO and Dulles-Cunha statement affirming Goa as an integral part of Portugal and, above all, military provocation caused by the Portuguese authorities in 1961 by shooting some merchants there. Thus, the three pockets of Portuguese colonialism (Goa, Daman, and Diu) were seized by India by means of 'police action' in the last week of December 1961.

However, Nehru's policy of non-alignment had the most serious jolt when China made a treacherous attack on our country in October, 1962. India gave recognition to China just after the establishment of the Communist state there in October, 1949 and signed a trade agreement with her in 1954. Nehru played an important role in bringing China into the comity of nations by ensuring her participation at the Bandung Conference in 1955. He declined to interfere in the affairs of Tibet by declaring this part under the sovereignty of China. But the slogan of 'Hindi-Chini Bhai Bhai' failed and in 1962 China captured some of the Indian territory in Ladakh and North-East Frontier Agency (now Arunachal Pradesh). Under such conditions, India had to take military aid from both the US and the USSR. It afforded another occasion for the critics to dub our policy as a shrewd strategy of 'double alignment'. Such an interpretation is totally baseless. National defence is an integral part of national interest and a state is required to take every possible step for this sake. The fact that the military aid was taken by India not from one super-power but from both the super-powers without joining their military alliances is enough to lay down that its requisition "did not bring about any fundamental change in its non-aligned position."[9]

---

9 K.P. Misra : "The Concept of Non-alignment" in his (ed.) : *Studies in India's Foreign Policy*, p. 104.

After the death of Nehru, Sahstri maintained the same tradition. In October, 1964 he represented India at the second summit of non-aligned nations held at Cairo. He laid stress on some new points to be incorporated into the programme of action as nuclear disarmament, peaceful settlement of border disputes, freedom from foreign domination and aggression, eradication of subversion of any kind and racial discrimination, acceleration of economic development through international cooperation, and full support to the United Nations and its programme for peaceful development. But what made Prime Minister Shastri popular was the victory of India in 1965. We defeated Pakistan and captured some of the strategic areas of Dera Ghazi Khan and Haji Pir Pass in the Lahore sector. It should be labelled as the first successful mark of our policy. And yet our foreign policy did not assume imperialistic overtones. At the Tashkent conference held in January, 1966 an agreement was signed whereby the two countries resolved to settle their disputes by means of bilateral negotiations. India withdrew its forces from the Lahore sector. It showed our magnanimity towards Pakistan.[10]

Indira Gandhi followed the same tradition. When the USSR interfered in the domestic affairs of Czechoslovakia in 1968, India took the same stand what had been taken earlier at the time of the Hungarian crisis. It afforded another occasion to the critics to dub our policy as one of 'selective alignment.' Undetererd by such allegations, Indira Gandhi went ahead. The outbreak of civil war in East Pakistan causing immigration of millions of refugees into our country posed a serious problem. Mrs. Gandhi's appeals to the dictator of Pakistan (Yahya Khan) failed. Foreseeing the consequences of events in time to come, she had to depend on the support of the USSR. Thus in August, 1971 India signed a pact of peace, friendship and cooperation with the USSR (known as Indo-Soviet Treaty) that paid dividends just a few months after. War broke out in December in which India defeated Pakistan. Bangladesh emerged as a separate sovereign country. President Bhutto of Pakistan came to India and signed the Shimla Agreement on 2 July, 1972 wherein the two countries again resolved to settle their disputes by means of bilateral negotiations.

A slight change of emphasis occurred in 1977 when the Janata Party formed government under the Prime Ministership of Morarji

---

10. See L.P. Singh: *India's Foreign Policy: The Shastri Period*, p. 111.

Desai with Atal Behari Vajpayee as the Foreign Minister. The new leaders labelled their policy as one of 'genuine' non-alignment. It implied nothing else than more and more tilt towards the United States. N.A. Palkhivala, a well-known friend of the Indian capitalist class, was sent to the United States as India's ambassador so as to improve our relations with America that had deteriorated to an unexpected extent during the days of Bangladesh war. However, nothing material could occur by way of change in the direction of, what the leaders in power called, positive or proper or genuine non-alignment. Though relations with the US improved, no setback could be given to Indo-Soviet relations. After some time, it appeared that the frequent use of certain adjectives preceding the term 'non-alignment' was "apparently a superfluity or at best a case of over-emphasis."[11]

Thus, there occurred a natural change when Mrs. Gandhi became the Prime Minister again in 1980. The experiment of Janata government could not survive after a couple of years. But now Mrs. Gandhi became very cautious in respect of our relations with the USSR. In clear contrast to the events of the past, she did not appreciate the intervention of the USSR in Afghanistan that occurred in the fall of 1979. But she bracketed this event with like events of interference in other countries of the world. In a statement given on 3 August, 1982, Foreign Minister P.V. Narsimha Rao said: "We cannot allow the non-aligned movement to be used as a vehicle or instrument for propagation of any single ideology or for promotion of the interest of any single great power directly or indirectly." Mrs. Gandhi strongly criticised the formation of military base at Diego Garcia and insisted on keeping Indian ocean as a zone of peace. She realised that the lack of capital equipment and financial resources was an important bottle-neck in the development of the Third World countries. So she supported the movement for North-South dialogue and South-South cooperation to usher in a better and more equitable international economic order.

Rajiv Gandhi became the Prime Minister after the assassination of Mrs. Gandhi in 1984. He adhered to the same course but with a vigour and dynamism of his own. In January, 1985 he hosted a summit of six nations (Mexico, Greece, Sweden, Tanzania, Argentina and India) in Delhi so as to lay special stress on the need for nuclear

---

11. S.C. Gangal: *India's Foreign Policy*, p. 6.

disarmament. At the Harare summit of the non-aligned nations held in September, 1986 he said that non-alignment "is an idea, a reality, a movement, a major force transforming history. We pledge ourselves a new to its central idea—coexistence and co-development in peace, honour and dignity." In New Delhi he signed a declaration with President Gorbachov of the USSR on 27 December, 1986 having these important points:

1. Peaceful coexistence must be the universal norm in international relations.
2. Human life must be recognised as supreme.
3. Non-violence should be the basis of community life.
4. Understanding and trust must replace fear and suspicion.
5. The right of every state to political and economic independence must be recognised and respected.
6. Resources being spent on armament must be channelled towards social and economic development.
7. Conditions must be guaranteed for the individual's harmonious development.
8. Mankind's material and intellectual potential must be used to solve global problems.
9. The 'balance of terror' must give way to comprehensive international security.
10. A nuclear weapon-free and non-violent world requires specific and immediate action for disarmament.

However, the most notable achivement of India'a foreign policy and diplomacy under the leadership of Rajiv Gandhi is the establishment of the South Asian Association for Regional Cooperation (SAARC) in 1985.

India's foreign policy lost its vigour when V.P. Singh became the Prime Minister, though his successor (Chandra Shekhar) could give a turn to the better side by criticising the action of Iraq in capturing Kuwait in August 1990 and thereby unleashing the Gulf war. He did not appreciate the view of the leftist forces that even in this situation of war, as per the resolutions of the U.N. Security Council, the United States should be condemned for an imperialistic action. Like his predecessors, he insisted that the problem of West Asia should be solved in a way that justice be done to the Palestinians. India appreciated the withdrawal of the Soviet forces from Afghanistan in 1989.

Non-Alignment Policy in the Post-Cold War Era

A new world came into being in 1991 as a result of the disintegration of the USSR. The phase of strained relationship between the two super-powers that had been in a state of decline since 1970 and that was given the name of 'detente', had its termination when the 'evil empire' (a name given by President Ronald Reagan to the Soviet Union) ended. To the critics of non-alignment policy it appeared that it lost its relevance altogether. In such a changed world, it was natural for the foreign policy of India to undergo a change in many directions which may be noted as under:

It is wrong to say that non-alignment policy has now become redundant. While its negative feature desiring aloofness from the military blocs of the super-powers became irrelevant, its positive feature of desiring a new international order having peace, security and cooperation among all countries of the world stiil stands. As such, the non-alignment policy would continue until the goal is achieved. Hence, India is still working for bringing about the new international order in all walks of life.

Prime Minister Rao added some new principles to the set of five principles already in operation since 1954. In a speech delivered in New Delhi at a seminar on Panch Sheel and Global Diplomacy on 27 June, 1994, he elaborated following principles to meet the requirements of the present age:

(*i*) Middle Path—adherence to the canons of mixed economy.

(*ii*) Technology and Tradition—bringing about harmony between tradition (old) and technology (new) for economic modernisation of the country without effacing the values of traditional system.

(*iii*) New World Order—strengthening the way of peaceful coexistence.

However, the most important shift finds place in the direction of economic liberalisation in response to the trend of globalisation of capital and technology. India is trying to improve her economic relations with as many countries of the world as possible. While delivering in augural address at the SAARC meet in New Delhi on 2 May , 1995, Prime Minister Rao said: "When we are opening up our markets to the world and inviting global competition, it stands to reason that we join forces and fortify our collective strength in support of our business communities."[12]

However, the most striking feature of India's foreign policy in the post-Cold War era should be noted in the increasingly important role played by her Finance Minister (Manmohan Singh). It showed that traditional diplomacy of avoiding conditions of war and rift had been replaced by the canons of desiring tangible economic gains. As a result, the Finance Minister usurped the role of the Foreign Minister to a considerable extent. A new kind of nexus developed between the bureaucrats acting at the behest of the politicians and the barons of Indian industry that track-two diplomacy came to occupy its own place in the making of our foreign policy and its implementation.[13] Several agencies controlled by the business magnates started playing their own part in refining and strengthening their relations with their counterparts in other countries of the world and thereby influencing the bureaucrats, the ministers and the diplomats of the concerned countries. The evolution of subtle synergy may be noticed in the fact that now there is a much greater degree of openness in government and deeper appreciation of the need for mutual reliance between business and government in the following directions :

1. The delegations of the Government of India visiting abroad for making economic or commercial agreements include leading figures of the business community. It in itself stands like close interface between the two. Preparations for these joint ventures are done in a way that very important areas of business are identified and fertile areas of partnership between the concerned nations are earmarked. Open and forthright discussions on the policy cliches and contentious diplomatic issues take place between government

---

12 *The Times of India* (New Delhi), 3 May, 1995

13 This is a new term that suggests the role of non-governmental agencies in exericising pressure either by themselves or through other multinational and international organisations on the decision-makers of a country in order to have favourable results.

and business so that the Indian business leaders are fully aware of the sensitivities before they venture into a new terrain. At the same time, the business leaders remain free to draw their own conclusions and chart out their own course of action. This new and welcome approach has already succeeded in breaking virgin grounds for India in a number of nations, the most glamorous of this is the signing of the Indo-US Commercial Alliance. In a unique move the governments of India and of the US have decided to allow business to be on the driver's seat.

2. It may also be noted in the relaxation of restrictions so that foreign capital may be attracted. The non-resident Indians as well as the foreign capitalists may now seek direct investment of their capital in our country.

3. There is also the emergence of an intellectual synergy between the world of business and the world of governance. For example, the Apex Chambers have now begun to make some contributions towards the formulation of 'country strategy' for India. For instance, a delegation of India led by the then Commerce Minister (Pranab Mukherji) to Johannesburg in South Africa in September, 1994 (that included some powerful business figures) broke new grounds there. It paved the way for the coming of President Nelson Mandela to India in January, 1995 who publicly appreciated the role of Indian businessmen in establishing bridges between the two nations.

4. Unlike the past, now many Indian missions abroad are emerging like a nodal point for foreign business visits to India. The final links in the chain are the Apex Chambers in Delhi who provide a firm platform for fulfilling the goals of these foreign delegations. In between lie layers of interface between the ministers of the Government of India and the business organisations working together to fructify the new policy objectives of globalisation.

5. Last, it may be noted in our desire to have a kind of regional common market on the lines of the European Union or the Association of South-East Asian Nations. Prime Minister Vapayee laid stress on such a development at the summit of the SAARC held at Islamabad in Pakistan in January, 2004 and the heads of the seven nation-states resolved to implement the South Asian Free Trade Agreement.

It is due to new realisation or awareness that India signed the Marrakesh agreement in 1994 and became one of the founder members of the World Trade Organisation formed on 1 January, 1995. The need of the time is to learn from economically powerful countries like Japan, Germany, South Korea and Israel so as to put our shattered economy back on the rails and add new dimensions to our foreign policy and diplomacy without having any obsession with our commitments made and observed in the past. We may make a sort of national consensus on optimal level of globalisation and then establish a happy and enduring relationship between our polity and economy, if we desire to be an economically powerful country in time to come.

India joined Indian Ocean Rim Association for Regional Cooperation (IORARC) formed in March 1997. Its aim is to bolster economic cooperation amongst the rim states of the Indian Ocean ranging from Mauritius and Madagaskar to Singapore, Malaysia and Australia. The formation of the Bangladesh, India, Sri Lanka and Thailand Economic Cooperation (also known as the Bay of Bengal Co-operation Forum) formed in June 1997 (Myanmar joined it after some time and so it is BIMST-EC) is another example in the same direction. Prime Minister Singh attended its meet at Bangkok in July 2004 where India and Thailand signed Free Trade Agreement.

Look-East Policy

In the post-Cold War era, India looked towards the countries of South-East and East Asia for improving her economic and cultural relations. When the ASEAN was formed in August, 1967 India had declined to join it as some of its members (like Philiphines and Thailand) were aligned with the military blocs of the United States. But now the milieu had changed and so India managed to have the status of a half-dialogue partner in the Asian Regional Forum (ARF) of this organisation in 1992 which was raised to the status of full dialogue partner in 1996. The Mekong-Ganga Cooperation came into being on 10 November, 1999 at a meet in Vientiane, capital of Laos, where the Foreign Ministers of India, Myanmar, Thailand, Laos, Cambodia and Vietnam focussed attention on the development of tourism, culture, education and communications amongst themselves. Prime Minister Vajpayee visited the countries of South-East Asia and he signed agreements with Cambodia, Malaysia, Vietnam and Indonesia covering economic and cultural spheres.

Not only this, Vajpayee paid visit to Japan and China and agreements covering scientific, cultural and economic matters were signed. Relations were revived with Myanmar as well.

The Look-East Policy implying improvement of relations with the countries of South-East and East Asia was initiated by Prime Minister Rao, but it saw its remarkable success during the tenure of Vajpayee. This policy was adopted in the wake of economic liberalisation emerged after the collapse of the USSR in 1991. It is a manifestation of India's desire to build strong relations with the 'economic tigers' of South-East Asia like Malaysia, Indonesia and Vietnam as well was with the great powers of East Asia like Japan and China. In this sphere the success of India's economic diplomacy has a fine track record. When Vajpayee visited Vietnam in January, 2001 he happily commented that it was not 'Look-East' but 'Re-Look-East Policy' of his government.

India has vigorously pursued its 'Look East Policy' and developed multi-faceted relationships as well as bilateral contacts with the countries of this region. She has been actively engaged with the Asian Regional Forum of the ASEAN as a full dialogue partner since 1996. India attended the East Asian summits held at Kuala Lumpur in December, 2005 and at Cebu in January, 2007. The India-ASEAN Partnership for peace, progress and shared prosperity was signed at the third summit of the ASEAN countries in November, 2004. It envisages strengthening of cooperation in the United Nations and other multilateral fora like the World Trade Organisation. India concluded a Comprehensive Economic Cooperation Agreement with Singapore in June, 2005 and established a Joint Study Group for examining the feasibility of a similar agreement with Malaysia. In July 2007, a new strategic partnership was established between India and Vietnam during the visit of the Prime Minister Dung to New Delhi. In September, 2007 India hosted the largest multilateral-naval exercises ever in the Bay of Bengal in which the navies of other countries like (USA, Japan, Australia and Singapore) participated. It shows that India's 'Look East Policy' is not limited to economic cooperation and cultural exchanges, now the security angle has also become very important.

Nuclear Policy

Prime Minister Nehru and his successors invariably laid stress on the need for time-bound universal disarmament and in very strong terms they condemned nuclear experiments made by the five great powers (USA, UK, France, USSR and China) known as the P-5. At the first non-aligned conference held at Belgrade in September, 1961, Nehru described such experiments as greatest menace to world peace. When the Partial Test Ban Treaty (PTBT) came into being in 1963, India signed it. It prohibited nuclear experiments above the ground, under the water, and in the atmosphere, but it exempted under-ground tests and so it was called Partial Test Ban Treaty. But when the Nuclear Non-proliferation Treaty (NPT) came into being in 1970, Indira Gandhi refused to sign it. Similar stand was taken by other Prime Ministers. it was a 25-years treaty, but when its period was extended indefinitely in May, 1995, Prime Minsiter Rao denounced it in very strong terms. The stand of the Indian leaders on this issue has been consistent that it is a discriminatory treaty in view of the fact that while it permits the 'big five' to exchange among themselves nuclear energy and technology, it prohibits the transfer of same to any other country by any of the P-5 powers. It also prohibits nuclear experiments for peaceful and constructive purposes.

As the draft of the Comprehensive Test Ban Treaty (CTBT) could not be passed at the Disarmament Conference held at Geneva in June, 1996 in the face of India's opposition, America managed to hijack it and get it passed by the General Assembly of the United Nations three months after. It bans all kinds of nuclear tests for any purpose whatsoever. So India refused to sign it.

While India has been critical of nuclear armament, her leaders have insisted on making peaceful nuclear explosions. Hence, Indira Gandhi justified the action of her government in making a successful nuclear test at Pokhran in May, 1974. Since Pakistan developed nuclear technology and produced nuclear weapons with the clandestine help of China, and as both countries had evil eyes towards India, Prime Minister Vajpayee realised threats to our security. Hence, in May 1998 successful nuclear tests were again made at Pokhran. America, Canada, Australia and Japan came forward with strong condemnation of such a move and they stopped their aid to our country. But the leaders of Britain, France and Russia expressed their reactions in a very cautious manner. It is a pity that even the leaders of the Indian National Congress, the CPI, and the CPM found fault with such a move of the Vajapyee. government on the plea that it would drag our country towards mad race for armaments.

Prime Minister Vajpayee dismissed all such criticisms on the plea that India could not make any compromise with her security concerns. But he also made it clear that India would not make use of such weapons in the first instance. It implied that if any country used such weapons against us, then we would retaliate in the like manner. On 17 August, 1999, the then National Security Adviser (Brijesh Mishra) presented draft of India's nuclear doctrine at a press conference highlighting these salient points.

1. India would use nuclear weapons as retaliatory instruments only against any state or entity that resorted to nuclear coercion against her.
2. The nuclear force would be effective, enduring, diverse, flexible and responsive, and would be based on a triad of aircraft, mobile land-based missiles, and sea-based missiles.
3. The production of nuclear weapons as to maintain the state of minimum credible deterrence was within the capacity of India.

Since India took a strong stand on these points, foreign powers like USA and Japan changed their views after a couple of years and the embargo put on assistance was lifted.

On 4th January, 2003 the Cabinet Committee on Security (consisting of the Prime Minister, Deputy Prime Minister and Finance and Foreign Ministers) declared the following points of its nuclear doctrine and command structure:

1. It said about the establishment of a National Command Authority in which a Political Council headed by the Prime Minister would be sole authority for ordering a nuclear strike. It would be done if India or its forces anywhere in the world were attacked with nuclear, chemical or biological weapons.
2. The Political Council would be advised by an executive council led by the National Security Adviser.[14] The executive council would give inputs to the political leadership and carry out its decisions.

---

14. The National Security Adviser would chair the executive council which would advise the Political Council after collecting inputs. The executive council would implement decisions taken by the political leadership.

3. The Cabinet Committee on Security also approved an all-services Strategic Forces Command (SFC) to manage and administer all strategic (nuclear) weapons and delivery systems.[15]
4. It also expressed its commitment to nuclear disarmament.
5. A retaliatory attack could also be authorised by this council which represented the civilian leadership. As the first among equals, the Prime Minister would symbolically have the finger on the nuclear button. An alternative chain of command had also been approved to take charge in case the command chain be disrupted in any way.
6. The Strategic Forces Command would be the custodian of all nuclear weapons and delivery system. It would formulate the strategy for retaliation and advise the change of staff committee and actually fire the nukes.
7. Once the committee received the inputs, it would provide military advice to the Political Council of the Nuclear Command Authority through the executive council.

It was, indeed, a timely step taken by the Government of India. It was a patent reality at that time that Pakistan openly valued nuclear blackmail as a shield to export terrorism to India and China continued to build up its weapons of mass destruction and covertly assist Pakistan.[16]

In short, India's nuclear policy is based on these relevant grounds. First, nuclear experiments for destructive purposes should be stopped, but there should be no ban on peaceful nuclear explosions. Second, each country has the right to defend herself. Hence, India cannot ignore her security concerns. When China and Pakistan have nuclear weapons, India must also have them. Third, though India is an economically backward country, production of nuclear weapons is within her capacity. Fourth, India may produce nuclear

---

15. It was considered necessary as India being a signatory to the Chemical and Biological Weapons Conventions does not possess such weapons.
16. Brahma Chellany, "Nuke Command: Better Late Than Never" in *The Hindustan Times* (New Delhi) 5 January, 2003.

weapons, but they would be used against a country as a retaliatory measure. Fifth, India would not tolerate any pressure from the side of any country to sign the NPT and the CTBT. Last, India invariably stands for a time-bound universal disarmament. In his first address to the nation on 24th June, 2004, Prime Minister Manmohan Singh reiterated that India "would maintain a credible minimum nuclear deterrence along with a policy of 'no first use' in its nuclear doctrine. India is a responsible nuclear power and we will continue to work to prevent proliferation of weapons of mass destruction. At the same time, we remain committed to the goal of universal nuclear disarmament."[17]

What we have said above shows that the basic concerns of India's foreign policy underwent a momentous change after the end of the Cold War and so the policy-makers had to refashion their options and endeavours which may be enumerated as under:

1. To restructure the basic orientation of foreign policy in the context of totally transformed paradigms and terms of reference born out of the change in the international situation. This had to be done in a manner ensuring fulfilment of India's national interest in every aspect.
2. To recast relations with each of the super-powers, such as the USA, Russia and China in the context of the end of the cold war.
3. To cope with threats to India's territorial integrity and stability generated by political developments and policies of India's immediate neighbours.
4. To diversify political and economic contacts so as to neutralise the impact of the disintegration of the Soviet Union on our sources of technology and defence supplier, important raw materials and other such inputs as were needed to sustain our defence capabilities.
5. To examine and decide upon options responsive to the new trends of multilateral pressures in spheres such as technology, space, nuclear capacities, environmental issues and human rights.
6. To generate international public opinion to support those steps

17. *The Times of India*, New Delhi, 25 June, 2004.

which India would have to undertake to maintain its territorial integrity and internal security.

7. To create new and positive equations with emerging centres of power and influence in the international community. This included fashioning of new patterns of relations with individual countries, establishing relations *ab initio* with some countries and opening up contacts with regional groupings and multilateral organisations whose policies and activities could impinge on India's interests.
8. To fashion an economic foreign policy responsive to the requirements of globalisation and to those of the mainstream free market economic trends. While responses to this category had to ensure an appropriate and creditable position for India in the international economic community, they also had to, at the same time, ensure domestic social and distributive justice.
9. To redefine political elements in India's strategic and defence doctrines in the context of the changed strategic equations at the global and regional levels.
10. To restructure policy responses to trends of international multilateralism on the part of the United Nations and other such agencies. This was to be a complex exercise in sustaining state sovereignty, while contributing to the creation of an international consensus on issues of trans-national concerns.
11. Above all, to reforge and recreate internal national consensus on India's foreign policy in all its dimensions and aspects—a consensus which had been previously eroded for almost two decades to the point of becoming almost extinct by mid-1991.[18]

India and the Non-Aligned Movement

Prime Minister Nehru not only clarified the implications of the term 'non-alignment' in the course of the prosecution of his foreign policy, he also started a movement with the support of leaders like President Tito of Yugoslavia, President Nasser of Egypt and President Soekarno of Indonesia. The support of other leaders like

18. J.N. Dixit : *India's Foreign Service : History of Challenges* (Delhi Konark, 2005), pp. 227-28

Prime Minister U Nu of Burma (now Myanmar), Prime Minister Bhandarnaike of Ceylon (now Sri Lanka) and President Nkrumah of Ghana should also be taken into account at this stage. The idea of calling a conference of the non-aligned nations was mooted by Nehru which received full support from Tito and Nasser. Hence, in June, 1964 a conference of the Foreign Ministers of these countries was held at Cairo where the criterion of non-alignment was laid down. It stipulated:

1. A country should follow an independent policy based on peaceful co-existence and non-alignment, or be showing a trend in favour of such a policy.
2. It should consistently have supported movements for national independence.
3. It should not be a member of a multilateral military alliance concluded in the context of Great Power conflicts.
4. If it has conceded military bases, these concessions should not have been made in the context of Great Power conflicts.
5. If it is a member of any bilateral or regional defence arrangement, this should not be in the context of Great Power conflicts.

The story of the non-alignment movement had its start when a conference of 25 such nations was held at Belgrade in September, 1961. Since then till now fourteen meets have taken place.

The track-record of the NAM shows that Indian made notable contributions on each occasion. At the first meet of 1961., Nehru apprised the world of the disastrous consequences of nuclear experiments. At the second meet of Cairo, Shastri condemned the course of cold war and hit at the futility of military alliances. Prime Minister Indira Gandhi made the same affirmations at the meets of Lusaka, Algiers and Colombo. It was at the Algiers conference that an important resolution was adopted for bringing about a new international economic order. At the Havana meet Foreign Minister S.N. Mishra made a very poor show of diplomacy. At the New Delhi meet, Indira Gandhi managed to control the situation with the help of President Castro of Cuba and thereby the issue of military intervention of the USSR in Afghanistan could not be allowed to blow up as desired by some members having pro-US leanings.

Conferences	*Year*	*Venues*	*Countries*
First	1961	Belgrade	Yugoslavia
Second	1964	Cairo	Egypt
Third	1970	Lusaka	Zambia
Fourth	1973	Algiers	Algeria
Fifth	1976	Colombo	Sri Lanka
Sixth	1979	Havana	Cuba
Seventh	1983	New Delhi	India
Eight	1986	Harare	Zimbabwe
Ninth	1989	Belgrade	Yugoslavia
Tenth	1992	Jakarta	Indonesia
Eleventh	1995	Cartegena	Colombia
Twelfth	1998	Durban	South Africa
Thirteenth	2003	Kuala Lumpur	Malaysia
Fourteenth	2006	Havana	Cuba
Fifteenth	2009	Sharmel-Sheikh	Egypt
Sixteenth	2012	Tehran	Iron
Fifteenh	2009	Sharam-al Sheikh	Egypt
Sixteenth	2012	Tehran	Iran

At the Harare and Belgrade summits, Rajiv Gandhi laid stress on the need for disarmament within a time-bound framework. Narsimha Rao represented India at the Jakarta and Cartegena meets. Vajpayee represented India at the Durban meet and he frankly registered his objection at the words of President Mandela of South Africa who touched the issue of Kashmir in his inaugural address. At the Kuala Lumpur meet, he advised that the NAM should 're-make' itself. Regretting at the mistakes of the past, he said that "ours is a story of missed huge opportunities." His idea of establishing a 300 million dollars corpus for Global Poverty Eradication Fund was appreciated. Since the clouds of American invasion on Iraq were hovering, Vajpayee and other members criticised such moves and insisted that any step in this direction should be taken in concurrence with the resolve of the Security Council of the United Nations. In his lecture on 'Changing Dimensions of Nehruism', Foreign Minister Natwar Singh well observed that 'NAM needs drastic reforms. It requires re-inventing, just like Tony Blair re-invented the Labour Party. And we should not mix 'non-alignment' with NAM."[19]

Prime Minister Manmohan Singh represented India at the XIV meet of the non-aligned nations held at Havana in Cuba in September, 2006. On this occasion, he put particular stress on the menace of global terrorism. He affirmed: "If the NAM is to be relevant in today's circumstances, it cannot afford to equivocate on the subject of terrorism. A message must

19. *The Times of India*, New Delhi, 12 July, 2004, p. 7.

emanate from us that we are united in our desire to fight and eliminate the scourge of terrorism. The forces of intolerance and extremism could not be allowed to distract the world's attention from the vital concerns such as poverty, ignorance and disease." While rejecting the notion of 'clash of civilisations', he "made a strong plea to the NAM to be seen as being central to global efforts to deal with urgent trans-national issues including terrorism. Today we again confront the danger of the world being split along an artificially created cultural and religious divide. The NAM encompasses, as it does, every religion professed by mankind, every ethnic groups and ideological persuasion is uniquely placed today once again, to play the role of a bridge of undestanding."[20]

India and the SAARC

Taking into his view the remarkable success of some regional organisations like the European Union (EU) and the Association of South-East Asian Nations (ASEAN), Prime Minister Rajiv Gandhi created the South Asian Association for Regional Cooperation (SAARC) with these objectives :

1. To promote the welfare of the peoples of South Asia and to improve the quality of life,
2. To achieve economic growth, social progress and cultural development of the region,
3. To promote and strengthen collective self-reliance among the countries of South Asia, and to provide all individuals the opportunity to live in dignity and to realise their full potential,
4. To contribute to mutual trust, understanding and appreciation of one another's problems,
5. To promote active collaboration and mutual assistance in economic, social, cultural and technical fields,
6. To strengthen cooperation among themselves in international forums on matters of common interest, and

---

20. *The Times of India* (New Delhi), 17 September, 2006. In a statement signed with President Musharraf of Pakistan, it was given that they condemned terrorism and agreed that it was a scourge that needed to be effectively dealt with. They decided to put in place an India-Pakistan anti-terrorism institutional mechanism to identify and implement counter-terrorism initiatives and investigations."

7. To cooperate with regional and international organisations with similar aims and purposes.

Formed on 8 December 1985, this regional organisation had seven members, namely, India, Pakistan, Bangladesh, Nepal, Bhutan, Sri Lanka and Maldives. Afghanistan joined it in 2006. Now it has 8 members. Since its inception the SAARC summits have been held from time to time as is evident from the tabular illustration.

It is an association based on the realisation of the fact that in an increasingly interdependent world, the objectives of peace, friendship, cooperation, social justice and economic prosperity in the under-developed region can be achieved by means of fostering mutual understanding, good neighbourly relations and meaningful cooperation among the members of this region which are bound together by close historical and cultural ties. Decisions are taken on the basis of unanimity. Bilateral and contentious issues are excluded from the range of deliberations. Important discussions take place at the summit meetings of the heads of the states/ governments, which are held every year or with a gap of one year or so. But the meetings of the Foreign Ministers of the member-states take place from time to time to formulate policies, review progress, explore new areas of cooperation, establish additional mechanisms as deemed necessary, and take up other matters of common interest. Its secretariat is located at Kathmandu. It coordinates and monitors implementation of its activities and serves as a channel of communication between it and other regional organisations and inter-governmental institutions.

A notable achievement of this organisation should be seen in the creation of the SAARC Preferential Trading Arrangement (SAPTA). Its agreement was signed on 11 April, 1993 but is came into effect on 7 December 1995. Its underlying principles are :

(*i*) Over-all reciprocity and mutuality of advantages so as to benefit equitably all the contracting states, while taking into account their respective levels of industrial and economic development, the patterns of their external trade, including trade and tariff policies and systems,

(*ii*) Step by step negotiations of tariff reforms, improved and extended in successive stages through periodic reviews, (*iii*) Recognition of the special needs of the least developed contracting states and agreement on concrete preferential measures in their favour, and

(*iv*) Inclusion of products, manufactured goods and commodities in their raw, semi-processed and processed forms.

At the Colombo meet (1998) it was decided to set up a committee of experts to draft a comprehensive treaty framework for creating a free trade area within the region, taking into consideration the asymmetries in development within the region and bearing in mind the need to fix realistic and achievable targets. Progress in this direction has been very tardy owing to the unhelpful and uncooperative attitude of some members, particularly Pakistan. However, the achievements of this organisation may be seen in adopting conventions on the suppression of terrorism, detection and prevention of Narcotic drugs and psychotropic substances, combating trafficking in women and children, and promotion of child welfare in this region. It has undertaken high level regional

SAARC Meets

Conferences	*Year*	*Venues*	*Countries*
First	1985	Dhaka	Bangladesh
Second	1986	Bangalore	India
Third	1987	Kathmandu	Nepal
Fourth	1988	Islamabad	Pakistan
Fifth	1990	Male	Maldives
Sixth	1991	Colombo	Sri Lanka
Seventh	1993	Dhaka	Bangladesh
Eight	1995	New Delhi	India
Ninth	1997	Male	Maldives
Tenth	1998	Colombo	Sri Lanka
Eleventh	2002	Kathmandu	Nepal
Twelfth	2004	Islamabad	Pakistan
Thirteenth	2005	Dhaka	Bangladesh
Fourteenth	2007	New Delhi	India
Fifteenth	2008	Colombo	Sri Lanka
Sixteenth	2010	Thimpu	Bhutan
Seventeenth	2011	Male	Maldives

studies in the spheres of trade, environment and eradication of poverty.[21]

The XIII meet of the SAARC was held at Dhaka on 12-13 November, 2005. On this occasion, Prime Minister Manmohan Singh put a number of measures for consideration as:

1. Reciprocal transit facilities to connect all the member-States as well as other countries of the Gulf, the Central Asia and South-East Asia,
2. Establishment of a South Asian university as a centre of excellence in any country of South Asia.
3. Establishment of a regional food bank on contributory basis to meet shortages and losses caused by natural disaster in any South Asian country.
4. Exercise of zero tolerance for cross-border terrorism and no member of this organisation to allow its territory to be used against the interest of another member, and
5. Establishment of a High Economic Council to promote initiatives for the creation of South Asian Economic Union by 2020.

At this meet, three important agreements were signed—on mutual Administrative Assistance in customs matters, on the establishment of a SAARC Arbitration Council, and Limited Agreement on avoidance of double taxation and mutual administrative assistance in tax matters.

At the end, as declaration was adopted that pledged to make this body an effective instrument for cooperation to visibly improve the quality of life in South Asia. It accepted the entry of Afghanistan as the eighth member, the request of China and Japan for having the

21. SAFTA came into operation on 1 January, 2006. Now all the members will bring down their customs duties to 0.5% upto 2013, while the LDCs or least developed countries (Nepal, Bhutan, Banladesh and Maldives) will do it by 2018. India has a sensitive list of 884 items for non-LDCs and 765 for LDCs. India being the larger and relatively developed country will be providing concessions to least developing countries including a mechanism for compensation of revenue loss due to reduction in duties and technical assistance.

status of 'observers' was also accepted in principle. It was given in the Dhaka Declaration that the scope of SAFTA shall be expanded to include trade in services, enhanced investment and harmonised standards. "Unfortunately, in spite of all the rhetoric and noble declarations, this seven countries' forum has failed to realise the SAFTA till now."

Unfortunately, the SAARC has not been able to achieve the desired results. It may be due to some pertinent reasons. First, it is an association of unequal partners. The European Union has many partners of equal rank as France, Germany and the United Kingdom and so in the ASEAN Malaysia, Indonesia and Vietnam have the same place. But in this organisation India is the only major partner. Second, the attitude of Pakistan has ever been unhelpful and it becomes more so when anti-India elements come to power in Bangladesh. It is due to this that the issue of SAPTA lingered on and nothing notable could occur in this direction in spite of the fact that a decision to this effect was taken at the New Delhi meet held in the summer of 1995. Certainly, due to such reasons, India's Foreign Minister Gujral advanced the idea of having closer relations with other small members of the SAARC like Nepal, Bhutan and Bangladesh. He even suggested that India should give all possible assistance to these countries without expecting anything from them in return. It came to be known as the Gujral doctrine and it led his critics to remark that India's Foreign Minister desired to make a mini-SAARC.

Cross-border terrorism is another factor in this regard. India raised this issue at the Kathmandu conference in 2002 and President Musharraf had to share his concern with the magnitude of this problem just for the sake of diplomatic reasons. But the Islamabad Summit of 2004 has its own importance where a decision was taken to combat this menace collectively. The Prime Minister of Bhutan took the opportunity to inform all the members that his government had adopted the policy of flushing out all such elements (as ULFA and Bodo militants) from his country which had taken shelter there. The heads of different stages/governments endorsed the proposal of Prime Minister Vajpayee that by the end of the next year (2005) South Asian Free Trade Agreement (SAFTA) should come into operation. No doubt, this was the first successful meet of this regional organisation since its birth in 1985. What is, however, appreciable in this regard is that the Foreign Ministers of India and Pakistan signed a memorandum and agreed to have a composite dialogue so as to sort out mutual problems.

Critical Appreciation

A critical evaluation of India's foreign policy, particularly in the post-cold war era, enables us to highlight its success in these important directions :[22]

1. Despite enormous diversities and centrifugal forces affecting us, we have remained a united country.
2. We have safeguarded our territorial integrity against external threats and pressures which we have faced in the form of subversion, military threats and internal and external political and military challenges.
3. Though subject to negative perceptions by our neighbours (however insignificant they may be), we have maintained a working relationship with all our neighbours in over-all terms, whatever the interim ups and downs might have been.
4. It is also to be noted that there has not been a single instance where we have shown tendencies of territorial aggrandisements or political hegemony with regard to our neighbours despite there being fundamental disputes affecting our relations with Pakistan, Bangladesh, Nepal and China.
5. We have retained our foreign policy and our nuclear, space and technological options, successfully restoring continuous negative pressures on us to fall in line with discriminatory arrangements and regimes which would have been detrimental to our national interests.
6. We have managed to structure a working relationship with all the major powers of the world on a continuous basis over the last 50 years, or during the profound transition witnessed by the world after the end of the cold war.
7. We are active members of most multilateral for a dealing with global issues even if we are not given the role and position due to us because of global power equations.

---

22. J.N. Dixit : *Across Borders : Fifty Years of India's Foreign Policy*, pp. 380-81

8. We have managed our defence and foreign economic relations with sufficient flexibility to meet basic interests, to ensure the security and well-being of our people in a complex world in constant ferment and change.

The success of a foreign policy is measured by the result of efforts it makes for the protection and promotion of its national interest. As such, our foreign policy has seen the marks of success as well as failure on many counts. On the positive side by following the policy of non-alignment India could create a third force that lessened the fears of another great war. Nehru showed a new way that was followed by more and more countries of the world. They left the military alliances of the super-powers and joined the non-aligned movement. With such a stand the bloc of the Afro-Asian nations could establish its hold over the General Assembly of the United Nations that was once regarded as 'American club'. The policy of non-alignment reinforced the demand for the creation of a new and just international order in social, economic and political spheres.

On the other side, the weak points of India's foreign policy may be counted as under :

1. India has to suffer on account of the element of 'idealism' in her foreign policy. We were cheated by Communist China in 1962. We have created complications by adhering to the path of idealism in keeping our relations with Pakistan particularly on the issue of Kashmir. By leaning too much on the side of the USSR, we provided a handle to our critics to dub our policy as one of 'selective alignment'. By throwing out the hold of Portugal over the pockets of Goa, Daman and Diu by force, we provided another handle to our critics to find fault with our commitment to the way of pacific settlement of international disputes. Foreign Minister Gujral advanced the idea of giving all help to some of our neighbours (as Nepal, Bhutan and Bangladesh) without expecting anything in return from them. It shows contradiction between our moral professions and political activities. As a seasoned diplomat observes : "The contradictions betwen our moral, professional and political necessities has been a continuous aberration in our foreign policy. We have not been able to strike the necessary balance to meet the endemic amorality characterising international relations. Our moral professionas and our civilisational claims result in our assuming a hectoring,

pontification and sometimes insensitive stance in negotiations and exchanges of views, which offends our foreign policy interlocutors."[23]

2. Now pragmatism is the hallmark of India's foreign policy and diplomacy as a result of which the feature of consistency coming since the times of Nehru has lost its place. In the name of studying each issue on its merit, the policy-makers try to sail with the wind of time. It is true that the new issues (like cross-border terrorism, nuclear proliferation and restructuring of the international agencies) have replaced the old issues (as condemnation of the military blocks of the super-powers, termination of colonialism and elimination racial discrimination), but the deplorable fact remains that the stand of the policy-makers looks like wavering from time to time. Non-interference in the internal affairs of a state has been one of the cardinal features of our foreign policy, and yet our policy-makers and implementers showed hesitancy in criticising American intervention in the internal affairs of Iraq and Iran. Once, our leaders openly criticised the role of a big military blocks like the NATO, but now their successors preferred to remain mute when the NATO forces arrived in Kosovo, Afghanistan and Iran in the name of 'peace mission'. While advocating the case of nuclear non-priliferation like his predecessors, Prime Minister Vajpayee appreciated the National Missile Defence System of American President Bill Clinton.

3. By yielding to the pressures of international agencies like International Monetary Fund and World Bank, Prime Minister Rao and his successors removed restrictions on the entry of foreign capital and multi-national companies. Moreover, by taking huge loans from such international agencies, the leaders in power virtually mortgaged the country that might have its adverse effect on our economic sovereignty. The official argument that it has been done due to the compulsions of a globalised economy is not very sound. In the name of liberalisation, market has been opened for foreign and native capitalists who are in league with each other. As a result of this, official diplomacy has been overshadowed by track-two diplmacy.

Keeping all these point in view, a perceptive analyst of India's foreign policy critically comments : "There was once a national

23. J.N. Dixit : *Across Borders : Fifty Years of India's Foreign Policy*, pp. 379

consensus on 'motherhood and apple pie' concept and on principles describing our national interests, namely, India's sovereignty sould not be challenged, India's territorial integrity should be maintained, India's economy should be sustained, India should not brook any political or military intervention in its internal affairs by any country, and India's technological capacities in all respects, especially its nuclear and space technology capacities, should grow untramelled by any external pressures. "But when it has come to policy options to ensure these interests, taking into account the complex factors which could affect the options, India has become somewhat of a Towel of Babel".[24]

But such points of criticism have no weight if we measure them against the positive achievements of our foreign policy. The elimination of colonialism and eradication of racial segregation from the world should be attributed to the successful prosecution of such a foreign policy. India has consistently maintained her stand that nuclear energy should invariably be used for peaceful and constructive purposes alone. She has ever taken the view that the Nuclear Non-Proliferation Treaty is unequal, unjust and discriminatory and now its extension for an indefinite period (as resolved at the Review Conference held at New York in April-May, 1995) is like legitimisation of hypocrisy committed by 178 states of the world at the behest of the US. Foreign Minister Pranab Mukherjee frankly said in the Rajya Sabha on 18 May, 1995 that this was a flawed treaty, because it legitimised nuclear weapons in the hands of five nations of the world.

24. J.N. Dixit : *India's Foreign Service*, pp. 228-29.

22

Miscellaneous Topics

Procedure of Amending the Constitution

It is really a unique feature of our Constitution that Art. 368 does not cover its process of amendment as a whole. A thorough study of the provisions of the Constitutions shows that while most of them may be amended by the unilateral action of the Parliament and by simple majority in each House, others may be amended by the unilateral action of the Parliament by special majority. It is only in respect of some specific items given in Art. 368 where the bill of amendment passed in each House of Parliament by special majority further requires to be ratified by the Legislatures of at least half of the States of the Indian Union. As such, the three categories may be put as under:

In the first place, we may enumerate those provisions of our Constitution which may be amended by the unilateral action of the Parliament. Here the procedure of passing a bill is exactly like that of passing an ordinary bill. That is, a bill may be introduced in either House of Parliament and, if passed in each House by the majority of the members present and voting, it shall be presented to the President who shall give his assent. The same legislative procedure shall be followed in respect of the adoption of a bill of constitutional amendent if it, for example, deals with the following provisions:

1. Creation of new States or making a change in the boundaries or name of any State or States of the Indian Union;
2. Indian Citizenship;
3. Quorum in Parliament, privileges of the members of Parliament, salaries and allowances of the members of Parliament;
4. Creation or abolition of second chamber in a State Legislature;
5. Administration of Union Territories or Scheduled and Tribal Areas.

In the second place, we may refer to some of the provisions (as Fundamental Rights contained in Part III and Directive Principles of State Policy contained in Part IV) where it is required that a bill of amendment must be passed in each House by its absolute majority coupled with two-thirds majority of the members, present and voting. Then, it shall be presented to the President who shall give his assent. Here the same legislative process is to be followed. The only requirement is that of a special majority.

Finally, we may refer to those items that have been specifically given in Art. 368 where a bill of constitutional amendment must be passed by both the Houses of Parliament by special majority (as in the above category) and then be referred to the States for ratification. In this case, a resolution of approval shall be passed by the State legislature by simple majority, *i.e.* majority of the members present and voting. This category includes:

(*a*) Articles 54 and 55 relating to the election of the President;

(*b*) Articles 73 and 162 relating to the extent of the executive power of the Union and the States respectively;

(*c*) Chapter IV of Part V relating to the Supreme Court of India;

(*d*) Chapter V of Part VI relating to the High Court of the States;

(*e*) Schedule VII showing distribution of powers between the Union and the States;

(*f*) Schedule IV specifying number of seats allocated to States in the Rajya Sabha;

(*g*) Art. 368 itself.

Apart from this, a reference should also be made to Art, 249 which empowers the Rajya Sabha to shift an item of the State List to the Union List or to the Concurrent List on the ground that it is expedient in the national interest. Such a resolution shall be passed by two-thirds majority of the members present and voting. It shall remain in force for one year, but the House may readopt it again and again. This may be termed as an *ad hoc* constitutional amendment.

As already pointed out, Art, 368 is inexhaustive in the sense that it does not constitute a 'complete code.' That is, it does not cover the amendment of all provisions of the Constitution and that its implications are not clear at each stage. When we refer to the word 'law' in this context, another point of debate arises as to whether it means an ordinary law made by the Parliament or a law of constitutional amendment made by the Parliament (in concurrence with the State legislatures in a special category as discussed above) whose validity can be looked into by the Courts. In the *Golak Nath Case*, the Supreme Court took a different view that the word 'law' as used in Art. 13(2) and the word 'law' used in Art. 368 had the same meaning and, as such, Parliament had no power to make a law of constitutional amendment that was inconsistent with the exercise and enjoyment of our fundamental rights. The 24th Amendment of 1971 re-empowered the Parliament to make any amendment in any part of the Constitution, including Part III.

A critic may also hold the view that the procedure of amending the Indian Constitution flouts the norms of a federal polity. Most of the provisions are amendable by the unilateral action of the Parliament. It is only in respect of certain items touching the federal system where ratification by half of the State legislatures is needed. The States have no right to initiate a bill of constitutional amendment. Moreover, the work of ratification of a bill of constitutional amendent is to be done by only half of the State Legislatures and that a resolution to this effect is to be adopted by the simple majority of members, present and voting. There is no provision for ratification of a bill by means of referendum as we see in Switzerland, France and Australia. Even in respect of a bill making alteration in the boundary lines of State, the will of the Centre shall prevail. As a matter of fact, the fundamental law of our country has been given a flexible nature with subsidiary touches of a rigid constitution so far as the amendment of its provisions relating to formal federal structure is concerned. Ambedkar well visualised that it "is difficult to conceive of a simpler method of amending the Constitution"[1]

Recent Constitution Amendment Acts

1. *The Eighty-seventh Amendment 2003* : The words '2001 census' as mentioned in Articles 82, 170 and 330 be read as '2026 census' which means that the number of Lok Sabha and Vidhan Sabha constituencies shall remain unchanged till 2026.

2. *The Eighty-eight Amendment 2003* : It inserts Art. 268 A and also entry 92 C in the Union List and thereby empowers the Government of India to impose service tax that may be collected and appropriated by the Union and the States.

3. *The Eighty-ninth Amendment 2003* : It inserts Art. 238A whereby the President shall appoint a National Commission for

1. *Constituent Assembly Debates*, Vol. VII, p. 43

Scheduled Tribes, while Art. 238 provides for the appointment of a National Commission for Scheduled Castes. Both the Commissions shall have a chairman, a vice-chairman and three members. Art. 238 had provided for the appointment of a National Commission for Scheduled Castes and Scheduled Tribes, but now the Commission has been bifurcated.

4. *The Ninetieth Amendment 2003 :* It adds a provision to Art. 332 which says that for elections to the Legislative Assembly of the States of Assam, the representatives of the Scheduled Tribes and non-Scheduled Tribes in the constitution of the Bodoland Territorial Areas District shall be maintained.

5. *The Ninety-first Amendment 2003 :* It inserts Clauses 1A and 1B into Art. 75. The former says that number of the ministers at the Centre, including the Prime Minister, shall not exceed 15% of the total strength of the Lok Sabha the latter says that a defector cannot be appointed as a minister. Likewise, it inserts Clauses 1A and 1B into Art. 164 which provide that the number of ministers in the States, including the Chief Minister, shall not exceed 15% of the total strength of the Vidhan Sabha and that a defector cannot be appointed as a minister. It also provides that there must be at least 12 ministers in a State. It is also given that the charge of being a defector shall be removed if he is re-elected, or the House of which he was a member is dissolved, whichever earlier. Then, it adds Art. 361B which says that a defector cannot be appointed on a political post where the salary and allowances are to be paid by the Union or State government. Finally, it deletes Sec. 3 of the Anti-defection Act (Schedule X of the Constitution) which had exempted defection as a crime in the event of split in a legislature party.

6. *The Ninety-second Amendent 2003 :* It incorporates four more languages into Eighth Schedule of the Constitution—Bodo, Dogri, Maithli, and Santhali.

7. *The Ninety-third Amendment (2006):*It empowers the state to make reservation of seats for the members of the Scheduled Castes, Scheduled Tribes and Other Backward Classes in private and unaided educational institutions excluding minority institutions.

Comptroller and Auditor-General of India

Chapter V of Part V of the Constitution provides for a high officer to act as the financial watch-dog of the Parliament in matters of exercising vigilance over the expenditure of public money in a way sanctioned by it. Thus, Art. 148 lays down:

That the Comptroller and Auditor-General of India shall be appointed by the President by a warrant under his hand and seal and shall only be removed from office in the manner and on the like ground as a Judge of the Supreme Court.

Every person appointed to be the Comptroller and Auditor-General of India shall, before he enters upon his office make and subscribe before the President, or some person appointed in that behalf by him, an oath or affirmation according to the form set out in the Third Schedule.

The salary and other conditions of service of the Comptroller and Auditor-General shall be such as may be determined by a law of Parliament and, until they are so determined, shall be as specified in the Second Schedule.

The term of the Comptroller and Auditor-General of India shall be of six years or until the completion of 65 years of age, whichever earlier, the time to be computed from the date on which he assumes his office. He may submit his resignation to the President of India at any time. He may be removed by the process of impeachment as applicable to a judge of the Supreme Court. His salary shall be equal to that of the judge of Supreme Court and on retirement he shall be entitled for a pension. In other matters his conditions of service shall be determined by the rules applicable to a member of the Indian Administrative Service holding the rank of a Secretary to the Government of India.

The duties of the Comptroller and Auditor-General of India relate to audit and report on all expenditures from the Consolidated Fund of India and of each State and Union Territory or from the Contingency Fund and Public Accounts of the Union and of the States, or on all trading, manufacture, profit and loss accounts etc. maintained by any Department of the Union or State Government, and of all bodies and authorities 'substantially financed' from the Union or State revenues, or Government companies, other corporate bodies or corporations or bodies. The CAG has to satisfy himself that rules and procedures are designed to secure an effective check on the assessment, collection and proper allocation of revenues.

The Constitution has made several arrangements to secure and ensure the independence of this important functionary. He is appointed by the President by a warrant under his hand and seal and can be removed by the tedious process of impeachment as applicable to a judge of the Supreme Court. His salary and allowances are a charge on the Consolidated Fund of India and they cannot be varied to his disadvantage during his term of office. Last, he remains in office for a fixed duration and he cannot be engaged in any other service by the Government of India after his retirement. This bar shall not apply to an international appointment as the first CAG (V. Narhari Rao) was appointed as the Executive Director of the International Bank in 1956. It is, however, for the Government to interpret the meaning of the bar of post-retirement service in the case of the CAG as we find that the second holder of this great office (A.K. Chanda) was appointed as the Chairman of the third Fianance Commission; T.N. Chaturvedi became an elected member of the Rajya Sabha and then he was appointed as the Governor of Karnataka.

Attorney-General of India

The Attorney-General, formerly known as the Advocate-General, is the highest law officer of the Government of India. He is appointed by the President and holds office during his pleasure. The Constitution says that he must possess the same qualifications that are necessary for a judge of the Supreme Court. That is, he must be a citizen of India, and that he must have served as a judge in some High Court or Courts for a period of at least 5 years, or that he must have worked as an advocate in some High Court or High Courts for a period of not less than 10 years, or that he must be a distinguished jurist in the view of the President. He may quit his office by submitting his resignation to the President. He may be removed by the President. He is entitled to all the privileges and immunities allowed for a Member of Parliament. When he presents himself in the House, he occupies a seat on the Government benches.

The functions and powers of the Attorney-General may be enumerated as under:

1. He advises the Government of India in such matters of legal and constitutional significance as are referred to him by the Government; he also performs such other duties of a legal character as are assigned to him by the President from time to time.
2. He has to appear on behalf of the Government in all cases, including suits and appeals, in the Supreme Court or in any

High Court in which the Government is a party. He is also required to appear in a court on behalf of the Parliament or its presiding officers.

3. It is also his duty to appear in matters of reference made by the President to the Supreme Court for having its advisory opinion. In such a case, he represents the Government of India.
4. He has the right of audience in all courts of India. However, he cannot hold briefs for any party except the Government of India, or some State Governments, or some other establishments maintained by the Union or State Governments.
5. While he appears in the Supreme Court, he has precedence over all other advocates; the Supreme Court has the right to issue notice of any proceedings to the Attorney-General and the latter may also apply to be heard in any of them.
6. He may be invited by the Speaker to speak in the House in order to give his opinion on matters of legal and constitutional importance. The members may bring a motion to invite him for enlightening the House with regard to legal and constitutional aspects of an important matter and the Speaker will make arrangements for his address if such a motion is adopted. The Speaker may also give advance notice to the Attorney-General of the questions that the members would like to ask him during the course of his attendance in the House. It should, however, be mentioned at this stage that the members may ask questions for the sake of having some clarifications, but they cannot cross-examine him, nor is any discussion permissible on a statement made by him there.
7. The Speaker may obtain the opinion of the Attorney-General on some matter of legal or constitutional significance, though he is not bound to act upon it.

In fine, the Attorney-General is the principal officer of law whose main function is to advise the Government of India in legal and constitutional matters and to represent it in a court of law on its behalf. He may carry on his private legal practice. It is, however, required that he cannot plead a case against the Government of India.

Anti-Defection Law

In 1985 the Parliament made a law so as to put a ban on political defections that was incorporated into the Constitution as Schedule

X. Known as the Fifty-second Amendment, it has these important provisions:

1. A member of any House of the Union Parliament (Rajya Sabha or Lok Sabha) or of any State legislature (Vidhan Sabha or Vidhan Parishad) elected on the ticket of a political party shall be disqualified from being a member of the House in case (*a*) he voluntarily gives up the membership of that political party on whose ticket he had won the election; or (*b*) if he votes or abstains from voting in such a House contrary to any direction issued by the whip of the political party to which he belonged, or by any person or authority authorised by him in this behalf, without obtaining in either case the permission of such political party, person, or authority and such voting or abstention from voting has not been condoned by such political party, person or authority within 15 days from the date of such voting or abstention.

2. It is also given that an elected independent member shall be disqualified from the membership of the House in the event of joining any political party, but a nominated independent member of the House may join many political party within six months.

3. The penalty clause of this law shall not apply in the event of a 'merger' when at least two-third members of a legislature party merge themselves with another political party.

4. The penalty clause of this law shall not apply to a person who resigns the membership of his party voluntarily after being elected as the presiding officer of the House and he rejoins that party after leaving the office of the presiding officer. It is required that on getting the office of the presiding officer of the House, he may live like a non-partyman or rejoin his party on whose ticket he was elected after relinquishing the post of the presiding officer.

5. Any matter relating to the disqualification of a member of the Union or State Legislature shall be decided by the presiding officer of the House. In case the presiding officer himself is invlved, then it shall be decided by his immediate successor. The decision of the presiding officer shall be final.

6. The Chairman or Speaker of the House may make rules for giving effect to the provisions of this Schedule.

7. The Chairman or the Speaker of the House may, without

prejudice to the provisions of article 105 or, as the case may be, article 194, and to any other power which he may have under this Constitution, direct that any wilful contravention by any person of the rules made under this paragraph may be dealt with in the same manner as a breach of privilege of the House.

In pursuance of this law, the Chairman of the Rajya Sabha and the Speaker of the Lok Sabha have made these rules:

1. The question whether a member of Parliament has incurred disqualifications under this law shall be considered after a petition is submitted by some member or members of the House. Such a petition must be addressed to the Secretary-General of the House and be accompanied by a concise statement of the material facts on which it relies.
2. The presiding officer of the House may either dismiss such a petition on some valid grounds, or he may refer it to the leader of the concerned party for his comments to be received within 7 days of the receipt of such communication, though he may extend this duration. After receiving the comments, he may either take a decision in the matter, or he may refer it to some committee of the House (Committee of Privileges) for making preliminary inquiries and then submit a report to him.
3. The final decision in this matter shall be taken after the member concerned has been given a chance to submit his explanation within a specific time.

It is true that this law has been able to put a check on the malady of political defections. Now the defectors cannot take benefit of the situation of a split in their legislature party and no defector can be given a political post where his salary and allowances are to be paid by the Union or State Government.[2] The Supreme Court has struck down Section 7 of this Act that bars jurisdiction of the Courts to look into the constitutional validity of the decision of the presiding officer of the House. It also ruled that as the presiding officer of the House would act like a 'tribunal' in such a matter, his decision would be subject to scrutiny by the highest court of the land.

❑❑❑

2. The 91st Amendment of 2003 has omitted Sec. 3 of this Act which had exempted defection in the event of a split in a legislature party. The penalty of defection could not be imposed if at least 1/3 members of a legislature party had defected as a bloc.

Appendix

Overseas Citizenship of India

Keeping in view persistent demand for dual nationality from the Indian people scattered all over the world, particularly in the United States, Canada, Britain, France, Germany, Australia and New Zealand and the firm commitment of the Government of India in engaging persons of Indian origin with the land of their ancestors in a mutually beneficial relationship, the Overseas Citizenship of India Scheme was launched in 2005 by amending the Indian Citizenship Act of 1955. It provides for the registration of the overseas citizens of India of all persons of Indian origin who were the citizens of India on or after 26 January 1950, and who are citizens of other countries excluding Pakistan and Bangladesh.

The scheme was introduced in the financial year 2006-07. It envisages issue of overseas citizen of India documents consisting of OCI registration certificate and universal visa sticker to Persons of Indian Origin. This scheme has been operational since January 2006 and as on 30 June 2011, a total number of 8, 61, 726 PIOs have been registered as OCIs. A registered OCI is granted multiple entry, multi-purpose life-long visa for visiting India, and is exempted from registration with Foregeniners Regional Registration Office for any length of stay in India. As mandated under the Allocation of Business Rules, the Ministry has issued notifications granting registered OCIs further benefits as under:

1. Parity with non-Resident Indians in the matter of inter-country adoption of Indian children.
2. Parity with resident Indian nationals in matters of tariffs in domestic airfares.
3. Parity with domestic Indian visitors in respect of entry fee for visiting national parks and wild life sanctuaries in India.

4. Parity with NRIs in respect of
   (a) entry fee for visiting the national monuments, historical sites and museums in India
   (b) Practising the following professions in India in pursuance of the provisions contained in the relevant Acts, namely, (i) doctors, dentists, nurses and pharmacists, (ii) advocates, (iii) architects, (iv) chartered accountants, and (v) entitlement to appear for the all-India pre-medical test or such other tests to make them eligible for admission in pursuance of the provisions contained in the relevant Acts.

However, the OCI is not dual nationality. It does not confer political rights.

Voting Rights to NRIs

The Representation of the People Act of 1951, as amended in 2010, gives voting rights to overseas Indian passport holders. A notification dated 9 February 2011 has been issued allowing overseas electors for their names to be included in the roll pertaining to the locality in which his place of residence in India mentioned in his passport is located. Overseas electors are required to apply in the requisite form along with copies of all the documents mentioned in the said form to the concerned registration officer directly or send the application to him by post. The rules allow self-attestation of documents.

Punchhi Commission Report (2010)

This Commission was set up by the Government of India on 28 April, 2007 under the chairmanship of Madan Mohan Punchhi, former Chief Justice of the Supreme Court of India, to look at the relative roles and responsibilities of the various levels of government and their inter-relations. As per its terms of reference, it was asked to examine and review the working of the existing arrangements between the Union and the States as per the Constitution of India, the healthy precedents being followed, various pronouncements of the Courts in regard to powers, functions and responsibilities in all spheres including legislative relations, administrative relations, financial relations, role of the Governors, emergency provisions, economic and social planning, Panchayati raj institutions, sharing

---

1. *India—Reference Annual, 2012*, pp. 656-69.

of resources including inter-state river water and recommend such changes or other measures as may be appropriate in view of the practical difficulties. The Commission submitted its report on 20 April, 2010. Its main recommendations are as follows:

1. There should be an amendment in Articles 355 and 356 to enable the Centre to bring specific trouble-torn areas under its rule for a limited period. It has proposed 'localising emergency provisions' covering not the State as a whole but only its specific part like a district to be placed under the rule of the Governor for a period of not more than three months. In the event of communal violence, the Centre must have the power to deploy its forces without the consent of the State government. It should continue for a week and then post-facto consent be taken from the concerned State.
2. It has laid down clear guidelines which the Governor of a State must follow while appointing the Chief Minister in the event of a hung House. This order should be as:
   (*a*) To call the leader of the pre-poll alliance commanding largest number of seats.
   (*b*) To call leader of single largest party claiming majority with the support of others.
   (*c*) To call the leader of the post-electoral coalition with parties joining the government.
   (*d*) To call the leader of the post-electoral alliance with some parties joining the government and others, including the independents, supporting from outside.
3. It has made some important recommendations about the office of the Governor. A person to be appointed for this post must not have been in active politics at any level for at least a couple of years; he must be an eminent person; and that he must not be a domicile of that State. This appointment should be made on the recommendation of a committee consisting of the Prime Minister, Union Home Minister, Speaker of the Lok Sabha, also preferably the Vice-President of India, and the Chief Minister of the concerned State. He must enjoy a fixed tenure of five years and that he may be removed by the process of impeachment by State Legislative Assembly. Art. 163 of the Constitution should be amended in a way that he may not be able to exercise his discretionary powers in an arbitrary manner. He should have the power to sanction prosecution of a working or former minister without or against the advice of

the Council of Ministers. The Governor should not be treated as a 'political football' and that he must not act as the Chancellor of State Universities.

4. The working of the National Integration Council should be streamlined. It should be restructured along the lines of the US Homeland Security Department. It must meet at least once a year. A committee of its five eminent members should visit the area affected by communal riots within two days and then submit its fact-finding report. Action must be taken on such a report expeditiously.
5. The working of the National Investigation Agency should also be streamlined so as to ensure effective cooperation of the State governments for dealing with the acts of terrorism.

Ninety-Seventh Constitution Amendment Act of 2012*

It accords constitutional recognition to the formation and operation of cooperative societies in any State or States of the Indian Union. In order to give to it the status of a fundamental right, it amends Art. 19 (1)(C) which says that all citizens have the right to form 'cooperative societies', other than associations or unions as enshrined in the original text. It inserts a new article 43(B) in the list of Directive Principles of State Policy specifying that the "state shall endeavour to promote voluntary formation, autonomous functioning, democratic control and professional management of cooperative societies." It inserts Part IXB titled 'Cooperative Societies' having 13 articles from 243 ZH to 243 ZT. Its main features may be noted as under:

1. A cooperative society means a society registered or deemed to be registered under any law relating to cooperative societies for the time being in force in any State. A 'multi-state cooperative society' means a society with objects not confined to one State and registered or deemed to be registered under any law for the time being in force relating to such cooperative.

---

* The ninety-fourth constitutional amendment omits the word 'Bihar' in Art. 164 (1) and puts the names of Chhattisgarh and Jharkhand there. It means that there shall be a minister for tribal welfare in these States. The ninety-fifth constitutional amendment of 2009 says about the extension of period for next 10 years for reservation of seats in favour of Scheduled Castes, Scheduled Tribls and Anglo-Indians in the Lok Sabha and Vidhan Sabhas. The ninety-sixth constitutional amendment of 2010 changes the names of Orissa as Odisha and Oriya as Odisha language.

2. The legislature of a State may by its law make provisions with respect to the incorporation, regulation and winding up of cooperative societies based on the principles of voluntary formation, democratic member-control, member-economic participation and autonomous functioning.
3. The law of the State legislature shall specify the number of directors of the board of a cooperative society whose number shall not exceed 21. Provisions may be made for the reservation of one seat for the Scheduled Castes or the Scheduled Tribes and two seats for women despite having members from such class or category of persons.
4. The term of the office of the elected members of the board and its office bearers shall be of five years from the date of the election and the term of the office bearers shall be coterminous with the term of the board. Provided that the board may fill a casual vacancy by nomination out of the same class of members in respect of which the casual vacancy has arisen, if the term of the board is less than half of its original term.
5. The legislature of a State shall by its law make provisions for cooperation of persons to be members of the board having experience in the field of banking, management, finance or specialisation in any other field relating to the objects and activities undertaken by the cooperative society, as members of the board of such society. Provided that such coopted members shall not have the right to vote in any election of the cooperative society in their capacity as such member or to be eligible to be elected as office bearers of the board. Provided also that the functional directors of a cooperative society shall also be the members of the board and such members shall be excluded for the purpose of counting the total number of the directors.
6. The election of a board shall be conducted before the expiry of its term so as to ensure that the newly elected members assume office immediately on the expiry of office of the members of the outgoing board. The suprintendence, direction and control of the preparation of electoral rolls for and the conduct of all elections to a cooperative society shall vest in such authority or body as provided in the law of the State that may also provide for the procedure and guidelines for the conduct of such election.

7. No board shall be superseded or kept under suspension for a period exceeding six months in certain situations as (*i*) persistent default, (*ii*) negligence in the performance of its duties, (*iii*) commitment of any act prejudicial to the interests of the cooperative society or its members, (*iv*) stalemate in the constitution or functions of the board, (*v*) failure of the concerned body or authority to conduct elections according to the law of the State. But it is subject to some conditions. First, it shall not be done where there is no Government shareholding or loan or financial assistance or any guarantee by the government. Second, in the case of a cooperative society, carrying on the business of banking, the provisions of the Banking Regulation Act of 1949 shall also apply. Third, in the case of a cooperative society, other than a multi-state cooperative society, carrying on the business of banking, the provisions of this clause shall have an effect as if for the words 'six months', the words 'one year' had been substituted. Fourth, in the event of the supersession of a board, the administrator appointed to manage the affairs of such cooperative society shall arrange for the conduct of elections within the specified period and hand over the management to the conditions of service of the administrator.
8. The law of State may also make provisions with respect to the maintenance of accounts by the cooperative societies and the auditing of such accounts at least once in each financial year. Such a law shall also lay down the minimum qualifications and experience of the auditors and auditing firms that shall be eligible for auditing accounts of the cooperative societies. The general body of the cooperative society shall appoint the auditors or auditing firm out of a panel approved by the State government or any authority so designated by it to act on its behalf. The accounts of every cooperative body shall be audited within six months and that its report shall be laid before the State legislature.
9. The annual general body meeting of every cooperative society shall be convened within a period of six months of the close of the financial year to transact its business. Each member of the cooperative society shall have access to its books, records and accounts.
10. Every cooperative society shall file returns within six months of the close of every financial year to the State government

containing its annual report of activities, audited statement of accounts, plan for surplus disposal as approved in the general body meeting, conduct of elections etc.

11. The members of a cooperative society may be penalised for committing an offence like wilfully making a false return or furnishing false information, disobeying any summons, refusal to submit documents as required to an authorised person, or involved in any corrupt practice.
12. The provisions of this act may apply to a multi-state cooperative society formed and operating under a law made by the Parliament or of the legislature or the government of a State or Union Territory. It may be done with the concurrence of the President of India.
13. The law of a State relating to the formation and working of cooperative society shall remain in force, despite being inconsistent with this Constitution Amendment Act for one year at the most after its notification by the Central Government in the Official Gazette, or the State government may suitably amend its law whichever earlier.

By according constitutional status to the formation and operation of cooperative societies, this constitution amendment act has sought to achieve what has already been successfully achieved by the seventy-third and seventy-fourth amendments of 1992 relating respectively to the organisation and working of village panchayats and municipal boards. Now the formation and operation of a cooperative society is a 'fundamental right' guaranteed to the citizens; it is also a Directive Principle of State Policy to be treated by the state as 'nevertheless fundamental in the governance of the country'. Part IXB has elaborate provisions which empower the legislatures of the States (including a Union Territory) to regulate the existing system by their laws after suitably modifying them in the light of this constitution amendment act. Provisions relating to the composition of a board of 21 members, auditing of annual accounts of the cooperative societies by the auditors approved by the State government and penalty for the wrong doers deserve due appreciation. Equally striking is the fact that multi-State cooperative societies may be formed and operated covering a State and some other State or States, including a Union Territory. A big idea could see light of the day in 2012 which was being celebrated as international cooperative year.

Fourteenth Presidential Election (2012)

States and Union Territories (Vidhan Sabhas and Parliament)	*Total No. of elected members*	*Value of each vote*	*Pranab Mukherjee*		*Purno A Sangma*	
			Votes	*Value*	*Votes*	*Value*
Andhra Pradesh	294	148	182	26,936	3	44
Arunachal Pradesh	60	3	54	162	2	6
Assam	126	116	110	14,616	13	1,508
Bihar	243	173	146	25,258	90	15,570
Chhattisgarh	90	129	39	4,831	50	6450
Goa	40	20	9	180	31	620
Gujarat	182	147`	59	8,673	123	18,081
Haryana	90	112	53	3,696	29	3,248
Himachal Pradesh	68	51	23	1,163	14	714
Jammu-Kashmir	87	72	68	4,896	15	1,080
Jharkhand	81	176	60	10,560	20	3,520
Karanataka	224	131	117	15,327	103	13,493
Kerala	140	152	124	18,848	0	0
Madhya Pradesh	230	131	74	4,694	149	19,519
Maharashtra	288	175	225	39,375	47	8,225
Manipur	60	18	58	1,044	1	18
Meghalaya	60	17	34	578	23	391
Mizoram	40	8	32	256	7	56
Nagaland	60	9	58	522	0	0
Odisha	147	149	26	3876	115	17,135
Punjab	117	116	44	5,104	70	7,120
Rajasthan	200	129	113	14,577	85	10,965
Sikkim	32	7	28	196	1	7
Tamilnadu	234	276	45	7,820	149	26,224
Tripura	60	26	56	1,456	1	26
Uttarakhand	70	64	39	1,106	30	1,920
West Bengal	294	151	275	29,125	3	453
Delhi	70	58	45	3,150	23	1,610
Pondicherry	30	16	23	368	5	80
Parliament	776	708	527	3,73,116	206	1,45,848
Total	4,896		3,108	7,13,763	1,454	3,15,987

4,659 votes were polled; 4,578 were valid, 81 votes were declared invalid. Mulayam Singh Yadav's vote was cancelled for breach of secrecy.

Panchayats (Extension to the Scheduled Areas) Act (1996)

The Seventy-third Constitution Amendment Act (1992) incorporated provisions relating to Village Panchayats in Part IX of the constitution. It was later found to have some shortcomings for whose removal this Act (PESA) came into effect in 1996. It was felt necessary that the provisions of this Part IX be extended to the Scheduled Areas subject to some additions and modifications so as to cover the administration and control of the Scheduled Areas and Scheduled Tribes in the States of the Indian Union other than Assam, Meghalaya, Mizoram and Tripura. Its main provisions may be enumerated as under:

1. A law made by the State legislature must be in consonance with customary laws, social and religious practices, and traditional management practices of the community resources.
2. Every village shall have a Gram Sabha consisting of persons whose names are included in the electoral rolls for the Panchayats at the village level. It shall be competent to safeguard and preserve the traditions and customs of the people, their cultural identity, community resources and the customary mode of the resolution of disputes.
3. Every Gram Sabha shall approve the plans, programmes and projects for social and economic development before they are taken up by the Panchayat at the village level for implementation. It shall be responsible for identification or selection of persons as beneficiaries under the poverty alleviation and other programmes.
4. Every Panchayat at; the village level shall be required to obtain from the Gram Sabha a certificate of utilisation of funds by the Panchayat for the plans, programmes and projects.
5. The reservation of seats in the Scheduled Areas at every Panchayat shall be in proportion to the population of the communities in that Panchayat for whose reservation is sought to be given in Part IX of the Constitution, provided that such reservation shall not be less than one-half of the total number or seats, provided further that all seats of Chairpersons of Panchayats at all levels shall be reserved for the Scheduled Tribes.
6. The State Government may nominate persons belonging to such Scheduled Tribes as have no representation in the

Panchayat at the intermediate level or the Panchayats at the district level provided that such nominations shall not exceed one-tenth of the total members to be elected in that Panchayat.

7. The Gram Sabha or the Panchayat at the appropriate level shall be consulted before making the acquisition of land in the Scheduled Areas for development projects and before re-settling or rehabilitating persons affected by such projects in the Scheduled Areas shall be coordinated at the State level. Planning and management of minor water bodies in the Scheduled Areas shall be entrusted to the Panchayats at the appropriate level.
8. The recommendations of the Gram Sabha or the Panchayats at the appropriate level shall be made mandatory prior to the grant of prospecting license or mining lease for minor minerals in the Scheduled Areas.
9. The law of the State Government may endow Panchayats with powers and authority as may be necessary to enable them to function as institutions of self-government and shall contain safeguards to ensure that the Panchayats at the higher level do not assume the powers and authority of any Panchayat at the lower level or of the Gram Sabha.
10. The State legislature shall endeavour to follow the pattern of the Sixth Schedule of the Constitution while designing the administrative arrangements in the Panchayats at district level in the Scheduled Areas.

The main object of these provisions is to ensure certain privileges and safeguards to the institutions of rural self-government in all the sates of the Indian Union on the pattern of such special arrangements guaranteed to the States of Assam, Meghalaya, Mizoram and Tripura.

Lok Pal Act (2013)

Ever since Dr. L.M. Singhvi initiated a debate in the Lok Sabha on 3rd April, 1963 to establish the institution of the Ombudsman (Anti-corrupion Officer) in India as prevailing in the Scandinavian and other countries of the world, the issue gained more and more significance. The Administrative Reforms Cammission headed by Morarji Desai recommended it in its report of 1966. It was recommended in more strong terms by the National Constitution Review Commission headed by Justice Venkatachelliah in its report of 2002. Then, it was recommended in equally powerful terms by the Second Administrative Reforms Commission headed by Veerappa Moily in its report of 2005. Tke Group of Ministers headed by the then Finance Minister (Pranab Mukherjee) reiterated it in its report of 2011. However, the satyagraha launched by Anna Hazare in Delhi in August 2011 made it the most important issue of the day.

The Morarji Commission Report (1966) renamed Ombudsman as the Lok Pal to be set up at the Centre with similar authorities in the States to be called Lok Ayuktas. A bill to establish this institution was introduced in the Lok Sabha in 1968 that lapsed with the dissolution of the House. Such attempts were made in 1971, 1977, 1985, 1989, 1996, 1998 and 1999, but all had the same fate. Happily, the ninth attempt came to have a successful end when the Parliament passed the Lok Pal Bill in 2013 that found its place on the statute book after receiving assent of the President. Its main features may be noted as under:

1. The Lok Pal shall consist of a Chairperson and at the most nine other members, half of whom must have judicial background, and the other half must be from the Scheduled Castes, Scheduled Tribes, Other Socially and Educationally Backward Classes, Minorities and Women.
2. The Chairperson and other members of this body shall be appointed by the President on the recommendation of a high-powered committee consisting of the Prime Minister, Lok Sabha Speaker, Leader of the Opposition in the Lok Sabha, Chief Justice of India or any sitting judge of the Supreme Court as his nominee; and an eminent jurist chosen by these four members by consensus. This committee shall also recommend the name of the Director of the Central Bureau of Investigation.
3. The Lok Pal shall have jurisdiction over all levels of public servants including the Prime Minister, politicians, ministers, public servants and bureaucrats. A matter may be investigated against the Prime Minister with the consent of its 2/3 majority. However, there shall be no probe against the Prime Minister on complaints relating to international relations, security, public order, atomic energy and space.
4. No prior permission is required for launching prosecution in cases probed by the Lok Pal or investigated at its instance.

The Lok Pal shall have the power to confiscate or attach provisionally any illgotten wealth even while prosecution is pending. This confiscation or attachment shall be subject to the jurisdiction of the Court.

5. The Lok Pal shall have its own wing for preliminary inquiry. If a prima facie case is established, the Lok Pal may refer the case for investigation to any agency, including the CBI. Moreover, it shall have the power of superintendence and direction over any investigating agency in all cases referred to it.
6. The Lok Pal shall have an independent prosecution wing of the agency concerned to initiate the prosecution. This law separates the investigation and prosecution functions of the CBI. It creates a Directorate of Prosecution linked to the agency. It shall be headed by a prosecutor reporting to the CBI Director.
7. It enhances the maximum conviction for persons guilty of corruption from 7 to 10 years and minimum conviction in such a case of 2 years.
8. The Directorate of Prosecution shall be under the over-all control of the CBI Director and his appointment shall be made on the recommendation of the Central Vigilance Commission. The Director of the CBI and the Director of Prosecution shall have a term of 2 years. The transfer of the CBI officers investigating cases referred to them shall be done with the approval of the Lok Pal.
9. It lays down the time limit for any preliminary inquiry, investigation and trial. Special courts may be set up for such purposes. The public servants will not present their views before preliminary inquiry if the matter involves some element of surprise like raids and searches. It empowers the Lok Pal to sanction prosecution against public servants. It cannot look into a case that is more than seven years old.
10. The CBI may appoint a panel of advocates with the approval of the Lok Pal and thereby not depend on the government advocates.
11. All entities including the NGOs (Non-Governmental Organisations) receiving donations from a foreign source in the context of the Foreign Contribution Regulation Act in

excess of Rs. 10 lakh per year are under the jurisdition of the Lok Pal.

12. Any person filing a false complaint to the Lok Pal shall be liable for punishment in the form of a fine of at least one lakh rupees or conviction for a term of five years at the most.
13. The Chairperson or any member of this body may be removed on the basis of a complaint filed by the Government or at least 100 MPs to the Supreme Court.
14. This law makes it mandatory for all States to set up Lok Ayuktas within a year of its implementation.

This statute may be appreciated for being a very important step taken by the Government of India to check the evil of rampant corruption. But it has same weak points as well. The Lok Pal cannot look into the actions of the MPs in respect of their speeches and vote in the House or its committees. It affords no protection to the whistleblowers. The selection committee to recommend the names of the Chairperson and other members has the majority of persons involved in politics. The CBI is not under the control of the Lok Pal. Above all, this statute says nothing about Citizens Charter. We shall be able to judge its real worth after its implementation in time to come.

Members of Parliament Involved in Criminal Cases

States/Union Terr.	Cases	States/Union Terr.	Cases
1. Delhi	5	2. Bihar	27
3. Maharashtra	30	4. Andhra Pradesh	20
5. Kerala	9	6. Union Terr. and Goa	3
7. Uttar Pradesh	28	8. Gujarat	9
9. Karnataka	9	10. Jharkhand	4
11. Assam	4	12. Himachal Pradesh	1
13. Madhya Pradesh	7	14. Uttarakhand	1
15. West Bengal	8	16. Odisha	4
17. Tamilnadu	7	18. Jammu-Kashmir	1
19. Haryana	1	20. Chhattisgarh	1
21. North-East States	1	22. Punjab	1
23. Rajasthan	1		

The Times of India (New Delhi), 19 May, 2014, p. 7.

Lok Sabha Election (2014)

Political Parties	Seats	Political Parties	Seats
1. Bharatiya Janata Party	282	20. Indian National Lok Dal	2
2. Indian National Congress	44	21. Indian Union Muslim League	2
3. A-I Anna Dravida Munnetra Kazhgam	37	22. Janata Dal (S)	2
4. Trinamool Congress	34	23. Janata Dal (U)	2
5. Biju Janata Dal	20	24. Apna Dal	2
6. Shiva Sena	18	25. Jharkhand Mukti Morcha	2
7. Telugu Desam Party	16	26. Communist Party	1
8. Telangana Rashtra Samiti	11	27. A.I.N.R. Congress	1
9. Communist Party-Marxist	9	28. Kerala Congress (M)	1
10. Y.S.R. Congress	9	29. Naga People's Front	1
11. Nationalist Congress Party	6	30. Pattali Makkal Kazhgam	1
12. Lok Jan Shakti Party	6	31. Sikkim Democratic Front	1
13. Samajwadi Party	5	32. A-I Majlis-i-Ittehad ul-Musalmeen	1
14. Aam Aadmi Party	4	33. Swabhimani Paksh	1
15. Rashtriya Janata Dal	4	34. National People's Party	1
16. Shromani Akali Dal	4	35. Revolutionary Socialist Party	1
17. United Democratic Front	3	36. Independents	3
18. J-K People's Democratic Party	3	Total	543
19. Rashtriya Lok Samta Party	3		